Fodor's 5th Edition

Provence and the Côte d'Azur

By Nancy Coons

D1302074

Fodor's Travel Publications • New York, Toronto, London, Sydney, Auckland

CONTENTS

MAPS

Circled letters in text correspond to the photographs. For more information on the sights pictured, turn to the indicated page number **Ⓐ** on each photograph.

DESTINATION
PROVENCE AND
THE CÔTE D'AZUR

Arid, rocky, windswept, its honey-gold hillsides silvered with olive trees, this primordial coastal landscape is so quintessentially Mediterranean that when the Greeks first landed at Marseille 4,000 years ago, they felt right at home. Here in Provence and on its famous coast, you too will feel the touch of the primeval, whether you climb into perched medieval villages; squeeze warm melons in an open-air market; or slip, seal-like, into the sea. Open your senses to the smell of thyme underfoot, the sound of Romanesque church bells, the taste of crushed garlic, the touch of balmy salt breezes, and the sight of the almost blinding beauty of bougainvillea, hot pink against the turquoise sea. Like the Greeks, Romans, feudal lords, and Sardinian kings who claimed a piece of this coveted land, you'll be seduced.

THE ALPILLES, ARLES AND THE CAMARGUE

On the marshy flatlands of the Rhône River delta and the raw-rock hills of the Alpilles that divert the river west, this region has been a major crossroads since the Romans first profited from the river, the coast, and an Alpine route. Nowhere in France will you find such a concentration of antiquities, so superbly preserved: Roman arenas, still in use, at Ⓐ**Arles** and Nîmes; a complete Greco-Roman village outside St-Rémy; and the spectacular triple-tier aqueduct called the Pont du Gard. It is a region of haunting natural beauty, too, with the Ⓒ**Camargue**'s hypnotic plane of marsh grass stretch-

Ⓑ⟩ 48

ing to the sea, interrupted only by an explosion of flying flamingos or a modest stampede of stocky bulls led by latter-day cowboys. The craggy Alpilles to the northeast are filled with feathery olive trees (this is one of Provence's main sources of olive oil) and with time-weathered *mas*, or farmhouses. The scenery is surpassed only by the cities: feisty, tatty, Latin Nîmes; graceful, golden Arles, still resonant with the memory of van Gogh; and cosmopolitan Ⓑ**St-Rémy-de-Provence**, a haven for chic urbanites and a mellow retreat dappled with the shade of ancient plane trees.

Ⓒ⟩ 29

Anchored by the former papal stronghold of **⑧Avignon,** with its mammoth medieval palace and crenellated city walls, the Vaucluse spreads luxuriantly north into the Rhône vineyards of Châteauneuf-du-Pape and east into mountain country quilted with olive and cherry orchards and fields purpling with laven-

THE VAUCLUSE

der. There are fields of Roman ruins in Vaison-la-Romaine and a Roman theater in Orange. But thanks in part to the tantalizing descriptions of British author Peter Mayle, the world beats a path to the Luberon, a long, low mountain, patchworked with vineyards and olive groves and punctuated by medieval hilltop villages: Bonnieux, Ménerbes, Roussillon, and Gordes. Like Mayle, others seek the sun-blessed lifestyle of cool stone farmhouses and warm feet. On Sunday they flock to the antiques market at Ⓐ**L'Isle-sur-la-Sorgue** to bargain for pastis glasses, quilts, and aspiring Old Masters.

AIX, MARSEILLE, AND THE CENTRAL COAST

Ⓐ❯ **118**

This is inspirational country, both for the austere beauty of its scenery and the rhythm of its cities, including the cosmopolitan shipping port of ⒺⒻ**Marseille**—bold, ancient, larger than life. The best of the Mediterranean is captured here in a savory bouillabaisse. Sleek, smart Ⓒ **Aix-en-Provence** burgeons with international students and the arts. Cézanne lived and died in Aix and painted its rugged countryside in rough-hewn daubs of russet and green, especially his beloved Ⓐ**Montagne de Ste-Victoire.** Marcel Pagnol, filmmaker and author of *Jean de Florette* and *Manon*

Ⓑ❯ **140**

Ⓔ **122**

des Sources, spent a lifetime capturing the scent of thyme and the roar of the fish market in his native territory around Marseille. In Ⓑ**Aubagne,** his hometown, Pagnol's characters come to life in sweet, slightly kitsch terracotta figurines called *santons*. The central coast is a well-kept secret, with pockets of natural beauty that could pass for an Aegean island. The rocky Ⓓ**Calanques,** fjord-like bays between Marseille and the picture-perfect port of Cassis, make for some of the prettiest coastline in France. Also stretched along this quiet underbelly are local beaches and spectacular views from the coastal highway. Farther east lie Bandol, as well known for its beaches as for its pink wine, and the brawny shipyard city of Toulon. And at the end of the world, the Presqu'île de Giens, ferries leave hourly for the car-free paradise of the Iles d'Hyères. The loveliest of these islands is Porquerolles, protected as a national park.

Ⓕ **130**

This is where the legend begins: palm trees, parasol pines, crystalline sun, a sea improbably blue, all framed against the green Massif des

Maures and the red-rock ⒟**Massif de l'Esterel** and backed by the wild Haut Var. Above-title credit goes to ⒷⒸ**St-Tropez**,

THE WESTERN CÔTE D'AZUR

with its white-sand beaches and its port cafés thick with young gentry hoping for a glimpse of a movie star... or a wanna-be. Also in the area are family-beach towns such as Ste-Maxime and Fréjus, and sportif resorts like St-Raphaël and Mandelieu. Just an hour's drive inland, Old Provence awaits in Cotignac, Mons, Seillans, and Fayence, palpable in crumbling ocher, heavy-leafed plane trees, and the chink of metal balls in a sandlot game of pétanque. Venture even farther and you'll enter the wild and woolly backcountry of Haute Provence, winding on mountain roads until you reach one of France's greatest natural wonders: the Gorges du Verdon, a Grand Canyon–like chasm roaring with milky green water and edged by some of Europe's most hair-

Ⓑ⟩158

Ⓒ⟩162

D⟩ 163

raising roads. At its west
end, the faïence center of
Ⓐ**Moustiers-Ste-Marie** proffers elegant pottery on either
side of a mountain torrent.

NICE AND THE EASTERN CÔTE D'AZUR

Ⓐ 231

Ⓑ 195

Cosseted by Mediterranean breezes and sheltered by green cliffs and silver Alps, this part of the Côte d'Azur has charmed the world, and it's easy to see why. Here are glamour capitals like ⒷⒹ**Cannes,** where palatial hotels such as the Carlton pamper the stars during the film festival, and Ⓒ**Monaco,** a principality with money to burn in its casinos. At the region's heart, Ⓔ**Nice** drapes along the Baie des Anges, rich with local museums and cuisine. All along the coast you'll experience the scenery and light that seduced Matisse, Picasso, Renoir, and Cocteau. Works by Matisse grace the region, including a life-spanning

Ⓒ 252

E〉228

collection in the Ⓐ**Musée Matisse** above Nice. Explore the noble old bastion of Antibes and its luxurious peninsula, the Cap d'Antibes; the pretty fishing port of Villefranche-sur-Mer; the yacht port of St-Jean on tropical Cap Ferrat; and the lemon-scented seaside resort of Menton. From the coast you can drive up into the hills to picturesque Vence, Mougins, and the perfume-making center of Grasse. Above the perched village of St-Paul, the Ⓕ**Fondation Maeght** has an extraordinary collection of contemporary art. Or you can plunge into the *arrière-pays* (backcountry), a world of forest gorges and isolated mountain towns.

D〉198

F〉218

GREAT ITINERARIES

Vaison-la-Romaine

CÔTE-DU-RHÔNE

HAUT VAUCLUSE

D977

N7

Pont-du-Gard

N100

Avignon

A51

D22

D109 · Lacoste

Ménerbes · Bonnieux

St-Rémy

D99

Les Baux

D17

Arles

Ⓐ 22

BOUCHES-DU-RHÔNE

A8

Aix · le Tholonet

CAMARGUE

A52

Marseille

A50

First-Time Tour
14 days

To hit the highlights of this sun-blessed region and mix the best of the arid hills of Provence with the tropical glamour of the Côte d'Azur, settle into one central town for a few nights at a time and make local trips from there.

AVIGNON
4 days. Explore the monuments and back streets, starting with the magnificent Popes' Palace. Spend the next morning in a museum, then make a half-day run out to the majestic Roman aqueduct, the Ⓐ Pont du Gard. On the third day, head east to the honey-tone village of Bonnieux, exploring Ménerbes and Lacoste along the way. The fourth day, veer north to the ancient Roman crossroads of Vaison-la-Romaine; wander the foundations of 1st-century villages and climb into the otherworldly Old Town.
☞ *Avignon, Haut Vaucluse, and the Luberon in Chapter 2.*

ARLES
3 days. Soak in the old-Provence atmosphere and golden light that drove van Gogh to distraction. Visit the Roman monuments and take in a bullfight in the 2nd-century arena. Spend a day exploring the chateau ruins in Les Baux and the Greek and Roman antiquities in St-Rémy.
☞ *Arles and the Alpilles in Chapter 1.*

ANTIBES
3 days. Experience the history and beauty of the Côte d'Azur in this fortified city and walk along the lush jungle peninsula of Cap d'Antibes. The next day, either venture into the backcountry to visit perfume factories in Grasse or stroll the palm-lined Croisette in Cannes. The third day leads you into the medieval town of St-Paul; spend the morning studying contemporary masterpieces in the Fondation Maeght and later peruse galleries along the village's cobbled streets.
☞ *Between Cannes and Nice; Cannes; Into the Pays Grassois; and St-Paul, Vence, and Backcountry Hill Towns in Chapter 5.*

VILLEFRANCHE-SUR-MER
4 days. Settle into the Mediterranean pace of this mellow port, visiting Cocteau's painted chapel and walking the Citadelle ramparts. Spend a day in St-Jean-Cap-Ferrat and swan through the sumptuous gardens at Villa Ephrussi. The third day, visit prosperous Monaco, exploring the Oceanography Museum and the famous casino. On your last day, wander Nice's exotic Old Town and stroll the Promenade des Anglais, bidding farewell to the azure waters.
☞ *Monaco and the Corniches Resorts and Nice in Chapter 5.*

Transportation
Rail service connects Avignon and Arles, and most of the ports and coastal resorts are easily reached by the scenic rail line. A bus leaves Avignon for the Pont du Gard, but the hill towns require car travel.

BORDERS

**BORDERS
BOOKS AND MUSIC**
11301 ROCKVILLE PIKE
KENSINGTON MD
(301) 816-1067

STORE: 0010   REG: 06/06 TRAN#: 2082
SALE   12/21/2002 EMP: 00142

FODORS PROVENCE & COTE DAZ-E05
     6417966 QP T   16.00

        Subtotal   16.00
        MARYLAND 5%   .80
1 Item   Total   16.80
        VISA   16.80
ACCT # /S XXXXXXXXXXXX4821
          AUTH: 021797
NAME: TRISCO/ROBERT F

CUSTOMER COPY

12/21/2002 03:53PM

THANK YOU FOR SHOPPING AT BORDERS
PLEASE ASK ABOUT OUR SPECIAL EVENTS

Visit our website @ www.borders.com!

(B) 118

20th-Century Art Tour
10 days

Perhaps even more than Paris, Provence and its sun-drenched coast was a lightning rod to modern artists and a crucible for the forging of modernism. It's easy to make a pilgrimage to the land that inspired many of the 20th century's greatest artists.

ARLES
2 days. After van Gogh slashed his ear here, his neighbors had him evicted and declared dangerous; thus this city he loved neither bought nor inherited his work. Yet Arles bears the traces of his productive days here, including Roman monuments, cafés, and landmarks he painted. It's a day trip to St-Rémy, where the artist had himself committed to a cloistered asylum.
☞ *Arles and the Alpilles in Chapter 1.*

AIX
2 days. Make a pilgrimage to Cézanne's perfectly preserved studio; the cours Mirabeau shop where his father sold hats; and the Musée Granet, where a few of his paintings remain. Drive into the pine-and-ocher countryside to visit Le Tholonet at the foot of **(B)**Ste-Victoire, the mountain Cézanne immortalized in myriad paintings.
☞ *Aix-en-Provence in Chapter 3.*

ST-TROPEZ
1 day. This famous port and the sugared-almond hues of the surrounding row houses inspired Paul Signac and a procession of visiting artists. At the Annonciade, a collection of their resulting work foreshadows a century of pointillism, fauvism, expressionism, and ultimately pure abstraction.
☞ *St-Tropez and the Massif des Maures in Chapter 4.*

ANTIBES
3 days. Visit the château where Picasso experimented on a grand scale and explore the resulting museum of his works. Then head to Vallauris, where he painted a chapel with a powerful war-and-peace fresco and revived the village's ancient ceramics tradition. At Mougins, the hermitage where he spent his last years still lords over the valley at the foot of Notre-Dame-de-Vie. The next day, drive to Biot, where Fernand Léger left a legacy of bold mosaics, ceramics, and stained glass. In Cagnes, visit Renoir's last home and its garden. Head inland on the third day to ©St-Paul, to contemplate the contemporary masterpieces at the Fondation Maeght.
☞ *Between Cannes and Nice; Into the Pays Grassois; and St-Paul, Vence, and Backcountry Hill Towns in Chapter 5.*

NICE
2 days. Hike or take the bus up to the Cimiez neighborhood to tour the exuberant collection of epic biblical paintings by Chagall in a museum devoted to his work. Then head to the top of the Cimiez hill to an Italianate villa brimming with Matisse masterworks. The next day, drive or take a train to Menton to see Cocteau's decorated beach-bastion and his murals in the Hôtel de Ville; on the way, consider stopping at Villefranche-sur-

Menton
Roquebrune/Cap Martin
Villefranche-sur-Mer
St-Paul
Monaco
St-Jean-Cap-Ferrat
Grasse
D36 **N98** **Nice**
Biot
N85 Vallauris **Cagnes**
Mougins
Antibes
A8
Cannes
N98
A8 220km
St-Tropez
N98 **D98A**
A57 **N98**
Toulon

© 218

Mer to view his frescoed chapel St-Pierre. And, like the designer, seek inspiration along Cap Martin on the rocky terraces of Le Corbusier's unassuming *cabanon*, and lay a flower on his grave in the adjoining medieval village of Roquebrune.
☞ *Nice and Monaco and the Corniches Resorts in Chapter 5.*

Transportation
The coastal rail line links Nice, Cannes, Antibes, Monaco, and Menton, but you'll need a car to cover all the ground here.

1 THE ALPILLES, ARLES, AND THE CAMARGUE

THE PONT DU GARD, NÎMES, THE RHÔNE DELTA, AND THE LANGUEDOC FRONTIER

From the spare, rugged flatlands in the Languedoc west of the Rhône, through the lunar landscape of the Camargue marshlands and into the painterly highlands known as the Alpilles, this is the region where the Romans left their surest mark. Astonishingly well-preserved arenas in Nîmes and Arles, the traces of the entire Greco-Roman village of Glanum outside St-Rémy, and the miraculous Pont du Gard aqueduct attest to the vibrancy of the Latin civilization found equal only in Rome.

S COURED BY THE MISTRAL and leveled to prairie flatlands by eons of earth deposits carried south by the Rhône, this is Provence in its rawest form. Only the rude rock outcrops called the Alpilles interrupt the horizon, dusted with silvery olives and bristling with somber cypress spears. To the west, where the Provençal dialect gives way to Languedoc, the ancient language of the southwest, vineyards swathe the countryside in rows of green and black. Along the southern coast, the Camargue's monotonous landscape of reeds and cane secrets exotic wildlife—rich-plumed egrets, rare black storks, clownish flamingos—as well as domestic oddities: dappled white horses and lyre-horned bulls descended from ancient, indigenous species.

The scenery is only surpassed by the cities: feisty, tatty Nîmes, its raffish urban lifestyle surging obliviously through a ramshackle, gritty-chic old town; graceful, artsy Arles, in harmonious van Gogh hues; chic St-Rémy, a gracious retreat for cosmopolitan regulars, the Hamptons of Provence.

Each of these cities would be fascinating to explore without their trump card: classical antiquities, superbly preserved, unsurpassed in northern Europe. The Colosseum-like arenas in Nîmes and Arles are virtually intact, solid enough to serve their original purpose as stadiums; they date from the time of Christ. The mausoleum and *arc de triomphe* outside St-Rémy are still so richly detailed, they look like reproductions, but they're signed by the children of Caesar Augustus. And across the street, the vivid high-relief ruins of Glanum trace back to the Hellenism of the 3rd century BC.

Add to these attractions Romanesque châteaux and abbeys, seaside fortresses that launched crusades, and sun-sharpened landscapes seen through the tortured eyes of van Gogh and Gauguin, and you have a region worth exploring in depth.

Pleasures and Pastimes

Architecture and Antiquities

Churches, châteaux, and abbeys sprinkle the countryside of western Provence, a surprising concentration of them pure Romanesque—that is, built in the solid progression of arches and barrel vaults that marked Roman engineering and was mimicked in the hinterlands by architects through the 12th and 13th centuries. Signs here point to ÉGLISE ROMANE XIIIÈME—meaning Romanesque. *Romain* refers to Roman remains—just as prolific in the region.

Although you'll find Roman traces throughout Provence (and indeed France), the most beautifully preserved are concentrated around the Rhône. With two arenas (at Arles and Nîmes), the ancient Hellenistic settlement outside St-Rémy, the miraculously preserved temple in Nîmes (Maison Carrée), and traces of Roman life scattered over the region, this is the place to concentrate if your taste runs to the classical. (You'll also want to run up to Orange and Vaison-la-Romaine; ☞ Chapter 2.)

Bird-Watching

The Camargue marshlands produce a nutty rice much prized by French gastronomes, as well as by birds who migrate through and feast on its chewy grains. A day's walk through the nearly car-free zone around the Etang du Vaccarès may reveal bitterns, egrets, a handful of tern species, hoopoes, and—a thrill even if you're not a birder—great flocks of gawky flamingos.

Dining

If eating is the national pastime in France, it is a vocation in Provence. And the pleasure of relaxing in a shady square over a pitcher of local rosé, a bowl of olives, and a regional *plat du jour* is only enhanced in western Provence by quirky local specialties. Consider nibbling tiny *tellines,* salty clams the size of your thumbnail, fresh from the Camargue coast. Or try a crockery bowl of steaming bull stew (*gardianne*), a sinewy daube of lean-and-mean beef from the harsh Camargue prairies, ladled over a scoop of chewy red Camargue rice. The mouth-watering oddity called *brandade* (salt cod pestled with olive oil and milk into a creamy spread) has a peculiar history; cod isn't even native to Nîmes but was traded, in its leathery salt-dried form, by medieval Breton fishermen in exchange for south-coast salt. The Nîmois mixed in local olive oil and created a regional staple.

CATEGORY	COST*
$$$$	over 400 frs/€61
$$$	250 frs–400 frs/€38–€61
$$	125 frs–250 frs/€19–€38
$	under 125 frs/€19

per person for a three-course meal, including tax (20.6%) and tip but not wine

Horseback Riding

The wild glamour of the ancient race of Camargue horses becomes downright pedestrian when the now-domesticated beauties are saddled en masse and led single-file through the marsh trails. Rent-a-horse stands proliferate along the marshland highways, and trails are thick with gringos plodding along in subservient lines. But since much of the preserve is limited to walkers and riders, a trip on horseback will let you experience the austerity of the landscape without getting your feet wet.

Lodging

Although Arles, Les Baux, and St-Rémy have stylish, competitive hotels with all the requisite comforts and Provençal touches from wrought iron to *folklorique* cottons, Nîmes doesn't attract—or much merit—the overnight crowds; thus its hotels, with rare exception, have little in the way of charm. But throughout the region and well outside the towns you'll find lovely converted *mas* (farmhouses), blending into the landscape as if they'd been there a thousand years—but offering modern pleasures: gardens, swimming pools, and sophisticated cooking.

If you plan on spending a week or more in the region, a *gîte* (vacation rental) opens up new ways to appreciate local life, such as market browsing and the sampling of area specialties *comme chez soi* (home style). The local branches of Gîtes-de-France, the national network for vacation rentals, are divided by *départements* (administrative regions). The Hérault offices serve much of the Camargue; the Gard offices handle Nîmes and environs, and the Bouches-du-Rhône branch covers the area including Arles, St-Rémy, and the Alpilles. For addresses, *see* Vacation Rentals *in* The Alpilles, Arles, and the Camargue A to Z, *below*.

CATEGORY	COST*
$$$$	over 800 frs/€122
$$$	550 frs–800 frs/€84–€122
$$	300 frs–550 frs/€46–€84
$	under 300 frs/€46

All prices are for a standard double room for two, including tax (20.6%) and service charge.

✑ *following the text of a review is your signal that the property has a Web site, where you will find details and, usually, images; for a link, visit www.fodors.com/urls.*

Wine

Though all of Provence is known for its rosés, some wines produced west of the Rhône merit special mention. Lirac and Tavel, world-famous and highly commercial rosés, come from the Rhône Valley just up the road from the Pont du Gard. The robust red *costières de Nîmes* grows in stony dry vineyards west of its namesake.

Exploring the Alpilles, Arles, and the Camargue

This is the kind of country that inspires a Latin latitude (if not lassitude), so with all the ruins and châteaux to visit, allow yourself time to wander through food markets and to sit on a shady terrace watching the painterly changes in light.

Great Itineraries

Although Nîmes belongs in spirit to the Languedoc, its proximity to the Camargue and Arles makes it a logical travel package with them. With their rugged hills and rich olive groves, the Alpilles are a world apart, but easily accessible from Arles and environs. You can move from site to site, or choose a central base—say, Arles—and explore them all without driving more than an hour to any one attraction. A couple of days passing through the region allows you to see world-class antiquities; five days allows time to wander the Camargue; a week lets you see the principal sites, enjoy a nature tour, and take a break by the sea. And don't forget that the ravishing old city of Avignon (☞ Chapter 2) is just an hour's easy run up from Arles.

Numbers in the text correspond to numbers in the margin and on the Alpilles, the Camargue, and the Languedoc Frontier, Nîmes, and Arles maps.

IF YOU HAVE 3 DAYS

Consider basing yourself in ⬚ **Arles** ⑭–㉕ to see the Roman treasures (including the Musée de l'Arles Antique), visit the Romanesque Église St-Trophime and its cloister, and wander the old-town streets and squares, as Vincent van Gogh did. Then on Day 2 head up to **Nîmes** ②–⑪ for a look at the Maison Carrée and the arena. From Nîmes you can drive to the ancient fortress-port of **Aigues-Mortes** ⑫ and through the austere Camargue. Or if you prefer culture to nature, head north from Nîmes to the magnificent Roman aqueduct called the **Pont du Gard** ①. Spend the third day in the hills, visiting the spectacular hilltop château-village of **Les Baux-de-Provence** ㉙ and serene and fashionable **St-Rémy-de-Provence** ㉛.

IF YOU HAVE 5 DAYS

Expand the above itinerary to include a night in ⬚ **Les Baux-de-Provence** ㉙ or ⬚ **St-Rémy-de-Provence** ㉛. Out of ⬚ **Arles** ⑭–㉕, you can make a day trip to the medieval fortress rivals **Tarascon** ㉖ and **Beaucaire** ㉗.

IF YOU HAVE 7 DAYS

Base yourself for three nights in ⬚ **Arles** ⑭–㉕ and invest a day enjoying its museums, ruins, and Latin ambience. Then spend a half-day visiting the antiquities in ⬚ **Nîmes** ②–⑪ and head north to the **Pont du Gard** ①. Devote Day 3 to exploring the **Camargue**, where you can stop in both **Aigues-Mortes** ⑫ and the resort town of **Stes-Maries-de-la-Mer** ⑬,

The Alpilles, the Camargue, and the Languedoc Frontier

which draws Gypsies to the shrine in its Romanesque church and tourists to its beaches. Then break camp for three nights in 🏨 **St-Rémy-de-Provence** ㉛, from where you can explore **Les Baux-de-Provence** ㉙ and make excursions to **Tarascon** ㉖, **Beaucaire** ㉗, and **Fontvieille** ㉘, whose windmill inspired writer Alphonse Daudet (*Letters from My Mill*). Allow a half-day for the magnificent **Abbaye de Montmajour,** just north of Arles.

When to Tour

July and August are very much the high season, especially along the coast, and are best avoided if possible, both because of the crushing crowds and the grilling heat. In winter (from November through February, even into March) you'll find a lot of tourist services closed, including hotels and restaurants, and much of the terrace life driven indoors by rain and wind. Around Easter, the plane trees begin to leaf out and the café tables to sprout. This easy midseason period maintains its lazy, pleasant pace from Easter through June and September to late October.

THE LANGUEDOC FRONTIER

Nîmes and its famous aqueduct hold forth in the *département* of Gard, considered more a part of the Languedoc culture than that of Provence. Yet because of its proximity to the heart of Provence and its similar climate, terrain, and architecture, it is included as a kindred southern spirit. Center of gaily printed *indienne* cottons, Camargue-style bullfights, and spectacular Roman ruins, it cannot be isolated from its Provençal neighbors. After all, the *langue d'oc* (language of oc) refers to the ancient southern language Occitane, which evolved from Latin; northern parts developed their own *langue d'oïl*. Their names derive from their manner of saying yes: *oc* in the south and *oïl* in the north.

By an edict from Paris, the *oïls* had it in the 16th century, and *oui* and its northern dialect became standard French. Languedocien and Provençal merely went underground, however, and still crop up in gesticulating disputes at farmers' markets today.

Pont du Gard

★ ❶ *24 km (15 mi) northeast of Nîmes, 25 km (16 mi) north of Arles, 25 km (16 mi) west of Avignon.*

No other sight in Provence rivals the Pont du Gard, a mighty, three-tiered aqueduct midway between Nîmes and Avignon (☞ Chapter 2). Erected some 2,000 years ago as part of a 48-km (30-mi) canal supplying water to Roman Nîmes, it is astonishingly well preserved.

If you come to the Pont du Gard very early in the morning—before dawn is ideal—you can discover Provence in its purest blend of natural beauty and antiquity. As the silhouettes of olives emerge from the darkness and the diamond-sharp air wells up slowly with birdsong, you can see the ancient tiers as they were in the days when they carried water to Nîmes. The aqueduct is shockingly noble in its symmetry, the rhythmic repetition of arches resonant with strength, testimony to an engineering concept that was relatively new in the 1st century AD, when it first was built under Emperor Claudius. And, unsullied by tourists and by the vendors of postcards and Popsicles that dominate the site later in the day, the natural setting is just as resonant, with the river flowing through its rocky gorge unperturbed by the work of master engineering that straddles it.

Later in the day, however, crowds become a problem, even off-season; no one wants to miss this wonder of the world. You can approach the aqueduct from either side of the Gardon River. If you choose the north side (Rive Gauche), you'll be charged 22 francs/€3.35 to park (stay as close to the booth as possible because unfortunately break-ins are a problem). The walk to the *pont* is shorter, and the views arguably better from here. It costs less (18 francs/€2.74) to park on the south side (Rive Droite), and there's a tourist office with information and postcards—but this is also the side the tour buses prefer. Access to the spectacular walkway along the top is indefinitely blocked for restoration work.

Nîmes

24 km (15 mi) southwest of Pont du Gard, 29 km (18 mi) northwest of Arles.

If you have come to the south to seek out Roman treasures, you need look no further than Nîmes (pronounced neem), for the Arènes and Maison Carrée are among continental Europe's best-preserved antiquities. But if you have come to seek out a more modern mythology—of lazy, graceful Provence—give Nîmes wide berth. It's a feisty, run-down rat race of a town, with jalopies and Vespas roaring irreverently around the ancient temple, and rock bands blasting sound tests into the arena's wooden stands. Its medieval old town has none of the gentrified grace of those in Arles or St-Rémy. Yet its rumpled and rebellious ways trace directly back to its Roman incarnation, when its population swelled with soldiers, arrogant and newly victorious after their conquest of Egypt in 31 BC.

Already anchoring a fiefdom of pre-Roman *oppidums* (elevated fortresses) before ceding to the empire in the 1st century BC, this ancient city bloomed to formidable proportions under the Pax Romana. A 24,000-seat coliseum, a thriving forum with a magnificent temple patterned after Rome's temple to Apollo, and a public water network fed by the Pont du Gard attest to its classical prosperity. Its next golden age bloomed under the Protestants, who established an anti-Catholic stronghold here and wreaked havoc on iconic architectural treasures—not to mention the papist minority. Their massacre of some 200 Catholic citizens is remembered as the Michelade; many of them were priests sheltered in the *évêché* (bishop's house), now the Musée du Vieux Nîmes (Museum of Old Nîmes). Chapels throughout the surrounding countryside were damaged by Calvin's righteous rebels.

A locally produced lightweight serge brought fame to Nîmes more than once. Legend has it that Christopher Columbus admired its durability and used it for sails; its reputation spread, and it was exported worldwide from the ports of Genoa (Gênes in French). Levi Strauss found its sturdy texture strong enough for gold miners' pants and Americanized its name from *bleu de Gênes*. The now-ubiquitous fabric's name traces back to its origins: de Nîmes.

Perhaps inspired by the influx of architects who studied its antique treasures, Nîmes has opted against becoming a lazy, atmospheric Provençal market town and has invested in progressive modern architecture. Smack-dab across from the Maison Carrée stands the city's contemporary answer, the modern-art museum dubbed the Carré d'Art (Art Square) after its ruthlessly modernist four-square form—a pillared, symmetrical glass reflection of its ancient twin. Other investments in contemporary art and architecture confirm Nîmes's commitment to modern ways.

★ ❷ The **Arènes** (Arena) is considered the world's best-preserved Roman amphitheater. A miniature of the Colosseum in Rome, it stands more than 520 ft long and 330 ft wide, with a seating capacity of 24,000. Bloody gladiator battles and theatrical wild-boar hunts drew crowds to its bleachers. As barbarian invasions closed in on Nîmes, it was transformed into a fortress by the Visigoths. Later, medieval residents found comfort and protection for tight-packed thatch-and-timber houses (as well as a small château and chapel). Nowadays the amphitheater has been restored almost to its original look, including exit signs marked VOMITORIUM (from the Latin for "to go out"). An inflatable roof covers it in winter, when various exhibits and shows occupy the space, and concerts and tennis tournaments are held here in summer. Its most colorful event is the *corrida,* the bullfight that transforms the arena (and all of Nîmes) into a sangria-flushed homage to Spain (☞ Outdoor Activities and Sports, *below*). ⊠ *bd. Victor-Hugo,* ☎ *04–66–76–72–77.* ⌨ *28 frs/€4.27; joint ticket to Arènes and Tour Magne 34 frs/€5.18.* ⊙ *May–Sept., daily 9–6:30; Oct.–Apr., daily 9–noon and 2–5.*

❸ At the **Musée des Beaux-Arts** (Fine Arts Museum), a few blocks south of the Arènes, you can admire a vast Roman mosaic; the marriage ceremony depicted provides intriguing insights into the Roman aristocratic lifestyle. Old-master paintings (by Nicolas Poussin, Pieter Brueghel, Peter Paul Rubens) and sculpture (by Auguste Rodin) form the mainstay of the collection. ⊠ *rue de la Cité-Foulc,* ☎ *04–66–67–38–21.* ⌨ *26 frs/€3.96.* ⊙ *Tues.–Sun. 11–6.*

❹ The **Musée Archéologique et d'Histoire Naturelle** (Museum of Archaeology and Natural History), a few blocks northeast of the Arènes, occupies a restored Jesuit college. Relics from local digs range from the Iron Age to the Roman period, with a plethora of artifacts from daily life over the ages: coins, dice, earrings, and crockery. There is also a rich variety of Roman artworks, including the Marbacum torso, dug up at the foot of the Tour Magne. ⊠ *bd. de l'Amiral-Courbet,* ☎ *04–66–67–25–57.* ⌨ *28 frs/€4.27.* ⊙ *Tues.–Sun. 11–6.*

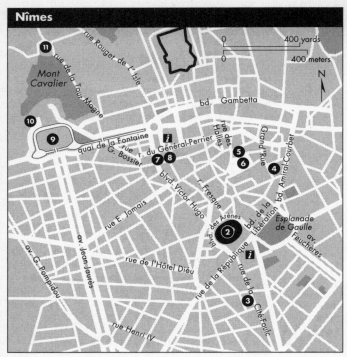

⑤ Destroyed and rebuilt in several stages, with particular damage by rampaging Protestants who slaughtered eight priests from the neighboring *évêché*, the **Cathédrale Notre-Dame et St-Castor** still shows traces of its construction in 1096. Is that fragment of classically symmetrical pediment an 11th-century reference to the Maison Carrée? Within its fluted lines, a miraculously preserved Romanesque frieze dates, for the most part, from the year of construction. Its lively Old Testament portraiture—reminiscent in style to its contemporary, the Bayeux tapestry—portrays Adam and Eve's cowering shame, the gory slaughter of Abel, a flood-weary Noah. Inside, look for the 4th-century sarcophagus (third chapel on the right) and a magnificent 17th-century chapel (in the apse), recently restored. ⊠ *pl. aux Herbes.*

⑥ The **Musée du Vieux Nîmes** (Museum of Old Nîmes), opposite the cathedral in the 17th-century Bishop's Palace, has embroidered garments in exotic and vibrant displays, including a reconstruction of a dressmaker's workshop. Look for the 14th-century jeans jacket made of blue serge "de Nîmes." There are evocative interiors of 17th-century bourgeois homes, complete with painted-wood paneling and local pottery. Don't miss the gift shop, where you can buy a piece of pottery or fabric copied from period examples. ⊠ *pl. aux Herbes,* ☎ *04–66–36–00–64.* ⌨ *28 frs/€4.27.* ⊙ *Tues.–Sun. 11–6.*

★ ⑦ Lovely and forlorn in the middle of a busy downtown square, the exquisitely preserved **Maison Carrée** (Square House) strikes a timeless balance between symmetry and whimsy, purity of line and richness of decor. Built around 5 BC and dedicated to Caius Caesar and his grandson Lucius, it has survived subsequent use as a medieval meeting hall, an Augustine church, a storehouse for Revolutionary archives, and a horse shed. It was modeled on the Temple to Apollo in Rome, and so inspired Thomas Jefferson that he had its chaste line of columns copied for the Virginia state capitol in Richmond. Alas, its interior now serves as a slapdash display space for temporary exhibitions. ✉ *bd. Victor-Hugo,* ☎ *04–66–36–26–76.* ✉ *Free.* ☉ *May–Oct., daily 9–noon and 2–7; Nov.–Apr., daily 9–7.*

The glass-fronted Carré d'Art (it's directly opposite the Maison Carrée) was designed in 1993 by British architect Sir Norman Foster as its neighbor's stark contemporary mirror. It literally reflects the Maison Carrée's creamy symmetry and figuratively answers it with a featherlight deconstructed colonnade. Homages aside, it looks like an airport

⑧ terminal. It serves as home to a library, archives, and the **Musée d'Art Contemporain** (Contemporary Art Museum). The permanent collection falls into three categories: French painting and sculpture; English, American, and German work; and Mediterranean styles, all dating from 1960 onward. There are often temporary exhibits of new work. ✉ *pl. de la Maison Carrée,* ☎ *04–66–76–35–70.* ✉ *28 frs/€4.27.* ☉ *Tues.– Sun. 10–6.*

⑨ The **Jardin de la Fontaine** (Fountain Garden), an elaborate formal garden, was landscaped on the site of the Roman baths in the 18th century, when the Source de Nemausus, a once-sacred spring, was channeled into pools and a canal. It's a shady haven of mature trees and graceful stonework, and a testimony to the taste of the Age of Reason. It makes for a lovely approach to the Temple of Diana and the Tour Magne. ✉ *Corner of quai de la Fontaine and av. Jean-Jaurès.* ☉ *Mid-Sept.– Mar., daily 7:30 AM–6:30 PM; Apr.–mid-Sept., daily 7:30 AM–10 PM.*

Just northwest of the Jardin de la Fontaine is the shattered Roman ruin

⑩ known as the **Temple de Diane,** which dates from the 2nd century BC. The temple's function is unknown, though it is thought to be part of a larger Roman complex that is still unexcavated. In the Middle Ages Benedictine nuns occupied the building before it was converted into a church. Destruction came during the Wars of Religion.

⑪ At the far end of the Jardin de la Fontaine is the **Tour Magne** (Magne Tower)—the remains of a tower that the emperor Augustus had built on Gallic foundations; it was probably used as a lookout post. Despite having lost 30 ft during the course of time, it still provides fine views of Nîmes for anyone energetic enough to climb the 140 steps. ✉ *quai de la Fontaine,* ☎ *04–66–67–29–11.* ✉ *Tour Magne 15 frs/€2.28, joint ticket with Arènes 34 frs/€5.18.* ☉ *May–Oct., daily 9–7; Nov.–Apr., daily 9–5.*

Dining and Lodging

$$–$$$ ✗ **L'Enclos de la Fontaine.** Nîmes's most fashionable post-corrida gathering spot is in the Impérator hotel (☞ *below*), with warm-weather dining in an idyllic garden court. Chef Jean-Michel Nigon provides such inventive luxuries as lobster salad with citrus vinaigrette, sole rolled with truffles, and Charolais beef sautéed with cèpes. Have an after-dinner drink in the bar Hemingway loved; they named it for him. ✉ *15 rue Gaston-Boissier,* ☎ *04–66–21–90–30. AE, DC, MC, V.*

$$ ✗ **Le Jardin d'Hadrien.** This chic enclave, with its quarried white stone, ancient plank-and-beam ceiling, and open fireplace, would be a culinary haven even without its lovely hidden garden, a shady retreat for summer meals. Generous portions of simple but sophisticated dishes seem like so much gravy when the setting's this nice. Mussel soup with saffron and cream, cod crisped in salt with peppers, or zucchini flowers filled with *brandade* (the creamy, light paste of salt cod and olive oil), and a frozen parfait perfumed with licorice all show Chef Alain Vinouze's subtle skills. ✉ *11 rue Enclos Rey,* ☎ *04–66–21–86– 65. AE, MC, V.*

$ ✕ **Chez Jacotte.** Duck into an old-town back alley and into this cross-
★ vaulted grotto that embodies Nîmes's Spanish-bohemian flair. Candlelight
flickering on rich tones of oxblood, cobalt, and ocher enhance the warm
welcome of red-haired owner Jacotte Friand, who coddles her guests
and artist friends with blackboard specials. Mouth-watering goat-
cheese-and-fig gratin, mullet crisped in olive oil and basil, herb-crusted
lamb, and seasonal fruit crumbles show off chef Christophe Ciantar's
flair with local ingredients. The homemade cakes and pastries are irresistible. ⊠ *15 rue Fresque (Impasse),* ☎ *04–66–21–64–59. MC, V.
Closed Sun.–Mon. No lunch Sat.*

$ ✕ **Nicolas.** You'll hear the noise of this homey place before you open
the door. A friendly, frazzled staff serves up delicious *bourride* (a thick
fish soup) and other local specialties at tightly packed tables, with plastic menus—and at low prices. ⊠ *1 rue Poise,* ☎ *04–66–67–50–47. AE,
DC, MC, V. No lunch Sat. and Mon.*

$ ✕ **Vintage Café.** This popular old-town wine bar draws a loyal crowd
of oenophiles for serious tastings and simple, compatible foods—hot
lentil salad with smoked haddock, beef stewed with capers and pick-
les, and a pressed-goat-cheese terrine. The bar still dominates—all the
better for bellying up to a glass of *côstières de Nîmes*—but the dining
room has expanded to embrace the neighboring building. Bright ceramics and warm lamplight enhance the warm-ocher Mediterranean
decor. Summer nights on the terrace are idyllic. ⊠ *7 rue de Bernis,* ☎
04–66–21–04–45. MC, V. Closed Sun. and Mon. No lunch Sat.

$ ✕ **Le Wine Bar/Chez Michel.** This classic mahogany-and-brass wine bar,
owned and managed by a former sommelier, features good seafood—
including *brandade de morue* (salt-cod paste)—as well as brasserie classics: foie gras salad, fried calamari, simple steaks. You may opt to dine
on the sidewalk terrace, adjacent to the square. Menus start at 80
francs/€12.19. ⊠ *11 square de la Couronne,* ☎ *04–66–76–19–59. AE,
MC, V. Closed Sun., no lunch Mon.*

$$–$$$ ⊞ **Impérator.** Despite its standing as the top hotel in Nîmes, this mem-
ber of the Concorde group has a bourgeois, businessy feel about it, without the luxurious excesses of more glamorous top hotels. Still, the newest
room decors have a pampered, Laura Ashley look, and those overlooking
the lovely garden court need no further frills. ⊠ *15 rue Gaston-Boissier,
30900,* ☎ *04–66–21–90–30,* ℻ *04–66–67–70–25. 60 rooms. Restaurant, bar, air-conditioning. AE, DC, MC, V.* ✍

$$ ⊞ **La Baume.** In the heart of scruffy old Nîmes, this noble 17th-cen-
tury *hôtel particulier* (mansion) has been reincarnated as a chic hotel
with an architect's eye for mixing ancient detail with modern design.
The balustraded stone staircase is a protected historic monument, and
stenciled beam ceilings, cross vaults, and archways counterbalance
hot ocher tones, swagged raw cotton, leather, and halogen lights. The
hip decor dates from 1992 but already shows wear and tear. See if one
of the wood-ceiling rooms (the largest and prettiest) is available instead.
⊠ *21 rue Nationale, 30000,* ☎ *04–66–76–28–42,* ℻ *04-66-76–28–
45. 33 rooms. Breakfast room, air-conditioning. AE, DC, MC, V.* ✍

$$ ⊞ **Clarine Plazza.** Despite a modular '80s look (lacquered wood, geometric prints), the scruffy, familial clutter that marks Nîmes has crept
in to make this chain hotel feel comfortably local; unframed bullfight
posters are taped to the walls, and hats and magazines clutter the lobby
bar. The breakfast is unusually generous, with eggs, cereal, and yogurt.
⊠ *10 rue Roussy, 30000,* ☎ *04–66–76–16–20,* ℻ *04–66–67–65–99.
28 rooms. Breakfast room, air-conditioning. AE, DC, MC, V.* ✍

$$ ⊞ **Royal Hôtel.** Jazz, Art Deco ironwork, and caged birds set the Latin
★ tone at this bohemian, shabby-chic urban hotel. Whitewash and
scrubbed concrete set off 1930s details and trendy flea-market finds.
Bathrooms have newish tiles, and amenities are reasonably up to date.

Its Spanish restaurant serves tapas on the pedestrian place d'Assas, but the lobby bar is where you'd expect to run across Picasso slumming over absinthe. ✉ *3 bd. Alphonse Daudet, 30000,* ☎ *04–66–58–28–27,* FAX *04–66–58–28–27. 27 rooms. Restaurant, bar. AE, MC, V.*

$ ⊞ **Amphithéâtre.** Just behind the arena, this big, solid old private home has fortunately fallen into the hands of a loving owner, who has stripped 18th-century double doors and fitted rooms with restored-wood details and antique bedroom sets. A generous breakfast buffet is served in the dining room. Ask for one of the two rooms overlooking the place du Marché, where you can observe café life from your balcony. ✉ *4 rue des Arènes, 30420,* ☎ *04–66–67–28–51,* FAX *04–66–67–07–79. 17 rooms. Breakfast room. AE, MC, V.*

Outdoor Activities and Sports

☙ The *corrida* (bullfight) is the quintessential Nîmes experience, taking place as it does in the ancient Roman arena, and is worth working into your schedule. There are usually three opportunities a year, always during the carnival-like citywide *férias* (festivals): in early spring (mid-February), at Pentecost (end of May), and during the wine harvest (end of September). These include parades, a running of the bulls, and gentle Camargue-style bullfights (where competitors pluck a ring from the bull's horns). But the focal point is a twice-daily Spanish-style bullfight, complete with *l'estocade* (the final killing) and the traditional cutting of the ear. For tickets and advance information, contact the Arena's **bureau de location** (ticket office; ✉ 1 rue A. Ducros, Nîmes 30900, ☎ 04–66–67–28–02).

☙ **Aquatropic** (✉ 39 rue de la Hostellerie, ☎ 04–66–38–31–00) is a swimming spot with a difference: an indoor and an outdoor pool, wave machines, slides, water cannons, and whirlpools add to the fun for kids and adults. It's open weekdays 10–8 and weekends 11–7 for a cost of 40 francs/€6.10 (10 francs/€1.52 children under 10). Since it's south of the city, it's best to exit the autoroute at Nîmes Ouest.

Shopping

The Monday-morning *marché* (market; ✉ bd. Jean-Jaurès) stretches the length of the boulevard Jean-Jaurès and features bright regional fabrics, linens, pottery, and *brocante* (collectibles). The permanent covered market called **Les Halles** is at the heart of the city and puts on a mouthwatering show of olives, fresh fish, cheeses, and produce. The colorful *marché aux fleurs* (flower market; parking in the Stades des Costières), though far from the center, is worth seeking out by car.

The only authentic commercial maker of brandade, Nîmes's signature salt-cod-and-olive-oil paste, is **Raymond** (✉ 24 rue Nationale, ☎ 04–66–67–20–47). It's paddled fresh into a plastic carton or sold in sealed jars so you can take it home. Brush toast points with olive oil, and spread it on.

In Nîmes's old town, you'll find interior-design **boutiques** and fabric shops selling the Provençal cottons that used to be produced here en masse (Les Indiennes de Nîmes, Les Olivades, Souleiado). **Antiques** and collectibles are found in tiny shops throughout the city's back streets, especially in the old town.

THE CAMARGUE

For 777 square km (300 square mi), the vast alluvial delta of the Rhône River known as the Camargue stretches to the horizon, an austere marshland unrelievedly flat, scoured by the mistral, swarmed over by mosquitoes. Between the endless flow of sediment from the Rhône and the erosive force of the sea, its shape is constantly changing. Even the Provençal poet Frederic Mistral described it in bleak terms: *"Ni arbre, ni ombre, ni âme"* (Neither tree, nor shade, nor a soul).

Yet its harsh landscape harbors a concentration of exotic wildlife unique in Europe, and its isolation has given birth to an ascetic and ancient way of life that transcends national stereotype. It is a strange region, one worth discovering slowly, either on foot or by horseback—especially as its wildest reaches are inaccessible by car.

If people find the Camargue interesting, birds find it irresistible. Its protected marshes lure some 400 species, including more than 160 in migration. Not only will you come across pockets of little egrets, gray herons, spoonbills, bitterns, cormorants, redshanks, and grebes, but also ivory-pink flamingos, which are as common as pigeons on a city square. Their gangly height, dodolike bill, and stilty legs give them a cartoonish air, and their flight style—the long neck slumping downward, legs trailing heavily—seems comic up close. But the sight of a few hundred—or a few thousand—of these broad-winged creatures taking flight in unison is one you won't forget.

All this nature surrounds a few far-flung villages, rich in the region's odd history and all good launching points for forays into the marshlands.

Aigues-Mortes

★ ⑫ *39 km (24 mi) south of Nîmes, 45 km (28 mi) southwest of Arles.*

Like a tiny illumination in a medieval manuscript, Aigues-Mortes (pronounced ay-guh-*mort*-uh) is a precise and perfect miniature fortress-town, contained within perfectly symmetrical castellated walls, with streets laid out in geometric grids. Now awash in a flat wasteland of sand, salt, and monotonous marsh, it once was a major port town from whence no less than St-Louis himself (Louis IX) set sail to conquer Jerusalem in the 13th century. In 1248 some 35,000 zealous men launched 1,500 ships for Cyprus, engaging the infidel on his own turf and suffering swift defeat; Louis himself was briefly taken prisoner. A second launching in 1270 led to more crushing loss, and Louis succumbed to the plague.

Despite his lack of success in the crusades, Louis's **fortress-port** flourished and grew stronger still, its massive stone walls rising double-thick. Completed in 1300, they remain intact and astonishingly well preserved in salt sea winds. Within now lies a small Provençal village milling with tourists, but the visit is more than justified by the impressive scale of the original structure.

If you're driving, park in one of the lots outside the formidable walls and enter by the main **Porte de la Gardette;** the tourist office is left of the entrance. To your right, you'll see the town's stronghold, called the **Tour de Constance.** Its 20-ft-thick walls date from 1241–44, when it was built to protect a larger building lost to history. Enter via the 17th-century **Logis du Gouverneur** (Governor's Lodging), itself a conglomerate of several centuries' construction. The tower still contains a small votive chapel dedicated to St-Louis and an upper hall that served as prison to generations of political outcasts. (One Protestant, the heroic Marie Durand, survived 38 years in the tower without relinquishing her faith; she carved the word *résister*—resist—on her cell wall. Her endurance and courage so impressed the Languedoc governor, he had her released along with a handful of her colleagues.) You can climb all the way to the top of the steepled tower, which once served as a lighthouse lantern. From here you can appreciate the rigorous geometry of the fortifications and imagine medieval fleets surging out to sea. ✉ *Porte de la Gardette,* ☎ *04–66–53–61–55.* 🎫 *32 frs/€4.88.* ☉ *Easter–late May, daily 10–6; late May–mid-Sept., daily 9:30–8; mid-Sept.–Easter, daily 10–5.*

It's not surprising that the town within the rampart walls has become tourist oriented, with the usual plethora of gift shops and postcard stands. But **place St-Louis,** where a 19th-century statue of the father of the fleur-de-lis reigns under shady pollards, has a mellow village feel, and the pretty bare-bones **Église Notre-Dame des Sablons** that corners it has a timeless air (it dates from the 13th century, but the stained glass is ultramodern).

Dining and Lodging

$$$ ✕🍽 **Les Arcades.** Long a success as an upscale seafood restaurant, this
★ beautifully preserved 16th-century house now offers big, airy rooms, some with tall windows overlooking a green courtyard. Pristine white-stone walls, color-stained woodwork, and rubbed-ocher walls frame antiques and lush fabrics, and bathrooms are all new, in white tile. There's even a little courtyard terrace with small pool. Classic cooking features lotte (monkfish) in saffron and poached turbot in hollandaise. ✉ *23 bd. Gambetta, 30220,* ☎ *04–66–53–81–13,* ℻ *04–66–53–75–46. 9 rooms. Restaurant, air-conditioning, pool. AE, DC, MC, V.*

$$ 🍽 **St-Louis.** Within the rampart walls, close to the Tour de Constance and just off place St-Louis, this homey little hotel warms its medieval construction of cool stone with Provençal charm and comfort. Rooms, which are pleasantly decorated if not stylish, look out on the garden below the ramparts or on to the sunny street. In winter dinner is served in the beamed restaurant, and in summer, in the shady garden. ✉ *10 rue Amiral Courbet, 30220,* ☎ *04–66–53–72–68,* ℻ *04–66–53–75–92. 22 rooms. Restaurant. AE, DC, MC, V.*

$$ 🍽 **Les Templiers.** In a 17th-century residence within the ramparts, this delightful hotel sets the stage with stone, stucco, and terra-cotta floors. Furnishings are classically simple and softened with antiques. On the ground floor are two small, cozy sitting areas; breakfast, weather permitting, is served in the small courtyard. ✉ *23 rue de la République, 30220,* ☎ *04–66–53–66–56,* ℻ *04–66–53–69–61. 11 rooms. Air-conditioning. MC, V. Closed Nov.–Feb.*

Festivals

At the end of August, Aigues-Mortes celebrates the **Fêtes du St-Louis** with a town fair, including a medieval pageant and market, strolling musicians, and fire-eaters. In early October, the **Fêtes Votive d'Aigues-Mortes** (town festival) features bull races, parades, and dancing in the main square.

Parc Regional de Camargue

As you drive the scarce roads that barely crisscross the Camargue, you'll usually be within the boundaries of the **Parc Regional de Camargue.** Unlike state and national parks in the United States, this area is privately owned and utilized within rules imposed by the state. The principal owners, the famous *manadiers* (the Camargue equivalent of a small-scale rancher), with the help of their *gardians* (a kind of open-range cowboy), keep it for grazing their wide-horned bulls and their broad-bellied, dappled-white horses. It is thought that these beasts are the descendents of ancient, indigenous wild animals, and though they're positively bovine in their placidity today, they still bear the noble marks of their ancestors. The strong, heavy-tailed Camargue horse has been traced to the Paleolithic period (though some claim the Moors imported an Arab strain) and is prized for its stolid endurance and tough hooves. The curved-horned *taureau* (bull), if not indigenous, may have been imported by Attila the Hun. When it's not participating in a blood-less bullfight (mounted players try to hook a ribbon from the base of its horns), a bull may well end up in the wine-rich regional stew, called *gardianne de taureau.*

Riding through the marshlands in leather pants and wide-rimmed black hats and wielding long prongs to prod their cattle, the gardians themselves are as fascinating as the wildlife. Their homes—tiny white-washed, cane-thatched huts with the north end raked and curved apse-like against the vicious mistral—dot the countryside. The signature wrought-iron crosses at the gable invoke holy protection, and if God isn't watching over this treeless plain, they ground lightning.

The easiest place to view bird life is in a private reserve just outside the regional park called the **Parc Ornithologique du Pont de Gau** (Or-nithological Park of the Pont de Gau). On some 150 acres of marsh and salt lands, birds are welcomed and protected (but in no way confined); injured birds are treated and kept in large pens, to be re-leased if and when able. Boardwalks (including a short, child-friendly inner loop past the easy-viewing invalids) snake over the wetlands, the longest leading to a blind where a half hour of silence, binocu-lars in hand, can reveal unsuspected treasures. ⊠ *Pont-de-Gau, 5 km (3 mi) north of Stes-Maries-de-la-Mer on D570,* ☎ *04–90–97–82–62.* 🎫 *35 frs/€5.33.* ☉ *Oct.–Mar., daily 10–sunset; Apr.–Sept., daily 9–sunset.*

If you're an even more committed nature lover, venture into the inner sanctum of the Camargue, the **Réserve Nationale de Camargue.** This intensely protected area contains the central pond called **Le Vaccarès,** mostly used for approved scientific research. The wildlife—birds, nu-tria, fish—is virtually undisturbed here, but you won't come across the cabins and herds of bulls and horses that most people expect from the Camargue. Pick up maps and information at the **Centre d'Information** (☎ 04–90–97–86–32, 🅵🅰🆇 04–90–97–70–82), open April–September, daily 9–6, October–March, Saturday–Thursday 9:30–5; it is located just up the D570 from the Parc Ornithologique at Pont de Gau. To ex-plore this area, you'll have to strike out on foot, bicycle, or horseback (the **Association Camarguaise de Tourisme Equestre** publishes a list of stables where you can rent horses, available at the centre d'informa-tion or the Stes-Maries tourist office). Note that you are not allowed to diverge from marked trails.

There's another good visitor's center at La Capelière, at the eastern-most point of the Etang du Vaccarès. The **Centre d'Information Na-ture** offers maps as well as exhibits on wildlife. There are three trails radiating from its pond-side position, each leading to small observa-tories. ⊠ *5 km (3 mi) south of Villeneuve/Romieu, off D37,* ☎ *04–90–97–00–97.* ☉ *Mon.–Sat. 9–noon and 2–5.*

Dining

$$ ✕ **Chez Bob.** In a smoky, isolated stone farmhouse chockablock with ★ old posters, you'll taste Camargue cooking at its rustic best. One daily menu features *anchoïade* (whole crudités with hard-cooked egg—still in the shell—and anchovy vinaigrette), homemade duck paté thick with peppercorns, and the pièce de résistance: a thick, sizzling slab of bull steak grilled in the roaring fireplace. Sprinkle on hand-skimmed sea salt and dig in. ⊠ *At Villeneuve/Romieu intersection of D37 and D36 (watch for tiny sign),* ☎ *04–90–97–00–29. No credit cards.* ☉ *Closed Mon.–Tues.*

Outdoor Activities and Sports

To penetrate the isolation of the Camargue beyond the limited access available to cars, rent a VTT (mountain bike) at Stes-Maries-de-la-Mer and follow one of the itineraries in the booklet "Camargue Naturellement." Rentals are available through **Le Vélo Santois** (⊠ 19 av. de la République, ☎ 04–90–97–74–56) or at two outlets of **Le Vélociste** (⊠ pl. des Remparts, ☎ 04–90–97–83–26; ⊠ 7 av. de la République, ☎ 04–90–97–86–44).

The most popular transport, of course, is the Camargue horse, and some 30 places rent them for a *promenade equestre* (horseback tour). The **Association Camarguaise de Tourisme Equestre** publishes a list of names and numbers, available at the **Stes-Maries tourist office** (⊠ 5 av. van Gogh) or by writing to the association (⊠ Centre de Gènes, Pont de Gau, 13460 Stes-Maries-de-la-Mer). It's easy to find a stable; they line the roads throughout the Camargue. Several are concentrated along D570 north of Stes-Maries as well as along the eastern loop D85. An hour's ride averages 70 or 80 frs/€10.67 or €12.20, a whole day 350 frs/€53.36. If you are not a seasoned rider, don't take on too long a trip. The horses, unlike American tourist plodders, require some degree of guidance and skill with the reins, and the saddle is unique, without the Western-style horn for gringos to cling to. An hour's promenade should suffice for beginners who want to get a sense of the backcountry—and be able to walk in the morning. Leave the camera at home—photos will inevitably be jiggly, with a pair of pointy ears framing the shot—but consider bringing mosquito repellent in summer.

Stes-Maries-de-la-Mer

⑬ *31 km (19 mi) southeast of Aigues-Mortes, 40 km (25 mi) southwest of Arles.*

The principal town within the confines of the Parc Régional de Camargue, Stes-Maries is a beach resort with a fascinating history. Provençal legend has it that around 45 AD a band of the very first Christians was rounded up and set adrift at sea in a boat without a sail and without provisions. Their stellar ranks included Mary Magdalene, Martha, and Mary Salome, mother of apostles James and John; Mary Jacoby, sister of the Virgin; and Lazarus, risen from the dead (or another Lazarus, depending on whom you ask). Joining them in their fate: a dark-skinned servant girl named Sarah. Miraculously, their boat washed ashore at this ancient site, and the grateful Marys built a chapel in thanks. Martha moved on to Tarascon (☞ *below*) to tackle dragons, and Lazarus founded the church in Marseille. But Mary Jacoby and Mary Salome remained in their old age, and Sarah stayed with them, begging in the streets to support them in their ministry. The three women died at the same time and were buried together at the site of their chapel.

A cult grew up around this legendary spot, and a church was built around it. When in the 15th century a stone memorial and two female bodies were found under the original chapel, the miracle was for all practical purposes confirmed, and the Romanesque church expanded to receive a new influx of pilgrims.

But the pilgrims attracted to Stes-Maries aren't all lighting candles to the two St. Marys: the servant girl Sarah has been adopted as an honorary saint by the Gypsies of the world, who blacken the crypt's domed ceiling with the soot of their votive candles lighted in her honor.

Two extraordinary festivals take place every year in Stes-Maries, one May 24–25 and the other on the Sunday nearest to October 22. On

May 24 Gypsy pilgrims gather from across Europe and carry the wooden statue of Sarah from her crypt, through the streets of the village, and down to the sea to be washed. The next day they carry a wooden statue of the two St. Marys, kneeling in their wooden boat, to the sea for their own holy bath. The same ritual is repeated by a less colorful crowd of non-Gypsy pilgrims in October, who carry the two Marys back to the sea.

★ On entering the damp, dark, and forbidding fortress-church, **Église des Stes-Maries** (Church of the St. Marys), what is most striking is its novel character. Almost devoid of windows, its tall, barren single nave is cluttered with florid and sentimental ex-votos (tokens of blessings, prayers, and thanks) and primitive and sentimental artworks of the famous trio. On the wall to your left, you'll see the wooden statue of the Marys in their boat; in the crypt below, Sarah glows to the light of dozens of candles.

Another oddity brings you back to this century: a sign on the door forbids visitors to come *torso nu* (topless). For outside its otherworldly role, Stes-Maries is first and foremost a beach resort, dead-flat, whitewashed, and more than a little tacky. (Although Aigues-Mortes's access to the sea has silted in over the centuries, Stes-Maries, once more than 3 mi from the coast, finds itself smack on the waterfront these days. Indeed, the encroaching Mediterranean has to be held off with concrete.) Unless you've made a pilgrimage to the sun and sand, don't spend much time in the town center; if you've chosen Stes-Maries as a base for viewing the Camargue, stay in one of the discreet *mas* (country inns) outside its city limits.

Lodging

$$ ⚏ **Mas de Cacharel.** On 170 acres of private marshland, many of
★ them bordering the Réserve Départementale de Camargue, this low-slung, low-keyed haven greets you with a flutter of egrets as you roll up the drive. Made up of a group of whitewashed buildings, set back from D85 just north of Stes-Maries, this is a simple retreat for nature lovers. It has a lodgelike central dining hall (really just a gathering spot for breakfast, drinks, or cold cuts) complete with Provençal furniture and a pleasantly smoky grand fireplace. Rooms are arranged motor-court style, so most have windows that overlook the eternal stretch of reeds and birds; their furnishings are spartan (electricity was added only in the 1960s), with terra-cotta tiles, jute rugs, and cotton throws. Even the pool is enclosed in glass walls to cut the wind but not the view toward the resident horses. You can arrange for a guided tour on horseback into the marshes, though you might be more content to curl up by the pool with binoculars next to your drink. ✉ *13460 Stes-Maries de la Mer, 4 km (2½ mi) north of town on D85,* ☎ *04–90–97–95–44,* 𝔽𝔸𝕏 *04–90–97–87–97. 15 rooms. Bar, breakfast room, pool, horseback riding. MC, V.* ✆

ARLES

29 km (18 mi) southeast of Nîmes, 40 km (25 mi) northwest of Stes-Maries.

Reigning over the bleak but evocative landscape of the marshlands of the Camargue, the small city of Arles is fiercely Provençal, nurturing its heritage and parading its culture at every colorful opportunity. Warming the wetlands with its atmosphere, animation, and culture, it is a patch of hot color in a sepia landscape—and an excellent home base for sorties into the raw natural beauty and eccentric villages of the Rhône delta.

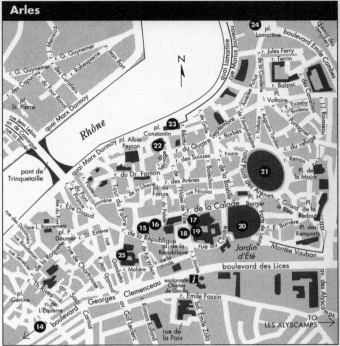

Arles

If you were obliged to choose just one city to visit in Provence, lovely little Arles would give Avignon and Aix a run for their money. It's too chic to become museumlike yet has a wealth of classical antiquities and Romanesque stonework; quarried-stone edifices and shuttered town houses shading graceful old-town streets and squares; and pageantry, festivals, and cutting-edge arts events. Its variety of atmospheric restaurants and picturesque small hotels makes it the ideal headquarters for forays into the Alpilles and the Camargue.

Yet compared to Avignon and Aix, it's a small town. You can zip into the center in five minutes without crossing a half hour's worth of urban sprawl. And its monuments and pretty old neighborhoods are conveniently concentrated between the main artery boulevard des Lices and the broad, lazy Rhône.

It wasn't always such a mellow site. A Greek colony since the 6th century BC, little Arles took a giant step forward when Julius Caesar defeated Marseille in the 1st century BC. The emperor-to-be designated Arles a Roman colony and lavished funds and engineering know-how on it, transforming it into a formidable civilization—by some accounts, the Rome of the north. Fed by aqueducts, canals, and solid roads, it profited from all the Romans' modern conveniences: straight paved streets and sidewalks, sewers and latrines, thermal baths, a forum, a stadium, a theater, and an arena. It became an international crossroads by sea and land and a market to the world, with goods from Africa, Arabia, and the Far East. The emperor Constantine himself moved to Arles and brought with him Christianity.

The remains of this golden age are reason enough to visit Arles today. Yet its character nowadays is as gracious and low-key as it once was cutting edge. Seated in the shade of the plane trees on the place du Forum, sunning at the foot of the obelisk on the place de la République, meditating in the cloister of St-Trophime, or strolling the rampart walkway along the sparkling Rhône, you'll see what enchanted Gauguin and drove van Gogh mad with inspiration. It's the light: intense, vivid, crystalline, setting off planes of color and shadow with prismatic concentration. As a foil to this famous light, multihued Arles—with its red and gold ocher, cool gray stone, and blue-black shade—is unsurpassed.

Note: If you plan to visit many of the monuments and museums in Arles, buy a *visite generale* ticket for 55 francs/€8.38. This covers the 35-franc entry fee to the Musée de l'Arles Antique and any and all of the other museums and monuments (except the independent Museon Arlaten), which normally charge 15 francs/€2.29 each per visit. It's good for the length of your stay.

A Good Walk
The best of Arles is enclosed in the inner maze of streets and alleyways known as the old town, nestled along the Rhône, where you'll find noble 18th-century architecture cheek-by-jowl with antiquities. Only the museum of antiquities lies across the Rhône, easily accessed by shuttle bus.

★ Though it's a hike from the center, a good place to set the tone and context for your exploration of Arles is at the state-of-the-art **Musée de l'Arles Antique** ⑭. From here, take advantage of the free museum shuttle; there's an adjacent parking lot if you're day-tripping by car. Get off at the boulevard Clemenceau and arm yourself with literature at the **tourist information center** just up the road, on boulevard des Lices. Then walk up rue Gambetta, right on rue Molière, and left up rue Rey to the **Espace van Gogh** ㉕, the hospital where van Gogh repaired for his decline into insanity. Continue up rue du President Wilson to the rue de la République and the intensely local **Museon Arlaten** ⑮. Just behind on rue Balze, explore the underground Roman galleries called the **Cryptoportiques** ⑯.

Follow rue Balze to the broad **place de la République** ⑱, where you'll study the extraordinary Romanesque facade of the **Église St-Trophime** ⑰. Next door, enter the hidden oasis of the **Cloître St-Trophime** ⑲. Continue up rue du Cloître to the **Théâtre Antique** ⑳, now in Byronesque ruins. Just above rears the **Arènes** ㉑, site of gladiator battles and modern bullfights.

Now wander down evocative backstreets to the river and the **Thermes Constantin** ㉒, the ruins of Roman baths. On rue du Grand Prieuré, stop into the **Musée Réattu** ㉓, which glorifies native-son painter Jacques Réattu and 20th-century peers. Not van Gogh, alas. Pay homage to that painter by walking up rue du Quatre Septembre and rue Amédée Pichot to **place Lamartine** ㉔, where the star-crossed artist lived in his famous Maison Jaune, destroyed in the second World War.

TIMING
This is an easy day's tour, including time to browse through the Arlaten Museum and trace a few van Gogh landmarks. If there's an event in the Arena, go and experience Arles's modern and Roman history all in one. But don't "do" Arles. Take the time to laze in a café, wander through the Alyscamps, sit on a park bench, and absorb its sweetly winning combination of warm light, cool shade, and Provençal textures.

Sights to See
★ ㉑ **Arènes** (Arena). Rivaled only by the even better-preserved version in Nîmes, this amazingly functional Roman arena dominates old Arles. Its four medieval towers are testimony to its transformation from clas-

sical sports arena to feudal fortification in the Middle Ages—at the sacrifice of a full row of arches and much of the original structure. Younger than Arles's theater, it dates from the 1st century AD and, unlike the theater, seats 20,000 to this day. Its primary function: as a venue for the traditional spectacle of the corridas, or bullfights, which take place annually during the *feria pascale*, or Easter festival. Climb to the top of the tallest medieval tower, by the entry, to see the arena as a whole and take in old Arles. ⊠ *Rond Point des Arènes*, ☎ 04–90–49–36–74. ⌨ *15 frs/€2.29.* ⊗ *Apr.–Sept. daily 9–7; Oct.–Mar. daily 10–4:30.*

★ ⑲ **Cloître St-Trophime** (St-Trophime Cloister). Tucked discreetly behind St-Trophime, this pillared enclosure is a peaceful haven, a Romanesque treasure worthy of the church and one of the loveliest cloisters in Provence. Next to the church portals, enter via broad wooden doors that open onto the place de la République and cross a peaceful courtyard to the entrance. The slender elegance of its pillars contrasts gracefully with the florid decorations of the capitals, each carved with fine detail and a painterly hand. Even drapery and feathers pop into high relief. The clear dichotomy of Gothic and Romanesque styles—curving vaults versus delicate cross vaults—harmonizes beautifully, as does the cloister as a whole: You wouldn't be surprised to come upon Cyrano's Roxanne embroidering quietly in the light dappling through the oleander. ⊠ *Off place de la République*, ☎ 04–90–49–36–74. ⌨ *15 frs/€2.29.* ⊗ *Apr.–Sept., daily 9–7; Oct.–Mar., daily 10–4:30.*

⑯ **Cryptoportiques.** At the entrance to a 17th-century Jesuit college, you can access these ancient and evocative underground galleries. Dating from 30 BC to 20 BC, this horseshoe of vaults and pillars buttressed the ancient forum from underneath. Yet openings let in natural daylight, and artworks of considerable merit and worth were unearthed here, including the extraordinary bust long thought to be a portrait of young Octavius wearing the whiskers of mourning for the murdered Julius Caesar. (Current research, alas, traces it to his grandson Caius.) ⊠ *rue Balze*, ☎ 04–90–49–36–74. ⌨ *15 frs/€2.29.* ⊗ *Apr.–Sept., daily 9–7, Oct.–Mar., daily 10–4:30.*

⑰ **Église St-Trophime** (St-Trophime Church). Classed as a world treasure by UNESCO, this extraordinary Romanesque church alone would justify a visit to Arles, though it's continually upstaged by the antiquities around it. Its transepts date from the 11th century and its nave from the 12th; the church's austere symmetry and ancient artworks (including a stunningly Roman-style 4th-century sarcophagus) are fascinating in themselves. But it is the church's 12th-century **portal**—its ★ entry facade—that earns it international respect. Superbly preserved and restored sculptures with high-relief modeling, complex layers of drapery, and a detail of expression that are nearly classical embellish every inch of the portal's surface. Indeed, it is that classicism that marks it as late Romanesque; Chartres Cathedral, of the same era, had long since ventured into fluid Gothicism. The **tympanum** (the half-moon over the door) tells the story of the Last Judgment, inherently symmetrical, with its separation of the blessed who surge toward Christ and the damned who skulk, naked and in chains, toward hell. Christ is flanked by his chroniclers, the evangelists: the eagle (John), the bull (Luke), the angel (Matthew), and the lion (Mark). ⊠ *pl. de la République.*

㉕ **Espace van Gogh.** For van Gogh pilgrims, the most strikingly resonant site, impeccably restored and landscaped to match one of van Gogh's paintings, is the courtyard garden shown in *Le Jardin de l'Hôtel-Dieu*. Now a complex called the Espace van Gogh, this was the hospital to which the tortured artist repaired after cutting off his ear, and its cloistered grounds have become something of a shrine for visitors. The hospital has been divided up into a municipal library, book shops, and a gift shop—none of them directly related to van Gogh, all of them reasonably discreet (☞ Shopping, *below*). ⊠ *pl. Dr. Félix Rey.*

★ ⓮ **Musée de l'Arles Antique** (Museum of Ancient Arles). This is the place to steep yourself in Arles's spectacular classical history. The building itself is anything but ancient: A bold, modern triangular-shape structure, it was built in 1995 on the site of an enormous Roman *cirque* (chariot-racing stadium). It secrets its prehistoric collections in a womblike interior but bathes displays of the Roman renaissance in wall-to-wall daylight. Natural materials and earth colors provide counterpoint to the high culture on display, and a preconceived viewing plan enhances the narrative flow of history (ask for the English-language guidebook). And there's more here than glass cases full of toga buckles. You'll learn about all the aspects of Arles in its heyday, from the development of its monuments to the details of daily life in Roman times. Perhaps the most instructive and fascinating aspect of this museum is its collection of tiny, precise models: a miniature cirque shows tiny chariots charging around its track, with an unfinished cross section that demonstrates building techniques; the amphitheater, forum, and theater as they were used; and a sophisticated 16-wheel water mill used to grind grain. The quantity of art treasures gives an idea of the extent of Arles's importance. Seven superb floor mosaics can be viewed from an elevated platform, and you exit via a hall packed tight with magnificently detailed paleo-Christian sarcophagi. As you leave you will see the belt of St-Césaire, the last bishop of Arles, who died in 542 AD as the countryside was overwhelmed by the Franks and the Roman era met its end. ⊠ *Presqu'île du Cirque Romain (follow bd. Clemenceau to N113 and cross over),* ☎ *04–90–18–88–88.* ☜ *35 frs/€5.33.* ☉ *Apr.–mid-Oct., daily 9–7; mid-Sept.–Mar., daily 10–5.*

⓴ **Musée Réattu** (Réattu Museum). Arles can't boast a single van Gogh painting—excusable, given that his works sell for $20 million today—but did they have to name their art museum after Jacques Réattu, a local painter of dazzling mediocrity? This very local art museum lavishes three rooms on his turn-of-the-19th-century ephemera but redeems itself with a decent collection of 20th-century works, including paintings by Léger, Vlaminck, and Rousseau, and a gathering of bits and pieces by Picasso, all dating from 1971. The best thing about the Réattu may be the building, a Knights of Malta priory dating from the 15th century, with its fortress-facade overlooking the Rhône. ⊠ *rue Grand Prieuré,* ☎ *04–90–49–36–74.* ☜ *15 frs/€2.29.* ☉ *Apr.–Sept., daily 9–7; Oct.–Mar., daily 10–4:30.*

⓯ **Museon Arlaten** (Museum of Arles). Take the time to comb leisurely through the quirky old collection of local paraphernalia housed in this grand 17th-century town house. Created by the father of the Provençal revival, turn-of-the-century poet Frédéric Mistral (he paid for it with his Nobel Prize winnings), it enshrines a seemingly bottomless collection of regional treasures. There are spindled-oak bread boxes (mounted high on the wall like bird cages); the signature Arlésienne costumes, with their pretty shoulder scarves crossed at the waist; dolls and miniatures; an entire Camargue gardian hut, with reconstructed interior; and dioramas with mannequins—tiny tableaux of Provençal life. Following Mistral's wishes, women in full Arlésienne costume oversee the labyrinth of lovely 16th-century halls. ⊠ *29 rue de la République,* ☎ *04–90–93–58–11.* ☜ *25 frs/€3.81.* ☉ *April–Sept., daily 9:30–12:30 and 2–6; Oct.–Mar., Tues.–Sun. 10–12:30 and 2–5:30.*

⓴ **Place Lamartine.** Between the rail station and the Rhône ramparts, this is the square where van Gogh lived in the famous Maison Jaune (Yellow House). The house was destroyed by bombs in 1944.

⑱ Place de la République. The slender, expressive saints of St-Trophime overlook the wide steps that attract sunners and foot-weary travelers who enjoy the modern perspective over this broad urban square, flanked by the classical symmetry of the 17th-century **Hôtel de Ville**. This noble Italianate landmark is the work of the great 17th-century Parisian architect François Mansart (as in mansard roofs); a passageway allows you to cut through its graceful vestibule from rue Balze. The **obelisk**, of Turkish marble, used to stand in the Gallo-Roman cirque and was hauled here in the 18th century.

⑳ Théâtre Antique (Amphitheater). Between the place de la République and the Arena, you'll come across the picturesque ruins of the amphitheater built by the Romans under Augustus in the 1st century BC. Now overgrown and a pleasant, parklike retreat, it once served as an entertainment venue to some 20,000 spectators. None of its stage walls and only one row of arches remain of its once high-curved back (it was not a natural amphitheater); its fine local stone was borrowed to build early Christian churches. Nonetheless, it serves today as a concert stage for the Festival d'Arles (in July and August) and a venue for the Recontres Internationales de la Photographie (Photography Festival). ✉ *rue du Cloître*, ☎ *04–90–49–36–74.* ⌨ *15 frs/€2.29. Apr.– Sept., daily 9–7; Oct.–Mar., daily 10–4:30.*

㉒ Thermes Constantin (Constantine Baths). Along the riverfront stand the remains of vast and sophisticated Roman baths, luxurious social centers that once included sports facilities and a library—the Barnes & Noble of the 4th century. *pl. Constantin at the corner of rue de l'Hôtel de Ville,* ☎ *04–90–49–36–74.* ⌨ *15 frs/€2.29.* ⏱ *Apr.–Sept., daily 9–7; Oct.–Mar., daily 10–4:30.*

OFF THE BEATEN PATH — Though **Les Alyscamps,** the romantically melancholy Roman cemetery, lie away from the old town, it's worth the hike if you're in a reflective mood. Follow the boulevard des Lices past the Jardin d'Été, the post office, and the *gendarmerie* (police station), then cut right. This long necropolis amassed the remains of the dead from antiquity to the Middle Ages; bodies were shipped up the Rhône to this prestigious resting place. Greek, Roman, and Christian tombs line the long shady road that was once the entry to Arles—the Aurelian Way—and the ruins of chapels and churches are scattered among the sarcophagi. The finest of these stone coffins were offered as gifts in feudal times, and tombstones were mined for building stone. Thus no one work of surpassing beauty remains, but the ensemble has an aura of eternity. ☎ *04–90–49–36–74.* ⌨ *15 frs/€2.29.* ⏱ *Apr.–Sept., daily 9–7; Oct.–Mar., daily 10–4:30.*

Dining and Lodging

$$$ ✕ **Lou Marguès.** Whether you dine indoors, surrounded by glowing woodwork and rich Provençal fabrics, or amid the greenery of this former Carmelite cloister, atmosphere figures large in your evening at this Arles institution, in the Jules César Hotel. Chefs Pascal Renaud and Joseph Kriz mix classical grandeur with Provençal rusticity: scallop and truffle risotto, roast pigeon with turnip confit, salsify with bacon and truffled polenta, and rice pudding with honey and orange. The wine list is as ambitious as Caesar himself. ✉ *Jules César Hotel, bd. des Lices,* ☎ *04–90–52–52–52. Reservations essential. AE, DC, MC, V. Closed mid-Nov.–Dec.*

$$ ✕ **Brasserie Nord-Pinus.** With its tile-and-ironwork interior straight
★ out of a design magazine and its place du Forum terrace packed with all the right people, this cozy-chic retro brasserie features light, simple, and purely Provençal cooking. And wasn't that Christian Lacroix

VAN GOGH IN ARLES AND ST-RÉMY "...WHAT A LOVELY COUNTRY, AND WHAT LOVELY BLUE AND WHAT A SUN!"

I T WAS THE LIGHT THAT DREW VINCENT van Gogh to Arles. For a man raised under the iron-gray skies of the Netherlands and the gaslight pall of Paris, Provence's clean, clear sun was a revelation. In his last years he turned his frenzied efforts to capture the resonance of ". . . golden tones of every hue: green gold, yellow gold, pink gold, bronze or copper colored gold, and even from the yellow of lemons to the matte, lusterless yellow of threshed grain."

Arles, however, was not drawn to van Gogh. Though it makes every effort today to make up for its misjudgment, Arles treated the artist very badly during the time he passed here near the end of his life—a time when his creativity, productivity, and madness all reached a climax. It was 1888 when he settled in to work in Arles with an intensity and tempestuousness that first drew, then drove away his companion Paul Gauguin, with whom he had dreamed of founding an artists' colony. Frenziedly productive—he applied a pigment-loaded palette knife to some 200 canvases in that year alone— he nonetheless lived within intense isolation, counting his sous, and writing his visions in lengthy letters to his long-suffering, infinitely patient brother Theo. Often heavy-drinking, occasionally whoring, Vincent alienated his neighbors, driving them to distraction and ultimately goading them to action.

In 1889 the people of Arles circulated a petition to have him evicted, a shock that left him more and more at a loss to cope with life and led to his eventual self-commitment to an asylum in nearby St-Rémy. The houses he lived in are no longer standing, though many of his subjects remain as he saw them (or are restored to a similar condition). The paintings he daubed and splashed with such passion have been auctioned elsewhere.

Thus you have to go to Amsterdam or Moscow to view van Gogh's work. But with a little imagination, you can glean something of van Gogh's Arles from a tour of the modern town. In fact, the city has provided helpful markers and a numbered itinerary to guide you between landmarks. You can stand on the place Lamartine, where his famous Maison Jaune stood until it was destroyed by World War II bombs. *Starry Night* may have been painted from the quai du Rhône just off place Lamartine, though another was completed at St-Rémy. The Café La Nuit on place Forum is an exact match for the terrace platform, scattered with tables and bathed in gaslight under the stars, from the painting *Terrace de café le Soir*; Gauguin and van Gogh used to drink here. (Current owners have determinedly maintained the fauve color scheme to keep the atmosphere.) Both the Arènes and Les Alyscamps were featured in paintings, and the hospital where he broke down and cut off his ear is now a kind of shrine, its garden reconstructed exactly as it figured in *Le Jardin de l'Hôtel-Dieu*. The drawbridge in *Le pont de Langlois aux Lavandières* has been reconstructed outside of town, at Port-de-Bouc, 3 km (2 mi) south on D35.

About 25 km (15½ mi) away is St-Rémy-de-Provence, where van Gogh retreated to the asylum St-Paul-de-Mausolée. Here he spent hours in silence, painting the cloisters. On his ventures into town, he painted the dappled lime trees at the intersection of boulevard Mirabeau and boulevard Gambetta.

And on route between the towns and, in fact, in traveling anywhere nearby, you'll see the orchards whose spring blooms ignite joyous explosions of yellow and cream, olive groves twisting like dancers in silver and green, ocher houses and red roofs, star-spangled crystalline skies—the stuff of inspiration.

(or Kate Moss or Juliette Binoche. . .) under those Ray-Bans? ✉ *pl.
du Forum,* ☎ *04–90–93–44–44. Reservations essential. AE, DC, MC,
V. Closed Feb. and Wed. Nov.–Mar.*

$$ ✕ **La Gueule du Loup.** Serving as hosts, waiters, and chefs, the ambi-
tious couple who own this restaurant tackle serious cooking—monk-
fish and squid in saffron, lamb in pastry lined with *tapenade*
(olive-and-caper spread), and crème brûlée perfumed with orange blos-
soms—and maintain a supercool ambience. Jazz music and vintage magic
posters bring the old Arles stone-and-beam setting up to date. ✉ *39
rue des Arènes,* ☎ *04–90–96–96–69. MC, V. Closed Sun. and Mon.
Oct.–Mar.; Apr.–Sept. closed Sun., no lunch Mon.*

$ ✕ **L'Affenage.** A vast smorgasbord of Provençal hors d'oeuvres draws
★ loyal locals to this former fire-horse shed. They come here for heap-
ing plates of fried eggplant, green tapenade, chickpeas in cumin, and
a slab of ham carved off the bone—followed by roasted potatoes and
lamb chops grilled in the great stone fireplace. In summer you can opt
for just the first-course buffet and go back for thirds; reserve a terrace
table out front. ✉ *4 rue Molière,* ☎ *04–90–96–07–67. AE, MC, V.
Closed Sun. and 3 wks in Aug.*

$ ✕ **Lou Caleu.** In a charming 16th-century building behind the Arena,
this popular, unpretentious place serves regional specialties—homemade
salt-cod brandade in profiteroles, *pintade* (guinea fowl) with a tang of
tapenade, and tough but authentic bull steak—at good prices. The lunch
deals are terrific, and you can gaze at the arena's arches if you dine on
the terrace. ✉ *27 rue Porte de Laure,* ☎ *04–90–49–71–77. AE, DC,
MC, V. Closed Thurs. Oct.–Easter.*

$ ✕ **Vitamine.** If you're unaccustomed to French-scale eating (even the
lighter southern cuisine), you'll be relieved to find this pretty, Provençal-
looking eatery that puts all its energy into fresh, crisp full-meal salads—
50 varieties for under 50 francs/€7.62 each. There are 15 pasta options,
too, and a friendly, laid-back staff. ✉ *16 rue du Docteur Fanton,* ☎
04–90–93–77–36. MC, V. Closed Sun. No dinner Sat. Sept.–June.

$$$$ ✕⊡ **Le Mas de Peint.** This may be the ultimate mas experience, set as
★ it is in a 17th-century farmhouse on some 500 hectares (1,250 acres)
of Camargue ranch land. Luxurious Provençal fabrics and antiques grace
the old stone floors, and burnished beams warm the firelit salon and
library. Rooms are lavished with brass beds, monogrammed linens, even
canopied bathtubs. At dinner time, guests gather in the kitchen to chat
with the cook and settle in for sophisticated specialties using home-
grown products (ratatouille and lamb dishes as well as Camargue rice
and bull). Diners not staying in the hotel are welcomed into the kitchen,
too, just for lunch or dinner; the restaurant ($$) is closed Wednesday
and advance reservations are required. In summer (mid-June–mid-
September) a light lunch is served by the pool. You're only 20 km (12
mi) south of Arles here, but you should plan on a relaxing immersion
in the country rather than a heavy sightseeing itinerary, as other towns
are well out of the way. But who would want to leave when you can
ride the private grounds on Camargue horses, or take a tour in a four-
wheel drive? ✉ *Le Sambuc, 13200 Arles,* ☎ *04–90–97–20–62,* FAX *04–
90–97–22–20. 8 rooms, 3 suites. Restaurant, air-conditioning, pool,
horseback riding. AE, DC, MC, V. Closed mid-Nov.–mid-Dec. and mid-
Jan.–mid-Mar.* 🕭

$$$$ ⊡ **Jules César.** This elegant landmark, once a Carmelite convent but
styled like a Roman palace, anchors the lively boulevard des Lices. Low-
slung, with rooms on the small side, it's not a grand luxury palace; rather,
it's an intimate, traditional hotel, conservatively decorated with richly
printed fabrics and burnished woodwork. Rooms are pure Souleiado,
from the flower-sprigged wallpaper to the bathroom tiles; the antiques
are classic, curvy Provençal. Some windows look over the pool and some

over the pretty cloister, where breakfast is served under a vaulted stone arcade. ⊠ *bd. des Lices, 13200,* ☎ *04–90–52–52–52,* FAX *04–90–52–52–53. 49 rooms, 5 suites. Restaurant, air-conditioning, pool. AE, DC, MC, V. Closed mid-Nov.–late Dec.* ✎

$$$$ 🏨 **Nord-Pinus.** J. Peterman would feel right at home in this quintessen-
★ tially Mediterranean hotel on the place du Forum; Hemingway and Picasso did. Travel relics, kilims, oil jars, angular wrought iron, and colorful
ceramics create a richly atmospheric stage-set for literati (or literary
poseurs), decor-magazine shoots, and people who refer to themselves
as "travelers." Its scruffy insider-chic is not for everyone; traditional-
ists should head for the mainstream luxuries of the Jules César. But
this is where you might brush past a *Vogue* editor on the way to breakfast, and the brasserie is the *dernier cri* (last word) in shoulder-rub-
bing (☞ *above*). ⊠ *pl. du Forum, 13200,* ☎ *04–90–93–44–44,* FAX *04–90–93–34–00. 24 rooms. Brasserie, bar. AE, DC, MC, V.* ✎

$$$ 🏨 **Arlatan.** Once home to the counts of Arlatan, this noble 15th-cen-
★ tury stone house stands on the site of a 4th-century basilica, and a glass
floor reveals the excavated vestiges under the lobby. Digging an exca-
vation in your lobby is just another aristocratic pastime for the friendly
owners of this jewel of a hotel, with rows of rooms that horseshoe around
a lovely fountain courtyard. Rooms are decorated with a chic, light
hand, with quarry tiles and Pierre Frey fabrics; seven modern rooms
were added in 1999, and a swimming pool is in the works. The inti-
mate lobby bar is a cool, quiet haven. Breakfast is served in pretty new
court-side salons. ⊠ *26 rue du Sauvage, 13200,* ☎ *04–90–93–56–66,* FAX *04–90–49–68–45. 39 rooms, 7 suites. AE, DC, MC, V.*

$–$$ 🏨 **Le Calendal.** The cheery Provençal colors of this small hotel next to
the Arènes reflect the spirit of the hotel and its staff, most of whom speak
English. Rooms overlook the amphitheater or the idyllic courtyard gar-
den; some sleep four. Light meals are served in the cozy tearoom. ⊠ *22 pl. du Docteur Pomme, 13200,* ☎ *04–90–96–11–89,* FAX *04–90–96–05–84. 27 rooms. Restaurant, air-conditioning. AE, MC, V.*

$ 🏨 **Le Cloître.** Built as the private home for the head of the Cloisters,
★ this grand old medieval building has luckily fallen into the hands of a
friendly, multilingual couple devoted to making the most of its historic
details—with their own bare hands. They've chipped away plaster
from pristine quarried stone walls, cleaned massive beams, restored tile
stairs, and mixed natural chalk and ocher to plaster the walls, which
are prettily decorated with stencils. Bargain hunters should opt for the
sweet little top-floor rooms, with bath but sans WC, with views over
the ancient rooftops. ⊠ *16 rue du Cloître, 13200,* ☎ *04–90–96–29–50,* FAX *04–90–96–02–88. 30 rooms. AE, MC, V.*

$ 🏨 **Hôtel Gauguin.** Of several concrete budget hotels that sprang up in
this section of the old town after World War II erased its original
structures, this is the nicest. The rooms, well scrubbed and decked in
pretty olive prints and sponge-paint, are small, but so is the price; those
with full bathrooms are a little more. Ask for a room in front; they
look onto the square. The welcoming owner, Madame Dugand, is
happy to try her English. ⊠ *5 pl. Voltaire, 13200,* ☎ *04–90–96–14–35,* FAX *04–90–18–98–87. 18 rooms, 12 with bath. MC, V.*

$ 🏨 **Muette.** With 12th-century exposed stone walls, a 15th-century spi-
★ ral stair, weathered wood, and an old-town setting, a hotelier would-
n't have to try very hard to please. But the couple who own this place
do. Hand-stripped doors, antiques, fresh white-and-blue–tiled baths,
hair dryers, good mattresses, Provençal prints, and fresh sunflowers
in every room show that Alain and Brigitte Deplancke care. ⊠ *15 rue des Suisses, 13200,* ☎ *04–90–96–15–39,* FAX *04–90–49–73–16. 18 rooms. AE, MC, V.* ✎

$ ⊡ **Le Rhône.** Simple and plain, with fresh pastel paint and a few balconies overlooking the place Voltaire, this small hotel's main attraction is its value for money. The most expensive doubles are 210 francs/€32.01, and those without bathrooms (sink and bidet only) cost 130 francs/€19.82. The young, friendly owners offer a warm welcome. ⊠ *11 pl. Voltaire,* ☎ *04–90–96–43–70,* FAX *04–90–93–87–03. 12 rooms, 5 with bath. AE, DC, MC, V.*

Festivals

Arles is a true festival town, offering a stimulating mix of folklorique and contemporary arts events. The **férias,** with traditional corridas, or bullfights, vie with the **Fêtes du Riz** (with corrida) in September and the **Fêtes d'Arles** from the end of June to the beginning of July. All feature traditional games and races in the Arena, parades, folk-dance events, and—their raison d'être—the beautiful traditional costumes of Arles.

In July, the famous **Rencontres Internationales de la Photographie** (Photography Festival) brings movers and shakers in international photography into the théâtre antique for five days of highly specialized colloquiums and homages. Ordinary folks can profit, too, by attending the photography exhibits displayed in some 17 venues in Arles, open to the public throughout July and August. If you're under age 25 with an I.D., you can get in free. For information, call ☎ 04–90–96–76–06 or write to ⊠ 10 rond-point des Arènes, BP 96, 13632 Arles Cedex.

Nightlife and the Arts

To find out what's happening in and around Arles (even as far away as Nîmes and Avignon), the free weekly **Le César** lists films, plays, cabaret, jazz, and rock events. It's distributed at the tourist office, in bars, clubs, and cinemas. Or consult its Web-site agenda at www.cesar.fr.

Though Arles seems to be one big sidewalk café in warm weather, the place to drink is the hip bar **Le Cintra,** in the also-hip hotel Nord-Pinus (☞ *above*); it's decorated with bullfight paraphernalia. In high season, the cafés stay lively till the wee hours; in winter, the streets empty out by 11. **Le Cargo de Nuit** (⊠ 7 av. Sadi-Carnot, ☎ 04–90–49–55–99) is the main venue for live jazz, reggae, and rock, with a dance floor next to the stage. There are three concerts per week (Thursday, Friday, and Saturday), and the restaurant serves food until 2 AM.

Shopping

Despite being chic and popular, Arles hasn't sprouted the rows of designer shops found in Aix-en-Provence and St-Rémy. Its stores remain small and eccentric and feature an overwhelming variety of Provençal goods. Regional fabric is available at every turn (☞ Close-Up Box: Those Ubiquitous Provençal Cottons, *below*), including boutiques for the principal makers (and rivals) **Les Olivades** (⊠ 2 rue Jean Jaurès) and **Souleiado** (⊠ 18 bd. des Lices).

Though the charming terra-cotta folk miniatures called *santons* originate from around Marseille, the **Maison Chave** (⊠ 14 Rond Point des Arènes), across from the Arena, is a good place to find them. There's always someone painting impossibly tiny fingernails or Barbie-scale kerchiefs, and you're welcome to watch without buying.

Arles's colorful **markets,** with produce, regional products, clothes, fabrics, wallets, frying pans, and other miscellaneous items, take place every Saturday morning along the boulevard des Lices, which flows into the boulevard Clemenceau. On the first Wednesday of the month there's a **brocante market** where you can find antiques and collectibles, many of them regional.

THOSE UBIQUITOUS PROVENÇAL COTTONS

VIVID MEDALLION PRINTS, SOFT floral sprigs, assertive paisley borders—they've come to define the Provençal Experience, these bright-patterned fabrics, with their sunny colors, naive prints, and country themes redolent of sunflowers and olive groves. And the southern tourist industry is eager to fulfill that expectation, swagging hotel rooms and restaurant dining rooms with gay Provençal patterns in counterpoint to the cool yellow stucco and burnished terra-cotta tiles. Nowadays, both in Provence and on the coast, it's all about country—back to the land with a vengeance.

These ubiquitous cottons are actually Indian prints *(indiennes)*, first shipped into the ports of Marseille from exotic trade routes in the 16th century. Ancient Chinese lost-wax techniques—indigo dyes taking hold where the wax wasn't applied—evolved into wood-block stamps, their surfaces painted with mixed colors, then pressed carefully onto bare cotton. The colors were richer, the patterns more varied than any fabrics then available—and, what's more, they were easily reproduced.

They caught on like a wildfire in a mistral, and soon mills in Provence were creating local versions en masse. Too well, it seems. By the end of the 17th century, the popular cottons were competing with royal textile manufacturers. In 1686, under Louis XIV, the manufacture and marketing of Provençal cottons was banned.

All the ban did was contain the industry to Provence, where it developed in Marseille (franchised for local production despite the ban) and in Avignon, where the Papal possessions were above royal law. Their rarity and their prohibition made them all the sexier, and fashionable Parisians—even insiders in the Versaille court—flaunted the coveted contraband.

By 1734, Louis XV cracked down on the hypocrisy, and the ban was sustained across France. The people protested. The cottons were affordable, practical, and brought a glimmer of color into the commoner's daily life. The king relented in 1758, and the peasants were free to swath their windows, tables, and hips with a limitless variety of color and print.

But because of the 72-year ban and that brief burgeoning of the southern countermarket, the tight-printed style and vivid colors remained allied in the public consciousness with the name "Provençal," and the region has embraced them as its own. If once they trimmed the windows of basic stone farmhouses and lined the quilted petticoats of peasants to keep off the chill, nowadays the fabrics drape the beveled-glass French doors of the finest *hôtel particuliers* (private mansions) and grandest Riviera hotels.

Two franchises dominate the market and maintain high-visibility boutiques in all the best southern towns: Souleiado and Les Olivades. Fierce rivals, each claims exclusive authenticity—regional production, original techniques. Yet every tourist thoroughfare presents a hallucinatory array of goods, sewn into every salable form from lavender sachets to place mats to swirling skirts and bolero jackets. There are bread bags and bun warmers, undershorts and toilet kits, even olive-sprigged toilet-paper holders.

But this folklorique fabric hasn't disintegrated into tourist kitsch yet. If you're lucky enough to witness a village festival, the townspeople proudly unpack their thick quilted skirts, vivid paisley shawls, and jaunty kerchiefs. And at the *corrida* (bullfights), even the most sophisticated Arlesiennes parade their regional finery, proud to confirm the tradition of the rare beauty of Arles' women.

Abbaye de Montmajour

★ *6 km (4 mi) north of Arles, direction Fontvieille.*

An extraordinary structure looming over the marshlands north of Arles, this magnificent Romanesque abbey stands in partial ruin, with shrieking rooks ducking in and out of its empty stone-framed windows. Begun in the 12th-century by a handful of Benedictine monks, it grew according to an ambitious plan of church, crypt, and cloister; under corrupt lay monks in the 17th century, it grew more sumptuous; when those lay monks were ejected by the church, they sacked the place. When, after the Revolution, it was sold to a junkman, he tried to pay the mortgage by stripping off and selling its goods. A 19th-century medieval revival spurred its partial restoration, but its 18th-century portions remain in ruins.

Ironically, because of this mercenary history, what remains is a spare and beautiful piece of Romanesque architecture, bare of furniture and art—an abstraction of massive stone arches, vaults and flowing curves that seem to be poured and molded instead of quarried and fitted in chunks. And its **cloister** rivals that of St-Trophime in Arles for its balance, elegance, and air of mystical peace: van Gogh was drawn to its womblike isolation, and came often to the abbey to paint and reflect. ⊠ *On D17 northeast of Arles, direction Fontvieille,* ☎ *04–90–54–64–17.* ▨ *35 frs/€5.33.* ☺ *Apr.–Sept., daily 9–7; Oct.–Mar., Wed.–Mon. 10–1 and 2–5.*

Tarascon

❷❻ *18 km (11 mi) north of Arles, 16 km (10 mi) west of St-Rémy.*

Tarascon's claim to fame is as home to the mythical Tarasque, a monster that would emerge from the Rhône to gobble up children and cattle. Luckily, Saint Martha (Ste-Marthe), who washed up at Stes-Maries-de-la-Mer, tamed the beast with a sprinkle of holy water, after which the inhabitants slashed it to pieces. This dramatic event is celebrated on the last weekend in June with a parade and immortalized by Alphonse Daudet, who lived in nearby Fontvieille, in his tales of a folk hero known to all French schoolchildren as *Tartarin de Tarascon.* Unfortunately, a saint has not yet been born who can vanquish the fumes that emanate from Tarascon's enormous paper mill, and the hotel industry is suffering for it.

★ Despite the town's modern-day drawbacks, with the walls of its formidable **Château** plunging straight into the roaring Rhône, this ancient city on the river presents a daunting challenge to Beaucaire, its traditional enemy across the water. Begun in the 13th century by the noble Anjou family on the site of a Roman *castellum,* the castle grew through the generations into a splendid structure, crowned with both round and square towers and elegantly furnished. René the Good (1409–80) held court here, entertaining luminaries of the age. Nowadays the castle owes its superb preservation to its use, through the ensuing centuries, as a prison. It first served as such in the 17th century, and released its last prisoner in 1926. Complete with a moat, a drawbridge, and a lovely faceted spiral staircase, it retains its beautiful decorative stonework and original window frames. ⊠ *D970 at the riverfront, direction Beaucaire.* ☎ *04–90–91–01–93.* ▨ *32 frs/€4.88.* ☺ *Apr.–Sept., daily 9–7; Oct.–Mar., Wed.–Mon. 9–noon and 2–5.*

Beaucaire

❷❼ *19 km (12 mi) north of Arles, 2 km (1 mi) northwest of Tarascon.*

Though Beaucaire's castle glowering across the Rhône at its ancient enemy Tarascon doesn't hold a candle to its neighbor, this riverside town has an ambience all its own. Virtually unvisited by tourists, its labyrinthine old town retains an ancient, empty air—with superb old buildings. The town's **Hôtel de Ville** (Town Hall; ⊠ pl. Clemenceau) is by 17th-century architect François Mansard. The fabulous **Hôtel de Margailler** (⊠ 23 rue de la République) dating from 1675 is graced with a porch supported by caryatids. Pick up a "Guide du Patrimoine" at the **tourist office** (⊠ quai Général de Gaulle) and wander at will.

Beaucaire's **Château** was built on the site of a Roman camp in the 11th century but was remodeled 200 years later and then dismantled in the 17th century on the orders of Cardinal Richelieu. What is left are the ramparts, two towers, the restored Romanesque chapel, and the barbican that defended the castle's entrance. You can visit the remains freely and wander in the peaceful garden, stopping in briefly to tour the **Musée Auguste Jacquet,** a collection of archeological finds from the castle and environs. For another way to experience the château, you might attend the spectacle called Les Aigles de Beaucaire—when birds of prey are handled by falconers in medieval costume. ⊠ *pl. du Château,* ☎ 04–66–59–47–61. ☼ *Museum and château grounds: Wed.–Mon. 10–noon and 2–6 (late Mar.– early Nov., Thurs.–Tues.), with bird shows at 2, 3, 4, 5 (July–Aug. 3, 4, 5, 6).* ☜ *Château free; museum 13 frs/€1.98; bird show 45 frs/€6.86.*

Lodging

$$ 🏠 **Domaine des Clos.** In this roomy 18th-century farmhouse in the windswept countryside southwest of Beaucaire, Sandrine and David Ausset offer a warm welcome to families. Guests share a communal breakfast and have access as well to the kitchen and barbecue. (Reserve a table-d'hôte meal well in advance.) Rooms have brass beds and homemade white linens, and bathrooms are fresh. ⊠ *On D38, 6 km southwest of Beaucaire, route de Bellegarde, 30300,* ☎ *04–66–01–14–61,* ℻ *04–66– 01–00–47. 5 rooms, 4 apartments. Breakfast room. AE, DC, MC, V.* ✍

Shopping
Beaucaire's picturesque **markets** hold forth Thursday and Sunday mornings in front of the Hôtel de Ville (produce) and along the Canal du Rhône à Sète (dry goods), with boats bobbing alongside the fabric stands.

THE ALPILLES

Whether approaching from the damp lowlands of Arles and the Camargue or the pebbled vineyards around Avignon, the countryside changes dramatically as you climb into the arid heights of the low mountain range called the Alpilles (pronounced ahl-*pee*-yuh). A rough-hewn, rocky landscape rises into nearly barren limestone hills, the fields silvered with ranks of twisted olive trees and alleys of gnarled *amandiers* (almond trees). It's the heart of Provence and is appealing not only for the antiquities in St-Rémy and the feudal ruins in Les Baux, but also for its mellow pace when the day's touring is done. Here, as much as anywhere in the south, is the place to slip into espadrilles, nibble from a bowl of olives, and attempt nothing more taxing than a lazy game of *pétanque* (lawn bowling). Hence, the countryside around St-Rémy is peppered with gentrified gîtes and mas, and is one of the most sought-after sites for Parisiens' (and Londoners') summer homes.

Fontvieille

28 *19 km (12 mi) northeast of Arles, 20 km (12½ mi) southeast of Tarascon.*

The village of Fontvieille (pronounced fohn-*vyay*-uh), among the lime-stone hills, is best known as the home of 19th-century writer Alphonse Daudet. Summering in the Château de Montauban, Daudet frequently climbed the windswept, pine-studded hilltop to the rustic old wind-mill that ground the local grain from 1814 to 1915. There the sweep-ing views of the Rhône valley and the Alpilles inspired his famous, folkloric short stories called *Lettres de Mon Moulin*. Today you can visit the well-preserved **Moulin de Daudet** (Daudet's Windmill), where there's a small museum devoted to his writings; you can walk upstairs to see the original milling system. ☎ *04–90–54–60–78.* 🎫 *10 frs/€1.52.* ⊙ *Apr.–Sept., daily 9–7; Oct.–Mar., daily 10–noon and 2–5.*

Dining and Lodging

$$$–$$$$ 🏨 **La Regalido.** In an old olive-oil mill covered with vines, this mod-est Relais & Châteaux property overlooks a stone-terraced garden full of flowering plants, despite its position in the village center. Its status as a landmark luxury inn sustains it despite a somewhat stuffy, faded decor. The best room is the top-floor suite with beams and its own ter-race with rooftop views. The restaurant continues to get mixed reviews for its concentration on the raw, new olive oil of the region, featured to the point of saturation; there's even a summer menu devoted to it. ⊠ *rue F. Mistral, 13990,* ☎ *04–90–54–60–22,* 𝔽𝔸𝕏 *04–90–54–64–29. 13 rooms, 2 suites. Restaurant. AE, DC, MC, V. Closed Jan.–mid-Feb.*

Les Baux-de-Provence

★ ㉙ *9 km (5½ mi) east of Fontvieille, 19 km (12 mi) northeast of Arles.*

When you first search the craggy hilltops for signs of Les Baux-de-Provence (pronounced boh), you may not quite be able to distinguish between bedrock and building, so naturally do the ragged skyline of tow-ers and crenellation blend into the sawtooth jags of stone. As dramatic in its perched isolation as Mont-St-Michel and St-Paul-de-Vence, this tiny château-village ranks as one of the most visited tourist sites in France. Its car-free main street (almost its *only* street) is thus jammed with shops and galleries and, by day, overwhelmed with the smell of scented sou-venirs. But don't deprive yourself for fear of crowds. Stay late in the day, after the tour buses leave; spend the night in one of its modest hotels; or come off-season, and you'll experience its spectacular character—a tour-de-force blend of medieval ambience and astonishing natural beauty.

From this intimidating vantage point, the lords of Baux ruled through-out the 11th and 12th centuries over one of the largest fiefdoms in the south, commanding some 80 towns and villages. Mistral called them "a race of eagles, never vassals," and their virtually unchallenged power led to the flourishing of a rich medieval culture: courtly love, troubadour songs, and knightly gallantry. By the 13th century the lords of Baux had fallen from power, their stronghold destroyed. Though Les Baux expe-rienced a brief renaissance and reconstruction in the 16th century, the final indignity followed hard upon that. Richelieu decided to eliminate the threatening eagle's nest once and for all and had the castle and walls demolished in 1632. Its citizens themselves were required to pay the cost.

Only in the 19th century did Les Baux find new purpose. The mineral bauxite, valued as an alloy in aluminum production, was discovered in its hills and named for its source. A profitable industry sprang up that lasted into the 20th century before fading into history, like the lords of Baux themselves.

Today Les Baux offers two faces to the world: its beautifully preserved medieval village and the ghostly ruins of its fortress, once referred to as the *ville morte* (dead town). In the village, lovely 12th-century stone houses, even their window frames still intact, shelter the shops, cafés, and galleries that line the steep cobbled streets.

Vestiges of the Renaissance remain in Les Baux, including the pretty **Hôtel de Manville,** built at the end of the 16th century by a wealthy Protestant family. Step into its inner court to admire the mullioned (stone-framed) windows, Renaissance-style stained glass, and vaulted arcades. Today it serves as the *mairie* (town hall). Up and across the street, the striking remains of the 16th-century Protestant temple still bear a quote from Jean Calvin: POST TENEBRAS LUX, or "after the shadows, light."

In the Hôtel des Porcelet, which dates from the 16th century, the **Musée Yves-Brayer** (Yves-Brayer Museum) shelters this local 20th-century artist's works. Figurative and accessible to the point of naivete, his paintings feature Italy, Spain, even Asia, but demonstrate most of all his love of Provence. Brayer's grave lies in the château cemetery. ⊠ *pl. Hervain,* ☎ *04-90-54-36-99.* ⊠ *25 frs/€3.81.* ☉ *Apr.–Sept., daily 10–12:30 and 2–6:30; Oct.–Mar., Wed.–Mon. 10–12:30 and 2–5:30.*

The main site to visit in town is the 17-acre cliff-top sprawl of ruins contained under the umbrella name **Château des Baux.** Climb the rue Neuve and continue up rue Trancat to the Tour du Brau, which contains the **Musée d'Histoire des Baux.** Entry to this small collection of relics and models gives access to the wide and varied grounds, where Romanesque chapels and towers mingle with skeletal ruins. A numbered program (available in English) guides you from site to site—the 16th-century hospital, the windmill, the 13th-century donjon—many of which are recognizable only by their names. Kids are especially fascinated by reconstructions of gigantic medieval siege machines. But be sure to stop into the cemetery; a more dramatic resting place would be hard to find. And the tiny **Chapelle St-Blaise** shelters a permanent music-and-slide show, *Van Gogh, Gauguin, Cézanne au Pays de l'Olivier,* of artworks depicting olive orchards in their infinite variety. You can see painterly views over patchwork olive orchards, as well as vineyards, almond orchards, and low-slung farmhouses, from every angle of the château cliff top—reason enough alone to pay entry. ☎ *04-90-54-55-56.* ⊠ *36 frs/€5.49.* ☉ *Mar.–June and Sept.–Oct., daily 9–7:30; July–Aug., daily 9–8:30; Nov. and Feb., daily 9–6; Dec.–Jan., daily 9–5.*

About half a mile north of Les Baux, off D27, you'll find the unusual **Cathédrale d'Images** (Cathedral of Images), in the majestic setting of the old limestone quarries. Towering rock faces and stone pillars are transformed into a series of colossal screens for evocative slide shows, complete with music and occasional voiceover. You walk through the series of towering halls, following a 30-minute spectacle. Bring a sweater. ⊠ *route de Maillane,* ☎ *04-90-54-38-65.* ⊠ *43 frs/€6.56.* ☉ *Mid-Mar.–mid-Nov., daily 10–7; winter, daily 10–6.*

Dining and Lodging

$ ✕ **Café Cinarca.** The tiny dining room is nice enough, but the garden courtyard of this small, unpretentious restaurant is a shady haven from the steady flow of tourists climbing the hill. A limited blackboard menu features a simple fixed-price meal, including *tartes* and salads embellishing one or two hearty meat dishes: beef *daube* (stew), or *caillette aux herbes* (pork meat loaf) served hot or cold. It's also worth coming for afternoon tea, as the cakes and pastries are homemade and delicious. ⊠ *rue Trencat,* ☎ *04-90-54-33-94. MC, V. Closed Tues. Sept.–June.*

$$$$ ✕▥ **L'Oustau de la Baumanière.** Sheltered by rocky cliffs below the village of Les Baux, this fabled country inn, with its formal, landscaped ★ terrace and broad swimming pool, has the air of a Roman palazzo. Chef

Jean-André Charial continues to attract culinary pilgrims for a reverent meal. There may be turbot steak roasted on the bone with chestnuts, sautéed foie gras with mango chutney, a boneless pigeon stuffed with truffles and wild mushrooms, and pineapple raviolis with licorice sauce. (Be sure to make reservations and note that the restaurant is closed Thursday lunch and all day Wednesday from November to Christmas, then closed altogether in January and February.) Breezy, private rooms are scattered through three buildings and are beautifully furnished with antiques. Those in the main house convey grandeur—enormous chimneys, heavy beams, four-poster beds and four-legged tubs, and everywhere sumptuous fabrics. A few hundred yards away are nine less formal rooms, and in a third, small, vine-covered building are five more simple but charming ones. Or consider its less formal, garden-bower sister inn a few meters farther, **La Cabro d'Or** ($$$). ✉ *Val d'Enfer, 13520,* ☎ *04–90–54–33–07,* FAX *04–90–54–40–46. 22 rooms. Restaurant, pool, 2 tennis courts, horseback riding. AE, DC, MC, V. Closed Jan.–Feb.*

$ ✕🏠 **La Reine Jeanne.** Sartre and de Beauvoir had separate rooms but a shared balcony—and what a balcony. Jacques Brel and Winston Churchill, too, were happy clients of this modest but majestically placed inn and stood on its balconies looking over rugged views worthy of the châteaux up the street. The inn is located right at the entrance to the village and offers rooms that are small, simple, and—despite the white, vinyl-padded furniture—fondly decorated with terra-cotta tiles and stencil prints. Reserve in advance for one of the two rooms with a balcony, though even one of the tiny interior rooms gives you the right to spend a quiet evening in lovely Les Baux after the tourists have drained away. Good home-style cooking and a fine plat du jour are served in the restaurant, which offers views from both the panoramic dining room and a pretty terrace; it's the best setting for a meal in Les Baux. ✉ *13520,* ☎ *04–90–54–32–06,* FAX *04–90–54–32–33. 10 rooms. Restaurant. MC, V. Closed end Nov.–end Dec. and 3 wks Jan.*

$$$ 🏠 **La Benvengudo.** With manicured grounds shaded by tall pines, this graceful shuttered mas feels centuries old but was built to look that way some 30 years ago. Its heavy old beams, stone fireplace, and terra-cotta tiles enhance the homey, old-fashioned decor (though bathrooms date from the '70s). The resident dogs greet you just before the friendly owners do. Dinner is served by the olive-shaded pool, or you can have a drink on the stone-tabled terrace. ✉ *Vallon de l'Arcoule, 13520 (below Les Baux, direction Fontvieille),* ☎ *04–90–54–32–54,* FAX *04–90–54–42–58. 24 rooms. Restaurant, air-conditioning, pool, tennis. AE, MC, V. Closed Nov.–Feb.*

$$$ 🏠 **Mas de L'Oulivié.** Another mas built to look ancient, with recycled roof tiles and hand-waxed chalk walls, the Oulivié is clarity itself, with a cool, clean look and a low-key ambience. There's no upscale restaurant—just easy and unpretentious lunches by the pool (grilled meats, salads, and goat cheese seasoned with the house-label olive oil); you can dabble your feet with an aperitif in hand. Eight rooms on the upper floor of the main house are pretty enough, with floral-print curtains and rich carpet, but ask for one with doors opening onto the lavender gardens and olive groves; there's even one with a private terrace and access to the pool. ✉ *Les Arcoules, 13520 (below Les Baux, direction Fontvieille),* ☎ *04–90–54–35–78,* FAX *04–90–54–44–31. 22 rooms, 1 suite. Restaurant, air-conditioning, pool, tennis. AE, DC, MC, V. Closed Nov.–Feb.* ✍

$ 🏠 **Mas de la Fontaine.** This 15th-century mas, under gorgeous cliffs and ancient pines, is the poor man's Oustau de la Baumanière (☞ *above*). Modest and *familiale* instead of deluxe, it has all the basics, plus exposed beams, a vaulted breakfast room, and a pool. Rooms are spare with dated bathrooms, but have fresh carpet and wallpaper. Ask for the upstairs room with private roof terrace. ⊠ *Val d'Enfer 13520, (below Les Baux on D78, direction Fontvieille),* ☎ *04–90–54–34–13. 7 rooms, 6 with bath. Breakfast room, pool. No credit cards. Closed Nov.–Easter.*

Outdoor Activities and Sports

Les Baux has a serious 18 holes of golf at **Domaine des Manville** (☎ 04–90–54–37–02), on D27 south of town. At Mouriès north of D17, the **Golf de Servannes** (04–90–47–59–95) has a complete 18-hole course.

Shopping

An extravagant choice of souvenirs ranging from kitsch (Provençal-print toilet-paper holders) to class (silk challis shawls from Les Olivades) virtually reach out and grab you as you climb the hill lined with tempting (and not-so) shops. But come with cash: Only the post office is equipped to change money, and there's no bank.

Maussane

③ *11 km (7 mi) south of Les Baux, 30 km (18½ mi) northeast of Arles.*

An unassuming Alpilles village, Maussane is widely known as the capital of olive-oil production within the territory lumped under the title La Vallée des Baux. This is where the wagons roll in, heaped with green and black olives, combed and raked from the silver trees that pepper the surrounding hills. At the local cooperative mill, the farmers' harvest will be crushed and pressed, then sold worldwide in fancy-food boutiques—and by the 5-litre plastic jug to locals. The streets of the town are quiet, with a few cafés full of farmers and landowners. Just up the road 2 km (1 mi), Maussane blurs into its neighboring village Paradou, which has an unusual concentration of good restaurants. Summer people make a day of coming to Maussane to top up their oil jug and to lunch in plane-shaded Paradou.

Dining

$$ ✕ **Le Bistro de Paradou.** This local institution, wholeheartedly adopted by the summer people, has become so self-conscious it's a caricature of itself with its antique posters, exposed stone, glittering aperitif bottles over the bar, and bantering waiters so egalitarian you half expect them to *"tu"* you. There's still just one menu per day, with decent food—a thick daube, a slab of leg of lamb, good fruit tarts, and excellent local goat cheese. But 180 francs (about €27) seems steep for the down-home style. ⊠ *57 av. de la Vallée-des-Baux,* ☎ *04–90–54–32–70. MC, V. Closed Sun.*

$$ ✕ **La Petite France.** This 18th-century former bakery serves a refined and elegant Provençal cuisine and has the local Maussane oil set on each white-linened table. On the daily menu there may be green-olive ravioli with sage, a tidy pocket of pigs' feet with morrel mushrooms, and a hot chocolate soup. Summer evening meals on the hedge-enclosed garden terrace live up to the cooking. ⊠ *route de Maussane, Paradous,* ☎ *04–90–54–41–91. MC, V. Closed Wed. No lunch Thurs.*

St-Rémy-de-Provence

③ *11 km (7 mi) northeast of Les Baux, 25 km (15½ mi) northeast of Arles, 24 km (15 mi) south of Avignon.*

There are other towns as pretty as St-Rémy-de-Provence, and others in more dramatic or picturesque settings. Ruins can be found throughout the south, and so can authentic village life. Yet something felicitous has happened in this market town in the heart of the Alpilles—a steady infusion of style, of art, of imagination—all brought by people with a respect for local traditions and a love of Provençal ways. Here more than anywhere you can meditate quietly on antiquity, browse redolent markets with basket in hand, peer down the very row of plane trees you remember from a van Gogh, and also enjoy urbane galleries, cosmopolitan shops, and specialty food boutiques. An abundance of chic choices in restaurants, mas, and even châteaux awaits you; the almond and olive groves conceal dozens of stone-and-terra-cotta gîtes, many with pools. In short, St-Rémy has been gentrified through and through, and is now a sort of arid, southern Martha's Vineyard or, perhaps, the Hamptons of Provence.

St-Rémy has always attracted the right sort of people. First established by an indigenous Celtic-Ligurian people who worshiped the god Glan, the village Glanum was adopted and gentrified by the Greeks of Marseille in the 2nd and 3rd centuries before Christ. They brought in sophisticated building techniques—superbly cut stone, fitted without mortar, and classical colonnades. Rome moved in to help ward off Hannibal, and by the 1st century BC Caesar had taken full control. The Via Domitia, linking Italy to Spain, passed by its doors, and the main trans-Alpine pass emptied into its entrance gate. Under the Pax Romana there developed a veritable city, complete with temples and forum, luxurious villas and baths.

The Romans eventually fell, but a town grew up next to their ruins, taking its name from their protectorate abbey St-Remi in Reims. It grew to be an important market town, and wealthy families built fine hôtels (mansions) in its center—among them the family De Sade (whose distant black-sheep relation held forth in the Lubéron at Lacoste). Another famous native son, the eccentric doctor, scholar, and astrologer Michel Nostradamus (1503–66), is credited by some as having predicted much of the modern age; Catherine de Medici consulted him on every life decision.

Perhaps the best known of St-Rémy's visitors was the ill-fated Vincent van Gogh. Shipped unceremoniously out of Arles at the height of his madness (and creativity), he had himself committed to the asylum St-Paul-de-Mausolé and wandered through the ruins of Glanum during the last year of his life. It is his eerily peaceful retreat as well as the ruins that draw visitors by the busload to the outskirts of modern St-Rémy, but the bulk of them snap their pictures and move on to Les Baux for the day, leaving St-Rémy to its serene, sophisticated ways.

To approach Glanum, you must park in a dusty roadside lot on D5 south of town (in the direction of Les Baux). But before crossing, you'll be confronted with two of the most miraculously preserved ★ classical monuments in France, simply called **Les Antiques** (The Antiquities). Though dating from the era of the Caesars, they could be taken for Romanesque, so perfectly intact are their carvings and architectural details. The **Mausolée** (Mausoleum), a wedding-cake stack of arches and columns built about 30 BC, lacks nothing but its finial on top, yet it is dedicated to a Julian (as in Julius Caesar), probably Caesar Augustus. Allegorical scenes in bas-relief represent myths of Greek origin but most likely refer to Julius Caesar's military triumphs. Two sculptured figures, framed in its column-ringed crown, must surely be the honorees; the dedication reads SEX. L.M. IVLIEI C.F. PARENTIBUS SUEIS, or "Sextius, Lucius, Carcus son of Caius, of the family of Julii, to their parents." A few yards away stands another marvel: the **Arc Triomphal,** most likely dating from around AD 20. All who crossed the Alps entered Roman Glanum through this gate, decorated with reliefs of battle scenes depicting Caesar's defeat and the capture of the Gauls.

Across the street from Les Antiques, a slick visitor center, set back from ★ D5, prepares you for entry into **Glanum** with scale models of the site in its various heydays. A good map and an English brochure guide you stone by stone through the maze of foundations, walls, towers, and columns that spread across a broad field; Greek sites are helpfully noted by numbers, Roman by letters. At the base of rugged white cliffs and shaded with black-green pines, it is an extraordinarily evocative site and inspires contemplation in even the rowdiest busload of schoolchildren. ⊠ *Off D5, direction Les Baux, info phone at Hôtel de Sade (☞ below),* ☎ *04–90–92–64–04.* ▦ *32 frs/€4.88 (36 frs/€5.49 includes entry to Hôtel de Sade).* ⊙ *Apr.–Sept., daily 9–7; Oct.–Mar., daily 9–noon and 2–5.*

You can cut across the fields from Glanum to **St-Paul-de-Mausolée,** the lovely, isolated asylum where van Gogh spent the last year of his life (1889–90), but enter it quietly. It shelters psychiatric patients to this day—all of them women. You're free to walk up the beautifully manicured garden path to the church and its jewel-box Romanesque **cloister** where the artist found womblike peace. A small boutique features works of current patients—*art brut* reminiscent of Munch and Basquiat—for sale. You can climb a stairway to a memorial bust of van Gogh and a picture window that frames a garden view he loved and painted. ⊠ *Next to Glanum, off D5 direction Les Baux,* ☎ *04–90–92–77–00.* ▦ *15 frs/€2.29.* ⊙ *May–Sept., daily 8–7; Oct.–Apr., daily 8–5.*

St-Rémy is wrapped by a lively commercial boulevard, lined with shops and cafés and anchored by its 19th-century church **Collégiale St-Martin.** Step inside to see the magnificent organ, one of the loveliest in Europe. Rebuilt to 18th-century specifications in the early '80s, it has the flexibility to interpret new and old music with pure French panache; you can listen to it Saturday afternoon at 5:30 from July through September. ⊠ *pl. de la République.*

Within St-Rémy's fast-moving traffic loop, a labyrinth of narrow streets leads you away from the action and into the slow-moving inner sanctum of the **Vieille Ville** (old town). Here high-end, trendy shops mingle pleasantly with local life, and the buildings, if gentrified, blend unobtrusively.

Make your way to the **Hôtel de Sade,** a 15th- and 16th-century private manor now housing the phenomenal abundance of treasure unearthed with the ruins of Glanum. There is a statue of Hercules and a graceful bas-relief of Hermes, funeral urns and crystal jewelry, and surprisingly sophisticated tools. There are also the remains of gallo-Roman funeral obelisks, early Christian altars, and a baptismal font from the 5th century, when St-Remy first flourished. The De Sade family built the house around remains of 4th-century baths and a 5th-century baptistery, now nestled in its courtyard. ⊠ *rue du Parage,* ☎ *04–90–92–64–04.* ▦ *15 frs/€2.29 (36 frs/€5.49 includes Glanum entry).* ⊙ *Feb.–Mar. and Oct., Tues.–Sun. 10–noon and 2–5; Apr.–Sept., Tues.–Sun. 10–noon and 2–6; Nov.–Dec., Wed. and Sat.–Sun. 10–noon and 2–5.*

Dining and Lodging

$$–$$$ ✕ **Maison Jaune.** This modern retreat in the old town draws crowds of summer people to its pretty roof terrace. The decor of sober stone and lively contemporary furniture, both indoors and out, reflects the cuisine. With vivid flavors and a cool, contained touch, chef François Perraud prepares grilled sardines with crunchy fennel and lemon confit, ham-cured duck on lentils with vinaigrette, and veal lightly flavored with olives, capers, and celery. Prices are high but one bargain lunch menu offers a minimalist smorgasbord of tastes, and wine is included. ⊠ *15 rue Carnot,* ☎ *04–90–92–56–14. Reservations essential. MC, V. Closed Mon. No dinner Sun.*

$$ ✕ **Le Bistrot des Alpilles.** This popular institution has a broad sidewalk terrace, glassed in brasserie-style in winter, and an ambience of easy-going professionalism. Cheap lunch menus and a reasonable evening menu make the good, traditional cooking a bargain: There's a melt-in-your-mouth gratin of salt-cod brandade, a daily fish specialty, and local roast lamb. ⊠ *15 blvd. Mirabeau,* ☎ *04–90–92–09–17. Reservations essential. AE, MC, V. Closed Sun.*

$–$$ ✕ **L'Assiette de Marie.** Though life is lived outdoors in St-Rémy, ★ there are rainy days and winter winds, and this is the place to retreat. Marie Ricco is a collector, and she's turned her tiny restaurant into an art-directed bower of attic treasures—unscrubbed, unrestored, as is. Fringed lamp shades are artfully askew, ancient wallpaper curls from a door, the coatrack sags with woolen uniforms, and classic jazz and candlelight complete the scene. Seated at an old school desk, you choose from the day's specials, all made with Marie's Corsican-Italian touch—marinated vegetables with tapenade, a cast-iron casserole of superb pasta (made in Marie's neighboring shop; ☞ Shopping, *below*), satiny *panetone* (flan). The house red is Corsican, but there's a wide choice of St-Rémy wines as well. ⊠ *1 rue Jaume Roux,* ☎ *04–90–92–32–14. Reservations essential. MC, V. Closed Mon. Nov.– Easter. No lunch Tues., and sometimes Thurs. in summer (except July– Aug.).*

$ ✕ **La Gousse d'Ail.** An intimate, indoor old-town hideaway, this family-run bistro lives up to its name (The Garlic Clove), serving robust, highly flavored southern dishes in hearty portions: eggplant and zucchini timbale in a shower of cumin, rich homemade pasta in powerful pesto with almonds, vegetarian couscous, and homemade nougat ice cream pungent with honey. A ceramic pitcher of ice water and a thick flask of house wine offer counterbalance, and the bill is delivered with much-needed mints. The cozy decor (dark timbers, niches full of puppets) matches the warm welcome. Aim for Thursday night when there is Gypsy music and jazz. ⊠ *25 rue Carnot,* ☎ *04–90–92–16–87. AE, MC, V. Closed Jan.–Feb. except occasional weekends.*

$$$$ ✕🏠 **Domaine de Valmouriane.** This genteel mas-cum-resort, beauti-★ fully isolated on a broad park, offers guests a panoply of entertainment, from billiards to a Jacuzzi. Inside, soft, overstuffed English-country decor mixes cozily with cool Provençal stone and timber, and massive stone fireplaces warm public spaces. The restaurant features chef Pierre Walter, who vies to please with fresh game, seafood, local oils, and truffles; his desserts have won him national standing. But it's the personal welcome from English owner Judith McHugo that makes clients feel like weekend guests in a manor house. ⊠ *Petite rte. des Baux (D27), 13210,* ☎ *04–90–92–44–62,* 𝖥𝖠𝖷 *04–90–92–37–32. 14 rooms. Restaurant, pool, hot tub, steam room, tennis court, billiards. AE, DC, MC, V.* 🐾

$$$$ ✕🏠 **Vallon de Valrugues.** This luxurious villa, replete with uniformed footmen and canopy beds, makes no bones about its pretensions to aristocracy, but you might like it for its beguiling views into the Alpilles and the olive groves. Chefs come and go, all with stellar resumés; at press time Laurent Chouviat was manning the kitchen. The restaurant atmosphere is formal, pampered, and a trifle stuffy; the bill a blow. ⊠ *chemin Canto-Cigalo, 13210,* ☎ *04–90–92–04–40,* 𝖥𝖠𝖷 *04–90–92– 44–01. 35 rooms, 15 suites. Restaurant, pool, hot tub, sauna. AE, MC, V. Closed Feb.* 🐾

$ ✕🏠 **Auberge de la Reine Jeanne.** With all the luxurious mas and châteaux to choose from, you don't have to be scared away if you're on a budget: This charming Logis-de-France property, in a 17th-century stone building that surrounds a green courtyard, offers more-conventional lodgings, right in the heart of town. Its strong point is its restaurant, where modestly priced, mainstream French cooking is served in the courtyard in summer and in a firelighted, dark-timber hall in winter. Room decor isn't up to St-Rémy style (blue carpeting, polyester quilts), but the best rooms overlook the court and are clean and comfortable. ✉ *12 bd. Mirabeau, 13210,* ☎ *04–90–92–15–33,* 𝔽𝔸𝕏 *04–90–92–49–65. 11 rooms. Restaurant. AE, DC, MC, V.*

$$$$ 🏨 **Château des Alpilles.** At the end of an alley of grand old plane trees, this early 19th-century manor house lords over a vast park off D31. If public spaces and atmosphere are cool and spare to the point of sparseness, rooms are warm and fussy, with lush Provençal prints and polished antiques. Outer buildings offer jazzy–modern apartments with kitchenettes, and the poolside grill gives you a noble perspective over the park. ✉ *Ancienne rte. du Grès, 13210,* ☎ *04–90–92–03–33,* 𝔽𝔸𝕏 *04–90–92–45–17. 15 rooms, 4 suites. Pool, sauna, tennis. AE, DC, MC, V. Closed mid-Nov.–mid-Dec. and Jan.–mid-Feb.*

$$$ 🏨 **Les Ateliers de l'Image.** Only in artsy St-Rémy: a hotel with its own black-and-white photo lab, workshops, a photo-supply shop, and photo expos and sales (you can even buy those displayed in your room). Naturally the decor has a contemporary edginess—cool white linens, halogen lights reflecting on exposed rafters—but there's a little pool and billiards for the laid-back. It's just outside the center, on the way to Les Antiques. ✉ *5 av. Pasteur, 13210,* ☎ *04–90–92–51–50,* 𝔽𝔸𝕏 *04–90–92–43–52. 16 rooms. Dining room, pool, billiards. AE, MC, V.*

$$$ 🏨 **Mas de Cornud.** An American mans the wine cellar and an Egyptian runs the professional kitchen (by request only), but the attitude is pure Provence. David and Nito Carpita have turned their farmhouse, just outside St-Rémy, into a bed-and-breakfast filled with French country furniture and objects from around the world. Guests and hosts unwind with a nightly pastis and a pétanque match. Without drop-in clients barging in (rooms must be reserved), guests feel like . . . well, guests. Table d'hôte dinners, cooking classes, and tours can be arranged. Breakfast is included. ✉ *rte. de Mas-Blanc, 13210,* ☎ *04–90–92–39–32,* 𝔽𝔸𝕏 *04–90–92–55–99. 5 rooms, 1 suite. Dining room, pool. No credit cards. Closed Jan.–Feb.*

$$ 🏨 **Château de Roussan.** In a majestic park shaded by ancient plane trees (themselves protected landmarks), its ponds and canals graced by swans and birdsong, this extraordinary 18th-century château is being valiantly preserved by managers who (without a rich owner to back them) are lovingly restoring it, squatter style. Glorious period furnishings and details are buttressed by brocante and bric-a-brac, and the bathrooms, toggled into various corners, have an afterthought air. Cats outnumber the staff. Yet if you're the right sort for this place— backpackers, romantic couples on a budget, lovers of atmosphere over luxury—you'll blossom in this three-dimensional costume drama. ✉ *rte. de Tarascon, 13210,* ☎ *04–90–92–11–63,* 𝔽𝔸𝕏 *04–90–92–50–59. 22 rooms. Restaurant. MC, V.*

Festivals

St-Rémy is fond of festivals, borrowing traditions of bull-races and ferias from its lowland neighbors and creating a few of its own. On Pentecost Monday (the end of May), the **Fête de la Transhumance** celebrates the passage of the sheep from Provence into the Alps, and costumed shepherds lead some 4,000 sheep, goats, and donkeys through the streets. The **Grande Feria,** in mid-August, brings the Camargue to the hills, with bull games, fireworks, and flamenco guitar. Three weekends a year (Ascension in May, late June, and mid-September) are devoted to the

Fête de la Route des Peintres de la Lumière en Provence (Festival of the Route of Painters of Light in Provence), an enormous contemporary-art fair.

Nightlife and the Arts

La Forge des Trinitaires (⊠ ave. de la Libération, ☎ 04–90–92–31–52) draws the young, the restless, and the trendily dressed for African and Antillaise music every Friday and Saturday night 11 PM–4:30 AM. At **La Haute Galine** (chemin Cante Perdrix et Galine, ☎ 04–90–92–00–03) a very young crowd gathers (on Friday and Saturday nights only) to eat by the pool and dance into the night. On the second Friday of the month, **Pégomas** (3 av. Jean Moulin, ☎ 04–32–60–01–90) is the site of a live jazz concert.

At 5:30 every Saturday in July, August, and September, you can hear the magnificent **organ of St-Martin Collégiale** (☞ *above*) in a free recital, often featuring the boy-wonder *organiste-titulaire* Jean-Pierre Lecaudey.

Shopping

Every Wednesday morning St-Rémy hosts one of the most popular and picturesque **markets** in Provence, during which the place de la République and narrow old-town streets overflow with fresh produce, herbs and spices, olive oil by the vat, and tapenade by the scoop, as well as fabrics and *brocante* (collectibles). There's a smaller version Saturday mornings.

Interior design is a niche market in this region of summer homes, so **decor shops** abound, not only featuring Provençal pottery and fabrics but also a cosmopolitan blend of Asian fabrics, English garden furniture, and Italian high-design items. Individual artisans fill gallery-style boutiques with their photography, picture frames, and wrought-iron furniture. The common denominator is high here, so good taste has stonewalled tourist kitsch. **Souleiado** (⊠ place de l'Église, 2 av. de la Résistance, ☎ 04–90–92–45–90) and **Les Olivades** (⊠ 28 rue Lafayette, ☎ 04–90–92–00–80) outdo themselves displaying their highest-end, least-souvenir-like clothes and linens. The design shops, fabric shops and art-gallery-cum-gift-shops are scattered throughout the Vieille Ville and along the boulevards that surround it. At **Tempera** (⊠ 45 rue Carnot, ☎ 04–90–92–03–91), Mireille Garcin stocks her interior-design gallery with an exotic collection of lamps, linens, and antique bric-a-brac. At **La Boutique des Jardins** (⊠ 1 bd. Mirabeau, ☎ 04–90–92–11–60), Françoise Gérin displays the booty she trolls on her Asian and African travels, from Egyptian cottons to Indian hanging lamps and tooled metal frames. **Big Bain** (⊠ 34 bd. Mirabeau, ☎ 04–90–92–59–53) is a bath-lover's dreamland, full of gorgeous fixtures and highly portable bath accessories. **Le Grand Magasin** (⊠ 24 rue Commune, ☎ 04–90–92–18–79) mixes handcrafted jewelry, glass sculpture, pottery, and scarves.

With all the summer people, food shops and *traiteurs* (take-out caterers) do big business in St-Rémy. Olive oils are sold like fine old wines, and the breads heaped in boulangerie windows are as knobby and rough-hewn as they should be. The best food shops are concentrated in the Vieille Ville. Local goat cheeses are displayed like jewels and wrapped like fine pastries at **Fromagerie du Mistral** (⊠ 1 pl. Joseph-Hilaire). **L'Épicerie de Marie** (⊠ 1 pl. Isidore Gilles) features the Corsican-Italian homemade pastas of Marie Ricco. At **Chocolaterie Joel Durand** (⊠ pl. Jean de Renaud), the chocolates are numbered to indicate the various flavors, from rose petal to Camargue saffron.

THE ALPILLES, ARLES, AND THE CAMARGUE A TO Z

Arriving and Departing

By Car

The A6/A7 toll expressway (*péage*) channels all traffic from Paris toward the south. It's called the Autoroute du Soleil (Highway of the Sun) and leads directly to Provence. From Orange, A9 (La Languedocienne) heads southwest to Nîmes. Arles is a quick jaunt from Nîmes via A54.

By Plane

Marseille (an hour's drive from Arles) is served by frequent flights from Paris and London, and daily flights from Paris arrive at the smaller airport in Nîmes. In summer, Delta Airlines flies direct from New York to Nice, 200 km (124 mi) from Arles.

By Train

There's regular rail service from all points north to Avignon and then to nearby towns, and the TGV (Trains à Grande Vitesse) connects Paris to Avignon in 3½ hours, stopping at Orange as well. From these cities you must transfer to local trains to get to Nîmes, Tarascon, or Arles, the only other cities served by rail lines. Overnight trains run daily to Avignon from Paris, Strasbourg, and other cloud-bound cities, allowing soggy travelers to stretch out on a couchette and wake up to indigo skies (☞ Train Travel *in* Smart Travel Tips A to Z).

Getting Around

By Bus

A moderately good network of private bus services links places not served, or badly served, by trains. Out of Arles, **Les Cars de Camargue** (1 rue Jean-Mathieu Artaud, ☎ 04–90–96–36–25) carries visitors on round-trip excursions into the Camargue. **Ceyte Tourisme Mediterranée** in Arles (14 bd. Georges Clemenceau, ☎ 04–90–18–96–33) runs into the far reaches of the Camargue and the Alpilles. In Nîmes, **Cars Fort** (27 bd. Jean Jaurès, ☎ 04–66–36–60–80) runs you into the deep country and offers tourist circuits as well. Throughout the region, ask for bus schedules at train stations and tourist offices, and head for the *gare routière* (bus station).

By Car

With its swift autoroute network, it's a breeze traveling from city to city by car in this region. But some of the best of Provence is experienced on back roads and byways, including the isolated Camargue and the Alpilles. Navigating the flatlands of the Camargue can feel unearthly, with roads sailing over terrain uninterrupted by hills or forests; despite this, roads don't always run as the crow flies and can wander wide of a clean trajectory, so don't expect to make time. Rocky outcrops and switchbacks keep you a captive audience to the arid scenery in the Alpilles; to hurry—impossible as it is—would be a waste.

By Train

Although good rail service connects Avignon to Nîmes, Tarascon, and Arles, trains don't penetrate the Alpilles; connections to St-Rémy and Les Baux must be made by bus.

Contacts and Resources

Bed-and-Breakfasts

Chambres d'hôtes (bed-and-breakfasts) offer simple lodging, usually in the hosts' home, with breakfast and a warm, regional welcome often included. There are lots to be found in this region, especially in the Alpilles around St-Rémy. The French national network **Gîtes de France** (☞ Lodging *in* Smart Travel Tips A to Z) lists B&Bs that have been rated. For chambres d'hôtes regulated by the national network, contact the local branches, divided by *départements*. Addresses are listed under Vacation Rentals, *below.*

Car Rentals

ARLES

Avis (⊠ at the train station, ☎ 04–90–96–82–42). **Europcar** (⊠ 2 bis av. Victor Hugo, ☎ 04–90–93–23–24). **Hertz** (⊠ 4 av. Victor-Hugo, ☎ 04–90–96–75–23).

NÎMES

Avis (⊠ 1800 av. Mar. Juin, ☎ 04–66–29–05–33). **Budget** (⊠ 225 rte. Rouquairol, ☎ 04–66–38–01–69). **Europcar** (⊠ 1 bis rue de la République, ☎ 04–66–21–31–35). **Hertz** (⊠ 5 bd. Prague, 04–66–21–25–90).

Guided Tours

The **Arles tourist office** (☎ 04–90–18–41–21) offers individual tours of the town, including visits to the Roman monuments, during the summer season. Dates and times vary depending on demand; check with them regarding English-speaking guides.

To learn more about Nîmes's monuments and old town and to arrange a guided tour in English, contact the **Service des Guides** at the tourist office (☎ 04–66–67–29–11). For about 150 francs/€23, you can tour the town in a taxi for an hour; when you stop in front of a monument, the driver slips in a cassette with commentary in the language of your choice. For 300 francs/€45.73, **Taxis T.R.A.N.** (☎ 04–66–29–40–11) can take you on a round-trip ride from Nîmes to the Pont du Gard (ask the taxi to wait while you explore for 30 minutes).

Travel Agencies

ARLES

Havas Voyages (⊠ 4 bd. des Lices, 13200 Arles, ☎ 04–90–18–31–31); **Provence-Camargue Tours** (⊠ 1 rue Émile Fassin, 13200 Arles, ☎ 04–90–49–85–58).

NÎMES

Cap Horizons (⊠ 3 bd. Amiral Courbet, 3000 Nîmes, ☎ 04–66–36–19–90); **Havas Voyages** (⊠ 44 bd. Victor Hugo, 3000 Nîmes, ☎ 04–66–36–99–99).

Vacation Rentals

Gîtes de France (☞ Vacation Rentals *in* Smart Travel Tips A to Z) is the national network of vacation rentals, many of them in restored buildings with real regional character. The region west of Nîmes, including some parts of the Camargue, lies in the département of Hérault. Gîtes de France offices for this department are based in Montpellier (⊠ B.P. 3070, 34034 Montpellier Cedex 1, ☎ 04–67–67–62–62, 𝕱𝕬𝕏 04–67–67–71–69). Nîmes itself and environs are processed by the Gard office (⊠ 3 pl. des Arènes, B.P. 59, 30007 Nîmes Cedex 4, ☎ 04–66–27–94–94, 𝕱𝕬𝕏 04–66–27–94–95). Arles and the Alpilles gîtes are handled by the Bouches-du-Rhône departmental office (⊠ Domaine du Vergon, B.P. 26, 13370 Mallemort, ☎ 04–90–59–49–39, 𝕱𝕬𝕏 04–90–59–16–75).

Each of the tourist offices for towns in the region usually publishes lists of independent rentals (*locations meublés*), many of them inspected and classified by the tourist office itself.

Visitor Information

Regional tourist offices prefer written queries only. The **Comité Régional du Tourisme du Languedoc-Roussillon** (✉ 20 rue République, Montpellier 34000, ☎ 04–67–22–81–00, FAX 04–67–22–80–27) provides information on all towns west of the Rhône. The remainder of towns covered in this chapter are handled by the **Comité Regional du Tourisme de Provence-Alpes-Côte d'Azur** (✉ 12 pl. Joliette, 13002 Marseille, ☎ 04–91–56–47–00, FAX 04–91–56–47–01). For information on the area around Arles and St-Rémy, contact the **Comité Départemental du Tourisme des Bouches-du-Rhône** (✉ 13 rue Roux de Brignole, 13006 Marseille, ☎ 04–91–13–84–13, FAX 04–91–33–01–82).

Local **tourist offices** for major towns covered in this chapter can be phoned, faxed, or addressed by mail. **Aigues-Mortes** (✉ Porte de la Gardette, 30220, ☎ 04–66–53–73–00, FAX 04–66–53–65–94). **Arles** (✉ 43 bd. de Craponne, 13200, ☎ 04–90–18–41–20, FAX 04–90–18–41–29). **Les Baux** (✉ 30 Grand-rue, 13520, ☎ 04–90–54–34–39, FAX 04–90–54–51–15). **Nîmes** (✉ 6 rue Auguste, 3000, ☎ 04–66–67–29–11, FAX 04–66–21–81–04). **Stes-Maries-de-la-Mer** (✉ 5 av. Van Gogh, 13460, ☎ 04–90–97–82–55, FAX 04–90–97–82–55). **St-Rémy** (✉ pl. Jean-Jaurès, 13210, ☎ 04–90–92–05–22, FAX 04–90–92–38–52). **Tarascon** (✉ 59 rue Halles, 13150, ☎ 04–90–91–03–52, FAX 04–90–91–22–96).

2 THE VAUCLUSE

AVIGNON, THE LUBERON, AND MONT VENTOUX

Anchored by the magnificent papal stronghold of Avignon, the Vaucluse spreads luxuriantly east of the Rhône. Its famous vineyards seduce connoisseurs, and its Roman ruins in Orange and Vaison-la-Romaine draw scholars and arts lovers. Plains dotted with orchards of olives, apricots, and cherries give way to a rich and wild mountain terrain around formidable Mont Ventoux and flow into the primeval Luberon, made a household name by Peter Mayle.

F OR MANY, this is the only true Provence, with its sun-bleached hills and fields that are tapestries of green-and-black grapevines and silver-gray olives, and its rolling rows of lavender that harmonize with the mountains looming purple against the indigo sky. It is here, in his beloved Luberon, that British author Peter Mayle discovered and described the simple pleasures of breakfasting on melons still warm from the sun, buying fresh-dug truffles from furtive farmers in smoke-filled bars, and life without socks. The world shared his epiphany, and vacationers now flock here in search of the same sensual way of life, some retreating to lavishly renovated farmhouses with cypress-shaded pools, others making pilgrimages to the luxurious inns that cater to refugees from city smog.

Thus the golden *villages perchés* (perched villages) that lord over the patchwork valleys—Gordes, Bonnieux, Ménerbes—have become bijou boutique towns, and the markets have become must-do events. A ticket to the summer opera festival in the Roman theater in Orange is as recherché as a case of 1982 Châteauneuf-du-Pâpe. But there are still quiet trails that leave the gentrification behind, winding up labyrinthine back alleys to pollard-shaded squares resonant with the splashing of ancient fountains, climbing into misty blue-black forests unaltered in spirit since the time of the Gauls.

And all this lies a stone's throw from thriving Avignon, its feudal fortifications sheltering a lively arts scene and a culture determinedly young.

Pleasures and Pastimes

Dining

The Vaucluse is the home of the famous Cavaillon melon, that globe of juicy pulchritude that hefts in the hand of marketing matrons, turned and sniffed and squeezed with the expertise of an Antwerp jeweler. The right melon, once found and sliced, yields like butter, pours a rich, perfumed nectar onto the cutting board, and melts on the tongue. Half the size of a cantaloupe and twice as flavorful, these melons are labeled, tissue-wrapped, and stacked in market pyramids of acrobatic proportion. Eating them, whether draped with a veil of musky *jambon cru* (cured ham) or cupping a pool of ruby port, is a summer ritual throughout Europe, but especially on the melon's native turf, where they're sold so fresh and unshippably ripe they're practically bursting at the seams.

When the undulating rows of green that spread through the Sorgue Valley's fertile fields aren't yielding melons, they're nurturing prize asparagus, fat stalks of purple-tipped white bound in bands of red, white, and blue. Pampered under mounds of cool earth from the rays of light that would cause photosynthesis and ruinous traces of green, these albino beauties retain a pure, sweet flavor and enough juice to run down your chin. Unlike the shriveled exports that wither in city supermarkets around the world, the local product is smooth and plump, and once its barky skin is stripped off (time-consuming but indispensable), it's as tender as, well, melon. In season (early March–May) restaurants go asparagus-crazy, some offering multicourse menus based entirely on this regional treasure.

Olives, of course, figure large in the Vaucluse culinary scene, from the ubiquitous *tapenade* (olive and caper spread) on toast to the requisite bowl of the pungent black ovals served with your aperitif. But the real attention getter here is the truffle, snuffled up beneath Luberon oaks by trained pigs and dogs driven wild by their smell. The Vaucluse produces 74% of all truffles sold commercially in France; even more are sold like smuggled drugs in backroom deals. Vaucluse chefs showcase the truffle in humble ways, the better to highlight its redolent charms. The classic vehicle is a simple *omelette aux truffes*.

CATEGORY	COST*
$$$$	over 400 frs/€61
$$$	250 frs–400 frs/€38–€61
$$	125 frs–250 frs/€19–€38
$	under 125 frs/€19

per person for a three-course meal, including tax (20.6%) and tip but not wine

Lodging

One of the most popular vacation regions in France outside the seaside, the Vaucluse has a plethora of sleek and fashionable converted *mas* (farmhouses), landscaped in lavender, cypress, and oil-jars full of vivid flowers. Given the crushing heat in high summer, the majority have swimming pools and, these days, air-conditioning (but it's wise to check ahead if you're counting on it). However, only a few provide *moustiquaires,* mosquito netting put over the bed or window screens to keep out troublesome flies. Reservations are essential most of the year, and many hotels close down altogether in winter.

Because of the pleasures of simple Provençal cooking and the joys of going to the market, as well as the privacy and independence that come with having a house of your own, booking a *gîte* (vacation rental) for your stay (by the week only) makes a lot of sense. Many in the luxury category are adding swimming pools to their comforts. All bookings for Gîtes-de-France rentals are handled through the Vaucluse branch (☞ The Vaucluse A to Z, *below*).

CATEGORY	COST*
$$$$	over 800 frs/€122
$$$	550 frs–800 frs/€84–€122
$$	300 frs–550 frs/€46–€84
$	under 300 frs/€46

All prices are for a standard double room for two, including tax (20.6%) and service charge.

✑ *following the text of a review is your signal that the property has a Web site, where you will find details and, usually, images; for a link, visit www.fodors.com/urls.*

Markets

Browsing through the *marché couvert* (covered food market) in Avignon is enough to make you regret all the tempting restaurants around; its seafood, free-range poultry, olives, and produce cry out to be gathered in a basket and cooked in their purest form. And the village open-air markets, which are carefully organized to cover in turn all the days of the week, are a visual feast as well.

But at one of the most famous markets in Provence, food plays second fiddle. L'Isle-sur-la-Sorgue draws crowds of bargain hunters and collectors to its Sunday antiques and *brocante* (collectibles) fair, strung in picturesque disarray along its water mills and canals. Some of the best pickings in linen sheets, silverware, engravings, pewter, oak furniture, and quirky collectibles can be had if you arrive early, though the after-lunch stroll-and-browse is a fashionable tradition.

Perched Villages

Although there are pretty hilltop villages throughout the south of France, the Luberon has a surprising concentration of them, some less gentrified (and more atmospheric) than others. Gordes, Ménerbes, Roussillon, and Bonnieux have become boomtowns in real estate and tourism but still retain their original honey-gold stone and the majesty of their extraordinary positions overlooking the countryside. Others that are less well-known—Seguret, Le Barroux, Mormoiron, Caromb—offer less to buy and eat, but allow you to experience the quiet isolation of these ancient retreats; around Mont Ventoux, it's worth it to turn off toward whatever cluster of hilltop houses catches your eye. Trust your instincts and wander.

Vestiges of the Past

The best Roman ruins in this region are in Vaison-la-Romaine, where a theater, grand villas, and an entire village complete with boutiques and toilets remain in skeletal form. In Orange the magnificent theater has retained its great stone stage wall and still serves as an inspiring venue for the summer opera festival.

Avignon's old town still stands within the 14th-century wall that protected its rebellious popes from angry skeptics; the popes' luxurious palace crowns the city center. And the magnificently preserved Romanesque Abbaye de Sénanque, outside Roussillon, floats in a sea of lavender.

But the most unusual and fascinating antiquities in the Vaucluse are the tiny stone beehive–huts called *bories,* of mysterious origin but built in the same fashion, it is thought, since the Iron Age. Some 3,000 are scattered over the hillsides of the Luberon and environs, and an entire village has been reconstructed outside Gordes.

Wine

The most serious wine center in the south of France is the southern portion of the Côtes du Rhône, home to the muscular reds of Gigondas, Vacqueyras, Rasteau, and of their more famous neighbor Châteauneuf-du-Pape, as well as the fruity Grenache-based rosé of Tavel. Nearby Beaumes-de-Venise is famous for its sweet, light muscat. But not to be overlooked are the wines of the Côtes du Ventoux and the Côtes du Luberon, with drinkable and inexpensive reds and rosés and a notable white from Lourmarin.

Exploring the Vaucluse

Avignon as well as the Roman centers and papal vineyards to its north lie in arid lowlands, and getting from point to point through these flats can be uninspiring. It's to the east that the real Vaucluse rises up into the green-studded slopes of Mont Ventoux and the Luberon. Here, the back roads are beautiful—the temptation to abandon your rental car and go on foot is often irresistible. Give in; the smells of wild thyme, lavender, wet stone, and dry pine are as heady as a Châteauneuf-du-Pape.

Great Itineraries

Avignon is a must, and if you're a wine lover, you'll enjoy exploring the vineyards north of it. If you're a fan of things Roman, you need to see Vaison-la-Romaine and Orange. The antiques market in L'Isle-sur-la-Sorgue makes for a terrific Sunday excursion, as does the nearby Fontaine-de-Vaucluse, a dramatic spring cascade (outside drought season). But the Luberon and its villages perched high up in the hills are a world of their own and worth allowing time for—perhaps even your whole vacation. Note that the Pont de Gard, the superbly preserved Gallo-Roman aqueduct, is just a 30-minute drive west of Avignon, and that Arles, Nîmes, and the windswept Camargue are only a stone's throw to the south and west (☞ Chapter 1).

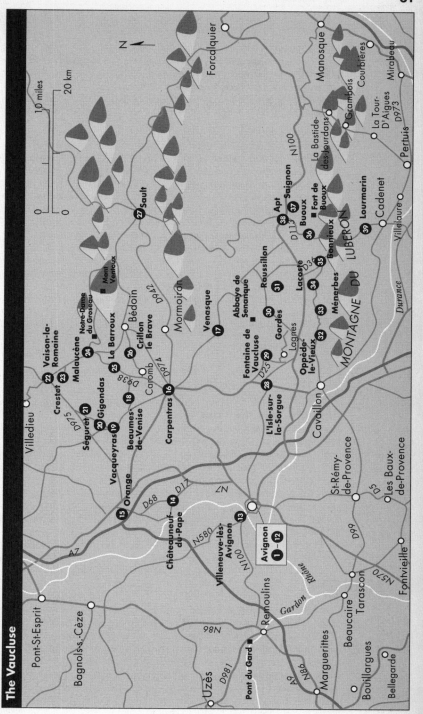

Numbers in the text correspond to numbers in the margin and on the Vaucluse and Avignon maps.

IF YOU HAVE 3 DAYS

Base yourself in the old town of ⌂ **Avignon** ①–⑫. Make excursions to **L'Isle-sur-la-Sorgue** ㉘ and **Fontaine de Vaucluse** ㉙ on the first day, and to **Gordes** ㉚ or **Bonnieux** ㉟ in the Luberon, the next day. On the third day, head up to see the antiquities in **Orange** ⑮ and **Vaison-la-Romaine** ㉒.

IF YOU HAVE 7 DAYS

Spend three nights in ⌂ **Avignon** ①–⑫, exploring its museums and making a day trip into **Châteauneuf-du-Pape** ⑭ and on to **Gigondas** ⑳, **Beaumes-de-Venise** ⑱, and **Vacqueyras** ⑲ for door-to-door tastings (the designated driver must sniff, rinse, and spit, of course). On day four, head up to **Orange** ⑮ and spend the night at ⌂ **Vaison-la-Romaine** ㉒, then dawdle along the scenic roads at the base of Mont Ventoux, wandering up into any hill villages that look intriguing. On the fifth day, press on to ⌂ **L'Isle-sur-la-Sorgue** ㉘ or ⌂ **Fontaine de Vaucluse** ㉙. Then head into the Luberon, stopping to explore **Roussillon** ㉛ and the Abbaye de Sénanque, spending night five in ⌂ **Gordes** ㉚. The next day meander through Peter Mayle country: **Oppède-le-Vieux** ㉜, **Ménerbes** ㉝, **Lacoste** ㉞, and ⌂ **Bonnieux** ㉟, where you can spend night six overlooking the countryside. From here it's easy to cut over the crest and head south to Aix-en-Provence and Marseille (☞ Chapter 3), or head west via Cavaillon to Les Alpilles or Nîmes (☞ Chapter 1).

IF YOU HAVE 10 DAYS

Take more time in each of the places in the seven-day itinerary, checking on concert tickets in ⌂ **Avignon** ①–⑫ or ⌂ **Orange** ⑮ and spending a night or two in one of the Mont Ventoux hill towns, such as ⌂ **Le Barroux** ㉕.

When to Tour the Vaucluse

High heat and high season hit in July and August with wallop: This lovely region is anything but undiscovered, thanks in part to Peter Mayle's revelations (he took a break from Provence to avoid the crowds he inspired, then relocated to the quieter south face of the Luberon). June and September are still intense but better. Low season falls between mid-November and mid-March, when many restaurants and hotels take two or three months off. That leaves spring and fall: If you arrive after Easter, the flowers are in full bloom, the air cool, and the sun warm, and you'll still be able to book a table on the terrace. The same goes for October and early November, when the hills of the Luberon turn rust and gold, and game figures on every menu.

AVIGNON

Of all the monuments in France—cathedrals, châteaux, fortresses—the ancient city of Avignon (pronounced ah-veen-*yonh*) is one of the most dramatic. Wrapped in a crenellated wall punctuated by towers and Gothic slit windows, its old center stands distinct from modern extensions, crowned by the Palais des Papes (Popes' Palace), a 14th-century fortress-castle that's nothing short of spectacular. Standing on the place du Palais under the gaze of the gigantic Virgin that reigns from the cathedral tower, with the palace sprawling to one side, the bishops' Petit Palais to the other, and the long, low bridge of childhood song fame stretching over the river ("Sur le pont d'Avignon on y danse tous en rond . . ."), you can beam yourself briefly into the 14th century, so complete is the context, so evocative the setting.

Yet you'll soon be brought back with a jolt by the skateboarders leaping over the smooth-paved square. Avignon is anything but a museum; it surges with modern ideas and energy and thrives within its ramparts as it did in the heyday of the popes—like those radical church lords, sensual, cultivated, cosmopolitan, with a taste for lay pleasures.

Avignon was transformed into the Vatican of the north when political infighting in the Eternal City drove Pope Clement V to accept Philippe the Good's invitation to start afresh. In 1309 his entourage arrived, preferring digs in nearby priories and châteaux; in 1316 he was replaced by Pope Jean XXII, who moved into the bishop's palace (today the Petit Palais). It was his successor Pope Benoit XII who undertook construction of the magnificent palace that was to house a series of popes through the 14th century.

During this holy reign Avignon evolved into a sophisticated, cosmopolitan capital, attracting artists and thinkers and stylish hangers-on. Founded in 1303, the university burgeoned, with thousands of students making the pilgrimage from across Europe. As the popes' wealth and power expanded, so did their formidable palace. And its sumptuous decor was legendary, inspiring horror and disdain from the poet Petrarch, who wrote of "towers both useless and absurd that our pride may mount skyward, whence it is sure to fall in ruins." The abandoned Italians dubbed Avignon a "second Babylon."

After a dispute with the king, Pope Gregory XI packed up for Rome in 1376, but Avignon held its ground. On his death in 1378, they elected their own pope, Clement VII, and the Great Schism divided the Christian world. Popes and antipopes abused, insulted, and excommunicated each other to no avail, though the real object of dispute was the vast power and wealth of the papacy. When the king himself turned on the last antipope, Avignon lost to Rome and the extravagant court dispersed.

Though it's merely the capital of the Vaucluse these days, Avignon's lively street life, active university, and colorful markets present a year-round spectacle. Every summer its arts life steps up to world-class status with the famous Avignon Theater Festival, which fills the city with devotees of its 300-plus stage productions, some "in," some "off," all on the cutting edge.

The Historic Center

A Good Walk

Begin your walk at the train station (there's a good parking garage). Crossing the busy ring road, walk through the Porte de la République, an opening in **Les Remparts** ①, the magnificent ramparts surrounding the entire old town. Head straight north up rue de la République. Past the post office on your left, duck left into a backstreet and peek into the **Hospice St-Louis** ②, a 17th- and 18th-century retreat that retains its magnificent courtyard shaded by gigantic plane trees. Today it's home to the Centre National du Théâtre (National Theater Center) and the hotel-restaurant Cloître St-Louis.

At the corner of rue Joseph-Vernet, stop in at the tourist office for maps and information. A block up from the tourist office, a lovely little 17th-century Jesuit chapel shelters a fascinating jumble of classical stonework in the **Musée Lapidaire** ③. Double back and turn right (west) onto rue Joseph-Vernet; two blocks up, you can stop into the tiny, eccentric **Musée Requien** ④, with its very personal displays on natural history. Next door, don't miss the **Musée Calvet** ⑤, a neoclassic stone mansion housing a collection of 17th- and 18th-century French art, much of it created in Avignon. Continue up Joseph-Vernet to rue St-Agricol, then follow it

64

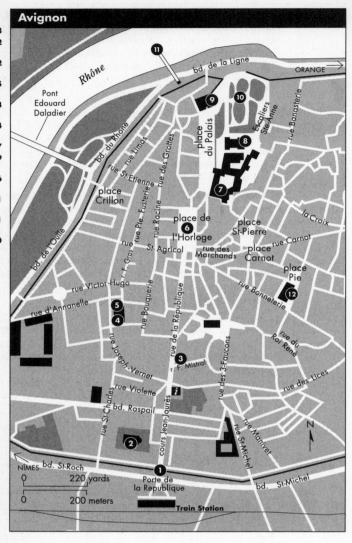

right into the animated heart of the city, the **place de l'Horloge** ⑥, anchored by the imposing 19th-century Hôtel de Ville and its Gothic Tour de l'Horloge (Clock Tower).

Tear yourself away from the sidewalk cafés, merry-go-round, jugglers, and mimes on the square and continue north to Place du Palais. Walk straight up the square and bear left until you're opposite the entry gate, so you can take in the full, wide-angle view of the magnificent **Palais des Papes** ⑦. After an hour or two touring the awesome interior, recross the square to study the magnificent facade of the Hôtel des Monnaies, a heavily sculpted Baroque masterpiece from the 17th century. Then cut across to the relatively humble but evocative **Cathédrale Notre-Dame-des-Doms** ⑧.

At the far end of Place du Palais, the **Petit Palais** ⑨—once home to Avignon's bishops and the first of its resident popes—houses a marvelous collection of Italian paintings, much of it (coincidentally) from the era of the popes and antipopes themselves.

Leave the square and climb up Montée du Moulin into the **Rocher des Doms** ⑩, a serene hilltop garden park replete with sculptures and black swans. From here you can look out over the city, the palace, and the river to the ancient enemy of papal Avignon, the fortified town of Villeneuve. Above all, you'll be able to take in the famous **Pont St-Bénézet** ⑪ in its stunted state and imagine dancers turning *tous en rond* (round and round). From the park, you can climb down past the Tour de Chiens in the ramparts to reach the bridge; or cut behind the Petit Palais.

Follow the scenic Escaliers Ste-Anne down and head right on rue Banasterie, but don't let the shops lining the winding backstreets around place Carnot keep you from stopping in to salivate over the delicious goods in **Les Halles** ⑫, the indoor market on place Pie (pronounced *pee*).

TIMING

If you spend the morning in the Popes' Palace and visit either the Musée Calvet or the Petit Palais in the afternoon, you can see these basics in a light day's sightseeing. (Note that the Petit Palais is closed on Tuesday.) If you're pressed, make a beeline for the Palace, then climb the Rocher des Doms for an overview that takes in the famous bridge.

Sights to See

❽ Cathédrale Notre-Dame-des-Doms. First built in a pure Provençal Romanesque style in the 12th century, then dwarfed by the extravagant palace beside it, this relatively humble church rallied in the 14th century with a cupola—that promptly collapsed. As rebuilt in 1425, it's a marvel of stacked arches with a strong Byzantine flavor and is topped nowadays with a gargantuan Virgin Mary lantern—a 19th-century afterthought—that glows for miles around. The Baroque styling in the nave dates from 1670. That's the tomb of Pope Jean XXII in the center-left chapel—but not his likeness, as his *gisant* (recumbent funeral statue) was wrecked in the Revolution and replaced with the likeness of a mere bishop, which he was before his rise to infamy. ✉ *pl. du Palais,* ☎ *04–90–86–81–01.* ☉ *Mon.–Sat. 7–7, Sun. 9–7.*

⑫ Les Halles. By seven every morning the merchants and artisans have stacked their herbed cheeses and arranged their vine-ripened tomatoes with surgical precision in pyramids and designs that please the eye before they tease the salivary glands. This permanent covered market is as far from a farmers' market as you can get, each booth a designer boutique of *haute gamme* (top-quality) goods, from jewel-like olives to silvery mackerel to racks of hanging hares worthy of a Flemish still life. Even if you don't have a kitchen to stock, consider enjoying a cup of coffee or a glass of (breakfast) wine while you take in the sights and smells and spectacle. ✉ *pl. Pie,* ☎ *04–90–27–15–15.* ☉ 6 AM–1 PM.

❷ Hospice St-Louis. Though not officially open to tourists, you can slip in for a peek at this graceful old 17th-century Jesuit cloister, converted for use as a hospital in the 19th century. Its symmetrical arches (now enclosed as a sleek hotel) are shaded by ancient plane trees. ✉ *20 rue du Portail Boquier.*

❺ Musée Calvet. Worth a visit for the beauty and balance of its architecture alone, this fine old museum holds a rich collection of art, acquired and donated by an 18th-century Avignon doctor with a hunger for antiquities and an eye for the classically inspired. Later acquisitions are neoclassic and Romantic, and almost entirely French, including works by Manet, Daumier, and David, such as *La Mort du Jeune Bara* (The Death of Young Bara). The main building itself is a Palladian-style jewel in pale Gard stone dating from the 1740s; the garden is so lovely that it may distract you from the paintings. ✉ *65 rue Joseph-Vernet,* ☎ *04–90–86–33–84.* 🎟 *30 frs/€4.57.* ☉ *Wed.–Mon. 10–1 and 2–6.*

❸ Musée Lapidaire. Housed indefinitely in a pretty little Jesuit chapel on the main shopping street (it will move eventually to a wing of the Musée Calvet), this collection of classical sculpture and stonework features funeral stones and works from Gallo-Roman times (1st and 2nd centuries), as well as items from the Musée Calvet's collection of Greek and Etruscan works. They are haphazardly labeled and insouciantly scattered throughout the noble chapel, itself slightly crumbling but awash with light. ✉ *27 rue de la République,* ☎ *04–90–85–75–38.* ✍ *10 frs/€1.52.* ☉ *Wed.–Mon. 10–1 and 2–6.*

❹ Musée Requien. Don't bother to rush to this eccentric little natural history museum, but since it's next door to the Calvet Museum and free, you might want to stop in and check out the petrified palm trunks, the dinosaur skeleton, the handful of local beetles and mammals, and the careful and evocative texts (French only) accompanying them. The museum is named for a local naturalist and functions as an entrance to the massive **library** of natural history upstairs. ✉ *67 rue Joseph-Vernet,* ☎ *04–90–82–43–51.* ✍ *Free.* ☉ *Tues.–Sat. 9–noon and 2–6.*

★ **❼ Palais des Papes** (Popes' Palace). The Renaissance chronicler Jean Froissart called this palace "the loveliest and strongest house in the world," while Petrarch sneered, "The houses of the apostles crumble as (popes) raise up their palaces of massy gold." Within these magnificent Gothic walls, one of the heydays (or low points) in French history took place, a period of extraordinary sacred and secular power and, to skeptics, outrageous wealth. Once densely decorated in tapestries, frescoes, and sumptuous fabrics, it hosted feasts of Romanesque extravagance and witnessed intrigues of Gothic proportion. The pope ruled within as half god, half prince, eating alone at an elevated table in the crowded dining hall, sleeping in a lavishly decorated bedroom distinctly devoid of sacred reference. His chamberlain's bedroom had eight hiding holes, complete with trapdoors concealed under carpets; who knows to what use they were put?

But don't expect to see eye-boggling luxury today. Resentful Revolutionaries hacked away most traces of excess in the 1780s, and ironically what remains has a monastic purity. Most of all you may be struck by the scale; either one of its two wings dwarfs the cathedral beside it, and between them they cover almost 50,000 ft of surface. The grand-scale interiors are evocative as well, with a massive wooden barrel vault arching over the dining hall like a boat belly and a kitchen with fireplaces big enough to house a family. The **Grande Audience** (Grand Audience Hall) and the **Grande Chapelle** are as vast as cathedrals.

From your first exterior view note the difference between the palace's two wings. The north end, toward the cathedral, is the Palais Vieux (Old Palace), a severe Cistercian bastion built by the sober Pope Benedict XII between 1334 and 1342; the south end was built over the next ten years with slightly airier fantasy by Pope Clement VI, who prized his creature comforts.

An enthusiastic patron of the arts, Clement VI brought in a team of artists from Italy to decorate his digs. It was led by no less than Simone Martini himself, imported from Siena and Assisi (where he had worked with Giotto). On his death, Mattheo Giovanetti took the lead, and the frescoes that covered every surface must have been one of the wonders of the world. Some of the finest traces remain in Clement's study, called the **Chambre du Cerf** (Stag's Room), where the walls still retain the lovely frescoes he commissioned in 1343. Unlike the Raphael masterpieces that decorate the Vatican chambers in Rome, which feature lofty classical themes and powerful Christian images, these paintings depict simple hunting scenes: a stag hunt, bird snaring, and fishing. They're graceful, almost naive in style, and intimate in scale, but the attempts at perspective in the deep window frames remind you that this was an advanced center of culture and learning in the 14th century, and perspective was then downright avant-garde, fresh from the sketchbooks of Giotto. Among many fragments, one other example of Giovanetti's work can be viewed in its entirety in **Chapelle St-Jean** (St. John's Chapel), a masterpiece of composition, in which the interplay of hands and the implied lines of gazes create a silent dialogue.

Though you may be anxious to see the more famous spaces, take time on entering to study the scale model of the palace in its medieval context. Only then can you take in its enormity, looming like Olympus over the tiny half-timber houses that crowded the place du Palais—a palace worthy of a royal dynasty and a temple to holy hubris.

A note of warning: This is one of those grand, must-see monuments that can be overwhelmed by shutter-popping bus tourists but should be seen nonetheless; aim for opening time, lunchtime, or evenings if you are there in the middle of summer. ✉ *pl. du Palais,* ☎ *04–90–27–50–00.* ✑ *45 frs/€6.86 includes choice of guided tour or individual audio guide; 55 frs/€8.38 for combination ticket with Pont St-Bénézet.* ☉ *Nov.–Mar., daily 9:30–5:45; Apr.–July and Oct., daily 9–7 (to 9 during theater festival in July); Aug.–Sept. daily 9–8.*

★ ⑨ **Petit Palais** (Small Palace). This former residence of bishops and cardinals houses a large collection of old-master paintings, the majority of them Italian works from the Renaissance schools of Siena, Florence, and Venice—styles with which the Avignon popes would have been familiar, but it's a coincidence. The paintings were acquired in the 19th century by the extravagant Italian marquis Campana and bought, on his bankruptcy, by Napoléon III. Divided among provincial museums throughout France, they remained scattered until after World War II; then the 300-some treasures were reunited under this historic roof. But even though the works weren't amassed by the popes, as you move through hall after hall of exquisite 14th-century imagery, you'll get a feel for the elevated tastes of the papal era. A key piece to seek out in the 15th-century rooms is Sandro Botticelli's *Virgin and Child,* a masterpiece of tenderness and lyric beauty created in his youth; 16th-century masterworks include Venetian works by Carpaccio and Giovanni Bellini. ✉ *pl. du Palais,* ☎ *04–90–86–44–58.* ✑ *30 frs/€4.57.* ☉ *Oct.–May, Wed.–Mon. 9:30–1 and 2–5:30; June–Sept., Wed.–Mon. 10–1 and 2–6.*

⑥ **Place de l'Horloge** (Clock Square). This square is the social nerve center of Avignon, where the concentration of bistros, brasseries, and restaurants draws swarms of locals and tourists to the shade of its plane trees. After a play, the doors of the **Théâtre Municipal** open onto the square and the audience spills into the nearest sidewalk café for a postperformance drink. The **Hôtel de Ville** (Town Hall) on the west side of the square was built in the 19th century around its dominating Gothic clock tower, from which the square gets its name.

★ ⑪ **Pont St-Bénézet** (St. Bénézet Bridge). "Sur le pont d'Avignon on y danse, on y danse . . ." Unlike London Bridge, this other fragment of childhood song still stretches its arches across the river, but only part way. After generations of war and flooding, only half remained by the 17th century. Its first stones allegedly laid with the miraculous strength granted St-Bénézet in the 12th century, it once reached all the way to Villeneuve. It's a bit narrow for dancing "tous en rond" (round and round) though the traditional place for dance and play was under the arches. For a fee, you may rent an audio guide and climb along its high platform for broad views of the old town ramparts. ⊠ *Port du Rocher.* 🎫 *19 frs/€2.90; 55 frs/€8.38 for combination ticket with Palais des Papes.* ⊙ *Apr.–Oct., daily 9–7; Nov.–Mar., daily 9:30–7:45.*

❶ Les Remparts (The Ramparts). More than 4 km (2½ mi) long, these protective crenellated walls and towers were built by the popes in the 14th century to keep out rampaging brigands and mercenary armies attracted by legends of papal wealth. It's extraordinarily well preserved, thanks in part to the efforts of architect Viollet-le-Duc, who restored the southern portion in the 19th century. Modern Avignon roars around its impervious walls on a noisy ring road that was once a moat.

❿ Rocher des Doms (Rock of the Domes). This ravishing hilltop garden, with statuary and swans under grand Mediterranean pines and subtropical greenery, would be a lovely retreat anywhere. But its views make it extraordinary. From side to side you can look over the palace, the rooftops of old Avignon, the St. Bénézet Bridge, and formidable Villeneuve across the Rhône. On the horizon looms Mont Ventoux, the Luberon, and Les Alpilles. ⊠ *Montée du Moulin, off pl. du Palais.* 🎫 *Free.*

Dining and Lodging

$$$$ ✕ **La Vieille Fontaine.** Summer-evening meals around the old fountain and boxwood-filled oil jars in the courtyard would be wonderful with *steak-frites* alone, but combine this romantic setting with stellar Southern French cuisine, and you have an event. Give yourself over to iced and truffled leek soup; pigeon roasted in lavender honey; the best regional wines; and an army of urbane servers—and hope for moonlight. It's in the lovely old Hôtel d'Europe. ⊠ *12 pl. Crillon,* 🕿 *04–90–14–76–76. Reservations essential. AE, MC, V.*

$$$ ✕ **La Mirande.** Whether you dine under the 14th-century coffered ceilings, surrounded by Renaissance tapestries, or in the intimate garden under the Popes' Palace walls, the restaurant of the luxurious Hôtel de la Mirande transports you to another time. Only the soigné cuisine of chef Daniel Hébet recalls the modern age with such delicacies as sea-snail ravioli in shellfish sauce, roast pigeon in ginger, and herbed saddle of lamb. Foodies take note: Hébet teams up with guest chefs to teach casual, multilingual cooking classes around the kitchen table, followed by a feast. ⊠ *pl. de la Mirande,* 🕿 *04–90–85–93–93. Reservations essential. AE, DC, MC, V.*

$$ ✕ **Brunel.** Stylishly decorated in "retro-bistro" style, this local favorite is helmed by Avignon-born and -bred chef Roger Brunel. Its down-home bistro cooking showcases a sophisticated larder: parchment-wrapped mullet with eggplant and tomatoes, chicken roasted with garlic confit (preserves), and caramelized apples in tender pastry. It's down a dull street just east of the Popes' Palace. ⊠ *46 rue de la Balance,* 🕿 *04–90–85–24–83. Reservations essential. MC, V.*

$$ ✕ **La Cuisine de Reine.** Glassed into the white-stone cloister of the trendy complex called Les Cloître des Arts, this chic bistro sports a theatrical dell'arte decor and a young, laid-back waitstaff. The blackboard lists eclectic dishes that are simple and sunny but serious in execution: duck in rosemary honey, rosy herbed lamb chops, and salmon tartare with eggplant caviar and citrus vinaigrette. Or join the cashmere-and-loafer set for the 120-franc (€ 18.30) Saturday brunch buffet. In summer, reserve a table in the elegant courtyard. ⊠ *83 rue Joseph-Vernet,* 🕿 *04–90–85–99–04. AE, DC, MC, V. Closed Sun.*

$$ ✕ **Hiély-Lucullus.** In the years since Pierre Hiély left the kitchen of this Avignon landmark, the cooking and ambience have faded. The upstairs

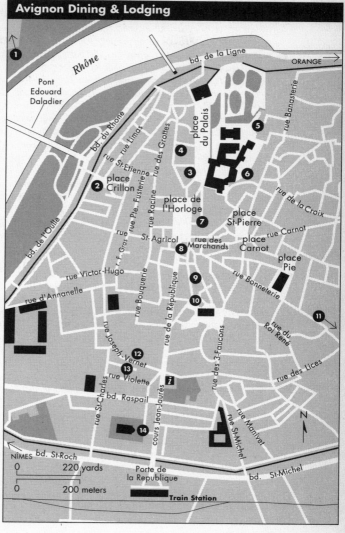

Avignon Dining & Lodging

dining room retains the quiet, dignified charm of old, but the cuisine is dependable bourgeois these days (look for the cod roasted with juniper, for instance). Prices have been graciously adjusted downward to compensate. ⊠ *5 rue de la République,* ☎ *04–90–86–17–07. Reservations essential. AE, MC, V. Closed late Jan., last 2 wks in June. No lunch Tues. Oct.–June.*

$ ✕ **Le Grand Café.** Behind the Popes' Palace, in a massive former factory—a setting of carefully preserved industrial decay—this hip entertainment complex combines an international cinema, a bar, and this popular bistro. Gigantic 18th-century mirrors and dance-festival posters hang on crumbling plaster and brick, and votive candles half-light the raw metal framework—an inspiring environment for intense film talk and a late supper of foie gras, goat cheese, or marinated artichokes, served in terra-cotta *tajines* (domed stew pots). ⊠ *La Manutention, 4 rue des Escaliers Ste-Anne,* ☎ *04–90–86–86–77. MC, V. Closed Mon. Aug.–June.*

$ ✕ **Maison Nani.** Crowded inside and out with trendy friends and young professionals, this pretty lunch spot serves stylish home-cooking in generous portion without the fuss of multiple courses—a comfortable Anglo-American approach. There are heaping dinner salads sizzling with fresh meat, enormous kebabs, and a creative quiche du jour. Rich desserts include fruit cobblers, chocolate cakes, and puddings. Prices are remarkable, averaging 55 francs/€8.38 for one large course. It's just off rue de la République. ⊠ *29 rue Théodore Aubanel,* ☎ *04-90-82-60-90. No credit cards. Closed Sun. No dinner Mon.–Thurs.*

$$$$ ✕🏨 **Hostellerie les Frênes.** This Relais & Châteaux hotel in a 19th-century country house underwent an extravagant face-lift in 1999, raising its style (and its prices) into the deluxe category. All rooms were renovated, from the formal Louis XV doubles in the main house to the bright, Southern-country rooms in the annexes. There are whirlpool baths in every room, a small spa with sauna and hot-water treatments, and—as always—lovely gardens and a pool surrounded by manicured greenery. ⊠ *645 av. des Vertes-Rives, 84140 Montfavet (5 km [3 mi] outside Avignon),* ☎ *04-90-31-17-93,* 𝔽𝔸𝕏 *04-90-23-95-03. 15 rooms. Restaurant, air-conditioning, pool, sauna, spa. AE, DC, MC, V. Closed Nov.–Easter.* ✺

$$$$ 🏨 **Hôtel de la Mirande.** Superbly restored and richly decorated with
★ exquisite reproduction fabrics and beeswaxed antiques, this designer's dream of a hotel is just below the Popes' Palace in a car-free zone. Its enclosed garden is a breakfast and dinner oasis, its central lounge a skylit and jazz-warmed haven. Rooms are both gorgeous and comfy, and the bathrooms, with their Victorian touches, are luxurious. Half the rooms face the garden, the other half the palace facade; a few even have tiny ultraprivate balconies with rooftop views. ⊠ *pl. de la Mirande, 84000,* ☎ *04-90-85-93-93,* 𝔽𝔸𝕏 *04-90-86-26-85. 19 rooms, 1 suite. Restaurant, bar. AE, DC, MC, V.* ✺

$$$–$$$$ 🏨 **Hôtel d'Europe.** Napoléon slept here, and so did Robert and Elizabeth Browning and any number of artists and writers right up to the theater luminaries who stay here today. This splendid 16th-century home, built by the Marquis of Graveson, resonates with history. With discreet, classic decor and a seasoned staff, this place will be lodging festival guests for centuries to come. Rooms are vast, with two suites overlooking the Popes' Palace. The restaurant, La Vieille Fontaine (☞ *above*), is one of Avignon's finest. ⊠ *12 pl. Crillon, 84000,* ☎ *04-90-14-76-76,* 𝔽𝔸𝕏 *04-90-14-76-71. 44 rooms. Restaurant. AE, DC, MC, V.* ✺

$$$ 🏨 **Cloître St-Louis.** Standing serene and noble within its sturdy 17th-
★ century walls, this sleek hotel encloses a cloistered square lined with grand old plane trees. The early Baroque building, erected by the Jesuits in 1611, was a theological school for novitiates and later a hospital before it became a hotel in the early 1990s. Now interiors are stripped and modernist, playing up the cool old stone. There's a small roof-top pool, and the hotel is a block's walk from the train station. ⊠ *20 rue du Portail-Boquier, 84000,* ☎ *04-90-27-55-55,* 𝔽𝔸𝕏 *04-90-82-24-01. 80 rooms. Restaurant, bar, pool. AE, DC, MC, V.* ✺

$$ 🏨 **L'Anastasy.** On the long, low island on the Rhône called Ile de la Barthelasse, this pretty farmhouse inn offers just five country-fresh rooms, home cooking, and an interesting social mix if you care to mingle: Madame Manguin lets guests withdraw or join in as they like, whether during meals, poolside chats, or while having drinks in the cozy kitchen–salon. Modest-priced meals (not included in the room price) must be reserved, and are prepared for guests on request only. ⊠ *Ile de la Barthelasse, 84000,* ☎ *04-90-85-55-94,* 𝔽𝔸𝕏 *04-90-82-59-40. 5 rooms. Pool. No credit cards.*

$$ ⊞ **Hôtel du Blauvac.** Just off rue de la République and place de l'Horloge, this 17th-century nobleman's home has been divided into 16 guest rooms, many with pristine exposed stonework, aged oak details, and lovely tall windows that look, alas, onto backstreet walls. Pretty fabrics and a warm, familial welcome more than compensate, however. It's a simple budget hotel (no elevator, no air-conditioning) and utterly charming. ⊠ *11 rue de la Bancasse, 84000,* ☎ *04–90–86–34–11,* FAX *04–90–86–27–41. 16 rooms. Breakfast room. AE, DC, MC, V.*

$$ ⊞ **Hôtel du Palais des Papes.** Though its two-star status might lead you to expect a modest lodging, this is a notably solid and comfortable hotel—all the better for its location just off the place du Palais. The room decor pairs exposed stone and beams, updated with ironwork furniture and rich fabrics, with modern tile baths. A film-set Louis XIII restaurant downstairs is more for honeymooners than gastronomes. ⊠ *1 rue Ge(ac)rard-Philippe, 84000,* ☎ *04–90–86–04–13,* FAX *04–90–27–91–17. 23 rooms. Restaurant, bar. AE, DC, MC, V.* ⊛

$ ⊞ **Hôtel Innova.** With the family living just off the breakfast room and Peter, the tiny shih tzu, sniffing at you as you breakfast, you'll feel like a student boarder in this modest budget lodging. But rooms are big and clean, freshly decorated, and equipped with phone and TV; miniature bathrooms fit neatly into closets. It's just up the street from the Musée Calvet. ⊠ *100 rue Joseph-Vernet, 84000,* ☎ *04–90–82–54–10,* FAX *04–90–82–52–39. 11 rooms, 5 with bath, 6 with shower only. Breakfast room. AE, DC, MC, V.*

$ ⊞ **Hôtel de Mons.** Tatty and decidedly eccentric, this is a neo-Gothic budget crash pad after Edward Gorey's heart. The 13th-century building was originally a chapel. Transformation took some maneuvering, but guest rooms with baths (and Brady Bunch decors) have been fitted into crooked nooks and crannies, while retaining some period detail such as quarried stone and a slanting spiral stair. Breakfast is served in a groin-vaulted crypt. Location is everything—it's two steps off place de l'Horloge. ⊠ *5 rue de Mons, 84000,* ☎ *04–90–82–57–16,* FAX *04–90–85–19–15. 11 rooms, 10 with bath. AE, MC, V.*

Nightlife and the Arts

Small though Avignon is, its inspiring art museums, strong university, and 60-some years of saturation in world-class theater have made the city an antenna for the arts south of Paris.

Held annually in July, the Avignon festival, known officially as the **Festival Annuel d'Art Dramatique** (Annual Festival of Dramatic Art), has brought the best of world theater to this ancient city since 1947. Some 300 productions—some official, some "off" and "off-off"—take place every year; the main performances are at the Palais des Papes. Overflowing with traveling players and audiences of every kind, the city takes on the look of a medieval festival or a grand party thrown by Clement VI. For tickets and information, call ☎ 04–90–27–66–50.

A winter festival known as **Les Hivernales** celebrates French dance here every January and February. Its central venue is the **Maison Jean Vilar** (⊠ 8 rue de Mons, ☎ 04–90–85–45–24).

For information on events and tickets, too, stop into the massive book-and-record chain **FNAC** (⊠ 19 rue de la République, ☎ 04–90–14–35–43).

NIGHTLIFE

Within its fusty old medieval walls, Avignon teems with modern nightlife well into the wee hours. At **Le Bistroquet** (⊠ Ile de la Barthelasse, ☎ 04–90–82–25–83), Saturday night brings rock concerts or dance music of all kinds. The **Bistrot du Cinéma** (⊠ 4 rue des Escaliers Ste-Anne, ☎ 04–

90–82–65–36) serves drinks in a dark, intimate space just outside the cinema in La Manutention (☞ The Arts, *below*). At the cabaret **Dolphin Blues** (✉ chemin de l'île Piot, ☎ 04–90–82–46–96), a hip mix of comedy and music dominates the repertoire. **Pub Z** (✉ 58 rue Bonneterie, ☎ 04–90–85–42–84) is the hot spot for rock, sometimes live; the black-and-white decor incorporates a zebra theme. **Le Rouge Gorge** (✉ 10 bis rue Peyrollerie, ☎ 04–90–14–02–54) presents a dinner show with singers, dancers, and comedians and after-dinner dancing every Friday and Saturday night. On other nights other comedy and music groups perform.

THE ARTS

Two cinema complexes show first-run, mainstream movies in *v.o.* (*version originale,* meaning in the original language with French subtitles) as well as hard-to-find international independent works: **Utopia Manutention** (✉ 4 rue des Escaliers Ste-Anne) and **République** (✉ 5 rue Figuière). For schedules call 04–90–82–65–36.

At **AJMI** (Association Pour le Jazz et la Musique Improvisée; ✉ 4 rue Escaliers Ste-Anne, ☎ 04–90–86–08–61), in La Manutention entertainment complex, you can hear jazz performed by artists of some renown.

Shopping

Avignon is too big and too resident oriented to be full of boutiques for tourists, so it doesn't have an unusual concentration of Provençal gifts and products. Rather it has a cosmopolitan mix of French chains, youthful clothing shops (it's a college town), and a few plummy dress shops. **Rue des Marchands,** off place Carnot, is one shopping stretch, but **rue de la République** is the main artery. Dominating the main drag is trendy, cheap-chic clothing store **Zara** (✉ 25 rue de la Republique, ☎ 04–90–80–64–40).

If you're hungry for books in English, find **Shakespeare** (✉ 155 rue Carreterie, ☎ 04–90–27–38–50); in addition to new and used books in English, it has a tearoom, café, and terrace.

If you're a fan of fine French cookware, head to **Jaffier-Parsi** (✉ 42 rue des Fourbisseurs, ☎ 04–90–86–08–85), a professional cooking supply store that has been stocking heavy copper pots, stainless steel ladles, mortar-and-pestle sets, and great knives since 1902. Among the myriad vendors of Provençal pottery throughout the region, **Terre è Provence** (✉ 26 rue République, ☎ 04–90–16–52–52) maintains a high esthetic standard, with lovely pitchers, platters, and tureens.

Excellent Provençal fabrics can be found at **Souleïado** (✉ 5 rue Joseph-Vernet, ☎ 04–90–86–47–67). More goods made from the signature printed fabrics can be found at Souleïado's competitor **Les Olivades** (✉ 28 rue Marchands, ☎ 04–90–86–13–42).

Mouret Chapelier (✉ 20 rue Marchands, ☎ 04–90–85–39–38) has a treasure trove of old-fashioned, Old-World, and marvelously eccentric hats in a jewel-box setting.

HAUT VAUCLUSE

North and northeast of Avignon, this land of rolling orchards and vineyards spreads lazily at the foot of Mont Ventoux, redolent of truffles, lavender, and fine wine. Perhaps that's why the Romans so firmly established themselves here, raising grand theaters and luxurious villas that still remain in part. From Avignon head north into the vineyards, making a brief tour of Châteauneuf-du-Pape, even if you don't stop to drink and buy wine. Orange is just up the highway; though the town isn't the most picturesque, its Roman theater is a must-see. Between Orange and Mont Ventoux are wine centers (Beaumes-de-Venise, Gigondas, Vacqueyras) and picturesque villages such as Crestet, Séguret, Le Barroux, and Malaucène, which the first French pope preferred to Avignon. Visit Vaison-la-Romaine for a strong concentration of Roman ruins.

Villeneuve-lès-Avignon

⓭ *2 km (1 mi) west of Avignon.*

Just across the Rhône from Avignon, this medieval town glowers over at its powerful neighbor to the east. Its abbey, fortress, and quiet streets offer a pleasant contrast to Avignon's bustle.

In the 14th century Villeneuve benefited enormously from the migration of the popes into Avignon as an accompanying flood of wealthy and influential cardinals poured over the river. No less than 15 of the status-seeking princes-of-the-church built magnificent homes on this neighboring hilltop. In addition, kings Jean le Bon and Charles V built up formidable defenses on the site to keep an eye on the papal territories.

However, it was the bounty and extravagance of the cardinals that nourished the abbey here, known as **Chartreuse du Val-de-Bénédiction** or, literally, the Chartreuse order of the Valley of Blessings. Inside the abbey are spare cells with panels illuminating monastic life, the vast 18th-century **cloître de cimetière** (cemetery cloister), a smaller Romanesque cloister, and, within the remains of the abbey church, the Gothic tomb of Pope Innocent VI. Theatrical events are staged here during Avignon's annual theatre festival. ☎ *04–90–15–24–24.* 🎟 *32 frs/€4.88.* ⊙ *Apr.–Sept., daily 9–6:30; Oct.–Mar., daily 9:30–5:30.*

At the top of the village is the **fort Saint-André,** which once ostensibly protected the town of St-André, now absorbed into Villeneuve. The fortress's true importance was as a show of power for the kingdom of France in the face of the all-too-close Avignon popes. You can explore the fortress grounds and the bare ruined walls of inner chambers for free; you can also climb (for a fee) into the twin towers for broad views over Avignon, the Luberon, and Mont Ventoux. Don't miss the fortress's formal Italianate **gardens** (☎ 04–90–25–55–95), littered with remains of the abbey that preceded the fortifications. Admission to the gardens, which are privately owned, is 20 francs/€3.05. They're open Tuesday through Sunday 10–12:30 and 2–6. ☎ *04–90–25–45–35.* 🎟 *Towers: 25 frs/€3.81.* ⊙ *Apr.–Sept., daily 10–1 and 2–6; Oct.–Mar., daily 10–1 and 2–5.*

Below the abbey, the **musée Pierre de Luxembourg** gives you access to one of the luxurious, 14th-century cardinals' manors. Here you'll find a collection of medieval and Renaissance art, including the spectacularly colorful and richly detailed *Couronnement de la Vierge* (Coronation of the Virgin), an altarpiece painted in 1453 by Enguerrand Quarton. ☎ *04–90–27–49–66.* 🎟 *20 frs/€3.05* ⊙ *Mid-June–mid-Sept., daily 10–12:30 and 3–7; Oct.–Mar., Tues.–Sun. 10–noon and 2–5:30; Apr.–mid-June, Tues.–Sun. 10–12:30 and 3–7.*

Châteauneuf-du-Pape

⓮ *18 km (11 mi) north of Avignon, 22 km (13½ mi) west of Carpentras.*

The countryside around this very famous wine center is a patchwork of rolling vineyards, of green and black furrows striping the landscape in endless, retreating perspective. Great gates and grand houses punctuate the scene, as symmetrical and finely detailed as the etching on a wine label, and signs—discreet but insistent—beckon you to follow the omnipresent smell of fermenting grapes to their source. Behind barn doors, under cellar traps, and in chilly caves beneath châteaux, colossal oak vats nurture this noble Rhône red to maturity.

Once the table wine of the Avignon popes, who kept a fortified summer house here (hence the name of the town, which means "new castle of the pope"), the vineyards of Châteauneuf-du-Pape had the good fortune to be wiped out by phylloxera in the 19th century. Its revival as a muscular and resilient mix of up to thirteen varietals moved it to the forefront of French wines, with an almost portlike intensity (it can reach 15% alcohol content). The whites, though less significant, are also to be reckoned with. To learn more, stop in at the **Musée des Outils de Vignerons Père Anselme,** a private collection of tools and equipment displayed in the *caveau* (wine cellar) of the Brotte family. ⊠ *rte. d'Avignon,* ☎ *04–90–83–70–07.* 🎫 *Free.* ☉ *Daily 9–noon and 2–6.*

In addition to the discreet *vignobles* on the edge of town, the center has become something of a tourist magnet, and storefront wineries invite tasters of every experience to sample their vintages. Feel free to enter and taste; most outlets are happy to let you try a few without pressure to purchase. Some of the top Châteauneufs come from Domaine de la Nerthe, Château de Vaudieu, and Château Fortia, and are priced accordingly. If you're not armed with the names of a few great houses, look for *medaille d'or* (gold medal) ratings from prestigious wine fairs; these are usually indicated with a gold sticker on the bottle.

If you're disinclined to spend your holiday sniffing and sipping in a dark basement, climb the hill to the ruins of the **Château.** Though it was destroyed in the Wars of Religion and its remaining donjon (keep) blasted by the Germans in World War II, it still commands a magnificent position. From this rise in the rolling vineyards, you can enjoy wraparound views of Avignon, the Luberon, and Mont Ventoux.

Dining and Lodging

$–$$ ✕ **Le Pistou.** Study the blackboard menu here for satisfying Provençal specialties, such as herb-roasted dorade (a whole, small Mediterranean fish) or a fricassée of rabbit livers and kidneys. The welcome is warm and the prix-fixe menus start cheap. ⊠ *15 rue Joseph-Ducos,* ☎ *04–90–83–71–75. MC, V. Closed Mon. No dinner Sun.*

$$ ✕🏨 **La Garbure.** With four modest rooms decked in vivid jewel tones upstairs and a tiny formal dining room downstairs, this intimate hotel offers a romantic, slightly old-fashioned stopover. The cooking aims for the haute rather than the hearty, with dishes like potted quail with Carpentras truffles, stuffed rabbit with a subtle thyme sauce, and a heady sorbet of marc de Châteauneuf-du-Pape, the eau-de-vie made of local grapes. The restaurant is closed on Sunday from October through June and for Sunday lunch July through August. ⊠ *3 rue Joseph-Ducos,* ☎ *04–90–83–75–08,* 🖷 *04–90–83–52–34. Air-conditioning. MC, V.*

Orange

⓯ *12 km (7 mi) north of Châteauneuf-du-Pape, 31 km (19 mi) north of Avignon.*

Even less touristy than Nîmes (☞ Chapter 1) and just as eccentric, the city of Orange (pronounced oh-*rawnzh*) sprawls somewhat gracelessly over the Rhône flatlands. Its hotels and restaurants have a vaguely bohemian air—eclectic decors, patchwork menus—and its insular ambience offers little of the easy grace of the rest of the Vaucluse. The air of the world having passed Orange by may be due in part to efforts to boycott it since it elected an extremely right-wing government. Nonetheless it draws thousands every year to its spectacular **Théâtre Antique,**

DU BON VAING POUR VOTRE SANGTÉ

AS MUCH AS IT IS IDENTIFIED with olives and cypress trees, the Provençal landscape is defined by the retreating perspective of row on rocky row of gnarled grapevines, their green shoots growing heavy through the summer and by fall sagging under the weight of ripe fruit.

Although Provence has a few fine wines—notably the lower Rhône greats such as Châteauneuf-du-Pape and Beaumes-de-Venise and a few excellent whites from Cassis, Bandol, and Palette—the majority of wine drunk here is unpretentious, sunny stuff, with the most by far being rosé. Red or rosé, it is usually drunk icy-cold, whether to quench arid thirsts or to hide a less than rounded finish.

There are several subregions of southern wines. In the eastern Languedoc, above the Camargue, spreads the region known as Costières-de-Nîmes, and a straightforward table wine from the Côtes-de-Luberon appears on every Vaucluse table, alongside the equally unpretentious Côtes-du-Ventoux. But generally from the Rhône eastward—most heavily focused in the Haut Var behind Saint-Tropez—the wines fall under the undemanding umbrella title of Côtes de Provence. Nowadays the demands of more-discerning palates are leading the vintners to tear out undistinguished, filler varietals and plant more Grenache, Cinsault, Cabernet, and Syrah.

Remember that in these parts the word *vin* (wine) twangs through the nose like a broken banjo string and sounds more like *vaing*. *Santé* (to your health)!

a colossal Roman theater built in the time of Caesar Augustus. Its vast stone stage wall, bouncing sound off the facing hillside, climbs four stories high, and the niche at center stage contains the original statue of Augustus, just as it reigned over centuries of productions of classical plays. Today this setting inspires and shelters world-class theater, as well as concerts of dance, classical music, poetry readings, and even rock. Orange's summer opera festival is one of Europe's best and one of its best known. ⊠ *pl. des Frères-Mounet,* ☎ *04–90–34–70–88.* ☜ *30 frs/€4.57; joint ticket with Musée Municipal.* ☉ *Apr.–Sept., daily 9:30–7; Oct.–Mar., daily 9:30–noon and 1:30–5:30.*

Across the street from the theater, the small **Musée Municipal** displays antiquities unearthed around Orange, including fragments of three detailed marble *cadastres* (land survey maps) dating from the 1st century. Upstairs a vivid series of 18th-century canvases show local mills producing Provençal fabrics, each aspect illustrated in careful detail. There are also personal objects from local aristocrats and a collection of faïence pharmacy jars. ⊠ *pl. des Frères-Mounet,* ☎ *04–90–34–70–88.* ☜ *30 frs/€4.57; joint ticket with theater.* ☉ *Apr.–Sept., daily 9:30–7; Oct.–Mar., daily 9:30–noon and 1:30–5:30.*

North of the city center and in the middle of modern-day traffic stands the notable **Arc de Triomphe** that once straddled the via Agrippa between Lyon and Arles. Three arches support a heavy double attic (horizontal top) floridly decorated with battle scenes and marine symbols, referring to Augustus's victories at Actium. The arch, which dates from about 20 BC, is superbly preserved, particularly the north side, but to view it on foot you'll have to cross a roundabout seething with traffic. ⊠ *North of the center on av. de l'Arc, direction Gap.*

Vieil Orange, the old-town neighborhood you must cross to hike from one Roman monument to the other, carries on peacefully when there's not a blockbuster spectacle in the theater. Lining its broad squares, under heavy-leaved plane trees, are a handful of shops and a few sidewalk cafés.

Dining and Lodging

$ ✕ **Aïgo Boulido.** The discreet but warm welcome makes a meal in this slightly crumbling town house all the more memorable. Flashy fabrics and artwork are juxtaposed with grand architectural detail. Even if the food is more sincere than sophisticated, you'll eat well here, choosing from dishes such as garlic soup (hence the restaurant's dialect name), local fish, and home-style desserts. ⊠ *20 pl. Sylvian,* ☎ *04–90–34–18–19. MC, V. Closed Sun.*

$ ✕ **La Yaca.** At this intimate, unpretentious bistro, you are greeted by the beaming owner/host/waiter, then pampered with an embarrassment of riches in menu choices. The home cooking draws local regulars. Specialties are emphatically *"style grandmère"*—slow cooked and heavily seasoned—and include rabbit stew, *caillette* (pork-liver meat loaf), and even canned peas with bacon. It's all in a charming stone-and-beam setting, complete with a Gothic archway. ⊠ *24 pl. Sylvian,* ☎ *04–90–34–70–03. MC, V. Closed Wed. and Nov. No dinner Tues.*

$$ ⌂ **Arène.** On a quiet square in the old center, this comfortable hotel is filled with a labyrinth of rooms densely decorated in rich colors and heavy fabrics. The nicest ones look out over the square. As it's built between several fine old houses strung together, there's no elevator, but a multitude of stairways instead. ⊠ *pl. de Langues, 84100,* ☎ *04–90–11–40–40,* 𝙵𝙰𝚇 *04–90–11–40–45. 30 rooms. Air-conditioning. AE, DC, MC, V.*

$–$$ ⌂ **Clarine-Cigaloun.** On a charmless backstreet just a block from the theater, this modest hotel offers basic rooms with white stucco and all-weather carpet. The breakfast room is brightened with olive-sprigged linens. Three rooms have air-conditioning. Now managed by the Clarine chain, it has traded some of its personal charm for efficiency. ⊠ *4 rue Caristie, 84100,* ☎ *04–90–34–10–07,* 𝙵𝙰𝚇 *04–90–34–89–76. 30 rooms. AE, DC, MC, V.* ✆

$–$$ ⌂ **L'Orangerie.** Hosts Micky and Gérard pour creative energy into this
★ auberge, just 4 km (2½ mi) north of Orange. His artwork, her flamboyant taste, and their mutual world travels result in an eclectic decor. The restaurant's menu reflects their wide-ranging interests as well, as influences from Asia and the Caribbean show up among the Provençal dishes. An annex, **La Mandarine,** is just up the road in the open country; the five-room stone mas has a fireplace, pool, and library. ⊠ *4 rue de l'Ormeau, 84420 Piolenc,* ☎ *04–90–29–59–88,* 𝙵𝙰𝚇 *04–90–29–67–74. 6 rooms. Restaurant. AE, DC, MC, V.* ✆

Nightlife and the Arts

To witness the torches of *Nabucco* or *Aida* flickering against a 2,000-year-old Roman wall and to hear the extraordinary sound play around the hemicycle of ancient seats is one of the great summer festival experiences in Europe. Every July, **Les Chorégies d'Orange** echo tradition and amass operatic and classical music spectacles under the summer stars. For information call ☎ 04–90–34–04–04; 𝙵𝙰𝚇 04–90–11–00–85; or write to ⊠ Chorégies, B.P. 205, 84107 Orange Cedex well in advance.

Carpentras

🔟 *24 km (15 mi) northeast of Avignon, 24 km (15 mi) southeast of Orange.*

Though its name figures in most highway directions and it serves as a major market crossroads, Carpentras is often bypassed en route to the Vaucluse's less prominent byways. Yet at its core lies an atmospheric old quarter that bursts into activity every Friday, when the sizable market takes over the narrow, circuitous inner streets. And on winter Fridays, Carpentras draws a steady stream of serious gastronomes in search of the perfect truffle.

Once the seat of the bishopric and blessed with gifts from the Avignon popes, old Carpentras tightly encircles the **cathédrale St-Siffrein,** whose expressive gargoyles loom halfway across the tiny streets around it. Construction on the cathedral began in 1404; the building included a high gallery where the bishop could slip in and out unobserved. The structure's pure Gothic style frames a startlingly Baroque **altarpiece,** which in turn surrounds a modern stained glass window. The 15th-century south portal, in a heavy and bombastic flamboyant Gothic style, is known as the **porte Juive** (Jewish door), through which converted Jews were said to pass on their way to their baptism.

There was, in fact, a sizable Jewish population in Carpentras from the Middle Ages until the Revolution, when the population was 1,500 strong. Banished from the Kingdom of France, the Jews of Provence were protected by the Avignon popes and thrived in relative liberty in Avignon, Cavaillon, and Carpentras. Relative indeed: They were constrained to live within a ghetto, called a *carrière,* whose portals were closed at night. That neighborhood was razed in the 19th century to create the place de l'Hôtel de Ville. Yet one treasure remains—the **synagogue.** Built in 1367, it's the oldest in France. Bathed in light from its clear arched windows, the second-story sanctuary exudes a cool simplicity, a strong contrast to the dark mysticism of its Christian contemporaries. In the basement are spring-fed pools for purification bathing; on the ground floor, there's an oven for baking unleavened bread. Closed to visitors during Jewish holidays. ⊠ *pl. de l'Hotel-de-Ville.* ☉ *Mon.–Thurs. 10– noon and 3–5; Fri. 10–noon and 3–4.*

Carpentras has a headily secular draw, too—its **truffle market.** From December through February, these perfumed black mushrooms, cultivated and dug in the surrounding oak woods, are brought to the place Aristide Briand and the Café l'Univers and sold in a tense, quiet street exchange, directly from the dealers' baskets. If you're ready to invest the 3,000 francs to 4,000 francs (about €460 to €610) per kilo they cost in high season, look for an honest face and pay in cash. But remember, you're not allowed to bring them out of the country.

Lodging

$–$$ ☐ **Hôtel du Fiacre.** Graced with tapestries, period furnishings, and a lovely garden courtyard, this 18th-century hôtel particulier is a grand place for an atmospheric overnight. There are sweet attic rooms with rooftop views across the old-town maze, plus a grand suite with high molded ceilings and French windows opening over the greenery. Though the plasterwork and bathrooms could use a face-lift, the welcome is warm, the setting distinctly regional, and the location for sorties into the Vaucluse ideal. ⊠ *153 rue Vigne, 84210,* ☎ *04–90–63–03–15,* FAX *04–90–60– 49–73. 19 rooms, 1 suite. Breakfast room. AE, DC, MC, V.*

Venasque

🄬 *12 km (7 mi) southeast of Carpentras, 35 km (22 mi) northeast of Avignon.*

Once the bishopric and capital of Comtat Venaissin, the large agricultural region east of Avignon, Venasque now only has a population of about

675 inhabitants. The village, tucked inside fortified walls, stands proudly on a hill overlooking the Carpentras Plain. With its sweeping views, stonework, and masses of flowers, it's pretty enough to visit for atmosphere alone.

★ But if you're interested in early churches, head straight for the stunning Merovingian **baptistery** behind the Église de Notre-Dame; it dates from the 6th century and is thus one of the oldest religious structures in France. Thought to be built on the site of a Roman temple, of which you can see columns recycled into chapel form, it retains its Greek-cross shape despite reconstruction in the 11th century. The pure curves of its arches and the simplicity of the decoration perfectly match the serenity of the cliff-top setting, and the ensemble as a whole surpasses its peers in Fréjus, Aix, and Riez. Besides the hours listed below, the church is open for services on Sunday morning. ☎ *10 frs/€1.52.* ☯ *Mid-Mar.–May and Oct.–mid-Nov., Mon., Tues. and Thurs.–Sat. 10–noon and 2–6; June–Sept., Mon., Tues. and Thurs.–Sat. 10–noon and 5–7; mid-Nov.–Jan., Mon., Tues. and Thurs.–Sat. 10–noon and 2–5.*

Dining and Lodging

$$$ ✕🏠 **Auberge de la Fontaine.** You'll climb winding stone stairs to
★ reach this graceful 18th-century house. It's been converted into a clever complex of stylish apartments, each with a bedroom, kitchenette, and fireplace salon. Don't cook in every night, though—the pretty, rustic restaurant merits your full attention. Chef-owner Christian Soehlke adds sunny Provençal flavors (truffles, thyme flowers) to local lamb and pigeon, and even knows the goats that provide his tiny cabri cheeses by name. There's a ground-floor bistro, too, for lighter meals (salads, airy pâtés, pastries) or the morning papers. ✉ *84210,* ☎ *04–90–66–02–96,* FAX *04–90–66–13–14. 5 apartments. 2 restaurants, air-conditioning, kitchenettes. MC, V.*

Beaumes-de-Venise

⑱ *23 km (14 mi) east of Orange, 9 km (5½ mi) north of Carpentras.*

Just west of the great mass of Mont Ventoux, surrounded by farmland and vineyards, is Beaumes-de-Venise, where streets of shuttered bourgeois homes slope steeply into a market center. This is the renowned source of a delicately sweet Muscat wine, but if you're tasting, don't overlook the local red wine. Look for **Domaine des Bernardins** (✉ av. Castaud, ☎ 04–90–62–94–13), a vineyard with a tasting cave, for both.

Beaumes lies at the foot of the **Dentelles de Montmirail,** a small range of rocky chalk cliffs eroded to lacy pinnacles—whence their name *dentelles* (lace). From tiny D21, east of town, you'll find dramatic views north to the ragged peaks and south over lush orchards and vineyards.

Vacqueyras

⑲ *5 km (3 mi) northwest of Beaumes-de-Venise, 16 km (10 mi) northwest of Carpentras.*

Smaller and more picturesque than Beaumes, with stone houses scattered along its gentle slopes, Vacqueyras gives its name to a robust, tannic red worthy of its more famous neighbors around Châteauneuf-du-Pape or Gigondas. Wine *domaines* beckon from the outskirts of town, and the center strikes a mellow balance of plane trees and draping wisteria, punctuated by discreet tasting shops. Thanks to its consistently rising quality, Vacqueyras was the latest of the Côte du Rhônes to earn its own appellation—the right to put its village name on the bottle instead of the less prestigious, more generic Côtes-du-Rhône label.

Gigondas

㉒ *3 km (2 mi) north of Vacqueyras, 19 km (12 mi) northwest of Carpentras.*

The prettiest of all the Mont Ventoux Côtes-du-Rhône wine villages, Gigondas is little more than a cluster of stone houses stacked gracefully up a hillside overlooking the broad sweep of the valley below. At the top a false-front Baroque church anchors a ring of medieval ramparts; from here you can take in views as far as the Cévennes.

Its few residents share one vocation: the production of the vigorous Grenache-based red that bears the village name. At the 41 *caveaux* (tasting caves) scattered through the village and its surrounding countryside, you're welcome to visit, taste, and buy without ceremony. Pick up a contact list from the tourist office at the village entrance. One of the biggest names is **Domaine Romane Machotte** (☎ 04–90–65–84–08), on the road from Vacqueyras. It stores its vast *recolte* (harvest) in an abandoned railroad tunnel.

Séguret

㉑ *8 km (5 mi) northeast of Gigondas, 23 km (14 mi) north of Carpentras.*

Nestled into the sharp rake of a rocky hillside and crowned with a ruined medieval castle, Séguret is a picture-book hill village that is only moderately commercialized. Its 14th-century clock tower, Romanesque St-Denis Church, and bubbling Renaissance fountain highlight steep little stone streets and lovely views of the Dentelles de Montmirail cliffs. Here, too, you'll find peppery Côte-du-Rhônes for the tasting.

Dining and Lodging

$$–$$$ ✕🏠 **La Table du Comtat.** Clinging to the top of the village and enjoying breathtaking valley views, this 15th-century former hospice now functions as a simple hotel and serious restaurant. Flamboyant chef Franck Gomez may present you with julienned truffle and scrambled eggs served in an eggshell, foie gras poached in anis consommé, or roast pigeon with licorice sauce. (The restaurant is closed Tuesday night and Wednesday from October through June.) Upstairs, eight plain, stucco rooms look over the valley or the pretty garden. The kidney-shape pool melts into a hillside terrace. ⊠ *Just after pl. de l'Église, 84110,* ☎ *04–90–46–91–49,* 𝔽𝔸𝕏 *04–90–46–94–27. 8 rooms. Restaurant, pool. AE, DC, MC, V. Closed Feb.*

$ ✕🏠 **La Bastide Bleue.** An idyllic youth hostel until a few years ago,
★ this old stone farmhouse is now an unpretentious but enchanting country inn. It's set in a pine-shaded garden court, and its blue-shuttered windows conceal pretty rooms done in stone, pine, and stucco, with bright, artisanal-tiled baths. Downstairs is a low-slung dining room with plank tables by a stone fireplace. Look for fluffy chicken liver terrine, garlic-roasted lamb, duck breast with a sweet tang of raspberries, and lavender-scented crème brûlée. ⊠ *La Bastide Bleue, 1 km (½ mi) south of Séguret on D23, 84110,* ☎ *04–90–46–83–43. 7 rooms. Restaurant, pool. MC, V. Closed Jan.*

Vaison-la-Romaine

㉒ *10 km (6 mi) northeast of Seguret, 27 km (17 mi) northeast of Orange.*

In a river valley green with orchards of almonds and apricots, this ancient town thrives as a modern market center. Yet it retains an irresistible Provençal charm, with medieval backstreets, lively squares lined with cafés and, as its name implies, remains of its Roman past. Vaison's well-established Celtic colony joined forces with Rome in the 2nd century BC and grew to powerful status in the empire's glory days. No gargantuan monuments were raised, yet the luxurious villas surpassed those of Pompeii.

There are two broad fields of **Roman ruins,** both in the center of town: Before you pay entry at either of the ticket booths, pick up a map (with English explanations) at the **Maison du Tourisme et des Vins** (☎ 04–90–36–02–11), which sits between them. It's open daily 9–12:30 and 2–6:45 from July through August, Monday through Saturday 9–noon and 2–5:45 from September through June..

Like a tiny Roman forum, the **Quartier de Puymin** spreads over the field and hillside in the heart of town, visible in passing from the city streets. Its skeletal ruins of villas, landscaped gardens, and museum lie below the ancient theater, all of which are accessed by the booth across from the tourist office. Closest to the entrance, the foundations of the **Maison des Messii** (Messii House) retain the outlines of its sumptuous design, complete with a vast gentleman's library, reception rooms, an atrium with a rain-fed pool, a large kitchen (the enormous stone vats are still there), and baths with hot, cold, and warm water. It requires imagination to reconstruct the rooms in your mind (remember all those toga movies from the '50s), but a tiny detail is enough to trigger a vivid image—the thresholds still show the hinge holds and scrape marks of swinging doors.

A formal garden echoes a similar landscape of the time; wander under its cypress and flowering shrubs to the **Musée Archéologique Théo-Desplans.** In this streamlined venue, the accoutrements of Roman life have been amassed and displayed by theme: pottery, weapons, gods and goddesses, jewelry, and, of course, sculpture, including full portraits of the emperor Claudius (1st century) and a strikingly noble nude Hadrian (2nd century). The findings of recent digs have been incorporated into new displays. Cross the park behind the museum to climb into the bleachers of the 1st-century **theater,** which is smaller than Orange's but is still used today for concerts and plays.

★ Across the parking lot is the **Quartier de la Villasse,** where the remains of a lively market town evoke images of main-street shops, public gardens, and grand private homes, complete with floor mosaics. The most evocative image of all is in the *thermes* (baths): a neat row of marble-seat toilets lined up over a raked trough that rinsed waste instantly away. Sic transit gloria mundi (thus passes the glory of the world). ⊠ *av. Gén. de Gaulle at pl. du 11 Novembre,* ☎ *04–90–36–02–11.* ✍ *Ruins, museum, and cloister 41 frs/€6.25.* ☉ *June–Sept., daily 9:30–6; Mar.–May and Oct., daily 10–12:30 and 2–6; Nov.–Feb., daily 10–noon and 2–4:30. Museum: June–Sept., daily 9:30–6; Mar.–May and Oct., daily 10–12:30 and 2:30–6; Nov.–Feb., daily 10–11:30 and 2–4. Quartier de la Villasse: June–Sept., daily 9:30–noon and 2–6; Mar.–May and Oct., daily 10–12:30 and 2–6; Nov.–Feb., daily 10–noon and 2–4:30.*

Take the time to climb up into the **Haute Ville,** a medieval neighborhood perched high above the river valley. Its 13th- and 14th-century houses owe some of their beauty to stone pillaged from the Roman ruins below, but their charm is from the Middle Ages: a trickling stone fountain, a bell tower with wrought-iron campanile, soft-color shutters, and blooming vines that create the feel of a film set of an old town.

If you're in a medieval mood, stop into the sober Romanesque **Cathédrale Notre-Dame-de-Nazareth,** based on recycled fragments and foundations of a Gallo-Roman basilica. Its cloister is the key attraction.

Created in the 12th and 13th centuries, it remains virtually unscarred, and its pairs of columns retain their deeply sculpted, richly varied capitals. ⊠ *av. Jules-Ferry.* ☉ *June–Sept., daily 9:30–noon and 2–5:30; Mar.–May and Oct., daily 10–noon and 2–5:30; Nov.–Feb., daily 10–noon and 2–4.*

The remarkable single-arch **Pont Romain** (Roman Bridge), built in the 1st century, stands firm across the River Ouvèze; it was one of the few structures to survive the devastating flood that roared through Vaison in 1992, destroying 150 homes and killing 37 people. It's a living testimony to Roman engineering and provokes reflection. Had it not been "quarried" for medieval projects, how much of Roman Vaison would still be standing today?

Dining and Lodging

$$–$$$ ✕🏨 **Le Beffroi.** Perched on a cliff top in the old town, this gracious ★ grouping of 16th-century mansions comes together as a fine hotel. The extravagant period salon leads to curving stone stairs and up to sizable rooms with beamed ceilings and antiques. The corner rooms have wonderful views. By day you can take a dip in the rooftop pool. In season, have dinner under the fig tree in the intimate enclosed garden court and savor rabbit terrine with hazelnuts and tarragon, garlicky lamb stew, rockfish perfumed with fennel and lemon, and a delicate lavender-scented crème brûlée. (The restaurant is open from April through October.) ⊠ *rue de l'Évêché, 84110,* ☎ *04–90–36–04–71,* FAX *04–90–36–24–78. 22 rooms. Restaurant, pool. AE, DC, MC, V. Closed Jan.–mid-Mar.* ☜

$$$ 🏨 **Château de la Baude.** Just outside town, this fortified medieval farm has been converted into a bed-and-breakfast retreat. Sleek, modern rooms feature beams, soft ocher shades, and quarry tiles. You won't lack for activities—you can swim, play tennis or pétanque, and explore the nine acres of grounds. There are table d'hôte dinners; breakfast is served under a grape trellis. ⊠ *6 km (4 mi) northwest of Vaison-la-Romaine, 84110 Villedieu,* ☎ *04–90–28–95–18,* FAX *04–90–28–91–05. 4 rooms, 2 suites. Restaurant, pool, whirlpool, tennis, Ping-Pong. AE, DC, MC, V.* ☜

$$ 🏨 **Évêché.** If you want to base yourself in the medieval part of town, stay in one of the four small rooms in this turreted 16th-century former bishop's palace, owned by the friendly Verdiers. The warm welcome and rustic charm—delicate fabrics, exposed beams, wooden bedsteads—have garnered a loyal following among travelers who prefer B&B character to modern luxury. In summer breakfast is served in a bower of greenery overlooking the Ouvèze Valley. Make sure to stop into the groin-vaulted art gallery across the street. Advance reservations are essential. ⊠ *rue de l'Évêché, 84110,* ☎ *04–90–36–13–46,* FAX *04–90–36–32–43. 4 rooms. No credit cards.*

Crestet

㉓ *7 km (4½ mi) south of Vaison-la Romaine.*

Another irresistible, souvenir-free aerie perched on a hilltop at the feet of the Dentelles de Montmirail cliffs and of Mont Ventoux, Crestet has it all—tinkling fountains, shuttered 15th-century houses, an arcaded *place* at the village's center, and a 12th-century castle crowning the lot. Views from its château terrace take in the concentric rings of tiled rooftops below, then the forest greenery and cultivated valleys below.

Malaucène

㉔ *9 km (5½ mi) southeast of Crestet, 10 km (6 mi) southeast of Vaison-la-Romaine.*

Yet another attractive composition of plane trees, fountains, and *lavoirs* (public laundry fountains), crowned by a church tower with campanile, this sizeable market town began as a fortified church-village. Its 14th-century church follows classic Provence Romanesque form (a broad, vaulted nave, a semicircle apse) and houses an ornate carved-oak organ from the 18th century. The town's nerve center is the cours des Isnards, where butchers, bakers, and cafés draw commerce from the tiny near-ghost-towns scattered through the countryside.

Just east of town, the **Chapelle Notre-Dame-du Groseau** is the only remains of the mighty 12th-century Benedictine abbey that Pope Clement V preferred as lodging before he settled into Avignon. The setting of cliffs and woodlands is just as wild and wonderful today. This is also a good place to launch a scenic circle drive over the crest of Mont Ventoux (☞ *below*). ⊠ *Off of D974 direction Col des Tempêtes.*

Dining and Lodging

$ ✕⊞ **L'Origan.** Directly on the tree-lined main commercial street, this family-run hotel/restaurant offers simple, comfortable rooms and straightforward, homey cooking. Crisp mesclun with hot goat-cheese toasts, daubes bristling with wild herbs, and homemade fruit tarts are served by the host, whose waxed mustache matches his flamboyant taste in color schemes. ⊠ *cours des Isnards, 84330,* ☎ *04–90–65–27–08,* FAX *04–90–65–12–92. 23 rooms. Restaurant. MC, V. Restaurant closed mid-Oct.–Mar.*

Le Barroux

㉕ *6 km (4 mi) southwest of Malaucène, 16 km (10 mi) south of Vaison-la-Romaine.*

Of all the marvelous hilltop villages stretching across the south of France, this tiny ziggurat of a town has a special charm. It has just one small church, one post office, and one tiny old *épicerie* (small grocery) selling canned goods, yellowed postcards, and today's *Le Provençal*. You are forced, therefore, to look around you and listen to the trickle of the ancient fountains at every labyrinthine turn.

Its **Château** is its main draw, though its Disney-perfect condition reflects a complete restoration after a World War II fire. Grand vaulted rooms and a chapel date from the 12th century; other halls serve as venues for contemporary art exhibits. Even if you don't go in, climb up to its terrace, where you can gaze across farmlands toward competing châteaux at Crillon and Caromb. ☎ *04–90–62–35–21.* 🎫 *20 frs/€3.05.* 🕙 *Apr.–May weekends 10–7; June, weekdays 2–7, weekends 10–7; July–Sept. daily 10–7; Oct. daily 2:30–7.*

Dining and Lodging

$ ✕⊞ **Les Géraniums.** The owner of this family-run auberge also wears the chef's toque. At the restaurant ($–$$), take a seat on the broad garden terrace stretching along the cliff side and sample herb-roasted rabbit, a truffle omelet, quail pâté, and local cheeses. Demi-pension is strongly encouraged and highly recommended. Spend the day sightseeing and come back to a modest, peaceful room. New rooms in the annex across the street take in panoramic views. ⊠ *pl. de la Croix, 84330,* ☎ *04–90–62–41–08,* FAX *04–90–62–56–48. 22 rooms. Restaurant, bar. AE, DC, MC, V. Closed Jan.–Feb.*

Crillon le Brave

㉖ *12 km (7 mi) south of Malaucène (via Caromb), 21 km (13 mi) southeast of Vaison-la-Romaine.*

The main reason to come to this minuscule hamlet, named after France's most notable soldier hero of the 16th century, is to stay or dine at its hotel, the Hostellerie de Crillon le Brave (☞ Dining and Lodging, *below*). But it's also pleasant—perched on a knoll in a valley shielded by Mont Ventoux, with the craggy hills of the Dentelles in one direction and the hills of the Luberon in another. Today the village still doesn't have even a *boulangerie* (bakery), let alone a souvenir boutique. The village makes a good base camp for exploring the region if you can afford to stay at the hotel; with no other commercial establishments in the village, and little more to visit than a tiny music-box museum and an ocher quarry, you're a captive audience.

Dining and Lodging

$$$$ ✕▥ **Hostellerie de Crillon le Brave.** The views from these Relais & Châteaux interconnected hilltop houses are as elevated as its prices, but for this you get a rarefied atmosphere of medieval luxury. A cozy-chic southern decor runs throughout, from the book-filled salons to the brocante-trimmed guest rooms. Some rooms have terraces looking out over the surrounding hills and plains. Fountains splash in the garden overlooking the pool. In the stone-vaulted dining room, sample Philippe Monti's stylish Mediterranean cooking—smoked dorade (sea bream) with stuffed zucchini flowers, monkfish with wild savory and eggplant caviar, quail roasted with figs, lamb with green anise— and consider signing up for a six-day cooking class. ⊠ *pl. de l'Église, 84410,* ☎ *04–90–65–61–61,* ℻ *04–90–65–62–86. 21 rooms. Restaurant, pool. AE, DC, MC, V. Closed Jan.–mid-Mar.*

Mont Ventoux

In addition to all the beautiful views *of* Mont Ventoux, there are equally spectacular views *from* Mont Ventoux. From Malaucène or any of the surrounding hill towns you can take an inspiring circle drive along the base and over the crest of the mountain, following the D974. This road winds through the extraordinarily lush south-facing greenery that Mont Ventoux protects from vicious mistral winds. Abundant orchards and olive groves peppered with stone farmhouses make this one of Provence's loveliest landscapes. Stop for a drink in busy **Bédoin,** with its 18th-century Jesuit church at the top of the old-town maze.

Reaching the summit itself (at 6,263 ft) requires a bit of legwork. From either Chalet Reynard or the tiny ski center Mont Serein you can leave your car and hike up to the peak's tall observatory tower. The climb is not overly taxing, and when you reach the top you are rewarded with gorgeous panoramic views of the Alps. And to the south, barring the possibility of high-summer haze, you'll take in views of the Rhône Valley, the Luberon, and even Marseille. Note that the summit is closed by snow from late fall to early spring.

Dining

$ ✕ **Le Chalet Reynard.** This is the spot for lunch and a bask in the sun on your way up the eastern slope of Mont Ventoux. Bikers, hikers, and car-tourists alike gather at plank tables on the wooden deck or warm themselves in the chalet-style dining area. The food is far beyond the merely acceptable: Rich homemade lasagne, truffled omelettes, hearty plats du jours, and slender, crispy frites justify the stop. ⊠ *At the easternmost elbow of D974,* ☎ *04–90–61–84–55. MC, V. Closed Tues. Oct.–June.*

Sault

★ ㉗ *41 km (25½ mi) southeast of Malaucène, 41 km (25½ mi) northeast of Carpentras.*

Though at the hub of no fewer than six *routes départementales*, Sault remains an utterly isolated market town floating on a stony hilltop in a valley of lavender. Accessed only by circuitous country roads, it remains virtually untouched by tourism. The landscape is traditional Provence at its best—wind-scoured, oak-forested hills and long, deep valleys purpled with the curving arcs of lavender. In the town itself, old painted storefronts exude the scent of honey and lavender. The damp church, Église Saint-Sauveur, dates from the 12th century; the long, lovely barrel nave was doubled in 1450.

From Sault all routes are scenic. You may head eastward into Haute Provence and Manosque (☞ Chapter 4), visiting (via D950) tiny **Banon**, source of the famed goat cheese. Wind up D942 to see pretty hilltop Aurel or down D30 to reach perched **Simiane-la-Rotonde**. Or head back toward Carpentras through the spectacular **Gorges de la Nesque**, snaking along narrow cliff-edge roads through dramatic canyons carpeted with wild boxwood and pine.

Dining and Lodging

$$$ ✕ ⬚ **Hostellerie du Val de Sault.** A holiday feel infiltrates this quiet retreat, once a summer camp. Five modern buildings range over the casually landscaped grounds, separated by low drystone walls and shaded by pines. Rooms are small and modular, with pine plank floors and private decks looking over the valley. Suites offer tiny sitting rooms (which can double as children's bedrooms) and whirlpool baths. Head to the main lodge for the rich regional cooking of owner-chef Yves Gattechaut, with dishes such as crème brûlée with asparagus and Parmesan, Camargue bull stew with juniper, and Carpentras strawberries in pastry with candied chestnuts. ⊠ *Ancien-Chemin-d'Aurel, 84390,* ☎ *04–90–64–01–41,* ⨳ *04–90–64–12–74. 11 rooms, 5 suites. Restaurant, bar, pool, tennis courts, bicycles. AE, DC, MC, V. Closed Nov.– Mar.* 🕮

THE SORGUE VALLEY

This gentle, rolling valley east of Avignon follows the course of the River Sorgue, which wells up from caverns below the arid hills of the Vaucluse plateau, gushes to the surface at Fontaine-de-Vaucluse, and rolls down to turn the mossy waterwheels in picturesque L'Isle-sur-la-Sorgue. It is a region of transition between the urban outskirts of Avignon and the wilds of the Luberon to the east.

L'Isle-sur-la-Sorgue

㉘ *23 km (14 mi) east of Avignon.*

Crisscrossed with lazy canals and alive with moss-covered waterwheels that once drove its silk, wool, and paper mills, this charming valley town retains its gentle appeal . . . except on Sunday. Then this easygoing old town transforms itself into a Marrakech of marketeers, its streets crammed with antiques and brocante, its cafés swelling with crowds of chic bargain browsers making a day of it. Even hard-core modernists inured to treasure hunts enjoy the show as urbane couples with sweaters over shoulders squint discerningly through half lenses at monogrammed linen sheets, zinc washstands, china spice sets, Art Deco perfume bottles, tinted engravings, and the paintings of modern almost-masters. There are also street musicians, food stands groaning under rustic breads, vats of tapenade, cloth-lined baskets of spices, and miles of café tables offering ring-side seats to the spectacle.

On a non-market day, life returns to its mellow pace. There are plenty of antiques dealers holding forth year-round, but also fabric and interior design shops, bookstores, and food stores to explore. People curl up with paperbacks on park benches by shaded fountains and read international papers in cafés.

If you want to explore the vestiges of L'Isle's 18th-century heyday, stop in the tourist office and pick up a brochure called "Vagabondages L'Isle-sur-la-Sorgue" (☞ Visitor Information *in* The Vaucluse A to Z, *below*). This map and commentary (in French only) will guide you to some of the town's grand old hôtels particuliers.

One of the finest of L'Isle's mansions, the **Hôtel Donadeï de Campredon**, has been restored and reinvented as a modern-art gallery, mounting temporary exhibitions of modern masters. ⊠ *20 rue du Docteur Tallet,* ☎ *04–90–38–17–41.* ⊙ *Tues.–Sun. 9:30–noon and 2–6.*

L'Isle's 17th-century church, the **Collégiale Notre-Dame-des-Anges,** is extravagantly decorated with gilt, faux marble, and sentimental frescoes. Its double-colonnaded facade commands the center of the old town. ⊠ *pl. de l'Église.*

Dining and Lodging

$$–$$$ ✕ **La Prévôté.** With all the money you saved bargaining on that chipped Quimper vase, splurge on lunch at this discreet, pristine *lavoir* (laundry fountain) hidden off a backstreet courtyard. Acclaimed chef Roland Mercier works with local flavors—try his assertive mackerel and dried tomato terrine, cod roasted in Camargue salt, or duckling in lavender honey, followed by lemon-and-basil sorbet. The wine list is succinct and favors reasonably priced local reds. But evening and à la carte meals are an investment best suited to buyers of antiques rather than brocante. ⊠ *4 rue Jean-Jacques-Rousseau,* ☎ *04–90–38–57–29. Reservations essential. MC, V. Closed Mon. (Dec.–June), Nov., and two wks in Feb. No dinner Sun.*

$$ ✕ **Le Carré d'Herbes.** Despite the garden furniture, the bucolic takes
★ a backseat to chic at this recherché dining spot. The restaurant hums with the rhythms of salsa, reggae, and clattering copper pans. The imaginative menu mixes vivid flavors; for instance, you could try a first-course *capon* (open-faced sandwich) of duck breast with apple and horseradish. Main courses include honey-glazed duck and whole fish and fennel roasted in rock salt. There are two seatings for Sunday (market day) lunch, but reserve ahead. ⊠ *13 av. des Quatre Otages,* ☎ *04–90–38–62–95. Reservations essential. MC, V. Closed Tues.–Wed.*

$ ✕ **Lou Nego Chin.** In winter you'll sit shoulder to shoulder in the cramped but atmospheric dining room (chinoiserie linens, brightly hued tiles), but in summer tables are strewn across the quiet street, on a wooden deck along the river. Ask for a spot at the edge so you can watch the ducks play, and order the inexpensive house wine and the three-course, 89-franc (€14) menu du jour, often a hot salad and a steak or a good and garlicky stew. ⊠ *12 quai Jean Jaurès,* ☎ *04–90–20–88–03. MC, V. Closed Mon. No dinner Sun.*

$–$$ ✕🖾 **Le Mas de Cure-Bourse.** This graceful old 18th-century postal-
★ coach stop is well outside the fray, snugly hedge-bound in the countryside amid fruit trees and fields. Here you can relax on six acres of green landscape, read by the large pool, and sleep in rooms freshly decked out in Provençal prints and painted country furniture. Meals are as memorable, whether taken by the grand old fireplace or on the terrace. The sophisticated cooking keeps a local touch with dishes such as stuffed zucchini flowers, pumpkin gnocchi, goat cheese with *pistou* (pesto) or tapenade, and deliciously gooey chocolate cake with cherries. The restaurant is closed Monday; there's no lunch Tuesday. ⊠ *Route de Cau-*

mont, 84800, ☎ *04–90–38–16–58,* FAX *04–90–38–52–31. 13 rooms. Restaurant, pool. MC, V. Closed 3 wks in Nov., first 2 wks in Jan.*

$ 🍽 **La Gueulardière.** After a Sunday glut of antiquing along the canals, you can dine and sleep in a setting full of collectible finds, from the school posters in the restaurant to the oak armoires and brass beds that furnish the simple lodgings, just up the street. Each room has French windows that open onto the enclosed garden courtyard, where you can enjoy a private breakfast in the shade. ⊠ *1 rue d'Apt, 84800,* ☎ *04–90–38–10–52,* FAX *04–90–20–83–70. 5 rooms. Restaurant. AE, DC, MC, V.*

Outdoor Activities and Sports

The **Provence Country Club** (⊠ Saumane, ☎ 04–90–20–20–65), standing idyllically in the valley between L'Isle and Fontaine de Vaucluse, has an 18-hole (par 72) golf course, as well as a "compact" with nine holes and both grass and carpet practice ranges. Take D25 in the direction of Fontaine.

Shopping

Throughout the pretty backstreets of L'Isle's old town (especially between place de l'Église and avenue de la Libération), there are boutiques spilling baskets full of tempting goods onto the sidewalk to lure you inside; most concentrate on home design and Provençal goods. **Sous l'Olivier** (⊠ 16 rue de la République, ☎ 04–90–20–68–90) is a food boutique crammed to the ceiling with bottles and jars of tapenade, fancy mustards, candies shaped like olives, and the house olive oil.

Of the dozens of antiques shops in L'Isle, one conglomerate concentrates some 40 dealers under the same roof: **L'Isle aux Brocantes** (⊠ 7 av. des Quatre Otages, ☎ 04–90–20–69–93). It's open Saturday through Monday. Higher-end antiques are concentrated next door at the twinned shops of **Xavier Nicod and Gérard Nicod** (⊠ 9 av. des Quatre Otages, ☎ 04–90–38–35–50 or 04–90–38–07–20). **Van Halewyck** (⊠ 15 quai de Rouget de L'Isle, ☎ 04–90–38–65–25) is a tiny shop crammed with old-masterly paintings.

Espace Béchard (⊠ 1 av. Jean-Charmasson, ☎ 04–90–20–81–40) throws 11 different dealers together, all with fabulously overscaled objects too big to carry home on the plane. **Maria Giancatarina** (⊠ across from the train station, 4 av. Julien Guigue, ☎ 04–90–38–58–02) features beautifully restored linens, including monogrammed linen sheets, lacy pillowcases, piqué throws, and *boutis* (Provençal quilts).

Fontaine de Vaucluse

㉙ *7 km (4½ mi) east of L'Isle sur la Sorgue, 30 km (19 mi) east of Avignon.*

Like the natural attraction for which it is named, this village has welled up and spilled over as a Niagara Falls–type tourist center; the rustic, pretty, and slightly tacky riverside town is full of shops, cafés, and restaurants, all built to serve the pilgrims who flock to its namesake. And neither town nor fountain should be missed if you're either a connoisseur of rushing water or a fan of foreign kitsch.

★ There's no exaggerating the magnificence of the **Fontaine de Vaucluse,** a mysterious spring that gushes from a deep underground source that has been explored to a depth of 1,010 ft . . . so far. Framed by towering cliffs, a broad, pure pool wells up and spews dramatically over massive rocks down a gorge to the village, where its roar soothes and cools the visitors who crowd the riverfront cafés.

You must pay to park, then run a gauntlet of souvenir shops and tourist traps on your way to the top. But even if you plan to make a

THE GÎTE WAY

YOU COME HOME FROM A HARD day's sightseeing, slip off your shoes, pull a pitcher of cold water from the fridge, pour a pastis and carry it out to the terrace. There's a basket heavy with goodies from the village market—a fresh rabbit, three different tubs of olives, a cup of fresh-scooped tapenade, apricots and melons warm from the sun. After your drink, you'll sort it all out and fix supper, French pop music playing gently on the radio. You'll eat as long and as late as you like, and carry the children to their twin beds in the back room before you take a stroll through the almond grove or crunch through the wild thyme to look at the city lights strung far below. Even doing the dishes in the sink seems okay in this faraway, summer-cottage mode, far from the mini-bars, lobby-lounges, and snotty waiters of the beaten tourist track.

This is the gîte way, the alternative to hotels and restaurants and even to the anonymous seaside vacation flats farmed out by agencies abroad. The national network known as Gîtes de France has organized and catalogued a vast assortment of rural houses, many of them restored farmhouses and old village bastides, most of them rich in regional character and set in the picturesque countryside. The participating houses are inspected and categorized by comfort level (for example, three stars includes a washing machine), with standardized lists of minimum furnishings (from corkscrews to salad spinners to vegetable peelers).

But the key to the charm is the personal touch: Gîtes de France owners greet their guests on arrival, and may pop by (discreetly, rarely) during the week with lettuce from their garden, a bottle from their vineyard, holiday candy for the kids. There's a cupboard full of maps and brochures on local museums, and often the name of a nearby restaurant if you're too sunburned to cook. And they'll come to collect the key a week later and wish you a bon voyage.

There are drawbacks, of course. You'll have to bring towels and linens, and make up the beds yourself (you can often rent linens from the host if you prefer), and you are requested to leave the house in the same condition in which you found it—which usually means impeccable, and requires some mopping and scrubbing.

But the privacy and independence counterbalance any drudgery, and you'll meet people far different from the tourists and supercilious concierges of standardized hotels: farmers, teachers, wine-makers, artists, anyone with the time to care for a cottage, a neighboring farmhouse, a converted stone barn.

Contact the headquarters of the département you plan to visit and request a catalogue of properties, then make a reservation by phone or fax. You must give them a 25% down payment with your reservation, then the rest when you return the contract, one month before your visit. The addresses of Gîte-de-France branches are listed in the Vacation Rentals of A to Z sections in every regional chapter; for more information on the gîte way, *see* Lodging *in* Smart Travel Tips A to Z.

beeline past the kitsch, do stop in at the legitimate and informative **Moulin Vallis-Clausa.** A working paper mill, it demonstrates a reconstruction of a 15th-century waterwheel that drives timber crankshafts to mix rag pulp, while artisans roll and dry thick paper *à l'ancienne* (in the old manner). The process is fascinating and free to watch, though it's almost impossible to resist buying note cards, posters, even lamp shades fashioned from the pretty stuff. Fontaine was once a great industrial mill center, but its seven factories were closed by strikes in 1968 and never recovered. All the better for you today, since now you can enjoy this marvelous natural setting in peace. ⊠ *On the riverbank walk up to the spring,* ☏ 04–90–20–34–14. ☉ *Sept.–June daily 9–noon and 2–6; July–Aug. 9–7 daily.*

Fontaine has its own ruined **Château,** perched romantically on a forested hilltop over the town and illuminated at night. First built around the year 1000 and embellished in the 13th century by the bishops of Cavaillon, it was destroyed in the 15th century and forms little more than a saw-tooth silhouette against the sky.

The Renaissance poet Petrarch, driven mad with unrequited love for a beautiful married woman named Laura, retreated to this valley to nurse his passion in a cabin with "one dog and only two servants." He had met her in the heady social scene at the papal court in Avignon, where she was to die years later of the plague. Sixteen years in this wild isolation didn't ease the pain, but the serene setting inspired him to poetry, and his *Canzoniera* were dedicated to Laura's memory. The small **Musée-Bibliothèque Pétrarch** (Petrarch Museum–Library), built on the site of his stay, displays prints and engravings of the virtuous lovers, both in Avignon and Fontaine de Vaucluse. ⊠ *On the left bank, direction Gordes,* ☏ 04–90–20–37–20. ☎ *20 frs/€3.05.* ☉ *Apr.–May, Wed.–Mon. 10–noon and 2–6; June–Sept., Wed.–Mon. 10–12:30 and 1:30–6; Oct., weekends 10–noon and 2–5.*

Dining and Lodging

$$ ✕🏠 **Le Parc.** In a spectacular riverside setting in the shadow of the ruined château, this solid old hotel has basic, comfortable rooms (whitewashed stucco, all-weather carpet) with clean baths and no creaks. Five take in river views. The restaurant (closed Wednesday) spreads along the river in a pretty park with tables shaded by trellises heavy with grapes and trumpet vine. Moderately priced daily menus include river-fresh salmon, de rigueur in this setting. ⊠ *rue de Bourgades, 84800,* ☏ 04–90–20–31–57, FAX 04–90–20–27–03. *12 rooms. Restaurant. AE, DC, MC, V. Closed Jan.–mid-Feb.*

$–$$ 🏠 **La Maison aux Fruits.** Even before you enter, you know an artist lives here and that this small B&B is no ordinary lodging. The carved front door and the painted woodwork set the tone for the faux marble, murals, painted ceilings, and the owner's art collection inside. An oval staircase takes you up to a sitting and dining room and a terrace. There are also two little apartments that you may rent by the week; some rooms overlook the roaring river. Some of the art works are for sale; aficionados may even be seduced to sign up for an art class here. ⊠ *rue de l'Isle de Sorgue, 84800,* ☏ 04–90–20–39–15, FAX 04–90–20–27–08. *2 rooms, 2 apartments. No credit cards.*

$ 🏠 **Le Grand Jas.** In a renovated farmhouse just outside the nearby village of Lagnes, this little B&B has four comfortable, rustic rooms with exposed beams and Provençal prints. There's also a pleasant, high-ceilinged common area. The new swimming pool is most inviting after a hot sightseeing day. Lagnes makes a good base—it's a sweet hilltop village with a couple of small restaurants and a café-bar. ⊠ *rue du Bariot, Lagnes (5 km [3 mi] from Fontaine de Vaucluse via D100) 84800,*

☎ *04–90–20–25–12,* ✆ *04–90–20–29–17. 4 rooms. Dining room, pool. No credit cards.* ✍

THE LUBERON

" 'Have you ever been to the Luberon? Between Avignon and Aix. It's getting a little chichi, specially in August, but it's beautiful—old villages, mountains, no crowds, fantastic light. . . Leave the autoroute at Cavaillon, and go towards Apt.'. . . Murat poured the red wine and raised his glass. '*Bonnes vacances,* my friend. I'm serious about the Luberon; it's a little special. You should try it.' "

After Peter Mayle, no doubt barefoot by the pool, typed these words in his first novel *Hotel Pastis*, the world took a map in hand. They had already taken note when his chronicles *A Year in Provence* and *Toujours Provence* painted a delicious picture of backcountry sunshine, copious feasts, and cartoonishly droll local rustics; now they had directions to get there.

They came. They climbed over Mayle's hedges for autographs. They built pink and yellow houses, booked his favorite restaurant tables, traced his footsteps with the book in hand. And not only the English. *A Year in Provence* sold 4 million copies and was translated into 20 languages, including French (where its sequel corrected his grammar to *Provence Toujours*). His name is a household word here (Peet-aire Mayeel) and doesn't always bring the oft-described grin and shrug from the locals. Perhaps that's why Mayle took a sabbatical from Provence, relinquishing the home with the famously immovable stone table. He has since returned, putting down new roots on the south face of the Luberon, in Lourmarin.

The dust has settled a bit, and despite the occasional Mayle Country bus tour rattling through from Cavaillon, the Luberon has returned to its former way of life. There were always Lacoste shirts here, and converted mas with pools (after all, Mayle's mas was already gentrified when they installed central heating), and sophisticated restaurants catering to seekers of the Simple Life. They're all still here, but so are the extraordinarily beautiful countryside, the golden perched villages, the blue-black forests, and the sun-bleached rocks.

The broad mountain called the Luberon is protected nowadays by the Parc Naturel Régional du Luberon, but that doesn't mean you should expect rangers, campsites, and his-and-hers outhouses. It has always been and remains private land, though building and forestry are allowed in moderation and hiking trails have been cleared.

The N100, anchored to the west by the market town of Cavaillon and to the east by industrial Apt, parallels the long, looming north face of the Luberon, and from it you can explore the hill towns and valley villages on either side. To its north, the red-ocher terrain around Roussillon, the Romanesque symmetry of the Abbaye de Sénanque, and the fashionable charms of Gordes punctuate a rugged countryside peppered with ancient stone *bories*. To its south lie Oppède-le-Vieux, Ménerbes, Lacoste, and pretty perched Bonnieux. From Bonnieux you can drive over the rugged crest through Lourmarin and explore the less gentrified south flank of the mountain. Although the Luberon is made up of two distinct regions, only the more civilized Petit Luberon, up to Apt, is covered in this chapter. If you're a nature lover, you may want to venture into the wilder Grand Luberon, especially to the summit called Mourre Nègre.

Gordes

③⓪ *10 km (6 mi) east of Fontaine de Vaucluse, 39 km (24 mi) east of Avignon.*

Gordes is only a short distance from Fontaine de Vaucluse, but you need to wind your way south, east, and then north on D100A, D100, D2, and D15 to skirt the impassable hillside. It's a lovely drive through dry, rocky country covered with wild lavender and scrub oak and may tempt you to a picnic or a walk. How surprising, then, to leave such wildness behind and enter resort country. Gordes was once a famous, unspoiled hilltop village; it has now become a famous, unspoiled hilltop village surrounded by luxury vacation homes, modern hotels, restaurants, and B&Bs. No matter. The ancient stone village still rises above the valley in painterly hues of honey gold, and its mosaiclike cobbled streets—lined with boutiques, galleries, and real-estate offices—still wind steep and narrow to its Renaissance château.

The only way to see the interior of the **Château** is to view its collection of mind-stretching photo paintings by pop artist Pol Mara, who spent his last years in Gordes. It's worth the price to look at the fabulously decorated stone fireplace, created in 1541; it covers an entire wall with neoclassic designs and stretches to frame two doors. ✉ *pl. du Château,* ☎ *04–90–72–02–75.* ✉ *25 frs/€3.81.* ☉ *Wed.–Mon. 10–noon and 2–6.*

Head downhill from the château and follow signs to the **belvédère** overlooking the miniature fields and farms below. From this height all those modern vacation homes blend in with the ancient mas—except for the aqua blue pools.

★ Just outside Gordes, on a lane heading north from D2, follow signs to the **Village des Bories.** Found throughout this region of Provence, the bizarre and fascinating little stone hovels called *bories* are concentrated some 20 strong in an ancient community. Their origins are provocatively vague. Built as shepherds' shelters with tight-fitting, mortarless stone in a hivelike form, they may date back to the Celts, the Ligurians, even the Iron Age—and were inhabited or used for sheep through the 18th century. This village was reconstructed from remains. ☎ *04–90–72–03–48.* ✉ *35 frs/€5.33.* ☉ *Daily 9–sunset or 8, whichever comes first.*

★ In a wild valley some 4 km (2½ mi) north of Gordes (via D177), the beautiful 12th-century **Abbaye de Sénanque** floats above a sea of lavender. (The flowers bloom in July and August.) An architecture student's dream of neat cubes, cylinders, and pyramids, its pure Romanesque form alone is worth contemplating in any context. But in this arid, rocky setting the gray stone building seems to have special resonance—ancient, organic, with a bit of the borie about it. Its **church** is a model of symmetry and balance. Begun in 1150 and completed at the start of the 13th century, it has no decoration but still touches the soul with its chaste beauty. The adjoining **cloister,** from the 12th century, is almost as pure. Its barrel-vaulted galleries frame double rows of discreet, abstract columns and pillars; you'll find no child-devouring demons or lurid biblical tales here. Next door, the enormous vaulted **dormitory** contains an exhibition on the abbey's construction, and the **refectory** shelters a display on the history of Cistercian abbeys. In 1969 the abbey's Cistercian monks moved to St-Honorat Island, off the shore of Cannes, and the buildings here, under the stewardship of a few remaining monks, are now part of a cultural center presenting concerts and exhibitions. The bookshop is one of the best in Provence; in addition to carrying wonderful and obscure religious books, it also has a huge collection of Provencaliana (lots of English), plus architecture, gardening, and cooking titles. ☎ 04–90–72–05–72. ⬚ 30 frs/€4.57. ☉ Mar.–Oct., Mon.–Sat. 10–noon and 2–6, Sun. 2–6; Nov.–Feb., weekdays 2–5, weekends 2–6.

Dining and Lodging

$$$ ✕ **Comptoir du Victuailler.** Directly across from the château, this tiny but deluxe bistro serves an international clientele without a trace of condescension. At lunch time, when tables spill out onto the square, the menu features daily aïoli, a smorgasbord of fresh cod and lightly steamed vegetables crowned with pestled garlic mayonnaise. Evenings are reserved for intimate, formal indoor meals à la carte–roast Luberon lamb, beef with truffle sauce, or a salty-sweet raspberry-sauced *pintade* (guinea fowl). Leave room for the chocolate cake and St-Honoré (airy vanilla-cream pastry), and take the owner's advice on lesser known, local finds in wine. The '30s-style bistro tables and architectural lines are a relief from Gordes' ubiquitous rustic–chic. ⬚ *pl. du Château,* ☎ 04–90–72–01–31. Reservations essential. MC, V. Closed mid-Nov.–Easter and Wed. Sept.–May. No dinner Tues. Sept.–May.

$$ ✕⬚ **Ferme de la Huppe.** This 17th-century stone farmhouse, with a well in the courtyard, a swimming pool in the garden, and rooms decked with pretty prints and secondhand finds, is all alone in the lavender-scented countryside outside Gordes. What more could you want? How about roast guinea fowl in saffron and ginger and an icy bottle of local rosé? The family chef will be glad to serve you by the poolside terrace, but reserve ahead; the restaurant (closed Thursday) is as popular as the hotel. ✉ *84220 Les Pourquiers (3 km [2 mi] east of Gordes),* ☎ 04–90–72–12–25, 🖷 04–90–72–01–83. 8 rooms. Restaurant, pool. MC, V. Closed Nov.–Mar.

$–$$ ✕⬚ **La Renaissance.** Whether you eat in the grand beamed dining hall, complete with Renaissance fireplace, or lounge under the plane trees by the fountain, you'll find an easy mix of city bistro and country Provençal. A blackboard menu lists regional specialties—aïoli, bourride—and live piano jazz livens things up at night. Six rooms upstairs have quarry tile, pristine white quilts, and double windows that open over the place du Château, but two of them share a toilet down the hall. Top-floor rooms are slick and modern, but windows are low and cheat the view. ⬚ *pl. du Château, 84220,* ☎ 04–90–72–02–02, 🖷 04–90–72–05–11. 6 rooms, 4 with bath. Restaurant, bar. MC, V. Closed Jan.–mid-Feb.

$$$ ⬚ **Domaine de l'Enclos.** Though this cluster of private stone cottages has had a face-lift, antique tiles and faux patinas keep it looking fashionably old. There are panoramic views and a pool, baby-sitting services and swing sets, and a welcome that is surprisingly warm and familial for an inn of this sophistication. Half-board arrangements (even for one night stays) keep costs down; in winter, when the popular restaurant calms down, the demi-pension guests are treated like house guests. ✉ *rte. de Sénanque, 84220,* ☎ 04–90–72–71–00, 🖷 04–90–72–03–03. 12 rooms, 5 apartments. Restaurant, pool. AE, MC, V. ✎

$$–$$$ ⬚ **Les Romarins.** At this 18th-century *bastide* (country house) on a hilltop crossroads on the outskirts of town, you can gaze across the valley at Gordes while you breakfast on a sheltered terrace. Rooms are clean, well lighted, and feel spacious. Be sure to ask for a room with a valley view, especially No. 1, in the main building, from whose white-curtained windows you can see forever. Another good pick is the atelier room with a terrace; front rooms overlook a busy road. Warm Oriental rugs, antique furniture around the fireplace in the sitting room, and a pool surrounded by borie-like stone add to your contentment. ⬚ *rte. de Sénanque,*

84220, ☎ *04–90–72–12–13,* FAX *04–90–72–13–13. 10 rooms. Pool. AE,*
MC, V. Closed mid-Jan.–mid-Feb.

Roussillon

❸❶ *14 km (9 mi) southeast of Gordes, 43 km (27 mi) southeast of Avi-*
gnon.

In shades of deep rose and russet, this hilltop cluster of houses blends
into the red-ocher cliffs from which its stone was quarried. The ensemble
of buildings and jagged, hand-cut slopes are equally dramatic, and views
from the top look over a landscape of artfully eroded bluffs that Geor-
gia O'Keeffe would have loved.

Unlike neighboring hill villages, there's little of historic architectural
detail here; the pleasure of a visit lies in the richly varied colors that
change with the light of day, and in the views of the contrasting countryside, where dense-shadowed greenery sets off the red stone with
Cézanne-esque severity. There are pleasant *placettes* (tiny squares) to
linger in nonetheless, and a Renaissance fortress tower crowned with
a clock in the 19th century; just past it, you can take in expansive panoramas of forest and ocher cliffs.

This famous vein of natural ocher, which spreads some 25 km (15½
mi) along the foot of the Vaucluse plateau, has been mined for centuries. You can visit the old **Usine Mathieu de Roussillon** (Roussillon's
Mathieu Ocher Works) to learn more about ocher's extraction and its
modern uses; though it has long since been closed as a mine, it functions today as the Conservatoire des Ocres et Pigments Appliqués
(Conservatory of Ochers and Applied Pigments). There are explana-
tory exhibits, ocher powders for sale, and guided tours in English with
advance request. ✉ *On D104 southeast of town,* ☎ *04–90–05–66–*
69. ⏱ *Mar.–Nov. daily 10–7.*

Lodging

$$–$$$ 🏨 **Ma Maison.** The artist-owners have infused this isolated 1850 *mas*
★   (farmhouse) in the valley below Roussillon with a laid-back, barefoot,
cosmopolitan style acquired, in part, in California. Their personality
and imagination show in every corner, from the big saltwater pool that's
surrounded with brass beds (instead of lounge chairs) to the mosquito
netting draped over the beds to the artworks—mostly their own—hanging on every surface. Rooms are big and private, some with fireplaces
and separate entrances onto the grounds. Breakfast, with homegrown,
homemade marmalade, is served from a massive blue-tile country
kitchen. The idyllic, all organic garden spans 3 hectares (7½ acres), much
of it in shade in the afternoon, with views toward Bonnieux and the
Luberon. ✉ *Quartier Les Devens, 4 km (2½ mi) south of Roussillon,*
84220, ☎ *04–90–05–74–17,* FAX *04–90–05–74–63. 6 rooms. Pool. MC,*
V. Closed Nov.–mid-Mar. ✍

Oppède-le-Vieux

❸❷ *25 km (15½ mi) southeast of Avignon, 15 km (9 mi) southwest of Gordes.*

Heading toward Apt on D22 out of Avignon, follow signs right into
the vineyards, toward Oppède. You'll occasionally be required to follow signs for Oppède-le-Village, but your goal will be marked with the
symbol of *monuments historiques*: Oppède-le-Vieux. A Byronesque tumble of ruins arranged against an overgrown rocky hillside, Oppède's
charm—or part of it—lies in its preservation. Taken over by writers
and artists who choose to live here and restore but not develop it, the
village offers a café or two but little more.

OLD AS THE HILLS

SINCE THE CAVE PAINTINGS of Lascaux, man has extracted ocher from the earth, using its extraordinary palette of colors to make the most of nature's play between earth and light. Grounded in these earth-based pigments, the frescoes of Giotto and Michelangelo glow from within, and the houses of Tuscany and Provence seem to draw color from the land itself—and to drink light from the sky. Says Barbara Barrois of the Conservatoire des Ocres et Pigments Appliqués at Roussillon, "Ça vibre à l'oeil!" (literally, "It vibrates to your eyes.")

The rusty hues of iron hydroxide are the source of all this luminosity, intimately allied with the purest of clays. Extracted from the ground in chunks and washed to separate it from its quartz-sand base, it is ground to fine powder and mixed as a binder with chalk and sand. Applied to the stone walls of Provençal houses, this ancient blend gives the region its quintessential repertoire of warm yellows and golds, brick, sienna, and umber.

In answer to the acrylic imitations slathered on new constructions in garish shades of hot pink and canary yellow (following a Côte d'Azur trend), there is an ocher revival under way, and you can easily spot the difference in the way naturally stuccoed buildings blend organically with their setting. Even the fashionable faux-weathered facades created by London and Paris designers can't hold a candle to the refracted light and velvety matte tones of the real thing.

Cross the village square, pass through the old city gate, and climb up steep trails past restored houses to the church known as **Notre-Dame-d'Alydon.** First built in the 13th century, its blunt buttresses were framed into side chapels in the 16th century; you can still see the points of stoned-in Gothic windows above. The marvelous hexagonal belltower sprouts a lean, mean gargoyle from each angle. It once served as part of the village's fortifications; the views from the plateau it dominates overlook the broad valley toward Ménerbes.

You can also clamber up to the ruins of the **Château,** first built in the 13th century and transformed in the 15th century. From the left side of its great square tower, look down into the dense fir forests of the Luberon's north face.

Ménerbes

🗿 *5 km (3 mi) east of Oppède-le-Vieux, 30 km (19 mi) southeast of Avignon.*

As you drive along D188 between Oppède and Ménerbes, the rolling rows of grapevines are punctuated by stone farmhouses. But something is different. These farmhouses have electric gates, tall arborvitae hedges, and swimming pools. Peter Mayle isn't the only outsider to have vacationed here and contrived to stay.

The town of Ménerbes itself clings to a long, thin hilltop over this sought-after valley, looming over the surrounding forests like a great stone ship. At its prow juts the **Castellet,** a 15th-century fortress. At its stern rears up the 13th-century **citadelle.** These redoubtable fortifications served the Protestants well during the War of Religions—until the Catholics wore them down with a 15-month siege.

A campanile tops the Hôtel de Ville (Town Hall) on pretty **place de l'Horloge** (Clock Square), where you can admire the delicate stonework on the arched portal and mullioned windows of a Renaissance house. Just past the tower on the right, you'll reach an overlook taking in views towards Gordes, Roussillon, and Mont Ventoux.

But what you really came to see is **Peter Mayle's house,** right? Do its current owners a favor and give it a wide berth. After years of tour buses spilling the curious into the private driveway to crane their necks and snap pictures, the heirs to the stone picnic table, the pool, and Faustin's grapevines wish the books had never been written. And besides, Peter Mayle has moved now, to the other side of the mountain. Do leave him in peace.

Dining and Lodging

$$$ 🏨 **Le Roy Soleil.** In the imposing shadow of the Luberon and the hilltop village of Ménerbes, this luxurious country inn has pulled out all stops on comfort and decor. (Think wrought-iron beds and marble and granite bathrooms.) But the integrity of its 17th-century building, with thick stone walls and groin vaults and beams, redeems it just short of pretentiousness and makes it a wonderful place to escape to. ⊠ *rte. des Beaumettes, 84560,* ☎ *04–90–72–25–61,* FAX *04–90–72–36–55. 19 rooms. Restaurant, bar, pool, tennis court. AE, MC, V. Closed mid-Nov.–mid-Mar.* 🐾

Lacoste

❸❹ *7 km (4½ mi) east of Ménerbes, 37 km (23 mi) southeast of Avignon.*

Like Ménerbes, gentrified hilltop Lacoste owes its fame to an infamous literary resident. Little but jagged ruins remain of the once magnificent **Château de Sade,** where the Marquis de Sade (1740–1814) spent some 30 years of his life, mostly hiding out. Exploits both literary and real, judged obscene by various European courts, kept him in and out of prison despite a series of escapes. His mother-in-law finally turned him in to authorities, and he was locked away in the Paris Bastille, where he passed the time writing stories and plays. Written during his time in the Bastille, *120 journées de Sodome* (*120 Days of Sodom*) featured a Black-Forest château suspiciously similar in form and design to his Lacoste home. The once-sumptuous château was destroyed with particular relish in the Revolution. It is privately owned now, and being restored wall by wall; you can only view it from the outside. But the village itself is worth a side trip for its pretty car-free streets and eagle's-nest views.

Bonnieux

★ ❸❺ *5 km (3 mi) southeast of Lacoste, 42 km (26 mi) southeast of Avignon.*

The most impressive of the Luberon's hilltop villages, Bonnieux (pronounced Bun-*yer*) rises out of the arid hills in a jumble of honey-color cubes that change color subtly as the day progresses. The village is wrapped in crumbling ramparts and dug into bedrock and cliff. Most of its sharply raked streets take in wide-angle valley views, though you'll get the best view from the pine-shaded grounds of the 12th-century church, reached by stone steps that wind past tiny niche houses. Shops, galleries, cafés, and fashionable restaurants abound here, but they don't dominate. It's possible to lose yourself in a back *ruelle* (small street) most of the year.

PERCHED VILLAGES

IN THE MIDDLE AGES, village life was driven by pirates and brigands, Saracens, and acquisitive lords to put its wagons, as it were, in a circle—and well above the fray. Thus the whole of Provence and its coast sprouted dense stone *villages perchés* (perched villages) from the hilltops, Babel-like towers of canted cubes and blunt cylinders in shades of dove-gray and honey-gold. Built with the stone beneath them, they seem to grow out of the rock, organic and somehow alive. Houses mount several levels, with rooms sometimes covering seven or eight floors. The tiniest of streets weave between these rakish building blocks, and the houses seem tied together by arching overpasses and rhythmic arcades. The whole of the ensemble is often wrapped in a wall and crowned with the two strongest assurances of protection, sacred and secular: a steeple and a watchtower.

Nowadays many of the hill towns are nearly ghost towns, though more and more are tapping into the tourist boom. Those closest to the coast and to urban centers—in the Luberon and in Nice's backcountry, in particular—have become souvenir malls choked with galleries of dubious quality. Yet as the tourist packs rove on in search of authenticity, the other hill towns develop their commerce and find new life. In these, you can still wander aimlessly through the maze of tunnel-like *ruelles* (alleys) and feel the isolation—often idyllic, sometimes harsh—of these eagle's-nest enclaves, high above the world.

Dining and Lodging

$$–$$$ ✕ **Le Fournil.** In a natural grotto deep in stone, lighted by candles and arty torchères, this restaurant would be memorable even without trendy decor (jade and gold cement tiles, mix-and-match jacquard linens) and stylishly-presented Provençal cuisine. But add adventurous dishes such as tomato-crisped pigs'-feet *galette* (patty), subtle seafood, an informed wine list, and the option of sitting on the terrace by the fountain, and you have an experience to note in your travel diary. ⊠ *5 pl. Carnot,* ☎ *04-90-75-83-62. MC, V. Closed mid-Nov.–mid-Dec., mid-Jan.–mid-Feb., and Mon. No lunch Sat. July–Aug.*

$$–$$$ 🏨 **Hostellerie du Prieuré.** Not every hotel has its own private chapel, ★ but this gracious inn holds forth in an 18th-century abbey and has kept its noble details. The decor is vivid and warm, from the saffron-color bar to the leather chairs in the firelighted salon to the dining room glowing with Roussillon ocher. Summer meals and breakfasts are served in the enclosed garden, which makes you feel like you're no longer in the village center. Rooms have plush carpets and antiques; one has a very small, sheltered terrace overlooking the chapel bell. Ask about the tiny, low-priced room with a toilet down the hall. Its double windows open over the garden. The Coutaz family has been in the hotel business since Napoléon III, and it shows. ⊠ *In center of village, 84480,* ☎ *04-90-75-80-78,* 𝔉𝔄𝔛 *04-90-75-96-00. 10 rooms. Restaurant. MC, V. Closed Nov.–Feb.* ✿

$$ 🏨 **Le Clos du Buis.** At this Gîtes de France B&B, whitewash and quarry ★ tiles, lovely tiled baths, and carefully juxtaposed antiques create a regional look in rooms. Relaxed, homey public spaces, with scrubbed floorboards, a fireplace, and exposed stone, invite you to hang around barefoot, like lodgers or weekend guests. It even has a pool and a pretty garden, and it's all overlooking the valley from the village center. ✉ *rue Victor Hugo, 84480,* ☎ *04–90–75–88–48,* FAX *04–90–75–88–57. 6 rooms. Pool. MC, V.* ✍

BUOUX

③⑥ *8 km (5 mi) northeast of Bonnieux, 9 km (5½ mi) south of Apt.*

To really get into back-country Luberon, crawl along serpentine one-lane roads below Apt, past orchards and lavender fields studded with bories. Deeply ensconced in the countryside, the tiny hamlet of Buoux (pronounced Bu-*ooks*) offers little more than a hotel and a café, sheltered by white brush-carpeted cliffs. If you squint you can just make out the dozens of rock-climbers dangling, spider-like, from slender cables along the cliff face.

An even tinier road can take you to the **Fort de Buoux,** the ruins of an ancient village and a fortification that has defended the valley since Ligurian and Roman times. Several houses and an entire staircase were chiseled directly into the stone; it's uncertain whether they're prehistoric or medieval. Louis XIV dismantled the ancient fortifications in the 17th century, leaving Turneresque ruins to grow over with wild box and ivy. ☎ *04–90–74–25–75.* ☞ *15 frs/€2.2.* ☉ *Daily sunrise–sunset.*

Lodging

$$ **✕▥ Auberge des Seguins.** Delve deep into this romantic valley to find ★ this fabulous hideaway, at the foot of an imposing white-rock cliff. The *dortoires* (shared public bunk rooms) and simple tile-and-stucco rooms make it a terrific retreat for families, hikers, and rock-climbers. Better yet, meals at the restaurant are several cuts above summer-camp chow. The owner is passionately Provençal and thus insists on wonderful regional food: äoli, tapenade, curried chickpeas, lamb stews, delicate goat cheese, and local wines. This is where the French come for reunions and weekends with friends, to lounge in lawn chairs or dip in the stream-fed swimming pool. In high season, make a dining reservation ahead of time. Half-board is mandatory for overnight guests. ✉ *3 km below downtown Buoux, 84480,* ☎ *04–90–74–16–37,* FAX *04–90–74–03–26. 27 rooms, 27 bunks. Restaurant, pool. MC, V.*

Saignon

③⑦ *15 km (9 mi) northeast of Buoux, 5 km (3 mi) southeast of Apt.*

Draped just below the crest of an arid hillside covered with olive groves, lavender, and stone farms, Saignon is an appealing hill town anchored by a heavy-set Romanesque church. Neat cobbled streets wind between flower-festooned stone houses and surround a central *placette* (small square) with a burbling fountain. Yes, it's been gentrified with a few boutiques and restaurants, but the escapist feel hasn't been erased.

Dining and Lodging

$–$$ **✕▥ Auberge du Presbytère.** Three stone houses on the village's central *place* join to make this graceful inn. Their country roots show in the exposed rafters, vaulted ceilings, weathered quarry tiles, and blue-shuttered windows. Two bargain rooms share a bathroom down the hall; two others offer spectacular valley views from private terraces. The restaurant (closed Wednesday) aims high with a pair of regional menus. Look for delicate goat cheese mousse in a tomato-basil coulis, milk-fed lamb with thyme flowers, and a summery watermelon sorbet. ✉ *pl. de la Fontaine, 84400,* ☎ *04–90–74–11–50,* FAX *04–90–04–68–51. 10 rooms, 8 with bath. Restaurant. AE, DC, MC, V. Closed 2 wks in Nov., 2 wks in Jan.* ✍

Apt

⊕ *40 km (25 mi) east of Avignon.*

Actively ugly from a distance, with a rash of modern apartment blocks and industrial buildings, Apt doesn't attract the tourism it deserves. Its central old town, with tight, narrow streets shaded with noble stone houses and strings of fluttering laundry, seethes with activity. The best time to visit is Saturday, when the old town buzzes with a vibrant Provençal market, selling crafts, clothing, carpets, jewelry, and—not incidentally—all the finest food products of the Luberon and Haut Provence.

Dining

$ ✕ **Dame Tartine.** Sit in the shade of an old plane tree on this pretty square and enjoy a light lunch of salads, homemade quiches, and fruit tarts. The choices are all fresh and imaginative, such as the tarts (or quiches) with tangy Roquefort or fresh spinach, and desserts made with market-fresh berries. ✉ *pl. du Septier,* ☎ *04–90–74–27–97. No credit cards. Closed Mon., evenings by 6:30 PM.*

En Route Between Apt and Lourmarin, the *départemental* road D943 winds dramatically through deep backcountry, offering the only passage over the spine of the Luberon. Bone-dry and bristling with scrub oak, pine, coarse broom, and wild lavender, it's a landscape reminiscent of Greece or Sicily. If you climb into the hills, you won't get views; this is landlocked, isolated terrain, but it's wildly beautiful.

Lourmarin

⊕ *12 km (7 mi) southeast of Bonnieux, 54 km (33 mi) southeast of Avignon.*

The highly gentrified village of Lourmarin lies low-slung in the hollow of the Luberon's south face, a sprawl of manicured green. Its **Château** is its main draw, privately restored in the 1920s to appealing near-perfection. Of the old wing (15th century) and the new (begun in 1525), the latter is prettiest, with a broad-ranging art collection, rare old furniture, and ornate stone fireplaces—including one with exotic Aztec caryatids. ☎ *04–90–68–15–23.* ▧ *30 frs/€4.57.* ☉ *Guided tours (in French; 45 mins long) daily 11, 2:30, 3:30, and 4:30; July–Aug. every half hour.*

Albert Camus loved Lourmarin from the moment he discovered it in the 1930s. After he won his Nobel prize in 1957 he bought a house here and lived in it until his death in 1960. He is buried in the village **cemetery.**

THE VAUCLUSE A TO Z

Arriving and Departing

By Bus

Major bus transport companies carry travelers from surrounding cities into towns not accessible by rail; bus and rail services usually dovetail. Avignon's **gare routière** (bus station; ☎ 04–90–82–07–35), has the heaviest interregional traffic.

By Car

The A6/A7 toll (*péage*) expressway channels all traffic from Paris to the south. At Orange A7 splits to the southeast and leads directly to Avignon and N100 (in the direction of Apt), which dives straight east into the Luberon. To reach Vaison and the Mont Ventoux region from

Avignon, head northeast toward Carpentras on D942. D36 jags south from N100 and leads you on a gorgeous chase over the backbone of the Luberon, via Bonnieux and Lourmarin; from there it's a straight shot to Aix and Marseille or to the Côte d'Azur. Or you can shoot back west up D973 to Cavaillon and Avignon.

By Plane

Marseille's **Marignane airport** (☎ 04–42–14–14–14) is served by frequent flights from Paris and London; it's about an hour's drive from Avignon (☞ Chapter 3). The smaller **aeroport Avignon Caumont** (southeast of Avignon, ☎ 04–90–81–51–51) has frequent daily flights from Paris.

By Train

Trains arrive from all points north—Paris, Strasbourg, Nantes, and Bordeaux—in Marseille. Those from Paris and Strasbourg pass through Orange and Avignon. Many of these routes have overnight runs, with *couchettes* (sleeper bunks) and, sometimes, *wagons-lits* (minicabins with hotel-like service). A high-speed TGV (Trains à Grande Vitesse) line connects Paris and Orange (3 hrs 20 mins) and then Avignon (3 hrs 30 mins). After that, secondary connections in this area are slim to nonexistent: L'Isle-sur-la-Sorgue is the farthest you'll get into the Luberon. (☞ Train Travel *in* Smart Travel Tips A to Z for more information.)

Getting Around

By Bus

A reasonable network of private bus services (called, confusingly enough, *cars*) links places not served or poorly served by trains. Ask for bus schedules at train stations and tourist offices, or head for Avignon's **gare routière** (bus station; ☎ 04–90–82–07–35), next to the train station. Avignon has a sizable station, with posted schedules; buses branch out into every corner of the Vaucluse from here. **Cars Lieutaud** (☎ 04–90–86–36–75) has a booth just outside the Avignon train station, offering daily bus excursions into different regions—for instance, the Luberon, Vaison, and the Alpilles. Some of them are one-way runs, useful as simple transport; others are round-trip guided tours.

By Car

With spokes shooting out in every direction from Avignon and A7, you'll have no problem accessing the Vaucluse. The main *routes nationales* (national routes, or secondary highways) offer fairly direct links via D942 toward Orange and Mont Ventoux and via N100 into the Luberon. Negotiating the roads to L'Isle-sur-la-Sorgue and Fontaine de la Vaucluse requires a careful mix of map and sign reading, often at high speeds around suburban *giratoires* (rotaries). But by the time you strike out into the hills and the tiny roads—one of the best parts of the Vaucluse—give yourself over to road signs and pure faith. As is the case throughout France, directions are indicated by village name only, with route numbers given as a small-print afterthought. Of course, this means you have to recognize the minor villages en route.

By Train

The Vaucluse is not a territory to explore in depth by train, though if you're passing through, you can venture out of Avignon as far as Orange, L'Isle-sur-la-Sorgue, and Cavaillon; buses connect from Cavaillon into the Luberon.

Contacts and Resources

Bed & Breakfasts

Chambres d'hôtes (bed-and-breakfasts) offer simple lodging, usually in the hosts' home, with breakfast and a warm, regional welcome often included. This region has a plethora of B&Bs, perhaps because of the onslaught of English and Americans looking for a simpler way of life and all that extra space in the barn; if you prefer to speak English, there's a good chance you'll find a lodging owned by an "Anglo-Saxon." The French national network, **Gîtes de France** (☞ Lodging *in* Smart Travel Tips A to Z) lists B&Bs that have been rated. For chambres d'hôtes regulated by the national network, contact **Vaucluse Gîtes de France** (✉ pl. Campana, by the Papal Palace in Avignon; B.P. 164, 84008 Avignon cedex 1, ☎ 04–90–85–45–00).

Car Rental

AVIGNON

Avignon, as a major rail crossroads and springboard for the Vaucluse, has plenty of car-rental agencies, and it's fairly easy to get out of town toward other destinations. **Avis** (✉ bd. St-Roche, ☎ 04–90–27–96–10) has an office at the Avignon rail station. **Budget** (✉ bd. St-Roch, ☎ 04–90–27–94–95) is to your left just as you leave the train station. **Hertz** (✉ 2A av. Monclar, ☎ 04–90–14–26–90) is on the station's right, by the bus station.

L'ISLE-SUR-LA-SORGUE

You can penetrate as far as L'Isle-sur-la-Sorgue by train and then rent from **Avis** (✉ 58 Zone Industrielle Grande Marine, ☎ 04–90–38–03–60) or **Budget** (✉ rue André Autheman, ☎ 04–90–20–64–13).

ORANGE

In Orange, **Avis** (✉ 19 av. Charles de Gaulle, ☎ 04–90–34–11–00) has a location by the train station; cars must be reserved in advance. If you telephone **Budget** (✉ 42 bd. Edouard Daladier, ☎ 04–90–34–00–34), they'll pick you up at the station and transport you to the office.

Guided Tours

An accompanied tour of **Avignon's old town** is given by the tourist office from April through October, leaving from its headquarters Tuesday and Thursday at 10 AM (English on request; ☞ Visitor Information, *below*).

Daily **bus excursions** into different regions, with commentary, are offered by Cars Lieutaud (☎ 04–90–86–36–75); there's a booth just outside the Avignon train station. Some offer English commentary; ask in advance.

Outdoor Activities and Sports

Two *grandes randonnées* (national hiking trails GR9-97 and GR92) follow the slopes and crest of the Luberon; head out from Oppède, in the northwest, or Lourmarin, in the southeast. The GR91 clambers over the south face of Mont Ventoux, reaching its razorback crest overlooking the Alps. For regional information, write to the **Comité Départemental de la Randonnée Pédestre** (✉ 307 av. Foch, Orange, ☎ 04–90–51–14–86). *See also* Hiking *in* Smart Travel Tips A to Z.

If you want to see the countryside by bike, **Vélo Loisir en Luberon** (✉ B.P. 14, 04280 Cereste, ☎ 04–92–79–05–82) suggests itineraries (principally between Cavaillon and Forcalquier) and accommodations; they will even transport your luggage.

Travel Agencies

AVIGNON

Havas/American Express (✉ 35 rue de la République, ☎ 04–90–80–66–80). **Nouvelles Frontières** (✉ 14 rue Carnot, ☎ 04–90–82–31–32).

L'ISLE-SUR-LA-SORGUE

Rév'Alizés Voyages (✉ 25 quai Jean Jaurès, ☎ 04–90–20–80–40).

Havas (⊠ 34 rue de la République, ☎ 04–90–11–44–44).

Lieutaud Voyages (⊠ av. Choralies, ☎ 04–90–36–09–90).

Vacation Rentals

Gîtes de France is a nationwide organization that rents vacation housing, often of exceptional regional charm (☞ Lodging *in* Smart Travel Tips A to Z). The Vaucluse is especially well disposed to rentals, as part of the appeal of a visit here means escaping from the usual rush of obligatory sightseeing to enjoy mouthwatering produce markets and low-key walks through the countryside. A few houses even have private pools (and cost up to 7,000 francs, or €1,070, per week), but most are reasonably priced compared to hotel stays, even for two people. For information about rentals in this region, contact the **Vaucluse Gîtes de France** (⊠ pl. Campana, by the Popes' Palace in Avignon; B.P. 164, 84008 Avignon cedex 1, ☎ 04–90–85–45–00); you can get a catalog at the office (for next time) or request one in writing or by phone.

Visitor Information

The **Comité Départemental du Tourisme de Vaucluse** (⊠ B.P. 147, 84008 Avignon Cedex 1) accepts written queries only; streamline your request and specify your needs by category (lodging, restaurants, general sights, biking).

Apt (⊠ av. Ph.-de-Girard, 84400). **Avignon** (⊠ 41 cours Jean-Jaurès, 84008, ☎ 04–90–82–65–11, FAX 04–90–82–95–03). **Bonnieux** (⊠ 7 pl. Carnot, 84480, ☎ 04–90–75–91–90). **Carpentras** (⊠ 170 allée Jean-Jaurès, 84200, ☎ 04–90–63–00–78, FAX 04–90–60–41–02). **Cavaillon** (for information on smaller villages in the Luberon; ⊠ pl. François Tourel, 84300, ☎ 04–90–71–32–01). **Châteauneuf-du-Pape** (⊠ pl. du Portail, 84230, ☎ 04–90–83–71–08, FAX 04–90–83–50–34). **Fontaine de Vaucluse** (⊠ chemin Fontaine, 84800, ☎ 04–90–20–32–22, FAX 04–90–20–21–37). **Gigondas** (⊠ rue du Portail, 84190, ☎ 04–90–65–85–46, FAX 04–90–65–88–42). **Gordes** (⊠ Salle des Gardes du Château, 84220, ☎ 04–90–72–02–26, FAX 04–90–72–04–39). **L'Isle-sur-la-Sorgue** (⊠ pl. de l'Église, 84800, ☎ 04–90–38–04–78, FAX 04–90–38–35–43). **Orange** (⊠ 5 cours A. Briand, 84100, ☎ 04–90–34–70–88, FAX 04–90–34–99–62). **Roussillon** (⊠ pl. de la Poste, 84220, ☎ 04–90–05–60–25, FAX 04–90–05–63–31). **Sault** (⊠ av. Promenade, 84390, ☎ 04–90–64–01–21, FAX 04–90–64–15–03). **Vaison-la-Romaine** (⊠ Vaison-la-Romaine, 84110, ☎ 04–90–36–02–11, FAX 04–90–28–76–04). **Villeneuve-lès-Avignon** (⊠ 1 pl. Charles David, 30400, ☎ 04–90–25–61–33, FAX 04–90–25–61–55).

3 AIX, MARSEILLE, AND THE CENTRAL COAST

AUBAGNE, CASSIS, AND THE ILES D'HYÈRES

This is the land of Cézanne and Pagnol—a rough-hewn and fiercely beautiful landscape that tapers to a coastline of pine-studded cliffs and enchanting fishing ports. Sophisticated Aix-en-Provence stands aloof from Marseille, tough, gorgeous, and larger than life, yet the backcountry between them ambles along at a 19th-century pace of boules, pastis, and country markets. Cassis and Bandol mean wine to some and waterfronts to others. Off the mainland, the Iles d'Hyères are a car-free paradise.

CÉZANNE PAINTED THIS COUNTRYSIDE in daubs of russet and black-green, the rough-cut structure of bluff and twisted pine inspiring a building-block approach to painting that for others jelled into Cubism. Marcel Pagnol painted pictures with words: the smells of thyme and rosemary crunching underfoot, the sounds of thunder rumbling behind rain-starved hills, the quiet joy of opening shutters at dawn to a chorus of blackbirds in the olive grove. Both Cézanne and Pagnol were native sons of this region east of the Rhône who were inspired to eloquence by the primordial landscape and its echoes of antiquity—and the world continues to seek out the understated wonders they described.

A visit to this region involves the best of urban culture, seaside, and arid backcountry. Aix is a small, manageable city with a leisurely pace and a concentration of arts, due in part to its university life. Marseille offers the yang to Aix's yin. Its brash style, bold monuments, and spectacular sun-washed waterfront center are reminiscent of Naples or modern Athens; it is much maligned and unfairly neglected by visitors. Up in the dry inland hills, Pagnol's hometown of Aubagne gives a glimpse of local life, with a big farmers' market in the plane-tree-lined town center and makers of *santons* (terra-cotta figurines) at every turn. The lovely port-village of Cassis and the busy beach town of Bandol allow time to watch the tides come and go, though for the ultimate ocean retreat, take the boat that leaves for the almost tropical Iles d'Hyères.

Pleasures and Pastimes

Beaches
Wherever there's water in France, beaches of every shape and substance fill with sun lovers from June to September. The most popular beach resort is Bandol, but for a quieter retreat, head for genteel Cassis, where you can perch on rocky promontories along the *calanques* (coves). The shipbuilding port town of La Ciotat has the most sandy-beach surface at the Clos des Plages, just beyond the pleasure-boat port.

Boat Rides
If you find yourself without a yacht on this wild and lovely coastline, it's easy to jump on a tourist cruiser, whether you putter from calanque to calanque between Marseille and Cassis or commute to the car-free Iles d'Hyères. Many boats are glass-bottomed for underwater viewing, and most allow you to climb onto the top deck and face the bracing wind as you buck the waves.

Dining
Aix is one of the capitals of olive-oil production in Provence, and its market tables groan with the weight of industrial-scale jugs of the stuff. Far more than a medium here, it takes center stage at the table: a pool of chartreuse encircles goat cheese, a fillet of sea bass shimmers on a mirror of green-gold. The olives themselves—gleaming beads of briny salt fruit—figure everywhere, in every degree of ripeness and marinade imaginable, scooped from vats into tiny bowls to accompany the aperitif. Ground into a caviarlike spread called *tapenade,* made even more pungent by the mix of capers, anchovies, and garlic, the local olives appear on toast or grace a rosy leg of lamb.

But it's in leaving the highlands that you come upon the star cuisine of this region. Marseille and its environs have some of the finest seafood dishes in France, cooked robustly with garlic and flush with the fruits of the adjacent sea. It's here, more than anywhere on the southern coast, that you find authentic bouillabaisse, the quintessential fish stew of Provence. In it, chunks of Mediterranean fish otherwise too small and, frankly, ugly to market—*rascasse, congre, grondin*—float with shellfish in a powerful broth of tomato-red fish stock, perfumed with garlic, onion, fennel, herbs, and—a must—orange peel and saffron. The simmered concoction (*bouillir,* for boiled, and *abaisser,* for reduced) is served in two courses: First the broth is poured over bread slices; it is then followed by a parade of tender fish. A dollop of *rouille* (chili peppers and garlic whipped into olive-oil paste) gives an extra jolt to the broth. Because of the price of fresh seafood, an authentic bouillabaisse will set you back from 200 francs to 250 francs/€30.49 to €38.11; order a bottle of chilled Cassis and enjoy the ritual.

If bouillabaisse is too rich for your blood, the ubiquitous *soupe de poisson* (fish soup) is an affordable alternative: Less subtly seasoned and stirred to a thick velouté, it appears as a first-course option on just about every regional menu. Spread the oil-brushed croutons with rouille and float them in the soup with a sprinkle of ground cheese.

Where you eat in this region is often as wonderful as what you eat: Outdoor tables pepper the sidewalks of Marseille and Aix nearly year-round, and coastal restaurants vie to give you the best sea views.

CATEGORY	COST*
$$$$	over 400 frs/€61
$$$	250 frs–400 frs/€38–€61
$$	125 frs–250 frs/€19–€38
$	under 125 frs/€19

*per person for a three-course meal, including tax (20.6%) and tip but not wine

Hiking

The walk from Cassis to the Calanques is one of the most dramatic in France, with cliff-top views over the ocean and clambering descents to intimate inlet beaches. In the hills above Marseille, so beloved by Pagnol, you can still follow his childhood trails and stand on the spot from which Ugolin screamed, *"Manon, je t'aime!"* (Manon, I love you!) in *Manon des Sources* (*Manon of the Springs*). The mountain called Ste-Victoire, often painted by Cézanne, affords beautiful hikes and views despite being burned by wildfires in 1989. Contact the Bouches-du-Rhône departmental tourist office (☞ Aix, Marseille, and the Central Coast A to Z, *below*) for information about hikes in the area.

Lodging

This is no longer converted *mas* (farmhouse) country. Nonetheless, hotels in this region favor Provençal decor and aim to provide outdoor space at its loveliest, from gardens where breakfast is served to parasol pines shading pools. As in all of France, hotels book up well in advance for July and August. If you plan to spend at least a week in the region, look into a *gîte* (vacation rental); those managed by Gîtes de France in the Bouches-du-Rhône and Var are often in inviting old houses and are always in rural settings (☞ Close Up: The Gîte Way *in* Chapter 2 *and* Smart Travel Tips A to Z for more information).

CATEGORY	COST*
$$$$	over 800 frs/€122
$$$	550 frs–800 frs/€84–€122
$$	300 frs–550 frs/€46–€84
$	under 300 frs/€46

*All prices are for a standard double room for two, including tax (20.6%) and service charge.

✎ following the text of a review is your signal that the property has a Web site, where you will find details and, usually, images; for a link, visit www.fodors.com/urls.

Wine

In the heart of the **Côtes de Provence** region, this area is summer wine country, with its fresh, unpretentious rosés chilling in buckets at every table. There are also reds, rather Italian in their hearty, fruity strength, and negligible whites, too, but the category always conjures rosés first and foremost. The smaller **Côteaux d'Aix** region, surrounding Aix-en-Provence, produces highly drinkable, unsensational rosés, as well as minor reds and whites. Yet this region concentrates the very best of Provence, indeed its only fine wines, labeled by their place name rather than the umbrella title of Côtes de Provence. **Bandol,** famous as the best-rounded and most viable of all the rosés, makes a crisp white and a strong red, too. **Cassis** (not to be confused with the black-currant liqueur produced in Burgundy) creates marvelous whites with distinct shades of almond; it's the wine of choice with a spicy bouillabaisse, and it won't overwhelm a simple fillet. But the lone contender for the title of Great Wine comes from a tiny region around Aix, called **Palette.** Here Château Simone produces a magnificent red redolent of *garrigue,* the wild thyme, rosemary, and pine that flavor its soil, as well as a wonderful, substantial white; by all means, splurge.

Exploring Aix, Marseille, and the Central Coast

Aix lies at a major crossroads of autoroutes: one coming in from Bordeaux and Toulouse, then leading up into the Alps toward Grenoble; the other a direct line from Lyon and Paris. Aix is extremely well placed for trips to the Luberon, Avignon, and Arles, and it's only a quick half hour from Marseille. All of the coastal towns line up for easy access between Marseille and Toulon, so you can cruise along A50, which follows the coastline, and take in all the sights. Although Marseille is one of the biggest cities in France, it's a matter of minutes before you're lost in deep backcountry on winding, picturesque roads that lead to Cassis or Aubagne and beyond.

Great Itineraries

To make the most of your time in this region, plan to divide your days between big-city culture, backcountry tours, and waterfront leisure. You can "do" Marseille in an impressive day trip, but its backstreets and tiny ports reward a more leisurely approach. Aix is as much a way of life as a city charged with tourist must-sees; allow time to hang out in a cours Mirabeau café and shop the backstreets. Aubagne must be seen on a market day (Monday, Tuesday, Saturday, or Sunday) to make the most of its charms. Cassis merits a whole day if you want to explore the calanques and enjoy a seaside lunch; Bandol is less appealing unless you're committed to beach time. The complete seaside experience, with rocky shoreline, isolated beaches, a picturesque port, and luxurious near-tropical greenery, can be found on the island of Porquerolles, one of the Îles d'Hyères; if your budget and schedule allow, spend a night or two in one of its few hotels and have much of the island to yourself.

Numbers in the text correspond to numbers in the margin and on the Aix and the Central Coast, Aix-en-Provence, and Marseille maps.

IF YOU HAVE 3 DAYS
With limited time, base yourself in ⊞ **Aix-en-Provence** ①–㉓ and explore the city first and foremost. Make a day trip to **Aubagne** ㊸, for the morning market, and **Cassis** ㊹, for an afternoon cruise to the

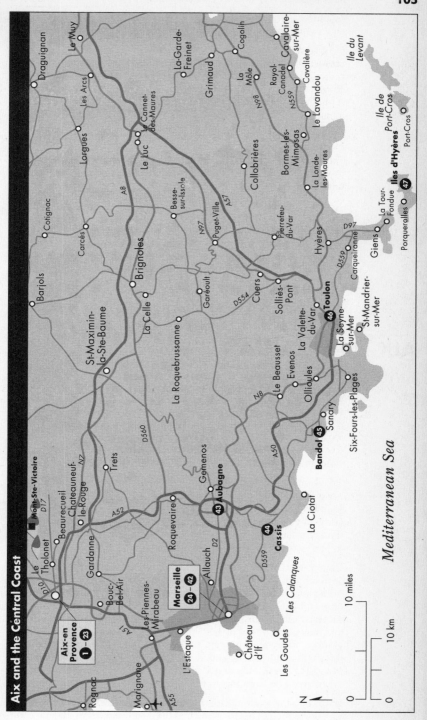

Aix and the Central Coast

Draguignan
Le Muy
Les Arcs
Lorgues
Cotignac
Carcès
Barjols
St-Maximin-la-Ste-Baume
La Celle
Brignoles
Besse-sur-Issole
Le Luc
Le Cannet-des-Maures
La-Garde-Freinet
Grimaud
Cogolin
Cavalaire-sur-Mer
Cavalière
La Môle
Rayol-Canadel
Le Lavandou
Collobrières
Bormes-les-Mimosas
la Londe-les-Maures
Puget-Ville
Pierrefeu-du-Var
Hyères
Giens
Carqueiranne
La Tour-Fondue
Porquerolles
Iles d'Hyères **47**
Ile de Port-Cros
Port-Cros
Ile du Levant
Garéoult
La Roquebrussanne
Cuers
Solliès-Pont
Toulon **46**
La Valette-du-Var
La Seyne-sur-Mer
St-Mandrier-sur-Mer
Le Beausset
Evenos
Ollioules
Sanary
Six-Fours-les-Plages
Bandol **45**
La Ciotat
Cassis **44**
Aubagne **43**
Gémenos
Roquevaire
Allauch
Marseille **24–42**
Les Calanques
Château d'If
Les Goudes
L'Estaque
Les-Pennes-Mirabeau
Bouc-Bel-Air
Gardanne
Trets
Beaurecueil
Chateauneuf-le-Rouge
Le Tholonet
Mont-Ste-Victoire
Aix-en-Provence **1** **23**
Rognac
Marignane

Mediterranean Sea

N

0   10 miles
0   10 km

calanques. You could make a foray into **Marseille** ㉔–㊷; consider taking the train from Aix to avoid the traffic and having to find parking.

IF YOU HAVE 7 DAYS
Spend two nights in ⛺ **Aix-en-Provence** ①–㉓, seeing the old town and cathedral, and two nights in ⛺ **Cassis** ㊹, exploring the calanques and going to the market in **Aubagne** ㊸. Two nights in ⛺ **Marseille** ㉔–㊷ should give you time to wander its colorful neighborhoods and visit its museums. A seventh night could be well spent in a hotel (and an evening bike ride) on the ⛺ **Iles d'Hyères** ㊼.

IF YOU HAVE 10 DAYS
Tackle all of the sights in the seven-day itinerary and take extra time to wander Pagnol country above **Aubagne** ㊸, to taste wines around **Bandol** ㊺, and visit the hilltop village of Le Castellet. If you're brave enough to cross the traffic-clogged city of **Toulon** ㊻ you'll find that its old town is full of picturesque backstreets (just avoid them at night).

When to Tour Aix, Marseille, and the Central Coast

High season falls between Easter and October, but if you come in the winter, you may be pampered with warm sun and cool breezes. When the mistral attacks (and it can happen year-round), it channels all its forces down the Rhône Valley and blasts into Marseille like a one-way tornado. But, happily, the assault may only last one day. This is not the day, however, to opt for a boat ride from Cassis or Porquerolles; aim instead for the sheltered streets of Aix.

AIX-EN-PROVENCE

Gracious, cultivated, and made all the more cosmopolitan by the presence of some 40,000 university students, the lovely old town of Aix-en-Provence (pronounced ex) was once the capital of Provence. The vestiges of that influence and power—fine art, noble architecture, and graceful urban design—remain beautifully preserved today. That and its thriving market, vibrant café life, and world-class music festival, makes Aix tie with Arles and Avignon as one of the towns in Provence that shouldn't be missed.

The Romans were first drawn here by mild thermal baths, naming the town Aquae Sextiae (Waters of Sextius) in honor of the consul who founded a camp nearby in 123 BC. Just 20 years later some 200,000 German invaders besieged Aix, but the great Roman general Marius flanked them and pinned them against the mountain known ever since as Ste-Victoire. Marius is a popular first name to this day.

Under the wise and generous guidance of Roi René (King René) in the 15th century, Aix became a center of Renaissance arts and letters. Under his auspices and discerning eye, a veritable army of artists flourished here and left a handful of masterpieces, including Nicolas Froment's Triptych of the Burning Bush. At the height of its political, judicial, and ecclesiastic power in the 17th and 18th centuries, Aix profited from a surge of private building, each grand *hôtel particulier* (mansion) meant to outdo its neighbor. Its signature *cours* (promenade) and *places* (squares), punctuated by grand fountains and intriguing passageways, date from this time.

It was into this exalting elegance that artist Paul Cézanne (1839–1906) was born, though he drew much of his inspiration from the raw countryside around the city and often painted Ste-Victoire. A writer and poet as well as a painter, he was barely recognized in his native Aix but drew the admiration of Impressionists on frequent trips to Paris. If he dabbled briefly in Impressionism, he moved quickly on to paint

Aix-en-Provence

in bold, building-block strokes, deconstructing the colors into multi-hued patches. It was this geometric dissection of form and color that laid the way for the 20th-century art revolution; Cubism, Fauvism, Constructivism, and all abstract modern-art styles have been dismissed, by his most zealous admirers, as "Cézanne misunderstood."

A schoolmate of Cézanne's made equal inroads on modern society: the journalist and novelist Emile Zola (1840–1902) attended the Collège Bourbon with Cézanne and described their friendship as well as Aix itself in several of his works.

You can sense something of the ambience that nurtured these two geniuses in the streets of modern Aix, not only charged with its large university population but continually injected with new blood from exchange programs: Vanderbilt, California State, Michigan, and Wisconsin all send students to this stimulating city. There's also a British-American Institute and an American Center: in short, enough students and intellectuals to keep the crêperies and cafés crowded into the wee hours and to sustain a branch of The Gap.

It's not just the universities that keep Aix young: its famous Festival International d'Art Lyrique (International Festival of Opera) has imported and created world-class opera productions as well as related concerts and recitals since 1948. Most of the performances take place in elegant, old-Aix settings, and during this time the cafés, restaurants, and hotels spill over with *beau monde* who've come to Aix especially for the July event.

The Historic Heart

The famous cours Mirabeau, a broad, shady avenue that stretches from one grand fountain to another, bisects old Aix into two distinct neighborhoods. Below the cours, the carefully planned and imminently rational Quartier Mazarin is lined with fine 17th- and 18th-century hôtels particuliers. Above, the old town twists and turns from square to fountain to square, each mysterious turn leading to another row of urbane boutiques and another cluster of café tables. If you turn a blind eye to these enticing distractions, you can see the best of Aix in a day's tour—but you'll be missing the point. The music of the fountains, the theater of the café crowds, and the painterly shade of the plane trees are what Aix is all about.

Note: At press time, the cours Mirabeau was well into a two-year renovation project, which was scheduled for completion in May 2002.

A Good Walk
Begin at the tourist office, which anchors the cours Mirabeau at place du Général de Gaulle. The spiraling traffic, kiosks, newsstands, events posters, and crowds of students contrast sharply with **La Rotonde** ①, the monumental sculpture-fountain that towers over the swirl of modernity. Walk up the **cours Mirabeau** ② itself. With vibrant café life to your left and grand old mansions to your right, you pass a series of fountains, including the magnificently mossy **Fontaine d'Eau Chaude** ③. At No. 55 are traces of the hat shop founded by Cézanne's father, now worn away by time: The sign still reads CHAPELLERIE DU COURS MIRABEAU, GROS ET DÉTAIL (Hatshop of the Cours Mirabeau, wholesale and retail). Cézanne himself hung out at the **Café les Deux Garçons** ④, the landmark café-restaurant that still serves gold-rimmed cups of espresso to artists and dreamers, nowadays armed with mobile phones. If you want to explore Cézanne sites in-depth, pick up a map of the Circuit Cézanne at the tourist office; a series of brass plaques right on the sidewalks mark the itinerary.

Now cut right down the lively market street rue d'Italie and turn left at the **Église St-Jean-de-Malte** ⑤, once the chapel for a Knights of Malta priory. Just across the way, the **Musée Granet** ⑥ houses a formidable collection of French art and archaeology. Follow rue Cardinale to the **Fontaine des Quatre Dauphins** ⑦, a graceful obelisk framed by curving dolphins; it sets off the patrician symmetry of the lofty homes around it. Turn right up rue du 4 Septembre to the **Musée Paul Arbaud** ⑧, with its highly personal collection of faïence and regional books. Then continue west down rue Goyrand to rue Cabassol; No. 3 is the imposing **Hôtel de Caumont** ⑨, now home to the Conservatoire de Musique Darius-Milhaud. Head down rue Cabassol (away from cours Mirabeau) to rue Cardinale, and you may see students of the Lycée Mignet crossing the courtyard of the former **Collège Royal-Bourbon** ⑩, just as alumni Cézanne and Zola once did.

Now head back up rue Cabassol and cross cours Mirabeau to enter the lovely labyrinth above it. Plunge straight in and veer left; on your right is the graceful **place d'Albertas** ⑪, lined with fine old shuttered mansions. The **Muséum d'Histoire Naturelle** ⑫, with its collection of dinosaur fossils, is just behind you in the Hôtel Boyer d'Eguilles. Follow rue Espariat to place de Verdun, where the Palais de Justice looms over an antiques market held three times a week. Walk the length of the square and the adjoining place des Prêcheurs to the **Église de la Madeleine** ⑬, where you'll find the Flemish Annunciation Triptych.

Next wind your way back via rue de Montigny to place Richelme and the **Ancienne Halle aux Grains** ⑭, these days a post office. Walk around to the front and admire its allegorical frieze of the rivers Rhône and Durance. Up and to the left stands the **Hôtel de Ville** ⑮ with its imposing clock tower.

Continue up rue Gaston de Saporta to the **Musée du Vieil Aix** ⑯, which houses eclectic memorabilia from Aix's past. Just beyond it on the left is the **Hôtel de Châteaurenard** ⑰, where fabulous trompe-l'oeil murals are concealed around a grand staircase; peek in, as it's a public building. Next door in the **Hôtel Maynier d'Oppède** ⑱ is a French-language school; its courtyard is where concerts are held during the July opera festival. Across the street, the luxurious Palais de l'Archevêché (Bishop's Palace) houses the **Musée des Tapisseries** ⑲, containing a rich collection of Beauvais tapestries. Next to it, the **Cathédrale St-Sauveur** ⑳ provides a survey course in architectural history, from its 5th-century baptistery to its Gothic-Romanesque double nave, and shelters the magnificent *Triptyque du Buisson Ardent*.

You're not far now from the very last traces of the medieval ramparts that once surrounded this ancient city; they're just up from the cathedral and to the left. Continue past this old stone wall, and you'll reach an even older landmark: the **Thermes Sextius** ㉑, now a high-tech treatment center. Just behind, turn left along the busy boulevard Jean-Jaurès and continue to the **Pavillon de Vendôme** ㉒, a rather grand 17th-century country house displaying regional furniture and art. From here, you may want to make a pilgrimage across the busy boulevard to the **Atelier Cézanne** ㉓, built by the artist when the beloved country house in which he worked was sold.

TIMING

If you only want to take in the big picture, you can easily stroll this broad circuit in a half day, browsing through shops and morning markets in the old town, then crossing cours Mirabeau to the Quartier Mazarin to admire the fine old architecture. (If you're here while construction on the cours Mirabeau is still in progress, however, you're likely to be slowed down somewhat.) If you want to visit one of the Mazarin's museums, spend a half day in this neighborhood, then devote the afternoon to the old town and the cathedral north of cours Mirabeau. A visit to Cézanne's Atelier requires extra walking time beyond the town center.

Sights to See

⑭ **Ancienne Halle aux Grains** (Old Grain Market). Built in 1761, this former grain market serves as a post office today—a rather spectacular building for a humble service. The frieze, portraying an allegory of the Rhône and Durance rivers, is the work of Aix sculptor Jean Chaste (1726–1793); he also created the fountain out front. That's a real Roman column at the fountain's top. ✉ *pl. Richelme.*

㉓ **Atelier Cézanne** (Cézanne's Studio). After the death of his mother forced the sale of Paul Cézanne's (1839–1906) beloved country retreat known as Jas de Bouffan, he had this studio built just above the town center. In the upstairs work space, the artist created some of his finest paintings, including *Les Grandes Baigneuses* (*The Large Bathers*). The latter was so large, in fact, that the artist had a special slot built into the studio wall, as the canvas was too broad to carry downstairs. But what is most striking is the collection of simple objects that once featured prominently in the still lifes he created: the tin milk can, the ginger jar, the flowered crockery, bottles and glasses from *La Nature Morte aux Oignons* (*Still Life with Onions*), and a tin coffee pot from *La Femme à la Cafétière* (*The Woman with the Coffee Pot*). Also here are Cézanne's redingote and bowler hat, hanging from pegs as he left them; brushes, paint tubes, and the engravings with which he surrounded himself—works by Courbet, Delacroix, and Poussin. The atelier is behind an obscure garden gate on the left as you climb the avenue Paul-Cézanne. ✉ *9 av. Paul-Cézanne,* ☎ *04–42–21–06–53.* ✉ *25 frs/€3.81.*

⊘ *Apr.–Sept., daily 10–noon and 2:30–6; Oct.–Mar., daily 10–noon and 2–5:30. Guided tours.*

❹ Café les Deux Garçons. Cézanne enjoyed his coffee and papers here, as have generations of *beau monde,* intellectuals, and neighborhood *habitués* (regulars) since its founding in 1792. The gilt-and-muraled decor inside is original, but you may not see it unless you're on your way to the bathroom: The *très récherché* (much sought-after) sidewalk terrace is *the* place to sit to see and be seen. (☞ Dining and Lodging, *below.*) ⊠ *53 cours Mirabeau.*

★ ⑳ Cathédrale St-Sauveur. This marvelous hodgepodge juxtaposes so many eras of architectural history, all clearly delineated and preserved, it's a survey course in itself. There's a double nave, Romanesque and Gothic side by side, and an extraordinary Merovingian (5th-century) **baptistery,** its colonnade mostly recovered from Roman temples to other gods. Shutters hide the ornate 16th-century carvings on the **portals,** opened by a guide on request. The guide can also lead you into the tranquil Romanesque cloisters next door so you can admire the carved pillars and slender columns.

As if these treasures weren't enough, the cathedral also contains a remarkable 15th-century triptych, painted by Nicolas Froment in the heat of inspiration from his travels in Italy and Flanders. Entitled *Triptyque du Buisson Ardent* (Burning Bush Triptych), it depicts the generous art patrons King René and Queen Jeanne kneeling on each side of the Virgin, who is poised above a burning bush. The extraordinary details are charged with biblical references—for example, the imperfect mirror in the Virgin's hand (Saint Paul to the Corinthians: "For now we see through a glass, darkly") and Moses barefoot in the thorns and thistles (the burning bush to Moses: "Put off thy shoes from off thy feet, for the place whereon thou standest is holy ground"). There's even a complete trio of Adam, Eve, and a serpent in an angel's cameo. Froment was eager to show off his newly acquired perspective technique in the rippling planes of red drapery and the juxtaposition of the king and queen: If you imagine the side panels fitted together at a 45-degree angle, the background detail falls into one plane—and the king and queen kneel side by side before the Virgin. The painting owes its extraordinary condition to being hidden away in a Carmelite convent for centuries and opened only once a year. It's just as delicate today, and there's the rub—now it's kept closed indefinitely to prevent its oil and tempera mix from being damaged. If you care passionately about seeing it (as you should), make your needs known to the porters and administration and even the tourist office. An impassioned plea could open doors—or protective shutters. ⊠ *rue Gaston de Saporta.*

❿ Collège Royal-Bourbon. It's within these walls, which now belong to the Lycée Mignet, that Cézanne and his schoolmate Emile Zola discussed their ideas. Cézanne received his baccalauréat *cum laude* here in 1858 and went on to attend a year of law school to please his father. ⊠ *rue Cardinale at rue Joseph-Cabassol.*

NEED A BREAK?   Wander into the beautifully proportioned place de l'Hôtel de Ville and settle under a parasol at the **Café de l'Horloge** (⊠ pl. de l'Hotel de Ville) for a coffee or, in the late afternoon, for an aperitif and a saucer of spicy curried chickpeas.

★ ❷ Cours Mirabeau. In the deep shade of tall plane trees interlacing their heavy leaves over the street, cours Mirabeau is the social nerve center of Aix. One side of the street is lined with dignified 18th-century hôtels particuliers; you can view them from a seat in one of the dozen or

so cafés and restaurants that spill onto the sidewalk on the other side. (At press time, the cours was under construction, with completion scheduled for May 2002. The renovation includes a transformation of the cours, from four lanes with parking on both sides to two lanes with no parking. Depending on the construction phase during your visit, you may not want to spend much time at a sidewalk café.)

The street is named for the Count de Mirabeau, a rake in his youth who scandalized the world by leaving his carriage—*all night*—outside the home of his fiancée before their wedding. He went on, despite this extraordinary lapse in judgment, to be elected to the quasi-noble Third Estate in Aix in 1789.

⓫ **Église de la Madeleine.** Though the facade is modern now, this small 17th-century church still contains the center panel of the fine 15th-century *Triptych of the Annunciation,* attributed to the father of Jan Van Eyck. Some say the massive painting on the left side of the transept is a Rubens. ⊠ *pl. des Prêcheurs.*

❺ **Église St-Jean-de-Malte.** This 12th-century chapel of the Knights of Malta, a medieval order of friars devoted to hospital care, was Aix's first attempt at the Gothic style, and its delicately groin-vaulted ceilings and tall windows have a touching purity of style. It was here that the counts of Provence were buried throughout the 18th century; their tombs (in the upper left) were attacked during the Revolution and only partially repaired. ⊠ *At intersection of rue Cardinale and rue d'Italie.*

❸ **Fontaine d'Eau Chaude** (Hot Water Fountain). Deliciously thick with dripping moss, this 18th-century fountain is fed by Sextius's own thermal source. It seems representative of Aix at its artfully negligent best. ⊠ *cours Mirabeau.*

❼ **Fontaine des Quatre Dauphins** (Four Dolphins Fountain). Within a tiny square at a symmetrical crossroads in the Quartier Mazarin, this lovely 17th-century fountain features four graceful dolphins at the foot of a pine-cone–topped obelisk. Under the shade of a chestnut tree and framed by broad, shuttered mansions, it makes an elegant ensemble worth contemplating from the park bench. ⊠ *pl. des Quatre Dauphins.*

❾ **Hôtel de Caumont.** The elegant facade of this mansion built in 1720 contains the **Conservatoire de Musique Darius-Milhaud** (Darius-Milhaud Music Conservatory). A native of Marseille, the composer Milhaud (1892–1974) spent several years of his childhood in Aix and returned here to die. He was a member of the group of French composers known as Les Six and created fine-boned, transparent works influenced by jazz and Hebrew chant. Aix has yet to make a museum of his memorabilia. ⊠ *3 rue Joseph-Cabassol,* ☎ *04-42-26-38-70.*

⓱ **Hôtel de Châteaurenard.** Across from a commercial gallery that calls itself the Petit Musée Cézanne (actually more of a tourist trap), this 17th-century mansion once hosted Louis XIV—and now houses government offices. This means that during business hours you can slip in and peek at the fabulous 18th-century stairwell, decorated in flamboyant trompe-l'oeil. Pseudostone *putti* (cherubs) and caryatids pop into three-dimensions—as does the false balustrade that mirrors the real one in stone. ⊠ *19 rue Gaston de Saporta.* ☉ *Weekdays, 9–4.*

⓲ **Hôtel Maynier d'Oppède.** This ornately decorated mansion houses the **Institut d'Etudes Françaises** (Institute of French Studies), where foreign students take French classes. During the July opera festival, its courtyard serves as venue to a series of classical concerts. ⊠ *23 rue Gaston de Saporta.*

⑮ **Hôtel de Ville** (City Hall). This 1655 landmark sports elaborate iron-work and frames a pretty pebble-paved courtyard. But it's the 16th-century **tour d'horloge** (clock tower) with an open ironwork belfry that draws the eye: It used to serve as the town's bell tower. The tree-lined square in front—with cafés setting up tables right into the center of the square—is a major gathering place. ⊠ *pl. de Hotel-de-Ville.*

❻ **Musée Granet.** Once the Ecole de Dessin (Art School) that granted Cézanne a second prize in 1856, this former priory of the Église St-Jean-de-Malte is now an art museum of some substance. Cézanne's draw-ings and watercolors have been moved here from his studio, and there are eight of his paintings as well. You'll also find Rubens, David, In-gres, and a group of sentimental works by the museum's namesake, François Granet (1775–1849). In the archeology section are statues and busts recovered from the early Roman settlement. ⊠ *pl. St-Jean-de-Malte,* ☎ *04–42–38–14–70.* 🎟 *10 frs/€1.52.* ⏰ *Wed.–Mon., 10–noon and 2–6.*

❽ **Musée Paul Arbaud.** A rich and varied collection of Provençal faïence is displayed in this grand mansion in the Mazarin quarter. It also con-tains a library full of books on Provençal culture (only open to the pub-lic on Tuesday and Thursday from 2 to 5). ⊠ *2 rue du 4-Septembre,* ☎ *04–42–38–38–95.* 🎟 *15 frs/€2.29.* ⏰ *Mon.–Sat. 2–5.*

⑲ **Musée des Tapisseries** (Tapestries Museum). Housed in the 17th-cen-tury **Palais de l'Archevêché** (Archbishop's Palace), this sumptuous col-lection of tapestries actually decorated the walls of the bishops' quarters. Their taste was excellent: There are 17 magnificent hangings from Beau-vais and a series on the life of Don Quixote from Compiègne. In the broad courtyard, the main opera productions of the Festival Interna-tional d'Art Lyrique take place. ⊠ *pl. de l'Ancien-Archevêché,* ☎ *04–42–23–09–91.* 🎟 *10 frs/€1.52.* ⏰ *Wed.–Mon., 10–noon and 2–5:45.*

⑯ **Musée du Vieil Aix** (Museum of Old Aix). An eclectic assortment of local treasures resides in this 17th-century mansion, from faïence to *santons* (terra-cotta figurines). There are 19th-century puppets displayed in historic tableaux, and ornately painted furniture. The building it-self is lovely, too, from the dramatic stairwell to the painted beams and frescoes. The lovely boudoir is capped with a cupola decked with gar-lands of flowers, painted by artists who worked on the trompe l'oeil in the Châteaurenard. ⊠ *17 rue Gaston de Saporta,* ☎ *04–42–21–43–55.* 🎟 *15 frs/€2.29.* ⏰ *Apr.–Oct., Tues.–Sun. 10–noon and 2:30–6; Nov.–Mar., Tues.–Sun. 10–noon and 2–5.*

⑫ **Muséum d'Histoire Naturelle** (Natural History Museum). The unusual collection of dinosaur eggs is this museum's claim to fame. Even if these don't interest you, the 17th-century Hôtel Boyer d'Eguilles's interiors are magnificent, with ornate woodwork and sculpture scattered among the fossilized bones. ⊠ *6 rue Espariat,* ☎ *04–42–26–23–67.* 🎟 *10 frs/€1.52.* ⏰ *June–Oct., daily 10–6; Nov.–May, daily 10–noon and 1–5.*

㉒ **Pavillon de Vendôme.** This extravagant Baroque villa was first built in 1665 as a "country" house for the Duke of Vendome; its position just outside the city's inner circle allowed the duke to commute dis-creetly from his official home on the cours Mirabeau to this love nest, where his mistress, La Belle du Canet, was comfortably installed. Though never officially inhabited, it was expanded and heightened in the 18th century to showcase the classical orders—ionic, doric, and corinthian—in its parade of neo-Grecian columns. Inside its cool, broad chambers you'll find a collection of Provençal furniture and art-works. ⊠ *13 rue de la Molle,* ☎ *04–42–21–05–78.* 🎟 *10 frs/€1.52.* ⏰ *Open Wed.–Mon. 10–noon and 2–5.*

⑪ Place d'Albertas. Of all the elegant squares in Aix, this one is the most evocative and otherworldly. Set back from the city's fashionable shopping streets, it forms a horseshoe of shuttered mansions, with cobbles radiating from a simple turn-of-the-century fountain. No wonder chamber music concerts are held here in summer. ⊠ *Intersection of rue Espariat and rue Aude.*

❶ La Rotonde. If you've just arrived in Aix's center, this sculpture-fountain is a spectacular introduction to the town's rare mix of elegance and urban bustle. It's a towering mass of 19th-century attitude. That's Agriculture yearning toward Marseille, Art leaning toward Avignon, and Justice looking down on the cours Mirabeau. But don't study it too closely; you'll likely be sideswiped by a speeding Vespa. ⊠ *pl. de Gaulle.*

㉑ Thermes Sextius (Thermal Baths of Sextius). First discovered under the leadership of Sextius, the Roman city's founding father, in the 2nd century BC, these warm springs are still popular with modern clients. The original site is now covered by a posh, high-tech treatment center called Les Thermes Sextius; it was recently (1999) remodeled to incorporate pressure showers, mud treatments, and underwater massage. Call or write for an appointment. ⊠ *55 cours Sextius, B.P. 30, 13101 cedex 1,* ☎ *04–42–23–81–81,* FAX *04–42–95–11–33.* ☉ *Sun.–Fri. 8:30–7:30; Sat. 8:30–1:30 and 2:30–6:30.*

Dining and Lodging

$$$$ ✕ **Le Clos de la Violette.** Whether you dine in the shade of the broad
★ chestnut trees or in the airy, pastel dining room of this noble old house, you'll taste the Mediterranean mixed-blood cuisine of Chef Jean-Marc Banzo, whose Spanish father and Italian mother imprint his famously colorful cooking. Banzo spins tradition into gold, from a chilled artichoke-heart *barigoule* (stewed in white wine with bacon) with coriander-perfumed mussels to *langoustine* (prawn) tails on shortbread with coral ravioli, from rabbit confit with caramelized turnips to a stunning sheeps'-cheese charlotte. The wine list is devoted to the best of the region, too. The restaurant isn't far from the Atelier Cézanne, outside the old-town ring. ⊠ *10 av. de la Violette,* ☎ *04–42–23–30–71. Jacket required. AE, MC, V. No lunch Mon.*

$$ ✕ **Les Bacchanales.** Despite a slightly self-important air—upheld by the waitstaff—and a position on a tourist-trap street off cours Mirabeau, this is a pleasant, intimate restaurant with inviting decor of daub-filled beams, yellow-ocher stucco, and Louis XIII chairs. The broad range of fixed-price menus may include a delicate octopus salad, classic garlic-roasted lamb, *rouget* (red mullet) perfumed with sage and fennel, and caramelized pears over pistachio ice cream. As the name implies, wine figures large here, and the list is extensive. ⊠ *10 rue de la Couronne,* ☎ *04–42–27–21–06. AE, MC, V.*

$$ ✕ **Brasserie Les Deux Garçons.** The food is rather ordinary—stick to the *coquillages* (oysters and clams) or the copious hot salads—but eating isn't what you come here for. It's the linen-decked sidewalk tables facing onto the cours Mirabeau, the fresh flowers, the frosted ice buckets, the white-swathed waiters snaking between the chairs, the blackboard menu, and the little gilt-edged espressos at the end of an atmospheric meal. Dining inside is less glamorous, but the murals and gilt-ivory decor date to the restaurant's founding, in 1792. Cézanne, Zola, and Cocteau were devoted regulars; call it the 2G (and remember to pronounce that *zhay*), and everyone will think you're a regular, too. ⊠ *53 cours Mirabeau,* ☎ *04–42–26–00–51. MC, V.*

Close-Up

PASTIS AND PÉTANQUE

I N EVERY VILLAGE from the Rhône Valley to the Italian border, underevery deep-shaded *allée* of plane trees, the theater of Provençal life plays itself out slowly, serenely, and sociably. The café is a way of life in Provence, a cool outdoor living room where friends gather like family and share the ritual of the long, slow drink, the discussion of the weather (hot), and an amble over to the *pétanque* (lawn bowling) court. The players stand, somber and intense, hands folded behind backs, and watch the intricate play of heavy metal balls rolling and clicking. A knot of onlookers gathers, disperses, is reinforced. In this region of the animated debate, the waving gesture, the forefinger punching to chest, it is a surprisingly quiet pastime.

Just as refined a ritual is the drinking of the requisite pastis. The server arrives with a tray loaded with the appropriate props: a carafe of water emblazoned with "Ricard" or "51"; a bowl with an ice cube or two; a bowl of olives, black as jet; and a stubby glass cradling two fingers of amber liquid redolent of anis and licorice. Plop an ice cube into the liquor, then slowly pour a rope of cool water into the glass, watching for the magic moment when the amber transforms itself to milky white. Sip slowly, mop your forehead, and settle in.

$$ \times $$ **Brasserie Léopold.** If you're more interested in food than regional atmosphere, this is the brasserie of choice in Aix. The cuisine is classic—steak tartare, *choucroute* (sausage and sauerkraut), and chocolate mousse—and the portions generous. Alas, the look of the place is contrived Art Deco—done to the hilt, as a good theme restaurant should. Provence this is not, but it's French through and through. It's across from La Rotonde, by the tourist office. ⊠ *Hôtel St-Christophe, 2 av. Victor-Hugo,* ☎ *04–42–26–01–24. AE, MC, V.*

$$ \times $$ **Chez Thomé.** At a crossroads deep in Cézanne country east of Aix, near the Château Noir and in the shadow of Montagne de Ste-Victoire, this ramshackle, fashionably bohemian hunting lodge conceals a series of intimate dining rooms and a broad terrace shaded by massive chestnut trees. Service is young and laid-back, and portions are more than generous: lamb roasted in tangy tapenade, grilled pepper terrine, and crème brûlée perfumed with lavender. ⊠ *D12 5 km east of Aix, La Plantation, Le Tholonet,* ☎ *04–42–66–90–43. MC, V. Closed Sun., no lunch Mon. Oct.–Apr.*

$$ \times $$ **L'Etape des Frères Lani.** This classic *auberge* (inn) serves familiale cuisine with a thick Provençal twang and garden-fresh ingredients. The blackboard menu may change before your eyes as something new comes in from the market: asparagus soup with a frizzle of julienned prosciutto, garlic-roasted farm pigeon, fresh goat cheese in a drizzle of emerald olive oil. Fresh flowers, creamy linens, and bright crockery match the family's warm welcome. ⊠ *route de Gardanne, Bouc-Bel-Air (east of N8, 16 km south of Aix),* ☎ *04–42–22–61–90. MC, V.*

$$ \times $$ **Le Grillon.** Another contender for the mobile-phone set on the lively stretch of cours Mirabeau, this brasserie gives sun baskers and hair tossers a place to preen and be seen (when the cours isn't under construction). It also has waiters in black and white, crisp linens, and—inciden-

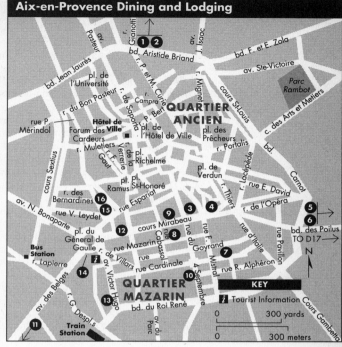

Aix-en-Provence Dining and Lodging

KEY

i Tourist Information

0   300 yards

0   300 meters

---

tally—a varied menu that's especially strong at lunch. Items include the hors d'oeuvre buffet (a salad bar of crudités, anchovies, and beans), and a sliding scale of fixed-price menus featuring salmon tartare, lamb, and simple grilled fish. For a more intimate atmosphere, slip upstairs to the tiny jewel-box dining parlor with cozy banquettes and an ornate wedding-cake decor. ⊠ *49 cours Mirabeau,* ☎ *04–42–27–58–81. MC, V.*

$–$$ ✕ **Le Bistro Latin.** Making the most of Aix's abundant markets, this unpretentious little restaurant has only two menus, both working with fresh ingredients and equally fresh ideas. Consider a subtle terrine of chickpeas and fresh cheese with balsamic vinegar, a hearty lamb *daube* (stew) perfumed with juniper berries, or a novel flan of rabbit with crisp grilled pistachios. The two dining rooms, upstairs and down, are downright intimate, the ambience is laid-back, and the waiters are easygoing to an almost American degree. ⊠ *18 rue de la Couronne,* ☎ *04–42–38–22–88. AE, MC, V. Closed Sun. No lunch Mon.*

$ ✕ **Le Verre Bouteille.** If you're keen on tasting rare local wines that you can't find at home, consider a simple lunch at this low-key bistro. Come here for a token platter of cold meats or cheeses to accompany the wine of the day. One or two home-cooked dishes—a fresh quiche, a pasta, or stew, as well as good cakes and fruit tarts—are served by the owners with a smile. A local clientele lunches here daily, a sure sign that it's top quality. ⊠ *1 bis rue Joseph-Cabassol,* ☎ *04–42–27–96–66. MC, V. Closed Sun. No dinner Mon.–Thurs.*

$$ ✕▥ **Relais Ste-Victoire.** In this isolated country inn, nestled at the foot
★ of Ste-Victoire, you can lose yourself in Chef René Bergès's impeccably fresh Provençal cuisine: poached eggs with truffles, sardine *rillettes* (spread), and duck breast with fresh figs and gnocchi. The intimate, formal atmosphere captures the essence of country-auberge dining, and there's a beautiful collection of glazed ceramics. (The restaurant [$$$]

is closed Monday and has no lunch Friday or dinner Sunday.) Though sizable, guest rooms are something of an afterthought, in '70s-style beige with catalog furniture, but you wake up to birds singing in a wooded grove. From Aix take scenic D17 toward Le Tholonet and Cézanne country; turn right on D46 into Beaurecueil. ⊠ *13100 Beaurecueil,* ☎ *04–42–66–94–98,* ℻ *04–42–66–85–96. 10 rooms. Restaurant, pool. AE, DC, MC, V. Closed 1st wk Jan., 2 wks Feb., and 1st 2 wks Nov.*

$$$$ 🏨 **Villa Gallici.** Shaded by ancient cypress and plane trees and land-
★   scaped with jars of laurel and topiary boxwood, this luxurious hilltop garden retreat stands serenely apart from the city center—yet it's only steps away. Have breakfast on the shaded terrace, tea by the pool, then retreat to your extravagantly decorated room swagged with rich flo-rals or plaids. The salons are design-magazine gorgeous, too. Hotel guests can enjoy light, unpretentious meals. ⊠ *av. de la Violette, 13100,* ☎ *04–42–23–29–23,* ℻ *04–42–96–30–45. 18 rooms, 4 suites. Restau-rant, pool. AE, DC, MC, V.* 🐾

$$$ 🏨 **Augustins.** The best aspect of this old-town hotel, just a half block back from cours Mirabeau, is its reception area. The groin-vaulted stone, stained glass, and ironwork banister date from the 15th century, when the house was an Augustinian convent (Martin Luther was once a guest). The rooms are perfectly nice but a bit of a letdown. Instead of monas-tic oak and pristine linens, you get heavy carpeting and fabric-covered walls. Bathrooms are all-white tile and marble, and a few rooms have private balcony-terraces with views of the steeple of St-Esprit. The staff is efficient and eager to please. ⊠ *3 rue de la Masse, 13100,* ☎ *04–42–27–28–59,* ℻ *04–42–26–74–87. 29 rooms. Breakfast room, air-conditioning. AE, DC, MC, V.*

$$–$$$ 🏨 **Nègre-Coste.** Its prominent cours Mirabeau position and its lavish
★   public areas make this 18th-century town house a popular hotel. Long neglected, the guest rooms now live up to the entryway and the loca-tion. Bathrooms are freshly tiled, and wallpaper and fabrics in bright Provençal golds now brighten the once-shabby rooms. It's worth the price to open your shutters in the morning and lean out over the cours Mirabeau with a cup of café crème in hand—just not while the cours is under construction (autumn 2001 is when work was to be concen-trated in front of the hotel). ⊠ *33 cours Mirabeau, 13100,* ☎ *04–42–27–74–22,* ℻ *04–42–26–80–93. 37 rooms. Breakfast room, air-con-ditioning. AE, DC, MC, V.*

$$ 🏨 **Cardinal.** In a lovely 18th-century house in the Quartier Mazarin, this eccentric and slightly threadbare inn is the antithesis of slick. Its large rooms are furnished gracefully enough with secondhand finds, and major renovations refreshed the carpet and brought most bath-rooms up to date. But if you're blinded by charm, you may only no-tice the novel furniture, the elegance of the structure, and the music of the bells of St-Jean-de-Malte. Of two large kitchenette "suites" across from the Musée Granet, the ground-floor one has a private garden. ⊠ *22–24 rue Cardinale, 13100,* ☎ *04–42–38–32–30,* ℻ *04–42–26–39–05. 30 rooms. Breakfast room. MC, V.*

$$ 🏨 **Mercure–Paul Cézanne.** A block from cours Mirabeau and the train station, this small, low-key hotel has a friendly, efficient staff. Rooms vary enormously, from the cozy (with four-poster beds) to the wildly modern, and bathrooms are just as unpredictable. But the little lobby bar, with a mural of Provençal greenery and a TV, is a reassuringly homey spot for a nightcap. ⊠ *40 av. Victor-Hugo, 13100,* ☎ *04–42–91–11–11,* ℻ *04–42–91–11–10. 55 rooms. Bar. AE, DC, MC, V.*

$$ 🏨 **Saint Christophe.** With so few midprice *hôtels de charme* in Aix, you
★   might as well opt for this glossy Art Deco–style hotel, where the com-fort and services are remarkable for the price. The Roaring '20s look dates from 1994, but the Cézannesque murals, burled-wood curves, and

Constructivist leather chairs carry you back to the Jazz Age. Rooms are slickly done in deep jewel tones, and the top-floor rooms have artisanal tiles in the bathrooms. For a pittance more, you can have a junior suite with a sleeping loft. The Brasserie Léopold (☞ *above*), though lacking cours Mirabeau chic, is the best of its kind in Aix. ⊠ *2 av. Victor-Hugo, 13100,* ☎ *04–42–26–01–24,* FAX *04–42–38–53–17. 58 rooms, 6 suites. Restaurant, air-conditioning, parking (fee). AE, MC, V.* ✎

$–$$ 🏨 **Quatre Dauphins.** In the quiet Mazarin neighborhood below the cours
★ Mirabeau, this modest but impeccable lodging inhabits a noble hôtel particulier. Its pretty, comfortable little rooms have been spruced up with *boutis* (Provençal quilts), Les Olivades fabrics, quarry tiles, jute carpets, and hand-painted furniture. The top-floor rooms are even more charming but can be hot in the height of summer. The house-proud but unassuming owner-host bends over backward to please. ⊠ *55 rue Roux Alphéran, 13100,* ☎ *04–42–38–16–39,* FAX *04–42–38–60–19. 13 rooms. MC, V.*

Nightlife and the Arts

To find out what's going on in town, pick up a copy of the events calendar *Le Mois à Aix* or the bilingual city guide *Aix Bienvenue* at the tourist office.

Hot Brass (⊠ rte. d'Eguilles, Celony, ☎ 04–42–21–05–57) draws an older, car-owning crowd to the suburbs for live concerts of blues, rock, and soul. **Le Mistral** (⊠ 3 rue Frédéric-Mistral, ☎ 04–42–38–16–49) is a dance club where students of every nationality meet. **Le Richelme** (⊠ 24 rue de la Verrerie, ☎ 04–42–23–49–29) draws a twenty-something crowd for dancing. **Le Scat Club** (⊠ 11 rue de la Verrerie, ☎ 04–42–23–00–23) is the place for live soul, funk, reggae, rock, blues, and jazz.

For a night of playing roulette and the slot machines, head for the **Casino Municipal** (⊠ 2 bis av. N.-Bonaparte, ☎ 04–42–26–30–33).

The **Cézanne** (⊠ rue Marcel Guillaume, ☎ 08–36–68–72–70) and **Renoir** (⊠ 24 cours Mirabeau, ☎ 08–36–68–72–70) cinemas both show some films in *v.o.* (*version originale,* i.e., not dubbed).

Every July during the **Festival International d'Art Lyrique** (International Opera Festival; ☎ 04–42–17–34–00 for information), you can see world-class opera productions in the courtyard of the Palais de l'Archevêché. It is one of the most important opera festivals in Europe, and cutting-edge productions involve the best artists available—recent guests have included director Peter Brook, choreographers Trisha Brown and Pina Bausch, and conductor Claudio Abbado. The repertoire is varied and often offbeat, featuring works like Britten's Curlew River and Bartok's Bluebeard's Castle as well as the usual Mozart, Puccini, and Verdi. Most of the singers, however, are not celebrities, but rather an elite group of students who spend the summer with the Academie Européenne de Musique, training and performing under the tutelage of stars like Robert Tear and Yo-Yo Ma. Tickets can be purchased as early as November for the following summer, but it's usually possible to find seats a month in advance. After that, seats are scarce.

The stunningly inventive choreography of **Le Ballet Preljocaj** (rue Allumettes, ☎ 04–42–93–48–00) can be seen September to May in Aix, their home base.

Outdoor Activities and Sports

Because it's there, in part, and because it looms in striking isolation above the plain east of Aix, its heights catching the sun long after the valley lies in shadow, **Montagne de Ste-Victoire** inspires climbers to conquest. The Grande Randonée stretches along its long, rocky crest from the village of Le Bouquet at its western end all the way east to Puyloubier. Its alternate route climbs the milder north slope from Les Cabassols. Along the way it peaks at 1,011 m (3,316 ft) at Pic des Mouches, from where the view stretches around the compass. But the real draw lies to the east at the **Croix de Provence** (945 m/3,100 ft), a gargantuan cross rising 28 m (92 ft) above the mountain top. You'll have sweeping views over the whole of Provence from the Luberon to the Alps. From Les Cabassols to the Cross, allow 3½ hours round-trip for this fairly strenuous hike. A bus from Aix's *gare routière* (bus station) carries hikers toward Vauvenargues and Les Cabassols departure point. Pick up detailed maps at the tourist office.

The **Club Hippique Ste-Victoire** (⊠ Chemin des Sauvaires, Meyreuil, ☎ 04–42–51–47–66) is an equestrian center from where you can take horseback sorties into the rugged countryside around Mont Ste-Victoire.

Just south of Aix, off D9 (in the direction of Aeroport Marignane), the **Golf Club Aix-Marseille** (⊠ Domaine de Riquetti, Les Milles, ☎ 04–42–24–20–41) has an 18-hole course.

For swimming, head to the **Piscine Municipale Plein Ciel** (⊠ av. Marcel-Pagnol, Jas de Bouffan, ☎ 04–42–20–00–78), a public indoor-outdoor pool open year round near Cézanne's country house west of town.

The **Thermes Sextius,** natural baths on the original site first discovered by Sextius himself, offer every kind of treatment and indulgence for weary bones. There are high-pressure showers, mud-wraps, scented whirlpools, and underwater massage. Call or write for an appointment. ⊠ *55 cours Sextius, 13101 cedex 1,* ☎ *04–42–23–81–81,* FAX *04–42–95–11–33.*

Shopping

Aix is a market town, and unlike the straightforward, country-fair atmosphere of nearby Aubagne, a trip to the market here is a gourmet event, with rarefied, high-end delicacies shoulder to shoulder with garlic braids. You'll find fine olive oils from the Pays d'Aix (Aix region), barrels glistening with olives of every hue and blend, and vats of *tapenade* (crushed olive, caper, and anchovy paste). Melons, asparagus, and mesclun salad are piled high, and dried sausages bristling with Provençal herbs hang from stands. A **food and produce market** takes place every morning on place Richelme; just up the street on place Verdun is a good, high-end *brocante* (collectibles) market Tuesday, Thursday, and Saturday mornings.

Another famous Aixois delicacy is *calissons*. A blend of almond paste and glazed melon, they are cut into geometric almond shapes and stacked high in *confiserie* windows. The most picturesque of the pretty shops specializing in calissons are **Leonard Parli** (⊠ 35 av. Victor-Hugo), by the train station, and **Bechard** (⊠ 12 cours Mirabeau).

In addition to its old-style markets and jewel-box candy shops, Aix is a modern shopping town—perhaps the best in Provence. The winding streets of the Vieille Ville above cours Mirabeau—focused around **rue Clemenceau, rue Marius Reinaud, rue Espariat, rue Aude,** and **rue Maréchal Foch**—have a head-turning array of goods, from high-end designer clothes, such as Sonia Rykiel, Escada, and Yves Saint Laurent, to Max Mara, Laura Ashley, and The Gap. Fabric and pottery also figure large at shops such as Les Olivades, Souleiado, and Terres de Provence. Between these chain shops are dozens of fascinating one-of-a-kind boutiques, with antique and artisan jewelry, old-style hats, trendy shoes, and arts and crafts.

Particularly noteworthy is **Bleu Marine** (✉ 8 rue Maréchal Foch, ☎ 04–42–27–26–94), which sells its utterly French collection of nautical-style blazers, navy cardigans, and fisherman's stripe shirts. **Gérard Darel** (✉ 13 rue Fabrot, ☎ 04–42–26–38–45) is the shop for classic French tailoring. **Tehen** (✉ 6 rue Clemenceau, ☎ 04–42–26–85–50) sells soft, draped knits.

Mephisto (✉ 16 bis pl. Verdun, ☎ 04–42–38–23–23) sells its signature walking shoes and boots to a mostly foreign clientele, as French women find them unaesthetic. **Jacadi** (✉ 33 rue Espariat, ☎ 04–42–26–14–45) stocks upscale, gentrified children's clothing. **Catimini** (✉ 9 pl. Chapeliers, ☎ 04–42–27–51–14) offers an imaginative, jazzy stock of kids' sweaters, jackets, and dresses.

MARSEILLE

Much maligned as a dirty urban sprawl plagued with impoverished immigrant neighborhoods and slightly louche politics, Marseille is often given wide berth by travelers in search of a Provençal idyll. What a waste: Its Cubist jumbles of white stone rise up over a picture-book seaport, bathed in light of blinding clarity, crowned by larger-than-life neo-Byzantine churches, and framed by massive fortifications. Its neighborhoods teem with multiethnic life, its souklike African markets reek deliciously of spices and coffees, its labyrinthine old town radiates bright shades of saffron, cinnamon, and robin's-egg blue. Feisty and fond of broad gestures, Marseille is a dynamic city, as cosmopolitan now as when the Phocaeans first founded it, and with all the exoticism of the international shipping port it has been for 2,600 years.

The Phocaeans, an ancient people shipping out of Asia Minor some 600 years before Christ, sailed into the hill-framed inlet that is today's Vieux Port. Its white stone and dazzling sun reminded them of home, and they settled in to stay. Legend has it that their leader, Protis, paid a state visit to the Ligurians who occupied the land. It was the day of their traditional feast, where all the suitors of the princess Gyptis lined up for her to choose. When she entered, she raised her goblet to the handsome visitor, and Protis and Gyptis were married. Thus was founded Massalia, which grew to be the most important continental shipping port of antiquity.

Massalia flourished for some 500 years as a typically Greek city, enjoying the full flush of Classical culture, its gods and mores, its democratic political system, its sports and theater, its naval prowess. On the Panier hill there were temples to Athena, Apollo, and Artemis. This cosmopolitan city built a temple at Delphi, offered by the citizens of Massalia in the 6th century BC, and sent learned ambassadors to England and Africa. Under Roman rule it flourished as well; in the time of Christ, its university was the finest preserve of Classical culture in the West and rivaled Athens for prestige.

Vital to the Crusades in the Middle Ages and crucial to Louis XIV as a military port, Marseille continued to flourish as France's market to the world. But not all its imports were good. In 1720 a Syrian ship sailed into harbor with a cargo of the plague; several of its sailors had succumbed en route. Though it was quarantined and held at bay, a greedy merchant slipped ashore to sell off the rich goods the ship carried. The infection spread through the narrow streets of Marseille, reaching as far as Arles and Toulon. More than 100,000 died in Provence—50,000

120

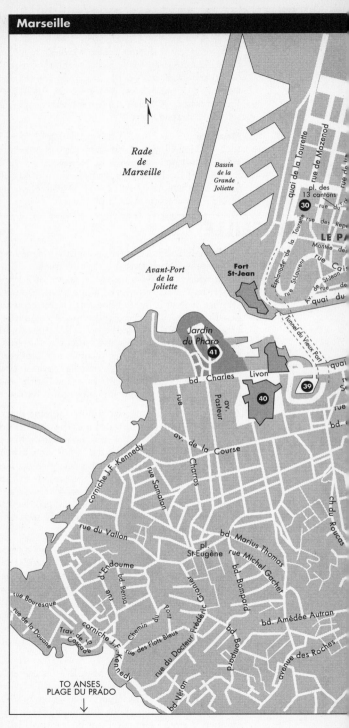

Marseille

rue Montolieu
av. C. Pelletan
rue Duverger
rue Bon Pasteur
autoroute Nord
rue de Turenne
av. du Gal. LeClerc
bd. Charles Nédélec
rue de la Joliette
bd. des Dames
pl. J. Guesde
rue Bernard du Bois
Gare St-Charles
rue Honnorat
bd. National
bd. Camille Flammarion
rue de l'Evêché
rue de Lorette
Passage de Lorette
rue St-Antoine
29
du Petit Puits
du Panier
pl. Sadi Carnot
rue Colbert
rue F. de Pressensé
rue des Petites Maries
rue des Dominicaines
bd. d'Athènes
bd. Voltaire
pl. Alex Labadié
rue Puvis de Chavannes
rue d'Aix
rue H. Barbusse
la République
rue Mary Teyssère
Grand Rue
pl. Daviel
Repenties
E PANIER
des Accoules
Coisserie
jean F. de Lacydon
de la Loge
32
pl. Victor Gelu
31
rue Coutellerie
26
28
quai des Belges
25
27
cours Belsunce
La Canebière
rue St. Savournin
rue Terrusse
pl. J. Jaurès
bd. Chave
bd. Garibaldi
du Port
33
Ferry Boat
Vieux Port
24
pl. du Général de Gaulle
r. St-Ferréol
r. St-Saëns
rue d'Aubagne
rue de Rome
r. Saint Pierre
quai de Rive
Pl. aux Huiles
Cours H.
Pl. Neuve Thiars
d'Estienne d'Orves
r. F. Davso
cours
36
34
rue Nueve Sainte Catherine
37
Pl. Huiles
35
Ballard
rue Sainte
bd. de la Corderie
cours Pierre Puget
rue Montgrand
cours Lieutaud
r. de la Loubière
Jardin P. Puget
bd. André Aune
bd. Notre-Dame
rue Jules Moulet
rue Breteuil
rue Paradis
rue Saint Suffren
avenue du Prado
bd. Baille
av. de Toulon
av. Jules Cantini
38
r. Fort du Sanctuaire
bd. Vauban
rue Breteuil
rue du Rouet
ch. du Roucas

0   400 yards

0   400 meters

in Marseille alone—before the ship was unceremoniously sunk in the harbor now known as the Bout du Monde (End of the World).

The graceful architecture of Marseille sustained heavy damage during the Second World War, the most brutal of which was Hitler's decision to tear down a broad swath of 18th-century buildings that lined the Vieux Port. It has been tastefully reconstructed in a discreet postmodern style, and the city's ensemble of urban architecture continues to be restored and renewed as Marseille makes a valiant effort to overturn its ugly reputation and show itself to the world for what it really is: a spirited international city in a spectacular setting.

The Quai du Port and Le Panier

Though Marseille is the second-largest city in France, it functions as a conglomerate of distinct neighborhoods—almost little villages. One of these microcosms—the Neapolitan-style maze of laundry-lined lanes called Le Panier—merits intimate exploration and the will to wander. There are also myriad museums tied into Marseille's nautical history, and the striking museum complex of the Vieille Charité, all worth a browse.

A Good Walk

Begin at the tourist office at the base of the Vieux Port, known as the quai des Belges. Be sure to start early because this is the stage for the first of a series of theatrical scenes that are part of Marseille's daily life: the **Marché aux Poissons** ㉔. The port behind them is a show in itself, with its colorful mix of gleaming white pleasure boats, scruffy blue and green fishing boats, and even a couple of restored schooners, all bobbing together in the vast horseshoe of water. Don't bother to come if the mistral has been roaring over the water; then the fishermen keep their boats safely tied in port.

Walk up La Canebière to the **Musée de la Marine** ㉕, where you can learn about the port's history through miniatures, paintings, and engravings. Just past the port is the unusual **Musée de la Mode** ㉖, where high-fashion clothes from the 1930s to today are on display. Head a half block over into the mall to enter the **Musée d'Histoire de Marseille** ㉗, which illustrates the classical history of this ancient city. Then wander into the adjoining **Jardin des Vestiges** ㉘ to see the foundations of Greek fortifications.

Next, head up broad rue de la République, past grand old apartment buildings and place Sadi Carnot. Just past the square, on the left, the elegant passage de Lorette leads you into a claustrophobic courtyard with laundry fluttering like medieval banners overhead, typical of Marseille. From here climb the steep stairs that lead into the famous neighborhood known as **Le Panier.** The anchor of the revitalization of this decaying but appealing neighborhood is the **Centre de la Vieille Charité** ㉙, once a hospice, now the home of two museums.

Follow rue du Petit Puits to place des 13 Cantons, head left on rue Ste-Françoise, then cross avenue Robert Schuman to the neo-Byzantine **Cathédrale de la Major** ㉚. Then wind back down the Montée des Accoules to place Daviel, turn right and double back right down rue du Lacydon to the **Musée du Vieux Marseille** ㉛. Housed in the Maison Diamantée, it features collections of pottery, furniture, costumes, and *santons* (terra-cotta figurines). Just a block up the port, the **Musée des Docks Romains** ㉜ displays the remains of 1st-century waterfront warehouses that lined this busy port.

Go down to the quai du Port and past the Baroque Hôtel de Ville (City Hall). At the water's edge, wait for the picturesque **Ferry Boat** ㉝ (pronounced fay-ree bow-aht) and ride across the port in style.

<u>TIMING</u>

Allow at least a half day to explore the backstreets of Le Panier, a whole day if you intend to visit any of the fascinating museums at the foot of its hill; you could easily spend a morning appreciating the wonders (both architectural and archeological) of the Vieille Charité museum complex. Wear good walking shoes and be prepared to climb: Much of this district is spread over steep slopes.

Sights to See

㉚ **Cathédrale de la Major (Cathedral of the Major).** This gargantuan, neo-Byzantine, 19th-century fantasy was built under Napoléon III, but not before he'd ordered the partial destruction of the lovely 11th-century original, once a perfect example of the Provençal Romanesque style. All that remain of that now are the choir and transept. Restoration is under way to correct this gaffe; the medieval church was closed at press time for renovations. You can view the flashy decor—marble and rich red porphyry inlay—in the newer of the two churches. ✉ *pl. de la Major.*

★ ㉙ **Centre de la Vieille Charité** (Center of the Old Charity). Designed as a hospice for the homeless, this superb ensemble of 17th- and 18th-century architecture stands at the top of Le Panier, a jewel of reason and symmetry in the midst of a romantic muddle. Even if you don't visit the museums inside, walk around its inner court, studying the retreating perspective of triple arcades and admiring the Baroque chapel with its novel egg-peaked dome. The ensemble is the work of the Marseillais artist/architects Pierre and Jean Puget. A new restaurant and *salon de thé* (tea salon) serve drinks and light meals al fresco in the courtyard or under the lovely arcades.

Under this complex's extensive roofs are two excellent museums. The larger is the **Musée d'Archéologie Méditerranéenne** (Museum of Mediterranean Archaeology), with a sizable collection of ceramics, bronzes, funeral stelae, amphorae, and sculptures from ancient Egypt, Cyprus, Greece, the Romans, and the Etruscans—in short, the whole of classical Mediterranean civilization. Unfortunately the lovely objects are erratically labeled, sometimes with appalling opacity (e.g., "Pot"). There's also a display on the mysterious Celt-like Ligurians who first peopled the coast, cryptically presented with more emphasis on the digs (and diggers) than the findings themselves. The best of the lot is the evocatively mounted Egyptian collection, the second biggest in France after the Louvre. There are mummies, hieroglyphics, and gorgeous sarcophagi in an evocative tomb-like setting. Also upstairs, the **Musée d'Arts Africains, Océaniens et Amérindiens** (Museum of African, Oceanian, and American Indian Art) provides a theatrical foil for the works' intrinsic drama. The spectacular masks and sculptures are mounted along a pure black wall, lighted indirectly, with labels and explanations across the aisle. ✉ *2 rue de la Charité,* ☎ *04–91–14–58–80.* ✉ *12 frs/€1.83 per museum.* ☉ *May–Sept., Tues.–Sun. 11–6; Oct.–Apr., Tues.–Sun. 10–5.*

㉝ **Ferry Boat.** To hear the natives say "fer-ry bo-at" (they've adopted the English) is one of the joys of a visit to Marseille. For a pittance you can file onto this little wooden barge and chug across the Vieux Port, which serves as handy mass transit just as it did in Marcel Pagnol's play *Marius.* It travels between place des Huiles on the quai de Rive Neuve side and the Hôtel de Ville on the quai du Port. ✉ *3 frs/50 European cents.*

㉘ Jardin des Vestiges (Garden of Remains). This garden is the site of the original waterfront in Marseille's classical prime—when it was Massalia—and there are still remains of the Greek fortifications, 1st-century loading docks, paved streets, and a necropolis. It was discovered in 1967 when roadwork was being done next to the Bourse (Stock Exchange). It's now part of the Musée d'Histoire de Marseille. ⊠ *Centre Bourse*, ☎ *04–91–90–42–22*. ⛦ *12 frs/€1.83 includes entry to Musée d'Histoire de Marseille.* ☉ *Mon.–Sat. noon–7.*

★ **㉔ Marché aux Poissons** (Fish Market). Up and going by 8 AM every day, this market puts on a vivid and aromatic show of waving fists, jostling chefs, and heaps of fish from the night's catch still twitching. You'll hear the thick soup of the Marseillais accent as blue-clad fishermen and silk-clad matrons bicker over prices, and you'll wonder at the rainbow of Mediterranean creatures swimming in plastic vats before you, each uglier than the last: the spiny-headed *rascasse* (scorpion fish), dog-nosed *grondin* (red gurnet) the monstrous *baudroie*, or *lotte de mer* (monkfish), and the eel-like *congre*,. (Now you'll understand why the slackjawed, bug-eyed Ugolin in *Jean de Florette* was nicknamed "*Galinette.*") "Bouillabaisse" as sold here is a mix of fish too tiny to sell otherwise; the only problem with coming for the early morning show is that you have to wait so long for your bouillabaisse lunch. ⊠ *quai des Belges.* ☉ *Daily 8–1.*

㉜ Musée des Docks Romains (Roman Docks Museum). In 1943 Hitler had the neighborhood along the quai du Port destroyed—some 2,000 houses, displacing some 20,000 citizens. This act of brutal urban renewal, ironically, laid open the ground for new discoveries. When Marseille began to rebuild in 1947, workers dug up remains of a Roman shipping warehouse, full of terra-cotta jars and amphorae that once lay in the bellies of low-slung ships. The museum created around the site demonstrates the scale and range of Massalia's shipping prowess. ⊠ *pl. de Vivaux*, ☎ *04–91–91–24–62*. ⛦ *12 frs/€1.83.* ☉ *Oct.–May, Tues.–Sun. 10–5; June–Sept., Tues.–Sun. 11–6.*

★ **㉗ Musée d'Histoire de Marseille** (Marseille History Museum). With the Jardin des Vestiges in its backyard and its front door in a shopping mall, this modern, open-spaced exhibition illuminates Massalia's history by mounting its treasure of archeological finds in didactic displays. You can learn about ancient metallurgy, Gallo-Roman pottery making, and shipbuilding. There's a section on Medieval Marseille, and some background on the marks Louis XIV and Vauban left on the city. Best by far is the presentation of Marseille's Classical halcyon days. There's a recovered wreck of a Roman cargo boat, its 3rd-century wood amazingly preserved, and the hull of a Greek boat dating from the 4th century BC. And that model of the Greek city should be authentic—it's based on the eyewitness description of Aristotle. ⊠ *Centre Bourse, entrance on rue de Bir-Hakeim*, ☎ *04–91–90–42–22*. ⛦ *12 frs/€1.83 (includes Jardin des Vestiges).* ☉ *Mon.–Sat. noon–7.*

㉕ Musée de la Marine (Marine Museum). One of many museums devoted to Marseille's history as a shipping port, this one concentrates on recent times, from the 17th century to today. It's all about boats, and a model lover's dream. There are steamboats and sailboats and schooners in miniature, as well as a collection of paintings and prints of the port in action. ⊠ *Palais de la Bourse, 7 La Canebière*, ☎ *04–91–39–33–33*. ⛦ *10 frs/€1.52.* ☉ *Daily 10–6.*

✍ **㉖ Musée de la Mode** (Fashion Museum). This museum is not about boats or Greeks—it's about clothes. Temporary exhibitions may feature a star designer, the contents of a fashion maven's closet, or focus on changes in male plumage. In between, displays from the permanent collection (some 5,000 dresses and accessories from the 1700s to the present) are executed with panache and mounted, naturally, with style. ⊠ *11 La Canebière,* ☎ *04–91–56–59–57.* ⌧ *18 frs/€2.57.* ⊘ *Tues.–Sun. noon–7.*

❸❶ **Musée du Vieux Marseille** (Museum of Old Marseille). In the 16th-century **Maison Diamantée** (Diamond House; one of few buildings in this quarter that would be spared by Hitler), so called because of its beveled-stone facade, this history museum concentrates on Marseille's Provençal personality and its more prosaic traditions of recent centuries. The collection includes beautifully carved wooden furniture, crèches and santons, and 19th-century clothes. Of particular interest: a display of locally made playing cards, as Marseille was one of the medieval ports of entry for this novelty from the East, and its citizens took to it in spades. Closed at press time for renovations, it should be open by early 2001. Check with the tourist office for new hours. ⊠ *rue de la Prison,* ☎ *04–91–13–89–00 info.*

★ **Le Panier.** This louche and scruffy *quartier* is the old heart of Marseille, a maze of high-shuttered houses looming over narrow cobbled streets, *montées* (stone stairways), and tiny squares. Le Panier is the principal focus of the city's efforts at urban renewal, with plans for the restoration of more than 1,500 houses over the next few years, and every season more houses take on the soft glow of new ocher. It was once home to seamen, fishermen, and every kind of craftsman and laborer, all drawing a living from the sea. There were women, too, who made a living from making themselves available to sailors in port, so many that a Maison de Refuge was founded—half prison, half convent. The "fallen women" entered via the rue Déshonneur (Dishonor Street), now tactfully renamed the rue des Honneurs. Once "reformed," they left via the rue des Repenties (Repented Street). You'll enter Le Panier through rue de Lorette and place de Lorette; an old Provençal saying had it that "the girls of Lorette can't sleep alone." Wander this seedy, atmospheric neighborhood at will, making sure to stroll along rue du Panier, the montée des Accoules, rue du Petit-Puits, and rue des Muettes; take in the smells of garlic and soap and the infinite spectrum of colors in the peeling shutters and crumbling stucco.

The Quai de Rive Neuve

If in your exploration of Le Panier and the quai du Port you examined Marseille's history in miniature via myriad museums, this walk will give you the "big picture." From either the crow's-nest perspective of Notre-Dame-de-la-Garde or the vast green Jardin du Pharo, you'll take in spectacular Cinemascope views of this great city and its ports and monuments. Wear good walking shoes and bring your wide-angle lens.

A Good Walk

From the quai des Belges, head left and up the quai de Rive Neuve, then head away from the port up rue Fortia. To your right opens **place Thiars** ㉞, a lively center with restaurants and cafés. Back on rue Fortia, continue a block over to cours d'Estienne d'Orves and **Les Arcenaulx** ㉟, a high-textured, state-of-the-art shop-and-restaurant complex in the old armory and a prime example of Marseille's commitment to renewal. Now head back to the waterfront and stop in for a pastis at the **Bar de la Marine** ㊱, scene of the salty barkeeper's saga in Pagnol's trilogy of plays and films *Marius, Fanny,* and *César.* All along the waterfront there are popular bars, and the alleys are peppered with small theaters. Continue up the quai to the **Théâtre National de Marseille La Criée** ㊲, where the city's prestigious state theater company performs in a former fish-auction house.

If you're willing and able to tackle the steep (and seemingly endless) climb to the city's sentimental landmark, **Notre-Dame-de-la-Garde** ㊳, you'll be rewarded with one of the best views in Provence, panning over the brilliant white stone of the city, its complex of ports, islands, and neighboring mountains. (Hint: Bus 60 makes the run regularly from the cours Jean Ballard, between the quai des Belges and the parking Estienne d'Orves, and on the descent you can get off at the Abbaye St-Victor if you like.) The church itself, another testimony to Napoléon III's megalomaniac passion for overscaled kitsch, conceals quirky treasures.

A more modest climb up rue Robert and rue Neuve Ste-Catherine brings you to the **Abbaye St-Victor** ㊴, a splendid Romanesque church-fortress. Walk past the looming walls of **Fort St-Nicolas** ㊵ to get across the boulevard and up to the **Jardin du Pharo** ㊶: From this vast green hilltop, you can take in dramatic views of the fort and its opposing **Fort St-Jean.**

TIMING

This walk involves about a half-day's worth of heavy hiking, half of it uphill. If you opt for a bus ride, you can make a beeline straight up to Notre-Dame-de-la-Garde and take in the spectacular views, all in a couple of hours.

Sights to See

★ ㊴ **Abbaye St-Victor.** Founded in the 4th century by St-Cassien, who sailed into Marseille's port full of fresh ideas on monasticism acquired in Palestine and Egypt, this ancient abbey grew to formidable proportions and influence from its vantage point on a ledge overlooking the sea. With its severe exterior of crenellated stone and the spare geometry of its Romanesque church, the structure would be as at home in the Middle East as its founder. The Saracens destroyed his first structure, so the abbey was rebuilt in the 11th century and fortified against further onslaught in the 14th. Its crudely peaked windows demonstrate the dawning transition from Romanesque arches to Gothic points; in the nave the early attempts at groin vaulting were among the first in Provence.

By far the best reason to come: the **crypt,** St-Cassien's original, which lay buried under the medieval church's new structure. In evocative nooks and crannies you'll find eerie early medieval sarcophagi, including the 5th-century sarcophagus that allegedly holds the martyr's remains. Upstairs look for the reliquary containing what's left of St-Victor himself, who was ground to death between millstones, probably by Romans. There's a passage into tiny **catacombs** here, where early Christians worshiped St. Lazarus and Mary Magdalene, said to have washed ashore at Stes-Maries-de-la-Mer and carried their message inland. The boat in which they landed is reproduced in canoe-shape cookies called *navettes,* sold for an annual procession for Candlemas in February as well as year round (☞ Shopping, *below*). *Crypt entry: 10 frs/€1.52. Daily 8:30–7:15.*

㉟ **Les Arcenaulx** (The Arsenal). In this broad, elegant stone armory, first built for Louis XIV, a complex of upscale shops and restaurants has given the building—and neighborhood—new life. Its bookstore features a large collection of publications on Marseille (as well as art, photography, history, and rare books); a boutique sells high-end cooking (and serving) goods with a southern accent; and a book-lined restaurant serves sophisticated cuisine. It's worth a peek to remind yourself that Marseille is not the squalid backwater people continue to expect. ✉ *25 cours d'Estienne d'Orves. Bookstore Mon.–Sat. 10 AM–midnight; boutique 10:30–6:30; salon de thé 3–6.*

㊱ **Bar de la Marine.** Even if you've never read or seen Marcel Pagnol's trilogy of plays and films *Marius, Fanny,* and *César* (think of it as a three-part French *Casablanca*), you can get a feel for its earthy, old-Marseille atmosphere by stopping into the bar it was set in. (Note that the bar was temporarily closed at press time but should reopen by 2001.) It's been, well, "retrovated"—that is, redecorated with murals and old café chairs—to evoke the place as it was in the days the bartender César, his restless son Marius, and Fanny, the shellfish girl, lived out their salty drama of love, honor and the call of the sea. The ferry boat still putts away from the quai, just as it once carried Fanny to her wedding at the Hôtel de Ville. Pagnol grew up in Marseille, and summered in the hills above Aubagne. ⊠ *15 quai Rive Neuve.*

40 **Fort St-Nicolas and Fort St-Jean.** This complex of brawny fortresses encloses the Vieux Port's entry from both sides. In order to keep the feisty, rebellious Marseillais under his thumb, Louis XIV had the fortresses built with the guns pointing *inward.* They're best viewed from the Jardin du Pharo.

41 **Jardin du Pharo** (Pharo Garden). The Pharo, another larger-than-life edifice built to Napoléon III's epic tastes, was a gift to his wife, Eugenie. It's a conference center now, but its green park has become a mecca for city strollers who want to take in panoramic views of the ports and fortifications. ⊠ *Above bd. Charles-Livon.*

38 **Notre-Dame-de-la-Garde.** This preposterously overscaled neo-Byzantine monument was erected in 1853 by the ever-tasteful Napoléon III. Its interior is a Technicolor bonanza of red-and-beige stripes and glittering mosaics; the gargantuan Madonna and Child on the steeple (almost 30 ft high) are covered in real gold leaf. It's bread and circus for the people, who pour in (more than a million a year) to thank the Virgin for sparing them (and their ancestors before them) from cholera (and equivalent modern plagues). The results give this otherwise contrived showpiece its profound and quirky charm. The walls of the nave are covered with a boggling array of ex-votos, stilted but passionate naive art offered in thanks for the Virgin's eleventh-hour intervention, most of them concerning shipwrecks and sea storms survived. ⊠ *On foot climb up cours Pierre Puget, cross the Jardin Pierre Puget, cross a bridge to rue Vauvenargues, and hike up to pl. Edon. Or catch Bus 60 from cours Jean-Ballard.* ☎ *04–91–13–40–80.* ☉ *May–Sept., daily 7 AM–8 PM; Oct.–Apr., daily 7–7.*

34 **Place Thiars.** An ensemble of Italianate 18th-century buildings frame this popular center of activity, where one sidewalk café spills into another, and every kind of bouillabaisse is yours for the asking. At night, the neighborhood is a fashionable hangout for young professionals on their way to and from the theaters and clubs on quai de Rive Neuve. *Framed by quai Neuve, rue Fortia, rue de la Paix Marcel-Paul, and cours d'Estienne d'Orves.*

37 **Théâtre National de Marseille La Criée** (National Theater of Marseille at "The Fish Auction"). Behind the floridly decorated facade of this grand old fish auction house, a prestigious, cutting-edge state theater company holds forth. La Criée (literally, "the screaming") is the traditional means of auctioning off the fishermen's daily catch to wholesalers; the real auction now takes place near L'Estaque. ⊠ *32 quai de Rive Neuve,* ☎ *04–91–54–70–54 for reservations.* ☉ *Box office Tues.–Sat. 11–6.*

....

OFF THE BEATEN PATH **CHÂTEAU D'IF** – This wildly romantic island fortress, its thick towers and crenellated walls looming in the seaspray just off Marseille's coast, is the stuff of history—and legend. François I, in the 16th century, recognized the strategic advantage of an island fortress surveying the mouth of Marseille's vast harbor, so he had one built. Its effect as deterrent was so successful, it never saw combat and was eventually converted to a prison. It was here that Alexandre Dumas locked up his most famous character, the Count of Monte Cristo. Though he was fictional, the hole Dumas had him escape through is real enough, and it's visible in the cell today. (On the other hand, the real-life Man in the Iron Mask, whose cell is still being shown, was not actually imprisoned here.) As you walk from cell to cell, each labeled for the noble (or ignoble) prisoner it held, video monitors replay scenes from film versions of the Dumas tale, including the Count's Houdini-like underwater escape from a body bag thrown from the tower. One camera actually projects *you* into his dreary cell. Even the jaded and castle-weary will find themselves playing nightwatch from the ramparts. The boat ride (from the quai des Belges, 50 frs/€7.62) and the views from the broad terrace alone are worth the trip. ☎ 04–91–59–02–30. ⌧ *Château 25 frs/€3.81.* ⊘ *Apr.–Sept., daily 9–7; Oct.–Mar., Tues.–Sun. 9–5:30.* ⊗

La Canebière

This famous avenue cuts a straight line east from the Vieux Port. It's easy to make forays from it through the North-African neighborhood along rue Longue-des-Capucins and rue d'Aubagne to the bohemian cours Julien and on to the elegant Palais Longchamp, containing a fine-arts museum.

A Good Walk

The famous **La Canebière** was the louche and lively nerve center of Marseille between the wars. From the Vieux Port, head up La Canebière and turn right on **rue Longue-des-Capucins,** narrow, lively, and crammed with tiny North African shops opening onto the street. Across from the Noaille métro station, near the intersection with La Canebière, place du Marché des Capucins concentrates the best of the North African influence in this city. Continue up the street and make a jaunt to the right down rue Vacon, where miles of Provençal cottons are sold from heavy bolts. Then double back and go right up **rue d'Aubagne,** cross the cours Lieutaud, and climb up to the **cours Julien.** At its upper end, this popular pedestrian thoroughfare opens out into a sea of restaurants, shops, and cafés, with people sunning by the modern fountain and musicians busking from table to table.

To browse through grand old museums of art and natural history in a mega-monumental public building, hike the length of La Canebière to the **Palais de Longchamp** ㊷, where there's the Musée des Beaux Arts and the Musée d'Histoire Naturelle. It's some 3 km (2 mi) slightly uphill, but it's possible to walk it in about 45 minutes; if you wear out, catch Bus 41 from anywhere on La Canebière. It's an easy run on Bus 81 from quai des Belges.

TIMING

Allow an hour to wander through the market and streets around place du Marché des Capucins. Aim for lunch or a coffee break along cours Julien. Give yourself about half a day for the Palais de Longchamp—it takes time to get there and back and to visit one of its two museums.

Sights to See

La Canebière. This wide avenue leading from the port, known affectionately as the "Can o' Beer" by American sailors, was crammed with cafés, theaters, bars, and tempting stores full of zoot suits and swell hats, and figured in popular songs and operettas. It's noisy but dull today, yet you may take pleasure in studying the grand old 19th-century mansions lining it.

Cours Julien. A center of Bohemian *flanerie* (hanging out), this is a lovely place to relax by the fountain, in the shade of plane trees, or under a café umbrella. Its low-key and painterly tableau is framed by graceful 18th-century buildings.

㊷ Palais de Longchamp. This extravagantly overscaled 19th-century palace splays gracefully, symmetrically, and more than a little pompously around fountain-ponds to honor the confluence of the Provençal river Durance with the open sea. It houses a museum in each broad wing. The **Musée des Beaux-Arts** displays 16th- and 17th-century paintings, including several Rubens, as well as fine marble sculptures and drawings by the Baroque architect Pierre Puget, a native of Marseille. The collection of French 19th-century paintings is strong (Courbet, Millet, Ingres, and David), and there's a delightful group of sculptures by the caricaturist Honoré Daumier. In the right wing of the Palais, the **Musée d'Histoire Naturelle** (Natural History Museum) contains a collection of every kind of flora and fauna from Provence, even those in fossilized form. There's also an aquarium of fish from around the world. ⊠ *End of Boulevard Longchamp,* ☎ *04–91–14–59–50.* 🎫 *12 frs/€1.83 per museum.* ☾ *May–Sept., Tues.–Sun. 11–6; Oct.–Apr., Tues.–Sun. 10–5.*

Rue Longue-des-Capucins/rue d'Aubagne. Stepping into this atmospheric neighborhood, you may feel you have suddenly been transported to a Moroccan souk. Shops with open bins of olives and coffee beans and tea and spices and dried beans and chickpeas and couscous and peppers and salted sardines serve the needs of Marseille's large and vibrant North African community. Tiny shoebox cafés proffer exotic sweets. Like lots of cities with large immigrant populations, there's been an unfortunate political swing to the racist right by many in Marseille, but this attitude doesn't take into account the city's 2,500-year history of input and enhancement from the outside world.

Anses East of Town

Along the coastline east of Marseille's center, a series of pretty little *anses* (ports) lead to the more famous and far-flung Calanques (☞ Cassis, *below*). These miniature inlets are really tiny villages, with pretty, balconied, boxy houses (called *cabanons*) clustered around bright-painted fishing boats. Don't even think about buying a cabanon of your own, however; they are part of the fishing community's heritage and are protected from gentrification by the outside world.

A Good Drive

Drive up the quai de Rive Neuve to the Corniche J.-F. Kennedy, which roars along the dramatic cliff top over the Mediterranean. The Art Deco **Monument aux Héros de l'Armée d'Orient et des Terres Lointaines** (Monument to the Heroes of the Army of the East and Faraway Lands) marks your turning point. Head left into the picture-perfect little fishing port called the **Vallon des Auffes.** You could paddle across it in two strokes, but this miniature inlet concentrates all the color (blue, red, and green fishing boats, azure water) of a Rossellini film set.

Continue past the wealthy **Roucas-Blanc** neighborhood and the full-scale 19th-century reproduction of Michelangelo's *David,* standing incongruously at the center of avenue du Prado. When the Marseillais do something, they do it big. The city's main beaches lie at David's feet in the **Parc Balnéaire** du Prado, including the Plage de David. From the sands, you'll have breathtaking views of the Iles de Frioul (Frioul Islands), which you can visit by boat from Marseille's port (☞ Outdoor Activities and Sports, *below*).

After David and the beaches, continue up the road to **Port de Plaisance de la Pointe Rouge** and then **La Madrague,** both postcard-pretty anses wedged with bobbing boats and toy-block cabanons in saturated tints. Pursue the road to its dead end at **Les Goudes** and climb over boulders and tidal pools to the extraordinary **Anse Croisette,** a rough inlet paradise of crashing waves and rock. It was near here, known to the Marseillais as the Bout du Monde (End of the World), where the *Grand St-Antoine*—the ship that brought the plague to Marseille in 1720—was sunk, but too late to save the 100,000 who died from its deadly cargo.

TIMING

Allow a half day for this dramatic drive—longer if you succumb to the temptation to clamber around on barnacle-covered rocks, to sip a pastis while watching the fishing boats come in at dusk, or to settle in for a full-out bouillabaisse.

OFF THE
BEATEN PATH

L'ESTAQUE – At this famous village north of Marseille, Cézanne led an influx of artists eager to capture its cliff-top views over the harbor. Braque, Derain, and Renoir all put its red rooftops, rugged cliffs, and factory smokestacks on canvas. Pick up the English-language itinerary "L'Estaque and the Painters" from the Marseille tourist office and hunt down the sites and views they immortalized. It's a little seedy these days, but there are cafés and a few fish shops making the most of the nearby Criée (fisherman's auction). This is where the real wholesale auction moved from Marseille's quai de Rive Neuve. A novel way to see Cézanne's famous scenery is to take a standard SNCF train trip from the Gare St-Charles to Martigue; it follows the L'Estaque waterfront and (with the exception of a few tunnels) offers magnificent views.

Dining and Lodging

$$$ ✕ **Chez Fonfon.** Tucked into a storybook film set of the tiny fishing
★ port east of the center called Vallon des Auffes, this landmark still draws the Marseillais for classic bouillabaisse served with all the bells and whistles—broth, chili-hot rouille, and flamboyant tableside filleting. A variety of plain, fresh seafood, impeccably grilled, steamed, or roasted in salt crust, are also served, and two pretty pink dining rooms with picture windows overlook the fishing boats that supply your dinner. Since Alexandre Pinna, the owner's son, has taken over for the late, great Chef Fonfon, the restaurant's quality and reputation have slipped some, but the setting remains the loveliest in greater Marseille. ✉ *140 rue du Vallon des Auffes,* ☎ *04–91–52–14–38. Reservations essential. AE, DC, MC, V. Closed 2 wks in Jan. No dinner Sun.*

$$$ ✕ **L'Epuisette.** If Chez Fonfon (☞ *above*) is fading, this neighboring rival's star is rising. At the sea end of the storybook port Vallon des Auffes, half overlooking the boats, half overlooking the crashing surf, this classic bastion of seafood offers a spectacular setting and a successful new chef, Guillaume Sourrieu. Yes, the bouillabaisse is terrific, but so are the sophisticated alternatives, each with a Mediterranean accent, like mullet fillets on a bed of peppers and eggplant and sauced with peppery rouille. ✉ *Vallon des Auffes,* ☎ *04–91–52–17–82. AE, MC, V. Closed Mon. No lunch Sat. No dinner Sun.*

$$$ ✕ **Mets de Provence.** Climb up the sleazy wharf-side stair and enter a cosseted Provençal world. With the boats bobbing in the Vieux Port below the picture window and a landlubbing country decor, this extraordinarily romantic restaurant makes the most of Marseille's dual personality, split between land and sea. Classic Provençal hors d'oeuvres—tapenade, brandade, aïoli—lead into sophisticated seafood (dorade roasted with fennel and licorice) and meats (rack of lamb in herb

pastry). There's a four-course lunch (200 frs/€31 including wine) and a six-course dinner (295 frs/€45), artfully orchestrated but with plenty of choice. ☒ *18 quai de Rive Neuve,* ☎ *04–91–35–33–38. AE, MC, V. Closed Sun. No lunch Mon.*

$$$ ✕ **Miramar.** Of the dozens of seafood restaurants that actively court you as you stroll the horseshoe of the Vieux Port, this is the lodestone, a Marseille institution. It maintains a '60s kind of red-velvet-and-wood-paneling elegance (you almost expect to spot Jackie in a pillbox at the next table) but the sacred bouillabaisse ritual is preserved—deliciously. Unlike many seafood restaurants here, bouillabaisse is always on the menu and you don't have to order in advance. Portside terrace tables cut the stuffiness. Desserts are spectacular, thanks to the super pastry chef. Order a bottle of Cassis and give in to the ultimate dining event. ☒ *12 quai du Port,* ☎ *04–91–91–10–40. AE, MC, V. Closed Sun. No lunch Mon.*

$$–$$$ ✕ **L'Escale.** If you're not up to the formality of a grand-style bouillabaisse, seek out this simple village landmark, where Serge Zarokian has brought his experience as a fisherman and fishmonger to the kitchen. Order his hearty, earthy bouillabaisse in advance, or opt for a catch of the day, simply grilled. The terrace and broad dining room look over the village port and out to sea. ☒ *2 bd. Alexandre Delabre, Les Goudes,* ☎ *04–91–73–16–78. MC, V. No dinner Mon.–Sun. Oct.–Apr.*

$$ ✕ **Les Arcenaulx.** At this book-lined, red-walled haven in the stylish book-and-boutique complex of the renovated arsenal, you can have a sophisticated regional lunch—and read while you're waiting. Seafood figures large, with garlic-perfumed octopus stew and *baudroie* (monkfish) from the market two blocks away. Look for mussels in saffron with buckwheat crêpes, carpaccio of cod with crushed olives, or rabbit with garlic confit. That diners enter via the bookstore and pass rows of burnished leather-bound antique tomes appeals to Marseille's finer side, and you'll find politicians, professors, and actors soaking in the ambience. The terrace (on the classically proportioned cours d'Estienne d'Orves) is as pleasant as the interior. ☒ *25 cours d'Estienne d'Orves,* ☎ *04–91–59–80–30. AE, DC, MC, V. Closed Sun. evening.*

$$ ✕ **Baie des Singes.** On a tiny rock-ringed lagoon as isolated from the
★ nearby city as if it were a desert island, this cinematic corner of paradise was once a customs house under Napoléon III. You can rent a mattress and lounge chair, dive into the turquoise water, and shower off for the only kind of meal worthy of such a setting: fresh fish. There's bouillabaisse, of course, but also fresh-grilled sardines, mullet, and baudroie; and crabs, lobster, and local *cigales de mer* (shrimplike "sea locusts"). It's all served at terrace tables overlooking the water. The expansive owner, son of a fishmonger and grandson of a fisherman, knows his craft, and boasts—literally—Jacques Chirac and Catherine Deneuve among his loyal clientele. Mattress and shower access costs 50 francs/€7.62 extra. ☒ *Anse des Croisettes, Les Goudes,* ☎ *04–91–73–68–87. AE, DC, MC, V. Closed Oct.–Mar.*

$$ ✕ **Le Kahena.** In an easygoing, familial setting far from the ethnic ambience of the North African neighborhoods, this Tunisian restaurant offers unconquerably generous mounds of couscous crowned with red-hot sausage and tender lamb. Affordable plats du jour and succulent *mechouï* (spit-roasted lamb) round out the menu, and there's a good choice of Tunisian wines. The melting-pot clientele is a cross section of all Marseille. ☒ *2 rue de la République,* ☎ *04–91–90–61–93. MC, V. Closed Mon., no dinner Sun.*

$$ ✕ **L'Oliveraie.** It's hard to find serious food in this touristy nightlife neighborhood, just off the quai Rive Neuve, but this easygoing bistro comes through with style. Provençal fabrics and sanded brick add to the warm

132

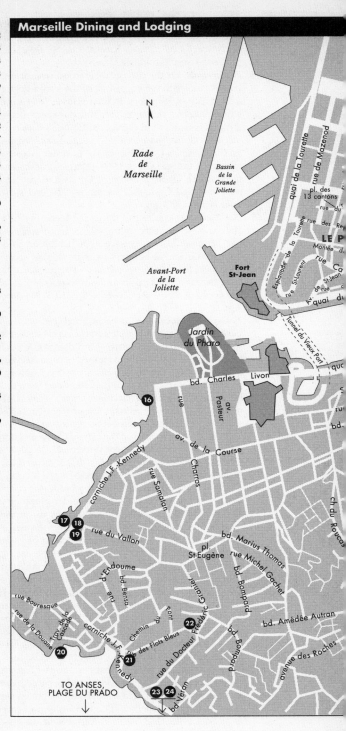

Marseille Dining and Lodging

bd.

rue Honnorat

National

bd. Camille Flammarion

av. C. Pelletan

av. du Gal. LeClerc

rue de l'Turenne

Nord

rue Montolieu

rue Duverger

rue de la Joliette

bd. des Dames

pl. J. Guesde

bd. Charles Nédélec

Gare St-Charles

rue Bernard du Bois

bd. Voltaire

pl. Alex. Labadié

rue de l'Evêché

rue de Lorette

Passage de Lorette

Petit Puits

rue St-Antoine

1

2

de

pl. Sadi Carnot

rue de

rue Mère

rue F. de Pressensé

rue des Petites Maries

rue d'Aix

rue des Dominicaines

bd. d'Athènes

Repenties

Puvis de Chavannes

rue Colbert

cours Belsunce

rue longue des Capucins

La Canebière

rue St. Savournin

PANIER

pl. Daviel

des Accoules

Coisserie

r. de Lacydon

Loge

Grand'Rue

pl. Victor Gélu

rue Coutellerie

6

rue H. Barbusse

3 **4** **5**

7

pl. du Général de Gaulle

cours St-Louis

8

rue d'Aubagne

bd. Garibaldi

rue Terrusse

pl. J. Jaurès

bd. Chave

du Port

quai des Belges

10

11

rue St-Ferréol

Beauvau

Vacon

9

r. Saint Pierre

Vieux Port

Ferry Boat

cours Jean Ballard

r. St-Saëns

r. F. Davso

de

Rome

Pl. aux Huiles

15

13

Pl. Neuve Thiars

d'Estienne d'Orves

12

rue Montgrand

cours Lieutaud

r. de la Loubière

quai de Rive

14

rue Nueve Sainte Catherine

Pl. Huiles

Pagnol

rue Sainte

bd. de la Corderie

cours Pierre Puget

Jardin P. Puget

bd. André Aune

bd. Notre-Dame

rue Jules-Moulet

rue Breteuil

rue Paradis

rue Saint Suffren

bd. Baille

av. de Toulon

avenue du Prado

av. Jules Cantini

r. Fort du Sanctuaire

bd. Vauban

rue Breteuil

rue du Rouet

0   400 yards

0   400 meters

ambience and friendly welcome. Try sausage-stuffed zucchini, delicate seafood mille-feuille pastry, lightly sauced St-Julien with pasta, and hope for a licorice parfait. Most fixed-price menus include Vaucluse wine. This is the lunch spot of choice for young neighborhood professionals. ⊠ *10 pl. aux Huiles*, ☎ *04–91–33–34–41. AE, DC, MC, V.*

$$ ✕ Le Panier des Arts. Behind a saffron-color facade and lace-covered windows, this sophisticated little neighborhood bistro has been taken over by its chef. If the welcome is less personal, the cooking remains straightforward but soigné—a basket of crudités with aïoli, a simple steak with shallots, and a modest local wine—and served on unpretentious olive-print oilcloths. It's all a part of the salvation and inevitable gentrification of the *quartier.* ⊠ *3 rue du Petit-Puits*, ☎ *04–91–56–02–32. MC, V. Closed Sun.*

$ ✕ César's Place. This tiny but cheery hole-in-the-wall, one of a gazillion dinner spots beckoning to tourists south of the quai Rive Neuve, offers a warm Midi-accented welcome and a good selection of Provençal specialties, from grilled peppers to roast lamb. Naturally the Pagnol theme figures heavily in the decor, and the catch of the day might as well have been delivered by Fanny herself. ⊠ *21 pl. auxs Huiles*, ☎ *04–91–33–25–22. MC, V. Closed Sun. No lunch Sat., Mon.*

$ ✕ Chez Jeannot. This is the poor man's Chez Fonfon, around the port from the prestigious restaurant and run by a member of the same family. It's so popular that it's become something of a theme-restaurant version of itself (plastic menus, wedding-banquet-style dining rooms), but it's a wonderful place to get away from town and enjoy a casual meal in an idyllic setting. The pizzas are heavy and there are towering platters of shellfish still twitching—but you're here for the film-set scenery as much as for the food. Terrace tables overlooking the fishing boats justify taxi fare from the center, but reserve in advance or you'll end up in the smoky interior. ⊠ *129 Vallon des Auffes*, ☎ *04–91–52–11–28. MC, V. Closed Mon. No dinner Sun.*

$ ✕ Etienne. This historic Le Panier hole-in-the-wall could be full of Pag-
★   nol characters, but nowadays it overflows with politicos and young professionals who enjoy bathing in the abuse and rich patois of the chef. Brace yourself for an epic, multifaceted meal. Start with a good fresh-anchovy pizza from the wood-burning oven. Then dig into fried squid, eggplant gratin, and a slab of rare-grilled beef big enough for one, two, or three. And if you're still hungry, there's always the quintessential *pieds et paquets,* Marseille's earthy classic of sheeps' feet and stuffed tripe. Orders are negotiated course by course with the waitresses. ⊠ *43 rue de la Lorette*, ☎ *no phone. No credit cards.*

$ ✕ Pizzeria des Catalans. Even closer to town than the Vallon des Auffes, the idyllic Anse des Catalans shelters a sliver of sandy beach, which, in turn, shelters this popular pizzeria, the summer address of choice for urban suncatchers. Stretch out on the broad terrace and gaze out to the Château d'If. Though you'd happily settle for less, there are excellent, light pizzas and fresh salads. ⊠ *3 rue des Catalans*, ☎ *04–91–52–37–82. MC, V. No dinner mid-Sept.–mid-May.*

$ ✕ Toinou. You can join the crowd at the outdoor stand and split a few oysters on the hoof. But it's more comfortable settling into a brasserie booth at this landmark shellfish joint, where you can get tiers and heaps of Cassis urchins, cream-filled *violets* (a kind of monstrous sea slug), clams, and mussels and, of course, oysters. Try the hot sauce—this is North African country, right?—or opt for the powerful aïoli. ⊠ *cours St-Louis*, ☎ *04–91–54–08–79. MC, V.*

$$$$ ✕ ⚷ Le Petit Nice. Despite its name, this extraordinarily glamorous hide-
★   away out-Rivieras anything in Nice. On a rocky promontory overlooking the harbor and the Iles de Frioul, this fantasy villa was bought from a countess in 1917 and converted to a hotel/restaurant, in anticipation

of the Jazz Age rush to the Côte d'Azur. The Passédat family has been getting it right ever since. Now father and son man the exceptional kitchen (one of the coast's best), creating truffled brandade, sea anemone beignets, fresh fish cooked whole, and licorice soufflé. In summer, meals are served by the saltwater pool overlooking the crashing surf. (The restaurant is closed Sunday.) Most rooms are sleek and minimalist, with some Art Deco-cum-postmodern touches. All in all, it's a Hollywood set for the South of France of your dreams. ⊠ *Anse de Maldormé, corniche J.-F. Kennedy, 13007,* ☎ *04–91–59–25–92,* FAX *04–91–59–28–08. 15 rooms. Restaurant, air-conditioning, pool. AE, DC, MC, V.* ✆

$$$ 🏨 **Mercure Beauvau Vieux Port.** The antiques are real, the woodwork
★ burnished with age; add a little marble, a touch of brass, and deep carpet underfoot, and you'll have an idea of this intimate urban hotel's genuine old-world charm. George Sand kept a suite here—knowing that makes the plush retro look in the rooms, with paisleys and moiré, seem all the more appropriate. Port-view rooms with balconies high over the fish market more than justify the splurge. The extensive breakfast is served in the cosseted salon overlooking the port. ⊠ *4 rue Beauvau, 13001,* ☎ *04–91–54–91–00; 800–MERCURE for U.S. reservations,* FAX *04–91–54–15–76. 71 rooms. Bar, breakfast room, air-conditioning. AE, DC, MC, V.*

$$$ 🏨 **Residence du Vieux Port.** The anonymous glass-and-concrete facade of this post-war structure grants all 40 rooms broad picture-window views and balconies over the old port. Bright prints and antiques soften the edges on the upper floors; lower rooms are classic pastel-modern. There's a generous breakfast buffet. ⊠ *18 quai du Port, 13002,* ☎ *04–91–91–91–22,* FAX *04–91–56–60–88. 40 rooms, 6 suites. Air-conditioning. AE, DC, MC, V.*

$$ 🏨 **New Hotel Bompard.** Removed from the center but accessible by bus, this oasis perches on a residential hillside above the corniche highway, its garden and rooms wrapped around a swimming pool. Several rooms opening directly onto the central court, motel-style, also have kitchenettes. ⊠ *2 rue des Flots Bleus, 13007,* ☎ *04–91–52–10–93,* FAX *04–91–31–02–14. 46 rooms. Air-conditioning, pool. AE, DC, MC, V.* ✆

$$ 🏨 **New Hotel Vieux Port.** In the heart of things at the crossroads of the quai du Port and the quai des Belges, this old, urban hotel has been slicked up. Now the cage elevator and weathered marble stairs lead up to spare, modern rooms with new tile baths. Ask for a corner room overlooking the ports. ⊠ *3 bis rue Reine-Elisabeth, 13001,* ☎ *04–91–90–51–42,* FAX *04–91–90–76–24. 47 rooms. Air-conditioning. AE, DC, MC, V.* ✆

$$ 🏨 **Le Rhul.** This is the Petit Nice for ordinary people: a broad, '60s-style roadside inn *left* of the corniche highway but still taking in spectacular sea views. Okay, so the stark architecture is cozied up with doilies and overstuffed chairs and the rooms have beige built-in laminate. Nonetheless, all but three rooms overlook the sea, and three have little balustraded balconies from which you can thumb your nose at the more famous inn below. ⊠ *269 corniche J.-F. Kennedy, 13007,* ☎ *04–91–52–01–77,* FAX *04–91–52–49–82. 16 rooms. Restaurant, air-conditioning. AE, MC, V.*

$$ 🏨 **Saint Ferréol.** Set back from the port in the heart of the shopping district, this cozy little hotel offers a warm reception and a homey feel in the breakfast room–cum–bar. Rooms are heavily decked in homage to various artists—Picasso in red, black and gilt, for example, with jazzy Cubist curtains. ⊠ *19 rue Pisançon at rue St-Ferréol, 13001,* ☎ *04–91–33–12–21,* FAX *04–91–54–29–97. 19 rooms. Air-conditioning. MC, V.* ✆

$–$$ 🏨 **Alizé.** On the Vieux Port, its front rooms taking in postcard views, this straightforward lodging has been modernized to include tight double windows, slick modular baths, and a laminate-and-all-weather-carpet look. Public spaces have exposed stone and preserved details, and a glass elevator whisks you to your floor. It's an excellent value and location for the price range. ⊠ *35 quai des Belges, 13001,* ☎ *04–91–33–66–97,* ℻ *04–91–54–80–06. 37 rooms. Air-conditioning. AE, DC, MC, V.*

$–$$ 🏨 **Hermès.** Just around the corner from the quai du Port, this modest
★ city hotel has been smartly renovated. Rooms are snug and modular and have new baths. Ask for one of the fifth-floor rooms with tiny balconies overlooking the port—or the crow's-nest "nuptiale" double with a private rooftop terrace. ⊠ *2 rue Bonneterie, 13002,* ☎ *04–96–11–63–63,* ℻ *04–96–11–63–64. 29 rooms. Air-conditioning. AE, DC, MC, V.*

Nightlife and the Arts

With a population of more than 800,000, Marseille is a big city by French standards, with all the nightlife the name entails. Arm yourself with *Marseille Poche,* a glossy monthly events minimagazine; the monthly *In Situ,* a free guide to music, theater and galleries; *Sortir,* a weekly about film, art, and concerts in southern Provence; or *TakTik,* a hip weekly on theater and new art. They're all in French.

The dance club **Monkey Club** (⊠ 20 rue Fortia, ☎ 04–91–54–03–03) is the place where local celebrities and sports stars hang out. **Le Trolleybus** (⊠ 24 quai de Rive Neuve, ☎ 04–91–54–30–45) is the hottest disco in town, with live concerts, three dance "grottoes," and a young, *branché* (hip) crowd. The music is a mix of techno, funk, and salsa.

The Red Lion (⊠ 231 av. Pierre Mendès France, ☎ 04–91–25–17–17) packs in Anglo-Saxons; they even pour onto the sidewalk, pints in hand, pub-style. There's happy hour daily (5 to 8) and live music Wednesdays that features everything from rock to blues to country.

Marseille's vibrant multicultural mix, with its enormous population of young North Africans, has evolved a genre of music that fuses all the soul of Arabic music with rhythms of Provence, Corsica, and Southern Italy and douses it with reggae and rap. To hear it, head for **L'Intermediaire** (⊠ 63 pl. Jean Jaurès, ☎ 04–91–47–01–25). For rap and soul try **L'Affranchi** (⊠ 212 bd. de St-Marcel, ☎ 04–91–35–09–19). Rock, jazz, and reggae concerts are held at the **Espace Julien** (⊠ 39 cours Julien, ☎ 04–91–24–34–15). **Le May Be Blues** (⊠ 2 rue André Poggioli, ☎ 04–91–42–41–00) is the best venue for live jazz, blues, and rock.

In a beautifully restored 1901 setting, **Le Café Parisien** (⊠ 1 place Sadi Carnot, up rue de la République, ☎ 04–91–90–05–77) is a dynamic melting pot where workers take their breakfast and intellectuals and the BCBG mingle at night over drinks and Latin music. Thursdays and Fridays from 6 to 9 there's a veritable smorgasbord of tapas for 25 francs/€3.81. **Le Pelle Mêle** (⊠ 45 pl. aux Huiles, ☎ 04–91–54–85–26) has a piano bar and, on Tuesday, Wednesday, and Thursday nights, jazz combos. For a traditional nightcap, have a cognac in the fine old oak-paneled **Le Cintra** bar (⊠ Hôtel Mercure Beauvau, 4 rue Beauvau, ☎ 04–91–54–91–00).

Classical-music concerts are held in the **Abbaye St-Victor** (☎ 04–96–11–20–60 for information). Operas and orchestral concerts take place at the **Opéra Municipal** (⊠ 2 rue Molière, pl. Ernest Reyer, ☎ 04–91–55–00–70).

At the **Théâtre National de Marseille La Criée** (⊠ quai de Rive Neuve, ☎ 04–91–54–74–54), a strong and solid repertoire of classical and contemporary works is performed. **Théâtre Off** (✉ quai de Rive Neuve, ☎ 04–91–33–12–92) presents alternative productions of classics. Celebrity-cast road shows and operettas are performed in the Théâtre Municipal's **Espace Odéon** (✉ 163 La Canebière, 04–91–92–79–44).

At **Badaboum** (✉ quai de Rive Neuve, ☎ 04–91–54–40–71), adventurous, accessible productions for children are performed. The **Théâtre des Marionettes** (✉ Theatre Massalia, 41 rue Jobin, ☎ 04–91–11–45–65) entertains a young audience with puppets, dance, and music—occasionally in foreign languages. It's by the Gare St-Charles.

Outdoor Activities and Sports

Marseille's waterfront position makes it easy to swim and sunbathe within the city sprawl. From the Vieux Port, Bus 83 or Bus 19 takes you to the vast green spread of reclaimed land called the **Parc Balnéaire du Prado.** Its waterfront is divided into beaches, all of them public and well-equipped with showers, toilets, and first-aid stations. The beach surface varies between sand and gravel. You can also find your own little beach on the tiny, rocky **Iles de Frioul**; boats leave from the Vieux Port and cost 50 francs/€7.62.

If you want to venture into wilder coastal country, and have a car, drive it to the end of the world. Head out the coastal road to Les Goudes, then penetrate even farther (up the road marked "sans issue" or dead end) until you reach Callelongue. From here you can strike out on foot, following the GR 98 to the idyllic **Calanque de Marseilleveyvre,** a rocky finger-inlet perfect for an isolated swim. From this point, the famous Calanques continue all the way to Cassis; though most of them lie on Marseille's official turf, they are most often accessed from Cassis (☞ Cassis, *below,* for more information). You can visit them by boat from Marseille, too, on a 4-hour mini-cruise with the Groupement des Armateurs Cotiers Marseillais (G.A.C.M.; ✉ 1 quai des Belges, ☎ 04–91–55–50–09). Tours leave at 2 Wednesday, Saturday, and Sunday (except in mistrals).

Marseille is a major center for diving (*plongée),* with several organizations offering "baptêmes" ("baptisms," or first dives) to beginners. The coast is lined with rocky inlets, grottos, and ancient shipwrecks, not to mention thronging with aquatic life. For general information, contact the **Association Plongez Marseille** (✉ 32 rue Antoine Merille, 13005, ☎ 06–14–89–17–71). Two English-speaking private companies specializing in initiations and day trips that can rent you the necessary equipment and provide showers and storage are: **Océan 4** (✉ 83 av. de la Pointe-Rouge, 04–91–73–91–16) and **Palm Beach Plongée** (✉ 2 promenade de la Plage, ☎ 04–91–22–10–38).

Shopping

The locally famous bakery **Four des Navettes** (✉ 136 rue Sainte, ☎ 04-91-33-32–12), up the street from Notre-Dame-de-la-Garde, makes orange-spice, shuttle-shape navettes. These cookies are modeled on the little boat in which Mary Magdalene and Lazarus washed onto continental shores (☞ Stes-Maries-de-la-Mer *in* Chapter 1) before Lazarus worked his way over to Aix and Marseille.

Savon de Marseille (Marseille Soap) is a household expression in France, often sold as a satisfyingly crude and hefty block in odorless olive-oil green. There's a world market, though, for the chichi offspring of this earth mother: dainty pastel guest soaps in almond, lemon, vanilla, and other scents. If you're not one for lingering in the odoriferous boutiques that sell these in gilt gift boxes, consider the no-non-sense outlet of **La Compagnie de Provence** (✉ 1 rue Caisserie, ☎ 04–91–56–20–97), at the foot of Le Panier. Here blocks of soap are sold in plain brown boxes, but you can have them gift wrapped on request.

For every kind of nautical doo-dad, from brass fittings for your yacht's bathroom to sturdy peacoats and oilskins, head down the quai to **Castaldi** (✉ 25 quai de Rive Neuve, ☎ 04–91–33–30–49). For exotic food products shipped into this international port, browse in the **Maison Axa** (✉ 24–27 rue d'Aubagne, ☎ 04–91–54–11–50), crammed floor to ceiling with Armenian specialties and aromatic goodies from North Africa, China, and the Middle East.

For good old-fashioned big-city shopping, the rue St-Ferréol (four blocks back from the Vieux Port) is flanked with major department stores: **Galeries Lafayette** (✉ 40 rue St-Ferréol, ☎ 04–91–54–46–54) and **Marks & Spencer** (✉ 55 rue St-Ferréol, ☎ 04–91–54–46–54). **Nouvelles Galeries** (✉ Centre Bourse/Bir Hakeim, ☎ 04–91–56–82–12), a mid-price department store, anchors the corner one block back from the port and the tourist office. Off-beat designer clothing created in Marseille can be found on cours Julien, including the home-base for the trendy, high-texture clothes and jewelry made by **Madame Zaza of Marseille** (✉ 73 cours Julien, ☎ 04–91–48–05–57). At **Diable Noir** (✉ 69 cours Julien, ☎ 04–91–42–86–73), next door to Zaza on the cours Julien, you'll find glamorous, slightly retro evening gowns in extravagant tulles and taffeta. Diable Noir's "downtown" shop anchors the edgy new shopping district along **rue de la Tour,** across from the Centre Bourse off place du Général de Gaulle; dubbed "rue de la Mode," it parades the earthy creativity of Marseille's new fusion-fashion culture.

THE CENTRAL COAST

With the floods of vacationers pouring onto the beaches from St-Tropez to Menton every summer, it's surprising that the coast between Marseille and Hyères is often dismissed. Although a few industrial pockets exist around La Ciotat and Toulon, there are just as many sections of magnificent coastline—white cliffs peppered with ragged, wind-twisted pines.

Just inland, in the dry white hills, lies the peaceful market town of Aubagne; climb to the top of its outlying hills, and you can see the ocean sparkling below. Cassis is the jewel of this region, a harbor protected by the formidable Cap Canaille, 1,300 ft (396 m) high; between Cassis and Marseille stretch the extraordinary Calanques, a series of rocky fjords that probe deep into the coastline. Following the coastal highway, you come to La Ciotat, a gargantuan (but oddly picturesque) naval shipyard, and reach the popular beach resort of Bandol—incidentally the source of one of Provence's most famous wines. A popular rainy-day excursion from Bandol leads to the hilltop medieval village of Le Castellet; you may want to stop at some of the wineries along the way. Toulon is an enormous naval base and a tough big city with an interesting old town for the intrepid; just east of the city is where you catch the ferry to Porquerolles, the best of the wild and beautiful Iles d'Hyères.

Aubagne

43   *15 km (9 mi) east of Marseille, 10 km (6 mi) north of Cassis.*

This easygoing, plane-tree-shaded market town (pronounced Oh-*bahn*-yuh) is proud of its native son, the dramatist, filmmaker, and chronicler of all things Provençal, Marcel Pagnol, best known to Anglophones as author of *Jean de Florette* and *Manon des Sources* (*Manon of the Springs*). Here you can spend the morning exploring the animated market or digging through used Pagnol books and collectibles in the old town. You can study miniature dioramas of scenes from Pagnol stories at **Le Petit Monde de Marcel Pagnol** (The Small World of Marcel Pagnol). The characters are all santons, and there are superb portraits of a humpback Gerard Dépardieu and Yves Montand, resplendent in mustache, fedora, and velvet vest, just as they were featured in *Jean de Florette*. ✉ *esplanade de Gaulle.* 🎫 *Free.* ⊘ *Daily 9–noon and 2–6.*

Aubagne claims the title of the santon capital of Provence. The craft, originally from Marseille, was focused here at the turn of the 20th century when artisans moved inland to make the most of local clay (☞ Close-Up: Little Santons with Feet of Clay, *below*). The more than a dozen studios in town are set up for you to observe the production process. Daniel Scaturro is one of the best; in 1997 he was granted status as Meilleur Ouvrier de France (Best French Artisan), the country's highest honor for artisans in all fields (Paul Bocuse is another). He specializes in portraits, mostly of Pagnol's film characters—but you can have one made of yourself for 4,000 francs/€610. His main display studio, simply called **Daniel Scaturro** (✉ 20A av. de Verdun, ☎ 04–42–84–33–29), is on the edge of town in an industrial quarter. Scaturro's sons demonstrate the family craft on a smaller scale in a shop in the central old town (✉ bd. Jean-Jaurès/rue Martinot).

The history of the craft of santon making and other uses to which the local clay was put—faïence and hand-painted tiles—can be studied at the **Ateliers Thérèse Neveu,** named for Aubagne's first master *santonière* (santon maker). Also on display are excellent temporary exhibitions about pottery. ✉ *chemin Entrecasteaux, at the top of the old town hill,* ☎ *04–42–03–43–10.* 🎫 *Free.* ⊘ *Tues.–Sun. 10–noon and 2–6.*

Even if you haven't read Pagnol's works or seen his films, you can enjoy the **Circuit Pagnol,** a hike in the raw-hewn, arid *garrigues* (scrublands) behind Marseille and Aubagne. Here Pagnol spent his idyllic summers, described in his *Souvenirs d'un Enfance* (*Memories of a Childhood*), crunching through the rosemary, thyme, and scrub oak at the foot of his beloved Garlaban. When he grew up to be a famous playwright and filmmaker, he shot some of his best work in these hills, casting his wife, Jacqueline, as the first Manon of the springs. After Pagnol's death, Claude Berri came back to the Garlaban to find a location for his remake of *Manon des Sources* but found it so altered by brush fires and power cables that he chose to shoot farther east, around Cuges-les-Pine and Riboux instead. (The lovely village and Manon's well were filmed in Mirabeau, in the Luberon.) Although the trail may no longer shelter the pine-shaded olive orchards of its past, it still gives you the chance to walk through primeval Provençal countryside and rewards you with spectacular views of Marseille and the sea. *To access the marked trail by yourself, drive to La Treille northeast of Aubagne and follow the signs. For an accompanied tour with literary commentary, contact the Office du Tourisme (☎ 04–42–03–49–98).*

Make sure you visit Aubagne on a **market** day, when the sleepy center is transformed into a tableau of Provençal life. For sale are fresh local asparagus, plant-ripened tomatoes, melons, and mesclun scooped by the gnarled fingers of blue-aproned ladies in from the farm. The Tuesday market is the biggest, with clothing, purses, tools, and pots and pans spilling onto the esplanade, but the Saturday and Sunday markets make more of regional products; those labeled Pays d'Aubagne must be organically raised. You won't find the social scene you'll see in Aix, but this is a more authentic farmers' market.

LITTLE SAINTS WITH FEET OF CLAY

THEY BECKON FROM SHOP windows in every hill town, these miniatures called *santons*, from the dialect *santouns* for "little saints." But whatever commercial role they may play today, their roots run deep in Provence.

The Christmas crêche has been a part of Provençal tradition since the Middle Ages, when people reenacted the tableau of the birth of Christ, wise men, shepherds, and all. When the Revolution cracked down on these pastoral plays, a crafty Marseillais decided to substitute clay actors. The tiny terra-cotta figures caught on and soon upstaged their human counterparts for good.

A Marseille tradition that eventually migrated to Aubagne in the hills above (the clay was better), the delicate doll-like figurines spread throughout Provence, and are displayed every Christmas in church crêches that resemble a rustic backcountry hill village as much as they do Bethlehem. Against a miniature background of model stone houses, dried-moss olive groves, and glass creeks, quaint, familiar characters go about their daily tasks—the lumberjack hauling matchstick kindling, the fisherman toting a basket of waxy fish, the red-cheeked town drunk leering drolly at the pretty lavender-cutter, whose basket hangs heavy with real dried sprigs. The original cast from Bethlehem gets second billing to a charming crowd of gypsies, goat herds, and provincial passersby. And wait—isn't that Gerard Depardieu? And Raimu? And Yves Montand? Even beloved film actors have worked their way into the scene.

It's a highly competitive craft, and while artisans vie for the souvenir trade, some have raised it to an art form: Daniel Scaturro, of Aubagne, was named a Meilleur Ouvrier de France in 1997, one of the highest national honors granted to craftsmen.

Molded, dried, then scraped with sharp tools down to the finest detail—wrinkled foreheads and fingernails—the santons are baked at 1,000°C (1,832°F). Once cool, they are painted with a watchmaker's precision: eyelashes, nostrils, and gnarled knuckles. The larger ones have articulated limbs that are joined to allow for dressing; their hand-sewn costumes, Barbie-scaled, are lavished with as much fine detail as the painted features.

Many artisans maintain highly public studios so visitors can watch the process and acquire the taste for collecting. Little ones (about an inch high), without articulated limbs, run about 25 francs/€3.81; big ones (8 to 10 inches), dressed and painted by the best artists, cost around 250 francs/€38. Or you can splurge and commission a portrait of yourself for the mantel—4,000 francs/€610 at Scaturro's.

But the preferred format is the crêche tableau, and it's easy to get hooked on building a collection of Provençal rustics to be lovingly unwrapped and displayed every Christmas season.

Another claim to fame for Aubagne: It's the headquarters for the French Foreign Legion. The legion was created in 1831 and accepts recruits from all nations, no questions asked. The discipline and camaraderie instilled among its motley team of adventurers, criminals, and mercenaries have helped the legion forge a reputation for exceptional valor—a reputation romanticized by songs and films in which sweaty deeds of heroism are performed under the desert sun. The **Musée de la Légion Étrangère** (Museum of the Foreign Legion) does its best to polish the image by way of medals, uniforms, weapons, and photographs. ⊠ *Caserne Viénot (to get there, take a left off D2 onto D44A just before Aubagne)*, ☎ *04–42–18–82–41.* 🖼 *Free.* ☉ *June–Sept., Tues.–Thurs. and weekends 10–noon and 3–7, Fri. 10–noon; Oct.–May, Wed. and weekends 10–noon and 2–6.*

Dining and Lodging

$ ✕ **La Farandole.** In a rustic Provençal setting of lemon-print cloths, lace curtains, and the region's typical bow-legged chairs, you can enjoy good home cooking with the local regulars who claim the same table every day. The inexpensive daily menu may feature panfried chicken livers on a green salad, rascasse with sorrel, or garlicky steak and *frites* (fries); wine is included. Homemade cakes and friendly waitresses enhance the small-town spirit. ⊠ *6 rue Martino (off cours Maréchal, on a narrow street leading into the old town)*, ☎ *04–42–03–26–36. MC, V. Closed Sun. No dinner Mon.*

$ ✕ **Le Triskel.** This miniature shoebox of an old-town restaurant has a
★ living santon for a chef—mustache, toque, and broad gestures worthy of Pagnol. In full view of the loyal locals who crowd elbow to elbow, he hauls heavy daubes from the wood-fire oven, ladles pot-au-feu over duck-leg confit—gesticulating and bantering with the guests. There are kidneys grilled with thyme, homemade gnocchi, eggplant gratinée and, almost incidentally, pizzas. ⊠ *12 rue Jean-Jacques Rousseau*, ☎ *04–42–03–59–86. No credit cards. Closed Wed.*

$$ 🏠 **Hostellerie de la Source.** Too bad it's in a suburban setting 4 km (2½ mi) outside Aubagne. This 17th-century country house stands in vast boxwood gardens surrounding tennis courts and an indoor-outdoor pool. Inside there's a slick suburban feel well suited to banquets and conferences. Rooms are bright and tidy, entirely rebuilt in the late 1980s. ⊠ *St-Pierre-des-Aubagne, 13400*, ☎ *04–42–04–09–19*, FAX *04–42–04–58–72. 24 rooms, 1 suite. Restaurant, bar, pool. MC, V.*

Cassis

★ ㊹ *22 km (14 mi) southeast of Marseille, 10 km (6 mi) north of Aubagne.*

Surrounded by vineyards, flanked by monumental cliffs, guarded by the ruins of a medieval castle, and nestled around a picture-perfect fishing port, Cassis (pronounced cah-SEE) is the prettiest coastal town in Provence. Neighboring it are the wild Calanques that cut into the rock walls toward Marseille.

Stylish without being too recherché, it provides shelter to numerous pleasure-boaters, who restock their galleys at its market, replenish their Saint James nautical duds in its boutiques, and relax with a bottle of Cassis and a platter of urchins in one of its numerous waterfront cafés. Pastel houses at rakish angles frame the port, and the mild rash of parking-garage architecture that scars its outer neighborhoods can't spoil the general effect, which is one of unadulterated charm.

You can't visit Cassis without touring the **Calanques,** the fjord-like finger bays that probe the rocky coastline. Either take a sightseeing cruise on a double-decker, glass-bottom boat that travels across the open water and dips into each calanque in turn, or hike across the cliff tops, clambering down the steep sides to these barely accessible retreats. Or you can combine the two, going in by boat and hiking back; make arrangements at the port (☞ Outdoor Activities and Sports, *below*).

The Calanque closest to Cassis is the least attractive: **Port Miou** was a stone quarry until 1982, when the Calanques became protected sites. *Pierre de Cassis* (Cassis stone) is much sought-after in the building trade for its pink-gray whorls. Now this calanque is an active leisure and fishing port, and on the cliff top above it you can see the precarious GR98 that follows the Calanques to Marseille. **Calanque Port Pin** is prettier, with wind-twisted pines growing at angles from the white-rock cliffs. But it's the third calanque that's a corner of paradise: **Calanque En Vau** is a castaway's dream, with a tiny beach at its root and jagged cliffs looming overhead, covered with gnarled pine and scrub. Rock climbers love it. The series of massive cliffs and calanques stretch all the way to Marseille (most fall, in fact, within that city's limits) but will always be known as Les Calanques de Cassis.

The **Château de Cassis** has loomed over the harbor since the invasions of the Saracens in the 7th century, evolving over the centuries into a walled enclosure crowned with stout watch towers. It's private property today and best viewed from a port-side café.

If you're a wine lover, pick up a map and the brochure "Through the Vineyards" from the tourist office. There are 12 domains, all of them open for tasting and buying, but the most spectacularly sited is the **Clos Sainte Magdeleine** (⊠ av. du Revestel, ☎ 04–42–01–70–28), overlooking the sea from the slopes of the Cap Canaille.

Dining and Lodging

$$ ✕ **Monsieur Brun.** Though Cassis has many restaurants with linens and extensive menus, one of the most authentic meals you can have is a platter of raw shellfish, served a few yards from the port that supplied it. An unpretentious choice, this terrace brasserie sprawls along the west side of the port, inches from the bobbing boats and overlooking the château and Cap Canaille. A multitier tower of shellfish on a bed of kelp is served with nothing but bread, butter, and a finger towelette. Have the nutty little *bleues,* the local oyster, or *oursins* (sea urchins), a Cassis specialty brought in daily here by the chef's fisherman friend. Omelets and salads are an alternative. ⊠ *2 quai Calendal,* ☎ *04–42–01–82–66. No credit cards. Closed mid-Dec.–mid–Jan.*

$$ ✕🏠 **Jardin d'Emile.** Tucked back from the waterfront under quarried
★ cliffs and massive parasol pines, this stylish yet homey inn takes in views of the cape from the restaurant and half the rooms. View or not, rooms are intimate and welcoming, with rubbed-chalk walls, *boutis* (Provençal quilts), scrubbed pine, weathered stone, Salerne tiles, and dimmers to enhance the romantic atmosphere. The restaurant is atmospheric, on a permanently sheltered garden terrace surrounded by greenery and, by night, the illuminated cliffs. Regional specialties with a cosmopolitan twist—such as harbor-fresh tuna grilled with soy, or rascasse filled with goat cheese—are served on locally made pottery. ⊠ *Plage du Bestouan, 13260,* ☎ *04–42–01–80–55,* 𝔽𝔸𝕏 *04–42–01–80–70. 7 rooms. Restaurant. AE, DC, MC, V.* ✍

$$$ 🏠 **Les Roches Blanches.** First built as a private home in 1887, this cliffside villa takes in smashing views of the port and the Cap Canaille, both from the best rooms and from the panoramic dining hall. The beautifully landscaped terrace is shaded by massive pines, and the horizon-line pool seems to spill into the sea. Yet the ambience is far from snooty or deluxe; rather it's friendly, low-key, and pleasantly mainstream. A bland '60s-style annex compensates for its looks with full-

THE S IS (HARDLY EVER) SILENT

(Or, how to brag to your friends, "we stayed in a beautiful mas out-side Cassis" without mispronouncing a thing.)

THE RULE OF THUMB in Provence is to pronounce everything, even to the point of pronouncing letters that aren't there. *Pain*, in the north pronounced through the nose without a final consonant, becomes "peng" in the south. *Vin* becomes "veng," *enfin* "on feng," etc.

But there are words in constant dispute, especially among a people toilet-trained on the Academie Française, that holy arbiter of the French language. One of the words caught in the crossfire: *mas*. This old Provençal word for farmhouse is a "mahss" in the south, but Parisians hold out for a more refined Frenchification: "ma."

Cassis, on the other hand, is a booby trap. For one thing, there are two drinks named Cassis, one a black-currant liqueur made in Burgundy to be blended in white-wine *kirs*, the other the famous wine from the coastal country east of Marseille. The liqueur is always called "cass-*eess*," and northerners (who consume the most kirs) insist on pronouncing both the wine and the village "Cass-*eess*" as well. But ask the locals, and they'll snort in disdain. "C'est 'Cass-*EE*,' " they'll explain, as if all the words in Provence followed the pattern.

There you have it: In Paris, it's cass-eess but mah; in Provence, it's cass-ee but mahss.

length balconies facing the cape. ✉ *rte. des Calanques, 13260,* ☎ *04–42–01–09–30,* 🖷 *04–42–01–94–23. 19 rooms, 5 suites. 2 restaurants, pool. AE, MC, V.* ✍

Outdoor Activities and Sports

To go on a **boat ride** to Les Calanques, get to the port around 10 AM or 2 PM and look for a boat that's loading passengers. Two of the best choices are the **Moby Dick III** and the **Ville de Cassis**—they have glass-bottom views and full commentary (in French only). But a slew of alternative boats won't leave you stranded. Round-trips should include at least three calanques and average 65 francs/€9.90.

To **hike** the Calanques, gauge your skills: The GR98 (marked with red-and-white bands) is the most scenic but requires ambitious scrambling to get down the sheer walls of En Vau. The alternative is to follow the green markers and approach En Vau from behind. The markers could use revision nonetheless. If you're ambitious, you can hike the length of the GR98 between Marseille and Cassis, following the coastline, a distance of roughly 30 km (18 mi). Arrange in advance for a boat pickup or dropoff at En Vau.

En Route From Cassis head east out of town and cut sharply right up the **route des Crêtes.** This road takes you along a magnificent crest over the water and up to the very top of **Cap Canaille.** Venture out on the vertiginous trails to the edge, where nothing stands between you and infinity, and the whole coast stretches below. The altitude is only 1,310 ft (400 m), but that's straight up—literally—from sea level. From the **Semaphore du Bec d'Aigle,** a military lighthouse, go to the overlook that gives you the view from the cape's other side. This perspective plunges down to the impressive shipbuilding center of **La Ciotat.** Here the Lumière

144

HOW TO EAT A SEA URCHIN

" . . . But answer came there none—/And this was scarcely odd, because/They'd eaten every one," wrote Lewis Carroll in *Through the Looking Glass.*

URCHINS, THOSE SPINY LITTLE BALLS, are cracked open and served belly up on a platter of seaweed, usually six or a dozen at a time. To the uninitiated, they're not a pretty sight: Each black demiglobe comes with quills still . . . well, waving, but only slightly. Within this macabre natural bowl floats a dense puddle of (it must be said) muddy brown grit and bile-green slime. Supporting the rim with your left thumb and index finger (taking care not to impale yourself), scrape said slime to the sides with the point of your spoon. Here lies what the fuss is all about: there are six coral-pink strips of sea-perfumed stuff inside, more foam than flesh (you may have experienced a more substantial version in sushi). Scrape these gently up and spread them on a slice of baguette. Or just slide them into a spoon and bite. An ocean of milky-sweet flavor is concentrated in this rosy streak. Granted, a dozen won't make a meal, but keep the little guys company with oysters, mussels, clams, sea snails, a crock of butter, a basket of bread, and an icy bottle of Cassis.

brothers filmed the first moving picture, of a steam engine pulling into the train station, and screened their first film. Along the **Clos des Plages** are a series of good sand beaches. Continuing east, you'll cross out of the Bouches-du-Rhône département and into the Var, which stretches nearly to Cannes.

Bandol

45 *25 km (15½ mi) southeast of Cassis, 15 km (9 mi) west of Toulon.*

Although its name means wine to most of the world, Bandol is also a popular and highly developed seaside resort town. In the 1920s glory days, the glamorous social life of the Riviera stretched this far west, and grand seaside mansions rivaled Cap d'Antibes and Juan-les-Pins for high society and literati. Nowadays it has seafood snack shacks, generic brasseries, a harbor packed with yachts, and a waterfront promenade. Yet the east end of town still conceals lovely old villas framed in mimosas, bougainvillea, and pine. And a port-side stroll up the palm-lined allée Jean-Moulin feels downright Côte d'Azur. But be warned: the sheer concentration of high-summer crowds can't be exaggerated. If you're not a beach lover, pick up an itinerary from the tourist office and visit a few Bandol vineyards just outside of town.

Several sights around Bandol are worth pursuing. Follow D559 north of town toward **Le Castellet,** perched high above the Bandol vineyards. Its narrow streets, 17th-century stone houses, and (alas) touristy shops are designer-made for beach lovers on a rainy day.

Just east of town on D559 and past the smaller seaside resort of Sanary, turn left on D63 and follow signs to the small stone chapel of

Bureau de change

Cambio

外国為替

In this city, you can find money on almost any street.

NO-FEE FOREIGN EXCHANGE

The Chase Manhattan Bank has over 80 convenient locations near New York City destinations such as:
  Times Square
  Rockefeller Center
  Empire State Building
  2 World Trade Center
  United Nations Plaza
Exchange any of 75 foreign currencies

THE RIGHT RELATIONSHIP IS EVERYTHING.®

Notre-Dame de Pépiole, hemmed in by pines and cypresses. It's one of the oldest Christian buildings in France, dating from the 6th century and modeled on early churches in the Middle East. The simple interior has survived the years in remarkably good shape, although the colorful stained glass that fills the tiny windows is modern—composed mainly of broken bottles. ☉ *Most afternoons 3–5.*

From Notre-Dame de Pépiole, retrace your steps toward Sanary and head south on D616 around the **Cap Sicié** for broad panoramas and a tremendous view across the Bay of Toulon. Or head north on D11 to Ollioules; just past the village, follow N8 (in the direction of Le Beausset) through a 5-km (3-mi) route that twists its scenic way beneath the awesome chalky rock faces of the **Gorge d'Ollioules.** Even more spectacular: Take a left at Ollioules on D20 and follow the winding road along the crest of **Le Gros Cerveau.** You'll be rewarded first with inland mountain views, then an expansive panorama of the coast.

OFF THE
BEATEN PATH

BRIGNOLES – This rambling backcountry hill town, 86 km (53 mi) northwest of Bandol, is the market center for the wines of the Var and the crossroads of this green region. The main point of interest is the Abbaye de La Celle, a 12th-century Benedictine abbey that served as a convent until the 17th century. It was closed when the young nuns began to run wild, known less for their chastity than "the color of their petticoats and the name of their lover." There's a refectory and a ruined cloister; the simple Romanesque chapel still serves as the parish church. But this quiet, ungentrified setting may not last long. Real estate here has rocketed; *le tout* Paris whispers of "The Next Luberon." Who's behind the surge of interest? Superchef Alain Ducasse, who opened a country inn, **Hostellerie de l'Abbaye de La Celle** ($$$–$$$$), just up the road from the abbey. This beautifully restored 18th-century house has rooms overlooking vineyards and a park thick with chestnut and mulberry trees. Upstairs rooms look over the gardens; new duplex rooms have private vineyard entrances. Marie Antoinette and Charles de Gaulle have bequeathed names to rooms they once favored as house guests. Heading the formidable kitchen is Chef Benoît Witz (transferred from Ducasse's Bastide at Moustiers), whose creations glorify the rustic: wild mushrooms sautéed with crayfish, rabbit with olives and polenta, crisp French toast with strawberries. ✉ *pl. du Général de Gaulle, 83170 La Celle,* ☎ *04-98-05-14-14,* ℻ *04-98-05-14-15. 10 rooms. Restaurant, pool. AE, DC, MC, V.* 🍴

Toulon

 67 km (41½ mi) east of Marseille, 29 km (18 mi) northwest of La Tour Fondue (departure point for the Iles d'Hyères).

One of France's largest naval ports, Toulon is best known for the dark day in World War II when 75 French ships sunk themselves rather than fall into the hands of the attacking Germans. Though you may see nothing but monstrous apartment buildings and traffic jams in crossing through this dense and messy city of some 500,000 inhabitants, the **Vieille Ville** (Old Town) lurks behind; its nickname, "Petit Chicago," recalls the neighborhood's history (*almost* entirely in the past) as a crime-ridden, red-light district. Nowadays, it's merely run-down, with funky and quirkily appealing stretches of ruined medieval houses mixed with lurid neon.

Leave your car in the parking lot under place de la Liberté. Head along boulevard de Strasbourg and turn right after the theater into rue Berthelot. It leads into the pedestrians-only streets that constitute the heart of the old town. Wander through **place des Trois Dauphins,** with its mossy fountain sprouting ferns and shrubs. Walk along **cours Lafayette,** with its wonderfully animated, authentically Provençal morning market (daily except Sunday) shaded by rows of plane trees. And stroll past the **Hôtel de Ville,** with its Baroque figures evocatively carved by the Marseillais sculptor Pierre Puget.

Avenue de la République, an ugly array of concrete apartment blocks, runs parallel to the waterfront, where yachts and pleasure boats—some available for trips to the Iles d'Hyères or around the bay—add bright splashes of color. At the western edge of the gray is the **Musée National de la Marine** (Naval Museum), with large models of ships, figureheads, paintings, and other items related to Toulon's maritime history. Photographs of the WWII sinking bring the sickening story to life. ⊠ *pl. Monsenergue,* ☎ *04–94–02–02–01.* ⊡ *29 frs/€4.42.* ☉ *Apr.–Sept. daily 10–6:30; Oct.–Mar. Wed.–Mon. 10–noon and 2–6.*

Mighty hills surround Toulon, and **Mont Faron,** 1,600 ft, is the highest of all. Either drive to the top, taking the circular route du Faron in either direction, or make the six-minute ascent by cable car from boulevard de l'Amiral Jean-Vence. ☎ *04–94–92–68–25.* ⊡ *38 frs/€5.79 round-trip.* ☉ *July–Aug. Tues.–Sun. 9:30–7:45, Mon. 2:15–7:45; Sept.–June, Tues.–Sun. 9:30–noon and 2:15–6.*

Iles d'Hyères

47 *32 km (20 mi) off the coast south of Hyères.* Off the southeastern point of France's star and spanning some 32 km (20 mi), this archipelago of islands could be a set for a pirate movie; in fact, it has featured in several, thanks to a soothing microclimate and a wild and rocky coastline dotted with palms. And not only film pirates made their appearance. In the 16th century the islands were seeded with convicts to work the land. They soon ran amuck and used their adopted base to ambush ships heading into Toulon.

A more wholesome population claims the islands today, which consist of three main bodies: Levant, Port-Cros, and Porquerolles. **Port-Cros** is a national park, with both its surface and underwater environs protected. **Levant** has been taken over, for the most part, by nudists. ★ But **Porquerolles** (pronounced pork-uh-*rohl*) is the largest and best of the lot, and a popular escape from the modern world. Off-season, it's a castaway paradise of pine forests, sandy beaches, and vertiginous cliffs over rocky coastline. Inland, its preserved pine forests and orchards of olives and figs are crisscrossed with dirt roads to be explored on foot or on bikes; except for the occasional jeep or work truck, the island is car-free. In high season (April to October) day-trippers pour off the ferries and surge to the beaches, while soap boutiques and T-shirt shops appear out of the woodwork to suit vacationers' whims. During this busy season it's worth considering staying in one of the few hotels in order to have the island to yourself when everyone else heads back to mainland.

Porquerolles is a perfect spot for a honeymoon, but it made an even better wedding gift. At the turn of the 20th century a Belgian engineer named François-Joseph Fournier made a killing on the Panama Canal, then struck gold in Mexico. To please his English bride, he bought Porquerolles at an auction and decided to create a hacienda-ranch, importing workers and founding his own school and electric company. It was only in 1970 that France nationalized the island, leaving Fournier's widow with a quarter of her original inheritance; her granddaughter runs the luxurious Mas du Langoustier (☞ Dining and Lodging, *below*).

To get to the islands, follow the narrow Giens Peninsula to La Tour-Fondue, at its tip. Boats (leaving every half hour in summer, every 60 or 90 minutes the rest of the year for 80 francs/€12.20 round-trip) make a 20-minute beeline to Porquerolles. For Port-Cros and Levant, you'll depart from Port d'Hyères at Hyères-Plages. You can also get to all three islands from Port-de-Miramar or Le Lavandou—a longer boat ride to Porquerolles, but you avoid the maddening traffic bottleneck of the Giens Peninsula.

Dining and Lodging

$$$ ✕ 🏠 **Mas du Langoustier.** Amid stunningly lush terrain at the westernmost
★ point of the Ile de Porquerolles, 3 km (2 mi) from the harbor, this luxurious hideout is a popular getaway for the yacht-and-helicopter set and a standard day trip from high-season St-Tropez. Owner Madame Richard, the granddaughter of the lucky woman who was given this island as a wedding gift, picks you up at the port in her Dodge. Choose between big new California-modern rooms and cosseted old-style rooms in the original section. Chef Joël Guillet creates inspired southern French cuisine, to be accompanied by the rare island rosé. ✉ *Pointe du Langoustier, 83400 Ile de Porquerolles,* ☎ 04-94-58-30-09, ⨕ 04-94-58-36-02. *49 rooms. Restaurant, tennis court, beach, billiards. AE, DC, MC, V. Closed Nov.–Apr..* ❧

$$-$$$ ✕ 🏠 **Les Glycines.** In soft shades of yellow ocher and sky blue, this sleekly modernized little *bastide* (country house) has an idyllic enclosed courtyard, verdant with lemon trees, ivy, and an ancient *figuier* (fig tree). Back rooms look over a jungle of mimosa and eucalyptus. Public salons have Provençal chairs and fabrics. The restaurant, where food is served on the terrace or in the garden, features port-fresh tuna and sardines. In the summer season (April through September) half board is obligatory; children stay (and eat) for free. The inn is just back from the port in the village center. ✉ *pl. d'Armes, 83400 Ile de Porquerolles,* ☎ 04-94-58-30-36, ⨕ 04-94-58-35-22. *11 rooms. Restaurant, bar, air-conditioning. AE, MC, V.* ❧

Outdoor Activities and Sports

You can rent a mountain bike (*velo tout-terrain,* or VTT) for a day to pedal the paths and cliff-top trails of Porquerolles at **Cycle Porquerol** (✉ rue de la Ferme, ☎ 04-94-58-30-32) or **L'Indien** (✉ pl. d'Armes, ☎ 04-94-58-30-39).

If you prefer to explore on foot, pick up a map at the tourist kiosk on the landing docks, or simply follow the arrows. The main road back from the village leads over the island's forested crest to the Cap d'Arme, with dramatic views of the lighthouse. To its right you can strike out toward the Gorges du Loup; the precarious trail breaks out in the open over a spectacular rocky cove with crashing surf. If you head right of town you'll pass through a series of botanical-study orchards, full of hybrid figs and olives, with a series of inlets and rocky coves for picnics and reflection. If you head left you'll follow the broad stretch of beaches, first the popular Courtade, then the isolated, pine-shadowed Notre-Dame. Roads and trails are marked for difficulty, but only a few are narrower than Jeep-width.

Locamarine 75 (✉ on the port, ☎ 04-94-58-35-84) rents motor boats to amateurs with or without license. At the **Club de Plongée du Langoustier** (✉ 7 Carré du Port, ☎ 04-94-58-34-94) you can take a diving class, hire a guide, rent diving equipment, and refill scuba tanks.

AIX, MARSEILLE, AND THE CENTRAL COAST A TO Z

Arriving and Departing

By Car

The A6/A7 toll expressway (*péage*) channels all traffic from Paris toward the south. At Orange, A7 splits to the southeast and leads directly to Aix. From there A51 leads to Marseille. Also at Aix, you can take A52 south via Aubagne to Cassis and A50, the coastal autoroute tollway; running parallel but closer to the water is the slow (but occasionally scenic) highway D559. Either of these will give you access to the coastal towns (Bandol, Toulon), inland sights (Le Castellet, Ollioules), and the Giens Peninsula for ferries to the Iles d'Hyères.

By Plane

Marseille has the second-largest airport in France, in **Marignane** (☎ 04–42–14–14–14), about 20 km (12 mi) northwest of the city center. Regular flights come in daily from Paris and London. In summer Delta Airlines flies direct from New York to Nice (about 190 km [118 mi] from Marseille and about 150 km [93 mi] from Toulon).

Airport shuttle buses to Marseille center leave every 20 minutes 5:30 AM–9:30 PM daily (47 frs/€7.17). Shuttles to Aix leave hourly 8 AM–10 PM (44 frs/€6.71).

By Train

Regular rail service goes from Paris and most points north into Marseille's central station. The high-speed TGV (Train à Grande Vitesse) connects Paris and Marseille in four hours. It's also easy to take a night train from Paris and wake up in Marseille (☞ Train Travel *in* Smart Travel Tips A to Z). From Marseilles it's a brief jaunt up to Aix. The main rail line also continues from Marseille to Toulon.

Getting Around

By Bus

A good network of private bus services (confusingly called *cars*) strikes out from **Marseille's gare routière** (bus station; ⊠ 3 pl. Victor Hugo, ☎ 04–91–08–16–40) and carries you to points not served by train. Aix has a dense network of bus excursions; **C.A.P.** (Compagnie Autocars de Provence; ☎ 04–42–97–52–10) makes daily forays from 2 to 7 into Marseille, the Calanques by Cassis, Les Baux, the Luberon, and Arles, leaving from in front of the tourist office, at the foot of cours Mirabeau.

By Car

Although you can see this region by train, a car allows you greater freedom to visit vineyards, to drive along the vertiginous edge of Cassis's Cap Canaille, and to explore the gorges, hilltop villages, and scenic countryside around Bandol and Toulon.

The Aix-Marseille-Toulon triangle is well served by a network of autoroutes with a confusing profusion of segmented number-names (A-50, A-51, A-52, A-55). Hang onto your map and follow the direction signs.

As with any major metropolis, it pays to think hard before driving into Marseille: If you want to visit only the port neighborhoods, it may be easier to make a day trip by train. However, you'll need to drive to visit the smaller ports and bays outside the center. To approach downtown Marseille, try to aim for the A-51 that dovetails down from Aix; it plops you conveniently near the Vieux Port, while A-55 crawls through industrial dockside traffic.

The autoroute system collapses inconveniently just at Toulon, forcing you to drive right through downtown; allow time for traffic if you're aiming for a ferry to the Iles d'Hyères.

Beautiful backroads between Aix, Marseille, and Aubagne carry you through Cézanne and Pagnol country; the N96 between Aix and Aubagne is worth skipping the freeway for. The D559 follows the coast, more or less scenically, from Marseille through Cassis to Hyères.

You can drive straight to La Tour-Fondue to take a ferry trip to Porquerolles (pedestrians-only), one of the Iles d'Hyères; you must pay for parking, day and night. But remember, don't even think about leaving luggage in your car.

By Train
Local trains departing from the main stations at Marseille and Aix make stops at Aubagne and at Station de Cassis, about 5 km (3 mi) above the village. There are local stops in Bandol, too, and even in Hyères-Plages, where you can catch a boat to the Iles d'Hyères.

Contacts and Resources

Bed and Breakfasts
Chambres d'hôtes (bed-and-breakfasts) are simple accommodations, usually in the hosts' home, with breakfast and a warm regional welcome generally included. They are mostly concentrated around Aix, the most gentrified and touristy region in this chapter. Around Marseille and the coastal towns, they're somewhat rarer.

Gîtes de France, the French national network of vacation lodging, rate participating B&Bs for comfort and lists them in a catalog (☞ Lodging *in* Smart Travel Tips A to Z). Addresses for the local listings are available through the departmental offices of Bouches-du-Rhône and the Var (☞ Vacation Rentals, *below*). Village tourist offices also publish lists of chambres d'hôtes and often rate them by objective comfort standards (shower or bath, air-conditioning, private garden, etc.). Aix's tourist office has an in-depth list of such lodgings in and around the city.

Car Rentals
AIX-EN-PROVENCE
Avis (⊠ 11 bd. Gambetta, ☎ 04–42–21–64–16). **Budget** (⊠ 16 av. des Belges, ☎ 04–42–38–37–36). **Hertz** (⊠ 43 av. Victor Hugo, ☎ 04–42–27–91–32).

MARSEILLE
Avis (☎ 04–91–64–71–00). **Hertz** (☎ 04–91–90–14–03). Both are in the train station.

Guided Tours
Two-hour **Aix walking tours** are organized by the **tourist office** (⊠ 2 pl. du Général de Gaulle, ☎ 04–42–16–11–61); tours of the old town (in French) leave at 3 on Wednesday and Saturday (50 francs/€7.62). An entirely English-language tour takes place only on Saturday (9:30 AM July–Sept., 3 PM Oct.–June). A tour of Cézanne landmarks, including a stop at the Musée Granet (and an optional finish at his Atelier), leaves from the tourist office at 9:30 Saturday morning (50 francs/€7.62); it follows the bronze plaques in the city sidewalks. You can request the tour in English.

Calanques boat tours leave from Cassis, with bullhorn commentary in French and English. Even off season there are two departures a day (around 10 AM and 2 PM). The *Moby Dick III* and the *Ville de Cassis* boats have glass-bottom views and full commentary in French. Tours include at least three Calanques and cost about 65 frs/€9.91. For specific departure times, contact **La Visite des Calanques** (☎ 04–91–06–99–35). You also can visit the Calanques from Marseille's Vieux Port on a four-hour mini-cruise with the **Groupement des Armateurs Cotiers Marseillais** (G.A.C.M; 1 quai des Belges, ☎ 04–91–55–50–09, ✎). Tours leave at 2 every Wednesday, Saturday, and Sunday(except in mistrals).

Marseille walking tours are organized by the **tourist office** (✉ 4 La Canebière); these cover various neighborhoods and take place three times a week. In July and August they leave the tourist office on Monday, Wednesday, and Friday at 10 AM. The rest of the year the tour leaves at 2 PM on Monday and Wednesday and at 2:30 on Sunday. The tours cost 40 francs/€6.10 per person and you can request them in English.

If you're feeling flush, footsore, or overwhelmed by the city, splurge on a **Marseille taxi tour** with cassette commentary in English; each taxi holds three adults or two adults and two children under 10. The drivers are selected by the tourist office and the itineraries fixed. In one-and-a-half hours (170 francs/€25.92) you'll be whisked up to the hard-to-reach Notre-Dame-de-la-Garde and Palais du Pharo; on the two-hour trip (335 francs/€51) you'll also cruise the seaside cliff called the Corniche and duck into the picturesque fishing port Vallon des Auffes. Four hours (570 francs/€87) shows you more ports, more monuments, and more neighborhoods. It's a good introduction to a huge city; reserve at the tourist office.

Even if you don't choose to hike the 12-km (7-mi) or 20-km (12-mi) loop through the garrigues above Aubagne, there's a **bus tour of Marcel Pagnol landmarks** that leaves from the **tourist office** (✉ av. Antide Boyer, ☎ 04–42–03–49–98). It takes place in July and August on Wednesday and Saturday at 4; cost is 40 francs/€6.10. Request an English-speaking guide in advance.

Travel Agencies
American Express (✉ 15 cours Mirabeau, Aix-en-Provence, 04–42–26–93–93). **Havas Voyages** (✉ 20 La Canebière, Marseille, ☎ 04–96–11–26–26; ✉ 4 av. Belges, Aix-en-Provence, ☎ 04–42–93–67–47).

Vacation Rentals
Gîtes de France is a nationwide organization that rents vacation housing, usually in homes or farmhouses with authentic regional character (☞ Lodging *in* Smart Travel Tips A to Z *and* Close-Up: The Gîte Way *in* Chapter 2 for more information). Two regional branches cover the area discussed in this chapter, so you should contact them directly. One handles the **Bouches-du-Rhône** (✉ Domaine du Vergon, 13370 Mallemort, ☎ 04–90–59–49–39, 🆁🅰🆇 04–90–59–16–75), as well as the Arles and Alpilles area. The other covers the **Var** (✉ BP 215, Rond-Point du 04/12/1974, ☎ 04–94–50–93–93, 🆁🅰🆇 04–94–50–93–90). Many of the rental houses are in the wild and pretty countryside around Aix and north of Marseille.

Visitor Information
The regional tourist office, the **Comité Départemental du Tourisme du Var** (✉ 1 bd. Maréchal Foch, 83300 Draguignan, ☎ 04–94–50–55–50, 🆁🅰🆇 04–94–50–55–51) has extensive documentation on lodging, restaurants, rentals, hikes, and attractions in the Var. Written requests are preferred, with specific interests detailed. The same goes for the **Comité Départemental du Tourisme des Bouches-du-Rhône** (✉ 13 rue Roux de Brignole, 13006 Marseille, ☎ 04–91–13–84–13, 🆁🅰🆇 04–91–33–01–82, ✎).

Following are local **tourist offices** for towns covered in this chapter: **Aix** (⊠ 2 pl. du Général de Gaulle, B.P. 160, 13605 Aix cedex 1, ☎ 04–42–16–11–61, FAX 04–42–16–11–62, ✏). **Aubagne** (⊠ av. Antide Boyer, Aubagne, ☎ 04–42–03–49–98, FAX 04–42–03–83–62). **Bandol** (⊠ pavillon du tourisme, on the waterfront, 83150 Bandol, ☎ 04–94–29–41–35, FAX 04–94–32–50–39, ✏). **Cassis** (⊠ pl. Baragnon, 13260 Cassis, ☎ 04–42–01–71–17, FAX 04–42–01–28–31). **Ile de Porquerolles** (⊠ carré du Port, 83400 Ile de Porquerolles, ☎ 04–94–58–33–76, FAX 04–94–58–36–39, ✏). **Marseille** (⊠ 4 La Canebière, 13001 Marseille, ☎ 04–91–13–89–00, FAX 03–91–13–89–20, ✏). **Toulon** (⊠ sq. William et Catherine Booth, 83000 Toulon, ☎ 04–94–18–53–00, FAX 04–94–18–53–09).

4 THE WESTERN CÔTE D'AZUR

ST-TROPEZ TO THE ESTÉREL, THE HAUT VAR, AND THE GORGES DU VERDON

Between the watercolor port of St-Tropez and the rugged red rock of the Estérel, this captivating stretch of the Riviera has drawn sun lovers and socialites since the days of the Grand Tour. The coastal highway hugs the spectacular waterfront, snaking past sophisticated resort towns as well as a staggering concentration of restaurants, high-rise resorts, gas stations, tourist traps, and beach discos. Yet just a few miles inland, picturesque Provençal villages perch above the fray; penetrate farther still and you'll be rewarded with mountain scenery and serene little towns.

A SERIES OF PICTURE-BOOK GULFS scoops into this part of the French Mediterranean coastline, less famous and exotic than its other half to the east. Above the coastline of the Var *département* (county), the horizon is dominated from all directions by the rugged red-rock heights of the Massif de l'Estérel and the green-black bulk of the Massif des Maures. Blue-green waters lap at the foot of thriving resort towns—St-Tropez, of course, but also Fréjus, St-Raphaël, Mandelieu, and La Napoule. Each vies with its neighbor for vacationers craving the dependable sun and balmy temperatures. In winter these port towns are low-key, with minor pockets of glamour provided by the occasional yachtsman popping in for coffee in sleepy St-Tropez. But in high summer masses flood the beaches, feast on the fish, fill up the marinas, luxuriate in the spa treatments, and crowd the hotels and cafés. Bored, sunburned, or regarding each other in mutual disgust, they then take to the hills—the glorious village-crowned hills that back the coast as the continent climbs gently toward the Alps.

They are a virtual subculture, these *villages perchés* (perched villages) and historic towns, which live in touristic symbiosis with the coast. To the east lie the famous, gentrified tourist towns of Grasse, St-Paul, and Vence (☞ Chapter 5); to the north rises Fayence, a definitive 18th-century Provençal town that now lives as much off its souvenirs as its spectacular views.

These towns make great day trips from the coast, though they're often dominated in high season by busloads of excursion-takers out of Cannes or St-Raphaël. But if you have a car and the time to explore, you can plunge even deeper into the backcountry, past the coastal plateau into the Haut Var. Here the harsh and beautiful countryside—raw rock, pine, and scrub oak—is lightly peppered with little hill villages that are almost boutique-free. You can hear the *pétanque* (lawn bowling) balls thunk, the fountains trickle, and the bells toll in their wrought-iron campaniles. If you like what you see and press on, you'll be rewarded with one of France's most spectacular natural wonders: the Gorges du Verdon, a Grand Canyon–style chasm roaring with milky-green water and edged by one of Europe's most hair-raising drives.

Pleasures and Pastimes

Beaches

With their worldwide fame as the earth's most glamorous beaches, the real things often come as a shock to first-timers. Much of the Côte d'Azur is lined with rock and pebble, and the beaches are narrow swathes backed by city streets or roaring highways. Only St-Tropez, on this stretch of the Mediterranean, has the curving bands of sandy waterfront you've come to expect from all those '50s photographs—and even there, the 3-mi stretch of Pampalone Beach supports no fewer than 36 restaurants and private businesses, complete with thatched parasols and beach bars.

Dining

Typical throughout Provence is a garlicky mayonnaise called *aïoli,* a staple condiment that's especially at home with a cold slab of fresh coastal fish. In the words of poet Frédéric Mistral, "Aïoli sums up the heat, the strength, and the joy of the Provençal sun. Its other virtue: It drives off flies." Made of mortar-crushed raw garlic whipped with egg yolk and olive oil, aïoli can bring tears to your eyes—and later,

JUST WHAT IS THE CÔTE D'AZUR?

ASK FOUR FRENCHMEN to define the boundaries of the Côte d'Azur, and you'll get four (emphatic) answers. Purists will insist on limiting this stellar title to the subtropical stretch of seaside cliffs between Nice and the Italian border; this the Victorian English first called the French Riviera, and all other resorts are impostors. Another may stretch his definition to embrace palm-studded Cannes and the border of the department of Alpes-Maritimes (literally, Seaside Alps). But where does that leave sultry St-Tropez? *Alors,* expand southwest to include the democratic sandy beaches of St-Raphaël, Fréjus, and Ste-Maxime and reach the elite fishing port whose name everyone loves to drop. But why stop there? After all, the sandy coast east of Toulon has unsung enclaves, and the department of Var rolls beach by beach westward all the way to La Ciotat. Yet that political border cuts short of the pretty port of Cassis—and the lovely *calanques* (rocky coves) that feather the coastline all the way to Marseille.

Keep on going this way and you'll wind up in Barcelona. Suffice it to say that the resonant appellation of "Côte d'Azur" is coveted by all the coastal resorts on France's southeastern underbelly, and its application is subject to debate. Here, we have split the difference, lumping much of the Var coast into Chapter 4 (The Western Côte d'Azur) and the whole of the Alpes-Maritimes coast (Cannes to Menton) into Chapter 5 (Nice and the Eastern Côte d'Azur). The coastline west of St-Tropez—also seductively warm, and bordered with rugged pine, fig trees, and spiny succulents—we have loosely defined as the Central Coast (☞ Chapter 3). West of Marseille spans the Rhône delta, and the Languedoc coast lies beyond (☞ Chapter 1).

to those of your fellow travelers. Never mind: Heap it on hard-boiled eggs, poached salt cod, or raw vegetables. And watch for it as a Friday lunch special, when all of the above appear in a Provençal smorgasbord.

Even more pungent than aïoli is the powerful paste called *anchoïade.* Whether spread on tiny toasts or used as a dip for raw vegetables, its base of Mediterranean anchovies provides a kick of concentrated salt and strong fish.

Another staple of the region is *pistou,* the Provençal pesto (which originates from the Italian port of Genoa, nearby). Made of the same savory blend of basil, garlic, and pine nuts ground in olive oil, pistou's frequent appearance along the Mediterranean is due, in part, to the proliferation of *pin parasol* on the coast, from which the tender little nuts are produced. Although it's often served over pasta or wrapped in ravioli, its most delicious role is in the hearty vegetable *soupe au pistou,* a soup reminiscent of minestrone.

Restaurants in the coastal resorts are expensive and often a risky investment, as they cater to crowds en passage. St-Tropez prices can be higher than in Paris. Inland, you'll tap into a culture of cozy *auberges* (inns) in hilltop villages and have a better chance of finding good home-cooking for your money.

CATEGORY	COST*
$$$$	over 500 frs/€76
$$$	250–500 frs/€38–€76
$$	150–250 frs/€23–€38
$	under 150 frs/€23

*per person for a three-course meal, including tax (20.6%) and tip but not wine

Hiking

Despite the mix of flash and glamour along the coast, the Massif des Maures and the Massif de l'Estérel are crisscrossed with excellent trails leading into rugged backcountry, often with views toward the sea. Several *sentiers du littoral* (waterfront trails) follow the water's edge along the base of the Estérel; another goes around the St-Tropez Peninsula. From the heights of the Estérel, the *grande randonée* (national hiking trail) GR51 heads into the highlands east of Draguignan, and the GR49 strikes off for Fayence, giving wide berth to the crackling crossfire on the *camp militaire* (military camp) of Conjuers. North of the camp, the GR49 continues all the way to the Gorges du Verdon, where it intersects with France's most spectacular grande randonée, the GR4. Its star trail is the precarious Sentier Martel, which goes through the heart of the Gorges du Verdon.

Lodging

If you've come from other regions in France—even western Provence—you'll notice a sharp hike in hotel prices, costly by any standard but skyrocketing to dizzying heights in summer. St-Tropez's rates vie with those in Monaco. You'll also notice a difference in decor. Though more and more coastal hotels are attempting to import Provençal style—sunny cottons, wrought-iron furniture—the look still leans toward "le style Côte d'Azur," a slick, neo-Deco pastiche that smacks of Scott-and-Zelda, Jazz-Age glamour.

Up in the hills above the coast you'll find the charm you'd expect, both in sophisticated inns with gastronomic restaurants and in friendly mom-and-pop auberges; the farther north you drive, the lower the prices.

CATEGORY	COST*
$$$$	over 1,000 frs/€152
$$$	600–1,000 frs/€91–€152
$$	400–600 frs/€61–€91
$	under 400 frs/€61

*All prices are for a standard double room for two, including tax (20.6%) and service charge.

❧ following the text of a review is your signal that the property has a Web site, where you will find details and, usually, images; for a link, visit www.fodors.com/urls.

Shopping

On quaint old-town streets and up cobbled alleys in hilltop villages, you'll be bathed in the odor of soaps, sachets, and potpourris wafting out of souvenir shops. Provence in general, but the Riviera in particular, makes the most of the flowers—especially lavender—proliferating in its sun-favored climate. The most prestigious makers of Provençal fabrics have prominent spots in the main tourist centers. And Moustiers (by the Gorges du Verdon) still makes and sells its acclaimed faïence (glazed earthenware), as it has since the 17th century.

Wine

Along the coast and into the hills above, vines stripe the fields in patchwork rows, destined for the unpretentious, all-encompassing wines known as Côtes de Provence. Even St-Tropez has vineyards, and the wild backcountry west of Draguignan bristles with roadside signs luring you into their *caves* (wine cellars) for *dégustations* (tastings). Most wines produced here are rosés with a few strong red table wines thrown in. Of the region's myriad versions of Côtes de Provence, one in particular gets top billing: the rosé of Domaine des Marchandises, produced outside Roquebrune-sur-Argens, is subtler than the usual coral pink blends.

Exploring the Western Côte d'Azur

You can visit any spot between St-Tropez and Cannes (☞ Chapter 5) in an easy day trip, and the hilltop villages and towns on the coastal plateau are just as accessible. Thanks to the efficient raceway A8, you can whisk at high speeds to the exit nearest your destination up or down the coast; thus even if you like leisurely exploration, you can zoom back to your home base at day's end. Above the autoroute things slow down considerably, and you'll find the winding roads and overlooks between villages an experience in themselves. Venturing farther north, either by the route Napoléon or D995, is a bigger commitment, and to be fully enjoyed should include at least one overnight stop.

Great Itineraries

Numbers in the text correspond to numbers in the margin and on the Western Côte d'Azur and The Haut Var and into Haute Provence maps.

IF YOU HAVE 3 DAYS

Spend two nights in 🏨 **St-Tropez** ①, exploring the city the first day and passing the second (after a fashionably late St-Tropez breakfast) in the hill villages of **Ramatuelle** ② and **Gassin** ③. Day three can be spent cruising (or in high summer, crawling along) coastal highway N98, stopping to visit **Fréjus** ⑧. Still on N98, wind around the dramatic Corniche de l'Estérel and stop to dawdle by the castle and waterfront of **Mandelieu–La Napoule** ⑫.

IF YOU HAVE 5 DAYS

Follow the three-day itinerary, using 🏨 **St-Tropez** ① as a home base for excursions into **Ramatuelle** ② and **Gassin** ③. Spend your third night in 🏨 **Fréjus** ⑧ or 🏨 **St-Raphaël** ⑨. Then wrench yourself away from the water (or the beach crowds) and cruise through the Haut Var to the Gorges du Verdon, staying over in 🏨 **Moustiers-Ste-Marie** ㉑. On day five, wind your way back down to reality, visiting villages such as **Aups** ㉕ and **Seillans** ⑮, and have lunch in old-fashioned **Cotignac** ㉖.

IF YOU HAVE 7 DAYS

Follow the three- and five-day itineraries, with one more night in St-Tropez for a scenic day-trip up to **La Garde-Freinet** ④. On the tail end, spend more time in the backcountry—a night in 🏨 **Aups** ㉕ or 🏨 **Cotignac** ㉖, for instance. Alternatively, end your trip with a jaunt east to Cannes, St-Paul-de-Vence, Vence, Antibes, or even Nice (☞ Chapter 5). A8 makes the whole coastline accessible in a day's round-trip.

When to Tour

Unless you enjoy jacked-up prices, traffic jams, and sardine-style beach crowds, avoid the coast like the plague in July and August, especially the last week of July and first three weeks of August. Many of the better restaurants simply shut down to avoid the coconut-oil crowd. Another negative about July and August: the Estérel is closed to hikers during this flash-fire season. From Easter through October the café life is in full swing; May is mild and often lovely, but the best restaurants and hotels may be crowded with spillover from the Cannes film festival.

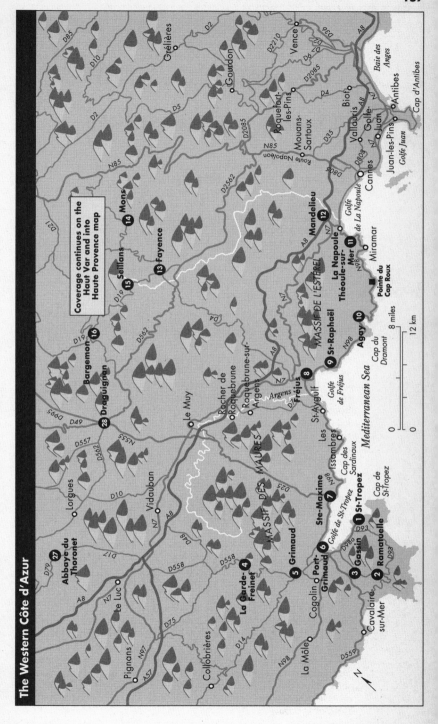

The Western Côte d'Azur

Coverage continues on the Haut Var and into Haute Provence map

- 14 Mons
- 13 Fayence
- 15 Seillans
- 16 Bargemon
- 28 Draguignan
- 27 Abbaye du Thoronet
- 4 La Garde-Freinet
- 5 Port-Grimaud
- 6 Grimaud
- 7 Ste-Maxime
- 1 St-Tropez
- 3 Gassin
- 2 Ramatuelle
- 8 Fréjus
- 9 St-Raphaël
- 10 Agay
- 11 Théoule-sur-Mer
- 12 Mandelieu
- La Napoule

Gréolières
Gourdon
Vence
Antibes
Cap d'Antibes
Baie des Anges
Roquefort-les-Pins
Mouans-Sartoux
Biot
Vallauris
Golfe Juan
Juan-les-Pins
Cannes
Golfe de La Napoule
Miramar
Pointe du Cap Roux
Cap du Dramont
MASSIF DE L'ESTÉREL
St-Aygulf
Golfe de Fréjus
Les Issambres
Cap des Sardinaux
Mediterranean Sea
Golfe de St-Tropez
Cap de St-Tropez
Cogolin
Port-Grimaud
Cavalaire-sur-Mer
La Môle
Collobrières
Pignans
Le Luc
Lorgues
Vidauban
Le Muy
Rocher de Roquebrune
Roquebrune-sur-Argens
Argens
MASSIF DES MAURES

8 miles
12 km

Route Napoléon

N

Once you move into the highlands, you won't feel the crush of summer crowds, though the Gorges du Verdon is a mecca for rock climbers
and hikers. Be prepared for late-spring and even late-summer snows
as altitudes average 3,280 ft and the region is far from the Mediterranean that warms the coast. To see the Gorges du Verdon in full fall
color, aim for early October, though the odds of rainy days increase
as the autumn advances.

ST-TROPEZ AND THE MASSIF DES MAURES

Shielded from the mistral by the broad, forested mass of the Massif
des Maures, this small expanse of pampered coastline is crowned by
the sparkling lights of St-Tropez, itself doubly protected by the hills of
the Paillas. A pretty pastel port in winter, in season it becomes glamorous "*St-Trop.*" For day trips you can escape to the simple life in the
hill towns of Ramatuelle and Gassin or delve deep into the Maures in
La Garde-Freinet. Ordinary mortals, especially vacationing families on
a budget, usually aim for Ste-Maxime, across the bay, where the hy-
perdevelopment typical of the Riviera begins.

St-Tropez

❶ *35 km (22 mi) southwest of Fréjus, 66 km (41 mi) northeast of Toulon.*

At first glance, it really doesn't look all that lovely. There's a pretty port,
but it's crammed with overscale yachts, double parking, and cafés
charging 25 frs/€3.81 for a coffee. There's a picturesque old town in
sugared-almond hues, but there are many prettier in the hills nearby.
There are sandy beaches, rare enough on the Riviera, and old-fashioned
squares with plane trees and pétanque players, but these are a dime a
dozen in Provence. So what made St-Tropez an internationally known
locale? Two words: Brigitte Bardot. When this *pulpeuse* (voluptuous)
teenager showed up in St-Tropez on the arm of Roger Vadim in 1956
to film *And God Created Woman*, the heads of the world snapped around.
Neither the gentle descriptions of writer Guy de Maupassant (1850–
93), nor the watercolor tones of Impressionist Paul Signac (1863–
1935), nor the stream of painters who followed (including Matisse and
Bonnard) could focus the world's attention on this seaside hamlet as
could one voluptuous woman in head scarf, Ray-Bans, and capris.

With the film world following in her footsteps, St-Tropez became the
hot spot it to some extent remains. The B. B. wannabes (not all of them
female)—who still strut along the port side in skintight leopard-skin,
toting leopard-collared terriers—now mix with a "BCBG" ("bon-chic-
bon-genre," or "well-bred yuppie") crowd in nautical togs and Gap
shirts (with only golden retrievers or dalmatians, please) and a plethora
of deeply tanned sixty-somethings in blazers and Gucci loafers. And
then there are the others, who come to see, snap photos, and say, "Oh,
we spent a few days in St-Tropez, though it isn't what it was. . . ." In
the heat of summer days tourist crowds are thick, gawking at the
golden boys swabbing yacht decks and perusing the array of art daubed
and painted along the port. By night, when the crowds thin and the
air softens, stylish couples make for the cafés, where they subtly preen
among others who share their creed: "One can never be too rich, too
thin, or too tan."

You're sure to see all these characters if you visit this gentrified old town—
and pay a steep price to do so. But it's worth it if you get up early (before the 11 o'clock breakfast rush at Le Gorille Café) and wander the

medieval backstreets and waterfront alone. Then you'll experience what the artists (who discovered St-Tropez before Bardot) first found to love and what remain the village's real charms: its soft light, its warm pastels, and the scent of the sea wafting in from the waterfront.

★ The legacy of the artists who loved St-Tropez has been preserved in the extraordinary **Musée de l'Annonciade** (Annunciation Museum), a 16th-century chapel converted to an art museum that alone merits a visit to St-Tropez. Located at the inner corner of the port so many painters admired, the museum traces the evolution of painting from impressionism to expressionism with works by Signac, Matisse, Signard, Braque, Dufy, Vuillard, and Rouault—many of them painted in (and about) St-Tropez. It was Signac who "discovered" the seductive light of this fishing village, using fine sprays of confetti dots to explore the vacillations of light and color on its pale-ocher houses and rippling water. Several of his port views may be on display at any given time, buttressed by those of lesser-known followers. A handful of bold fauvist paintings includes the moody *L'Estaque* by Braque, painted north of Marseille. Although there are only 50 or so paintings and a handful of sculptures, few small museums achieve such a balance of theme and concentration of quality. ✉ *quai de l'Épi/pl. Georges Grammont*, ☎ 04–94–97–04–01. ☒ *35 frs/€5.34.* ☉ *June–Sept., Wed.–Mon. 10–noon and 3–7; Oct. and Dec.–May, Wed.–Mon. 10–noon and 2–6; closed Nov.*

The **Vieux Port** (Old Port), bordered by the quai de l'Epi, the quai Bouchard, the quai Peri, the quai Suffren, and the quai Jean-Jaurès, is the nerve of this famous yachting center, a place for strolling and looking over the shoulders of artists daubing their versions of the view on easels along the water's edge. It's here, from folding director's chairs at the famous port-side cafés Le Gorille, Café de Paris, and Sénéquier's—which line quai Suffren and quai Jean-Jaurès—that the cast of St-Tropez's living theater plays out its colorful roles.

St-Tropez's 16th-century **citadelle** stands in a lovely hilltop park. Inside its *donjon* (defense tower), a **Musée Naval** (Naval Museum) displays ship models, cannons, and pictures of St-Tropez in its days as a naval port. The views from its terrace take in the whole of the gulf and the hills behind. ✉ *rue de la Citadelle*, ☎ 04–94–97–59–43. ☒ *25 frs/€3.81.* ☉ *Dec.–Easter, Wed.–Mon. 10–noon and 1–5; Easter–Oct., Wed.–Mon. 10–6; closed Nov.*

The **quartier de la Ponche,** just east of the quai Jean-Jaurès, is an oldtown maze of backstreets and old ramparts daubed in shades of gold, pink, ocher, and sky blue. Trellised jasmine and wrought-iron birdcages hang from the shuttered windows, and many of the tiny streets deadend at the sea.

You'll hear pétanque balls clicking in the sand square on **place des Lices**—together with the Vieux Port, the social center of St-Tropez. Lying two blocks inland, straight back from the quai Suffren, the square's symmetrical forest of plane trees shades rows of cafés and restaurants, skateboarders, children, and the grandfatherly pétanque players.

To experience St-Tropez's beautiful natural setting up close, consider walking the **sentier du littoral** (coastal path) around the peninsula. It's 12 km (7 mi) long and takes an average of four hours. Leave from the Tour du Portalet or the Tour Vieille at the edge of the quartier de la Ponche. Follow the footpath from Plage des Graniers along the beaches and cliffs overlooking the water, often with views toward the Estérel or out to the open sea. From Cavalaire, at the southwest root of the peninsula, you can catch a bus back to St-Tropez.

THE DOGS OF ST-TROPEZ

I **N AD 68 THE ROMAN EMPEROR NERO** had a centurion from Pisa decapitated for his Christian tendencies; to drive the lesson home for witnesses, he had the headless body placed in a boat with a cock and a dog, then set adrift at sea. When the boat washed ashore on St-Tropez's beach, the starving animals still kept their loyal vigil, refusing to touch the holy flesh.

Perhaps it's because of this heroic act of self-discipline that dogs are held in such high esteem in modern St-Tropez. They are clearly the companion (and accessory) of choice, as prevalent as mobile phones in the Vieux Port cafés. Whether tucked into handbags, strutted in pairs as beautifully matched as coach horses, dyed to match their mistress's hair, bounding nobly out of yachts, snarling at each other from under café tables, or lapping out of the ice bucket that chilled the champagne, they provide a spectacle almost as intriguing as their owners.

If you want to get the right port-front table at Le Gorille, consider borrowing a dog and accessorizing appropriately. Want to look like your yacht's being swabbed down for that lunch-run to Monte Carlo? A Lhasa Apso to match your ascot. Showing those canvases you daubed in the Alps last winter? Hot pants, hip-length hair, Timberlands, and an Afghan hound. Your bistro courting the Festival crowd out of Cannes? Green Lacoste sweater, red toupée, red German shepherd. Just drawn up a marriage contract to cover the London flat and Daddy's domain in Burgundy? Matching buckskin jackets, separate phones, and a twinned team of golden retrievers.

Dining and Lodging

$$$ ✕ **Leï Mouscardins.** Breton-born chef Laurent Tarridec has left the pétanque courts of the Bistrot des Lices for this spectacular new seaside ★ setting with 180-degree sea views, just on the edge of the quartier de la Ponche. Luckily, he's brought with him a sophisticated tradition of upscale Provençal cuisine: watch for a frothy mullet soup, an earthy *galette* (patty) of chestnuts and morel mushrooms, the house *bourride* (a fish, vegetable, and white wine stew served over bread), and tender, long-simmered veal. ✉ *Tour du Portalet,* ☎ *04–94–97–29–00. AE, DC, MC, V. Closed Mon., mid-Nov.–mid-Dec., and mid-Jan.–mid-Feb. No dinner Sun.*

$$ ✕ **Le Girelier.** Like his father before him, chef Yves Rouet makes an effort to prepare Mediterranean-only fish for his buffed and bronzed clientele, who enjoy the casual sea-shanty decor and the highly visible Vieux Port terrace tables. Grilling is the order of the day, with most fish sold by weight, but this is also a stronghold for bouillabaisse. If you're watching your pennies, try one of the reasonable daily specials, which cost between 90 and 140 frs/€13.72 and €21.34. ✉ *quai Jean-Jaurès,* ☎ *04–94–97–03–87. AE, DC, MC, V. Closed Oct.–Mar. (with the occasional exception).*

$ ✕ **Le Café.** This big, convivial brasserie on the place des Lices draws regulars for a generous plat du jour of classic bistro fare: *gigot* (leg of lamb) with *gratin dauphinois* (scalloped potatoes), salmon in juicy *poivrade* (red-pepper sauce), local seafood, and homemade desserts. Tables on the square provide courtside seats to the pétanque games. ✉ *pl. des Lices,* ☎ *04–94–97–44–69. AE, MC, V.*

$$$$ ✕⊞ **Byblos.** Arranged like a Provençal village, with ocher-stuccoed, cottagelike suites grouped around courtyards landscaped with palms, olive trees, and lavender, this landmark has undergone major renovations and changes since its days of kitschy glamour. Now it sports cool Mediterranean shades of blue and gold, and stresses fitness and beauty treatment more than ever. Chef Georges Pelissier creates artful classics with a Mediterranean touch: sea bass roasted with salsify and garlic chips, a light bouillabaisse, and rib-sticking beef tournedos with foie gras. Work on your waistline in the extensive exercise room, or sign up for a massage and skin treatment. ⊠ *av. Paul-Signac, 83990,* ☎ *04–94–56–68–00,* ℻ *04–94–56–68–01. 50 rooms, 48 suites. Restaurant, air-conditioning, pool, spa, exercise room, nightclub. AE, DC, MC, V. Closed mid-Oct.–Easter.* ⊛

$$$$ ⊞ **La Résidence de la Pinède.** This balustraded white villa and its broad annex sprawl elegantly along a private waterfront, wrapped around an isolated courtyard and pool shaded by parasol pines. Pay extra for the seaside rooms, where you can lean over the balustrade and take in broad views of the coast. Fair-sized rooms and sunny colors add to the charms of this cosmopolitan resort. The hotel's restaurant draws accolades for its herb-roasted St-Pierre (the equivalent of a John Dory, a white-fleshed fish, with tarragon sauce) and lavish desserts. ⊠ *Plage de la Bouillabaisse, 83991,* ☎ *04–94–55–91–00,* ℻ *04–94–97–73–64. 39 rooms, 4 suites. Restaurant, air-conditioning, pool. AE, DC, MC, V. Closed mid-Oct.–Mar.*

$$$–$$$$ ⊞ **Le Mas de Chastelas.** In a lush tropical garden full of mimosas and palms, set back from the main access road into St-Tropez, this 18th-century former silkworm farm offers rooms in a main house as well as a handful of apartments clustered around two tree-lined pools. Earth-tone decor, pretty stenciling, and kitchenettes make the apartments preferable to the bare-bones rooms. ⊠ *quartier Bertaud, 83580 Gassin,* ☎ *04–94–56–71–71,* ℻ *04–94–56–71–56. 19 rooms, 12 apartments. Restaurant, air-conditioning, 2 pools, 2 tennis courts. AE, DC, MC, V.*

$$–$$$ ⊞ **Ermitage.** Surrounded by mimosas and lemon trees, this big, old-fash-
★ ioned hotel stands on a hill above town and, from backrooms and garden, commands striking sea views. The fireplace and cozy armchairs in the bar, the light-bathed rooms in soft pastels, and owner Annie Bolloreis's friendly welcome make this a real charmer. ⊠ *av. Paul-Signac, 83990,* ☎ *04–94–97–52–33,* ℻ *04–94–97–10–43. 26 rooms. Bar. AE, MC, V.*

$$ ⊞ **Le Baron.** All the simple, small, brocante-furnished rooms overlook the citadelle's green park, some from tiny balconies. If you're more than two, ask for the pretty loft suite, with its private spiral-stair entrance. Breakfast is served in the cozy "library" bar. ⊠ *23 rue de l'Aïoli, 83990,* ☎ *04–94–97–06–57,* ℻ *04–94–97–58–72. 11 rooms. Breakfast room, bar. AE, DC, MC, V.* ⊛

$–$$ ⊞ **Lou Cagnard.** Inside an enclosed garden courtyard is this pretty lit-
★ tle hotel owned by an enthusiastic young couple, who have fixed it up room by room. Five ground-floor rooms open onto the lovely manicured garden, where breakfast is served in the shade of a fig tree. Most rooms have regional-tile baths, quarry-tile floors, and Provençal fabrics. If you're willing to share a toilet down the hall, five of the rooms are real bargains. ⊠ *18 av. Paul Roussel, 83900,* ☎ *04–94–97–04–24,* ℻ *04–94–97–09–44. 19 rooms, 14 with bath. Parking (free). MC, V. Closed Nov.–late Dec.*

Nightlife and the Arts

The most elite and sought-after nightspot in St-Tropez remains the evergreen **Les Caves du Roy,** a disco in the Byblos Hotel (⊠ av. Paul-Signac, ☎ 04–94–97–16–02); look your best if you want to get in. The vast

Le Papagayo disco (✉ Résidence du Port, ☎ 04–94–54–88–18) anchors the end of a commercial and residential building called the Résidence du Port, catering to a crowd of teens and twenty-somethings. The **VIP Room** (✉ Résidence du Port, just off the main parking lot, ☎ 04–94–97–14–70), across from Le Papagayo, was all the rage at press time, drawing a democratic mix of young clients and baby boomers. The scene peaks only after 2 AM, winding down around 6, and the club closes off-season (Oct.–Easter).

Every July and August, **classical music concerts** take place in the sultry gardens of the private manor house called the Château de la Moutte (✉ rte. des Salins). For ticket information, inquire at the tourist office (☞ The Western Côte d'Azur A to Z, *below*).

Outdoor Activities and Sports

Despite the hip-to-hip commerce and piped-in pop music, the *plages* (beaches) around St-Tropez are the most isolated on the Côte d'Azur, providing one of the rare stretches where your back doesn't lean up against the coastal highway. The closest to town, just at the base of the Citadelle, is the **Plage des Graniers**, easily accessible on foot. To the southwest of the port (and the vast expanse of parking lot that precedes it) stretch the beaches of **La Bouillabaisse**, in which you'll find the newly stylish private club **Golfe Azur.** But the best beaches lie on a long ribbon of white sand that wraps around the peninsula east of the center, reached by the route des Plages and its parallel fork, the route de Tahiti. From here you'll find signs pointing to the two principal beaches: the relatively unexploited **Les Salins** and the famous, highly commercialized **Plage de Pampelonne**. The 5-km-long (3-mi-long) sweep of the white Pampelonne is home to some 30 private beachside restaurants, including the dignified, chic **Moorea**, the celebrity hangout **Tahiti**, and the classic **Club 55**. Most notorious of all—famous for A-list debauches and a regular clientele of mega-movie-stars and nymphet wannabes—is **La Voile Rouge.** All of these beaches are divided into private turf right up to the waves, and you must pay an average of 60 to 120 francs/€9 to €18 per day to access their restaurants, colorful lounge chairs, hot showers, and mattress-side bar service. There are, however, a few public-access beaches between the private ones, many equipped with showers and toilets. There is cane-shaded parking sold near most of these beaches, though you might consider renting a bike for easy getaways at sundown.

Bicycles are an ideal way to get to the beach. **Holiday Bikes** (✉ 14 av. Général-Leclerc, ☎ 04–94–97–09–39) rents mountain bikes by the day or hour.

Sailboats can be rented from **Sportmer** (✉ 8 pl. Blanqui, ☎ 04–94–97–32–33).

Shopping

Rue Sibilli, behind the quai Suffren, is lined with all kinds of trendy boutiques, many featuring those all-important sunglasses. The **place des Lices** overflows with produce and regional foods, as well as clothing and *brocantes* (secondhand items), every Tuesday and Saturday morning. The picturesque little **fish market** holds forth on the place aux Herbes every morning.

Ramatuelle

❷ *12 km (7 mi) southwest of St-Tropez.*

A typical hilltop whorl of red-clay roofs and dense inner streets topped with arches and lined with arcades, this ancient market town was destroyed in the War of Religions and rebuilt as a harmonious whole in 1620. Now its souvenir shops and galleries attract day-trippers out of St-Tropez, who enjoy the pretty drive through the vineyards as much as the village itself.

En Route　From Ramatuelle, the lovely ride through vineyards and woods full of twisted cork oaks to the hilltop village of Gassin takes you over the highest point of the peninsula (1,070 ft).

Gassin

❸　*7 km (4 mi) northwest of Ramatuelle.*

Though not as picturesque as Ramatuelle, this hilltop village gives you spectacular views over the surrounding vineyards and St-Tropez's bay. In winter, before the summer haze drifts in and after the mistral has given the sky a good scrub, you may be able to make out a brilliant-white chain of Alps looming on the horizon. There's less commerce here to keep you distracted; for shops, head to Ramatuelle.

En Route　The dramatic forest scenery of D558 winding west and northwest of St-Tropez merits a drive even if you're not heading up to A8. This is the **Massif des Maures,** named for the Moors who retreated here from the Battle of Poitiers in 732 and profited from its strong position over the sea. The forest is dark with thick cork oaks, their ancient trunks girdled for cork only every 10 years or so, leaving exposed a broad band of sienna brown. Looming even darker and thicker above are the chestnut trees cultivated for their thick, sweet nuts; you're not allowed to gather them from the forest floor, as signs from the growers' cooperative warn. Between wine domains' vineyards, mushroom-shape parasol pines, unique to the Mediterranean, crowd the highway.

La Garde-Freinet

❹　*20 km (12 mi) northwest of St-Tropez.*

The Moors (Arabic North Africans defeated by Charles Martel at Poitiers in 732) created a stronghold on this hilltop, building a fortress of which only ruins remain. You can look out over the sea from there, as the Moors did, and enjoy this isolated village's quirky personality. Ramshackle but picturesque, with stacked stone visible under the ivy on some of the older buildings, it seems infinitely removed from the glamour of the coast.

Dining

$　✕ **La Colombe Joyeuse.** Those pigeon hutches you saw lining the forest cliffs to the north aren't just for sport—they provide the dinner on your plate at this novel restaurant, where the menu revolves around fresh pigeon, potted pigeon, pigeon terrine, and pigeon roasted in honey. The fauve-tone decor inside has its charms, but the terrace in the heart of the old village feels like real Provence. ⊠ *12 pl. Vieille,* ☎ *04–94–43–65–24. MC, V. Closed Tues. May–June and Sept.; closed Oct.–Mar.*

Grimaud

❺　*10 km (6 mi) west of St-Tropez.*

Once a formidable Grimaldi fiefdom and home to a massive Romanesque château, the hill-village of Grimaud is merely charming today, though the romantic castle ruins that crown its steep streets still command lordly views over the forests and coast. The labyrinth of cobbled streets is punctuated by pretty fountains, carved doorways, and artisans' gallery-boutiques. Wander along the Gothic arcades of the rue des Templiers to see the beautifully proportioned Romanesque Église St-Michel, built in the 11th century.

Dining

$$–$$$ ✕ **La Ferme du Magnan.** Just 10 km (6 mi) west of St-Tropez and 4 km (2½ mi) south of Grimaud and the village of Cogolin, this bucolic old farmhouse looms on a hillside over forests dense with cork oak and chestnuts. Whether you eat on the terrace or in the rustic dining room, the food tastes and smells of the surrounding country: snails with sharp, garlicky aïoli, mussels grilled on grape leaves, duck simmered with olives, and guinea fowl stewed in Bandol. ⊠ *rte. de la Mole, RN 98, Cogolin,* ☎ *04–94–49–57–54. MC, V. Closed Tues. and Oct.–Mar.*

Port-Grimaud

❻ *5 km (3 mi) east of Grimaud, 7 km (4½ mi) west of St-Tropez.*

Although much of the coast has been infected with new construction of extraordinary ugliness, this modern architect's version of a Provençal fishing village works. Begun in 1966, it has grown gracefully over the years, and offers hope for the pink-concrete-scarred coastal landscape. It's worth parking and wandering up the village's Venicelike canals to admire its old-Mediterranean, canal-tile roofs and pastel facades, already patinated with age. Even the church, though resolutely modern, feels Romanesque. There is, however, one modern touch some might appreciate: little electric boats that carry you from bar to shop to restaurant throughout the complex of pretty squares and bridges.

Ste-Maxime

❼ *8 km (5 mi) northeast of Port-Grimaud, 33 km (20 mi) northeast of St-Tropez.*

You may be put off by its heavily built-up waterfront, bristling with parking-garage-style apartments and hotels, and its position directly on the waterfront highway, but Ste-Maxime is an affordable family resort with fine sandy beaches. It even has a sliver of car-free old town and a stand of majestic plane trees sheltering the central place Victor-Hugo. Its main beach, north of town, is the wide and sandy **La Nartelle.**

En Route   As you cling to the coastline on dramatic N98 between Ste-Maxime and Fréjus, you'll see a peculiar mix: pretty beaches and fjordlike *calanques* (rocky coves) dipping in and out of view between luxury villas (and their burglar-wired hedges), trailer-park campsites, and the fast-food stands and beach discos that define much of the Riviera. The **Calanque des Louvans** and the **Calanque du Four à Chaux** are especially scenic, with sand beaches and rocks shaded by windblown pines; watch for signs.

FRÉJUS, ST-RAPHAËL, AND THE ESTÉREL RESORTS

Though the twin resorts of Fréjus and St-Raphaël have become somewhat overwhelmed by waterfront resort culture, Fréjus still harbors a small but charming enclave that evokes both the Roman and medieval periods. As you then follow the coast east, a massive red-rock wasteland rears high above the sparkling azure water, known as the Massif de l'Estérel. Made up of red volcanic rocks (porphyry) carved by the sea into dreamlike shapes, the harsh landscape is softened by patches of lavender, mimosa, scrub pine, and gorse. At the rocks' base churn azure waters, seething in and out of castaway coves, where a series of gentle resort bays punctuate the coastline. N98 leads to one of the coast's most spectacular drives, the Corniche de l'Estérel. And if you take N7, the mountain route to the north, you can lose yourself in the Estérel's desert landscape, far from the sea (☞ The Haut Var and into Haute Provence, *below*). The resorts that cluster at the foot of the Estérel are densely populated pleasure ports, with an agreeable combination of cool sea breezes and escapes into the near-desert behind.

Fréjus

8 *19 km (12 mi) northeast of Ste-Maxime, 37 km (23 mi) northeast of St-Tropez.*

Confronted with the gargantuan pink holiday high-rises that crowd the Fréjus–St-Raphaël waterfront, you may be tempted to forge onward. But after a stroll on the sandy curve in tacky, overcommercialized Fréjus-Plage (Fréjus Beach), turn your back on modern times and head uphill to Fréjus-Centre. Here you'll enter a maze of narrow streets lined with butcher shops, patisseries, and neighborhood stores barely touched by the cult of the lavender sachet. The farmers' market at the foot of the cathedral (Monday, Wednesday, and Saturday mornings) is as real and lively as any in Provence, and the cafés encircling the fountains and squares nourish an easygoing social scene.

Fréjus (pronounced fray-*zhooss*) also has the honor of possessing some of the most important historic monuments on the coast. Founded in 49 BC by Julius Caesar himself and named Forum Julii, this quiet town was once a thriving Roman shipbuilding port of 40,000 citizens, where Caesar had a fleet of galleys equipped to take on Cleopatra at Actium. In its heyday Roman Fréjus had a theater, baths, and an enormous aqueduct that carried water all the way from Mons in the mountains, 45 km (28 mi) north of town. Today you can see the remains: a series of detached arches that follow the main avenue du Quinzième Corps (leading up to the old town).

Just up northbound D37 from the old town is the Roman **theater**; its remaining rows of arches are mostly intact and much of its stage works are still visible at its center. The town's more impressive remains, however, are the **arènes** (often called the *amphithéâtre*), still used today for concerts and bullfights. To reach the arènes, follow avenue du Verdun west of the old town toward Puget.

NEED A BREAK?

To drink in the atmosphere of Old Fréjus, settle under the shade of the great plane trees and listen to the fern-heavy fountain at the **Bar du Marché** (✉ 5 pl. Liberté, ☎ 04-94-51-29-09). Here a *croque monsieur* (grilled ham and cheese toast), sundae, or apéritif will buy you time to watch the neighborhood putter through its daily rituals.

★ Fréjus is graced with one of the most impressive religious monuments in Provence: the **Groupe Épiscopal,** an enclosed ensemble of cathedral, cloisters, and baptistery. The early Gothic **cathedral** consists of two parallel naves, the narrower one from the 12th century (with barrel vaults) and the broader from the 13th century, with groin vaults supported by heavy pillars. The ensemble is spare and somber, with modern windows. Through the heavy arches of the 15th-century narthex you reach the entrance to the **baptistery,** which dates from the 5th century. This extraordinary structure retains the style of arches and columns that shows just how Roman these early Christians were. The bishop himself baptized them, washing their feet in the small pool to the side, then immersing them in the deep font at the room's center. Outside the baptistery, stairs lead up to the early Gothic **cloister,** redolent of boxwood and framing a stone well. There are two stories of pillared arcades, the lower ones pointed, the upper ones round (an odd effect, yet all were executed during one architectural period). The capitals on the lower pillars are graceful and abstract; the grotesques and caricatures you'd expect appear instead in the unusual and striking wooden roof covering the lower gallery, painted in the 15th century in sepia and earth tones with a phantasmagoric assortment of animals and biblical characters. Off the entrance and gift shop, you can peruse a small museum of findings from Roman Fréjus, including a complete mosaic and a sculpture of a two-headed Hermes. ⊠ *58 rue de Fleury,* ☎ *04–94–51–26–30.* ▣ *Cathedral free; cloister, museum, and baptistery 25 frs/€3.81.* ☉ *Cathedral: daily 8:30–noon and 2–6. Cloister, museum, and baptistery: Apr.–Sept., daily 9–7; Oct.–Mar., Tues.–Sun. 9–noon and 2–5.*

OFF THE BEATEN PATH	**ROCHER DE ROQUEBRUNE** – Follow N7 out of Fréjus and exit south toward Roquebrune-sur-Argens, then cut right toward this massive red-rock island looming over the Argens Valley. Rough-hewn and basically unpopulated, its pine-covered slopes provide deep-country drives and walks down primeval footpaths pounded firm by thousands of passing sheep. The village of Roquebrune and its environs provide endless possibilities for purchasing local wines and olive oil; the rosé from the Domaine de Marchandise is a cut above the rest.

Dining and Lodging

$ ✕▥ **L'Aréna.** At the edge of the old town, this slick central hotel offers gay Provençal colors, a pool surrounded by exotic greenery, and breakfast on the palm court. Too bad about the trains zipping below, but the windows are insulated and there's air-conditioning. Duplex rooms have sleeping lofts for the kids, and two rooms on the ground floor have views of the pool. The stylish garden restaurant features fish with a Provençal accent, from mullet sautéed with a spicy vinaigrette to roasted sea bass with artichokes *barigoule* (simmered in white wine with bacon). ⊠ *bd. Générale de Gaulle, 83615,* ☎ *04–94–17–09–40,* ℻ *04–94–52–01–52. Restaurant, air-conditioning, pool. 36 rooms. AE, DC, MC, V.* ✍

Outdoor Activities and Sports

Diving off the calanques between Fréjus and Ste-Maxime gives you interesting underwater insight into the marine life lurking in the rocks. Contact the **Centre International de Plongée** (International Diving Center; Port Fréjus, ☎ 04–94–52–34–99) for instruction, equipment rental, and guided outings.

The urban **beaches** draped at the foot of Fréjus are backed by a commercial sprawl of brasseries, beach-gear shops, and realtors (for sun-struck visitors who dream of buying a flat on the waterfront). The beaches outside the city, however, are public and wide open, with deep sandy stretches toward St-Aygulf. The calanques just south are particularly wild and pretty, with only tiny sand surfaces.

St-Raphaël

❾ *3 km (2 mi) east of Fréjus, 30 km (19 mi) southwest of Cannes.*

Right next door to Fréjus, with almost no division between, spreads St-Raphaël, a sprawling resort city with a busy downtown anchored by a casino. It's also a major sailing center, has five golf courses nearby, and draws the weary and indulgent to its seawater-based thalassotherapy. Along with Fréjus, it serves as a rail crossroads, the two being the closest stops to St-Tropez. The port has a rich history: Napoléon landed at St-Raphaël on his triumphant return from Egypt in 1799; it was also from here in 1814 that he cast off in disgrace for Elba. And it was here, too, that the Allied forces landed in their August 1944 offensive against the Germans.

Augmenting the Atlantic City atmosphere of this modern pleasure port is the gingerbread-and-gilt dome of the neo-Byzantine **Église Notre-Dame-de-la-Victoire** (✉ bd. Fèlix-Martin), which watches over the yachts and cruise boats sliding into the port. Those who do wish to gamble can head to **Le Grand Casino** (✉ bd. de la Libération, ☎ 04–98–11–17–77), open daily 11 AM–4 AM, which looks out over the waterfront, catering to the city's many conventioneers.

It's worth penetrating the dense city traffic and cutting inland past the train station and into the Vieille Ville (Old Town), a tiny enclave of charm crowned by the 12th-century **Église St-Pierre-des-Templiers** (✉ rue des Templiers), a miniature-scale Romanesque church.

On the same quiet square as St-Pierre, shaded by an old olive tree, the intimate little **Musée Archéologique** (Archaeology Museum) offers a quirky diversion. Its few rooms contain a concise and fascinating collection of ancient amphorae gleaned from the shoals offshore, where centuries' worth of shipwrecks have accumulated; by studying this chronological progression of jars and the accompanying sketches, you can visualize the coast as it was in its heyday as a Greek and Roman shipping center. The science of exploring these shipwrecks was relatively new when French divers began probing the depths; the underwater Leicas from the 1930s and the early scuba gear from the '50s on display are as fascinating as the spoils they helped to unearth. Upstairs, a few objects—jewelry, spearheads, pottery shards, and skulls—illustrate the Neolithic and Paleolithic eras and remind you of the dense population of Celto-Ligurians who claimed this region long before the Greeks and Phocaeans. A few of their dolmen and menhirs are still visible on the Estérel. ✉ *rue des Templiers,* ☎ *04–94–19–25–75.* ⏲ *June–Sept. Tues.–Sat. 9–noon and 3–6:30; Oct.–May Tues.–Sat. 9–noon and 2–5:30.*.

Dining and Lodging

$$ ✗ **La Bouillabaisse.** Enter through the beaded curtain covering the open doorway to a wood-paneled room decked out with starfish and the mounted head of a swordfish. This classic hole-in-the-wall has a brief, straightforward menu inspired by the fish markets in the neighborhood. You might have the half lobster with spicy *rouille* (peppers and garlic whipped with olive oil), the seafood-stuffed paella, or the generous house bouillabaisse. ✉ *50 pl. Victor-Hugo,* ☎ *04–94–95–03–57. AE, MC, V. Closed Mon.*

$$$ ⌂ **Excelsior.** This urban hotel has been under the careful management of one family for three generations. Its combination of straightforward comforts and a waterfront position in the center of town attract a regular clientele. Rooms are plush and pastel, bathrooms reasonably up to date. The café and restaurant attract nonguests for dependable fare and sea views. ✉ *Next to Le Grand Casino on the promenade Coty, 83700,* ☎ *04–94–95–02–42,* 📠 *04–94–95–33–82. 36 rooms. Restaurant, café, air-conditioning. AE, DC, MC, V.* ⌘

$ ⌂ **Le Thimotée.** The owners of this bargain lodging have thrown them-
★ selves wholeheartedly into improving an already attractive 19th-century villa (with double-glazing, brightly painted woodwork, and new carpets). In the garden, grand palms and pines shade the walk to a pretty little swimming pool. They're helpful, too: they will rent you a bike, book an excursion, pick you up at the train station, and give you seconds on coffee at breakfast. Though it's tucked away in a neighbor-

hood far from the waterfront, top-floor rooms have poster-perfect sea views. ☒ 375 bd. Christian-Lafon, 83700, ☎ 04–94–40–49–49. FAX 04–94–19–41–92. 12 rooms. Pool. AE, MC, V. ✍

Outdoor Sports and Activities

St-Raphaël's **beaches** form a snaking sliver of sand, starting just east of the port and finally petering off into the red cliffs of the Estérel. From that point on, you'll find tiny calanques and *criques* (coves and finger bays) for swimming and basking on the rocks.

Several picturesque golf courses are easily accessible. A green residential quarter called Valescure, north of town, frames the lovely 18-hole **Golf de Valescure** (☒ av. Paul l'Hermite, ☎ 04–94–82–40–46). Three kilometers east of town, the **Golf de l'Estérel** complex offers 18 holes surrounded by forest as well as a 9-hole practice course (☒ av. du Golf, ☎ 04–94–52–68–30). The spectacularly sited 9-hole **Golf de Cap Estérel** hovers directly over the sea behind Agay (☒ RN 98, Saint-Agay, ☎ 04–94–82–55–00).

St-Raphaël is a serious **sailing and boating** center, with nautical centers at four different sites along the coast: the Vieux Port, Santa Lucia (by Fréjus-Plage), Le Dramont (at the base of a dramatic little cape below the Estérel), and within Agay's quiet harbor. For information on boat rentals, training sessions, and diving lessons, contact the Club Nautique St-Raphaël (☎ 04–94–95–11–66).

To explore the wilds of the Estérel on foot, consider a guided **hike** led by a qualified staffer from the tourist office (☞ The Western Côte d'Azur A to Z, *below*).

Trails crisscross the Massif and are ideally suited for **mountain biking.** You can rent a bike in Agay at Mountain Bike (☒ Ferme du Grenouilley, Agay, ☎ 04–94–82–81–89). Rentals for Estérel mountain bike tours are available at Evolution 2 in the hamlet Cap du Dramont (☒ Cap du Dramont, ☎ 04–94–95–48–86).

The Corniche de l'Estérel

Stay on N98 and you'll find yourself careening along a stunning coastal drive, the Corniche de l'Estérel, which whips past tiny calanques and sheer rock faces plunging into the sea. At the dramatic Pointe de Cap Roux, an overlook allows you to pull off the narrow two-lane highway (where high-season sightseers can cause bumper-to-bumper traffic) and contemplate the spectacular view up and down the coast. Train travelers have the good fortune to snake along this cliffside for constant panoramas. It's also a hiker's paradise. Some 15 trails strike out from designated parking sites along the way, leading up into the jagged rock peaks for extraordinary sea views. (Don't leave valuables in the car as the sites are littered with glass from break-ins.) For trail maps, ask at the St-Raphaël tourist office across from the train station. There is also a *sentier du littoral* (waterfront trail), leaving from the St-Raphaël port and following the rocky coast all the way to Agay (☞ *below*); you'll see a mix of wild, rocky criques and glamorous villas.

Agay

❿ *10 km (6 mi) east of St-Raphaël.*

Surrounded by the red rock of the Estérel, as well as the growing clutter of its own development, Agay has the best protected harbor along the Estérel coast, amazingly isolated from the Riviera hubbub to its east and west. Traders from ancient Greece once used it as a deep-water anchorage. It was also near here that writer Antoine de St-Exupéry (*The Little Prince*) was shot down in July 1944, just after flying over his family castle in what would be his last mission.

Théoule-sur-Mer

⑪ *21 km (13 mi) northeast of Agay, 2 km (1 mi) south of La Napoule.*

Tucked into a tiny bay on the Golfe de Napoule, Théoule seems far removed from the major resorts around it. A sliver of beach, a few shops and villas, and magnificent views toward Cannes make it a pleasant home base for forays along the coast.

Dining

$–$$ ✕ **Nino's.** At the far southeast tip of Théoule's miniature bay, this unpretentious pizzeria serves simple Italian specialties—but oh, what a setting. A few tables line a wooden "boathouse" porch directly over the lapping water, and at night the whole glittering necklace of Cannes reflects its luxurious glow over the bay. Good wood-oven pizzas and pastas add superfluous pleasure. *6 chemin Débarcadère,* ☎ *04–92–97–61–11. MC, V. Closed Oct.–Apr.*

Mandelieu–La Napoule

⑫ *32 km (20 mi) northeast of St-Raphaël, 8 km (5 mi) southwest of Cannes.*

La Napoule is the small, old-fashioned port village, Mandelieu the big-fish resort town that devoured it. You can visit Mandelieu for a golf-and-sailing retreat, with its marinas full of luxury yachts and lovely, low-slung golf course shaded by a veritable forest of parasol pines. La Napoule offers the requisite quaintness, ideal for a port-side stroll, casual meal, beach siesta, or visit to its peculiar castle. Unless you're here for the sun-and-surf, however, these twinned towns mostly serve as a home base for outings to Cannes, Antibes, and the Estérel. In fact, the easternmost beach in Mandelieu dovetails with the first, most democratic beaches of its glamorous neighbor, Cannes (☞ Chapter 5).

The **Château de La Napoule,** looming over the sea and the port, is a bizarre hybrid of Romanesque, Gothic, Moroccan, and Hollywood cooked up during the Jazz Age by eccentric American sculptor Henry Clews. Working with his architect wife, Clews transformed the 14th-century bastion into something that suited his own expectations and then filled the place with his fantastical sculptures. If you visit, you'll see Clews's works in their context, as he designed them. You may also visit the gardens without the guided castle tour, from 2:30–6 March through October. ⊠ *av. Henry Clews,* ☎ *04–93–49–95–05.* ☞ *25 frs/€3.81.* ☺ *Guided visits Mar.–Jun. and Sep.–Nov., Wed.–Mon. at 3 and 4; July–Aug., Wed.–Mon. at 3, 4, and 5.*

Dining and Lodging

$$ ✕ **Le Boucanier.** The drab, low-ceilinged dining room is upstaged by ★ wraparound plate-glass views of the marina and château at this waterfront favorite. Locals gather here for mountains of oysters and whole fish, simply grilled and impeccably filleted table-side. The seafood, market-fresh, speaks for itself. No one interferes beyond a drizzle of fruity olive oil, a pinch of rock salt, or a brief flambé in pastis. ⊠ *Port La Napoule,* ☎ *04–93–49–80–51. AE, DC, MC, V. Closed mid-Nov.–mid-Dec.*

$$$$ ✕▥ **Royal Hôtel Casino.** As much a resort as a hotel, this modern waterfront complex has deluxe comforts on a grand scale, with a broad beach-terrace, indoor and outdoor pools, and vast conference facilities. Streamlined rooms in soft pastels have balconies and sea views

from all sides. At the informal yet glamorous restaurant-grill you can dine on such dishes as artichokes with scampi and lightly grilled *rouget* (red mullet) with kasha while you gaze out over the floodlit swimming pool. ⊠ *605 av. Général-de-Gaulle, 06210,* ☎ *04–92–97–70–00,* FAX *04–93–49–51–50. 211 rooms. 2 restaurants, bar, 2 pools, sauna, 2 tennis courts, exercise room, casino. AE, DC, MC, V.*

$$$ 🏨 **Le Domaine d'Olival.** Set back from the coast on its own vast landscaped grounds along the Siagne River, this charming inn has a Provençal feel that denies its waterfront-resort situation. The sleek apartment-like rooms have built-in furniture and small kitchenettes. Balconies, ideal for breakfast, overlook the semitropical garden. ⊠ *778 av. de la Mer, 06210,* ☎ *04–93–49–31–00,* FAX *04–92–97–69–28. 18 apartments. Air-conditioning, kitchenettes, tennis court. AE, DC, MC, V. Closed Dec.–mid.-Jan.*

$$ 🏨 **Villa Parisiana.** In the residential neighborhood of La Napoule, about 500 ft from the waterfront, this impeccably kept hotel offers simple comforts, chenille bedspreads, and a few updated bathrooms. A big balcony-terrace overlooks a jungle of a garden. ⊠ *rue de l'Argentière, 06210,* ☎ *04–93–49–93–02,* FAX *04–93–49–62–32. 13 rooms. AE, DC, MC, V.* 🕭

Outdoor Activities and Sports

The **Golf Club de Cannes-Mandelieu** (⊠ rte. du Golf, ☎ 04–93–49–55–39) is one of the most beautiful in the south of France and is famous for its 100-year-old parasol pines that shade the greens. Posh and eccentric, it features a grand clubhouse in half-timber Normandy style and ferries golfers over the River Siagne—between holes. There are two courses—one 18 holes (par 71) and one 9 holes (par 33). The golf club is closed Tuesday except July–August.

Classified as a *station voile* (sailing resort), Mandelieu–La Napoule is a major water-sports center. To rent a boat or—what the heck—charter a yacht, contact **Cayman Yachting** (☎ 04–93–93–27–67) or **Yacht Charter Egon Bender** (☎ 04–93–49–86–85). For windsurfing and small sailboats, contact **Centre Nautique** (☎ 04–92–97–07–70). Lessons and supplies for scuba diving are available from **Armand Ferrand Centre de Plongée** (⊠ Port de la Rague, ☎ 04–93–49–74–33).

Two private beaches—**La Voile d'Azur** (☎ 04–93–49–20–44) and **Le Sweet** (☎ 04–93–49–87–33)—have mattresses, restaurants, and bar service. The same fine sand can be found on the public beaches scattered between them, which provide toilets and showers.

THE HAUT VAR AND INTO HAUTE PROVENCE

The hills that back the Côte d'Azur are often called the *arrière-pays*, or backcountry, a catch-all term that applies to the hills and plateaus behind Nice as well (☞ Chapter 5). Yet this particular wedge of backcountry—north and west of Fréjus—has a character all its own. If the territory behind Nice has a strong Latin flavor, influenced for centuries by the Grimaldi dynasty and steeped in Italian culture, these westerly hills are deeply, unselfconsciously Provençal: wild lavender and thyme sprout in dry, rocky hillsides; the earth under scrub oaks is snuffled by rooting boars; and hilltop villages are so isolated and quiet you can hear pebbles drop in their mossy fountains.

The rocky swells behind Cannes and Fréjus are known as the Haut Var, the highlands of the département called Var. The untamed, beautiful, and sometimes harsh landscape beyond these hills lies over the thresh-

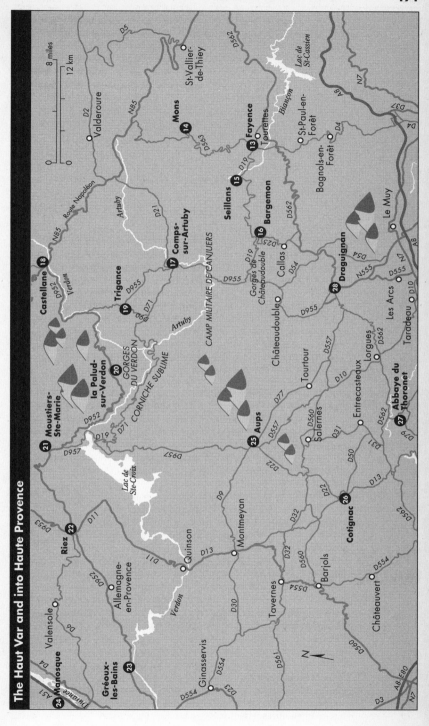

The Haut Var and into Haute Provence

old of Haute Provence—itself loosely defined, more a climate and terrain than a region. The author Jean Giono, born in Manosque, evokes its landscape as windswept and often brutal, directly vulnerable to the mistral and the winds whistling down from the Alps. Its environs include southern bits of the département of Drôme and much of the Alpes-de-Haute-Provence.

It's possible to get a small taste of this backcountry on a day trip out of Fréjus or Cannes. On your way north you may choose to trace the steps of Napoléon himself, who followed what is now N85, today named for him, on his tentative comeback from Elba Island in 1815. But if you give yourself time to wind through the back roads, stop for the views, and linger in shady perched-village squares, you may be tempted to cancel your waterfront plans and settle in for an otherworldly experience.

Fayence

⑬   *27 km (17 mi) west of Grasse, 30 km (19 mi) northwest of Cannes.*

The most touristy of all the hill towns in the Haut Var backcountry, Fayence is easiest to reach from the coast and often filled with busloads of day-trippers. Nonetheless, it has a pretty old town at the top, magnificent wraparound views from its 18th-century church down to the Massif des Maures and the Estérel, and a plethora of artisans' galleries and boutiques. If the development—villa-fication, if you will, or perhaps California-fication—that spreads wider each year along its slopes seems off-putting compared to serene Seillans or Bargemon, locals point out that it's a living town, with year-round residents and an active community life that extends well beyond tourism.

Dining and Lodging

$–$$ ✕ **Le Temps des Cerises.** Whether under the trellis at the gaily decked café tables or in the elegant, intimate beamed dining room, you'll find your *bonheur* (happiness) in this stylish, central restaurant. Fresh ravioli, truffled quail, and homemade tarts are served with surprising chic for the middle of a tourist town. Too bad about the trucks and motorcycles roaring past. ⊠ *pl. de la République,,* ☎ *04–94–76–01–19. MC, V. Closed Tues., no lunch Mon.*

$$–$$$ ✕🏨 **Moulin de la Camandoule.** On four hectares of stream-side green-
★   ery, this noble old olive mill has been turned into a lovely country inn, complete with beams, the original millwheel, and a *pressoir* (olive press) in the middle of the bar. Rooms are fresh and charming with quarry tiles, Persian rugs, and tiled baths. The restaurant serves elegant regional cooking—sea bass roasted in salt crust, quail on herbed fava bean salad, and a beef filet redolent of black olives. Half-board is obligatory in high season, so you can sightsee in the hill villages, languish by the garden pool, and then dress for your apéro on the terrace before a memorable evening meal. The relaxed, warm welcome of the Franco-British owners, whose faithful old dogs churn around their ankles, makes this feel like a weekend in a private country home. ⊠ *rte. de Notre-Dame-des-Cyprés, 83440,* ☎ *04–94–76–00–84,* 📠 *04–94–76–10–40. 10 rooms. Restaurant, pool. MC, V.* ☙

$ 🏨 **La Sousto.** Friendly, casual, and accommodating to families and bud-
★   get travelers, this cozy if spartan little old-town lodging house offers kitchenettes in every room. Mix-and-match flea-market furniture is backed by whitewashed stucco and polished quarry tiles; some rooms have showers in the kitchen. Room 4 has separate bedrooms and a dining room; Room 5 has a roof terrace overlooking the valley, where you can shower outdoors if you choose. ⊠ *pl. du Paty, 83440,* ☎ *04–94–76–02–16. 6 rooms. Kitchenettes. MC, V.*

Outdoor Activities and Sports

Because of its strategic position over the broad valley slope to the sea, Fayence is a mecca for hang gliders. Anxious to leap into the void yourself? Contact the **Centre de Vol à Voile de Fayence** (Fayence Hang Gliding Center; ✉ quai Malvoisin, ☎ 04–94–76–00–68). Also available are rides in glider planes, which are dragged by small prop planes into the heights and then released to free-wheel over the forested hills and valley.

Mons

⑭ *15 km (9 mi) north of Fayence, 46 km (28 ½ mi) west of Grasse, 44 km (27 mi) northwest of Cannes.*

Prettier than Fayence but just that much harder to reach, this serene hilltop village stands neatly framed on the flat top of a high plateau. The breadth of its magnificent views contrasts vividly with its tidy, self-contained houses, turned inward on a warp and woof of tiny streets, dipping under arches and through arcades, ducking into courts and up cobbled steps. It's easy to see how the plague overtook this intimate enclave more than once; and it's just as easy to see why, today, Mons (pronounced *mohnss*) is a popular summer-home retreat, not gentrified but quietly colonized. There are almost no shops and only one restaurant, but be sure to stop into the church to see its fabulous Baroque altarpieces, entirely covered in gold leaf.

Seillans

⑮ *7 km (4½ mi) northwest of Fayence, 36 km (22 mi) northwest of Cannes.*

With its ruined château and ramparts, fountains, flowers, and sunny maze of steeply raked cobblestone streets that suddenly break open over valley views, this is a charming old village that still smacks of the Côte d'Azur. Its church—a Renaissance remake of an 11th-century structure—is the best site for admiring the panorama; it's worth a pause to take in the musty Latin atmosphere. There are old-style, competitive bakers here, and an active café life on a miniature scale. The French opera composer Gounod and the surrealist Max Ernst were regulars in Seillans; Ernst retired here.

Just east of town on the route de Fayence is the Romanesque chapel **Notre-Dame-de-l'Ormeau,** which contains a remarkable altarpiece dating from the 16th century. Sculpted portraits of the wise men and shepherds adoring the Christ child, strikingly real in emotion and gesture, contrast sharply with the simple ex-votos that pepper the walls. ✉ *rte. de Fayence.* ◷ *Sun. 10:30–6.*

Dining and Lodging

$–$$ ✕ **La Chirane.** With a handful of parasoled tables perched on the side-
★ walk high over the old-town slopes, this looks like any old tourist stop at first glance. But crisp, creative pizzas (such as fresh roasted eggplant with tangy blue cheese), light raviolis, a hefty herring gratin, subtle stewed salt cod, and deliciously seasoned *daubes* (stews) show that the owners care about the food they prepare—and serve it with mellow smiles. Feel free to eat a one-course lunch, or settle into the tiny vaulted stone dining room for a more leisurely meal. Homemade tarts and fresh omelette *norvegienne* (baked alaska) round out an easy, pleasant meal à la Provençal. There's live jazz some Saturday nights. ✉ *4 rue de l'Hospice, 83440,* ☎ *04–94–76–96–20. MC, V. No lunch Wed. and Nov.–mid-Dec., Jan.–mid-Mar.*

$ X🏨 **Deux Rocs.** Picture a tiny square with a trickling fountain, ven-
★   erable plane trees, green valley views, and two massive rocks posing,
sculpturelike, where they fell aeons ago. This is a magical place for a
hotel. It's almost gilding the lily that the hotel should be small and personal to the point of eccentricity. From the fireplace in the salon to the
bright, mixed fabrics in the rooms to the dainty breakfast, this property exudes Provençal style. All bathrooms have been smartened up
with fresh tile and updated fixtures. Ask for Room 10, which offers
corner views of the idyllic place. At press time the kitchen was between
chefs, but guests can enjoy a lavish international brunch (daily except
Tuesday) or a generous tea break (complete with savory tarts and salads) in the romantic stone-and-beam restaurant or under the trees by
the fountain. ⊠ *pl. Font d'Amont, 83440,* ☎ *04–94–76–87–32,* FAX
04–94–76–88–68. 14 rooms. Restaurant. MC, V.

Bargemon

🔟   *13 km (8 mi) west of Seillans, 25 km (15½ mi) northeast of Draguignan, 49 km (30 mi) northwest of Cannes.*

By the time you reach this hill village, you'll feel the Côte d'Azur drop-
ping away and the highland winds curling over the mountains: Suddenly
you'll stop craving bouillabaisse and start thinking about trout. A few
mimosas and orange trees remain, but this is a mountain town, a cold
stone bastion of medieval strength surrounded by traces of ramparts. Its
ruined château, cobbled streets, and stone arches are softened by the fountains and plane trees of its slow, picturesque modern life. Settle into a
café or restaurant and climb its few back streets, and you'll feel your blood
pressure ease back. Study the ex-votos and the miraculous Virgin in Notre
Dame de Montaigu, just up from the central crossroads. Then step into
the imposing Gothic portal of Église Saint-Etienne, built into the village
walls. When your eyes adjust, search out the two exquisite angels at the
main altar, sculpted by Marseille artist/architect Pierre Puget.

Dining

$$ X **Chez Pierrot.** Inside, the cottage beams, lace curtains, and oversize
Armagnac on prominent display take you back to another, stuffier era,
as do the courtly service and classic cuisine (beef stew with olives, local
rabbit, and buttery trout). But sit at a table out front under the plane
trees, listen to the splashing fountain and chiming church tower, and
you'll understand why time stands still in Bargemon. ⊠ *pl. Philippe-
Chauvier,* ☎ *04–94–76–62–19. MC, V. Closed Mon. No dinner Sun.*

En Route   If you're feeling intrepid or you love the primeval, follow tiny D25,
which winds north from Bargemon. As you leave the olive groves and
lemon trees behind and approach the rocky, scrub-flecked highlands,
you'll cross the **Col du Bel-Homme** (Handsome Man Pass); it's only 3,120
ft above sea level, but it's a watershed of sorts between vastly differ-
ent terrains. From here you can take in the full panorama of the coast-
line and the blank blue horizon of the sea. Next, cross the barren,
quarantined **Camp Militaire de Canjuers,** riddled with tank trails and
crackling with distant gunfire; you are strongly advised not to leave
the road. The camp lies on land requisitioned from Var farmers in the
'70s, whose family *mas* (farmhouses) were used for artillery practice.
Gaping ruins pepper the arid hills. Ironically, the military camp has
preserved the dramatic landscape, abandoned but for flowing masses
of sheep and a few stone ghost towns. If you're inclined, you can cross
D21 and continue north briefly up to the noble little hill village of
Bargèmes, at 3,592 ft the highest in the Var. A bastion of fortified power
in the 16th century, nothing remains of the village but a few artfully
restored ruins and superb views.

Comps-sur-Artuby

⑰ *24 km (15 mi) northwest of Bargemon via Col du Bel-Homme, 26 km (16 mi) north of Draguignan.*

With D21 connecting from the Route Napoléon and D955 leading up from Draguignan and the coast, tiny Comps has long been something of a crossroads for travelers en route to the Gorges du Verdon. From here you can veer northwest on D71 and head for the famous south bank of the gorges, called the Route de la Corniche Sublime (☞ Moustiers-Ste-Marie, *below*). Lost in the isolated hills, with a few artisans' shops, it's mostly a pit stop for fuel and a memorable meal from another era.

Dining and Lodging

$-$$ ✕☒ **Grand Hôtel Bain.** A stagecoach stopover since 1737, this plain,
★   old-fashioned restaurant and hotel has been run by the same family for eight generations, with the chef's toque passing from father to son. Its broad back dining room overlooks the hills and valleys, and travelers in hunter's lodens, biker's spandex, and trailer-tour sweat suits equally enjoy the feasts of down-home, traditional fare. From the vast regional menu overseen by young Arnaud Bain, look for hearty herbed stew, roast rabbit and mountain lamb, tripe, and homemade cannelloni, followed by local cheeses and enormous homemade desserts. Truffles are a specialty, although the culinary level is considerably less lofty. Comfortable but simple rooms upstairs hark back to the '60s but are tidy and well-scrubbed. Many take in valley views. ⊠ *Off D21 in village center, 83840,* ☎ *04–94–76–90–06,* ℻ *04–94–76–92–24. 18 rooms. MC, V.*

Castellane

⑱ *26 km (16 km) north of Comps-sur-Artuby, 64 km (40 mi) northwest of Grasse, 81 km (50 mi) northwest of Cannes.*

Another juncture flanked by scenic roads, including the Route Napoléon, and a gateway to the Gorges du Verdon, this old-fashioned mountain town draws hikers, fishermen, and nature lovers. Its setting is extraordinary—curled around the roaring Verdon River and backed by a sheer rock cliff nearly 675 ft high—and its old-town streets are pleasant for strolling. In place Marcel-Sauvaire, the town's main rendezvous point, cafés, restaurants, and hotels encircle a splashing fountain.

If you like a challenge, consider climbing the trail that zigzags up the cliff face, past ruins of the original Roman settlement, to the top. Here stands the eagle's nest **Chapelle Notre-Dame-du-Roc,** an 18th-century shrine crowned with an overscaled Virgin and lined with ex-votos left by the pilgrims who made this penitential climb before you.

Trigance

⑲ *18 km (11 mi) southwest of Castellane, 90 km (56 mi) northwest of Cannes.*

With a handful of gray-stone houses and a few artists' studios, this infinitesimal hill village between Comps-sur-Artuby and the Gorges du Verdon wouldn't merit more than a glance from the road but for its extraordinary medieval **Château de Trigance.** The castle was restored with a free hand and open purse by Jean-Claude Thomas, who bought it in 1971 and had it rebuilt stone by stone; it functions as a hotel-restaurant today.

LA TRANSHUMANCE

IT **HAPPENS THROUGHOUT JUNE** for travelers in Haute Provence. Picture yourself sitting in a village café, hiking the arid hills, or perhaps driving around a tight switchback, when you suddenly hear the faint, ephemeral tonking-and-clonking of bells. Then, like lava pouring from a limitless source, come the sheep, in vast curving masses of fleece and a cacophony of bleats and baaahs. By the hundreds they flow, two thousandfold. Solemn shepherds in safety orange trudge beside them, guiding the eddies and whorls of wool. Onlookers gape, children reach out tentative hands. Can this be the 21st century, or is it a wrinkle in time?

It is the transhumance, the ancient, imperative spring ritual of guiding the herds from the dry lowlands to the juicy green meadows of the Alps. There they will gorge on mountain flowers until, fat and healthy, they descend back down again in autumn. The best ewes return year after year; the rest head for the dinner table as sizzling, herb-savory lamb chops.

Sheep raisers are reviving the tradition of transhumance, shunning trucks for the ways of old. To witness this primordial migration, station yourself at a Verdon-region crossroads—say, Comps-sur-Artuby or Castellane—in the early morning or late evening, when they walk to avoid the midday sun. Then watch for a wave from another world.

Dining and Lodging

$$$ ✕ 🏠 **Château de Trigance.** Here's a novelty for honeymooners and romantics: to stay in a restored medieval castle perched on a hilltop in the isolated countryside. Rooms are decked in festival style, with baldachin beds and severe oak furniture. Dine under a 10th-century stone barrel vault guarded by suits of armor and fleurs-de-lis, or on the broad terrace, wrapped by crenellated walls. Naturally, the restaurant is in the novelty-banquet business and features a hefty classic cuisine (smoked duck, oysters, quail, and lamb). Half board is obligatory, which is just as well: à la carte prices are high, and the nearest alternative can't be seen, even from the guard tower. It's a Relais & Château property but is not in its luxury class—after all, it's hard to find good serfs these days. ⊠ *Off D955, 83840,* ☎ *04–94–76–91–18,* 🖷 *04–94–85–68–99. 8 rooms. Restaurant, bar. AE, DC, MC, V. Closed Dec.–Feb.*

La Palud-sur-Verdon

㉚ *26 km (16 mi) southwest of Castellane, 27 km (17 mi) southeast of Moustiers.*

Though several towns bill themselves as *the* gateway to the Gorges du Verdon, this unassuming village stands in its center, on a plateau just north of the gorge's vertiginous drop. It's a hikers' and climbers' town, and—as the Germans and Dutch are more *sportif* than the French—has an international feel. You'll see more beards and Volkswagen vans here than anywhere in France, and you'll probably share a café terrace with backpackers clad in boots and fleece easing off a load of ropes, picks, and cleats. The friendly grocery store sells flashlights and *camping gaz* (cooking propane), and the central intersection flaunts six public telephones, the better to call a taxi to carry you to your hiking departure point.

★ You are here for one reason only: to explore the extraordinary **Gorges du Verdon,** also known as—with only slight exaggeration over another, more famous version—the Grand Canyon. Through the aeons the jewel green torrent of the Verdon River has chiseled away the limestone plateau and gouged a spectacular gorge lined with vertiginous white cliffs and sloping rock falls carpeted with green forest. The jagged rock bluffs, roaring water, and dense wild boxwood create a savage world of genuinely awe-inspiring beauty, whether viewed from dozens of cliff-top overlooks or explored from the wilderness below.

If you're driving from La Palud, follow the dramatic **Route des Crêtes** circuit (D23), a white-knuckle cliffhanger not for the faint of heart. When you approach and leave La Palud, you'll do it via D952 between Castellane and Moustiers, with several breathtaking overlooks. The best of these is the **Point Sublime,** at the east end; leave your car by the hotel-restaurant and walk to the edge, holding tight to dogs and children—that's a 2,834 ft drop to the bottom.

If you want to hike, there are several trails that converge in this prime territory. The most spectacular is the branch of the GR4 that follows
★ the bed of the canyon itself, along the **Sentier Martel.** This dramatic trail, beginning at the Chalet de la Maline and ending at the Point Sublime, was created in the 1930s by the Touring-Club de France and named for one of the gorges' first explorers (☞ Close-Up: A Tourist's Proving-Ground, *below*). Easier circuits leave from the Point Sublime on *sentiers de découverte* (trails with commentary) into the gorge known as Couloir Samson.

Dining

$ ✕ **Le Perroquet Vert.** In a restored house on La Palud's only street, a resourceful couple of rock climbers have opened an intimate restaurant over their sports-equipment shop. Think California 1970: incense, jazz, and Indian cotton in fauve colors; photos of the owners suspended over a chasm; and intense discussion of the threat of a new power line to be shaved straight through the local wilderness. The cooking is as evocative and sincere, with seafood smuggled in from coastal markets and local ingredients impeccably cooked and served by the owners: soup with tiny *favouilles* (coastal crabs), basil ravioli, and fresh goat cheese from up the road. Ask about their *chambres d'hôte* (guest rooms), which were in the works at press time. ✉ *rue Grande*, ☎ *04-92-77-33-39. MC, V. Closed Nov.–Mar.*

Moustiers-Ste-Marie

㉑ *63 km (39 mi) northwest of Draguignan, 45 km (28 mi) west of Castellane.*

At the edge of all this epic wilderness, it's a bit of a shock to find this picture-perfect village tucked into a spectacular cleft in vertical cliffs, its bluffs laced with bridges, draped with medieval stone houses, and crowned with church steeples. The Verdon gushes out of the rock at the village's heart, and between the two massive rocks that tower over the ensemble, a star swings suspended from a chain.

To most, the name *Moustiers* means faïence, the fine glazed earthenware that has been produced here since the 17th century, when a monk brought in the secret of enamel glazes from Faenza in Umbria. Its brilliant white finish caught the world's fancy, especially when the fashionable grotesques of Jean Berain, decorator to Louis XIV, were

A TOURIST'S PROVING-GROUND

To SEE THE GORGES DU VERDON UP close and personal, instead of gawking over its precipices from the safety-railed overlooks, consider tackling the Sentier Martel. But make sure you're in shape before you test your mettle—it's no Sunday-after-lunch promenade. The famous 14 km (9 mi) stretch of the GR4 follows a steep, narrow path flanked on one side by rock wall and the other by nothingness, sometimes passing over loose rubble and sometimes over slick, mossy limestone at a 45-degree rake. And those are the easy parts. One of the trail's many engineered challenges: a series of wrought-iron ladder-stairs (240, count them if you dare) bolted deep into rock cliff and suspended over the chasm below. The grand finale: two womb-dark tunnels through shoe-deep water, one of them 2,198 ft long. Yet, if you're an experienced hiker, you'll be able to take your eyes off your feet and appreciate the magnificence of the setting, one of the grandest canyons in Europe.

Because the Verdon is regulated by two dams, you'll often be confronted with not-so-comforting signs showing a human stick figure running for his life before a tidal wave. This is to warn you to stick to the trail and not to linger on the low, beachlike riverbed when the water is low, as it could rise suddenly at any moment. If you choose to peel off your socks and boots and wade during a much-needed break, keep an escape route in mind. Wandering in to drape yourself over a rock for a quick nap is not recommended, as you may wake to find your retreat cut off by rising, roiling waters. The trail itself stays above the danger line at all times, sometimes so well above it that the risk of drowning seems preferable to the risk of plunging 500 ft into the void.

The Sentier Martel takes anywhere from six to nine hours to complete. Wear good shoes with firm ankle support and textured soles. Carry plenty of water and a flashlight with good batteries; you won't be able to grope your way through the tunnels without it. Dogs and most children under six won't be able to handle the metal ladders. Follow the red-and-white GR marker, and don't leave the trail. You can arrange a taxi pickup at the Point Sublime based on a rough estimate of your own abilities, or leave a car at the final destination and ask a taxi to carry you to your take-off point. Most people depart from the Chalet de La Maline, striking out on the long descent and then working their way back up gradually to the Couloir du Samson and the Point Sublime.

The spelunker/explorer Edouard Martel (1859–1938) couldn't arrange a taxi, but first penetrated the Gorges in 1896 with a canvas canoe, an assistant, and two local trout fishermen. Despite repeated attempts, he didn't manage to negotiate the full canyon's length until 1905. Before that first traverse, the only humans who knew the canyons at all were woodcutters who rappelled down the cliffs to chop wild boxwood—which was made into prosaic, unadventurous boules (lawn-bowling balls).

It was in the 1930s that the Touring Club blasted fire-escape-style ladders and catwalks along the precarious rock walls, and drilled two tunnels through solid stone. They added occasional rope railings and steps, and buttressed the trail with rock supports. But much of it crosses rubble slides that shift and change with the years, and steady maintenance can't keep natural erosion from changing the limestone profile over the years. That's why it remains a challenge worthy of its intrepid namesake.

imitated and produced in exquisite detail. A colony of ceramists still creates Moustiers faïence today, from large commercial producers to independent artisans. The small but excellent **Musée de la Faïence** has concise audiovisual explanations of the craft and displays a chronology of fine pieces. Currently housed in a pretty 18th-century *hôtel particulier* (private mansion) with a lovely *salle de mariage* (wedding hall) lined in painted canvas, it will soon be expanded into a new building. ⊠ *pl. du Tricentenaire,* ☎ *04–92–74–61–64.* 🎫 *10 frs/€1.52.* ☉ *Apr.–Oct., daily 9–noon and 2–6; Nov.–Dec. and Feb.–Mar., weekends 2–6. Closed Jan.*

With all the faïence around, you may end up keeping your nose to the shop windows, where every form (and every quality) of the Moustiers product is for sale. But the walk through town is pretty, too, though it's little more than a double loop along the rushing stream, over a bridge or two, and a peek into the early Gothic church, with its sliver windows in pre-Raphaelite hues.

Moustiers was founded as a monastery in the 5th century, but it was in the Middle Ages that the **Chapelle Notre-Dame-de-Beauvoir** (first known as d'Entreroches, or "between rocks") became an important pilgrimage site. You can still climb the steep cobbled switchbacks, along with pilgrims, passing modern stations-of-the-cross panels in Moustiers faïence. From the porch of the 12th-century church, remodeled in the 16th century, you can look over the roofs of the village to the green valley, a patchwork of olive groves and red-tiled farmhouses. The forefather of the star that swings in the wind over the village was first hung, it is said, by a crusader grateful for his release from Saracen prison.

Despite its civilized airs, Moustiers is another gateway to the Gorges du Verdon, providing the best access to the southern bank and the famous drive along D71 called the **Route de la Corniche Sublime.** (You may also approach from the southeast at Comps-sur-Artuby.) Breathtaking views over withering drop-offs punctuate this vertiginous road that's just wide enough for two cars if you all hold your breath. The best of the vistas is called the **Balcons de la Mescla,** with viewpoints built into the cliff face overlooking the torrential whirlpool where the Verdon and the Artuby combine.

Dining and Lodging

$ ✕ **Jadis.** Whether you eat at sidewalk tables on the cobbled backstreet or climb downstairs to the tiny, cool, vaulted-stone dining room, you'll get a warm welcome at this simple, family-run restaurant/pizzeria. But don't limit yourself to the excellent wood-oven pizza. Also served are fresh crudités with *anchoïade* (anchovy dip), stuffed sardines, a puff pastry of chèvre with lavender honey, fish soup, baked pastas, and hefty beef daubes. ⊠ *rue Courtil,* ☎ *04–92–74–63–01. MC, V.*

$$$$ ✕ 🏠 **La Bastide de Moustiers.** From the whole baguette and switchblade on your table to the folksy, wisecracking waitstaff and the recorded birdsong for callers on hold, this neo-bucolic inn is far from the regal realms chef Alain Ducasse commands in Paris and Monte Carlo. He's happily slumming here, like Marie Antoinette on her miniature farm, creating a Provençal country life for himself and his guests. In the green valley below Moustiers, Ducasse has transformed a 17th-century *bastide* (country house) into a sleek and luxurious retreat surrounded by olive trees, chestnuts, cypress, lavender, and even a medicinal herb garden. The cuisine, under protégé Vincent Maillard, has that Ducasse-in-the-country touch: a froth of pea soup with bacon bits, vegetables from the *potager* (garden) steamed and served with olive oil and sea salt, beef roasted in the fireplace, and regional cheeses. (The restaurant is closed from early January through early March, except for guests

on half board.) The chestnut-shaded terrace is a small paradise. Rooms have a cool and eclectic mix of antiques and country prints without tipping into the realm of kitsch, and baths are state of the art. ✉ *chemin de Quinson, 04360,* ☎ *04–92–70–47–47,* 𝔽𝔸𝕏 *04–92–70–47–48. 11 rooms, 1 suite. Restaurant, air-conditioning, pool. AE, DC, MC, V.*👜

$$ 🏨 **La Ferme Rose.** This pretty pink farmhouse, hidden in verdure in a valley outside the village, overlooks Moustier's cliff-topped old town. Rooms are simple, with an easygoing mix of '50s kitsch and country-cozy. It's a poor man's La Bastide de Moustiers and, in its own way, just as charming. ✉ *04360 Moustiers-Ste.-Croix,* ☎ *04–92–74–69–47,* 𝔽𝔸𝕏 *04–92–74–60–76. 7 rooms. MC, V.*

$ 🏨 **Le Baldaquin.** This tiny, somewhat eccentric little hotel is in a solid 17th-century bastide in Moustiers's old center. Rooms are fussy and satin-frilled, with brightly decorated all-tile baths. The light and views are serene, however, and you can hear the water trickling in the *lavoir* (stone laundry fountain) across the street. One room overlooks roofs and the hill above, another the tiny closed courtyard with a thick lilac tree. Breakfast is served in a charming little kitchen-bar with a white-washed fireplace. ✉ *pl. Clérissy, 04360,* ☎ 𝔽𝔸𝕏 *04–92–74–67–28,* ☎ *06–08–06–49–95 mobile. 6 rooms. No credit cards.*

Riez

㉒ *15 km (9 mi) west of Moustiers on D952.*

Nowadays Riez (pronounced ree-*ehz*) is modest enough, but this little market town west of Moustiers was once a Gallo-Roman colony and a bishopric up through the Revolution. Its claim to fame is its 5th-century baptistery, its boxy exterior concealing the classic octagon and ring of columns that framed early Christian baptismal fonts. This scrap of antiquity stands alone on a corner outside the town center, a padlock on its door and its interior a jumble of broken statuary. Across the street some casual Roman ruins with scattered chunks of column attest to Riez's glory days. If you park next to the baptistery, you can cross a bridge to the field where a lone quartet of Corinthian columns stand, still supporting their architrave; they date from the 1st century AD.

It's worth puttering in the old town, too, passing through one of its 13th-century gates to enter the tangle of tiny streets. Riez's importance as a church center shows in the stature of its hôtels particuliers. Among the usual shuttered cubes, a handful of Renaissance showcases stand out with Gothic windows, jutting corbel bays, and florid decoration.

En Route   From Riez, head southeast on D11 and D111 to Ste-Croiz-de-Verdon, on the shores of the **Lac de Ste-Croix.** This vast man-made lake was created by a dam in 1975; though its waters are brilliant blue-green, its banks and verdure have yet to acquire the natural lines that grace an older lake—for instance, one that can trace its pedigree to the Ice Age. Like America's Lake Powell, it has nonetheless become a center for water sports and swimming, and trailer campgrounds have sprung up around its base. Follow D71 and D49 on south to D957, which leads to Aups, or continue on D952 west to Gréoux-les-Bains and Manosque.

Gréoux-les-Bains

㉓ *20 km (12 mi) southwest of Riez, 14 km (9 mi) southeast of Manosque.*

This modest old spa town still draws health-seeking travelers taking warm-water cures, so its whorl of an old-town blooms with pretty tourist boutiques as well as modern commerce. At the top, a bold four-square **château** is under restoration; from its grounds, you can take in valley views airbrushed with lavender.

Though you may think you've seen enough of the sweet, slightly kitschy *santons* (clay figurines) sold throughout Provence, venture to the edge of town where Martine and Gérard Moine have mounted a vast, highly detailed village of their own figurines called **La Crèche de Haute-Provence.** Constructed entirely with natural materials—houses of ocher and stone, miniature twig-trees, and mossy cliffs—their doll-scale village evokes life in the wind-swept north. Archetypal characters seem to live their daily rituals—the apricot picker, the goat girl, the baker, the cheese monger, the winemakers breaking bread over a keg, the village idiot with his goofy grin. Only in the deep background do your eyes discern the central theme, as the nativity scene seems a small part of the rural life churning around it. ⊠ *36 av. des Alpes (rte. de Vinon),* ☎ *04–92–77–61–08.* ⌷ *25 frs/€3.81.* ☉ *Mar.–Dec. daily 9:30–noon and 2:30–6.*

Manosque

㉔ *14 km (9 mi) northwest of Gréoux-les-Bains, 58 km (36 mi) northeast of Aix, 100 km (36 mi) east of Avignon.*

Once the bleak, wind-scrubbed Haute-Provence home of author Jean Giono and the rural culture he documented in his early 20th-century novels, today's Manosque is far from isolated and picturesque. Since the 1970s the town has evolved into a high-tech industrial capital, complete with a flourishing nuclear power station and a sprawl of concrete-block buildings and shopping strips. An enormous immigration of laborers has swelled Manosque to overflowing, with construction spreading into the Durance river valley. Even the hilltop old town has been buffed and modernized to contain the Manosquins. Nonetheless you can stroll the central cone of the old town, browsing in modern shops and feeling an urban pulse that's slightly quicker than those of its sleepy Provençal neighbors.

Aups

㉕ *23 km (14 mi) south of Moustiers, 30 km (19 mi) northwest of Draguignan.*

Not perched but rather nestled artfully in a valley of olive groves under imposing pine-covered hills, this village (pronounced *ohpss*) spills in a graceful delta of towers, campaniles, and tile-roofed cubes. Its old town, above the modern section, echoes with trickling fountains, and the square, under heavy plane trees, remains undisturbed by tourism. Many noble old town houses remain ungentrified, and the back streets are lined with unpretentious cafés. It has ruins, too, of a 12th-century château-fort with traces of the medieval ramparts that once surrounded it. Aups's claim to fame is the truffle, rooted up from the surrounding forests and sold in a Thursday market from November through April.

OFF THE BEATEN PATH   **TOURTOUR –** At the top of a pretty winding drive of D77, the hilltop town of Tourtour merits a side trip. Perched above the valley and crowned by two châteaux, it has a central square with ancient olive trees and steep-raked streets, some covered with vaulted arcades. Views from the Romanesque church sweep down to the coastal hills.

En Route   Between Aups and Cotignac, pull over for a brief turn through **Sillans-la-Cascade.** Only moderately gentrified, it has pretty backstreets and bits of old rampart walls, but its main attraction is a waterfall, the Cascade de Sillans. An easy 20-minute stroll from the village through woods and fields takes you to a viewpoint, from which you see a thick veil of water pouring over the green cliff side.

Cotignac

 36 km (22 mi) west of Draguignan, 66 km (41 mi) northwest of St-Raphaël.

The light changing on the stone bluff, revealing pockets of ancient stairs and dwellings tucked into shadowy hollows, give this old mountain town, nestled at the foot of a dramatic rock cliff crowned by two medieval towers, a Turner-esque quality. Life in the old town below plays out in tones of tinted sepia, in the quiet Renaissance center and along the lazy, deep-shaded cours Gambetta, where painted storefronts and cafés stand oblivious to time.

Though it's possible to make a running tour of hill villages, popping into churches, perusing the galleries, and drinking a quick one on the squares, Cotignac is a place to stop, stay, listen, and live—even briefly—the rhythm of a Provençal day. It is the place to drink a pastis slowly and practice your French with the couple at the neighboring table; they're likely to live here—and to welcome your attempts. The butcher is proud of his award-winning lamb, the bakers compete for your business, and the very few galleries maintain a low profile.

Take time to stroll through the old town, an inner sanctum within Baroque gates. On the place de la Mairie, noble houses from the 16th and 17th centuries encircle a fountain and a lovely ironwork bell tower. Farther in, rue Clastre is flanked by medieval houses with shutters painted in muted hues.

If you need a concrete goal, climb up the cliff face into one of the mysterious grottoes; these ancient hollows have served as refuges and lookouts for centuries. From this vantage point you can look down over the plane trees, elms, and red roofs of the otherworldly town.

OFF THE BEATEN PATH	**CHÂTEAU D'ENTRECASTEAUX** – This long, lean château, on the pretty country roads outside Cotignac (D50 and D31), is a jewel of a sight that offers a change from the stocky medieval style in neighboring villages and deserves a side trip. Built into a forest rock wall, it was first constructed in the 9th century as a fortress, then expanded into its Italian Baroque style in the 16th century. There are vaulted galleries, a grand kitchen and cooks' apartments, a lavoir, and even a small classical garden designed by Le Notre (of Versaille fame; it's owned by the commune). The most recent owner lives on site and has been restoring and furnishing it in period style, including paintings, tapestries, and 17th-century furniture. Nearby there's also a tiny old town with a fortified church. ☎ 04–94–04–43–95. ⌨ *Château: 35 francs/€5.34. Garden: free.* ◷ *June–Sept., guided tours daily at 11 and 4–6; Oct.–May, ring the doorbell or call for a rendezvous.*

Dining and Lodging

🏠 **Domaine de Nestuby.** Set in the countryside in the family vineyards, this familial bed-and-breakfast offers a warm, personal welcome from Jean-François and Natalie Roubaud. Taste their wine and reserve a home-cooked meal, redolent of the Haut Var countryside. Pretty pastel rooms have some regional furniture. Table d'hôte dinners evoke the Haut Var countryside. ✉ *D22, direction Brignoles, 83570,* ☎ *04–94–04–60–02,* FAX *04–94–04–79–22. 4 rooms. Restaurant. MC, V. Closed Nov.–Jan.*

Abbaye du Thoronet

 29 km (18 mi) southwest of Draguignan.

This 12th-century Cistercian abbey, an extraordinary example of Romanesque architecture at its most distilled, stands in an austere, isolated valley. The purity of the structure (or severity, if you will) was a reaction in its day to the luxurious extravagance of the Cluny abbey in Burgundy. Study the dense stonework and almost total lack of wooden support and admire the near-perfect symmetry of the church's ground plan and its gentle forays into Gothic style. The cloister is stark and stolid when compared to the delicate cloisters of Fréjus and Arles. ☎ 04–94–60–43–90. ⊠ 35 frs/€5.34. ⊙ Apr.–Sept., Mon.–Sat. 9–7, Sun. 9–noon and 2–7 (3–7 on Catholic holidays); Oct.–Mar., Mon.–Sat. 9:30–1 and 2–5, Sun. 10–noon and 2–5.

Draguignan

② 30 km (19 mi) northwest of Fréjus, 56 km (35 mi) west of Grasse, 64 km (40 mi) northwest of Cannes.

Long the capital of the Var, this broad sprawl of a city suffers from intense modernization, starting with the rigid 19th-century reorganization of Baron Haussmann, who ironed out much of its charm. He spared the pretty old town, though, and it's in this charming neighborhood of shuttered houses, sculpted doors, and bubbling fountains that the animated market takes place (on place du Marché) Wednesday and Saturday mornings. At the heart of the old town, the imposing 17th-century **Tour de l'Horloge** (Clock Tower) rears up, cornered by scroll-like guard towers and topped with an elaborate campanile.

En Route If you're heading north from Draguignan toward Comps and the Gorges du Verdun, you'll pass through the **Gorges de Châteaudouble,** a deep, winding forest canyon that prepares you for the wilderness ahead. En route you may choose to cut briefly north up to the tiny medieval hill town of **Châteaudouble,** where you can view the magnificent wooded gorge from above.

THE WESTERN CÔTE D'AZUR A TO Z

Arriving and Departing

By Car
A8 provides swift, easy access to Fréjus and other towns along the coast. To reach resorts along the Estérel, you must follow the coastal highway N98 east; to get to St-Tropez and the resorts at the foot of the Massif des Maures, follow N98 southwest from Fréjus. To explore the hill towns and the Gorges du Verdon, slow and scenic roads lead north and west from Fréjus and Cannes, including the famous Route Napoléon (D85).

By Train
The main rail crossroads from points north and west are at Fréjus and St-Raphaël, where the rail route begins its scenic crawl along the coast to Italy, stopping in La Napoule and Cannes. There is no rail access to St-Tropez; St-Raphaël and Fréjus are the nearest stops. The train station nearest the Haut Var and the Gorges du Verdon is at Les Arcs, below Draguignan. From there you have to rent a car or take local buses into the hills. The scenic little **Chemin de Fer de Provence** (Provence Railroad; ⊠ Gare du Sud, 33 av. Malausséna, 06000 Nice, ☎ 04–97–03–80–80) leads from Nice to Digne and makes a local stop at St-André-les-Alpes, about 20 km (12 mi) north of Castellane, the eastern gateway to the Gorges du Verdon.

Getting Around

By Bus

Local buses cover a network of routes along the coast and stop at many out-of-the-way places that can't be reached by train. Timetables are available from tourist offices, train stations, and local bus stations (*gares routières*). Ask for information on commercial bus excursions, too; there are several day-trip tours out of Fréjus and St-Raphaël into the more popular backcountry towns.

By Car

Sailing from Fréjus and St-Raphaël toward Cannes is a breeze on A8, but N98, which connects you to coastal resorts in between, can be extremely slow, though scenic. To the north and east of this region, you break into the country, and the roads are small, pokey, and pretty. If you want to explore any hill towns in depth and at will, a car is indispensable.

By Train

A good rail network follows the coast from St-Raphaël to Mandelieu, stopping at the coastal resorts. For further sightseeing you have to resort to renting a car or taking a bus excursion.

Contacts and Resources

Car Rental

If you fly into Nice, rent your car from the airport there (☞ Chapter 5). If you take the train to the coast, you'll probably stop in St-Raphaël and can rent a car from one of the following central locations: **Avis** (⊠ 190 pl. Pierre Coullet, ☎ 04–94–95–60–42); **Budget** (⊠ 40 rue Waldeck, ☎ 04–94–82–24–44); **Europcar** (⊠ 54 pl. Pierre Coullet, ☎ 04–94–95–56–87); **Hertz** (⊠ 32 rue Waldeck, ☎ 04–94–95–48–68).

Outdoor Activities and Sports

If you want to hike the hills and Grandes Randonnées of the Haut Var, contact the following agency for information and maps: **Comité Départemental de la Randonnée** (Pedestre du Var, ⊠ rue Ollivier, La Rode, 83000 Toulon, ☎ 04–94–42–15–01). For hiking around the Gorges du Verdon, contact the **Comité Départemental de la Randonnée Pedestre des Alpes-de-Haute-Provence** (⊠ L'Ubac de Chandourène, 04660 Champtercier).

Travel Agencies

ST-RAPHAËL
Havas (⊠ 64 av. Commandant Guilbaud, ☎ 04–94–19–82–20).

ST-TROPEZ
Havas (⊠ 17 bd. Louis Blanc, ☎ 04–94–56–64–64).

Vacation Rentals

Gîtes de France is a nationwide organization that rents vacation houses by the week that are outside urban areas and usually of exceptional charm and regional character. Very few of the houses are right on the coast, as they are by definition *gîtes ruraux* (rural lodgings). For information about houses in this area, contact: **Gîtes de France Var** (⊠ rond-point du 3 Décembre 1974, B.P. 215, 83006 Draguignan Cedex, ☎ 04–94–50–93–93, ℻ 04–94–50–93–90) and **Gîtes de France des Alpes-Maritimes** (⊠ 55 promenade des Anglais, B.P. 1602, 06011 Nice Cedex 01, ☎ 04–92–15–21–30, ℻ 04–93–86–01–06). For the Gorges du Verdon, contact **Gîtes de France des Alpes de Haute Provence** (⊠ B.P. 201, 04001 Dignes-les-Bains, ☎ 04–92–31–52–39, ℻ 04–92–32–32–63). Write or call for a catalog, then make a selection and reservation. (For more information about renting gîtes, *see* Close-Up: The

Gîte Way *in* Chapter 2 and Lodging *in* Smart Travel Tips.) The tourist offices of individual towns often publish lists of *locations meublés* (furnished rentals).

Visitor Information

For information on travel within the Var département (St-Tropez to La Napoule) write to the **Comité Départemental du Tourisme du Var** (⊠ 1 bd. Maréchal Foch, 83300 Draguignan, ☎ 03–94–50–55–50, FAX 04–94–50–55–51). For Cannes and environs, write to the **Comité Regional du Tourisme Riviera Côte d'Azur** (⊠ 55 promenade des Anglais, B.P. 1602, 06011 Nice Cedex, ☎ 04–93–37–78–78). For the Haute-Provence region between Moustiers and Manosque, contact the **Comité Départemental du Tourisme des Alpes de Haute Provence,** (⊠ 19 rue du Dr. Honnorat, B.P. 170, 04005 Digne-les-Bains, ☎ 04–92–31–57–29, FAX 04–92–32–24–84). For the Verdon, contact **Verdon Accueil** (⊠ rue Nationale, 04120 Castellane, ☎ 04–92–83–67–36, FAX 04–92–83–73–11).

Local **tourist offices** in major towns discussed in this chapter are as follows: **Fayence** (⊠ pl. Léon-Roux, 83440 Fayence, ☎ 04–94–76–20–08, FAX 04–94–84–71–86). **Fréjus** (⊠ 325 rue Jean-Jaurès, B.P. 8, 83601 Fréjus, ☎ 04–94–51–83–83, FAX 04–94–51–00–26, www.ville-frejus.fr). **Mandelieu–La Napoule** (⊠ 340 av. Jean-Monnet, 06210 Mandelieu-La Napoule, ☎ 04–93–49–95–31, FAX 04–93–64–66). **Moustiers** (⊠ Hôtel-Dieu, 04350 Moustiers, ☎ 04–92–74–67–84, FAX 04–92–74–60–65). **St-Raphaël** (⊠ rue Waldeck-Rousseau, 83700 St-Raphaël, ☎ 04–94–19–52–52, FAX 04–94–83–85–40, ✆). **St-Tropez** (⊠ quai Jean-Jaurès, B.P. 183, F-83992 St-Tropez, ☎ 04–94–97–45–21, FAX 04–94–97–82–66).

5 NICE AND THE EASTERN CÔTE D'AZUR

CANNES, ANTIBES, MONACO, AND THE ARRIÈRE-PAYS

This region is the heart and soul of the Côte d'Azur. Its waterfront resorts—Cannes, Antibes, Villefranche, and Menton—draw energy from the thriving city of Nice, while jutting tropical peninsulas—Cap Ferrat, Cap Martin—frame the tiny principality of Monaco. Just behind, medieval villages mushroom out of the nearby hills, offering refugees from the coastal crowds a token taste of old Provence. Deeper into the backcountry lie scattered wild, Latin-accented mountain towns, long cut off from the chic scene below. And backing it all, looming icy white on a clear day, rise the Alps, telephoto-close behind the palm trees.

WITH THE ALPS AND PRE-ALPS playing bodyguard against inland winds, and the sultry Mediterranean warming the sea breezes, the eastern slice of the Côte d'Azur is pampered by a nearly tropical climate that sets it apart from the rest of France's southern coast. This is where the real glamour begins: the dreamland of azure waters and indigo sky; white villas with balustrades edging the blue horizon; evening air perfumed with jasmine and mimosa; palm trees and parasol pines silhouetted against sunsets of apricot and gold. Ideal as a Jazz Age travel poster, this area lives up to the image of the Côte d'Azur, which seems to define happiness itself in the mind of the world.

Thus the dream confronts modern reality. On the hills that undulate along the azure water, every cliff, cranny, gully, and plain bristles with hot-pink cement-cube "villas" with balconies skewed toward the sea and the sun. Like a rosy rash they crawl and spread, outnumbering the trees and blocking each other's views. Their owners and the renters who stream southward at every school vacation—Easter, Christmas, Carnaval, and All Saints'—choke the tiered highways, and on a hot day in high summer the traffic to the beach—slow going any day—coagulates and blisters in the sun.

There has always been a rush to this prime slice of the Côte d'Azur, starting with the ancient Greeks who sailed eastward from Marseille to market their goods to the indigenes. From the 18th-century English aristocrats who claimed it as one vast treatment spa, to the 19th-century Russian nobles who transformed Nice into a tropical St-Petersburg, to the 20th-century American tycoons who cast themselves as sheikhs, the coast beckoned like a dreamscape, a blank slate for their whims. Like the modern vacationers who have followed in their footsteps, they all have left their mark on the coast: Moroccan palaces in Menton, a neo-Greek villa in Beaulieu, the promenade des Anglaises in Nice planted with tropical greenery introduced to suit English fancies—temples all to fantasy, inspired by the sensual pleasures of sun and sultry sea breeze.

The beauty of the coast, however, is only skin deep—a veneer of coddled glamour backed by a sharp ascent into relatively ascetic heights. True, the fantasy world spills slightly inland. Day-trippers seeking contrast have transfigured the hills behind the Baie des Anges into something of a Provençal theme park, filled with historic towns and *villages perchés* (perched villages). Towns such as Mougins, where Picasso spent his last years, and Grasse, with its factories that make perfume from the region's abundant flowers, have transformed themselves to fulfill visitors' dreams of backcountry villages, and galleries, souvenir shops, and snack stands crowd the cobblestones of old St-Paul, Vence, and Eze.

But the hills and deep gorges behind this hyperpopulated region, known as the *arrière-pays Niçoise* (Nice backcountry), have a character all their own—a world apart, not only from the coastal scene but from the hill towns of the Haut Var and Haute Provence (☞ Chapter 4). Long under the rule of the Dukes of Savoy and reminiscent of Alpine Italy, sprinkled with naively frescoed Baroque chapels and eagles'-nest villages in mellow ocher hues, they remain utterly isolated and retain their unique regional essence.

You could drive from Cannes to the Italian border in two hours and see the entire region, so small is this renowned stretch of Mediterranean coast; the swift A8 autoroute allows you to pick and choose your stopoffs. But like the artists and nobles who paved the way before you, you will likely be seduced to linger.

Pleasures and Pastimes

Architecture

Despite the view-hogging eyesores sprouting all over the coastal hills, the eastern Côte d'Azur retains many of the eccentric Belle Époque villas where wealthy sojourners gave their fantasies free rein. There are Moorish-style onion domes and cupolas, Gothic pastiche, glazed-tile roofs in whimsical jewel tones, friezes in Art Nouveau mosaic, and trompe l'oeil frescoes.

These pleasure domes stand cheek by jowl with the extravagant symmetry of grand waterfront hotels and the classical rigor of broad Italian-style squares. There's Italy in the air, too, in the urban old towns, with dark canyonlike alleys flanked by ocher walls, pastel shutters, and laundry flying like medieval banners.

Baroque churches anchor every town, some of extraordinary sumptuousness and extravagance of scale; there's one on nearly every corner in the old quarter of Nice. Gothic chapels in the medieval hill towns and deep pre-Alpine valleys—Vence, Peillon, La Brigue—and in the tiny perched villages above the Tinée and Vésubie river gorges have a purity of form offset by rich, often simple frescoes; their precedents inspired modern masters to decorate chapels of their own.

Art

Apart from the sun, 20th-century art is one of the main reasons to come to this region. Renoir, Picasso, Matisse, Chagall, Cocteau, Fernand Léger, and Raoul Dufy all left their marks here; museums devoted to their work are scattered along this section of the coast. Some of these artists threw themselves enthusiastically into the traditions of the region, decorating chapels in intensely personal styles, just as their Gothic predecessors had: Matisse painted one in Vence, Picasso in Vallauris, and Cocteau in Villefranche. Formidable collections of modern masters and contemporary works can be seen in the museums of Nice and at the Fondation Maeght, on a hilltop garden above St-Paul.

Beaches

Despite its reputation as a beach paradise, the eastern Côte d'Azur waterfront is mainly surfaced by stretches of smooth, round rocks the size of your fist; from Cagnes-sur-Mer to Menton, you'll spread a towel over cold lumps instead of nestling into sand. A thin foam mattress or an inflatable one can make all the difference in a day's stay. You might consider springing for a private beach, where you can lie on a lounge chair or mattress. From Cannes to Antibes and Cagnes, there are patches of sand between the ports and rocky shoreline. A few resorts and private beaches farther up the coast have made an effort to haul in sand to cater to the expectations of swimmers.

If you're lodging inland and plan to make a day trip to the beach, leave early. Traffic on N98, from which you'll access the waterfront throughout the length of the coast, grinds to a halt as others of like mind flow in from points north, east, and west.

Dining

This sunny, sea-warmed area mixes the best of Provençal specialties with fresh Mediterranean fish, including succulent fillets of *rouget* (mullet) and *loup* (sea bass), often served with pungent garlic sauce or grilled with a crunch of anise-perfumed fennel. Along the coast and into the hills, your plate will often be garnished with ratatouille, the garlicky vegetable stew of sun-plumped eggplant, zucchini, and tomato. Zucchini flowers appear on the table, too, stuffed and fried in batter.

But the last expanse of the Riviera between the Cap d'Antibes and the Italian border draws strong culinary influence from its central city, Nice. As a gateway port intimately allied with Genoa and Liguria and influenced by input from Corsica and North Africa, Nice developed a unique cuisine that is still a part of the region's daily life. In the old town off place Garibaldi, in street stands and *traiteurs* (food shops), you can sample Niçois specialties such as *salade Niçoise,* a confetti-bright mix of tomatoes, green beans, potatoes, eggs, anchovies or tuna, and the signature tiny, shiny black olives of Nice (the real thing is a far cry from the mainstreamed international version). Equally ubiquitous is the *pissaladière,* the father of modern pizza. Its oil-based pizza crust is topped with a golden heap of caramelized onions and garnished with a smear of *pissa* (herbed anchovy spread) and a handful of olives. It's a good picnic takeout, as is a hefty *pan bagnat,* a pita-like bun stuffed to bursting with tuna, hard-cooked eggs, tomatoes, and olives.

But venture farther to find backstreet exotica: *socca,* a paste of ground chickpeas spread on a griddle and scraped up like a gritty pancake, then eaten by hand with a generous shower of ground pepper; *petits farcis,* a selection of red peppers, zucchini, and eggplant stuffed with spicy sausage paste and roasted; and sardine *beignets,* fresh, whole sardines fried in a thick puff of spicy batter, crunched down bones and all. If you're a brave culinary adventurer, seek out *l'estocaficada* (pronounce it with an Italian accent, and you'll hear its roots in the word *stockfish,* or salt cod), an ammoniac dried fish soaked and simmered with olives and strong, fresh herbs. Accompany it all with delicate Bellet, a rare Côtes-de-Provence wine produced on the slopes around Nice that rates as one of the better rosés.

CATEGORY	COST*
$$$$	over 500 frs/€76
$$$	250–500 frs/€38–€76
$$	150–250 frs/€23–€38
$	under 150 frs/€23

*per person for a three-course meal, including tax (20.6%) and tip but not wine

Lodging

In this golden stretch you'll feel the prices rise, even beyond those of the Estérel. The atmosphere changes, too. In the coastal resorts the majority of visitors seem to value proximity to the sea over cachet, and you'll often find yourself far from the land of Provençal cottons and cozy country inns. The decor here is a peculiar hybrid—vaguely Jazz Age, a little Hollywood—that falls into a loose category known as Côte d'Azur style. In Cannes the grand hotels are big on prestige (waterfront position, awe-inspiring lobbies, high-price sea views) and weak on swimming pools, which are usually just big enough to dip in; their private beaches are on the other side of the busy street, and you'll have to pay for access, just as nonguests do. That said, there are a few treasures worth seeking out—and reserving well in advance. Inland, hilltop villages feature small and quiet inns, some in the center of the old towns; rooms are priced accordingly.

CATEGORY	COST*
$$$$	over 1,000 frs/€152
$$$	600–1,000 frs/€91–€152
$$	300–600 frs/€46–€91
$	under 300 frs/€46

*All prices are for a standard double room for two, including tax (20.6%) and service charge.

✑ following the text of a review is your signal that the property has a Web site, where you will find details and, usually, images; for a link, visit www.fodors.com/urls.

Shopping

As the commercialized hilltop villages behind the eastern coast—St-Paul, Vence, and Eze—try to create Provençal atmosphere for day-trippers, the heavy-sweet smell from the ubiquitous scented-soap shops wafts through the streets (with the exception of Peillon, whose citizens wisely voted to ban boutiques). Other souvenirs include Provençal cottons (which originated around the ancient ports of Arles and Nîmes, farther west), lavender potpourris (harvested from the hills of Haute Provence), and just about anything made of olive wood. All too familiar as these charming souvenirs may be, none of them can claim roots in the coastal region.

Perfume is more this region's forte. In Grasse, bottled scents are made from the flowers on neighboring hillsides, then funneled into industrial-looking vials in its tourist-friendly factories. Arts and crafts are another strong suit. Sculpture, glass, and contemporary art in vivid colors are sold in commercial galleries lining the streets of St-Paul and, to a lesser extent, Vence. But the place to go for artisanal products—sculptures, weavings, paintings—is Tourrettes-sur-Loup, where the artists have made a way of life for themselves on the tiny, raked backstreets of the old village.

Art glass and ceramics dominate the shops in two hill villages outside Antibes: Biot and Vallauris. Biot is home to the extremely popular and sought-after colored glassware that bears its name—La Verrerie de Biot. Its pitchers, goblets, and hurricane lamps are bubbled and pleasantly heavy in form as well as heft. In Vallauris, the streets are lined with ceramicists' studios, and pottery is sold in every form, from useful everyday pieces to works of art.

Exploring the Eastern Côte d'Azur

It's easy to explore this part of the coast, and you can do it in depth without retracing your steps too often. There are parallel roads, especially along the Corniches between Nice and Menton, that access different towns and reveal different points of view. A8, which parallels the coast, makes zipping back to home base a breeze.

Great Itineraries

Whether you settle into one coastal home base and make day trips from there or move from resort to city to hill village, this part of the coast has an enormous variety of places to see. It's worth it to visit different resort towns, as each has a distinct personality and its own sights. Even on a short trip, you'll want to make a foray into the hills to see one of the famous perched villages; you can visit one or two in an easy day trip, but a night or two in the backcountry offers a pleasant contrast to the seaside. On a longer sojourn, consider making a day trip—or a lengthier exploration—into the hills toward the Alps.

Numbers in the text correspond to numbers in the margin and on the Eastern Côte d'Azur, Cannes, Nice, and Monaco maps.

IF YOU HAVE 3 DAYS

Choose one waterfront resort town—🔟 **Cannes** ①–⑧, 🔟 **Antibes** ⑭, 🔟 **Villefranche-sur-Mer** ㊴, or 🔟 **Menton** ㉗—as your home base for three nights. Settle into the Mediterranean pace on your first day and explore your chosen town. For a big-city day, choose between the novelty of glamorous Monte Carlo in **Monaco** ⑥⓪–⑥⑤, with its landscaped

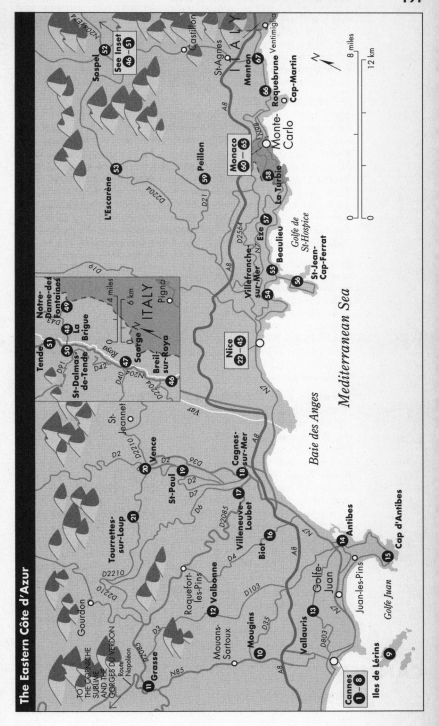

The Eastern Côte d'Azur

casino and cliff-top palace, or a tour of the old-town quarter of **Nice** ㉒–㊺, roving the backstreets and the market on the Cours Saleya and ambling along the waterfront on the promenade des Anglais. Spend your third day in the hill town of **St-Paul** ⑲, window-shopping along the cobbled streets and taking in the extraordinary sculpture garden and modern-art collection at the Fondation Maeght.

IF YOU HAVE 7 DAYS

Spend two nights in either urbane, upscale ⊞ **Cannes** ①–⑧ or time-burnished ⊞ **Antibes** ⑭. Make an afternoon outing to either **Vallauris** ⑬, to see its ceramics studios and a chapel decorated by Picasso, or **Biot** ⑯, to see its glass studios and a museum devoted to Fernand Léger. Move up into the hills for a night, visiting ⊞ **St-Paul** ⑲ and nearby ⊞ **Vence** ⑳, with its evocative walled old town; spend the night in either. Then move on to ⊞ **Nice** ㉒–㊺ for two nights, devoting your second day to art museums. On your sixth and seventh days settle into the picture-pretty port towns of ⊞ **Villefranche-sur-Mer** ㊿ or ⊞ **St-Jean-Cap-Ferrat** ㊻, making a foray into **Monaco** ⑥⓪–⑥⑤ and cruising the Corniche highways, or spending a morning at the **Menton** ㊿ market.

IF YOU HAVE 10 DAYS

Split the extra nights between ⊞ **Cannes** ①–⑧, ⊞ **Antibes** ⑭, or ⊞ **Menton** ㊿, and earlier on, when you're near Vence, head on up to **Tourrettes-sur-Loup** ㉑ for a taste of Haute Provence. Add visits to the extraordinary (and touristy) **Eze** ㊼, perched right on the coast above the sea, and drive up to the quiet, boutique-free zone in the hilltop village of **Peillon** ㊾. Devote at least a day to an excursion into the wild gorges of the Alpine foothills northeast of Nice, stopping in the otherworldly village of **Saorge** ㊹ and visiting the painted chapel in **Notre-Dame-des-Fontaines** ㊽.

When to Tour the Eastern Côte d'Azur

Naturally the coast is in its tropical prime in July and August, but that's no secret, and the seaside resorts and hill towns are overloaded to bursting with sun-seekers. If you're anxious to enjoy the beaches, aim for June or September, or you could even look for sheltered spots from March onward. Many hotels and restaurants close from November to Easter, though Nice and Monaco thrive year-round. Cannes books early for the film festival in May, so unless you're determined to hover outside the Farfalla with an autograph book, aim for another month (April, June, September, or October). But there are good times, even magical times, all year on the coast. The eastern Côte d'Azur enjoys a gentle microclimate, protected by the Estérel from the mistral that razors through Fréjus and St-Raphaël to the west and by the Alps from northern winds. So with a little luck you may stroll in shirtsleeves under the palm trees on a winter day (though many places close during the off season) and even swim—if you're deeply committed. If you're counting on exploring the mountain gorges in the arrière-pays, there may be snow in this Alpine region as late as June and as early as September; the roads are kept open all winter to allow access to the ski resorts at the heights of the Vésubie and Tinée valleys.

CANNES

Backed by gentle hills and flanked to the south by the heights of the Estérel, warmed by dependable sun but kept bearable in summer by the cool breeze that blows in from the Mediterranean, Cannes is pampered with the luxurious climate that has made it one of the most popular and glamorous resorts in Europe. Its graceful curve of wave-washed sand peppered with chic restaurants and prestigious private beaches,

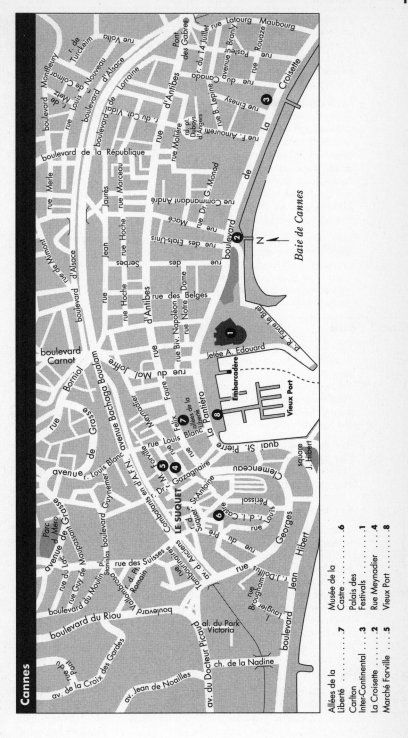

Cannes

Baie de Cannes

Vieux Port

LE SUQUET

its renowned waterfront promenade strewn with palm trees and poseurs, its status-symbol grand hotels vying for the custom of the Louis-Vuitton set, this legend is, to many, the heart and soul of the Côte d'Azur. For 150 years the mecca of sun worshippers, it has been further glamorized by the success of its film festival, as famous as (and, in the trade, more respected than) Hollywood's Academy Awards.

Settled first by the Ligurians and then dubbed Cannoïs by the Romans (after the cane that waved in its marshes), Cannes was an important sentinel site for the monks who established themselves on Ile St-Honorat in the Middle Ages. Its bay served as nothing more than a fishing port until in 1834 an English aristocrat, Lord Brougham, made an emergency stopover with his sick daughter and fell in love with the site. He had a home built here and returned every winter for a sun cure—a ritual quickly picked up by his peers. A railroad brought even more sunseekers, and by the turn of the century the bay glittered with the gaslight of some 50 hotels.

With the democratization of modern travel, Cannes has become a tourist and convention town, and the Croisette traffic jams slow 20 compact Twingos for every Rolls-Royce. But glamour—and the perception of glamour—is self-perpetuating, and as long as Cannes enjoys its ravishing climate and setting, it will maintain its incomparable panache.

A Good Walk

If you arrive by car, abandon it quickly in either the parking garage named La Pantiéro (on the port) or under the casino. Then pick up a map at the tourist office in the **Palais des Festivals** ①, the scene of the famous Festival International du Film, popularly known as the Cannes Film Festival. As you leave the information center, follow the Palais to your right to see the fountains, palm trees, and red-carpeted stairs where the stars ascend every year.

Through the palm trees and flowers and crowds of strolling poseurs (fur coats in tropical weather, mobile phones on Rollerblades, and sunglasses at night) follow the waterfront promenade known as **La Croisette** ② past the broad expanse of private beaches, glamorous shops, and luxurious hotels. The most famous of these is the wide, white-masonry wedding cake called the **Carlton Inter-Continental** ③.

After seeing the Carlton—have a drink in its see-and-be-seen terrace brasserie, or even, in season, lunch at one of the seductive beach restaurants—double back and right up rue Amouretti, through rond-point Duboys d'Angers, and left on rue Molière. Here you'll find an array of glittering big-name designer shops with prices that barely fit on the tag. Cut right up to rue d'Antibes, Cannes's main shopping street, and window-shop all the way back to rue du Maréchal Joffre. Turn right and immediately left on **rue Meynadier** ④, a lively pedestrian shopping street packed tight with trendy clothing boutiques cheek by jowl with fine food shops. Turn right briefly up rue Louis Blanc and then take a left into the covered **Marché Forville** ⑤, scene of the animated morning food market.

Leave the market via rue Dr. Gazagnaire, cut right briefly on rue Meynadier, and climb up rue St-Antoine into the picturesque old-town neighborhood known as **Le Suquet.** Wind up the steep and narrow rue du Suquet and climb the steps of avenue de la Tour to **place de la Castre.** Dominating the square is the Romanesque château known as La Castre (from the Latin *castrum*); within its chapel you'll find the **Musée de la Castre** ⑥, containing ethnological treasures.

On leaving the museum, angle down rue Louis Périssol, tiny rue de la Boucherie, and rue St-Antoine, and head down to the port, and the broad Provençal-style square called the **allées de la Liberté** ⑦, where there's a flower market every morning (but Monday). Across the road the **Vieux Port** ⑧ bobs with pleasure boats and magnificent yachts; here you can buy tickets for boat trips to the Iles de Lérins (☞ Side Trip from Cannes, *below*).

TIMING

You can easily walk this tour in a morning, or make a day of it, window-shopping, watching a pétanque game in the allées de la Liberté, or studying African masks in the Musée de la Castre. If you have an extra half day, consider the boat trip to one of the Iles de Lérins.

Sights to See

⑦ **Allées de la Liberté.** Shaded by plane trees and sheltering a sandy pétanque field (occupied round the clock by distinctly unglamorous grandfathers inured to the scene on La Croisette), this is a little piece of Provence in a big, glitzy resort town. Every morning but Monday a flower market paints the square in vivid colors.

③ **Carlton Inter-Continental.** Built in 1912, this was the first of the grand hotels to stake out the superb stretch of beach and greenery on La Croisette and thus is the best positioned. It is here that many of the film festival's grand banquets take place (☞ Lodging, *below*).

② **La Croisette.** For many this palm-studded promenade along the waterfront, backed by an imposing row of sumptuous apartment houses and hotels, is the epitome of the Côte d'Azur. Stretching from the Palais des Festivals to the eastern point that juts into the bay, it's the perfect spot to park on a bench overlooking the Golfe de Napoule, the beach restaurants serving wind-screened meals at the water's edge, and the rows of deck chairs under umbrellas advertising the luxury hotels that own them.

⑤ **Marché Forville** (Forville market). Under the permanent shelter that every morning draws the chefs, connoisseurs, and voyeurs of Cannes, you'll see showy displays of fresh fish still flipping and glossy vegetables piled high, cheeses carried down from the mountains, and sausages, olives, and flower stands. Real farmers sell real local produce here—hand-mixed mesclun, fat asparagus, cherries picked yesterday—but the whole scene is hosed down by 1 PM, so don't linger too long over breakfast.

⑥ **Musée de la Castre** (Castle Museum). In the château known as La Castre, built in the 11th century by the monks who inhabited the Iles de Lérins, this small museum is Cannes's token cultural attraction. In the vaulted Gothic chapel and a series of small castle rooms, the collection of 19th-century ethnological treasures—African drums, Asian flutes, and native clothing from America and Peru—seems out of place. But the handful of Impressionist paintings by Provençal artists shows landscapes you may recognize. ✉ *pl. de la Castre,* ☎ *04-93-38-55-26.* ☐ *10 frs/€1.52.* ☉ *Apr.–June, Wed.–Mon. 10–noon and 2–6; July–Sept., Wed.–Mon. 10–noon and 3–7; Oct.–Mar., Wed.–Mon. 10–noon and 2–5. Closed most of Jan.*

① **Palais des Festivals** (Festival Palace). This is where it all happens: When the Cannes Film Festival is in town, paparazzi jostle and crowd under the palm trees, popping flashbulbs at the glittering movie stars swanning up the broad, red-carpeted stairs to view a colleague's latest creation or, at last, to find out who has won the Palme d'Or (Golden Palm). Something of a shrine, these stairs are a popular spot for posing for souvenir snapshots. At the foot of the Palais and set into the surrounding pavement, the allée des Etoiles (Stars' Alley) enshrines some 300 autographed imprints of film stars' hands—Dépardieu, Streep, and Stallone, among others. ⊠ *East of the tourist office on La Croisette.*

④ Rue Meynadier. You may not notice the pretty 18th-century houses that once formed the main street of Cannes, so distracting are the boutiques they now contain. Here inexpensive and trendy clothes alternate with rarified food and wine shops, and some of the best butchers in town.

Le Suquet. On the site of the original Roman *castrum,* this ancient neighborhood seems to cling to the hill overlooking Cannes. Shops proffer crafts and Provençal goods and the atmospheric theme-restaurants give you a chance to catch your breath. The pretty pastel shutters, Gothic stonework, and narrow passageways are lovely distractions; take time to lose yourself awhile on the tiny backstreets, ducking under arches and peeking into courtyards. At the top is **place de la Castre**—from behind the square's Romanesque 16th-century Église Notre-Dame-d'Esperance, take in magnificent views over Cannes and the Ile Ste-Marguerite. The hill is crowned by the 11th-century château, housing the **Musée de la Castre** (☞ *above*), and the imposing four-sided **Tour du Suquet** (Suquet Tower), built in 1385 as a lookout against Saracen invasions.

⑧ Vieux Port (Old Port). Sparkling at the foot of Le Suquet, this narrow, well-protected port harbors a fascinating lineup of grand luxury yachts and slick little pleasure boats that creak and bob beside weathered-blue fishing barques. From the east corner, off La Pantiéro, you can catch a cruise to the Iles de Lérins.

Dining and Lodging

$$–$$$ ✕ **La Brouette de Grand'mère.** This tiny hole-in-the-wall, complete with lace curtains, painted-wood front, fireplace, and old posters, could be a set for one of the Festival's films. Yet it's a true-blue bistro, with a five-course menu that includes aperitif, wine, and coffee. There's chicken steamed with tarragon, pot-au-feu with beef, pork, and chicken, andouillettes crisped in sweet muscadet, and sharp-aged goat cheese. It's only open evenings and feels especially right in winter. ⊠ *9 rue d'Oran,* ☎ *04–93–39–12–10. AE, DC, MC, V. No lunch. Closed Sun.*

$$ ✕ **Auberge Provençal.** Of the plethora of slightly touristy restaurants lining the long hike up into Le Suquet, this ancient inn is most evocative of Old Provence. This is largely due to its age, as it claims to be the oldest restaurant in town, and the heavy old beams back up the claim. For maximum effect, reserve a table in the room with the stone fireplace that crackles pleasantly on cool days. In summer, terrace tables overlook the sea. Regional specialties dominate, including bouillabaisse, aïoli, farcis Niçoise, sea bass grilled with fennel, and a rich beef *estouffade* (stew). ⊠ *10 rue St-Antoine,* ☎ *04–92–99–27–17. AE, DC, MC, V.*

$$ ✕ **Chez Astoux.** For seafood, this popular spot stands out among the other restaurants overlooking the leisurely tableau of *boules* (lawn bowling), pigeons, and bandstand on allées de la Liberté. Linen-covered tables on the terrace sport showy, tiered platters of sparkling-fresh seafood, and bouillabaisse anchors the menu. You can also order seafood platters to go, with the shellfish pre-opened or not, from the same address (not to be confused with Brun, around the corner, which uses the Astoux name). ⊠ *43 rue Félix-Faure,* ☎ *04–93–39–06–22. AE, DC, MC, V.*

$$ ✕ **La Mère Besson.** This long-standing favorite continues to please a largely foreign clientele with regional specialties such as sweet-and-sour sardines *à l'escabeche* (marinated in white wine and vinegar), monkfish Provençal (with tomatoes, fennel, and onion), and roast lamb with garlic purée. The formal setting, with damask linens and still lifes,

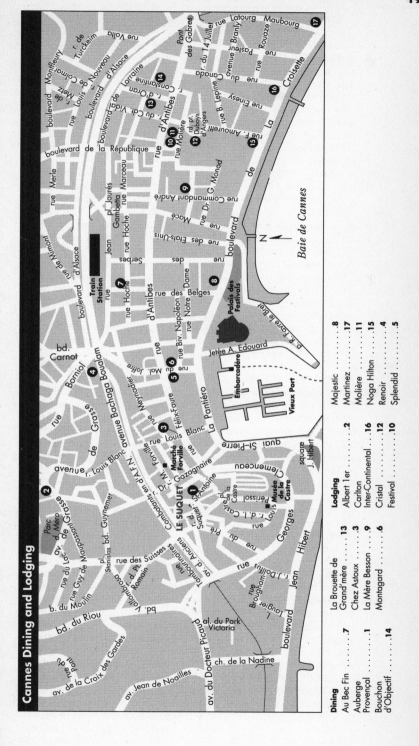

Cannes Dining and Lodging

Dining
Au Bec Fin **7**
Auberge
Provençal **1**
Bouchon
d'Objectif **14**
La Brouette de
Grand'mère **13**
Chez Astoux **3**
La Mère Besson **9**
Montagard **6**

Lodging
Albert 1er **2**
Carlton
Inter-Continental . . **16**
Cristal **12**
Festival **10**
Majestic **8**
Martinez **17**
Molière **11**
Noga Hilton **15**
Renoir **4**
Splendid **5**

is lightened up with clatter from the open kitchen. ✉ *13 rue des Frères-Pradignac,* ☎ *04–93–39–59–24. AE, DC, MC, V. Closed Sun. No lunch Sat. or Mon., though during festivals open daily for all meals.*

$ ✕ **Au Bec Fin.** Despite its spruced-up luncheonette decor, devoted regulars attest to the quality of this antichic, family-run bistro near the train station, distinguished by its steamy clatter, crowds of ordinary locals (old folks and kids, too), and homey food. The prix-fixe menus are a fantastic value for real food—grilled sardines and mesclun salad served with a liter bottle of olive oil, the day's catch grilled with fennel, and osso buco—even big, old-fashioned sundaes, a far cry from the chichi sorbets served along the waterfront. ✉ *12 rue du 24-Août,* ☎ *04–93–38–35–86. AE, MC, V. Closed Sun.*

$ ✕ **Bouchon d'Objectif.** Popular and unpretentious, this tiny bistro
★   serves inexpensive Provençal menus prepared with a sophisticated twist. Watch for anise-scented snails in pastry, rabbit terrine with raisins and pistachios, or a trio of fresh fish with aïoli. An ever-changing gallery display of photography adds a hip touch to the simple ocher-and-aqua setting. ✉ *10 rue Constantine,* ☎ *04–93–99–21–76. AE, MC, V. Closed Mon. Oct.–Easter.*

$ ✕ **Montagard.** Elegant, imaginative, all-organic vegetarian cuisine—
★   a movement just dawning in France—is served in a chic, low-key setting. Prices are surprisingly reasonable, especially the hot-and-cold lunch plate at 65 frs/€10. A complex orchestration of crudités may include avocado, spinach, lentils, walnuts, sultanas, and fresh currants; a turnover stuffed with pumpkin and chestnuts may be trimmed with deep-fried pumpkin rings and ruby-beet chips. Strains of Keith Jarrett waft through the artful mise-en-scene, with its high-design chairs and warm shades of ocher. ✉ *6 rue du Maréchal Joffre,* ☎ *04–93–39–98–38. MC, V. Closed Sun. and Mon.*

$$$$ ✕🖾 **Carlton Inter-Continental.** This neoclassical landmark staked out
★   the best position, with La Croisette seeming to radiate symmetrically from its figurehead waterfront site. No discreet setback here: the Carlton sits right on the sidewalk—the better for you to be seen on the popular brasserie's terrace, made even more noticeable by the gleaming, renovated facade. The main film festival banquets take place in its gilt-and-marble Grand Salon, as do, alas, year-round conferences. Seafront rooms have a retro Laura Ashley look; those on the back compensate with cheery Provençal prints. The restaurant **La Belle Otero**, next to the exclusive seventh-floor casino, is one of Cannes's finest. Chef Francis Cauveau applies a restrained and disciplined hand to risotto with morels and white asparagus, John Dory with chorizo and sherry, and Sisteron lamb roasted with pesto. La Belle Otero is closed Sunday and Monday; no lunch Tuesday. ✉ *58 bd. de la Croisette, 06414,* ☎ *04–93–06–40–06,* 𝖥𝖠𝖷 *04–93–06–40–25. 338 rooms, 28 suites. 4 restaurants, bar, air-conditioning, health club, beach, casino. AE, DC, MC, V.* ✍

$$$$ ✕🖾 **Majestic.** Classical statuary and tapestries set the aristocratic tone at this other La Croisette "palace"; it's grand but gracious, with a quieter feel than most of its neighbors. The (smallish) pool is behind a landscaped hillock so that guests breakfasting poolside can't be seen by passersby. In the restaurant, **Villa des Lys**, another of Cannes's gastronomic greats, young wonder-chef Bruno Oger plays with Provençal traditions at refined levels: tender pesto tart, lamb roasted in pungent tapenade. Its romantic poolside terrace and Egyptian/Art Deco bar give a nod to cinematic glamour. Though some rooms are fussy, most are done in subdued tones of gold and burgundy. Ask for one of the renovated ones, carefully redone in retro style. ✉ *14 bd. de la Croisette, 06400,* ☎ *04–92–98–77–00,* 𝖥𝖠𝖷 *04–93–38–97–90. 304 rooms, 24 apartments. Restaurant, bar, air-conditioning, pool, beauty salon, sauna, parking (fee). AE, DC, MC, V. Closed mid-Nov.–Dec..* ✍

$$$$ ✕⊞ **Martinez.** A Hollywood-style face-lift restored the Art Deco Martinez to a theatrical version of its original '30s glamour. Renovated rooms have a splashy neo-Deco look—be sure to ask for one of these, as well as one on the seaside with gorgeous views. Avoid those on the interior overlooking the grim parking lot. The **Palme d'Or** restaurant overlooking La Croisette has a plush, extravagant burled-wood and ebony decor worthy of Napoléon (or Joan Collins). But despite all that, chef Christian Willer draws lavish praise for his modern Mediterranean cuisine: fresh anchovies marinated in herbs, octopus and squid floating in a cassoulet of white beans. ⊠ *73 bd. de la Croisette, 06400,* ☎ *04–92–98–73–00,* 𝔽𝔸𝕏 *04–93–39–67–82. 369 rooms, 24 apartments. 3 restaurants, bar, air-conditioning, pool, beach. AE, DC, MC, V. Closed mid-Nov.–mid-Jan..* ✍

$$$$ ✕⊞ **Noga Hilton.** On the site of the old Palais des Festivals, the in-your-face modern white-and-glass facade of this relative newcomer gives way to interiors just as bold and glossy, with lipstick-red leather lobby chairs, a dizzying atrium design, and high-gloss wood, chrome, and mirrors, the better to reflect the geometric-print carpets. But in refusing to play movie-set retro, the hotel maintains a posh integrity, with a seamlessly professional staff and a sense of hushed luxury that denies the exuberance of the decor. The good Mediterranean restaurant La Scala (though not on the same culinary level as its palace peers) has tables high above La Croisette and the waterfront, from which you can enjoy refined pastas and grilled fish. Also don't miss the rooftop sun-bathing terrace, with grill and bar around the plunge pool. ⊠ *50 bd. de la Croisette, 06400,* ☎ *04–92–99–70–00,* 𝔽𝔸𝕏 *04–92–99–70–11. 180 rooms, 49 suites. 2 restaurants, 3 bars, air-conditioning, pool, exercise room, beach. AE, DC, MC, V.* ✍

$$$ ⊞ **Cristal.** This Best Western property has all the comfort and predictability the brand name implies, but with a touch of Côte-d'Azur glitz: all rooms have a neo-Deco look, and the best have marble-lined bathrooms. A rooftop whirlpool is fed by a stone fountain and surrounded by lemon trees, a bar, and a Provençal restaurant. ⊠ *13–15 rond-point Duboys-d'Angers, 06400,* ☎ *04–93–39–45–45,* 𝔽𝔸𝕏 *04–93–38–64–66. 50 rooms. Restaurant, 2 bars, air-conditioning. AE, DC, MC, V.* ✍

$$–$$$ ⊞ **Splendid.** If you covet a waterfront position but can't afford the grand hotels on La Croisette, consider this traditional 1873 palace overlooking La Pantiéro and the old port. Maintained in simple comfort, it offers freshly decorated rooms and bathrooms that are impeccably up-to-date. Small doubles take in spectacular seaside views; some first-floor rooms have terraces. It's family run and thus full of personal touches: flowers and fruit in rooms, robes and kitchenettes in those with sea views, and pretty Provençal furniture in the breakfast room. ⊠ *allées de la Liberté, entrance on 4–6 rue Félix-Faure, 06407,* ☎ *04–97–06–22–22,* 𝔽𝔸𝕏 *04–93–99–55–02. 64 rooms. Air-conditioning, kitchenettes. AE, DC, MC, V.*

$$ ⊞ **Festival.** This small, central property benefits from an owner who is eager to please. Rooms have full marble baths, postmodern pastel decor, and built-in Deco-style ash furnishings; five overlook the neighbor's lovely orange trees and palms. Ask for one of the two roomier doubles on the garden side, and make an appointment for the sauna and whirlpool, scheduled for maximum privacy. In addition to discount packages for long stays and reduced-price entry to several private beaches, the hotel arranges excursions to the islands and nearby tourist attractions. ⊠ *3 rue Molière, 06400,* ☎ *04–97–06–64–40,* 𝔽𝔸𝕏 *04–97–06–64–45. 14 rooms. Air-conditioning, sauna. AE, DC, MC, V.* ✍

$$ ⊞ **Molière.** Plush, intimate, and low-key, this hotel has pretty tile baths
★ and small rooms in cool shades of peach, indigo, and white-waxed oak. Nearly all overlook the vast, enclosed front garden, where palms and

cypress shade terrace tables, and breakfast is served alfresco most of the year. ✉ *5 rue Molière, 06400,* ☎ *04–93–38–16–16,* FAX *04–93–68–29–57. 24 rooms. AE, MC, V. Closed mid-Nov.–end Dec.*

$$ 🏨 **Renoir.** This graceful former mansion is on a quiet backstreet in a residential neighborhood only a few blocks back from the center and beach (some suites even have sea views), but it feels like another world. A highly charged sunflower-print decor (none of the ubiquitous pink Art Deco), the scent of lavender, and kitchenettes in every suite create a sense of a vacation in Provence instead of on the Côte d'Azur. Sea-view rooms overlook a busier street; for maximum quiet, ask for the backstreet side. ✉ *7 rue Edith Cavell, 06400,* ☎ *04–92–99–62–62,* FAX *04–92–99–62–82. 10 rooms, 17 suites. Bar, air-conditioning, kitchenettes. AE, DC, MC, V.* 🛏

$** 🏨 **Albert Ier. In a quiet residential area above the Forville market—a
★ 10-minute walk downhill to La Croisette and beaches—this neo-Deco mansion has pretty rooms in pastels as well as tidy tile baths and an enclosed garden setting. You can have breakfast on the flowered, shady terrace or in the family-style salon. The hotel has had one owner since 1980, and it shows in the details. ✉ *68 av. de Grasse, 06400,* ☎ *04–93–39–24–04,* FAX *04–93–38–83–75. 11 rooms. MC, V.*

Nightlife and the Arts

The Riviera's cultural calendar is splashy and star-studded, and never more so than during the **International Film Festival** in May. The film screenings are not open to the public, so unless you have a pass, your glimpses of celebs will be on the streets or in restaurants—though if you hang around in a tux, a stray ticket might come your way. The stars themselves no longer grace cafés, beaches, or the morning market; they hide in the privacy of the Hotel du Cap-Eden Roc on the Cap d'Antibes (☞ Cap d'Antibes, *below*).

As befits a glamorous seaside resort, Cannes has two casinos. The famous **Casino Croisette** (✉ Palais des Festivals, ☎ 04–92–98–78–00), which traces its pedigree to 1907, draws more crowds to its slot machines than any other casino in France. The **Carlton Casino Club** (✉ 58 bd. de la Croisette, ☎ 04–93–68–00–33), a relative newcomer to the Cannes nightlife scene, encourages an exclusive atmosphere in its posh seventh-floor hideaway.

To make the right entrance at the currently popular **Le Cat Corner** (✉ 22 rue Macé, ☎ 04–93–39–31–31) have yourself whisked by limo from the steakhouse Le Farfalla. **Jimmy'z** (✉ Palais des Festivals, ☎ 04–93–68–00–07) admits celebrities, stars, and starlets, but not necessarily everyone else; the cabaret shows are legendary. After many metamorphoses, **César Palace** (✉ 48 bd. de la République, ☎ 04–93–68–23–23) is once again one of the main disco draws.

Outdoor Activities and Sports

Most of the **beaches** along La Croisette are owned by hotels and/or restaurants, though this doesn't necessarily mean the hotels or restaurants front the beach. It does mean they own a patch of beachfront bearing their name, from which they rent chaise lounges, mats, and umbrellas to the public and hotel guests (who also have to pay). One of the most fashionable is the Carlton Hotel's beach (☞ *above*). Other beaches where you must pay a fee include the stretch belonging to the Martinez, which is the largest in Cannes, Long Beach, and Rado Plage. You can easily recognize public beaches by the crowds; they're interspliced between the color-coordinated private beach umbrellas, and offer simple open showers and basic toilets. To be slightly removed from the city traffic and crowds, head west of town; the open stretches of sand run uninterrupted toward Mandelieu.

Sailboats can be rented—along with the staff and skipper to sail them—at **Camper & Nicholson's** (✉ Port Canto, ☎ 04–93–43–16–75). The prestigious **Yacht Club de Cannes** encourages you to dine at its posh restaurant before taking a turn in your rented yacht (✉ Palm Beach Port, ☎ 04–93–43–05–90). Windsurfing equipment is available from **Le Club Nautique La Croisette** (✉ Plage Pointe Palm-Beach, ☎ 04–93–43–09–40). The **Centre Nautique Municipal** (✉ 9 rue Esprit-Violet, ☎ 04–93–47–40–55) has a private windsurfing base off Ile Ste-Marguerite, and organizes diving sorties. The **Majestic Ski Club** (Ponton du Majestic; ✉ at the Majestic private beach, ☎ 04–92–98–77–47) can take you waterskiing, or pull you on a ski-board, an inflatable chair, or up over the water on a parachute.

Bicycles can be rented from the train station (✉ pl. de la Gare).

Close to town are several golf courses. The venerable **Golf de la Bastide du Roy** (✉ La Bastide du Roy, ☎ 04–93–65–08–48), at the foot of the village of Biot, has 18 holes and par 67. **Golf de Royal Mougins** (✉ 424 av. du Roi, ☎ 04–93–92–49–69), beautifully landscaped and opened in 1993, has 18 holes and par 71. **Golf Cannes-Mandelieu** (✉ rte. du Golf, ☎ 04–92–97–32–00)—the pretty one with the parasol pines—has 18 holes at par 71 and 9 holes at par 33.

Shopping

Whether you're window-shopping or splurging on that little Galliano number in the Dior window, you'll find some of the best shopping outside Paris on the streets off La Croisette. For stores carrying designer names, try **rond-point Duboys-d'Angers** off **rue Amouretti, rue des Serbes,** and **rue des Belges,** all perpendicular to the waterfront. **Rue d'Antibes** is the town's main shopping drag, with every kind of clothing and shoe shop, as well as mouthwatering candy, fabric, and home-design stores. **Rue Meynadier** mixes trendy young clothes with high-end food specialties.

You can find almost any item, from moth-eaten uniforms to second-hand gravy boats, at the **brocante market** (✉ allées de la Liberté) that springs up every Saturday. The permanent **Marché Forville,** at the foot of Le Suquet, has every kind of fresh and regional food in its picturesque booths every morning but Monday, from 7 AM to 1 PM. On Mondays it fills up with flea-market wares and brocante from 8 to 6. On the first and third Saturday of each month, an array of old books, posters, and postcards is sold at the **Marché du Livre Ancien et des Vieux Papiers** (Antique Books and Paper Market; ✉ pl. de la Justice).

Side Trip from Cannes: Iles de Lérins

❾ *15–20 minutes by ferry off the coast of Cannes.*

When you're glutted on glamour and have had enough of dodging limos, skaters, and the leavings of dyed-to-match poodles, catch a boat from Cannes's Vieux Port to one of the two Iles de Lérins (Lérins Islands). On one of these two lovely getaways, you can find car-free peace and lose yourself in a tropical landscape of palms, pines, and tidal pools. Ste-Marguerite Island has more in the way of attractions: a ruined prison-fortress, a museum, and a handful of restaurants. Smaller and wilder, St-Honorat Island is dominated by its active monastery and the ruins of its 10th-century original.

Buy your tickets from one of the ferry companies at the booths on Cannes's Vieux Port; look for the **Horizon/Caribes Company** (✉ Jetée Edouard, ☎ 04–92–98–71–36), set back from the street, which has the most comfortable boats. You can also buy tix at the more visible **Estérel Chanteclair** (✉ promenade La Pantiéro, ☎ 04–93–39–11–82).

You must decide which island (if not both) you wish to visit before you buy your tickets. Allow at least a half day to enjoy either of these islands; you can see both if you get an early start but might regret the obligation to move on once you've arrived on the first one. Although Ste-Marguerite has some restaurants and snack shops, you would be wise to bring along a picnic and drinks; you'll have to do this if you spend the day on the noncommercial St-Honorat.

It's a 15-minute, 60-franc/€9.15 round-trip to **Ile Ste-Marguerite,** the larger of the Iles de Lérins, which is covered with dense growths of palms, pines, and eucalyptus. On arriving, head left up the tiny main street lined with restaurants and snack shops, or cut uphill and left toward **Fort Royal,** built by Richelieu in the 18th century and improved by Vauban. The views over the ramparts to the rocky island coast and the open sea are as evocative as the prison buildings, one of which supposedly locked up the Man in the Iron Mask. Behind the prison buildings you'll find the **Musée de la Mer** (Marine Museum; ☎ 04–93–43–18–17), with its Roman boat dating from the first century BC and its collection of amphorae and pottery recovered from ancient shipwrecks. The museum hours are: Wednesday through Monday, October through March 10:30–12:15 and 2:15–4:30 (it's closed three weeks in January); April through June 10:30–12:15 and 2:15–5:30; and July and August 10:30–12:15 and 2:15–6:30. Admission is 10 francs/€1.52. If you have time or prefer nature to history, head right from the port and follow the signs along the coast to the small **bird preserve,** with cormorants and gulls, and the quiet beach beyond, a paradise of tidal pools which seethe with marine life at low tide.

Ile St-Honorat can be reached in 20 minutes (60 frs/€9.15 round-trip) from the Vieux Port. Smaller and wilder than Ste-Marguerite, it is anchored by its active monastery, which traces its foundation here to the 4th century. That's when St-Honorat sought solitude on this island—and was swiftly followed by devotees also seeking solitude. The large 19th-century structure his heirs inhabit today encloses many older chapels and harbors a shop where the monks sell their herb liqueur, called Lerina. The majority of the island is covered with thick forests of pine and eucalyptus that belong to the monastery, punctuated by small chapels and crisscrossed by public paths. Wild and isolated rockbound shores surround the island. On the island's point farthest south, just below its modern replacement, the remains of the 11th-century fortified **monastery** send thick walls plunging into the sea; the walls were built to protect the monks from marauding pirates. The monastery's complex of chapels, courtyards, and views from the crenellated rampart is worth the climb. ☎ 04–93–39–61–41. 🖾 10 frs/€1.52 July–Aug.; free Sept.–June. ☉ Sept.–June, Mon.–Sat. 9–4; Sun. afternoon only; July–Aug., daily 10–noon and 2:30–4:30.

INTO THE PAYS GRASSOIS

Just behind Cannes, the hills that block the mountain winds rise, sunbleached and jungle-green. From the well-groomed Provençal village-cum-bedroom community of Mougins to the hill-city of Grasse, the hills are tiled with greenhouses that feed the region's perfume factories. Grasse itself supports modern industry and tourist industry with aplomb, offering a dense Italian-style old town as well. Beyond, you can head for the hills of the arrière-pays on the Route Napoléon.

Mougins

❿ *8 km (5 mi) north of Cannes, 11 km (7 mi) northwest of Antibes, 32 km (20 mi) southwest of Nice.*

Passing through Mougins, a popular summer-house community convenient to Cannes and Nice, you may perceive little more than sleek, upscale suburban sprawl. But in 1961 Picasso found more to admire and settled into a *mas* (farmhouse) that became a mecca for artists and art lovers; he died there in 1973. Despite overbuilding today, Mougins claims extraordinary views over the coast and an old town, on a hilltop above the fray, that has retained a pretty, ultra-gentrified charm.

You can find Picasso's final home and see why of all spots in the world, he chose this one, by following D35 to the ancient ecclesiastic site of **Notre-Dame-de-Vie.** This was the hermitage, or monastic retreat, of the Abbey of Lérins (☞ Cannes, *above*), and its 13th-century bell tower and arcaded chapel form a pretty ensemble in a magnificent setting. Approached through an alley of ancient cypress, the house Picasso shared with his wife, Jacqueline, overlooks the broad bowl of the countryside. It is, alas, enclosed in cane fencing by his heirs, who fight to preserve their privacy from art-loving pilgrims.

Dining and Lodging

$$$-$$$$ ✕🏨 **Moulin de Mougins.** In a 16th-century olive mill on a hill above
★ the coastal fray, this sophisticated inn houses one of the country's most famous restaurants. It's a de rigueur lunch trip out of Cannes, and hosts the stellar annual AIDS benefit Liz Taylor heads during the film festival. Celebrity chef Roger Vergé has ceded most responsibility to Serge Chollet in order to develop his nearby cooking school, but it's still one of the best restaurants in the region. The sun-drenched Mediterranean cuisine is redolent of the market: white asparagus, sweet garlic, the freshest fish. Inside there are intimate beamed dining rooms; in summer dine outside under the awnings. Reservations are essential for the restaurant, which is closed Monday. Rooms are elegantly rustic, with all-white linens and old wood; the apartments are small but comfortable, although not at Relais & Châteaux level of luxury—only the restaurant belongs to this high-end group. ✉ *Notre-Dame-de-Vie, 06250,* ☎ *04–93–75–78–24,* FAX *04–93–90–18–55. 3 rooms, 4 apartments. Restaurant. AE, DC, MC, V. Closed Feb..*🏖

$$$ 🏨 **Manoir de l'Etang.** An isolated paradise near Picasso's final hermitage that lords over a pond floating with lily pads, this is a real Provençal country inn. Rooms are rustic but patrician, with cheerful flowered fabrics and antiques. Landscaped grounds slope down from a grand hilltop position, and most windows open onto silent greenery. The pool takes in expansive valley views. ✉ *Bois de Fond Merle, rte. d'Antibes, 06250,* ☎ *04–92–28–36–00,* FAX *04–92–28–36–10. 15 rooms. Restaurant, pool. AE, MC, V.* 🏖

Grasse

⑪ *10 km (6 mi) northwest of Mougins, 17 km (10½ mi) northwest of Cannes, 22 km (14 mi) northwest of Antibes, 42 km (26 mi) southwest of Nice.*

High on a plateau over the coast, this busy, modern town is usually given wide berth by anyone who isn't interested in its prime tourist industry, the making of perfume. But its unusual art museum featuring works of the 18th-century artist Fragonard and the picturesque backstreets of its very Mediterranean old town round out a pleasant day trip from the coast.

It's the Côte d'Azur's hothouse climate, nurturing nearly year-round shows of tropical-hue flowers, that fosters Grasse's perfume industry. The heady, heavy scent of orange blossoms, pittosporum, roses, lavender, jasmine, and mimosa wraps around you like silk in gardens along the coast, especially on a sultry night, and since time immemorial people have tried to capture that seductive scent in a bottle. In the past, perfume makers laid blossoms facedown in a lard-smeared tray, then soaked the essence away in alcohol; nowadays the scents are condensed in vast copper stills. Only the essential oils are kept, and the water thrown away—except rose water and orange water, which find their way into delicately perfumed pastries.

It takes 10,000 flowers to produce 2.2 pounds of jasmine petals and nearly one ton of petals to distill one and a half quarts of essence; this helps justify the sky-high cost of perfumes, priced by the proportion of essence their final blend contains.

In Paris and on the outskirts of Grasse, these scents are blended by a professional *nez*, or "nose," who must distinguish some 500 distinct scents and may be able to discern 3,000. The products carry the household names of couturiers like Chanel and Dior, perfume houses like Guerlain. You can't visit the laboratories where these great blends are produced. But Grasse, to accommodate the crowds of visitors who come here wanting to know more, has met their needs with three functioning perfume factories that create simple blends and demonstrate their production techniques for free. You pass through a boutique of house perfumes on the way back to the bus and . . . well, you get the idea.

Fragonard (✉ rte. de Cannes "Les 4-Chemins," ☎ 04–93–36–44–65) holds forth in a factory built in 1782; it displays a small collection of stills, perfume bottles, and "necessaries" for women's—and men's—toilettes. **Galimard** (✉ 73 rte. de Cannes, ☎ 04–93–09–20–00) offers two-hour "studios des fragrances," during which the house "nose" will coach you in designing your own personally labeled scent (200 frs/€30, by reservation only). **Molinard** (✉ 60 bd. Victor-Hugo, ☎ 04–93–36–01–62) offers 90-minute workshops for visitors to blend their own scents (200 frs/€30 per person, reserve in advance).

The **Musée International de la Parfumerie** (International Museum of Perfume), not to be confused with the small museum in the Fragonard perfume factory that calls itself the Musée de la Parfumerie but feeds directly into the gift shop, traces the 3,000-year history of perfume making. The museum has a room equipped with pot-bellied copper stills and old machines, and labels guide you through the steps of production in different eras. It also has a series of displays of exquisite perfume bottles and toiletries. There's even Marie Antoinette's *nécessaire* (travel kit). ✉ 8 pl. du Cours, ☎ 04–93–36–80–20. ☎ 20 frs/€3.05. ☉ June–Sept., daily 10–7; Oct. and mid–Dec.–May., Wed.–Sun. 10–noon and 2–5. Closed Nov.–mid-Dec.

The **Musée Fragonard** isn't named for the perfume factory, rather, it's the other way around. The grand old Fragonard family of Grasse figured large in the town's 17th-century industry—that of making perfumed leather gloves. (The scents themselves eventually outstripped the gloves in popularity.) The family's most famous son, Jean-Honoré Fragonard (1732–1806), became one of the great French artists of the period, and during the Revolution lived in the family mansion that houses the museum today. The lovely villa, decorated with reproductions of the neoclassic panels he created (the originals are at the Frick Museum in New York), contains a collection of drawings, engravings, and paintings by the artist, including two graceful self-portraits. Other rooms in the mansion display works by Fragonard's son Alexandre-Evariste and his grandson Théophile. ✉ 23 bd. Fragonard, ☎ 04–93–36–02–71. ☎ 20 frs/€3.05. ☉ June–Sept., daily 10–7; Oct. and mid–Dec.–May, Wed.–Sun. 10–noon and 2–5. Closed Nov.–mid-Dec.

The **Musée d'Art et d'Histoire de Provence** (Museum of the Art and History of Provence), just down from the Fragonard perfumery, has a large collection of faïence from the region, including works from Moustiers, Biot, and Vallauris. Also on display in this noble 18th-century mansion are *santons* (terra-cotta figurines), furniture, local paintings, and folk costumes. ✉ *2 rue Mirabeau,* ☎ *04–93–36–01–61.* 💰 *20 frs/€3.05.* ☉ *June–Sept., daily 10–7; Oct. and mid-Dec.–May, Wed.–Sun. 10–noon and 2–5. Closed Nov.–mid-Dec.*

To lose yourself in the dense labyrinth of the **Vieille Ville** (Old Town), follow rue Ossola down into the steep, narrow streets, darkened on each side by shuttered houses five and six stories tall. Several little bakeries feature *fougassette à la fleur d'oranger,* a Grasse specialty profiting from the orange water created in its factories; the sweet, briochelike pastry is heavy with orange-blossom perfume.

On a cliff-top overlook at the old town's edge, the Romanesque **Cathédrale Notre-Dame-du-Puy** (✉ pl. du Petit Puy) contains no less than three paintings by Rubens, a triptych by the Provençal painter Louis Bréa, and *Lavement des Pieds* (*Washing of the Feet*), by the young Fragonard.

The picturesque **place aux Aires,** below the central cluster of museums and perfumeries, is lined with 17th- and 18th-century houses and their arcades. Every morning a flower market covers the square in Technicolor hues.

Dining

$ ✕ **Arnaud.** Just off place aux Aires, this easygoing corner bistro serves up inventive home cooking under a vaulted ceiling trimmed with grapevine stencils and pretty Provençal prints. Choose from an ambitious and sophisticated menu of à la carte specialties—a nouvelle arrangement of three kinds of fish in garlic sauce and a hearty *confit de canard* (preserved duck). At lunch there's an imaginative fixed-price regional menu, which might include tomato baked with herbed chèvre, veal with pasta, or *pieds et paquets* (pigs' feet and tripe). ✉ *10 pl. de la Foux,* ☎ *04–93–36–44–88. MC, V.*

Route Napoléon

Extends 176 km (109 mi) from Grasse to Sisteron.

One of the most famous and panoramic roads in France, the Route Napoléon was followed by Napoléon Bonaparte in 1815 after his escape from imprisonment on the Mediterranean island of Elba. Napoléon landed at Golfe-Juan, near Cannes, on March 1 and forged northwest to Grasse, then through dramatic, hilly countryside to Castellane, Digne, and Sisteron. In Napoléon's day, most of this road (now N85) was little more than a winding dirt track. Commemorative plaques bearing the imperial eagle stud the route, inspired by Napoléon's remark, "The eagle will fly from steeple to steeple until it reaches the towers of Notre-Dame." That prediction came true. Napoléon covered the 176 km (109 mi) from the coast to Sisteron in just four days, romped north through Grenoble and Burgundy, and entered Paris in triumph on May 20.

Though the mighty warrior officially started his journey through this region from the coast, the route between Golfe-Juan and Grasse is mostly urban tangle, with the Route Napoléon generally considered to start north of Grasse, when it opens into scenic countryside. Except for the occasional inn with the name Napoléon, there are no historical buildings or monuments, bar the plaques. There are a few lavender–honey stands and souvenir shacks, but they're few and far between. It is the panoramic views as the road winds its way up into the Alps that make this route so worth traveling.

Unless you are heading north to Grenoble, you can easily make a circular day trip along the Route Napoléon, starting from the coast at Grasse. Without stopping, you could reach **Sisteron** in 90 minutes, so take your time and stop for a picnic along the way. Sisteron, which is guarded by a medieval citadel perched 1,650 ft above the river, is the gateway between Provence and the Alpine region of Dauphine. It's also famous for its tender lamb, favored by Provençal chefs. If you forge all the way to Sisteron, pick up A51 down to Aix-en-Provence (☞ Chapter 3), and then join A6 to return to the Côte d'Azur.

You can make a beeline up the Route Napoléon to Castellane and west to the Gorges du Verdon, the main tourist goal in the region, or take your time winding through the hill towns to the west (☞ Haut Var and into Haute Provence *in* Chapter 4). The hill towns just east of Grasse—Vence and St-Paul—are much more developed and more frequented by tourists.

Valbonne

🄬 *18 km (11 mi) north of Cannes, 14 km (9 mi) northwest of Antibes.*

A kind of little-England-on-the-Brague (the river that flows through town), this fiercely Provençal hill town has been adopted by the British, especially those working at the nearby high-tech complex Sophia-Antipolis. Thus it exudes a peculiar kind of mixed-country charm, *plus Provençal que les Provençaux,* with a plethora of tasteful restorations. Its principal cachet is the novel layout of the old town, designed in a grid system in the 16th century by the monks of Lérins. A checkerboard of ruler-straight *ruelles* (little streets) lies within a sturdy rampart of wraparound houses; at the center, a grand *place* is framed by Renaissance arcades and shady elms.

BETWEEN CANNES AND NICE

The coastline spanning the brief distance from Cannes to Antibes and Nice has a personality all its own, combining some of the most accessible and democratic waterfront resorts (Juan-les-Pins, Villeneuve, and Cagnes) with one of the most elite (Cap d'Antibes). This is vacationland, with a culture of commercial entertainment that smacks of the worst of Florida in the '60s. Hot, poky N98, which goes from Antibes to Cagnes, crawls past a jungle of amusement parks, beach discos, and even a horse-racing track. The hill towns of Vallauris and Biot cater to souvenir hunting and lunch sorties. Juan-les-Pins is a party town, its cafés and brasseries thriving into the wee hours. And the glass highrise monstrosities curving over the waterfront below Cagnes and Villeneuve glow unnaturally bright until dawn. Yet minutes away on a peninsula jutting into the sea, the Cap d'Antibes floats aloof, its mansions and manicured gardens turning their backs on the cheaper real estate on the "mainland."

Everyone visiting this little piece of the Côte d'Azur, whether staying in a villa or a concrete cube, is after the same experience: to sit on a balcony, listening to the waves washing over the sand, and to watch the sun setting over the oil-painted backdrop of the Alps. Wherever you base yourself, you are always just a 20-minute zip to Cannes or Nice, and you can easily wend your way into the hills to visit the ancient villages of St-Paul, Vence, and beyond.

Vallauris

⓭ *6 km (4 mi) northeast of Cannes, 6 km (4 mi) west of Antibes.*

This ancient village in the low hills over the coast, dominated by a blocky Renaissance château, owes its four-square street plan to a form of medieval urban renewal. Ravaged and eventually wiped out by waves of the plague in the 14th century, the village was rebuilt by 70 Genovese families imported by the Abbaye de Lérins in the 16th century to repopulate the abandoned site. They brought with them a taste for Roman planning—hence the grid format in the old town—but more important, a knack for pottery making. Their skills and the fine clay of Vallauris were a marriage made in heaven, and the village thrived as a pottery center for hundreds of years. In the 1940s Picasso found inspiration in the malleable soil and settled here, giving the flagging industry new life. Nowadays, Vallauris has a split personality: the commercial, souvenir-shop tourist section vaunting bins of pottery below, the dense medieval gridwork of the old town looming barren and isolated above, with little to see but laundry and cats.

During his years here, sequestered in a simple stone house, Picasso created pottery art with a single-minded passion, sometimes dozens of works a day. But he was a painter first and foremost, and he returned to that medium in 1952 to create one of his masterworks in the château's barrel-vaulted Romanesque chapel, the vast multipaneled composition called *La Guerre et la Paix* (*War and Peace*)—a difficult and forceful work, created in broad, ruthlessly simplistic strokes in the heat of post-war
★ inspiration. Today the chapel is part of the **Musée National "La Guerre et la Paix,"** where several of Picasso's ceramic pieces are displayed along with a collection of pre-Columbian works. ⊠ *pl. de la Libération,* ☎ *04–93–64–16–05.* 🎟 *17 frs/€2.59.* 🕙 *June–Sept., Wed.–Mon. 10–6:30; Oct.–May, Wed.–Mon. 10–noon and 2–6.*

Shopping

Along **rue Hoche** and throughout the lower village are shops and galleries crammed with bright pottery and ceramic art. Look for the more elegant **Galerie Madoura** (⊠ av. Anciens Combattants, ☎ 04–93–64–66–39), owned by the ceramic house with which Picasso worked and still managed by descendants of his friends Georges and Suzanne Ramié. You can buy good limited-edition reproductions of his Madoura pieces here.

Antibes

★ **⓮** *11 km (7 mi) northeast of Cannes, 15 km (9 mi) southeast of Nice.*

With its broad stone ramparts scalloping in and out over the waves and backed by blunt medieval towers and a skew of tile roofs, Antibes (pronounced Awn-*teeb*) is one of the most romantic old towns on the Mediterranean coast. Stroll promenade Amiral-de-Grasse along the crest of Vauban's sea walls, watch the cormorants diving off jagged black rock and sleek yachts purring out to sea, and you'll understand why this place inspired Picasso to paint on a panoramic scale. A few steps inland you'll enter a souklike maze of old streets, its market filled with fresh fish and goat cheese, wild herbs, and exotic spices.

Named Antipolis—meaning across from (*anti*) the city (*polis*)—by the Greeks who founded it in the 4th century BC, Antibes has always been the antithesis of Nice, gazing quietly across the harbor at its powerful and vital neighbor. Antibes flourished under the Romans' aristocratic rule, with an amphitheater, aqueducts, and baths. The early Christians established their bishopric here, the site of the region's cathedral until the 13th century.

It was in the Middle Ages that the kings of France began fortifying this key port town, an effort that culminated in the recognizable star-shaped ramparts designed by Vauban. The young general Napoléon once headed this stronghold, living with his family in a humble house in the old town; his mother washed their clothes in a stream. There's still a *lavoir* (public laundry fountain) in the old town where locals, not unlike Signora Buonaparte, rinse their clothes and hang them like garlands over the narrow streets.

Antibes has its glamorous side, too. Whether you approach the waterfront from the train station or park along the avenue de Verdun, you'll first confront the awesome expanse of luxury yachts in the **Port Vauban.** Some of them stretch as much as 500 ft and swan back and forth at will between Greece, Saudi Arabia, and other ports of call. They won't find a more dramatic spot to anchor, with the tableau of snowy Alps looming behind and the formidable medieval block towers of the **Fort Carré** (Square Fort) guarding entry to the port. This superbly symmetrical island fortress was completed in 1565 and restored in 1967, but can only be admired from afar. Across the quai Rambaud, which juts into the harbor, a tiny crescent of soft sand beach called **La Gravette** offers swimmers one of the last soft spots on the coast before the famous Riviera pebble beaches begin.

To visit old Antibes, stroll the **cours Masséna,** where an exotic little sheltered market sells lemons, olives, and hand-stuffed sausages, and the vendors take breaks in the shoebox cafés flanking one side. Find the cours by passing through the Porte Marine, an arched gateway in the rampart wall that leads from the port into the town, then follow rue Aubernon.

The **Église de l'Immaculée-Conception,** located between the cours Masséna and the seafront, served as the region's cathedral until the bishopric was transferred to Grasse in 1244. Its stout medieval watchtower was built in the 11th century with stones "mined" from Roman structures—one reason the town has no amphitheater or ruins today. The church's 18th-century facade, a marvelously Latin mix of classical symmetry and fantasy, has been restored in shades of ocher and cream. Inside you'll find a Baroque altarpiece of the Virgin and Child draping a protective cloak and rosary over the people, humbly underscaled, below; this central composition and the 18 fascinating miniatures that surround it were painted by the Niçois artist Louis Bréa in 1515. A moving *gisant* (full-body death portrait) of Christ, carved in wood in 1447, stands to the altar's right. ⊠ *pl. de la Cathédrale.*

The medieval **Château Grimaldi** rises on a Roman foundation, in turn constructed on a Greek base. Its square watchtower, along with the bell tower of the neighboring church, defines Antibes' silhouette. The bishops lived here in the church's heyday, and the Grimaldi family until the Revolution. But this fine old castle, high over the water, was little more than a monument until in 1946 its curator offered use of its vast chambers to Picasso, where he was to work with a singular passion against the inspiring backdrop of mountains, village, and sea. Here Picasso experimented with techniques, scale, and mediums, creating vast paintings on wood, canvas, paper, and walls. This extraordinary collection of works, alive with nymphs, fauns, and centaurs, as well as earthy fishermen, forms the core of the **Musée Picasso.** A rotating display includes more than 300 works by the artist, as well as pieces by Miró, Calder, and Léger. On the second floor (third story) is a room dedicated to the works of Nicolas de Staël (1914–55), who spent the last winter of his life in Antibes creating more than 300 paintings before throwing himself from a window. These cool, lonely late works

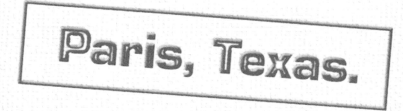

When it Comes to Getting Local Currency at an ATM, Same Thing.

Whether you're in Yosemite or Yemen, using your Visa® card or ATM card with the PLUS symbol is the easiest and most convenient way to get local currency. For example, let's say you're in France. When you make a withdrawal, using your secured PIN, it's dispensed in francs, but is debited from your account in U.S. dollars. This makes it easy to take advantage of favorable exchange rates. And if you need help finding one of Visa's 627,000 ATMs in 127 countries worldwide, visit **visa.com/pd/atm**. We'll make finding an ATM as easy as finding the Eiffel Tower, the Pyramids or even the Grand Canyon.

It's Everywhere You Want To Be.

SEE THE WORLD
IN FULL COLOR

Fodor's Exploring Guides bring all the great sights vividly to life with hundreds of photographs, fascinating historical background, and colorful anecdotes. Detailed maps and practical information keep you headed in the right direction.

Pair a **Fodor's** Exploring Guide with your trusted Gold Guide for a complete planning package.

offer a marked contrast to Picasso's sunny joie de vivre. ✉ *pl. du Château,* ☎ *04–92–90–54–20.* ✇ *30 frs/€4.57.* ☉ *June–Sept., Tues.–Sun. 10–6; Oct.–May, Tues.–Sun. 10–noon and 2–6.*

The old **Portail de l'Orme** (Gate of the Elm), built of quarried Roman stone and enlarged in the Middle Ages, leads visitors from the cours Massena and the market toward compelling seaside ramparts. Inside the tower next to the Portail de l'Orme is the tiny **Musée de la Tour des Arts et Traditions Populaire** (Tower Museum of Popular Arts and Traditions), which displays old photos and costumes from 18th- and 19th-century Antibes. There's even a pair of water skis, dating from 1931; the sport was invented in neighboring Juan-les-Pins. ✉ *Tour de l'Orme,* ☎ *04–93–34–50–91.* ☉ *Apr.–Sept., Wed., Thurs., and Sat. 4–7; Oct.–Mar., Wed., Thurs., and Sat. 3–5.*

The promenade Amiral de Grasse—a marvelous setting for pondering the mountains and tides—leads directly to the Bastion St-André, a squat Vauban fortress now home to the **Musée Archéologique** (Archaeology Museum). In its glory days this 17th-century stronghold sheltered a garrison; the bread oven is still visible in the vaulted central hall. The museum collection focuses on Antibes's classical history, displaying amphorae and sculptures found in local digs as well as in shipwrecks from the harbor. ✉ *av. Général-Maizières,* ☎ *04–92–90–54–35.* ✇ *20 frs/€3.05.* ☉ *Tues.–Sun. 10–noon and 2–6.*

★ Not far off the promenade and focused around the place du Safranier is the **Commune Libre du Safranier** (Free Commune of Safranier), a magical little neighborhood with a character all its own. Here the tiny houses hang heavy with flowers and vines, and neighbors carry on conversations from window to window across the stone-stepped rue du Bas-Castelet. It is said that place du Safranier was once a tiny fishing port; now it's the scene of this sub-village's festivals.

From the Commune quarter it's easy to drift farther into the old-town streets, exploring the mix of shops, galleries, restaurants, and bakeries. Aim to wind up on **place Nationale,** the site of the Roman forum. It's a pleasant place for a drink under the broad plane trees.

From old Antibes you can jump on a bus over the hill to **Juan-les-Pins,** the jazzy younger-sister resort town that, with Antibes, bracelets the wrist of the Cap d'Antibes. This stretch of beach was "discovered" by the Jazz-Age jet set, who adopted it with a vengeance; F. Scott and Zelda Fitzgerald lived in a seaside villa here in the early 1920s, dividing their idylls between what is now the Hotel Belle Rives (☞ Lodging, *below*) and the mansions on the Cap d'Antibes. Here they experimented with the newfangled fad of waterskiing, still practiced from the docks of the Belle Rives today. Ladies with bobbed hair and beach pajamas exposed lily-white skin to the sun, browning themselves like peasants and flaunting bare, tanned arms. American industrialists had swimming pools introduced to the seaside, and the last of the leisure class, weary of stateside bathtub gin, wallowed in Europe's alcoholic delights. Nowadays, the scene along Juan-les-Pins's waterfront is something to behold, with thousands of sun worshippers flowing up and down the promenade and lying flank to flank on the endless stretch of sand. Cafés and restaurants feed the mobs, many of them right on the beach. Yet the grand old pines and palm trees, now massive with age and proffering much-needed shade, remind visitors of the heyday of the Riviera.

Dining and Lodging

$$$ ✕ **La Jarre.** You can dine under the beams or the ancient fig tree at this lovely little garden hideaway, just off the ramparts and behind the cathedral. Open only for dinner, it has an ambitious menu of Provençal

specialties filtered through an international lens: sweetbreads sautéed with tender spinach sprouts, turbot sauced with basil and ginger, a chilled summer-fruit soup. As there's no fixed-price menu, the à la carte tally runs high. ⊠ *14 rue St-Esprit, Antibes,* ☎ *04–93–34–50–12. AE, MC, V. Closed mid-Oct.–Easter. No lunch.*

$$–$$$ ✗ **La Bonne Auberge.** In a graceful inn set back from the overbuilt sprawl along N7, chef Philippe Rostang cooks up classic, conservative specialties such as lamb slow-simmered in herbs for seven hours, lobster salad with tiny ravioli, and airy fish soufflés. The dining room is a pastel haven of exposed beams, fresh flowers, and soft light; huge glass windows allow you to view the inspired work in the kitchen. ⊠ *Quartier de la Brague (4 km [2½ mi] east of Antibes),* ☎ *04–93–33–36–65. MC, V. Closed Mon. and no dinner Sun. Sept.–mid-Nov. and mid-Dec.–June. Closed mid-Nov.–mid-Dec.*

$ ✗ **Le Brûlot.** One street back from the thriving market, this bistro remains one of the busiest in Antibes. Burly chef Christian Blancheri hoists anything from pigs to apple pies in and out of his roaring wood oven, and it's all delicious. Watch for the sardines *à l'escabèche* (in a tangy sweet-and-sour marinade), sizzling lamb chops, or grilled fresh fish. The decor is rustic and chaotic and the seating so close it's almost unavoidable to become part of one large, unruly crowd. ⊠ *3 rue Frédéric Isnard, Antibes,* ☎ *04–93–34–17–76. MC, V. Closed Sun., last 2 wks of Aug., and last wk Dec.–1st wk Jan. No lunch Mon.–Wed.*

$ ✗ **Taverne le Safranier.** Part of a tiny old-town enclave determined to resist the press of tourism, this casual tavern is headquarters for the Commune Libre du Safranier. A handful of tables scattered on the place Safranier hold locals and visitors relishing spicy fish soup, thick handmade ravioli, and whole *dorade,* a delicate Mediterranean fish that is unceremoniously split, fried, and garnished with lemon. A laid-back staff in shorts and rubber sandals shouts your order into the nautical-decor bar. Blackboard specials are cheap, homemade, and satisfying. ⊠ *pl. Safranier, Antibes,* ☎ *04–93–34–80–50. No credit cards. Closed Mon.*

$$$$ ✗⌂ **Juana.** This luxurious landmark, run by the Barrache family since
★   it opened in 1931, retains a Gatsby feel. There are striped awnings, white balustrades, gleaming brass, and ornate Deco ironwork trimming the lobby. Pine trees tower over the grounds and the white-marble pool, and rooms have a cool plain-pastel decor. Though it's two long blocks from the waterfront, the Juana has its own private sand beach there, with changing cabins, bar, and restaurant. But you'll want to save room for a serious dinner at La Terrasse, where chef Christian Morisset maintains top honors for some of the best cuisine on the Côte d'Azur. Try inky cannelloni stuffed with clams and squid, sea bass steamed with Menton lemon, lamb roasted in Vallauris clay, a sprig of batter-fried acacia, or hand-rolled truffles. ⊠ *av. Georges-Gallice, 06160 Juan-les-Pins,* ☎ *04–93–61–08–70,* ⅀⅍ *04–93–61–76–60. 45 rooms, 5 suites. Restaurant, bar, air-conditioning, pool. AE, MC, V. Closed Nov.–Mar..* ✑

$$$$ ⌂ **Belles Rives.** For dreamers and literary pilgrims who like to mix history with glamour, this is the place. F. Scott Fitzgerald lived here—in a delicate, pine-shaded villa that in 1930 was expanded into a grand and radical hotel. The Belles Rives pioneered the idea of an inn *pieds dans l'eau* (with its feet in the water), constructing terraces directly on the waterfront—something that disappointingly few hotels along the Côte d'Azur offer today. On these docks, the newly invented sport of waterskiing caught on like wildfire, and jazz giants mingled with royalty. The original Art Deco furniture remains, artfully preserved in an almost museum-like ambience, though the grand glass doors lead to a vivid and lively waterfront scene. Rooms are neither slick nor seedy, with fresh, updated fabrics, and sea views are poster-perfect. Cocktails and restaurant meals on the terrace, with the sunset framed over the

Estérel, make you want to dress for dinner. ⊠ *bd. Edouard Baudoin, 06160 Juan-les-Pins,* ☎ *04–93–61–02–79,* FAX *04–93–67–43–51. 30 rooms. Restaurant, bar, air-conditioning, beach, boating, waterskiing. AE, MC, V.* ☙

$$–$$$ ⊡ **Le Mas Djoliba.** Tucked into a residential neighborhood on the crest between Antibes and Juan-les-Pins, this cool, cozy inn feels like the private home it once was. Surrounded by greenery and well protected from traffic noise, the swimming pool is a haven for guests too relaxed to hike down to the beach. Rooms, decked in bright colors and floral prints, have either views of the garden or the sea; from the family room on the top that sleeps four, there's a balcony overlooking the Cap d'Antibes. Friendly, energetic hosts Stephanie and Sylvain prepare half-board meals, which are encouraged in high season. ⊠ *29 av. de Provence, 06600 Antibes,* ☎ *04–93–34–02–48,* FAX *04–93–34–05–81. 13 rooms. Restaurant, pool. AE, DC, MC, V. Closed Nov.–Jan..* ☙

$$ ⊡ **Les Mimosas.** This hotel's fabulous setting—in an enclosed hilltop garden studded with tall palms, mimosa, and tropical greenery—makes up for the trafficky hike down to the beach, although most guests lounge around the pool anyway. Rooms are small and modestly decorated in Victorian florals. Ask for one with a functioning balcony: many overlook the garden and pool, which is bigger than most. The lobby and lounge are doily-cozy, with Oriental rugs and bric-a-brac, but you'll probably be drawn to the palm-shaded lawns to relax. ⊠ *rue Pauline, 06160 Juan-les-Pins,* ☎ *04–93–61–04–16,* FAX *04–92–93–06–46. 34 rooms. Pool. AE, MC, V. Closed Oct.–Apr.*

Nightlife and the Arts

Though it's a poor heir to the grand casino of Scott-and-Zelda days, the modern glassed-in complex of the **Eden Casino** (⊠ bd. Baudoin, Juan-les-Pins, ☎ 04–92–93–71–71) houses restaurants, bars, dance clubs, and a casino, many with sea views. If you're ready to party all night, **La Siesta** (⊠ north of town on rte. du Bord de Mer, Antibes, ☎ 04–93–33–31–31) is the place; it's an enormous setup, with 11 open-air dance floors, bars, slot machines, and roulette; like most of neighboring Juan-les-Pins, it's only open in summer. At **Le Pam Pam** (⊠ 137 bd. Wilson, Juan-les-Pins, ☎ 04–93–61–11–05) the chic and restless sip exotic cocktails and sway and shout over live Brazilian music. There's no cover charge, but drinks are steep.

Every July the **Festival de Jazz d'Antibes-Juan-les-Pins** (☎ 04–92–90–50–00 for information) challenges Montreux for its stellar lineup and romantic venue under ancient pines. It's one of the oldest festivals in Europe and claims to have had the European debut performances of Miles Davis (pronounce that Meels Dah-*vees*) and Ray Charles. More recent jazz greats gracing the tropical nights include Herbie Hancock, Kyle Eastwood, and Joshua Redman.

Outdoor Activities and Sports

Antibes and Juan-les-Pins together claim 25 km (15½ mi) of coastline and 48 **beaches** (including Cap d'Antibes). In Antibes you can choose between small sandy inlets, such as **La Gravette,** below the port; the central **Plage du Ponteil;** and **Plage de la Salis** toward the Cap; rocky escarpments around the old town; or the vast stretch of sand above the Fort Carré. The Plage de la Salis may be one of the prettiest beach sites on the coast, with the dark pines of the cape to one side and the old stones of Antibes on the other, all against a backdrop of Alpine white. Juan-les-Pins is one big city beach, lined by a boulevard and promenade peppered with cafés and restaurants.

For information about deep-sea diving in the area, contact the **Centre Azuréen de Plongée** (Azurian Diving Center, ☎ 04–93–67–26–22).

Guigo Marine (⊠ 9 av. du 11 novembre, ☎ 04–93–34–17–17) arranges deep-sea fishing expeditions and rents boats. To study underwater life while circling the cape, contact **Visiobulle** (☎ 04–93–34–09–96), which organizes one-hour cruises in tiny yellow glass-bottom boats. Boats leave from the Ponton Courbet in Juan-les-Pins.

Shopping

At the **market** on Antibes's cours Masséna, you can buy fruits, vegetables, and a tempting array of other regional products daily until 1 PM. An **antiques and flea market** takes place Thursday and Saturday from 7 to 6 on place Nationale. You can also find plenty of eclectic little boutiques and gallery shops in the old town, especially along rue Sade and rue de la République.

Cap d'Antibes

⑮ *2 km (1 mi) south of Antibes.*

This idyllic peninsula, protected from the concrete plague infecting the mainland coast, has been carved up into luxurious estates perched high above the water and shaded by thick, tall pines. Since the 19th century its wild greenery and isolation have drawn a glittering assortment of aristocrats, artists, literati, and the merely fabulously wealthy. Among those claiming the prestigious Cap d'Antibes address over the years: Guy de Maupassant, Anatole France, Claude Monet, the Duke and Duchess of Windsor, the Greek arms tycoon Stavros Niarchos, and the cream of the Lost Generation, including Ernest Hemingway, John Dos Passos, Dorothy Parker, Alice B. Toklas, Gertrude Stein, and Scott and Zelda Fitzgerald. Now the focal point is the famous Hotel Eden Roc, rendezvous and weekend getaway of film stars from Madonna and Robert De Niro to Clint Eastwood and Alain Delon.

You can sample a little of what draws them to the site by walking up the chemin de Calvaire from the Plage de la Salis in Antibes (about 1.2 km [¾ mi]), and taking in the extraordinary views from the hill that supports the old lighthouse, called the **Phare de la Garoupe** (Garoupe Lighthouse).

Next to the Phare de la Garoupe, the 16th-century double chapel of **Notre-Dame-de-la-Garoupe** contain ex-votos and statues of the Virgin, all in the memory, and for the protection, of sailors. *Follow bd. du Cap, then follow signs to Phare,* ☎ 04–93–67–36–01. ⊙ *Easter–Sept., daily 9:30–noon and 2:30–7; Oct.–Easter, daily 10–noon and 2:30–5.*

Another lovely walk (about 1½ km [1 mi]), along the **Sentier Tirepoil,** begins at the cape's pretty Plage de la Garoupe and winds along dramatic rocky shores, magnificent at sunset. The final destination of the Sentier Tirepoil is the **Villa Eilenroc,** designed by Charles Garnier, who created the Paris Opera—which should give you some idea of its style. It commands the tip of the peninsula, from a grand and glamorous garden. You may swan around the grounds freely, but the house remains closed (unless the owners, on a good day, choose to open the first floor to visitors). ⊠ *At tip of Cap d'Antibes,* ☎ 04–93–67–74–33. 🎫 *Free.* ⊙ *Mid-Sept.–June, Tues.–Wed. 9–5.*

★ To fully experience the Riviera's heady, hothouse exoticism, visit the glorious **Jardin Thuret** (Thuret Garden), established by botanist Gustave Thuret in 1856 as a testing ground for subtropical plants and trees. Thuret was responsible for the introduction of the palm tree, forever changing the profile of the Côte d'Azur. On his death, the property was left to the Ministry of Agriculture, which continues to dabble in the

THE FEISTY FLORA
OF PROVENCE

ALTHOUGH THE HOTHOUSE crescent of the Côte d'Azur blooms extravagantly with palm and lemon trees and jungle flowers, the rest of Provence has a flora all its own—austere, hardy, and aromatic. The intense heat of the summer sun alternates with the razor-sharp winds of the mistral—a freight train of air blasting down the Rhône Valley. The vegetation battens down and lies low, turning thick, tiny, waxy leaves toward the assault of heat and wind—as if to say, the less surface exposed, the better. Boxwood and holly and dwarf scrub oak cling to the hillsides. Rosemary and lavender send out leaves matchstick thin and wrap themselves in woody bark dense with aromatic resin. Eucalyptus flutters long ribbon strips of aromatic leaves, and olive trees hang clusters of silver ovals, their twisted trunks staked deep into the earth with broad, strong roots. The cork oak develops a thick bark so resistant and watertight, it's harvested in sheets. And the pines define the landscape, the tall black–green silhouettes of the *pin d'alep* (a species of mediterranean pine) tortured into random forms, the mushroom-shape parasol pine spreading a thick, black dome over the earth.

Yet the plane tree is a paradox. Although its brothers tuck in like sumo wrestlers against heat and wind, these *grandes dames* spread glorious branches wide over city squares, their leaves broad and heavy as palms, creating their own deep shade in summer, then shedding all to let in the gentle winter sun.

But the cypress is the symbol of Provence, its tall evergreen spears flanking mansion and *mas* (farmhouse) and symbolizing hospitality. Tradition has it that one cypress symbolizes the proffering of a glass of water to passersby; two means water and a meal; and three means a night's sleep in the barn.

introduction of exotic species. ⊠ *bd. du Cap,* ☎ 04–93–67–88–00. ☜ *Free.* ☉ *Weekdays 8:30–5:30.*

At the southwest tip of the peninsula, an ancient battery is home to the **Musée Naval et Napoléonien** (Naval and Napoleonic Museum), where you can peruse a collection of watercolors of Antibes, lead soldiers, and scale models of military ships. ⊠ *Batterie du Grillon, av. Kennedy,* ☎ 04–93–61–45–32. ☜ *20 frs/€3.05.* ☉ *Weekdays 9:30–noon and 2:15–6, Sat. 9:30–noon.*

Dining and Lodging

$$$–$$$$ ✕ **Restaurant de Bacon.** Since 1948, this has been the spot for seafood
★ on the Côte d'Azur, carefully controlled by the Sordello brothers, who peruse the fish markets at dawn in Cannes and Antibes. The catch of the day is presented on a tray, silver raw and still twitching; it's your decision whether to have it minced in lemon ceviche, floating in a top-of-the-line bouillabaisse, or simply grilled with fennel, crisped with hillside herbs, or baked in parchment. Such purity doesn't come cheap, but fixed-price menus help keep the bill down. The warm welcome, discreet service, sunny dining room, and dreamy terrace over the Baie des Anges justify extravagance. ⊠ *bd. de Bacon,* ☎ 04–93–61–50–02. *Reservations essential. AE, DC, MC, V. Closed Mon. and Nov.–Jan.*

$$$$ 🏨 **La Baie Dorée.** Clinging to the waterfront and skewed toward the
★ open sea, this elegant little inn provides private sea-view terraces off
every room. The room decor is plush and subdued, the ambience discreet to the point of self-effacing, and the reception area is as small as
a coat check—yet even the standard doubles feel deluxe when you look
out the window. The public grounds and terraces fall in tiers down to
the water, from the shaded restaurant and bar to the boat dock to the
private beach on the Baie de la Garoupe. ✉ *579 bd. de la Garoupe,
06160*, ☎ *04–93–67–30–67*, FAX *04–92–93–76–39. 17 rooms. Restaurant, beach. AE, MC, V. Closed Nov.–mid-Dec..* 🍽

$$$$ 🏨 **Hôtel du Cap Eden Roc.** F. Scott Fitzgerald described the Eden Roc
★ as ". . . a large, proud, rose-colored hotel. Deferential palms cooled its
flushed facade, and before it stretched a short dazzling beach . . ." and
set much of *Tender Is the Night* within its luxurious confines. On 22
acres of immaculate tropical gardens bordered by rocky shoreline,
this extravagantly expensive hotel has long catered to the world's fantasy of a subtropical idyll on the Côte d'Azur. Today its broad, sun-
drenched rooms, thickly carpeted and furnished with antiques, are in
demand from celebrities and stars, from De Niro to Madonna. Ultraprivate waterfront cabanas with changing rooms, showers, and champagne buckets skew discreetly toward sea views, with cane screening
to keep one Euro power broker from peeking at another. The pool seems
to spill directly into the sea, and a sense of playful indulgence reigns,
with trapeze rings suspended over the water, a pontoon swimming dock
straight out of summer camp, and a diving board that invites you to
jackknife into the indigo sea. Tip heavily if you want to be treated like
"somebody," and bring wheelbarrows of cash as credit cards are not
accepted. ✉ *bd. Kennedy, 06160*, ☎ *04–93–61–39–01*, FAX *04–93–67–
76–04. 121 rooms, 9 suites. Restaurant, bar, pool, sauna, 5 tennis courts,
health club. No credit cards. Closed Nov.–Apr..* 🍽

$$ 🏨 **La Garoupe and La Gardiole.** Cool, simple, and accessible to non-
movie-stars, this pair of partnered hotels offers a chance to sleep on
the hallowed peninsula and bike or walk to the pretty Garoupe beach.
A sizable pool, framed by high walls and tall pines, offers cool-down
time. Rooms are comfortably furnished in both buildings, with the
Garoupe offering slightly newer decor. ✉ *60–74 chemin de la Garoupe,
06160*, ☎ *04–92–93–33–33*, FAX *04–93–67–61–87. 40 rooms. Restau-
rant, pool. AE, MC, V.*

Biot

16 *6 km (4 mi) northeast of Antibes, 15 km (9 mi) northeast of Cannes,
18 km (11 mi) southwest of Nice.*

Rising above an ugly commercial-industrial quarter up the coast from
Antibes, Biot (pronounced Bee-*otte*) sits neatly on a hilltop, welcom-
ing day-trippers into its self-consciously quaint center. For centuries
home to a pottery industry, known for its fine yellow clay that stretched
into massive, solid oil jars, it has in recent generations made a name
for itself as a glass-art town. Nowadays its cobbled streets are lined
with boutiques and galleries, their display windows flashing a staggering
variety of goods in vividly colored glass.

Yet despite the commercialism, traces of old Provence remain, espe-
cially in the evening after the busloads of shoppers leave and the deep-
shaded *placettes* (small squares) under the plane trees fall quiet. Then
you can meander around the edges of the old town to find the stone
arch-gates known as the **Porte des Tines** and the **Porte des Migraniers**;
they're the last of the 16th-century fortifications that once enclosed Biot.
Step into the 15th-century **église**, which contains an early 16th-cen-

tury altarpiece attributed to Louis Bréa depicting the Virgin Mary shielding humanity under her cloak; the surrounding portraits are as warmly detailed as the faces and hands in the central panel. **Place des Arcades,** between the tourist office and the church, just behind rue Barri, has an otherworldly grace, with its Gothic arcades and tall palm trees.

Long a regular on the Côte d'Azur, Fernand Léger fell under Biot's spell and bought a farmhouse here in 1955 to house an unwieldy collection of his sculptures. On his death his wife converted the house to a museum of his works, and in 1967 she donated it to France. The modernized structure of the **Musée National Fernand-Léger** is striking, its facade itself a vast mosaic in his signature style of heavily outlined color fields. Within you can trace the evolution of Léger's technique, from his fascination with the industrial to freewheeling abstractions. ⊠ *chemin du Val de Pomme,* ☎ *04–92–91–50–30.* 🎫 *38 frs/€5.79.* ⊙ *July–Sept., Wed.–Mon. 11–6; Oct.–June, Wed.–Mon. 10–12:30 and 2–5:30.*

On the edge of town, follow the pink signs to **La Verrerie de Biot** (Biot Glassworks), which has developed into something of a cult industry since its founding in the 1950s. Here you can observe the glassblowers at work, visit the extensive galleries of museum-quality art glass (which is of much better quality than the kitsch you find in the village shop windows), and start a collection of bubbled-glass goblets, cruets, or pitchers, just as Jackie Kennedy did when the rage first caught hold (she liked cobalt blue). The bubbles come from baking soda applied to the melted glass. Despite the extreme commercialism—there is a souvenir shop, a boutique of home decor, audio tours of the glassworks, a bar, and a restaurant—it's a one-of-a-kind artisanal industry, and the product is made before your eyes. ⊠ *5 chemin des Combes,* ☎ *04–93–65–03–00.* ⊙ *May–Sept., Mon.–Sat. 9–8, Sun. 10–1 and 3–7:30; Oct.–Apr., daily 10–1 and 3–7:30.*

🐋 Marketed under the umbrella title of **Parc de la Mer** (Sea Park), this extremely commercial amusement complex provides parents with bargaining leverage for a day of Picasso and pottery shopping. There's a small **Marineland,** with a lively scripted dolphin show, dancing killer whales, and a Plexiglass walk-through aquarium that allows sharks to swim over your head; it also has a surprisingly deep and fascinating collection of old sea paraphernalia in its museum. Next door the **Jungle des Papillons** (Butterfly Jungle) presents a fluttering Butterfly Ballet that must be seen to be believed; wear colored clothing to stimulate them into a wing-flapping frenzy. There's **Aquasplash,** with a wave pool and 12 slides, and beside that, **La Petite Ferme,** a petting zoo. It's only a short distance from Antibes and Biot; take N7 north, then head left at La Brague onto D4, toward Biot. ⊠ *309 rue Mozart,* ☎ *04–93–33–49–49.* 🎫 *Marineland 124 frs/€19, Papillons 46 frs/€7, Aquasplash 98 frs/€15, La Petite Ferme 54 frs/€8.23. Joint-ticket admission and two-day passport for all parks available on request.* ⊙ *Daily 10–dark.*

Dining and Lodging

$ ✕🏨 **Galerie des Arcades.** Tucked away behind the quiet palm-lined
★ place des Arcades in the old town, this combination hotel-restaurant-art gallery draws a chic and loyal clientele. They come to browse in the gallery, enjoy a weekend in one of the extraordinary guest rooms or dine on the serious, unpretentious, authentic Provençal food: rabbit sautéed in fresh herbs, stuffed sardines, or a Friday *aïoli* (fish and crudités served with garlic mayonnaise). Eat at the checked-cloth-covered tables, either under the arcades or under the cozy beams indoors. Then ask for one of the three *grandes chambres* (large rooms) and revel in antiquity: four-poster beds, stone sinks and fireplaces, beams, and a tapestry-rich color scheme. (The smaller rooms are nothing to write

home about.) ✉ *14 pl. des Arcades, 06410,* ☎ *04–93–65–01–04,* ℻
04–93–65–01–05. 12 rooms. Restaurant. AE, DC, MC, V.

Villeneuve-Loubet

🕗 *10 km (6 mi) north of Antibes.*

This tiny village, its medieval château heavily restored in the 19th century, is best known for its sprawl of overbuilt beachfront, heavily
charged with concrete high-rises and with all the architectural charm
of a parking ramp.

Yet, if you're a foodie, you may want to make a pilgrimage to the eccentric **Musée de l'Art Culinaire** (Museum of Culinary Arts), a shrine
to the career of the great chef Auguste Escoffier (1846–1935). The epitome of 19th-century culinary extravagance and revered by the French
as much as Joan of Arc and de Gaulle, Escoffier was the founding father
of the school of haute cuisine Calvin Trillin calls "stuff-stuff-with-heavy,"
where ingredients are stripped, simmered, stuffed, sauced, and generally intervened with, sometimes beyond recognition. His was the school
of food as sculpture—the famous *pièces montées,* wedding-cake spires
of spun sugar, and the world of menus of staggering length and com-
plexity. He wowed 'em at the Ritz in Paris and the Savoy and Carlton
in London and is a point of reference for every modern chef—if only
as a foil for rebellion. In his birthplace you'll view illustrations of his
creations and a collection of fantastical menus, including one featuring the meat of zoo animals killed in the war of 1870. ✉ *3 rue Escoffier,* ☎ *04–93–20–80–51.* ☒ *25 frs/€3.81.* ☉ *July–Aug., Tues.–Sun.
2–7; Sept.–Oct. and Dec.–June, Tues.–Sun. 2–6. Closed Nov.*

Cagnes-sur-Mer

🕗 *14 km (9 mi) southwest of Nice, 10 km (6 mi) north of Antibes.*

Although from N7 you may be tempted to give wide berth to Cagnes-
sur-Mer—with its congested sprawl of freeway overpasses, tacky
tourist-oriented stores, and beachfront pizzerias—follow the signs inland and up into **Haut-de-Cagnes,** with its steeply cobbled old town.
It's a pleasure to wander the old streets, some with cobbled steps, others
passing under vaulted arches. The houses are unusually pretty and well
preserved, many dating from the 14th and 15th centuries.

Crowning Haut-de-Cagnes is the fat, crenellated **Château de Cagnes.**
Built in 1310 by the Grimaldis and reinforced over the centuries, this
imposing fortress lords over the coastline, banners flying from its square
watchtower. Its balustraded stairway and the triangular Renaissance courtyard, with a triple row of classical arcades, are infinitely more graceful
than the exterior. Within are vaulted medieval chambers, a vast Renaissance fireplace, and a splendid 17th-century trompe l'oeil fresco of
the fall of Phaeton from his sun chariot. The château also contains three
highly specialized museums: the **Musée de l'Olivier** (Olive Tree Museum),
an introduction to the history and cultivation of this Provençal mainstay; the obscure and eccentric **Collection Suzy-Solidor,** a group of portraits of the cabaret chanteuse painted by her artist friends, including
Cocteau and Dufy; and the **Musée d'Art Moderne Méditerranéen**
(Mediterranean Museum of Modern Art), which contains paintings by
some of the 20th-century devotees of the Côte d'Azur, including Chagall, Cocteau, and Dufy. If you've climbed this far, continue to the
tower and look over the coastline views in the same way that the guards
once watched for Saracens. ✉ *pl. Grimaldi,* ☎ *04–93–20–87–29.* ☒
20 frs/€3.05. ☉ *Oct. and Dec.–Easter, Wed.–Sun. 10–noon and 2–5;
Easter–Sept., Wed.–Sun. 10–noon and 2–6. Closed Nov.*

The **Chapelle Notre-Dame-de-la-Protection,** with its Italianate bell tower, was first built in the 13th century after the fortress had been destroyed; as a hedge against further invasion, they placed this plea for Mary's protection at the village edge. In 1936 the *curé* (priest) discovered traces of fresco under the bubbling plaster; a full stripping revealed every inch of the apse to have been decorated in scenes of the life of the Virgin and Jesus, roughly executed late in the 16th century. From the chapel's porch are sweeping sea views. ⊠ *rue Hippolyte Guis.*

Auguste Renoir (1841–1919) was particularly fond of the Chapelle Notre-Dame-de-la-Protection, and of the whole town as well. After staying up and down the coast, Renoir settled in a house in Les Collettes, just east of the old town, now the **Musée Renoir.** Here he passed the last 12 years of his life, painting the landscape around him, working in bronze, and rolling his wheelchair through the luxuriant garden of olive, lemon, and orange trees. You can view his home as it was preserved by his children, including his bed, his wheelchair, and of course his paintbrushes and easel. You can also view 11 of his last paintings and a bronze Venus in the garden bearing testimony to his successful ventures into sculpture. On Thursdays in July and August there are English-language guided tours. ⊠ *av. des Collettes,* ☎ *04–93–20–61–07.* 🎫 *20 frs/€3.05.* ☉ *June–Oct., Wed.–Mon. 10–noon and 2–6; Dec.–May, Wed.–Mon. 10–noon and 2–5. Closed Nov.*

Dining and Lodging

$$$ ✕🏨 **Le Cagnard.** What better way to experience old Cagnes's grand castle views than to stay in a 13th-century manor perched on its ramparts? Maintaining a discreet sense of medieval atmosphere—pastel-rubbed beams, restored murals and vaulting, a few four-poster beds—this romantic inn offers regal comfort. Most rooms look out over the old town and on toward the sea. The restaurant (closed November through mid-December; no lunch Thursday) offers sophisticated Mediterranean cuisine, from black-truffle lasagne to sea bass sauteed with grapefruit, with summertime dining on the place du Château. ⊠ *rue du Pontis-Long, 06800,* ☎ *04–93–20–73–21,* 📠 *04–93–22–06–39. 21 rooms. Restaurant. AE, DC, MC, V.* ✍

ST-PAUL, VENCE, AND BACKCOUNTRY HILL TOWNS

High above the coastline rises a rank of sunbaked hills, which still retain the arid climate and rustic ambience of old Provence. Inspired—indeed, propelled—by the clutter and crowds of the coast, forays into the famous villages on the plateau behind are an important part of the ritual of visiting the Côte d'Azur. High in the hills they loom, parallel to the sea, smelling fragrantly of wild herbs and medieval history . . . and soap shops. So hungry have the hordes that flock to the Riviera become for a taste of Pagnol-and-Peter-Mayle that many of the hill towns have been only too happy to oblige. Many of these old stone villages, which once hunkered down against the onslaught of Moors, now open their pale-blue shutters wide to surges of day-trippers from the beach. Stooped stone rowhouses are now galleries and boutiques offering everything from neo-Van Gogh sofa art to assembly-line lavender sachets, and everywhere you'll hear the gentle *breet-breet* of mechanical souvenir *cigales* (cicadas).

As the most conveniently accessible of the famous hill villages, St-Paul and Vence have become commercialized to an almost overwhelming degree, especially in high season. If you're allergic to souvenir shops, artsy-craftsy boutiques, and middle-brow art galleries, aim to visit off-season or after hours, when the stone-paved alleys, backstreets, placettes, and rampart overlooks empty of tourists, and when the scent of strawberry potpourri is washed away by the natural perfume of bougainvillea and jasmine wafting from terra-cotta jars.

St-Paul

⑲ *18 km (11 mi) west of Nice.*

The most commercially developed of Provence's perched villages and second only to Mont-St-Michel for its influx of tourists, St-Paul (often called St-Paul-de-Vence) is nonetheless a magical place when the crowds thin. Artists—Chagall, Bonnard, and Miró—were drawn to its light, its pure air, its wraparound views, and its honey-colored stone walls, soothingly cool on a hot Provençal afternoon. Film stars loved its lazy yet genteel ways, lingering on the garden-bower terrace of the Auberge de la Colombe d'Or and challenging the locals to a game of pétanque under the shade of the plane trees.

In the Middle Ages St-Paul was basically a city-state, and it controlled its own political destiny for centuries. Its 16th-century ramparts curved boldly over the valley, challenging Vence, Cagnes, and even almighty Nice. But by the early 20th century St-Paul had faded to oblivion—until a few penniless artists began paying their drink bills at the local *auberge* (inn) with paintings. Nowadays art of a sort still dominates in the myriad tourist traps that divert your eyes from the beauty of its old stone houses.

It won't take you long to "do" St-Paul; a pedestrian circuit leads you inevitably through its rue-Grande to the *donjon* (fortress tower) and austere Gothic church. But break away and slip into a few mosaic-cobbled backstreets, little more than alleys; door after door, window after niche spill over with potted flowers and orange trees. The shuttered stone houses rear up over the streets, so close you could shake hands from window to window. And no matter which way you turn, you'll suddenly break into the open at the rampart walls; follow along the walkway to see the Tuscan-pretty landscape that quilts over the hills below, backed by an ivory sprawl of Alps.

On your way from the overpriced parking garages, you'll pass a Provençal scene played out with cinematic flair yet still authentic: the perpetual game of pétanque outside the **Café de la Place** (✉ pl. de Gaulle, ☎ 04–93–32–80–03). A sun-weathered pack of men in caps, cardigans, and workers' blues—occasionally joined by a passing professional with tie and rolled-up sleeves—gathers under the massive plane trees and stands serene, silent, and intent to roll metal balls across the dusty square. Until his death Yves Montand made regular appearances here, participating in this ultimate southern scenario.

★ Many people come to St-Paul just to visit the **Fondation Maeght,** a small modern-art museum founded in 1964 by art dealer Aimé Maeght. Set on a wooded cliff top high above the medieval town, the museum is an extraordinary marriage of the arc-and-plane architecture of José Sert; the looming sculptures of Miró, Moore, and Giacometti; and its humbling setting of pines, vines, and flowing planes of water. On display is an intriguing and ever-varying array of the work of modern masters, including the wise and funny late-life masterwork *La Vie* (*Life*) by Chagall. ✉ Colline des Gardettes, ☎ 04–93–32–81–63. 🎟 50 frs/€7.62. ☉ July–Sept., daily 10–7; Oct.–June, daily 10–12:30 and 2:30–6.

Dining and Lodging

$–$$ ✕ **Le Tilleul Menthe.** Before you plunge into the dense tangle of ruelles in old St-Paul, stop on the ramparts under the thick-trunked, broad-leaved plane trees for a light meal or snack at this atmospheric out-door café. Served here are a few hot, plain dishes—roast chicken, pastas, or a hot goat-cheese salad, for instance—as well as drinks and sorbets, and you can idle at a table looking over the stone walls, valley, and Alps. ⊠ *pl. Tilleul,* ☎ *04–93–32–80–36.*

$$$$ ✕🏨 **Le Saint-Paul.** Right in the center of the labyrinth of stone alleys, with views over the ancient ramparts, this luxurious inn (a Relais & Châteaux property) fills a noble 15th-century house with comfort and charm. Provençal furniture, golden quarried stone, and lush reproduction fabrics warm the salons and restaurant; rooms are decked in sleek pastels and sprig prints, and a few have balconies over the valley. The restaurant, serving sophisticated regional specialties such as eggplant terrine with *pistou* (Provençal pesto), and sole with bacon and pumpkin puree, is a cut above as well. And a candlelit meal on the terrace, where flowers spill from every niche, is a romantic's dream. (Off-season, the restaurant is closed Wednesday and lunch is not served on Tuesday.) To park, you may briefly defy the ACCÈS INTERDIT (entry forbidden) signs, follow the rampart road, and drop off your baggage before parking on the other side of the village. ⊠ *86 rue Grande, 06570,* ☎ *04–93–32–65–25,* 𝖥𝖠𝖷 *04–93–32–52–94. 19 rooms. Restaurant, bar, air-conditioning. AE, DC, MC, V. Closed early Jan.–mid-Feb..* 🐾

$$$–$$$$ ✕🏨 **La Colombe d'Or.** The art display here may cause a double take—are those really Mirós, Bonnards, Picassos, Légers, and Braques hanging on the rustic walls? Yes, it's true, they were indeed given in payment by the artists in hungrier days. This idyllic old auberge was the heart and soul of St-Paul's artistic revival, and the cream of 20th-century France lounged together under its fig trees—Picasso and Chagall, Maeterlinck and Kipling, Marcel Pagnol (*Manon des Sources*) and Jacques Prévert (*Les Enfants du Paradis*). Yves Montand and Simone Signoret met and married here, and current film stars make appearances from time to time. They do so more in homage to the inn's resonant history and *pastorale* atmosphere than for its food, which is unambitious bordering on the ordinary—rack of lamb, rabbit stew, aïoli and *petits farcis* (stuffed vegetables)—but high-priced nonetheless. Give in to the green-shaded loveliness of the terrace, the creamy manners of the waitstaff, and the sense of contemporary history. The pool is an idyllic garden bower, complete with a Calder, and there's a Braques by the fireplace in the bar. Rooms are spartan and don't live up to the luxury-level prices; they simply rent you access to this idyllic and legendary retreat. ⊠ *pl. Général-de-Gaulle, 06570,* ☎ *04–93–32–80–02. AE, DC, MC, V. Closed mid-Nov.–late Dec.*

$$ 🏨 **Le Hameau.** Less than a mile below tourist-packed St-Paul, with views
★ of the valley and the village, this lovely little inn is a jumble of terraces, trellises, archways, orange trees, olives, and heavy-scented honeysuckle vines. The main hotel, built in 1920, has good-size rooms and old Provençal furniture; you can also opt for the 18th-century farmhouse, with smaller, more modern rooms but wonderful views. One triple room even has a kitchenette; honeymooners take note. Each room seems to skew toward a private world, several with individual terraces for *grasses matinées* (late, lazy breakfasts). The beautiful new pool has hydro-massage. ⊠ *528 rte. de La Colle, 06570,* ☎ *04–93–32–80–24,* 𝖥𝖠𝖷 *04–93–32–55–75. 15 rooms. Pool. MC, V. Closed mid-Nov.–mid-Feb. (except Christmas–New Year's).* 🐾

Vence

㉚ *4 km (2½ mi) north of St-Paul, 22 km (14 mi) north of Nice.*

Encased behind stone walls inside a thriving modern market town, this jewel of an old town dates from the 15th century. Though crowded with boutiques and souvenir shops, it's slightly more conscious of its history than St-Paul—plaques guide you through its historic squares and *portes* (gates). Wander past the pretty place du Peyra with its fountains, and place Clemenceau, with its ocher-color Hôtel-de-Ville (Town Hall), to place du Frêne, with its ancient ash tree planted in the 16th century.

On place Godeau, in the old-town center, the **Cathédrale de la Nativité de la Vierge** (Cathedral of the Birth of the Virgin) was built on the Roman's Champ de Mars (military drilling field) and traces bits and pieces to Carolingian and even Roman times. It's a hybrid of Romanesque and Baroque styles, expanded and altered over the centuries. The carved-wood stalls are worth studying (if access to the loft isn't blocked); they were sculpted between 1463 and 1467 by the Grasse cabinetmaker Jacques Bellot, and their detail and characterizations border on the risqué. In the baptistery is a ceramic mosaic of Moses in the bulrushes by Chagall.

★ On the outskirts of Vence, toward St-Jeannet, it's easy to bypass a humble white chapel below the road, indistinguishable from a home except for its imposing cast-iron cross. But the **Chapelle du Rosaire** (Chapel of the Rosary), decorated with beguiling simplicity and clarity by Matisse between 1947 and 1951, reflects the reductivist style of the era: the walls, floor, and ceiling are gleaming white, and the small stained-glass windows are cool greens and blues. Stylized biblical characters are roughly sketched in thick black outline; in the annex behind the chapel you can see that earlier versions were more detailed. "Despite its imperfections I think it is my masterpiece . . . the result of a lifetime devoted to the search for truth," wrote Matisse, who designed and dedicated the chapel when he was in his eighties and nearly blind. ⊠ *av. Henri-Matisse,* ☎ *04–93–58–03–26.* ▭ *13 frs/€1.98.* ☉ *Mon., Wed., and Sat. 10–11:30; Tues. and Thurs. 10–11:30 and 2–5:30; Fri. 2–5:30 during school vacations.*

Dining and Lodging

$$$ × **Jacques Maximin.** Temperamental superchef Jacques Maximin has
★ found peace of mind in a gray-stone farmhouse covered with wisteria and flanked by spikes of cypress—his home and his own country restaurant. Having cut his teeth at La Bonne Auberge in Antibes and become a star at the Chantecler at the Negresco in Nice, he left it all for the arrière-pays. Here he devotes himself to creative country cooking, superbly prepared and unpretentiously priced—shellfish soup with crayfish ravioli, white beans in rich squid ink, Mediterranean fish grilled in rock salt and olive oil, and candied-eggplant sorbet. The yellow dining room is airy and uncluttered, with light pouring through saffron curtains; the garden, sheltered with creamy parasols, is a palm-shaded paradise. ⊠ *689 chemin de la Gaude,* ☎ *04–93–58–90–75. AE, MC, V. Closed Mon. and no dinner Sun. (Sept.–Oct. and Dec.–June). Closed Nov.*

$–$$ × **La Farigoule.** In a long, beamed dining room that opens onto a shady terrace, this is a fine place to enjoy sophisticated Provençal cooking in an easygoing atmosphere. Watch for tangy *pissaladieres* (pizza-like onion-and-anchovy tarts) with sardines marinated in ginger and lemon, salt-cod ravioli, lamb with olive polenta, and a crunchy parfait of honey and hazelnuts. ⊠ *15 rue Henri-Isnard,* ☎ *04–93–58–01–27. MC, V. Closed Wed., first 2 wks Nov., end Dec.–early Jan., two wks Feb. No lunch Tues. Oct.–Apr. and Thurs. May–Sept.*

$$ ☳ **Villa Roseraie.** Although it doesn't have a rose garden, this 100-year-old house has a giant magnolia that spreads its venerable branches over the terrace. Inside, owners Monsieur and Madame Martefon have

THE ROUTE DES CRÊTES

ON A SCENIC ALL-DAY DRIVE along the Route des Crêtes (Route of the Mountain Crests), you'll meander through hills woven with pine forests, needlepoint-neat olive orchards, and groves of waxy-green orange trees, punctuated by a string of picture-perfect perched villages.

Starting at Vence, continue past the Chapelle du Rosaire and follow D2210; it leads toward the medieval village of **St-Jeannet,** draped at the foot of the magnificent limestone cliff that rears 1,312 ft above, known as the *baou* (mesa, or butte). From the top you can look out over the Estérel and the Alps. Continue on to the tiny hilltop village of **Gattières,** taking a break to explore backstreets and ancient squares. Cut north on the narrow, wild D2209 to precariously perched **Carros-Villages,** spiraled at the base of a four-square medieval château. From the top you can look out over the string of villages and panorama of mountains.

Wind slowly ahead up the miniature D1 to **Le Broc,** once a sentinel point. Now you'll twist over the pine-darkened hills to Bouyon and ocher-gold **Bézaudun-les-Alpes,** which remains virtually untouched. Forge on to pretty **Coursegoules,** draped on a hill under a looming mountain, and peek into the church; it contains a 16th-century altarpiece attributed to Bréa. D2 will lead you south over the climactic 3,159 ft **Col de Vence** (Vence Pass), from where you can pan the vast Mediterranean coast before returning to Vence and civilization.

kept all the charming regional details: mix-and-match old furniture, fine local tiles and fabrics, even homemade bath salts and jams. You can enjoy a generous breakfast on the terrace and lounge by the pool much of the year, and it's a quick walk down to old Vence. ⊠ *51 av. Henri-Giraud, 06140,* ☎ *04–93–58–02–20,* Ⅷ *04–93–58–99–31. 14 rooms. Pool. AE, MC, V.*

$–$$ ☒ **Auberge des Seigneurs.** This extraordinary little inn holds forth in a wing of an old-town manor house overlooking the landmark ash tree reputedly planted by François I. Eccentrically decorated with antiques and modern art, it is personally managed by Madame Rodi and her daughter—the third generation. Rooms are spare but manorial, with dark antiques made cheery by Provençal fabrics. The restaurant is formal and a tad stuffy, but the fireplace-roasted rack of lamb is legendary. ⊠ *pl. du Frêne, 06140,* ☎ *04–93–58–04–24,* ⅧX *04–93–24–08–01. 6 rooms. Restaurant. AE, MC, V. Closed Nov.–mid-Mar.*

Tourrettes-sur-Loup

㉑ *5 km (3 mi) west of Vence, 24 km (15 mi) west of Nice.*

More accessible—and thus more touristy—than the little villages on the Route des Crêtes (☞ Close-Up, *above*), this steep-sloped old hill town stands over an invisible line that distinguishes it from the day-trip towns of Vence and St-Paul. The wind blows colder, the forest around is dense and arid, and the coast seems hours—and ages—away (though Tourrettes is less than an hour's drive from Nice). From the town square that doubles as a parking lot with an ongoing pétanque game on one side, to the quiet cafés lining it, to the sharply raked, torturously twisted streets snaking down the slopes of the old town, this is old Provence without the stage makeup. Yes, there are dozens of galleries and arts-and-crafts shops, but they're owned and run by real artists and artisans, who have made a life for themselves in this intimate community.

Built in the Middle Ages inside a rampart of stone houses and encircling a 15th-century church, Tourrettes's old town crowns a rocky plateau. At its feet the olive orchards are purple with violets in spring, which are cultivated for the perfume industry, candied in Toulouse, or tied into nosegays and sold in flower markets across France.

NICE

As the fifth-largest city in France, sprawling from its waterfront airport to the Cap Ferrat, this distended tangle of suburbs, modern apartment buildings, industry, and traffic is often avoided by travelers who expect a more leisurely experience from the south of France. Crawling into town from the airport or stepping off the train at the congested commercial quarter around Gare Nice-Ville, you may be tempted to bolt for the nearest city limit, where signs encircle and slash through the name Nice—as if to say "not Nice."

They couldn't be more wrong. The vast sprawl of urbanity south of the autoroute pours inevitably toward the sea, and the waterfront, paralleled by the famous promenade des Anglais and lined by grand hotels and mansions, is one of the noblest in France. It's capped by a dramatic promontory (called "the château") whose slopes plunge almost into the sea and at whose base unfolds a bewitching warren of ancient streets reminiscent of Italy, of Greece, of old Sardinia.

It was in this old quarter, now the Vieille Ville, that the Greeks established a market-port and named it Nikaia. Having already established Marseille as early as the 4th century BC, they branched out along the coast soon afterwards and founded the city that would become Marseille's chief coastal rival. The Romans established themselves a little later on the hills of Cimiez (Cemenelum) and quickly overshadowed the waterfront port. After falling to the Saracen invasions, Nice regained power as an independent state, developing into an important port in the early Middle Ages.

So cocksure did it become that in 1388, Nice, along with the hill towns behind, effectively seceded from the county of Provence, under Louis d'Anjou, and allied itself with Savoie. Thus began its intimate liaison with the House of Savoy, and through it with Piedmont and Sardinia, as the Comté de Nice (Nice County). It was a relationship that lasted some 500 years, tinting the culture, architecture, and dialect in rich Italian hues.

By the 19th century Nice was flourishing commercially, locked in rivalry with the neighboring shipping port of Genoa. Another source of income: the dawning of tourism, as first the English, then the Russian nobility discovered its extraordinary climate and superb waterfront position. A parade of fine stone mansions and hotels closed into a nearly solid wall of masonry, separated from the smooth-round rocks of the beach by the appropriately named promenade des Anglais (promenade of the English).

Today, Nice strikes an engaging balance between old-world grace, port-town exotica, urban energy, whimsy, and—in its extraordinary museums and thriving arts life—high culture. Thanks to its two universities, there's a healthy dose of the young and hip, too. You could easily spend your vacation here and emerge days or weeks later subtly Latinized, sensually and aesthetically engaged, attuned to Nice's quirks, its rhythms, and its Mediterranean tides.

FLOWERS, FLOATS, AND FATHEADS

F THE WORD CARNIVAL MEANS MASKED balls in Venice to most, or conjures images of feather-clad dancers writhing rhythmically through the streets of Rio, few people associate Nice with this pre-Lenten festival of excess and droll debauchery. Yet this most Latin of French cities is the capital of Carnaval in France, and transforms itself every February from a relatively sedate seaside metropolis into one vast party. The streets behind the waterfront and around place Masséna explode in bright lights and color, and parades, masks, and impromptu street celebrations are everyday sights. Confetti brightens the gutters and no one seems to mind having colored streamers caught in their hair.

It's a tradition that dates back to pagan times, when the Romans fêted the end of winter and the dawning of spring. The festival translated easily into Christian terms, when the church established the period of partial fasting before Easter. We call it Lent; the French call it Carême; but in church Latin it was *carne levare* (crudely translated, "take out the meat"), and easily evolved into the word *carnaval.* Thus *mardi gras* (fat Tuesday) was the last chance to indulge before Ash Wednesday and the deprivations of Lent.

It wasn't long, however, before the pleasures of Carnaval outstripped those of Mardi Gras and shook free of their sacred meaning. The festival these days lasts a good two weeks and often takes place smack in the middle of Lent.

Nice's Carnaval is extremely user friendly, with a published calendar of events and easy advance ticket sales for any seated events. There's the presentation of towering effigies of King and Queen Carnaval on place Masséna, which is transformed into an electric fantasy-land of music and blinking lights. There are parades of magnificently crafted *grosses têtes* (literally, "fatheads"), enormous puppetlike personages that make Macy's balloons look like so much rubber. And there are the famous *batailles des fleurs* (flower battles), really full-scale parades complete with marching bands, clowns, and samba troupes. Elaborate floats heaped with Côte d'Azur flowers cruise down the promenade des Anglais hauling a cargo of spectacularly costumed beauty queens who toss fresh flowers into the crowd. The crowds in the bleachers lining the promenade des Anglais toss back confetti, wave branches of lemon-yellow mimosa, and cheer for their favorite floats. Weaving between the floats are stilt-walkers, jugglers, and street-theater troupes dressed in phantasmagoric excess who leer at onlookers and tease gawking children. Imagination reigns and no image is too extreme, too bizarre, too extravagant.

The grand finale of Carnaval, which draws the days and nights of festivity to a close, takes on a solemn air. For the last time the towering dummy-king is paraded down avenue Jean-Médecin and stands, still and lonely, on the dark pebble beach below the promenade. A parade of torchbearers in friars' robes cut a glowing swath through the crowd and set fire to the royal puppet. A silence falls over the crowd, then a cheer—really a primal roar—rises. The flames glow across the water as they engulf the King and, from a boat hovering off shore, fireworks burst in confetti colors over the waterfront. The party's overat least until next year.Despite the theatrics of the grand finale, the whole of Carnaval strikes a wholesome tone, with revelry maintaining a polite and familial level that rarely breaks into rowdiness. This, the city claims, is due to a vigilant and discreet security source who see to it that despite the let-your-hair-down mood, things never get out of hand. For dates, schedules, and information, contact ☎ 04–92–14–48–14.

Nice

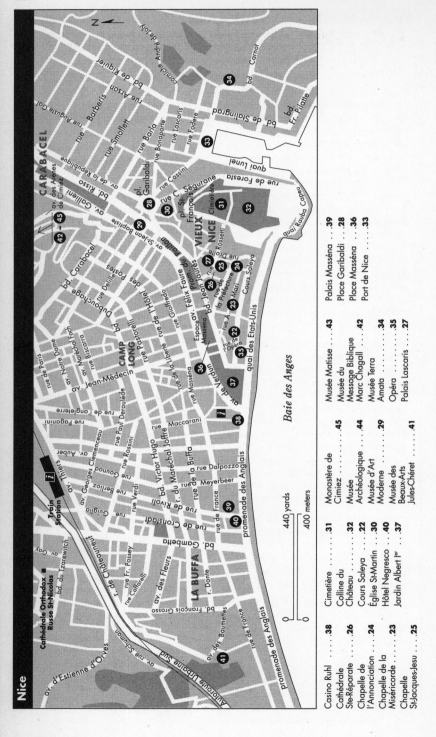

Vieux Nice

Framed by the "château"—really a rocky promontory—and cours Saleya, the old town of Nice is its strongest drawing point and, should you only be passing through, the best place to capture the city's historic atmosphere. Its grid of narrow streets, darkened by houses five and six stories high with bright splashes of laundry fluttering overhead and jewel-box Baroque churches on every other corner, creates a magic that seems utterly removed from the Côte d'Azur fast lane.

A Good Walk

Begin your exploration on **cours Saleya** ㉒, preferably in the morning so you can experience the market in full swing. Its cafés, restaurants, and market stalls throng with the sounds, smells, and sights of old Nice. At its center you'll find the florid Baroque **Chapelle de la Miséricorde** ㉓, worthy of a stop. Then make your way to the far end of the cours. The tall yellow-stone building at its end, its top floor wrapped around with a balcony, was home to Henri Matisse from 1921 to 1938; from the apartments on its top floors he took in magnificent views over the sea. Turn left up rue de la Poissonerie to find the extravagant **Chapelle de l'Annonciation** ㉔. Continue up Poissonerie to rue de la Place Vieille, then head right to rue Droite. The **Chapelle St-Jacques-Jesu** ㉕ looms large and spare in comparison with neighboring chapels. Turn left on rue Rossetti and cross the square to the **Cathédrale Ste-Réparate** ㉖, its restored ocher facade an inspired balance of Italianate arcs and lines.

NEED A BREAK?
For fresh, homemade gelato-style ice cream offered in a rainbow of flavors and colors, stop at **Glacier Fenocchio** (✉ 6 rue de la Poissonnerie, ☎ 04-93-62-88-80). There's even a choice of locally grown citrus flavors, including blood orange, mandarin, and Menton lemon.

Now take a break from the sacred, doubling back up rue Rossetti and continuing left up narrow rue Droite to the magnificent **Palais Lascaris** ㉗, whose broad classical facade squeezed onto this narrow street belies the Baroque extravagance within. Continue up rue Droite to **place St-François,** where a port-fresh fish market holds forth every morning.

Head up rue Pairolière, but take time to duck left and right up the tiny alleys and steep streets that plunge you into a concentration of popular cafés and restaurants, including the landmark street-food hang-out called Chez René (☞ Dining and Lodging, *below*). You'll emerge on boulevard Jean-Jaurès and empty onto the grand arcaded **place Garibaldi** ㉘, which would be at home in Milan or Turin. One of its five street-spokes points straight to the **Musée d'Art Moderne** ㉙, a bold sculpture of a building anchoring a sleek plaza.

From place Garibaldi and boulevard Jean-Jaurès, follow rue Neuve to the **Église St-Martin** ㉚, the oldest church. From here wind your way up rue de la Providence and rue Jouane Nicolas to the **Cimetière** ㉛ and ultimately the ruins of the castle, now a park called the **Colline du Château** ㉜, with a wraparound panorama of Nice and the coast. From here you can either follow the switchback steps down or take the *ascenseur* (elevator) to the foot of the fat Tour Bellanda (Bellanda Tower), where the French composer Hector Berlioz once lived.

Next, you can cross quai des Etats-Unis to the pebbled beach and rest your weary feet. Or, if you're still feeling energetic, swing left away from the old town and hike around the tidy rectangle of the **Port de Nice** ㉝, with its neat rows of pleasure boats, and from its end follow boulevard Carnot to the **Musée Terra Amata** ㉞, marking the settlement where man first flourished some 400,000 years ago.

TIMING

Aim for morning on this walk, so you'll see the markets on cours Saleya and place St-François at their liveliest. If you include a visit to the Palais Lascaris and a visit to the Musée Terra Amata, this would make a wonderful full-day's outing.

Sights to See

㉖ Cathédrale Ste-Réparate. Named for the 15-year-old Palestinian martyr whose body washed ashore at Nice to become the city's patron saint, this superb ensemble of columns, cupolas, and symmetrical ornaments dominates the old town, flanked by its own 18th-century bell tower and capped by a glossy ceramic tile dome. The cathedral's interior, restored to a bright color palette of ocher golds and rusts, has elaborate plasterwork and decorative frescoes on every surface. Look for the **Chapelle du St-Sacrement** in the north transept, dating from 1707; its twisted marble columns and exuberant sculpture are worthy of Bernini and St. Peter's in Rome. ⊠ *rue Ste-Réparate.*

㉔ Chapelle de l'Annonciation. Also known through typical Nice-lore obfuscation as St-Jaume, St-Giaume, or Ste-Rita, this 17th-century Carmelite chapel is a classic example of pure Niçoise Baroque, from its sculpted door to its extravagant marble work and the florid symmetry of its arches and cupolas. The interior concentrates every form of colored faux-stonework, rich marble inlay, gilt, and frescoes—a lot of bombast squeezed into a finite space. Though it's officially dedicated to St. James the Apostle, the people of Nice lavish flowers and candles on the statue of Ste-Rita in the first chapel on the left; having suffered from a leprous sore and a lifetime of isolation in the 14th century, she has come to represent help for the terminally ill. ⊠ *rue de la Poissonerie.*

★ ㉓ Chapelle de la Miséricorde. If you step inside only one Baroque chapel here, this superb 1740 structure on cours Saleya should be it. A superbly balanced pièce-montée of half domes and cupolas, decorated within an inch of its life with frescoes, faux marble, gilt, and crystal chandeliers, it's the ultimate example of Nice Baroque at its most excessive and successful. A magnificent Bréa altarpiece crowns the ensemble. ⊠ *cours Saleya.*

㉕ Chapelle St-Jacques-Jesu. If Nice's other chapels are jewel boxes, this is a barn. Broad, open, and ringing hollow after the intense concentration of sheer matter in the Miséricorde and Ste-Rita, it seems austere by comparison. That's only because the decoration is spread over a more expansive surface. If it's possible, this 17th-century Baroque chapel is even more theatrical and over the top than its peers. Angels throng in plaster and fresco, pillars spill over with extravagantly sculpted capitals, and from the pulpit (to the right, at the front), the crucifix is supported by a disembodied arm. ⊠ *Corner of rue Droite and rue Gesu.*

㉛ Cimetière (Cemetery). This solemn cluster of white tombs looms prominently over the city below, providing a serene or macabre detail of daily life, depending on your mood. Under Nice's blue skies, the gleaming white marble and Italian mix of melodrama and exuberance in the decorations, dedications, photo portraits, and sculptures are somehow oddly life-affirming. There are three sections, to this day segregating the Catholics, the Protestants, and the Jews. ⊠ *allée François-Aragon.*

㉜ Colline du Château (Château Hill). Though nothing remains of this once-massive medieval stronghold but a few ruins left after its 1706 dismantling, the name château still applies to this high plateaulike park, from which you can take in extraordinary views of the Baie des Anges, the length of the promenade des Anglais, and the red-ocher roofs of the old town. ⊠ *At east end of promenade des Anglais.* ☉ *Daily 7–7.*

★ ㉒ **Cours Saleya.** This long pedestrian thoroughfare, half street, half square, is the nerve center of old Nice, the heart of the Vieille Ville (Old Town), and the stage-set for the daily dramas of the marketplace and café life. Framed with 18th-century houses and shaded by plane trees, the long, narrow square bursts into a fireworks-show of color Tuesday through Sunday, when flower-market vendors roll armloads of mimosas, irises, roses, and orange blossoms into *cornets* (paper cones) and thrust them into the arms of shoppers (Tues.–Sat. 6 AM–5:30 PM, Sun. 6–noon). Cafés and restaurants, all more or less touristy, fill outdoor tables with onlookers who bask in the sun. At the far-east end, antiques and *brocante* (collectibles) draw avid junk-hounds every Monday morning. Just beyond, place Félix seems to lure the most fashionable crowd to see and be seen, perhaps because there are no market stands to get in the way of the most visible café tables, or because it provides clearest access to sun on cool winter days. ⊠ *2 blocks back from the quai des Etats-Unis, in the center of the old town.*

㉚ **Église St-Martin.** Also known as St-Augustin, this serene Baroque structure at the foot of the château anchors the oldest church-parish in Nice. Built in 1405, it was here that Martin Luther preached in 1510 and that Garibaldi was baptized in 1807. ⊠ *rue Sincaire.*

㉙ **Musée d'Art Moderne** (Modern Art Museum). Moored by four marble-front towers, joined by the transparent arcs of pedestrian bridges and dramatically framing a concourse decked with outdoor sculptures, this building is a bold and emphatic statement of Nice's presence in the modern world. The art collection inside focuses intently and thoroughly on contemporary art from the late 1950s onward, featuring works of the École de Nice (Nice School), the self-dubbed Nouveau Réalistes (New Realists) such as artists César, Bernar Venet, Ben, Yves Klein, Daniel Spoerri, Jean Tinguely, and Niki de Saint-Phalle. The collection includes international acquisitions, too, ranging from Jim Dine and Frank Stella to Miró and Giacometti. Be sure to climb along the rooftop sculpture terrace, a catwalk overlooking the whole of the city. ⊠ *promenade des Arts,* ☎ *04–93–62–61–62.* 🎟 *25 frs/€3.81.* ⊗ *Mon., Wed.–Thurs., and weekends 11–6; Fri. 11–10.*

㉞ **Musée Terra Amata.** During the digging of the foundation for a new building in 1966, the shovels revealed the remains of a temporary settlement once used by elephant hunters around 380,000 BC. They were perhaps the oldest known inhabitants of Europe. Now the site is a museum reconstructing the ancient beach-camp known as Terra Amata ("beloved land") as it was, lodgings and all—incorporating a real human footprint, calcified in the sand. There are recorded commentaries in English, and films explaining the lifestyle of these earliest Europeans. Don't expect a blockbuster anthropology expo; displays are small-scale and mainly limited to tiny models. ⊠ *25 bd. Carnot,* ☎ *04–93–55–59–93.* 🎟 *25 frs/€3.81.* ⊗ *Oct.–mid-Sept., Tues.–Sun. 9–noon and 2–6. Closed last 2 wks Sept.*

㉗ **Palais Lascaris** (Lascaris Palace). This aristocratic palace was built in 1648 for Jean-Baptiste Lascaris-Vintimille, marechal to the duke of Savoy, in a manner grand enough to put the neighboring chapels to shame. The magnificent vaulted staircase with its massive stone balustrade and niches filled with classical gods is only surpassed in grandeur by the Flemish tapestries (after Rubens) and the extraordinary trompe l'oeil fresco of the fall of Phaeton. On the ground floor an 18th-century pharmacy has been imported and reconstructed from Besançon, complete with built-in wooden cabinets and a lovely collection of faïence jars. There's also a collection of cookware and tools from daily life at the other end of the income scale. Like much of old Nice, this is a quirky, atmospheric museum, worth a stopover as you explore the backstreets. ⊠ *15 rue Droite,* ☎ *04–93–62–05–54.* 🎫 *Free.* ☉ *Tues.–Sun. 10–noon and 2–6.*

㉘ Place Garibaldi. Encircled by grand vaulted arcades stuccoed in rich yellow, this broad pentagon of a square could have been airlifted out of Turin. In the center the shrinelike fountain-sculpture of Garibaldi surveys the passersby, who stroll under the arcades and lounge in its cafés. Garibaldi is held in high esteem here: the Italian general fought beside his own sons in the French ranks during the war of 1870.

㉝ Port de Nice. In 1750 the Duke of Savoy ordered a port to be dug into the waterfront to shelter the approach of the freight ships, fishing boats, and yachts that still sail into its safety today. Surrounded in rhythmic symmetry by the ocher facades of 19th-century houses, it makes for a pleasant walk far from the beach crowds.

Along the Promenade des Anglais

Nice takes on a completely different character west of cours Saleya, with broad city blocks, vast neoclassic hotels and apartment houses, and a series of inviting parks dense with palm trees, greenery, and splashing fountains. From the Jardin Albert Ier, once the delta of the Paillon River, the famous promenade des Anglais stretches the length of the city's waterfront.

The original promenade was the brainchild of Lewis Way, an English minister in the growing community of British refugees drawn to Nice's climate. They needed a proper walkway to take the sea air and pooled resources to build a 2-m-wide (6½-ft-wide) road meandering through an alley of shade trees. Nowadays it's a wide multilane boulevard thick with traffic—in fact, it's the last gasp of the coastal highway N98. Beside it runs its charming parallel, the wide, sun-washed pedestrian walkway with intermittent steps leading down to the smooth-rock beach; its foundation is a seawall that keeps all but the wildest storm from sloshing waves over the promenade. A daily parade of *promeneurs,* rollerbladers, joggers, and sun-baskers strolls its broad pavement, looking out over the hypnotic blue expanse of the sea. Only in the wee hours is it possible to enjoy the waterfront stroll as the cream of Nice's international society did, when there were nothing more than hoof beats to compete with the roar of the waves.

A Good Walk

From the west end of cours Saleya, walk down rue St-François-de-Paule past the Belle-Époque **Opéra** ㉟, constructed in classic Italian tiered loggias. Continue up the street, then head right up rue de l'Opéra to **place Masséna** ㊱, framed in broad arcades and opening onto the vast, green **Jardin Albert Ier** ㊲. Three long blocks past the glamorous **Casino Ruhl** ㊳ you'll reach the gates and park of the imposing **Palais Masséna** ㊴; to peruse its eclectic collection of nuggets of Nice history, walk through the grounds to enter from the rue de France side. Next door, the landmark **Hôtel Negresco** ㊵ expands its colossal facade along the waterfront, crowned at the corner by its signature dome.

Walk along the waterfront for a few blocks, past the busy boulevard Gambetta, then head inland up tiny rue Sauvan. Cross boulevard Grosso and head diagonally up the hill on avenue des Baumettes. In this quiet, once luxurious neighborhood you'll climb to the **Musée des Beaux-Arts Jules-Chéret** ㊶, built by the Ukrainian princess Kotschoubey in extravagant Italianate style.

This walk covers a long stretch of waterfront, so it may take up to an hour to stroll the length of it. Allow a half day if you explore the Palais Masséna or the Musée des Beaux Arts.

Sights to See

③⑧ Casino Ruhl. Behind its gleaming all-glass 1970s facade, this casino thrives on summer vacationers and winter convention crowds. Some sign into the hushed gambling room for roulette and blackjack, others stand at one of the 300-some slot machines. ⊠ *1 promenade des Anglais*, ☎ *04–97–03–12–22.* ☉ *Daily 10 AM–dawn.*

④⓪ Hôtel Negresco. This vast neoclassic palace hotel dominates a full block of the promenade and remains, for many, an enduring symbol of Côte d'Azur luxury. Its famous Salon Royal, a broad rotunda at the hotel's center, is classed as a historic monument, with its Gustav Eiffel lead-glass dome, Aubusson carpet, and Baccarat chandelier commissioned by Czar Nicholas II. Like many grand hotels trying to make ends meet these days, it now caters to conferences and tour groups (☞ Lodging, *below*).

③⑦ Jardin Albert Iᵉʳ (Albert Iᵉʳ Garden). This luxurious garden of tropical greenery stands over the delta of the River Paillon, underground since 1882. Every kind of flower and palm tree grows here, thrown into exotic relief by nighttime illumination. This is a wonderful place to claim a bench for a shaded picnic, snooze, or cuddle, and to watch the Niçois do the same.

④① Musée des Beaux-Arts Jules-Chéret (Jules-Chéret Fine Arts Museum). Housed in a 19th-century Italianate mansion, this museum has a fine collection of paintings by Nice artists of the era, including works by the museum's namesake. A small collection of Impressionist works includes paintings by Alfred Sisley, Pierre Bonnard, and Edouard Vuillard. Two pieces by Rodin, including the original plaster of *Le Baiser* (*The Kiss*), and some ceramic pieces by Picasso round out an otherwise modest ensemble of works by lesser artists. ⊠ *33 av. des Baumettes*, ☎ *04–92–15–28–28.* ☝ *25 frs/€3.81.* ☉ *Oct.–Apr., Tues.–Sun. 10–noon and 2–5; May–Sept., Tues.–Sun. 10–noon and 2–6.*

③⑤ Opéra. Demolished by a devastating 1881 fire, the victims of which lie in the cemetery on the hillside of the château, this magnificent Italian-style opera house rose from the ashes in 1885. Charles Garnier, architect of the Paris Opéra, consulted on its design. It's home today to the Opéra de Nice, with a permanent chorus, orchestra, and ballet corps (☞ Nightlife and the Arts, *below*). ⊠ *4 rue St-François-de-Paul*, ☎ *04–92–17–40–40.*

③⑨ Palais Masséna (Masséna Palace). This handsome Belle Époque villa was built by a grandson of Napoléon's, Marechal Masséna; his great-grandson donated it to Nice on the grounds that it house a museum of the city's history. The resulting **Musée d'Art et d'Histoire** (Museum of Art and History) is a fascinating hodgepodge of private collections reflecting every aspect of Nice's past, from Garibaldi's death sheet to Asian jewelry collected in imperial days to Empress Josephine's tiara, carved entirely in cameo. It also contains extraordinary notebook sketches of Napoléon by neoclassic painter Louis David, as vivid and natural as snapshots, as well as relief models of Nice in the 1930s and 1954—a desert-island wasteland compared to today's congested overbuilding. There's even a Bréa polyptich of St-Marguerite. It's a must if you love the offbeat, the obscure, and the treasure hunt. Call before visiting: at press time the museum was closed for renovation that was expected to continue as long as to the end of 2001. ⊠ *Entrance at 65 rue de France*, ☎ *04–93–88–11–34.* ☝ *25 frs/€3.81.* ☉ *Wed.–Mon. 10–noon and 2–6.*

③⑥ **Place Masséna.** As cours Saleya is the heart of the old town, so this broad and noble square is the heart of the city as a whole. It's framed by an ensemble of Italian-style arcaded buildings first built in 1815, their facades stuccoed in rich red ocher. At its center is a heroic fountain in which thick-muscled bronze figures surge from the water. It's here that the central activities of the Carnaval unfold every February, when the square is transformed with flashing lights and monstrous, parade-scale balloon puppets. Behind the place and following the ancient riverbed, stretches the inviting **Escape Masséna**, a long public plaza with fountains, permanent performance spaces, grassy park grounds, and dozens of skateboarders at any given moment.

OFF THE
BEATEN PATH

CATHÉDRALE ORTHODOXE RUSSE ST-NICOLAS – From the promenade, hop Bus 7 up boulevard Gambetta and get off at either the Thiers-Gambetta or Parc Imperial stops, or walk west from the train station to visit this magnificent Russian Orthodox cathedral. Built in 1896 to accommodate the sizable population of Russian aristocrats who had adopted Nice as their winter home, this Byzantine fantasy is the largest of its kind outside the motherland. The church has no fewer than six gold-leaf onion domes, rich ceramic mosaics on its facade, and extraordinary icons framed in silver and jewels. The benefactor was Nicholas II himself, whose family attended the inauguration in 1912. ⊠ *av. Nicolas II,* ☏ *04–93–96–88–02.* ☉ *Apr.–Oct., Mon.–Sat. 9–noon and 2:30–6, Sun. 2:30–6; Nov.–Mar., Mon.–Sat. 9:30–noon and 2:30–5, Sun. 2:30–6.*

Cimiez

Once the site of the powerful Roman settlement Cemenelum, the hilltop neighborhood of Cimiez—4 km (2½ mi) north of cours Saleya—is Nice's most luxurious quarter. Villas seem in competition to outdo each other in opulence, and the combination of important art museums, Roman ruins, and a historic monastery make it worth a day's exploration.

To visit Cimiez and nearby museums, you need to combine a bus pass or taxi fare with strong legs and comfortable shoes. If you brave the route by car, arm yourself with a map and a navigator. Bus 15 from place Masséna or avenue Jean-Médecin takes you to both the Chagall and Matisse museums; from the latter you can visit the ruins and monastery.

A Good Walk

Begin your day at the **Musée du Message Biblique Marc Chagall** ㊷, which houses one of the finest collections of Chagall's works based on biblical themes. Then make the pilgrimage to the center of Cimiez and the **Musée Matisse** ㊸, where an important collection of Matisse's life work is amassed in an Italianate villa. Just behind, the **Musée Archéologique** ㊹ displays a wealth of Roman treasures unearthed on the site of the original colony. Slightly east of the museum is the thriving **Monastère de Cimiez** ㊺, a Franciscan monastery.

TIMING

Between bus connections and long walks from sight to sight, this walk is a half-day commitment at minimum. If you plan to stop into the Chagall Museum, really spend time in the Matisse Museum, and explore the ruins, this could easily be a day's outing.

Sights to See

㊺ **Monastère de Cimiez** (Cimiez Monastery). High over Nice and its château-bearing hill, this fully functioning monastery, originally established in the 16th century, is worth the pilgrimage. There's a lovely

garden, replanted following the original 16th-century lines. There's also the **Musée Franciscain** (Franciscan Museum), a didactic museum tracing the history of the Franciscan order, and a 15th-century **church.** The pretty, single-nave chapel contains three works of remarkable power and elegance by Bréa: the early *Pietà* (1475) flanked by portraits of high-Renaissance grace; the *Crucifixion* (1512); and the *Deposition* (1520), of intense suppressed emotion. ⊠ *pl. du Monastère,* ☎ *04–93–81–00–04.* ⊠ *Free.* ☉ *Mon.–Sat. 10–noon and 3–6.*

④ **Musée Archéologique** (Archaeology Museum). This contemporary building houses a dense and intriguing collection of objects extracted from the digs around the Roman city of Cemenelum, which flourished from the 1st to the 5th centuries and dwarfed its waterfront neighbor with a population of 20,000 in its prime. The examples of Greek and Italian treasures—ceramics, jewelry, and coins—attest to the cosmopolitan nature of coastal commerce. Behind the museum, you can wander through the **ruins** and digs, including the *thermes* (baths) and an early Christian baptistery. Just beyond, the Roman *arènes* (arena) seats 4,000 for the annual jazz festival. ⊠ *160 av. des Arènes-de-Cimiez,* ☎ *04–93–81–59–57.* ⊠ *25 frs/€3.81.* ☉ *Apr.–Sept., Tues.–Sun. 10–noon and 2–6; Oct.–Mar., Tues.–Sun. 10–1 and 2–5.*

★ **④** **Musée Matisse.** In the '60s, the city of Nice bought this lovely, light-bathed 17th-century villa, surrounded by the ruins of Roman civilization, and restored it to house a large collection of Henri Matisse's works. Matisse settled in Nice in 1917, seeking a sun cure after a bout with pneumonia, and remained here until his death in 1954. During his years on the Côte d'Azur, Matisse maintained intense friendships and artistic liaisons with Renoir, who lived in Cagnes, and with Picasso, who lived in Mougins and Antibes. Settling first along the waterfront, he eventually moved up to the rarified isolation of Cimiez and took an apartment in the Hotel Regina (now an apartment building), where he lived out the rest of his life. Matisse walked often in the parklands around the Roman remains and was buried in an olive grove outside the Cimiez Cemetery. The collection of artworks includes several pieces donated to the city by the artist himself before his death; the rest was donated by his family. In every medium and context—paintings, gouache cut-outs, engravings, and book illustrations—it represents the evolution of his art, from Cézanne-like still lifes to exuberant dancing paper dolls. Even the furniture and decor speak of Matisse, from the Chinese vases to the bold-printed fabrics with which he surrounded himself. A series of black-and-white photographs captures the artist at work, surrounded by personal—and telling—details. ⊠ *164 av. des Arènes-de-Cimiez,* ☎ *04–93–81–08–08.* ⊠ *25 frs/€3.81.* ☉ *Apr.–Sept., Wed.–Mon. 10–6; Oct.–Mar., Wed.–Mon. 10–5.*

★ **④** **Musée du Message Biblique Marc Chagall** (Marc Chagall Museum of Biblical Themes). Superbly displayed in a modern structure bathed in light and surrounded by coastal greenery, this is one of the finest permanent collections of the artist's late works. Included here are 17 vast canvases on biblical themes, each in emphatic and joyous color schemes; they celebrate the stories of Adam and Eve, Noah, Abraham, Moses, and the sensual, mystical Song of Solomon, dedicated to his wife. Preparatory sketches, sculptures, and ceramic pieces enhance the exhibit, as well as a tapestry and, outside, a mosaic. ⊠ *av. du Dr-Ménard (head up av. Thiers, then take a left onto av. Malausséna, cross the railway tracks, and take the first right up av. de l'Olivetto),* ☎ *04–93–53–87–20.* ⊠ *30 frs/€4.57 (in summer 38 frs/€5.79).* ☉ *July–Sept., Wed.–Mon. 10–6; Oct.–June, Wed.–Mon. 10–5.*

Dining and Lodging

$$$$ ✕ **Chantecler.** Under the leadership of two-star chef Alain Llorca, this
  ★ is the city's top restaurant, at the forefront of the Nice dining scene.
Grand gastronomy is served in formal, florid style—and with a Mediterranean touch. There may be puff pastry layered with tender green asparagus, tortellini with ricotta and wild arugula, or a mouth-melting
lamb shoulder cooked in a thick jam of sweet roasted garlic. Or gather
a group of friends and indulge in the famous Ronde des Tapas, with
11 courses of tidbits served in showy sequence. ⊠ *Hôtel Negresco, 37
promenade des Anglais,* ☎ *04–93–16–64–00. MC, V.*

$$–$$$ ✕ **L'Ane Rouge.** For years the best seafood restaurant in Nice, this old-
school culinary landmark maintains a loyal local clientele. Chef Michel
Devillers walks firmly down the middle, offering low-risk salads and
poached fish, occasionally venturing into newer turf: risotto with squid
and cardamom, cabbage lightly stuffed with rockfish in a pool of lobster butter. The context remains somewhat stuffy, frozen in the tradition of heavy linens, flame-stitch Louis XIII chairs, padded menus, and
patronizing service. ⊠ *7 quai des Deux-Emmanuel,* ☎ *04–93–89–49–
63. AE, DC, MC, V. Closed Wed. and 2 wks in Jan.*

$$ ✕ **Don Camillo.** Despite its staid and discreet atmosphere, this has
long been a lightning rod for young, experimental cuisine. It was from
this springboard that chef Franck Cerutti launched himself into Alain
Ducasse's Louis XV in Monaco. Now Stéphane Viano mans the kitchen,
and if the results are a hair less inspired, they're still worth your time.
Watch for artful compositions of Mediterranean dishes: goat cheese
layered with tapenade in a brick-like terrine, fresh sea bass or dorade
on a bed of sweet ratatouille, and confetti-colored nougat ice cream.
⊠ *5 rue des Ponchettes (just off cours Saleya, between the old town
and the sea),* ☎ *04–93–85–67–95. AE, DC, MC, V.*

$$ ✕ **Fleur de Sel.** In a fine old residential neighborhood between the waterfront and the train station, this peculiar little white cube of a restau-
rant may not look appealing from the outside. But its shape creates a
pretty rooftop terrace and a closed terrace, quiet oases where you can
enjoy a light, fresh meal with an emphasis on a healthy diet. The *menu
dietetique* (diet menu) clocks in at 600 calories: haddock ravioli with
delicate fennel and dill sauce, fish mousse with coriander, and a light
honey-filled puff pastry with a gentle counterpoint of thyme. ⊠ *10 bd.
Dubouchage,* ☎ *04–93–13–45–45. MC, V. Closed weekends.*

$$ ✕ **Grand Café de Turin.** Whether you crowd into a banquette in the
  ★ dark, low-ceilinged bar or win a coveted table under the arcaded por-
ticoes on place Garibaldi, this is *the* place to go for shellfish in Nice.
Order a bottle of something cold, spread butter on the sliced brown
bread, and dive into the platters set before you: sea snails, clams,
plump *fines de claires* and Mediterranean *bouzigue* oysters, salty snail-
like *violets,* and urchins by the dozen, their spines still waving. They've
all just been pried open at the refrigerator-counters on the sidewalk,
with dripping crates of fresh supplies standing by. It's packed noon and
night, and there's a thriving young-pro scene after work. ⊠ *5 pl.
Garibaldi,* ☎ *04–93–62–29–52. AE, DC, MC, V. Closed June.*

$$ ✕ **La Mérenda.** The back-to-bistro boom climaxed here when Do-
  ★ minique Le Stanc retired his crown at the Negresco to take over this tiny,
unpretentious landmark of Provençal cuisine. Now he and his wife work
in the miniature open kitchen creating the ultimate versions of stuffed
sardines, pistou, slow-simmered *daubes* (beef stews), and the quintessential stockfish (the local lutefisk). Despite the diner-scale room and the
crowded tables shared with well-heeled food-fans slumming, la cuisine
Niçoise is served with the same nostril-flaring, holier-than-thou service
as in any three-star restaurant. Don't dare ask for salt or Parmesan, and

Nice Dining and Lodging

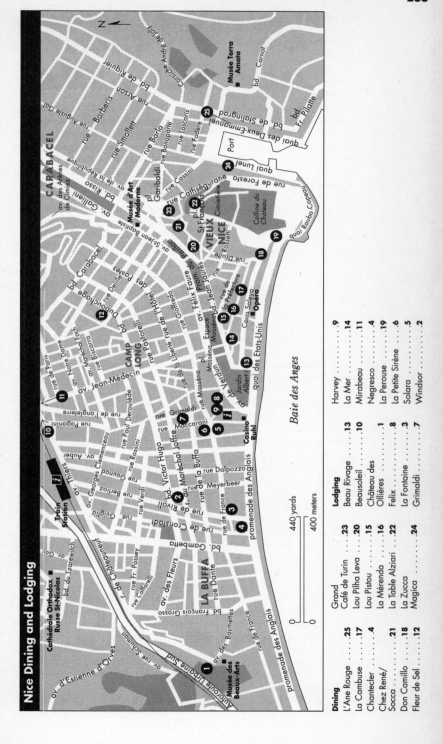

CARABACEL

Musée Terra Amata

bd. Fr. Pilatte

Port

Musée d'Art Moderne

Musée des Beaux-Arts

Cathédrale Orthodox Russe St-Nicolas

VIEUX NICE

Colline du Château

CAMP LONG

LA BUFFA

Train Station

Casino Ruhl

Baie des Anges

0 ____ 440 yards

0 ____ 400 meters

eat what the pony-tailed waiters—something like bodyguards to a superstar—tell you to eat. It's one man's private mission; stop by in person to reserve entry to the inner sanctum. The fact that there are two evening servings—at 7 and at 9—tells you something of the cynical ambience. ⊠ *4 rue de la Terrasse,* ☎ *no phone. No credit cards. Closed weekends, last wk in July, first 2 wks in Aug., and school holidays.*

$–$$ ✕ **La Cambuse.** A marketplace greasy spoon, this friendly joint on cours Saleya packs the sunny outside tables as well as the somber, spare barroom. The cooking is straightforward and the portions generous, from sardine beignets to sweet grilled peppers to classic *petits farcis* (eggplant, peppers, mushrooms, and zucchini stuffed with spicy meat and crumbs and drizzled with garlicky olive oil); watch for the fish du jour. ⊠ *5 cours Saleya,* ☎ *04–93–80–12–31. MC, V. Closed Sun.*

$–$$ ✕ **Lou Pistou.** If you want to explore Nice cuisine but in a more inti-
★   mate setting than a back-alley takeout stand, this mom-and-pop shoe box of a restaurant serves real, authentically prepared home cooking. Sit elbow to elbow at checked-cloth tables and browse through framed newspaper clippings praising the owners' campaign to preserve the old ways. There are *soupe au pistou* (minestrone with pesto), double-fried omelets with a touch of Parmesan, and little pissaladières, just for starters. Then choose between a rich stew or a heaping bowl of homemade pasta, and a fresh mesclun salad tossed in olive oil, followed by freshly baked fruit tarts. It's all served with sweet concern by the wife while the husband clatters and sizzles away beyond the kitchen door. Just next door to its superstar equivalent, the Mérenda, it's friendlier, cozier, and— dare we?—tastier. ⊠ *4 rue de la Terrasse (just off Espace Masséna),* ☎ *04–93–62–21–82. MC, V. Closed weekends.*

$–$$ ✕ **La Table Alziari.** Pick up the famous blue-and-yellow can of Alziari olive oil at the shop off cours Saleya (☞ Shopping, *below*), then taste it being used as it was intended: in fresh, simple Niçoise home cooking. Tucked behind the bewildering maze of touristy old-town restaurants, this backstreet hideaway features the fine cooking of the Alziari family, served in an unpretentious blackboard-menu setting. There are mouthwatering roasted eggplants and peppers, white beans in a drizzle of balsamic vinegar, crispy stuffed sardines, and the house tapenade— for starters. Then tackle a savory lamb *daube* (stew) or a saffron-spiked salt-cod stew. All are peppered with pinky-nail-size Niçoise olives, which the Alziaris have been harvesting for generations. ⊠ *4 rue François Zanin (just off rue de la Tour),* ☎ *04–93–80–34–03. MC, V. Closed Sun. and Mon.*

$ ✕ **Chez René/Socca.** This back-alley landmark, where rustic olivewood tables line the narrow street, is the most popular dive in town for the snack food unique to Nice. Curt waiters splash down your drink order, but you have to get in line for the food and carry it steaming to the table yourself. There's *socca,* of course, the grainy golden pancake of chickpea flour scraped with a palette knife straight off the griddle; spicy assortments of petits farcis; pissaladières heaped with caramelized onions and shiny black olives; and sweet, quiche-like *tourta de blea,* full of chopped Swiss chard and sprinkled with pine nuts. It's off place Garibaldi on the edge of the old town, across from the *gare routière* (bus station). ⊠ *2 rue Miralhetti,* ☎ *04–93–92–05–73. No credit cards.*

$ ✕ **Lou Pilha Leva.** Its name in dialect means "tu prend et tu t'en va"
★   (take and go), but you'll be tempted to stay a while and taste everything here. Not as well known as Chez René but much more serious about the food it serves, this street stand just south of place St-François offers good, fresh-cooked versions of petits farcis, tourta de blea, and pissaladières as well as full meals of homemade pasta, pizza, *moules-frites* (mussels with fries), soupe au pistou, polenta, stockfish, and

fruit tarts, all made on the premises. Order food at the window and drinks at the table. ☒ *10 rue du Collet on pl. Centrale,* ☎ *04–93–13–99–08. MC, V.*

$ ✕ **La Zucca Magica.** Tucked in a cozy, rustico shoe box along the port, this vegetarian-Italian bistro is all the rage, thanks to the imaginative cooking of Roman chef Marco Folicaldi. His Neapolitan *tourte piazella* is stuffed with steaming olives, pine nuts, and raisins; there's also a light lasagne with asparagus and lemon peel, ravioli with leeks and goat cheese, and airy strawberry zabaglione. The chef's gruff friendliness, the noisy camaraderie of crowded diners, and the surreal decor of pumpkins in every form make for a real dining event. ☒ *4 bis, quai Papacino,* ☎ *04–93–56–25–27. No credit cards. Closed Sun. and Mon.*

$$$$ ⊞ **Château des Ollières.** The genteel owner of this fantastic neo-Mo-
★ roccan palace, once the dream house of Prince Lobnov-Rostowsky, has restored it as a luxurious manor-house inn. Its eight rooms are furnished as in a private home, with period details—herringbone parquet, crown moldings, and chandeliers—in mint condition. Deluxe rooms have vast marble baths and fine old furniture; standard rooms bloom with toile de Jouy. The candlelit restaurant functions as a table d'hôte—one prix-fixe menu each day—and in summer expands into the extraordinary tropical garden-estate. Only the noise of the highway reminds you of the current epoch. ☒ *39 av. des Baumettes, 06000,* ☎ *04–92–15–77–99,* FAX *04–93–15–77–99. 8 rooms. Restaurant, air-conditioning. AE, DC, MC, V.* ☙

$$$$ ⊞ **Negresco.** Its pink cupola the symbol of Riviera glamour, this faded Belle Époque landmark retains much of its architectural excess, rescued by the eccentric vision of its owner of 40 years. Each floor is devoted to eras of French history, but the dominant one is the 1960s, from the plastic-glitter bathtubs to the Vasarely op-art carpet to the photos of Liz-and-Dick in the bar. Its grand restaurant Le Chantecler, however, still ranks among Nice's finest (☞ *above*). Indulge in a drink in the glorious walnut-and-velour bar, and you'll recapture some of the glamour of the old Riviera. ☒ *37 promenade des Anglais, 06000,* ☎ *04–93–31–16–64–00,* FAX *04–93–88–35–68. 122 rooms. 2 restaurants, bar, air-conditioning, beach. AE, DC, MC, V.*

$$$$ ⊞ **La Perouse.** Just past the old town, at the foot of the château, this
★ antipalace is a secret treasure cut into the cliff (an elevator takes you up to reception). Most rooms have breathtaking views of the Baie des Anges. Some of the best not only overlook the azure sea but also look down into an intimate garden with lemon trees and a cliff-side pool. A sundeck and sauna by the pool, as well as valet parking, add to the sense of private luxury. Rooms are fairly large; some sport somber plaids, others have painted Provençal furniture. The restaurant serves meals in the candlelit garden May through September. ☒ *11 quai Rauba-Capeau, 06300,* ☎ *04–93–62–34–63,* FAX *04–93–62–59–41. 64 rooms. Restaurant, air-conditioning, pool, sauna. AE, DC, MC, V.* ☙

$$$–$$$$ ⊞ **Beau Rivage.** Occupying an imposing late-19th-century town house near cours Saleya, this landmark hotel is just a few steps from the best parts of old Nice and the beach, though buildings have long since blocked its sea views. The room decor is standard and a bit stuffy, in pinks and teals; corner rooms have big windows and are by far the best. Le Bistrot, the house restaurant, moves to the beach every summer. Matisse lived here before moving to cours Saleya and then the hills of Cimiez. ☒ *24 rue St-François-de-Paule, 06000,* ☎ *04–92–47–82–82,* FAX *04–92–47–82–83. 118 rooms. Restaurant, air-conditioning, beach. AE, DC, MC, V.* ☙

$$–$$$ ⊞ **Grimaldi.** Small but stylish, this well-boned little city hotel, halfway between the train station and the waterfront, offers a discreet, personal welcome and a sense of southern charm. Rooms have vivid color schemes and imaginative, old-style bathrooms, and the sleek lobby bar encourages international mingling. Prices are low for this level of comfort. ⊠ *15 rue Grimaldi, 06000,* ☎ *04–93–16–00–24,* FAX *04–93–87– 00–24. 23 rooms. Bar, air-conditioning. AE, MC, V.* ⊛

$$–$$$ ⊡ **Windsor.** This is a memorably eccentric hotel with a vision: most
★ of its white-on-white rooms either have frescoes of mythical themes or are works of artists' whimsy. There's also a "relaxation room" on the top floor, where you can exercise, meditate, or have a steam bath and massage. But the real draw of this otherworldly place is its astonishing city-center garden—a tropical paradise of lemon, magnolia, and palm trees. Exotic finches flutter through the leaves, and a toucan caws beside the breakfast buffet; a small pool is screened by flowering shrubs. You can breakfast or dine here by candlelight (guests only). Book well ahead to immerse yourself in an exoticism that is particularly Niçois. ⊠ *11 rue Dalpozzo, 06000,* ☎ *04–93–88–59–35,* FAX *04– 93–88–94–57. 57 rooms. Restaurant, bar, air-conditioning, pool. AE, DC, MC, V.* ⊛

$$ ⊡ **La Fontaine.** Downtown and a block from the waterfront, this immaculate, simply designed hotel offers a friendly welcome from its house-proud owners. Rooms are small and comfortable, in cheery blues and yellows and with freshly tiled bathrooms. It even has a pretty little courtyard where breakfast is served. ⊠ *49 rue de France, 06000,* ☎ *04– 93–88–30–38,* FAX *04–93–88–98–11. 29 rooms. Breakfast room, air-conditioning. AE, DC, MC, V.* ⊛

$$ ⊡ **Mirabeau.** Two hundred yards above the train station on busy avenue Malausséna, and an easy bus ride from place Masséna and the beach, this slickly renovated urban hotel serves as a good home base for pilgrimages to the Chagall Museum and Cimiez. Fresh flowers and leather armchairs brighten the lobby breakfast area; rooms, with jazzy jewel-tone quilts and functional modern furniture, vary in size. The owners are friendly and always ready to assist. ⊠ *15 av. Malausséna, 06000,* ☎ *04–93–88–33–67,* FAX *04–93–16–14–08. 42 rooms. Bar, air-conditioning. AE, DC, MC, V.*

$$ ⊡ **La Petite Sirene.** Even an all-Danish hotel decorated à la Hans Christian Andersen can find a place in this Latin-blooded metropolis. The central location is key, and its cozy scale helps. Rooms are tidily furnished and plushly carpeted in sleek beige and cream. Downstairs, the restaurant features Scandinavian food and a Nordic, party-hearty ambience. It's good for young, international travelers craving an Anglophone retreat. ⊠ *8 rue Maccarani, 06000,* ☎ *04–97–03–03–40,* FAX *04–97–03–03–41. 14 rooms. Restaurant, bar, air-conditioning. AE, DC, MC, V.*

$–$$ ⊡ **Beausoleil.** This big old downtown hotel has a certain urban charm, with French windows, ironwork balconies, and an oak cage elevator that whisks you up to impeccably maintained pink-and-gray rooms. A small bar and a cozy living room with TV make you feel at home. With its location near the train station, this is a convenient home base for day trips by train up and down the coast. The hotel does a brisk business with bus groups, so book ahead. ⊠ *22 rue Assalit, 06000,* ☎ *04–93–85–18–54,* FAX *04–93–62–49–14. 53 rooms. Bar, air-conditioning. DC, MC, V.* ⊛

$–$$ ⊡ **Felix.** On popular, pedestrian rue Masséna and a block from the beach, this tiny budget hotel is owned by a hard-working couple (both fluent in English) who make you feel welcome. Rooms are slightly tatty— vinyl wallpaper, saggy beds—but four have tiny balconies with ringside seats over the pedestrian thoroughfare. In-room picnics are encouraged with cups and plates, and there's even TV with CNN. ⊠ *41 rue Masséna, 06000,* ☎ *04–93–88–67–73,* FAX *04–93–16–15–78. 14 rooms. Air-conditioning. AE, DC, MC, V.*

$–$$ ☷ **Harvey.** Location is everything: this big, blocky city hotel sits squarely off the Jardin Albert Ier, two blocks behind the casino and the promenade, and at the root of rue Masséna, the main pedestrian shopping street. Even if the rooms have a slightly dated '80s decor—white lacquer and brass—they're air-conditioned. Request Room 210, which is vast and has angle views, or one of the corner rooms. ✉ *18 av. de Suede (at rue Masséna), 06000,* ☎ *04–93–88–73–73,* FAX *04–93–82–53–55. 66 rooms. Air-conditioning. AE, DC, MC, V.*

$–$$ ☷ **La Mer.** Don't be frightened away by the grim street-level entrance; once upstairs, you'll find a warm welcome and rock-bottom prices. Though rooms are downright spartan (and carpets sometimes frayed), the location can't be beat: it's right on place Masséna, near the waterfront and the old town. Room rates are budget friendly, and the staff and owners are downright sweet. Ask for a room away from the square to be sure of a quiet night's sleep. ✉ *4 pl. Masséna, 06000,* ☎ *04–93–92–09–10,* FAX *04–93–85–00–64. 12 rooms. AE, MC, V.*

$–$$ ☷ **Solara.** One block from the beach and two from the place Masséna, this tiny budget hotel perches on the fourth and fifth floors, high above the main shopping street. Rooms are fresh and tidy with bright Provençal fabrics; some have kitchenettes and rooftop views. Don't be put off by the unsavory ground-floor entrance. ✉ *7 rue de France, 06000,* ☎ *04–93–88–09–96,* FAX *04–93–88–36–86. 12 rooms. Air-conditioning, kitchenettes. AE, DC, MC, V.* ✇

Nightlife and the Arts

Nice has the most-active café society and nightlife on the coast. If you want to explore in depth, pick up a copy of *Le Pitchoun,* a free, French-language guide to clubs, restaurants, and leisure activities.

The glamorous **Casino Ruhl** (✉ 1 promenade des Anglais, ☎ 04–97–03–12–22), gleaming neon-bright and modern, is a sophisticated Riviera landmark that's open daily 10 AM to dawn. If you're all dressed up and just won big, invest in a drink in the intimate walnut-and-velvet **Bar Anglais** in the Hôtel Negresco (✉ 39 promenade des Anglais).

L'Ascenseur (✉ 18 bis rue Emmanuel Philibert, ☎ 04–93–26–35–30), two blocks east of place Garibaldi, is the most popular gay and lesbian club in town. Young fans of Brit pop—especially Americans and English—drink and dance at **Chez Wayne** (✉ 15 rue de la Préfecture, ☎ 04–93–13–46–99). **Iguane Café** (✉ 5 quai Deux-Emmanuels, ☎ 04–93–56–83–83), along the port, pounds with Latin rhythms and techno until 4 AM.

L'Ambassade (✉ 18 rue du Congrès, ☎ 04–93–88–88–87) draws the crème-de-la-crème of the well-groomed, upscale Niçois young-and-restless. Dress well to get past the sharp-eyed screeners. At **Butterfly** (✉ 67 quai des Etats-Unis, ☎ 04–93–92–27–31), in the old town, dance and drink to contemporary pop with a young, laid-back crowd.

To stay in touch with friends and family back home, plug into the **Email Café** (✉ 8 rue Saint-Vincent) in the old town, which offers surf-and-salad options and Qwerty keyboards.

In July, the **Nice Jazz Festival** (☎ 04–92–17–77–77 for information) draws international performers from around the world for outdoor concerts in the Parc de Cimiez north of the center, some in the Matisse museum and some in the Roman arena. During past festivals, big-name jazz artists have gathered in the Madisson Lounge of the **Hotel Radisson SAS** (✉ 223 promenade des Anglais, ☎ 04–93–37–17–17) for impromptu jam sessions into the wee hours. The **Théâtre de Verdure** (✉ Jardin Albert Ier) is another spot for jazz and pop; concerts relocate to the **Arènes de Cimiez** in summer. Classical music and ballet performances take place at Nice's convention center, the **Acropolis** (✉ Palais des Congrès, Esplanade John F. Kennedy, ☎ 04–93–92–83–00).

The season at the **Opéra de Nice** (✉ 4 rue St-François-de-Paul, ☎ 04–92–17–40–40) runs from September to June. The **Théâtre Municipal Francis-Gag** (✉ 4 rue St-Joseph, ☎ 04–93–62–00–03) offers a wide and varied selection of independent theater productions. The **Théâtre de Nice** (✉ promenade des Arts, ☎ 04–93–13–90–90), headed by stage and screen star Jacques Weber, alternates productions imported from Paris with creative experiments of the Centre National Dramatique Nice Côte d'Azur.

Outdoor Activities and Sports

Nice's **beaches** extend all along the Baie des Anges, backed full-length by the promenade des Anglais and a thriving and sophisticated downtown. This leads to the peculiar phenomenon of seeing power-suited executives and secretaries stripping down to a band of Lycra, tanning over the lunch hour, then suiting back up for the afternoon's work, a block or two away. The absence of sand (there's nothing but those famous Riviera pebbles) helps maintain that dress-for-success look. The downside of the location: the otherwise stylish streets downtown tend to fill up with under-dressed, sunburned tourists caked with salt during beach season.

Posh private beaches feature full restaurants and bar service, color-coordinated mattresses and parasols, and ranks of tanners with phones glued to their ears. Several of the beaches lure clients with waterskiing, parasailing, windsurfing, and jet skiing; if you're looking for a particular sport, signs are posted at the entrance with the restaurant menus. One of the handiest private beaches is the **Beau Rivage** (☎ 04–92–47–82–83), across from the cours Saleya, which has jet skiing and a popular restaurant. Here 85 francs/€13 will rent you a cushy lounge chair, a parasol, and access to a changing room, hot showers, and bar service. At **Ruhl** (☎ 04–93–87–09–70), across from the casino, waterskiing and parasailing boats running steadily all day. Fees for private beaches average 60–85 francs/€9.15–€12.96 for a dressing room and mattress, 15 to 25 francs/€2.29–€3.81 for a parasol, and 25 to 35 francs/€3.81–€5.34 for a cabana to call your own. Private beaches alternate with open stretches of public frontage served by free toilets and open "showers" (a cold elevated faucet for rinsing off salt). Enterprising vendors cruise the waterfront, hawking ice cream, slabs of melon, coffee, ice-cold sodas, and beer.

Bicycles can be rented at the train station (✉ 17 av. Thiers). The entire promenade des Anglais is closed to traffic on the first Sunday of every month (except for July and August), making for a terrific 10-km (6-mi) ride along the waterfront.

In winter, good Alpine **skiing** is surprisingly accessible: Nice is only about 97 km (60 mi) from Valberg (4,600 to 6,300 ft), Auron (4,800 to 7,350 ft), and Isola (6,000 to 8,700 ft) in the Alps. You can practically ski into the sea.

Shopping

Nice's main shopping street, **avenue Jean-Médecin,** runs inland from place Masséna; all needs and most tastes are catered to in its big department stores (galeries Lafayette, Prisunic, and the split-level Étoile mall).

Olive oil by the gallon, in cans sporting colorful old-fashioned labels, is sold at tiny **Alziari** (✉ 14 rue St-François-de-Paule, ☎ 04–93–85–76–92). Tapenade, pistou, and olive-wood doodads are also sold here. From November to February you can witness the winter pressing at Alziari's oil mill (✉ 318 bd. de la Madeleine).

The venerable old **Henri Auer** (✉ 7 rue St-François-de-Paule, ☎ 04–93–85–77–98) has sold its beautiful selection of crystallized fruit, a Nice specialty, since 1820. Another good source for crystallized fruit is the **Confiserie du Vieux Nice** (✉ 14 quai Papacino, ☎ 04–93–55–43–50), on the west side of the port.

Seafood of all kinds is sold at the **fish market** on place St-François every morning except Monday. At the **flower market** on cours Saleya, you can find all kinds of plants and mounds of fruits and vegetables (Tues.–Sat. 6 AM–5:30 PM and Sun. 6–noon).

The **antiques and brocante market** (✉ pl. Robilante) by the old port is held Tuesday through Saturday. For brocante on Monday check out cours Saleya.

THE ARRIÈRE-PAYS NIÇOISE

When you're saturated with Côte d'Azur glamour—or crowds—and you've had enough of Nice's big-city downside, consider a car trip of a day or two deep into the hill country behind the coast. Within 10 minutes of cutting inland you enter a new universe—a wild, pre-Alpine terrain of rock gorges, black-green pine forests, and churning white-water rivers sending up soft veils of mist. Along N204 you parallel a remarkable railroad, an engineering miracle of vertiginous tinker-toy bridges and model-train tunnels that drill neatly through the shaggy green cliffs; and you visit isolated mountain villages with tiny Baroque chapels decorated with the fervor of an Alpine Bernini. You may want to hike or you may want to picnic. And you may want to toss out your vacation itinerary and settle into this lost, wild world for the duration.

This circuit is only a sample of the forays to be made into the arrière-pays; the region is riddled with a series of river valleys, which thread down from the Alps and the heavily protected Parc National du Mercantour. You may approach it from either end, either cutting immediately up into L'Escarène, the mountain town north of Nice, or starting, as suggested here, from the Italian border. It makes for a full day's drive, counting sorties into churches and villages, and could be difficult in heavy rain. To explore further, consider spending a night or two in St-Dalmas-de-Tende, just below Tende, the hiking center at the northernmost point covered here.

From Nice, hop on A8 and speed along the dramatic hills and in and out of tunnels. Just past the Italian customs booths (don't forget your passport) bear right toward Ventimiglia. Signs will point to Breil-sur-Roya and the Col de Tende. You'll be following E74 along the River Roya, driving only 15 km (9 mi) in Italy before crossing back into France. The territory is already radically different from the coast, resembling the mill valleys of West Virginia or the gorges of the Ozarks; the architecture, in stone and ocher stucco, seems to grow out of the rock that shores it up. At the first crossroads you'll arrive at Breil-sur-Roya, on the river's banks. Stop here and fuel up, as farther north gas stations are few and far between, then spend a little time exploring the town.

Breil-sur-Roya

46 *24 km (15 mi) northwest of Ventimiglia (just over the Italian border), 58 km (36 mi) northeast of Nice via N204.*

Draped at the foot of the forested mountains that separate it from Italy, and crowding gracefully along the wide River Roya, this peaceful mountain town (pronounced *bray*) has survived practically intact from the Middle Ages. Its dense inner streets, basically car-free, are lined with pretty old houses, still framed by bits and pieces of old fortifications.

The main square, place Brancion, is flanked by two churches, which, including a third church across the river, makes about 2% of the village's buildings sacred. On the square the town market proffers crops from local farmers' vegetable patches and the local cheese, made from cow's milk.

The facade of one of the churches, **Chapelle Ste-Catherine,** is pure Italian Renaissance, with sleek pairs of Corinthian columns flanking its portal. But step into the larger **Église Sancta-Maria-in-Albis,** a massive 17th-century Baroque structure turning a broad and windowless apse toward the river. The elaborate decor seems startling in these backwoods parts, especially the richly carved wood and gilt of the 17th-century organ.

Across the river rears a slender Romanesque bell tower, the last vestige of a Benedictine abbey destroyed in the 18th century. Just up the hill, the town's third church, **Notre-Dame-de-l'Assomption,** retains traces of its spare Romanesque origins, though its decoration is Baroque.

En Route   If you are heading from Roya to Saorge (☞ *below*), first get a view of the painterly perched village by continuing north on N204, past the turnoff, to **Fontan.** Then double back to climb up to Saorge.

Saorge

★ ㊇   *7 km (4½ mi) north of Breil-sur-Roya.*

An extraordinary composition of stacked pastel cubes clinging precariously to the dark forest cliffs over the Roya gorge, Saorge is one of the most spectacular and beautiful of southern France's myriad hilltop villages. Here you'll see the first flat, stone roof tiles that signal the retreat of Mediterranean tile and the beginning of the Piedmontese Alps.

Saorge was a key Roman military point for defending the river valley and the Alpine passes, and it remained important under the Grimaldis and the dukes of Savoy for centuries; it even figured in Alpine strategies of World War II. Yet its ancient stucco houses remain untouched by time, and its paved streets, which you must negotiate practically single file, lead to vertiginous views over the gorge. There are passageways arching over the cobblestones, and locals hauling goods home by skinny tractor-tricycles. It used to be mules: in the 16th century, they carried every stone up the precarious paths to build the **Église St-Sauveur,** an eagle's aerie of a church as sumptuously decorated and furnished as any on the coast. Despite this achievement, there's nary a boutique in sight, and one pizzeria and one simple "panoramic" restaurant to meet your needs. Much is written of the lovely painted chapel called Madonna del Poggio, just below the village, but it has been bought by a Niçois devotee of medieval art and visitors are no longer allowed. A sign on the door says "Don't even knock."

La Brigue

㊈   *13 km (8 mi) northeast of Saorge on D43.*

Once a powerful medieval stronghold, La Brigue was dominated by the Genovese Lascaris-Grimaldis, vestiges of whose wealth and influence still feature prominently in Nice and Monaco. The village nestles under the ruins of its château, in a pretty valley on the River Levense that gushes toward the Roya.

Like Breil, tiny La Brigue seems disproportionately blessed with wonderful old churches. In the village center, the **Collégial St-Martin** dates from the 15th century. It's a welcome relief from Baroque excess, yet the decor of its early Gothic structure is lavishly decorated with fine 16th-century art. Most of the works are influenced by, if not attributed to, Bréa, including a richly detailed triptych on the story of Ste-Marthe and a rare nativity scene. On the same square, two 17th-century chapels face off. The **Chapelle de l'Annonciation** flaunts a supremely Baroque facade and a startling ellipsoid shape. The **Chapelle de l'Assomption,** in contrast to the flamboyant Annonciation chapel it confronts, holds out for Renaissance purity.

Notre-Dame-des-Fontaines

★ ⑭ *4 km (2½ mi) east of La Brigue.*

If you make the pilgrimage to only one of the arrière-pays's famous painted chapels, this one would be a good choice. Above a roaring stream supposed to have curative powers, this spare Alpine-Gothic structure stands alone in the woods, a dead-end that's well removed from a few houses and cafés. Built in the 15th century, it was painted in a naïve but awe-inspiring series of frescoed panels, some Giotto-esque in their classical reserve, some seething with gore and the horrors of hell. The passion of Christ is depicted in 25 squares, one a vast crucifixion, another a ghastly image of Judas hanged with a demon ripping his damned soul from his bowels. The *Last Judgment* on the entrance wall combines the epic vision of Michelangelo with the morbid wit of Bosch. The works are attributed to a passionate Piedmontese named Jean Canavesio and to Jean Baleison, whose graceful Gothic style denies his provincial experience. Both worked in the mid-15th century. Bring a flashlight for viewing details, as the church is illuminated only by natural light. ⊠ *At end of D143, east of La Brigue.* ☉ *Daily 2:30–5, with guided tours leaving from the tourist office in La Brigue (French only).*

St-Dalmas-de-Tende

⑮ *7 km (4½ mi) west of Notre-Dame-des-Fontaines.*

This tiny mountain hamlet clusters around the crossroads between the main north–south highway N204 and D91 (direction Casterino), which winds up into the departure points—on foot or four-wheel-drive—for the **Vallée des Merveilles,** a valley with rocks carved with figures dating from 1800 BC (☞ Close-Up: Marvels in the Mercantour, *below*). There's one lonely train station, vastly overscaled for the setting; it was built for Mussolini as a statement of Italian sovereignty. Besides the listings below, there's only a pair of cafés, a baker and a grocer, and the sound of a mountain torrent competing with the roar of passing Italian speedsters on their way to Turin.

Dining and Lodging

$$$ ✕🏠 **Le Prieuré.** In a whitewashed Romanesque priory nestled on riverside gardens in the shadow of the mountains, this pretty inn offers comfort beyond its class. Thanks to an unusual arrangement, it's impeccably maintained and serviced: the staff is made up of people with disabilities who live and work on site. Thus the Centre d'Aide par le Travail (Center for Helping through Work) provides workers with an idyllic mountain home and on-the-job training—and guests are pampered with pristine rooms, scrubbed tile bathrooms, laundry service, immaculate grounds, and a friendly ambience. The restaurant serves good regional food—fresh meat terrines, poached fish, grilled duck breast—to passing diners, but focuses on half-board guests who've come to hike and compare exploits with their neighbors. The result: a staff and clientele of happy

campers. ⊠ *rue Jean Médicin, 06430,* ☎ *04–93–04–75–70,* FAX *04–93–04–71–58. 24 rooms. Restaurant, laundry service. AE, MC, V.* ♺

$$$ ✕▥ **Le Terminus.** Cozy and familial, with a mountain-inn ambience, this easygoing hotel offers simple rooms full of old-oak furniture and good home-cooking. Look for beef daube with olives, mountain trout, and homemade fruit tarts, all served in a dining hall full of adventure travelers. The hotel's specialty: packages that combine half-board lodging with one or two days' excursion by jeep into the Vallée des Merveilles. ⊠ *Across from the train station, 06430,* ☎ *04–93–04–96–96,* FAX *04–93–04–96–97. 20 rooms, 16 with bath. Restaurant. MC, V.*

Tende

🖂 *4 km (2½ mi) north of St-Dalmas-de-Tende.*

The last stop before the climb over the pass to Italy, Tende is a market town and a center for hikers and nature lovers who come to venture into the **Parc National du Mercantour** and the Vallée des Merveilles.

Tende's striking **vieille ville** (old town) skews gracefully down from the rocky, scrub-covered mountainside, under the macabre spire of the last stone vestige of the Lascaris château; the houses, many from the 15th and 16th centuries, are built of schist with slate-slab roofs.

★ The modern **Musée des Merveilles** (Museum of Marvels), its facade decked out with intriguing runes, can introduce you to the wonders of the nearby Vallée des Merveilles. Using reproductions of the valley's stone engravings, personal objects, and weapons discovered in the area, along with evocative dioramas of daily life in the Bronze Age, the display evokes and illuminates a context for the mysteries of Mont Bégo. It's a sober and scholarly approach to a subject that lends itself easily to wild conjecture of voodoo, death cults, and curses. ⊠ *av. du 16-septembre-1947,* ☎ *04–93–04–32–50.* ▥ *30 frs/€4.57.* ☉ *May–mid-Oct., Wed.–Mon. 10:30–6:30; mid–Oct.–Apr., Wed.–Mon. 10:30–5.*

The nearby **Vallée des Merveilles** (Valley of Marvels) is a high and isolated valley enclosed on all sides by mountains and dominated by the eery, storm-ridden Mont Bégo. Scattered throughout the valley's windswept crags and hollows lie rocks etched with thousands of Bronze Age petroglyphs depicting bulls' horns, spearheads, and lively dancers (☞ Close-Up: Marvels in the Mercantour, *below*). To experience the valley firsthand, you can hire a guide for an outing on horseback, on foot, or by jeep. For more information, contact the Tende-Roya tourist office (☞ Nice and the Eastern Côte d'Azur A to Z, *below*).

En Route From Tende, you've no choice: either double back south on the main highway or climb over the Col de Tende (Tende Pass; 6,136 ft) into Turin, Italy. If you opt to return south, just before you return to Breil-sur-Roya, cut sharply right on D2204, following directions to Sospel. Along narrow switchbacks (the signs count them for you) you climb over sparse heathered hills to the **Col de Brouis** (2,883 ft). Walk up to the overlook and you'll be rewarded with a panorama of snowcapped mountains. Over the crest is new terrain and a new climate; the hills are grassy, sheltered from the wind, with olive trees growing on ancient step-terraced slopes. There's scarcely a house or farm in sight; by the time you descend to the banks of the River Bevera, the small mountain town of Sospel seems downright cosmopolitan.

Sospel

🖂 *21 km (13 mi) southwest of Breil-sur-Roya, 40 km (25 mi) northeast of Nice.*

MARVELS IN THE MERCANTOUR

DEEP WITHIN THE PARC NATIONAL du Mercantour, a wild, isolated mountain preserve barely accessible by car, an even more isolated valley has intrigued, attracted, and possibly terrified man since the Iron Age. It is called the Vallée des Merveilles—the Valley of Marvels—and no one knows just how far back its wonders reach. But something inspired the region's first inhabitants to its nearly inaccessible heights—and they left their mark. Some 30,000 rock drawings, etched on flat, smooth stone, give witness to a cult of veneration, fear, and supplication.

You can only reach it by foot, horseback, or jeep, and the climb isn't easy. The forest hillsides, carpeted with wildflowers, are shin-splint steep, and four-wheel-drive access moves upward at a lurching crawl. But once standing in the bleak, treeless, rock-strewn valley bowl hemmed in on all sides by mountains, it's easy to see why Iron-Age man attributed mystical powers to this site. Winds curl over the surrounding peaks, and Mount Bégo itself—toward which the majority of drawings are oriented—rises impassive and vaguely monstrous above. Most afternoons, black clouds roll in heavy with rain, and lightning plays threateningly over the treeless terrain.

The drawings themselves are simple and repetitive: bull's horns, field grids, and phallic spears. Were the field images primitive maps inviting the gods to rain on the supplicant's crops? A few human forms with arms raised high make your neck hairs prickle: someone imploring? a witch doctor spreading fingers high and wide to the mountain gods? No one knows, though theories abound, and a good mountain guide can help.

On foot, you must make a long day of it to mount, explore, and return to St-Dalmas-de-Tende. Many opt to stay overnight at the Club Alpin Françaid Refuge des Merveilles, located at 2111 m (6,926 ft). Open mid-June to October, the refuge offers 30-bunk rooms, pension-style meals, and a bowl of hot chocolate to put under your belt before exploring the engravings (☎ 04–93–04–69–22). Others hop a jeep tour with a trained guide, who drives five or six explorers uphill for an hour and a half, then leads them from carving to carving, explaining the mythology and history as they hike. One entrepreneur even leads horseback tours from the village of Casterino, where a handful of hotels offer lodging.

The Vallée des Merveilles is only one of the marvels of the Mercantour national park, but gives you some idea of how protected these nature preserves are. While the national park laws allow farmers and shepherds to continue their cultivation, the flora and fauna are protected, and all fishing, hunting, and camping are fiercely controlled. The main difference between this park and its American counterparts is access. The Mercantour can barely be entered by car, as almost no roads have been cut into its mountainous terrain. Therefore it remains a true preserve for the intrepid few. Several well-developed resorts flourish around its nether regions—St-Martin-Vésubie, St-Etienne-de-Tinée, and a modern ski-resort called Isola 2000—but most branch roads rise to a full-stop on wilderness slopes, where you must double back to return to civilization.

To learn more about tours, lodging, and guides into the Vallée, contact the tourist office at Tende-Roya (☞ Nice and the Eastern Côte d'Azur A to Z, *below*). For a convenient and comfortable package-tour, stay at Le Terminus at St-Dalmas-de-Tende, then ride with driver-guide Luc Fioretti into the valley, where he'll regale you with hours of history and theory (☞ Lodging, St-Dalmas-de-Tende, *above*). For information about the Parc National du Mercantour, contact the Administration de l'Environment (✉ 103 av. 16-Septembre 1947, 06430 Tende, ☎ FAX 04–93–04–67–00).

With its cereal-box, six-story houses in rich-hued stucco flanking the banks of the River Bevera, its fine old fountains, and its florid Baroque church, Sospel is a picturesque old mountain town. It's difficult to imagine it as the second-largest city in the Comté de Nice and a center of medieval church power, which it was in the 13th century.

The most remarkable reminder of Sospel's fast-track past is the 11th-century **Vieux Pont** (Old Bridge), a sophisticated Romanesque bridge composed of two graceful arches spanning the waters, buttressed by a toll tower. This sturdy structure bore the steady stream of mules carrying salt from Nice to Turin along the 18th-century *route de sel* (salt route).

The **Église St-Michel** in place St-Michel is the largest church in the département Alpes-Maritimes. Once the cathedral in the days of the papal schism in the 14th century, it bears only the bell tower from Romanesque days; the rest was built in the early 18th century and dazzles with gilt and trompe-l'oeil frescoes. From the church you can climb up to the **Fort St-Roch** and other remains of the post-World-War-II Maginot Line.

En Route   From Sospel climb back into the heights on D2204 to cross the **Col de Braus** (3,287 ft), where the Alps rear back into view. The road descends sharply by *lacets,* switchbacks as tightly angled as the laces in a shoe. The perspective broadens and greenery thickens as you descend to L'Escarène, another pretty river town.

L'Escarène

53   *22 km (14 mi) southwest of Sospel, 18 km (11 mi) north of Nice.*

As you land safely from the switchbacks down from the Col de Braus, you roll into this serene and unassuming river town. L'Escarène is the access point for the pretty, snaking 7-km (4-mi) drive up D2566 to the lovely perched village of **Lucéram**. Draped high on a cliff and flanked by forested ravines, it has commanded a key sentinel position over the backcountry since the Middle Ages. Its remaining 13th-century guard tower and Romanesque church anchor a charming skew of stone-and-stucco houses and a maze of cobbled streets. The **Église St-Pierre,** with two Penitent chapels standing guard at its sides, seems remarkably florid for the humble setting, yet it was designed by the same architect as Nice's cathedral.

MONACO AND THE CORNICHES RESORTS

Purists and hard-core regional historians insist that this final sunny sliver of coast—from the Cap Ferrat to the Italian border—is the one and only, true Côte d'Azur. It is certainly the most dramatically endowed, backed by forested mountains and crystalline Alps, with Mediterranean breezes relieving the summer heat and radiant light soothing midwinter days. Banana trees and date palms, cactus and figs luxuriate in the climate, and the hills, bristling with wind-twisted parasol pines, are paved with hothouses where roses and carnations profit from the year-round sun.

The lay of the land is nearly vertical as the coastline is one great cliff, a *corniche* terraced by three parallel highways—the Basse Corniche, the Moyenne Corniche, and the Grande Corniche—that snake along its graduated crests. Woven between these panoramic routes lie the resorts, their names as evocative of luxury and glamour as a haute-couture logo: Cap Ferrat, Beaulieu, and Monte Carlo.

Yet it must be said: these pockets of elegance have long since overflowed, and it's a rare stretch of cliffside that hasn't sprouted a cluster of concrete cubes in cloying hues of pineapple, apricot, and Pepto-Bismol pink. The traffic along the Corniches routes—especially the Basse Corniche that follows the coast—is appalling, exacerbated by the manic Italian driving style and self-absorbed luxury roadsters that turn the pavement into a bumper-car battle.

But there are moments. Wrench your car out of the flow, pull over at a rare overlook on the Haute Corniche, and walk to the extremity. Like the ancient Ligurians who first built their settlements here, you can hang over the infinite expanse of teal blue sea and glittering waves and survey the resorts draped gracefully along the curves of the coast. It was from these cliffs that for 2,500 years castles and towers held watch over the waters, braced against the influx of new peoples—first the Greeks, then the Romans, the Saracens, trade ships from Genoa, battleships under Napoléon, Edwardian cruise ships on the Grand Tour, and the Allies in the Second World War. The influx continues today, of course, in the great waves of vacationers who storm the coast, summer and winter.

Villefranche-sur-Mer

★ 54 *10 km (6 mi) east of Nice.*

Nestled discreetly along the deep scoop of harbor between Nice and the Cap Ferrat, this pretty watercolor fishing port seems surreal, flanked as it is by the big city of Nice and the assertive wealth of Monaco. Genuine fishermen actually skim up to the docks here in weathered-blue barques, and the streets of the old town flow directly to the waterfront, much as they did in the 13th century.

A favorite as a film location for its old-world atmosphere, this tiny port has been featured in James Bond films and *The Jewel of the Nile*. Its deep harbor was preferred by Onassis and Niarchos, and royals on their yachts. But the character of the place was subtly shaped by the artists and authors who gathered at the **Hôtel Welcome** (☞ Dining and Lodging, *below*)—Diaghilev and Stravinsky, taking a break from the Ballet Russe in Monaco; Somerset Maugham and Evelyn Waugh; and, above all, Jean Cocteau, who came here to recover from the excesses of Paris life.

So enamored was Cocteau of this painterly fishing port that he decorated the 14th-century **Chapelle St-Pierre** with images from the life of St. Peter and dedicated it to the village's fishermen. Working in crayon and chalk fixed with paraffin, he covered the walls with earthy, simplistic drawings, heavily outlined and surprisingly—even disappointingly—realist for this master of the surreal. ⊠ *pl. Pollanais,* ☎ *04–93–76–90–70.* ⊠ *12 frs/€1.83.* ۞ *Mid-June–mid-Sept., Tues.–Sun. 10–noon and 4–8:30; mid-Sept.–mid-Nov., 9:30–noon and 2–6; end Dec.–Mar., 9:30–noon and 2–5:30; Apr.–mid-June, Tues.–Sun. 9:30–noon and 3–7.*

Villefranche's old town is made for wandering, with steeply stepped streets leading up into alleys and passageways arching over the cobbles. The extraordinary 13th-century **rue Obscure** (literally, "dark street") is entirely covered by vaulted arcades; it sheltered the town's residents when the Germans fired their parting shots—an artillery bombardment—near World War II's end.

The modest Baroque **Église St-Michel** (⊠ pl. Poullan), just above rue Obscure, contains a movingly realistic sculpture of Christ carved in fig wood by an anonymous 17th-century convict.

The stalwart 16th-century **Citadelle St-Elme,** restored to perfect condition, anchors the harbor with its broad, sloping stone walls. Beyond its drawbridge lie the city's offices and a group of minor gallery–museums. Whether or not you stop into these private collections of local art (all free of charge), you are welcome to stroll around the inner grounds and circle the imposing exterior.

Dining and Lodging

$$–$$$ ✕ **Hôtel Welcome.** When Villefranche harbored a community of
★   artists and writers, this waterfront landmark was their adopted headquarters. Somerset Maugham holed up in one of the tiny crow's-nest rooms at the top, and Jean Cocteau moved into one of the corners, with windows opening onto two balconies. Alec and Evelyn Waugh (and later, Liz and Dick) used to tie one on in the bar, and film directors shooting action scenes in the bay sent the guests flowers when special-effects explosions disturbed their repose. It's comfortable and modern, with the best rooms brightened with vivid colors and stenciled quotes from Cocteau, yet there's nothing glamorous about it—except that its rooms open over the port, the harbor nearby, and the sounds of ropes ticking against masts of gently rocking yachts. The casual brasserie Carpe Diem serves salads and pastas on the quai; the formal restaurant St-Pierre specializes, naturally enough, in fish. Look for plump scallops with langoustine tails, and St-Pierre roasted, oddly but successfully, with tomatoes and mozzarella. ✉ *quai Courbet, 06230,* ☎ *04–93–76–27–62,* 🅵🅰🆇 *04–93–76–27–66. 32 rooms. 2 restaurants, bar, air-conditioning. AE, DC, MC, V. Closed mid-Nov.– mid-Dec..* ✎

Beaulieu

🏵 *4 km (2½ mi) east of Villefranche, 14 km (9 mi) east of Nice.*

With its back pressed hard against the cliffs of the corniche and sheltered between the peninsulas of Cap Ferrat and Cap Roux, this once-grand resort basks in a tropical microclimate that earned its central neighborhood the name "Petite Afrique." The town was the pet of 19th-century society, and its grand hotels welcomed Empress Eugénie, the Prince of Wales, and Russian nobles.

One manifestation of its Belle Époque excess is the extravagant **Villa Kerylos,** a mansion built in 1902 in the style of classical Greece. It was the dream house of the amateur archeologist Théodore Reinach, who commissioned an Italian architect so he could surround himself with Grecian delights: cool Carrara marble, alabaster, rare fruitwoods, a mosaic-lined bath/pool worthy of a 1950s toga movie, and a dining room where guests draped themselves on the floor to eat, *à la Greque.* ✉ *rue Gustave-Eiffel,* ☎ *04–93–01–01–44.* 🖼 *43 frs/€6.56.* ☉ *Mid-Feb.– June, daily 10:30–6; July–Aug., daily 10:30–7; Sept.–mid-Nov., daily 10:30–6; mid-Dec.–mid-Feb., weekdays 2–6, weekends 10:30–6. Closed mid-Nov.–mid-Dec.*

Today Beaulieu is usually spoken of in the past tense and has taken on a rather stuffy ambience. But on the **promenade Maurice-Rouvier,** you can stroll the waterfront, past grand villas and their tropical gardens, all the way to St-Jean-Cap-Ferrat.

St-Jean-Cap-Ferrat

★ 🏵 *2 km (1 mi) south of Beaulieu on D25.*

This luxuriously sited pleasure port moors the peninsula of Cap Ferrat; from its port-side walkways and crescent of beach you can look

over the sparkling blue harbor to the graceful green bulk of the corniches. Yachts purr in and out of port, and their passengers scuttle into
cafés for take-out drinks to enjoy on their private decks.

★ Between the port and the mainland, the phenomenally beautiful **Villa
Ephrussi de Rothschild** stands as a testament to the wealth and worldly
taste of the Baroness Ephrussi de Rothschild, who had it built (though
she only stayed here a week or two per year). Constructed in 1905 and
donated to the Academy of Beaux Arts in 1934, the house was created
around the artworks, decorations, and furniture brought to Beatrice
de Rothschild's door by eager dealers (she rarely traveled herself). The
mansion is lavished with rare tapestries and fabrics and landscaped with
no fewer than seven theme gardens (she liked to collect). The extraordinary ensemble reigns over a hilltop at the crest of the peninsula,
taking in spectacular, symmetrical views of the coastline. On the ground
floor you can freely visit hall after hall exquisitely decorated with Go-
belins and Beauvais tapestries, Renaissance painted-wood furniture, and
wall panels painted in classical grotesques. In de Rothschild's bedroom
is a ravishing collection of gowns and her travel kit for a cruise on the
Ile-de-France; in the dining room the table is set with Sèvres tea things
ready for sipping. On a guided tour of the upstairs, you can see things,
things, and more things, including some fine little etchings by Fragonard, but allow yourself time to wander in the gardens. They are one
of the few places on the coast where you'll be allowed to experience
the lavish pleasures of the Belle Époque Côte d'Azur. Tea and light lunches
are served in a glassed-in porch overlooking the grounds. ✉ *av.
Ephrussi,* ☎ *04–93–01–33–09.* ✉ *Access to ground floor and gardens
49 frs/€7.47; guided tour upstairs 14 frs/€2.13 extra.* ☾ *Feb.–June
and Sept.–Nov., daily 10–6; July–Aug., daily 10–7; Nov.–Jan., weekdays 2–6, weekends 10–6.*

Cap Ferrat itself is fiercely protected from curious tourists by its residents; its grand old villas are, for the most part, hidden in the depths
of tropical gardens. You can nonetheless walk its entire **coastline promenade** if you strike out from the port; from the restaurant Capitaine
Cook, cut right up avenue des Fossés, turn right on avenue Vignon,
and follow the chemin de la Carrière. The 11-km (7-mi) walk passes
through rich tropical flora and, on the west side, over white cliffs buf-
feted by waves. When you've traced the full outline of the peninsula,
veer up the chemin du Roy past the fabulous gardens of the **Villa des
Cèdres,** once owned by Leopold II, king of Belgium at the turn of the
century; you'll reach the **Plage de Passable** and cut back across the peninsula's wrist.

A shorter loop takes you from town out to the **Pointe de St-Hospice,**
much of the walk shaded by wind-twisted pines. From the port, climb
avenue Jean Mermoz to place Paloma and follow the path closest to
the waterfront. At the point there's an 18th-century prison tower, a
19th-century chapel, and unobstructed views of Cap Martin.

Dining and Lodging

$$ ✕ **Le Sloop.** Among the touristy cafés and snack shops along the port,
this sleek blue-and-white restaurant caters to the yachting crowd and
sailors who cruise in to dock for lunch. The focus is fish, of course:
soupe de poisson (fish soup), St-Pierre (John Dory) steamed with as-
paragus, or whole sea bass roasted with olives and pistou. Its outdoor
tables surround a tiny "garden" of potted palms, and the view of the
cliffs and bobbing boats is mesmerizing. ✉ *Port de Plaisance,* ☎ *04–
93–01–48–63. AE, MC, V. Closed Wed. mid-Sept.–mid-Apr. No lunch
Wed. or Thurs. mid-Apr.–mid-Sept.*

$$$ 🏠 **Brise Marine.** This golden-ocher 1878 villa, brightened with sky-blue
★   shutters and a frieze of frescoed lemons, opens onto a broad balustraded
garden and unbroken views of the sea. Though it overlooks one of the
cape's many exclusive mansions, complete with vast garden and much-
vaunted *chien très méchant* (very nasty dog), *this* little mansion remains
unpretentious and accessible, with pretty little pastel guest rooms that
feel like bedrooms in a private home. The terraces are shared, the aper-
itif a social occasion, and the comforts first class, including hair dry-
ers, safes, and CNN (if you must). Honeymooners should ask for the
"villa," a small room set slightly apart, with a sizable private terrace
looking straight out to sea. ⊠ *58 av. Jean Mermoz, 06230,* ☎ *04–93–
76–04–36,* ℻ *04–93–76–11–49. 16 rooms. Bar, air-conditioning. AE,
DC, MC, V. Closed Nov.–Jan..* 🍃

Eze

❺ *2 km (1 mi) east of Beaulieu, 12 km (7 mi) east of Nice, 7 km (4½ mi)
west of Monte Carlo.*

Towering like an eagle's nest above the coast and crowned with ram-
parts and the ruins of a medieval château, Eze (pronounced *ehz*) is un-
fortunately the most accessible of all the perched villages. Consequently,
it's by far the most commercialized, surpassing St-Paul for the tacki-
ness of its souvenir shops and the indifference of its waiters. Even off-
season its streets pour with a lava flow of tourists, some not-so-fresh
from the beach, and it earns unique status as the only town to post
pictorial warnings that say, in effect, "No Shoes, No Shirt, No Service."
It is, nonetheless, spectacularly sited; if you can manage to shake the
crowds and duck off to a quiet overlook, the village commands splen-
did views up and down the coast.

From the crest-top **Jardin Exotique** (Tropical Garden), full of exotic
succulents, you can pan your video cam all the way around the hills
and waterfront. But if you want to have a prayer of a chance to enjoy
the magnificence of this lovely stone village, come at dawn or after sun-
set. Or (if you have the means) spend the night—and the day elsewhere.

Dining and Lodging

$$$$ ✕🏠 **Château de la Chèvre d'Or.** Though it's directly on the main
★   tourist thoroughfare—and you may be obliged to crisscross the pedes-
trian traffic to move from room to restaurant—this extraordinary con-
glomerate of weathered-stone houses allows you to turn your back on
the world and drink in unsurpassed sea views. More than half the creamy
white rooms look over the water, and the others compensate with ex-
posed stone, beams, and burnished antiques. The three restaurants—
from the casual, affordable grill to the very medieval grand dining
room—all take in the views, too, as does the Louis XIII–style bar. It is
the luxurious, if occasionally precious, main restaurant that draws kudos
for its delicate stuffed pastas and near-crunchy risotto, its buttery mul-
let filets, and its gingerbread soufflés. The swimming pool alone, cling-
ing like a swallow's nest to the hillside, justifies the investment. So do
the liveried footmen who greet you at the village entrance to wave you,
VIP style, past the cattle drive of tourists. It's a member of the Relais
& Châteaux group. ⊠ *rue du Barri, 06360,* ☎ *04–92–10–66–66,* ℻
*04–93–41–06–72. 22 rooms, 8 apartments. 3 restaurants, bar, pool.
AE, DC, MC, V. Closed Dec.–Feb..* 🍃

La Turbie

❻ *5 km (3 mi) northeast of Eze, 7 km (4½ mi) northwest of Monaco.*

Lying directly above Monaco, this village serves as a crossroads for both French and Monagesque commuters stopping for coffee, a pizza, or bread for dinner. A pretty old-town labyrinth weaves a quiet web just behind the main road, and at its base you can stroll into the Jardin Prince Albert Ier to take in spectacular views over all of Monaco.

★ La Turbie takes its name from its magnificent Roman monument, the Tropea Augusti, or Trophy of Augustus, now known as the **Trophée des Alpes** (Trophy of the Alps). Visible from miles around, this spectacular mass of columned white stone rears above the village, marking the Via Julia Augusta as well as Rome's authority over the alliance of Italy, Gaul, and Germania. It's impressive enough from a distance, but consider visiting it up close. Augustus meant for the trophy to command magnificent views of his turf, and the panorama from its terrace stretches from the Estérel to Bordighera in Italy. There's a film in French on its history and a small museum. ☎ 04–93–41–20–84. ✉ 25 frs/€3.81. ☼ July–Sept., daily 9:30–7; Oct.–Mar., Tues.–Sun. 10–5; Apr.–June, daily 9:30–6.

Peillon

★ 59 *15 km (9 mi) northeast of Nice via D2204 and D53.*

Perhaps because it's difficult to reach and not on the way to or from anything else, this idyllic village has maintained the magical ambience of its medieval origins. You can hear the bell toll here, walk in silence up its weathered cobblestones, and smell the thyme crunching underfoot if you step past its minuscule boundaries onto the unspoiled hillsides. And its streets are utterly and completely commerce-free; the citizens have voted to vaccinate themselves against the plague of boutiques, galleries, and cafés that have infected its peers along the coast.

Dining and Lodging

$–$$$ ★ ✕⌂ **Auberge de la Madone.** With its shaded garden terrace and its impeccable bright-colored rooms, this inn is a charming oasis on the perimeter of the village. Some windows open out over greenery, others over spectacular views. The restaurant revels in the best local ingredients and traditions, from sea bass in fennel to pigeon stuffed with figs to local goat cheese drizzled with green olive oil; a lunch on the flowery veranda is everything the south of France should be. Yet owner Christian Millo and his partner/sister Marie-José continue to improve things: now the inn has a tennis court on the slope above, and six little rooms in a village annex called Lou Pourtail, which offer shelter at bargain rates. ✉ *06440 Peillon Village*, ☎ *04–93–79–91–17*, FAX *04–93–79–99–36. 18 rooms, 2 suites in main house; 6 rooms without bath in village annex. Restaurant, tennis court. MC, V. Closed late Oct.–late Dec. and Jan.*

Monaco

7 km (4½ mi) east of Eze, 21 km (13 mi) east of Nice.

It's positively feudal, the idea that an ancient dynasty of aristocrats could still hold fast to its patch of coastline, the last scrap of a once-vast domain. But that's just what the Grimaldi family has done, clinging to a few acres of glory and maintaining their own license plates, their own telephone area code (377), and their own highly forgiving tax system. Yet the Principality of Monaco covers just 473 acres and would fit comfortably inside New York's Central Park or a family farm in Iowa. And its 5,000 pampered citizens would fill only a small fraction of the seats in Yankee Stadium.

The present ruler, Prince Rainier III, traces his ancestry to Otto Canella, who was born in 1070. The Grimaldi dynasty began with Otto's great-great-great-grandson, Francesco Grimaldi, also known as Frank the Rogue. Expelled from Genoa, Frank and his cronies disguised themselves as monks and in 1297 seized the fortified medieval town known today as Le Rocher (the Rock). Except for a short break under Napoléon, the Grimaldis have been here ever since, which makes them the oldest reigning family in Europe. On the Grimaldi coat of arms are two monks holding swords (look up, and you'll see them above the main door as you enter the palace).

In the 1850s a Grimaldi named Charles III made a decision that turned the Rock into a giant blue chip. Needing revenue but not wanting to impose additional taxes on his subjects, he contracted with a company to open a gambling facility. The first spin of the roulette wheel was on December 14, 1856. There was no easy way to reach Monaco then—no carriage roads or railroads—so no one came. Between March 15 and March 20, 1857, one person entered the casino—and won two francs. In 1868, however, the railroad reached Monaco, and it was filled with Englishmen who came to escape the London fog. The effects were immediate. Profits were so great that Charles eventually abolished all direct taxes.

Almost overnight, a threadbare principality became an elegant watering hole for European society. Dukes (and their mistresses) and duchesses (and their gigolos) danced and dined their way through a world of spinning roulette wheels and bubbling champagne—preening themselves for nights at the opera, where such artists as Vaslav Nijinsky, Sarah Bernhardt, and Enrico Caruso came to perform.

But it's the tax system, not the gambling, that's made Monaco one of the most sought-after addresses in the world—that and its sensational position on a broad, steep peninsula that bulges into the Mediterranean, its harbor sparkling with luxury cruisers, its posh mansions angling awnings toward the nearly perpetual sun. The population explosion here has allowed Monaco to break another French code, that of construction restraints. Thus it bristles with gleaming glass-and-concrete corncob-towers 20 and 30 stories high and with vast apartment complexes, their terraces landscaped like miniature gardens.

The Monagesques themselves add to the sense of flossy, flashy self-contentment. Nearly everything is dyed-to-match here, even the lap dog in the Vuitton bag, and fur coats flourish from September through May. Doormen and policemen dress in ice-cream-colored uniforms worthy of an operetta, and along the port yacht clubs host exclusive birthday parties for little-rich-girls in couture party dresses. Pleasure boats vie with luxury cruisers in their brash beauty and Titanic scale, and teams of handsome young men—themselves dyed blond and tanned-to-match—scour and polish every gleaming surface.

Thanks in part to the pervasive odor of money-to-burn, Monaco's **casino** remains the most famous in the world, long the playground of royalty, wealthy playboys, and glamorous film stars. One of the loveliest of the latter, in fact, became its princess when Hollywood darling Grace Kelly married Prince Rainier in 1956; their wedding, marriage, and her tragic death in a car accident have only added to the mythology of this fairy-tale mini-principality.

Monaco's gleaming profile is due, for the most part, to an entertainment organization called SBM: the Societé des Bains de Mer. Founders, in the 19th century, of the original casino, they have burgeoned to reign over a mega-complex of 23 restaurants, 4 hotels, nightclubs, cabarets,

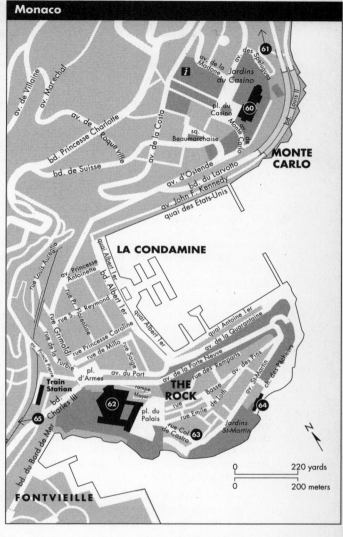

and all the casinos in town. In 1995 they added **Les Thermes Marins de Monte-Carlo** (Sea Baths of Monte-Carlo; ✉ 2 ave. de Monte-Carlo, ☎ 377/92–16–40–40), a seawater-therapy treatment center that stretches between the landmark Hôtel de Paris and its sister, the Hermitage. Within its sleek, multilevel complex you can pursue every creature comfort, from underwater massage to seaweed body wraps to light, elegant spa-style lunches—almost all with views over the port.

You may well gather that Monaco can be intimidating for budget travelers. Eating is expensive, and even the most modest hotels cost more here than in nearby Nice or Menton. For the frugal, Monaco is the ultimate day trip, although parking is as coveted as a room with a view. And its two far-flung tourist centers—the lovely casino grounds of Monte Carlo, surrounded by flossy shops, and Old Monaco, the medieval town on the Rock, topped by the palace, the cathedral, and the oceanography museum—are separated by a vast port, and shuttling between them is a daunting proposition for ordinary mortals without wings. Before starting off, arm yourself with a map and a bus schedule or an excellent pair of walking shoes and start at the **tourist office** (☞ Nice and the Eastern Côte d'Azur A to Z), just north of the casino gardens.

★ ⑥ Place du Casino is the center of Monte Carlo and the **casino** is a mustsee, even if you don't bet a sou. Into the gold-leaf splendor of the casino, where fortunes have been won, shirts lost, and any number of James Bond scenes filmed, the hopeful traipse from tour buses to tempt fate beneath the gilt-edged rococo ceiling.

In the true spirit of the town, it seems that the **Opéra** (⊠ pl. du Casino), with its 18-ton gilt-bronze chandelier and extravagant frescoes, is part of the casino complex. The designer, Charles Garnier, also built the Paris Opéra. Within this jewel-box are some of the coast's most significant performances of dance, opera, and orchestral music.

⑥ From place des Moulins there is an escalator down to the Larvotto Beach complex, artfully created with imported sand, and the **Musée National,** housed in a Garnier villa within a rose garden. There's a beguiling collection of 18th- and 19th-century dolls and mechanical automatons—more than 400 altogether. ⊠ *17 av. Princesse Grace,* ☎ *377/93–30–91–26.* ☞ *30 frs/€4.57.* ☉ *Easter–Aug., daily 10–6:30; Sept.–Easter, daily 10–12:15 and 2:30–6:30.*

It's a hike or a ride on bus No. 6 from Monte Carlo to the **port** along boulevard Albert Ier, where pleasure boats of every shape flash white and blue. It's here that they mount the stands for fans of the Grand Prix (☞ Outdoor Activities and Sports, *below*). And it's from the far corner of the port that the Institut Océanographique launches research boats to study aquatic life in the Mediterranean, as its late director Jacques Cousteau did for some 30 years.

On the broad plateau known as Le Rocher, or **the Rock,** the majority of Monaco's touristic sights are concentrated with tidy, self-conscious charm. This is the medieval heart of Monaco, and home to its cathedral, palace, and the Oceanography Museum. You can either climb up a raked *rampe* from the place d'Armes, behind the right corner of the port, or approach it by elevator from the seafront at the port's farthest end (past the Yacht Club).

At the center of the Rock's plateau, the broad place du Palais knots up with crowds at 11:55, when the poker-faded guards—in black in winter, white in summer—change shifts, or, as the French say, relieve ⑥ themselves. They are protecting hallowed ground: the **Palais Princier,** where the royal family resides, including, on occasion, Princess Stephanie. You can tell they're home if the family banner flies on the mast above the main tower. A 40-minute guided tour (summer only) of this sumptuous chunk of history, first built in the 13th century and expanded and enhanced over the centuries, reveals an extravagance of 16th- and 17th-century frescoes, as well as tapestries, gilt furniture, and paintings on a grand scale. One wing of the palace, open throughout the year, is taken up by the **Musée Napoléon,** filled with Napoleonic souvenirs—including The Hat and a tricolor scarf—and genealogical charts. (The Grimaldis and the Bonapartes were related, you see.) There is an abundance of military paraphernalia, from uniforms to medals, etchings and banners, all from the Prince's private collection. ⊠ *pl. du Palais,* ☎ *377/93–25–18–31.* ☞ *Palace apartments 30 frs/€4.57; Musée Napoléon 20 frs/€3.05; joint ticket 40 frs/€6.10.* ☉ *Palace apartments: June–Oct., daily 9:30–6:30. Museum: June–Sept., daily 9:30–6:30; Oct.–mid-Nov., 10–5; Dec.–May, Tues.–Sun. 10:30–12:30 and 2–5.*

Follow the flow of crowds down the last remaining streets of medieval
Monaco to the **Cathédrale de l'Immaculée-Conception** (⊠ av. St-Martin), an uninspired 19th-century version of Romanesque. It harbors
nonetheless some wonderful artworks, including an **altarpiece** painted
in 1500 by Bréa. Now shielded behind glass at the left transcepts, it
is, perhaps, his masterwork, depicting with tender detail the steady gaze
of St-Nicolas; he is flanked by small panels portraying other saints, graceful, chastened, and demure. Despite the humility innate to the work,
it's framed with unusual flamboyance in ornate gilt wood. Just beyond
the Bréa polyptich, enter the curve of the apse to see the tombs of the
Grimaldi clan. The first on entering the apse from the left is simply labeled *Gracia Patricain, Principis Rainerii*; Princess Grace's death date—
1982—figures in Roman numerals. It's easy to identify her tomb
without reading the inscription; even today, it's heaped with fresh
flowers.

At the prow of the Rock, the grand **Musée Océanographique** (Oceanography Museum) perches dramatically on a cliff, its many levels plunging dramatically to the sea. The splendid Edwardian structure was built
under Prince Albert Ier to house specimens collected on amateur explorations, and evokes the grandeur of the days of imperialist discovery and the old National Geographic Society. Both the museum and
its research organization, the Institut Océanographique (Oceanography Institute), were led by Jacques Cousteau (1910–97) from 1957 to
1988. Sumptuously decorated with mosaics of sea life, beveled-oak display cases, and gleaming brass, the museum contains a collection
somewhat pared down from its heyday. (Despite its extravagant wealth,
the Principality of Monaco contributes virtually nothing to the museum,
which subsists entirely on ticket sales.) The main floor displays skeletons and taxidermy of enormous sea creatures, including a 6½-ft-wide
Japanese crab, and a magnificent new life-scale model of a sperm
whale, created from first-hand observation by the museum's conservateur/artist Maurizio Würtz. There are interesting examples of early
submarines, diving gear dating to the Middle Ages, and a few interactive science displays. Upstairs you'll find boat models, including a
scale miniature of the Titanic sinking. But the reason the throngs pour
into this landmark is its famous **aquarium**, a vast complex of backlit
tanks at eye level containing every imaginable variety of fish, crab, and
eel. The wide-open piranha pond is a crowd pleaser. Watch for new
interactive programs between visitors and researchers on the open sea,
armed with two-way microphones. For a fine view and a restorative
drink, take the elevator to the roof terrace. ⊠ *av. St-Martin,* ☎ *377/
93–15–36–00.* ◨ *60 frs/€9.15.* ☉ *April–Sept., daily 9–7; Oct.–Mar.,
daily 10–6.*

Six hundred varieties of cacti and succulents cling to a sheer rock face
at the **Jardin Exotique** (Tropical Garden), a brisk half-hour walk west
from the palace. The garden traces its roots to days when Monaco's
near-tropical climate nurtured unheard-of exotica, amazing visitors from
the northlands as much as any zoo. The plants are of less interest today,
especially to Americans familiar with southwestern flora. The views
over the Rock and coastline, however, are spectacular. In the cavernous **grotte de l'Observatoire** (entered from the gardens; 40-minute
guided tours leave hourly), shapes of the stalactites and stalagmites resemble the cacti outside. From the gardens you can also enter the
Musée d'Anthropologie Préhistorique (Museum of Prehistoric Anthropology), which contains bones, tools, and other artifacts of early
man. ⊠ *bd. du Jardin Exotique,* ☎ *377/93–15–29–80.* ◨ *40 frs/€6.10.*
☉ *Daily 9–7 (till dusk in winter).*

Dining and Lodging

$$$$ ✕ **Le Louis XV.** This extravagantly showy restaurant, in the Hôtel de
★ Paris (☞ *below*), stuns with neo-Baroque decor, yet it manages to be
upstaged by its product: the superb cuisine of Alain Ducasse, one of
Europe's most celebrated chefs. With too many tokens on his Monopoly
board, Ducasse jets between his other, ever-growing interests—including his eponymous three-star in Paris, his country inns in Moustiers
and Brignoles, and his management of the entire Châteaux Independents hotel group; this leaves the Louis XV kitchen, for the most part,
in the capable hands of chef Franck Cerutti. No great loss. Glamorous
iced lobster consommé with caviar and risotto perfumed with Alba white
truffles slum happily with stockfish (stewed salt cod) and tripe. There
are sole sautéed with tender baby fennel, local sea bass trimmed with
sage-and-anchovy beignets, milk-fed lamb with hints of cardamom, and
dark-chocolate sorbet crunchy with ground coffee beans—in short, a
panoply of theatrical delights using the sensual flavors of the Mediterranean. ⊠ *Hôtel de Paris, pl. du Casino,* ☎ 377/92–16–30–01. *AE,
DC, MC, V. Closed Tues.–Wed. (except Wed. dinner mid-June–Aug.),
2 wks in Feb.–early Mar., and late Nov.–late Dec.*

$$ ✕ **Cafe de Paris.** This landmark Belle Époque brasserie, across from
the casino, offers a wide variety of classic dishes: shellfish, steak tartare,
match-stick frites, and fish boned tableside. Supercilious, super-pro wait-
ers fawn gracefully over Old World preeners, gentlemen, jet-setters, and
tourists alike, serving good hot food until 2 AM. ⊠ *pl. du Casino,* ☎
377/92–16–20–20. *AE, DC, MC, V.*

$$ ✕ **Castelroc.** With its tempting pine-shaded terrace just across from the
entrance to the Prince's Palace, you may take this for a tourist chaser,
but it's one of the more popular lunch spots in town with locals. The
cuisine is a mix of classic and regional flavors, from *anchoïade* (anchovy paste) with olive oil to stuffed artichokes, and garlicky *stocafi*
(stockfish) simmered with tomatoes and Provençal herbs. ⊠ *pl. du Palais,*
☎ 377/93–30–36–68. *MC, V. Closed Sat. and end-Nov.–Dec.*

$$ ✕ **Polpetta.** This popular little trattoria, a favorite with stars and
★ politicos since the 1970s, is close enough to the Italian border to pass
for the real thing, and the exuberant Guasco brothers who greet you
add to the authenticity. Enjoy a parade of antipasti, seafood risotto,
osso buco perfumed with saffron, or the house specialty, *trofie* (skinny
Ligurian-style gnocchi) with pesto and tomato sauce. There's a terrific
list of Italian wines. ⊠ *2 rue Paradis,* ☎ 377/93–50–67–84. *AE, MC,
V. Closed Tues. and June. No lunch Sat.*

$$ ✕ **Quai des Artistes.** This warehouse-scale neo-Deco bistro on the
★ port is the chic-est of the chic with Monagesque gentry, packing well-
heeled diners shoulder-to-shoulder at banquettes lined up for maximum
people-watching. Rich brasserie classics (grilled tongue, lentils with salt
pork) are counterbalanced with high-flavor international experiments
(mussels in a red-pepper ceviche, char-grilled salmon served sushi-
rare). Reservations are a must. ⊠ *4 quai Antoine Ier,* ☎ 377/97–97–
97–77. *Reservations essential. AE, DC, MC, V.*

$ ✕ **La Cigale.** With mom and pop serving, the ceiling draped in fishing
nets, a mounted TV, and timers that shut off the lights in the bathroom
if you linger too long, this is the other side of Monaco, where they struggle to make ends meet and to keep the prices low. Their efforts reward
you with fresh *fritto misto,* a crunchy platter of batter-fried baby fish
and squid rings; hearty minestrone thick with pesto; sardine beignets;
and homemade pastas sauced with a generous hand. ⊠ *18 rue Millo,*
☎ 377/93–30–16–14. *MC, V. Closed weekends.*

$ ✕ **Stars'n'Bars.** This American-style port-side bar/restaurant/entertainment center is such a phenomenal success with the Monagesque it's worth a stop for the culture shock alone. Fat, juicy burgers, cookie sundaes, real iced tea in thick glasses, and (gasp!) pitchers of ice water draw homesick ex-pats, burrito-starved backpackers—and mobs of locals wallowing in *la cuisine américaine*. Portside tables are low-key; inside, soft rock, arcade games, and a friendly international bar scene mingle all ages and nationalities. ✉ *6 quai Antoine Ier,* ☎ *377/93–50– 95–95. AE, DC, MC, V. Closed Mon.*

$$$$ ✕⊡ **Hermitage.** A riot of frescoes and plaster flourishes embellished with gleaming brass, this landmark 1900 hotel nonetheless maintains a relatively low profile, set back a block from the casino scene. This is where the mink-and-Vuarnets set comes *not* to be seen. Even if you're not staying, walk through the lobby to admire the glass-dome Art Nouveau vestibule, designed by Gustav Eiffel. The best rooms face the sea or angle toward the port. The formal, sophisticated restaurant **Vistamar** still buys its seafood from a local Monagesque fisherman, and serves it in a tailored, modern setting splashed with cobalt blue. Its broad, broad terrace offers one of the most glamorous dining settings in Monaco. ✉ *sq. Beaumarchais, 98005,* ☎ *377/92–16–40–00,* ⨏⨯ *377/ 92–16–38–52. 195 rooms, 14 junior suites, 18 suites. Restaurant, bar, air-conditioning, pool. AE, DC, MC, V.* ✍

$$$$ ✕⊡ **Hôtel de Paris.** Built in 1864 on an extravagant scale, this vestige of the Belle Époque has one of the most prestigious addresses in Europe. The cavernous lobby is a veritable crossroads of the buffed and befurred Euro-gentry, and rooms—fresh, pretty, and not in the least grandiose—overlook the casino, the gardens, and, from above, the sea. Looking for the ultimate indulgence? Book a suite directly overlooking the Grand Prix. The open-air grill, which takes in vast Monaco panoramas from the 8th floor, serves simple grilled meats and seafood with a Provençal accent. On the ground floor, Côté Jardin draws ladies-who-lunch for salads and light seafood specialties. Neither can compete, of course, with the granddaddy of haute cuisine that flanks the palatial entrance: **Louis XV** (☞ above). ✉ *pl. du Casino, 98000,* ☎ *377/92–16–30–00,* ⨏⨯ *377/92–16–38–50. 141 rooms, 40 suites, 19 junior suites. 4 restaurants, air-conditioning, 1 outdoor and 1 indoor pool, spa. AE, DC, MC, V.* ✍

$$$$ ⊡ **Monte Carlo Grand Hotel.** Sprawling long and low along the waterfront at Monte Carlo's base, this ultra-modern, airport-scale complex is so vast it commands a full-time staff of upholsterers. Bright rooms decked in vivid hues angle onto the open sea. The bars, casino, boutiques, and mall-size lobby easily contain megaconventions, but thanks to the friendly staff vacationers will feel at home, too. There's a veritable food court of restaurants: The Café de la Mer is coffee-shop comfortable but offers an eclectic choice of seafood and Provençal specialties—at all hours—and the casual rooftop Le Pistou makes the most of the Grand's exclusive position on the open sea. ✉ *12 av. des Spélugues, 98000,* ☎ *377/93–50–65–00,* ⨏⨯ *377/93–30–01–57. 619 rooms, 69 apartments. 3 restaurants, bar, air-conditioning, pool, hot tub, health club, casino. AE, DC, MC, V.* ✍

$$$ ⊡ **Alexandra.** The friendly proprietress, Madame Larouquie, makes you feel right at home at this central, comfortable spot, just north of the casino. Though the color schemes clash and the decor is spare, bathrooms are big and up-to-date, and insulated windows shut out traffic noise. ✉ *35 bd. Princesse-Charlotte, 98000,* ☎ *377/93–50–63–13,* ⨏⨯ *377/92–16–06–48. 56 rooms. Air-conditioning. AE, DC, MC, V.*

$$$ ⊡ **Balmoral.** This 100-year-old urban hotel makes no effort to please, keeping its walls stripped of art, its woodwork overpainted, and its bath-

rooms with '60s-style tiles and shower. The only reason to stay here is the view from its port-side rooms, some with wrought-iron balconies. The boats, blue water, and looming Rock make you forget the unmatched color scheme. ⊠ *12 av. de la Costa,* ☏ *377/93–50–62–37,* FAX *377/93–15–08–69. 75 rooms. Restaurant, air-conditioning in 50 rooms. AE, DC, MC, V.*

Nightlife and the Arts

There's no need to go to bed before dawn in Monte Carlo when you can go to the grand casinos, the American game rooms in the Café de Paris, or the night-glamour scene at Le Sporting. The casinos fix no closing times, but keep the doors open as long as the games are rolling.

The bastion and landmark of Monte Carlo gambling is, of course, the **Casino de Monte-Carlo.** The main gambling hall is the **Salle Européene** (European Room), where for a 50-franc/€7.60 entry fee you can play roulette, trente et quarante, or blackjack. The slot machines stand apart in the **Salle Blanche** (White Room) and the **Salon Rose** (Pink Salon), where unclad nymphs float about on the ceiling smoking cigarillos. The **Salles Privées** (Private Rooms) are for high rollers; pay another 100 francs/€15 to play for a minimum stake of 500 francs/€76. Jacket and tie are required in the back rooms, which open at 3 PM. Bring your passport (under-21s not admitted). ⊠ *pl. du Casino,* ☏ *377/92–16–20–00* ⊙ *3 PM–noon.*

Once owned by the rival Loews Hotel (now the Monte Carlo Grand) the **Sun Casino** has been absorbed by SBM, though its long, low hall remains inside the Monte Carlo Grand hotel and just beside the waterfront convention center. It features no fewer than 435 slot machines, as well as craps, blackjack, and *roulette américaine.* ⊠ *12 av. des Spélugues,* ☏ *377/92–16–21–23.* ⊙ *Tables open weekdays at 5 PM and weekends at 4 PM; slot machines open daily at 11 AM.*

Behind the dining room of the **Café de Paris** you'll find *les jeux améri-cains:* row upon row of slot machines as well as American roulette, craps, and blackjack. ⊠ *pl. du Casino,* ☏ *377/92–16–21–24.* ⊙ *Tables open daily at 5 PM; slot machines open daily at 10 AM.*

SBM's Le Sporting, a summer-only entertainment complex on the waterfront, has opened the **Salle des Palmiers** for the full panoply of European games, from English roulette to chemin de fer. Its games are open only at night. ⊠ *Le Sporting, av. Princess Grace,* ☏ *377/92–16–21–25.* ⊙ *Late June–mid-Sept. Tables open daily at 10 PM.*

The **Living Room** (⊠ 7 av. des Spélugues, ☏ 377/93–50–80–31) is a popular, crowded piano bar and discotheque open year-round. For a relatively low-key night, try **Sparco Café** (⊠ 19 av. Charles-III, ☏ 377/93–30–41–06), a piano bar that often attracts good jazz singers. **Tiffany's** (⊠ 3 av. des Spélugues) is a year-round hot spot for disco dancing from 11 PM into the wee hours.

Monte Carlo's **Printemps des Arts** (Spring Arts Festival) takes place from early April to mid-May and includes the world's top ballet, operatic, symphonic, and chamber performers. For schedules and information contact the Direction des Affaires Culturelles (⊠ 4 bd. des Moulins, ☏ 377/93–15–85–15). Year-round ballet and classical music can be enjoyed at the **Salle Garnier** (⊠ pl. du Casino, ☏ 377/92–16–22–99), the main venue of the Opéra de Monte-Carlo and the Orchestre Philharmonique de Monte-Carlo, both worthy of the magnificent hall. The **Théâtre Princesse Grace** (⊠ 12 av. d'Ostende, ☏ 377/93–25–32–27) stages a number of plays during the Spring Arts Festival; off-season there's usually a new show each week.

Outdoor Activities and Sports

Diving equipment can be rented from the **Club d'Exploration Sous-Marine de Monaco** (Underwater Exploration Club; ⌧ quai des Sanbarbani, ☎ 377/92–05–91–78). For golf, head to the 18-hole **Golf de Monte Carlo** (⌧ rte. du Mont-Agel, La Turbie, ☎ 0033/04–93–41–09–11), which is open to the public.

The **Monte Carlo Tennis Open** is held in late April in the Monte Carlo Country Club, which lies in the outskirts of Monaco in the French commune of Roquebrune-Cap-Martin (☎ 377/04–93–41–30–15 for information). When the tennis stops, the auto racing begins: the **Grand Prix de Monaco** (☎ 377/93–15–26–00 for information) takes place in mid-May.

Roquebrune–Cap-Martin

66 *5 km (3 mi) east of Monaco.*

In the midst of the frenzy of overbuilding that defines this last gasp of the coast before Italy, two twinned havens have survived, each in its own way: the perched old town of Roquebrune, which gives its name to the greater area, and Cap-Martin—luxurious, isolated, and exclusive.

With its tumble of skewed tile roofs and twisting streets, fountains, archways, and quiet squares, Roquebrune retains many of the charms of a hilltop village, although it's heavily gentrified and commercialized in a Bohemian kind of way. Its main attraction is the **Château Féodal** (Feudal Castle) at the top of the old town. Around the remains of a 10th-century tower, the Grimaldis erected an impregnable fortress that was state of the art in the 16th century, with crenellation, watch towers, and a broad moat. Nowadays this stronghold is besieged by tourists, who invade its restored halls and snap pictures from its wraparound walkway. ☎ 04–93–35–62–87. ⌧ *20 frs/€3.05.* ☉ *Oct.–Jan., daily 10–12:30 and 2–5; Feb.–May, 10–12:30 and 2–6; June–Sept., 10–12:30 and 3–7:30.*

In the **cemetery,** at the far eastern end of the old town, Swiss-French architect Le Corbusier lies buried with his wife in a tomb of his own design. He kept a humble *cabanot* (beach bungalow) on the rocky shores of the Cap-Martin, where he drowned while swimming in 1965.

★ You can visit Le Corbusier's bungalow and see the glorious flora of the cape by walking the **promenade Le Corbusier.** It leads over chalk cliffs and through dense Mediterranean flora to his tiny retreat, a cabin and series of terraces, landings, and walkways designed along the rigorous lines he preferred. Park at the tip of the cape on avenue Winston-Churchill and follow the signs.

Dining and Lodging

$$–$$$ ✕🏠 **Les Deux Frères.** Magnificently sited, eccentric, and oozing with
★ charm, this whitewashed 1854 schoolhouse has been transformed into an inn overlooking the sea. Every room is designed with a different theme—African safari, flower power, medieval castle, 1001 nights—and tied-in video cassettes stand by to back up the mood. It's not as silly as it sounds, but is executed with modern, high-tech style and quality materials. The restaurant (closed Sunday night and Monday, and mid-November through mid-December) offers ambitious and generous French cooking, either indoors by the crackling fireplace or on the terrace *place* overlooking the whole of the Côte d'Azur. Homemade terrines, herbed lamb, and good cheeses and pastries draw a local

clientele for picturesque culinary excursions. ✉ *Above D2254 in Roquebrune-village, 06190,* ☎ *04–93–28–99–00,* FAX *04–93–28–99–10. 10 rooms. Restaurant, bar. AE, MC, V.* ♨

Menton

 1 km (⅔ mi) east of Roquebrune, 9 km (5½ mi) east of Monaco.

Menton, the most Mediterranean of the French resort towns, rubs shoulders with the Italian border and owes some of its balmy climate to the protective curve of the Ligurian shore. Its Cubist skew of terra-cotta roofs and yellow-ocher houses, Baroque arabesques capping the church facades, and ceramic tiles glistening on their steeples, all evoke the villages of the Italian coast. Yet there's a whiff of influence from Spain, too, in its fantastical villas, exotic gardens, and whimsical patches of ceramic color, and a soupçon of Morocco, Corsica, and Greece. It is, in fact, the best of all Mediterranean worlds—and humble to boot: Menton is the least pretentious of the Côte d'Azur resorts, and all the more alluring for its modesty.

Its near-tropical climate nurtures orange and lemon trees that hang heavy with fruit in winter. There's another Florida parallel: the warmth attracts flocks of senior citizens who warm their bones far from northern fog and ice. Thus a large population of elderly visitors basks on its waterfront benches and browses its downtown shops. But Menton has a livelier, younger side, too, and the farther you penetrate toward the east, the more intriguing and colorful it becomes.

To get a feel for the territory, start your exploration at the far-east end of the Vieille Ville (Old City) and walk out to the end of the **Jetée Impératrice Eugénie** (Empress Eugenie Jetty), jutting far out into the water. Above the masts of pleasure boats, all of Menton spreads over the hills, and the mountains of Italy loom behind.

Up a set of grand tiered stairs that lead from the Quai Bonaparte and the Jetée lies the **Parvis St-Michel,** a broad plaza paved in round white and gray stones patterned in the coat of arms of the family Grimaldi. The plaza was created in the 17th century by Prince Honoré II; the letter H is mingled into the design as a kind of signature at the base of his great gift to the city.

The majestic, Baroque **Basilique St-Michel** (St-Michel Church), on Parvis St-Michel, dominates the skyline of Menton with its bell tower. A humbler Renaissance church was destroyed by order of the prince to make way for something on a grander scale, and its towering belfry secured its conspicuousness in 1701. Beyond the beautifully proportioned facade—a 19th-century addition—the richly frescoed nave and chapels contain several works by Genovese artists and a splendid 17th-century organ.

Just above the Basilique St-Michel, the smaller **Chapelle de l'Immaculée-Conception** answers with its own pure Baroque beauty, dating from 1687. Between 3 and 5 PM you can slip in to see the graceful trompel'oeil over the altar and the ornate gilt lanterns the penitents carried in processions.

High above the Parvis St-Michel, the **Cimetière du Vieux-Château** (Old Château Cemetery) lies on the terraced plateau where once stood a medieval castle. The Victorian graves here are arranged by nationality, with an entire section of Russian royalty. The birth and death dates often attest to the ugly truth: even Menton's balmy climate couldn't reverse the ravages of tuberculosis.

Two blocks below the plaza, **rue St-Michel** serves as the main commercial artery of the Vieille Ville, lined with shops, cafés, and orange trees. Between the lively pedestrian rue St-Michel and the waterfront, the marvelous **Marché Couvert** (Covered Market) sums up Menton style with its Belle Époque facade decorated in jewel-tone ceramics. Inside, it's just as appealing, with merchants vaunting chewy bread, mountain cheeses, oils, fruit, and Italian delicacies in Caravaggio-esque disarray. Outside its walls, other merchants bargain away their garden vegetables and hand-wound bundles of herbs. Right by the market, the pretty little **place aux Herbes** is a picturesque spot for a pause on a park bench, a drink, or a meal in the deep shade of the plane trees.

On the waterfront opposite the market, a squat medieval bastion crowned with four tiny watchtowers houses the **Musée Jean-Cocteau.** Built in 1636 to defend the port, the structure was spotted by the artist-poet-filmmaker Jean Cocteau (1889–1963) as the perfect site for a group of his works; he planned and supervised its reconstruction but never saw it finished. Outside its walls, a mosaic in round stone (an homage to the Parvis St-Michel) depicts a lizard; the inside floor answers with a salamander mosaic. There are bright, cartoonish pastels of fishermen and wenches in love, and a fantastical assortment of ceramic animals in the wrought-iron windows he designed himself. ⊠ *At the base of Quai Napoléon,* ☎ *04–93–57–72–30.* ▨ *20 frs/€3.05.* ۞ *Wed.–Mon. 10–noon and 2–6.*

Stroll the length of Menton's famous beachfront along the **promenade du Soleil,** broad, white, and studded with palm trees. The **Casino du Soleil** (⊠ av. Félix-Faure, ☎ 04–93–10–16–16) stakes out the middle of the promenade that shares its name; it's a modest, approachable, anti–Monte Carlo.

Directly behind the casino and perpendicular to the beach, the broad tropical **Jardins Biovès** (Biovès Gardens) stretch the breadth of the center, sandwiched between two avenues. Its symmetrical flower beds and spires of palms are the spiritual heart of town.

The 19th-century Italianate **Hôtel de Ville** (City Hall) conceals another Cocteau treasure: he decorated the **Salle des Mariages** (Marriage Room), the room in which civil marriages take place, with vibrant allegorical scenes. ⊠ *17 av. de la République,* ☎ *04–93–10–50–29.* ▨ *10 frs/€1.52.* ۞ *Weekdays 8:30–12:30 and 1:30–5.*

At the far west end of town, toward Roquebrune, stands the 18th-century **Palais Carnolès,** in vast gardens luxuriant with orange, lemon, and grapefruit trees. It was once the summer retreat of the princes of Monaco; today it contains a sizable collection of European paintings from the Renaissance to the present day. The halls of the palace themselves are as interesting as the artworks; the **Grand Salon d'Honneur** (Grand Salon of Honor) retains a rich ensemble of neoclassic grotesques and bas reliefs. ⊠ *3 av. de la Madone,* ☎ *04–93–35–49–71.* ▨ *Free.* ۞ *Wed.–Mon. 10–noon and 2–6.*

Dining and Lodging

$$–$$$ ✕▥ **Aiglon.** Sweep down the curving stone stairs to the terrazzo mosaic lobby of this lovely 1880 garden villa for a drink or a meal by the pool, or settle onto your little balcony overlooking the grounds and a tiny wedge of sea. There's a room for every whim, all soft-edged, comfortable, and romantic. The poolside restaurant, Le Riaumont, serves candlelit dinners of fresh, local fish lightly steamed and sauced with a Provençal accent; breakfast is served in a shady garden shelter. It's a three-minute walk to the beach. ⊠ *7 av. de la Madone, 06502,* ☎ *04–*

93–57–55–55, FAX *04–93–35–92–39. 28 rooms, 2 apartments. Restaurant, bar. AE, MC, V.* ✈

$$–$$$ 🏨 **Royal Westminster.** This Victorian waterfront palace hotel, beautifully restored inside and out in shades of lemon, mint, and robin's-egg blue, usually rents out its light-bathed, sea-view rooms to tour groups of seniors by the week. But you might get lucky on a standby basis, calling to reserve no sooner than 10 days in advance, or even dropping in. Beach mattresses and sun parasols are provided in the rooms. ✉ *1510 promenade du Soleil, 06500,* ☎ *04–93–28–69–69,* FAX *04–92–10–12–30. 92 rooms. Restaurant, bar, air-conditioning, billiards. AE, DC, MC, V.*

$–$$ 🏨 **Londres.** This modest, family-run hotel is on a small patch of greenery just a block from the beach and three blocks from the casino. It has an inexpensive traditional restaurant with outdoor tables and a tiny garden bar. Though the building dates from the turn of the 20th century, rooms have a '70s look, with all-weather carpeting, linoleum bathrooms, and acoustic tiles. But most have big French windows that open over the garden and just a sliver of sea view between the buildings, and seven now have air-conditioning. Small back rooms with shower only are a bargain. ✉ *15 av. Carnot, BP 73, 06502,* ☎ *04–93–35–74–62,* FAX *04–93–41–77–78. 27 rooms. Restaurant, bar. AE, MC, V.*

Nightlife and the Arts

The **casino** (✉ promenade de Soleil, ☎ 04–92–10–16–16) has the usual slot machines and roulette tables, as well as a disco and a cabaret in its Club 06. It's open daily 10–3AM.

In August the **Festival de Musique de Chambre** (Chamber Music Festival) takes place on the stone-paved plaza outside the St-Michel Church. The **Fête du Citron** (Lemon Festival), at the end of February, celebrates the lemon with Rose Bowl Parade–like floats and sculptures, all made of real fruit.

NICE AND THE EASTERN CÔTE D'AZUR A TO Z

Arriving and Departing

By Plane

The **Nice–Côte d'Azur Airport** (✉ 7 km [4½ mi] from Nice, ☎ 04–93–21–30–30) sits on a peninsula between Antibes and Nice. There are frequent flights between Paris and Nice on Air Liberté, AOM, and Air France as well as direct flights on Delta Airlines from New York. The flight time between Paris and Nice is about 1 hour.

A taxi from the airport into Nice proper—say, the train station or the place Masséna—costs about 130 francs/€20. Private shuttles leave every half hour or so until 11 PM (until 6 on Saturday). A city bus makes the run to and from the train station all day as well. Regular shuttle buses also serve the main coastal cities (Cannes, Antibes, Monaco, Menton), leaving from both terminals every half hour or so.

By Car

A8 flows briskly from Cannes to Antibes to Nice to the resorts on the Grand Corniche; N98 follows the coast more closely. From Paris, the main southbound artery is A6/A7, known as the Autoroute du Soleil; it passes through Provence and joins the eastbound A8 at Aix-en-Provence.

By Train

Nice is the major rail crossroads for trains arriving from Paris and other northern cities and from Italy, too. This coastal line, working eastward from Marseille and west from Ventimiglia, stops at Cannes, Antibes, Monaco, and Menton. To get from Paris to Nice (and with stops in most resorts along the coast), you can take the TGV, though it only maintains high speeds to Valence before returning to conventional rails and rates. Night trains arrive at Nice in the morning from Paris, Metz, and Strasbourg.

Getting Around

By Bus

If you want to penetrate deeper into villages and backcountry spots not on the rail line, you can take a bus out of Cannes, Nice, Antibes, or Menton to the most frequented spots. Pick up a schedule for local and commercial excursion buses at the train station, at tourist offices, and at the local *gare routière* (bus station). Many hotels and excursion companies organize day trips into St-Paul and Vence.

In Nice, the Sun Bus is a convenient way to cut across town; a one-way trip costs 8.50 francs/€1.30. Monaco's buses help stitch together the principality's widely dispersed neighborhoods. In both cases, maps and schedules are posted at the bus stops. Bus drivers give change and hand you a ticket, which must be validated in the composter.

By Car

The best way to explore the secondary sights in this region, especially the deep backcountry, is by car. A car also allows you the freedom to zip along A8 between the coastal resorts and to enjoy the tremendous views from the three Corniches that trace the coast from Nice to the Italian border. A car is, of course, a liability in downtown Cannes and Nice, with parking garages expensive and curbside spots virtually nonexistent. Drive defensively and stay alert. This is one of the most dangerous driving regions in Europe, and the speeds and aggressive Grand-Prix style of some drivers makes it impossible to let your guard down. On the A8 toward Italy, tight curves, hills, tunnels, and construction keep things interesting. For English-language traffic reports (as well as BBC news) tune to 86.4 FM.

By Train

You can easily move along the coast between Cannes, Nice, and Ventimiglia by train on the slick double-decker Côte d'Azur line, a dramatic and highly tourist-pleasing branch of the SNCF lines that offers panoramic views as it rolls from one famous resort to the next. But train travelers will have difficulty getting up to St-Paul, Vence, Peillon, and other backcountry villages; that you must accomplish by bus or car. It's still possible to climb up into the pre-Alpine arrière-pays via the tiny trestled Italian-French rail line that winds toylike from Ventimiglia in Italy to Breil-sur-Roya in the hills above Menton and on to Turin in Italy. You can catch it out of Nice.

Contacts and Resources

Car Rentals

Most likely you'll want to rent your car at one of the main rail stops, either Cannes, Nice, Monaco, or Menton, or at the airport in Nice, where all major companies are represented.

Avis (✉ 69 bd. Croisette, Cannes, ☎ 04–93–94–15–86; ✉ pl. de la Gare, Cannes, ☎ 04–93–39–26–38; ✉ 2 av. des Phocéens, Nice, ☎

04–93–80–63–52; ✉ Nice Airport, ☎ 04–93–21–42–80; ✉ 9 av. d'Ostende, Monaco, ☎ 377/93–30–17–53). **Budget** (✉ 160 rue Antibes, Cannes, ☎ 04–93–99–44–04; ✉ 23 rue de Belgique, Nice, ☎ 04–93–16–24–16; ✉ Nice Airport, ☎ 04–93–21–36–50). **Europcar Interrent** (✉ 3 rue Commandant Vidal, Cannes, ☎ 04–93–06–26–30; ✉ 3 av. Gustave, Nice, ☎ 04–92–14–44–50; ✉ Nice Airport, ☎ 04–93–21–43–54; ✉ 9 av. Thiers, Menton, ☎ 04–93–28–21–80; ✉ 47 av. de Grande-Bretagne, Monaco, ☎ 377/93–50–74–95). **Hertz** (✉ Eden Palace II, 147 rue Antibes, Cannes, ☎ 04–93–99–04–20; ✉ 1 promenade des Anglais, Nice, ☎ 04–93–87–11–87; ✉ Nice Airport, ☎ 04–93–21–36–72; ✉ 27 bd. Albert Iᵉʳ, Monaco, ☎ 377/93–50–79–60).

Guided Tours

Santa Azur (✉ 11 av. Jean-Médecin, Nice, ☎ 04–93–85–46–81) organizes full- or half-day bus excursions to sights near Nice, including Monaco and Cannes, either leaving from their offices or from several stops along the promenade des Anglais, mainly in front of the big hotels. English-language tours are available with advance request. In Antibes, **Phocéens Voyages** (✉ 8 pl. de Gaulle, Antibes, ☎ 04–93–34–15–98) organizes bus explorations of the region, with English tours on advance request.

The city of Nice arranges individual guided tours on an à la carte basis, according to your needs. For information contact the **Bureau d'Acceuil** (☎ 04–93–14–48–00) and specify your dates and language preferences. A small **tourist train** (☎ 04–93–92–45–59) goes along the waterfront from the Jardin Albert Iᵉʳ on the promenade des Anglais, along cours Saleya, and up to the Château.

Menton is particularly keen to introduce visitors to its rich architectural heritage by offering regular *visites du patrimoine* (heritage tours) to its gardens, cemetery, museums, and villas. Details on each visit and points and times of departure are published in the city's free *programme des manifestations* (events program), published bi-monthly by the tourist office. The tours cost 30 francs/€4.60 per person, or four visits for 60 francs/€9.15. For information contact the **Service du Patrimoine** (✉ 5 rue Ciapetta, Menton, ☎ 04–92–10–33–66).

In Antibes there are guided walking tours of the old town only on the first Tuesday of each month, leaving at 3 PM from the **Bibliotheque de l'Antiboulenc** (✉ 34 rue de la Tourraque,, Antibes, ☎ 04–93–34–27–60).

Outdoor Activities and Sports

This is golf country; for a complete listing of golf courses and facilities from St-Tropez to Monaco, pick up the brochure and map *Les Golfs du Soleil* (*Golf Courses of the Sun*) and *Destination Golf* at local tourist offices.

For information on hiking in the mountains above the coast, contact the **Comité Départemental de la Randonée Pedestre des Alpes-Maritimes** (Departmental Committee of Alpes-Maritimes Hiking; ✉ 83 av. Joseph Raybaud, 06300 Nice, ☎ 04–93–13–07–60), which can furnish itineraries and maps upon written request.

Travel Agencies

CANNES

American Express (✉ 8 rue des Belges, ☎ 04–93–38–15–87); **Nouvelles Frontières** (✉ 19 bd. de la République, ☎ 04–92–98–80–83).

MENTON
Havas Voyages (⊠ 11 av. Félix Faure, ☎ 04–92–10–54–04).

MONTE CARLO
American Express Voyages (⊠ 35 bd. Princess Charlotte, ☎ 377/93–25–74–45).

NICE
Havas Voyages (⊠ 12 av. Félix Faure, ☎ 04–93–62–76–30); **Thomas Cook** (⊠ 12 av. Thiers, ☎ 04–93–82–13–00); **American Express Voyages** (⊠ 11 promenade des Anglais, ☎ 04–93–16–53–51).

Vacation Rentals

Gîtes de France is a nationwide organization that rents vacation housing by the week, outside urban areas, and usually of outstanding regional character. There are very few directly on the coast, as they are by definition *gîte ruraux* (rural lodgings), but there are exceptions. The prettiest represent the Italian-style stucco mountain houses and farmhouses that cover the hills behind the coast; they provide easy access to the countryside, villages, churches, and markets that are part of the region's rhythm.

The headquarters for the region covered in this chapter is **Gîtes de France des Alpes-Maritimes** (⊠ 57 promenade des Anglais, B.P. 1602, 06011 Nice Cedex 01, ☎ 04–92–15–21–30, FAX 04–93–37–48–00, www.crt-riviera.fr/gites06). Write or call for a catalog, then make a selection and reservation. For general information on gîtes, *see* Close-Up: The Gîte Way *in* Chapter 2 *and* Lodging *in* Smart Travel Tips.

The tourist offices of individual towns often publish lists of *locations meublés* (furnished rentals), sometimes vouched for by the tourist office and rated for comfort. Select the town you'd like to be near and write or fax their tourist office (☞ Visitor Information, *below*) to a request a list.

Visitor Information

The **Comité Régional du Tourisme Riviera Côte d'Azur** (Regional Tourist Committee; ⊠ 55 promenade des Anglais, B.P. 1602, 06011 Nice Cedex 01, ☎ 04–93–37–78–78, ✆) provides information on tourism throughout the department of Alpes-Maritimes, from Cannes to the Italian border.

Local **tourist offices** in major towns discussed in this chapter are as follows: **Antibes/Juan-les-Pins** (⊠ 11 pl. de Gaulle, 06600 Antibes, ☎ 04–92–90–53–00, FAX 04–92–90–53–01). **Biot** (⊠ pl. de la Chapelle, 06410 Biot, ☎ 04–93–65–05–85). **Cagnes-sur-Mer** (⊠ 6 bd. Maréchal Juin, B.P. 48, 06800 Cagnes-sur-Mer, ☎ 04–93–20–61–64, FAX 04–92–20–52–63). **Cannes** (⊠ Palais des Festivals, Esplanade G. Pompidou, B.P. 272, 06400 Cannes, ☎ 04–93–39–01–01, FAX 04–93–99–37–34). **Grasse** (⊠ Palais des Congrés, 22 cours Honoré Cresp, 06130 Grasse, ☎ 04–93–36–66–66, FAX 04–93–36–86–36). **Menton** (⊠ Palais de l'Europe, av. Boyer, 06500 Menton, ☎ 04–92–41–76–76, FAX 04–92–41–76–78). **Monaco** (⊠ 2a bd. des Moulins, 98000 Monte Carlo, Monaco, ☎ 377/92–16–61–66, FAX 377/92–16–60–00). **Mougins** (⊠ 15 av. Jean-Charles Mallet, 06251 Mougins, ☎ 04–93–75–87–67, FAX 04–92–92–04–03). **Nice** (⊠ 5 promenade des Anglais, 06000 Nice, ☎ 04–92–14–48–00, FAX 04–92–14–48–03; or in person at the train station or airport). **Roquebrune–Cap Martin** (⊠ 20 av. Paul Doumer, 06190 Roquebrune–Cap Martin, ☎ 04–93–35–62–87, FAX 04–93–28–57–00). **St-Jean–Cap-Ferrat** (⊠ 59 av. Denis Semeria, 06230 St-Jean–Cap-Ferrat, ☎ 04–93–76–08–90, FAX 04–93–76–16–67). **St-Paul** (⊠ 2 rue Grande, 06570 St-Paul, ☎ 04–93–32–86–95, FAX 04–93–32–60–27).

Tende-Roya (✉ av. du 16-Septembre 1947, 06430 Tende-Roya, ☎ 04–93–04–73–71, FAX 04–93–04–35–09). **Vence** (✉ pl. du Grand Jardin, 06140 Vence, ☎ 04–93–58–06–38, FAX 04–93–58–91–81). **Villefranche-sur-Mer** (✉ Jardin François-Binon, 06230 Villefranche-sur-Mer, ☎ 04–93–01–73–68, FAX 04–93–76–63–65).

6 BACKGROUND & ESSENTIALS

Fodor's Choice

Provence and the Côte d'Azur at a Glance:
A Chronology

Portraits of Provence

Books and Videos

French Vocabulary

Smart Travel Tips A to Z

FAVORITES IN PROVENCE AND THE CÔTE D'AZUR

No two people will agree on what makes a perfect vacation, but it's fun and helpful to know what others think. We hope you'll have a chance to experience some Fodor's Choices yourself while visiting Provence and the Côte d'Azur. For detailed information about each, refer to the appropriate chapters.

Antiquities

Abbaye de Sénanque, near Gordes. With its rhythm of perfectly preserved Romanesque cubes, vaults, and domes, this abbey functions today in pure isolation, surrounded by fields of lavender.

Arenes, Arles. Though a hair less flawlessly preserved than its triple-tiered rival at Nîmes, this Colosseum-style Roman stadium stands at the heart of Arles's quiet old town, and is all the easier to appreciate without Nîmes's roaring traffic.

Les Antiques, St-Rémy. Just across the highway from the ruined Greco-Roman village of Glanum, these two superbly detailed Roman monuments date from 30 BC, when they marked an important trans-Alpine crossroads.

Pont du Gard. The granddaddy of Roman treasures in France and surely one of the wonders of the (classical) world, this imposing multitiered aqueduct–bridge deserves the awestruck crowds it attracts.

Quartier de la Villasse, Vaison-la-Romaine. At these skeletal remains of a Roman village, it's the toilets in the *thermes* (baths) that stick in the memory: they are so perfectly preserved and efficiently constructed, with fresh water used to sweep waste down raked troughs.

Beaches

Calanque en Vau, Cassis. You can reach this castaways' cove only by boat or by hiking the cliff top and clambering down the steep rocks, but it's worth it. Nowhere else on the coast can you find such a tiny slice of paradise, surrounded by massive cliffs and sheltered from the winds of the open sea.

Plage de Tahiti, St-Tropez. This popular beach club, on a pristine stretch of soft sand, looks out to the open sea and northeast at the whole of the Côte d'Azur.

Churches

Abbaye de Montmajour, north of Arles. All the more evocative because it stands empty and ruined on a hilltop at the foot of Les Alpilles, this Romanesque abbey retains its pure vaulting forms.

Cathédrale St-Sauveur, Aix-en-Provence. It's worth planning your visit to Aix around the weekly opening of the Nicolas de Froment triptych in this cathedral, itself a marvelous hodgepodge of Merovingian, Romanesque, Gothic, and Baroque styles.

Chapelle de la Miséricorde, Nice. Of the dozens of florid Baroque chapels scattered throughout Nice's old town, this one is the most magnificent; it's a superbly balanced *pièce-montée* (wedding cake) of half-domes and cupolas, decorated frescoes, faux marble, gilt, and crystal chandeliers.

Église St-Trophime, Arles. You won't find a more perfectly preserved Romanesque facade in the south of France—its arcing lines and superb figurative detail are enough to rivet you to the place de la République on which it stands.

Groupe Épiscopal, Fréjus. A superb 5th-century baptistery surrounded by Corinthian columns, a delicate Gothic cloister, and an austere cathedral make up this ensemble at the top of Fréjus's old town.

Notre-Dame-des-Fontaines, Vallée de la Roya. This tiny chapel, isolated in a wooded valley and surrounded by the roar of mountain streams, was decorated in the 15th century with moving, sometimes naively powerful, images of the life and death of Christ.

Dining

Le Louis XV, Monte Carlo. Crystal, gilt, and period pomp frame the extraordinary cuisine of Alain Ducasse—one of France's finest chefs, but holding forth in Monaco. *$$$$*

La Colombe d'Or, St-Paul. As much as the lovely mulberry-shaded terrace and the Provençal food, the ravishing modern-art collection left by hungry artists—Calder, Picasso, and Miró among them—continues to draw the glitterati to this backcountry institution. *$$$–$$$$*

La Ferme du Magnan, Cogolin (St-Tropez). Just 6 miles west of urbane St-Tropez, this hilltop farm overlooking dense forests serves sophisticated country cooking. *$$–$$$*

Le Fournil, Bonnieux. The food is fresh, light, and classic at this little niche, carved deep in a stone cliff, that's decorated with contemporary art and mismatched linens. *$$–$$$*

Baie des Singes, Marseille. This romantic seafood restaurant, perched on rocks over an isolated cove south of town, has lounge chairs and showers available if you choose to dive into the azure water before your meal. *$$*

Le Bistrot des Alpilles, St-Rémy. Striking a sophisticated balance between the cozy and the urbane, this Alpilles landmark serves terrific lamb and salt-cod gratin. *$$*

Le Carré d'Herbes, L'Isle-sur-la-Sorgue. With trendy Provençal specialties—open-face sandwiches, salt-baked fish—this popular lunch spot offers a contemporary antidote to antiques-market overload. *$$*

Chez Bob, Villeneuve (Camargue). In a well-hidden cottage behind the Etang du Vaccarès, Bob himself grills your bull steak in the grand stone fireplace. *$$*

Quai des Artistes, Monaco. *Le tout* Monaco flocks to this spacious, modern bistro to gaze at one another from crowded banquettes and to feast on seafood as well as classic specialties. *$$*

La Chirane, Seillans. Eat crisp eggplant pizzas and herb-savory daube in this cozy, vaulted hole-in-the-wall, or on its terrace looking over the valley. *$–$$*

Lou Pistou, Nice. Sample the classics of old-Nice cuisine—*soupe au pistou* (minestrone with pesto), *pissaladière* (a pizzalike dish topped with caramelized onions and anchovy spread), and *petits farcis* (red peppers, zucchini, and eggplant stuffed with spicy sausage)—in this friendly shoe-box–size mom-and-pop joint. *$–$$*

La Table Alziari, Nice. Great Provençal cooking and Niçoise specialties served in a comfortable old-town backroom—what else would you expect from one of Nice's oldest olive-oil families? *$–$$*

L'Affenage, Arles. A roaring fireplace grill and a parade of crockery bowls full of Provençal hors d'oeuvres (eggplant, tapenade, and chickpeas with cumin) make this a popular lunch spot. *$*

Auberge des Seguins, Buoux. Crawl down deep-country back roads to the end of the world, where this bucolic retreat offers rigorously authentic Provençal cooking and the arbored terrace as well as simple rooms. *$*

La Bastide Bleue, Séguret. This converted farmhouse not only offers country-fresh rooms with cotton prints and artisanal tiles, but it also serves superb Provençal food and local wine in a beamed cowshed. *$*

Etienne, Marseille. Favorite rendezvous of politicos and habitués in the old hilltop neighborhood called Le Panier, this landmark pizzeria heaps on the gratins, fried squid, and steak-for-two until you scream for mercy. *$*

Montagard, Cannes. This place is a rarity in France: it serves imaginative, stylishly prepared vegetarian cuisine in a cool, chic setting. *$*

Fodor's Choice

Drives

Corniche de l'Estérel (N98), from St-Raphaël to La Napoule. As you drive along this dramatic cliff-top coastline highway, with the red rock of the Estérel sloping spectacularly down to the azure water, you'll get a glimpse of the coast as it was before the building boom.

Route de la Corniche Sublime, Gorges du Verdon. Don't drive along here if you suffer from vertigo, because the views from the passenger side drop a cool mile to the seething green water below. That's why it's one of the most spectacular drives in Europe.

Routes des Crêtes, Cassis to La Ciotat. This extraordinary drive takes you to the top of the Cap Canaille, a massive cliff that soars above the rocky coast.

Gardens

Jardin Thuret, Cap d'Antibes. The botanist Gustave Thuret first introduced the exotic, subtropical greenery that now defines the Côte d'Azur in this garden; its position on a peninsula surrounded by the sea is magnificent.

Villa Ephrussi-Rothschild, St-Jean-Cap-Ferrat. No fewer than seven gardens designed by theme—rustic Provençal, serene Japanese, the severe symmetry of the French—crown this hilltop estate that takes in sea views from both sides.

Lodging

La Bastides de Moustiers, Moustiers. Alain Ducasse plays country gentleman here, supervising a protégé chef and tending his herb garden on the grounds of this lovely old stone country house. *$$$$*

Cap–Eden Roc, Cap d'Antibes. F. Scott Fitzgerald set scenes of Jazz Age decadence in this grand waterfront getaway, and it continues to draw the rich-and-the-restless to its unparalleled luxury. *$$$$*

Mas de Langoustier, Porquerolles, Iles d'Hyères. Extravagantly blessed with one end of the island, this elegant inn adds private beaches, rocky bays, and fine seafood to its long list of luxuries. *$$$$*

La Mirande, Avignon. Arguably the loveliest hotel in Provence, this grand but intimate hotel nestles at the foot of the Popes' Palace and is exquisitely decorated in rich fabrics. *$$$$*

Nord-Pinus, Arles. Design-magazine decor make this place Forum hotel the choice of literati and film stars. *$$$$*

Le Petit Nice, Marseille. Play Scott-and-Zelda in this beautiful cliff-top villa with a balustraded terrace over the sea. *$$$$*

Brise Marine, St-Jean-Cap-Ferrat. With unbroken views of the sea and homey guest rooms, this "sea-breeze" inn provides a chance for you to live like the other half who people Cap Ferrat. *$$$*

Ma Maison, Roussillon. Laid-back chic and an artist's eye in the decor and garden make this country *mas* below Roussillon a vacation in itself. *$$–$$$*

Windsor, Nice. Rooms are decorated by artists, and there's a meditation space upstairs, but it's the tropical garden that makes this downtown hotel a tiny paradise. *$$–$$$*

Auberge de la Madone, Peillon. High on a hill at the edge of a boutique-free perched village, this inn is the ultimate Provençal getaway—and it's just miles from the Côte d'Azur. *$–$$$*

Château de Roussan, St-Rémy. Maintained as is rather than modernized, this graciously proportioned 18th-century château has more cats than staff—and romance in its soul. *$$*

Le Clos du Buis, Bonnieux. This bed-and-breakfast has a pool with a valley view, impeccable regional-style rooms, and the ambience of a home with guests instead of paying customers. *$$*

Le Hameau, St-Paul. Serenely private, on a green hillside below the old town, this series of individually skewed, bungalow-like rooms drapes around a swimming pool. *$$*

Hôtel du Fiacre, Carpentras. In the heart of the old-town labyrinth, this patrician home has nobly proportioned rooms and mix-and-match decor. $$

Jardin d'Emile, Cassis. Parasol pines, chalk cliffs, and sea views add charm to this cozy–chic romantic retreat. $$

Mas de Cacharel, Stes-Maries-sur-Mer. Serene and isolated along the border of the Camargue's natural reserve, this simple retreat has wild egrets that flutter up when you drive in and white horses that gaze at you by the pool. $$

Moulin de la Camandoule, Fayence. The rooms in this former olive-oil mill, where fine Provençal cuisine is served around the old press, retain charming farmhouse details. $$

Hermès, Marseille. Just beyond the quai du Port, this tiny, tidy budget hotel offers three rooms with spectacular Vieux Port views, and one crow's nest of a room with its own roof terrace. $–$$

Lou Cagnard, St-Tropez. The young, enthusiastic owners have fixed up this bargain retreat with fresh tiles and a lovely garden. $–$$

Quatre Dauphins, Aix. In the noble old quarter below the cours Mirabeau, this pretty little hotel is brightened by Provençal fabrics, painted furniture, and a personal welcome. $–$$

Le Cloître, Arles. The result of the hard work and devotion of a friendly couple who love old architecture, this restored abbot's residence has quarried stone, hand-rubbed ocher walls, and massive beams. $

Markets

Antiques Market, Isle-sur-la-Sorgue. Lacy linens, crockery, oak washstands, and almost-old-master paintings crowd the banks of the Sorgue canals during this Sunday antiques market.

City Market, Aix. Every Provençal delicacy imaginable can be tucked into your basket at this chic city market, augmented by antiques on Tuesday, Thursday, and Saturday.

Cours Saleya Market, Nice. Flanked by cafés and overflowing with vivid flowers, this long stretch of stands vaunts olives, fresh crabs, *socca* (a pancake of chickpea flour), and mesclun salad mix.

Fish and North African Markets, Marseille. Both the theatrical fish market on the quai des Belges and the activity-filled North African market on place des Capucins make this big city feel like an international village.

Local Market, Aubagne. Authentic, atmospheric, and full of farm stands brimming with local produce, this is the real thing: a Provençal market, with pots, pillows, mesclun, and all.

Marché Couvert, Menton. In a Belle Époque shelter just in from the seaside, fruit, cheese, bread, fish, and game are arranged like jewels in an upscale boutique, but the spirit is pure Provençal.

Museums

Centre de la Vieille Charité, Marseille. Its extraordinary neoclassic architecture and fine ethnic and archaeology museums make this converted hospice a must-see.

Fondation Maeght, St-Paul-de-Vence. With its serene setting in a hilltop woods and its light-flooded displays of modern works, this gallery-museum is the best mixed-artist exhibition space in the south of France.

Musée de l'Arles Antique, Arles. This state-of-the-art shrine to antiquity has magnificent mosaics and rows of early Christian sarcophagi.

Musée Matisse, Nice. In a superb Italianate villa above Nice, Matisse's family has amassed a wide-ranging collection of the artist's works.

Musée National Message Biblique Marc Chagall, Nice. This passionate and personal collection of late works shows the artist at his life-affirming best.

Musée Océanographique, Monaco. With its atmosphere of Victorian adventure and its aquarium tanks full of exotic sea life, this museum is one of a kind.

Musée Picasso, Antibes. This noble old seaside château seems to struggle to contain the energy and inspiration Picasso brings to its walls.

Museon Arlaten, Arles. The quirky, personal collection of Provençaliana from Frédéric Mistral himself, the 19th-century poet and father of the Provençal revival, is here.

Natural Wonders

Fontaine de Vaucluse. Welling out of the center of the earth and sheltered by vertiginous cliffs, this phenomenal spring gushes down to a pretty riverside town.

Gorges du Verdon, Haute Provence. France's Grand Canyon mixes dizzying cliff-top views with roaring green water and the scent of wild boxwood.

Promenade Le Corbusier, Roquebrune-Cap Martin. Wander over rocks and through lush greenery on this contemplative cape-side trail that leads to what was once Le Corbusier's waterfront retreat.

Roussillon. The village seems to grow out of the stone around it, from which the earthy reds and golds of the local ocher are extracted.

Sentier Martel, Gorges du Verdon. This harrowing canyon trail, clinging to walls above the torrent of the Verdon river, over vertical iron ladders, and through tunnels ankle deep in water, has been called the best of France's Grande Randonées (Great Trails); if you dare take your eyes off your feet, the setting is spectacular.

Old Towns

Commune Libre du Safranier, Antibes. Narrow alley–streets, shutters, hanging laundry, and a riot of flowering vines make this neighborhood off Antibes's old town picture-book pretty.

Le Panier, Marseille. This dense maze of improbably tall row houses looms dark, exotic, and terribly Mediterranean above the old port.

Vieux Nice, Nice. Far from gentrified, this aromatic neighborhood seethes with unself-conscious life, the energy and texture that sets Nice apart; food stands selling Niçoise specialties and the jewel-box Baroque chapels on every corner add to its charm.

Perched Villages

Oppède-le-Vieux. Isolated above the Luberon, this village stands alone in the mist, lovingly cared for by its residents but utterly uncommercial.

Peillon. This perfect example of the eagle's-nest villages above the coast has been voted boutique-free forever by its citizens, and remains marvelously ancient, even primeval, in atmosphere.

Saorge. Watercolor tones and precarious cants over the forest gorge give the old houses of this mountain village surreal beauty.

Ports of Call

Anse Croisette/Les Goudes, Marseille. The end of the world, they call it, and it feels like it, on a rocky thrust between the city and the Calanques of Cassis.

Cassis. Under the imposing monolith of the Cap Canaille and the picturesque ruins of a medieval château, this pretty pleasure port mixes sophisticated yachts and brightly painted fishing boats.

St-Jean-Cap-Ferrat. Yachts sail into dock and passengers jump out for lunch at one of the port-side cafés that make this gateway to the cape all the more appealing.

Villefranche. With a portly citadel and a medieval old town that spills down to the waterfront cafés, this town is the most picturesque Mediterranean port on the Côte d'Azur.

PROVENCE AND THE CÔTE D'AZUR AT A GLANCE: A CHRONOLOGY

ca. 600 BC Greek colonists found Marseille.

after 500 BC Celts appear in France.

58–51 BC Julius Caesar conquers Gaul; writes up the war in *De Bello Gallico*.

52 BC Lutetia, later to become Paris, is built by the Gallo-Romans.

46 BC Roman amphitheater built at Arles.

14 BC The Pont du Gard aqueduct at Nîmes is erected.

AD 406 Invasion by the Vandals (Germanic tribes).

The Merovingian Dynasty

486–511 Clovis, king of the Franks (481–511), defeats the Roman governor of Gaul and founds the Merovingian dynasty. Great monasteries, such as those at Tours, Limoges, and Chartres, become centers of culture.

497 Franks converted to Christianity.

567 The Frankish kingdom is divided into three parts—the eastern countries (Austrasia), later to become Belgium and Germany; the western countries (Neustria), later to become France; and Burgundy.

The Carolingian Dynasty

768–778 Charlemagne (768–814) becomes king of the Franks (768), conquers northern Italy (774), and is defeated by the Moors at Roncesvalles, Spain, after which he consolidates the Pyrénées border (778).

800 The pope crowns Charlemagne Holy Roman Emperor in Rome. Charlemagne expands the French kingdom far beyond its present borders and establishes a center for learning at his capital, Aix-la-Chapelle (Aachen, in present-day Germany).

814–987 Death of Charlemagne. The Carolingian line continues through a dozen or so monarchs, with a batch called Charles (the Bald, the Fat, the Simple) and a sprinkling of Louises. Under the Treaty of Verdun (843), the empire is divided in two—the eastern half becoming Germany, the western half, France. Provence is given to Lothair I. The Kingdom of Provence is founded in 879, joins Arles in 933.

The Capetian Dynasty

987 Hugh Capet (987–996) is made king of France and establishes the principle of hereditary rule for his descendants.

1066 Norman conquest of England by William the Conqueror (1028–87).

ca. 1100	Development of European vernacular verse: *Chanson de Roland*. The Gothic style of architecture begins to appear.
1112–1245	Provence ruled by the counts of Barcelona.
ca. 1150	Struggle between the Anglo-Norman kings (Angevin Empire) and the French; when Eleanor of Aquitaine switches husbands (from Louis VII of France to Henry II of England), her extensive lands pass to English rule.
1245–1481	Provence ruled by the dukes of Anjou.
1270	Louis IX (1226–70), the only French king to achieve sainthood, dies in Tunis on the seventh and last Crusade.
1302–07	Philippe IV the Fair (1285–1314) calls together the first States-General, predecessor to the French Parliament. He disbands the Knights Templars to gain their wealth (1307).
1309	Pope, under pressure, leaves a corrupt and disorderly Rome for Avignon in southern France, seat of the papacy for nearly 70 years.

The Valois Dynasty

1337–1453	Hundred Years' War between France and England: fighting for control of those areas of France gained by the English crown following the marriage of Eleanor of Aquitaine and Henry II.
1348–50	The Black Death rages in France.
1428–31	Joan of Arc (1412–31), the Maid of Orléans, sparks the revival of French fortunes in the Hundred Years' War but is captured by the English and burned at the stake at Rouen.
1453	France finally defeats England, terminating the Hundred Years' War and English claims to the French throne.
1494	Italian wars: beginning of Franco-Habsburg struggle for hegemony in Europe.
1515–47	Reign of François I, who imports Italian artists, including Leonardo da Vinci (1452–1519), and brings the Renaissance to France. The Château of Fontainebleau is begun (1528).
1562–98	Wars of Religion: Catholics versus Huguenots (French Protestants).

The Bourbon Dynasty

1589	The first Bourbon king, Henri IV (1589–1610) is a Protestant who converts to Catholicism and achieves peace in France. He signs the Edict of Nantes, giving limited freedom of worship to Protestants.
ca. 1610	Scientific revolution in Europe begins, marked by the discoveries of mathematician and philosopher René Descartes (1596–1650).
1643–1715	Reign of Louis XIV, the Sun King, a monarch who builds the Baroque power base of Versailles and presents Europe with a glorious view of France. With his first minister, Colbert, Louis makes France, by force of arms, the most powerful nation-state in Europe. He persecutes the Huguenots, who emigrate in great numbers, nearly ruining the French economy.

1660 Classical period of French culture: dramatists Pierre Corneille (1606–84), Jean-Baptiste Molière (1622–73), and Jean Racine (1639–99), and painter Nicolas Poussin (1594–1665).

1700–onward Writer and pedagogue François-Marien Voltaire (1694–1778) is a central figure in the French Enlightenment, along with Jean-Jacques Rousseau (1712–78) and Denis Diderot (1713–84), who in 1751 compiles the first modern encyclopedia. The ideals of the Enlightenment—for reason and scientific method and against social and political injustices—pave the way for the French Revolution. In the arts, painter Jacques-Louis David (1748–1825) reinforces revolutionary creeds in his neoclassical works.

ca. 1715 Rococo art and decoration develop, typified by the painter Antoine Watteau (1684–1721) and, later, François Boucher (1703–70) and Jean-Honoré Fragonard (1732–1806).

1756–63 The Seven Years' War results in France's losing most of its overseas possessions and in England becoming a world power.

1776 The French assist in the American War of Independence. Ideals of liberty cross the Atlantic with the returning troops to reinforce new social concepts.

The French Revolution

1789–1804 The Bastille is stormed on July 14, 1789. Following early Republican ideals is the Reign of Terror and the administration of the Directory under Robespierre. There are widespread political executions—Louis XVI and Marie Antoinette are guillotined in 1793. Reaction sets in, and the instigators of the Terror are themselves executed (1794). Napoléon Bonaparte enters the Directory (1795–99) and is installed as First Consul during the Consulate (1799–1804).

1790 The départements of Bouches-du-Rhône, Var, and Basses-Alpes and the *parats* of Drôme, Alpes-Maritimes, and Vaucluse are formed from Provence.

The First Empire

1804 Napoléon crowns himself emperor of France at Notre-Dame in the presence of the pope.

1805–12 Napoléon conquers most of Europe. The Napoleonic Age is marked by a neoclassical artistic style called Empire as well as by the rise of Romanticism—characterized by such writers as François-Auguste-René de Chateaubriand (1768–1848) and Marie-Henri Stendhal (1783–1842), and the painters Eugène Delacroix (1798–1863) and Théodore Géricault (1791–1824)—which is to dominate the arts of the 19th century.

1812–14 Winter cold and Russian determination defeat Napoléon outside Moscow. The emperor abdicates and is transported to Elba.

Restoration of the Bourbons

1814–15 Louis XVIII, brother of the executed Louis XVI, regains the throne after the Congress of Vienna settles peace terms.

1815 The Hundred Days: Napoléon returns from Elba and musters an army on his march to the capital, but lacks national support. He is defeated at Waterloo (June 18) and exiled to the island of St. Helena in the south Atlantic.

1821 Napoléon dies in exile.

1830 Bourbon king Charles X, locked into a prerevolutionary state of mind, abdicates. A brief upheaval (Three Glorious Days) brings Louis-Philippe, the Citizen King, to the throne.

1840 Napoléon's remains are brought back to Paris.

1846–48 Severe industrial and farming depression contributes to Louis-Philippe's abdication (1848).

Second Republic and Second Empire

1848–52 Louis-Napoléon (nephew and step-grandson of Napoléon I) is elected president of the short-lived Second Republic. He makes a successful attempt to assume supreme power and is declared emperor of France, taking the title Napoléon III.

ca. 1850 The ensuing period is characterized in the arts by the emergence of realist painters—Jean-François Millet (1814–75), Honoré Daumier (1808–79), Gustave Courbet (1819–77)—and late-Romantic writers—Victor Hugo (1802–85), Honoré de Balzac (1799–1850), and Charles Baudelaire (1821–87).

1863 Napoléon III inaugurates the Salon des Refusés in response to critical opinion. It includes work by Édouard Manet (1832–83), Claude Monet (1840–1926), and Paul Cézanne (1839–1906) and is commonly regarded as the birthplace of Impressionism and of modern art in general.

The Third Republic

1870–71 The Franco-Prussian War sees Paris besieged by and fall to the Germans. Napoléon III takes refuge in England.

1871–1914 Before World War I, France expands its industries and builds vast colonial empires in North Africa and Southeast Asia. Sculptor Auguste Rodin (1840–1917), composers Maurice Ravel (1875–1937) and Claude Debussy (1862–1918), and poets such as Stéphane Mallarmé (1842–98) and Paul Verlaine (1844–96) set the stage for Modernism.

1874 Emergence of the Impressionist school of painting: Monet, Pierre Auguste Renoir (1841–1919), and Edgar Degas (1834–1917).

1894–1906 Franco-Russian Alliance (1894). Dreyfus affair: The spy trial and its anti-Semitic backlash shock France.

1904 The Entente Cordiale: England and France become firm allies.

1914–18 During World War I, France fights with the Allies, opposing Germany, Austria-Hungary, and Turkey. Germany invades France.

1918–39 Between wars, France attracts artists and writers, including Americans Ernest Hemingway (1899–1961) and Gertrude Stein (1874–1946). The country nourishes major artistic and philosophical movements: Constructivism, Dadaism, Surrealism, and Existentialism.

1939–45 At the beginning of World War II, France fights with the Allies until invaded and defeated by Germany in 1940. The French government, under Marshal Philippe Pétain (1856–1951), moves to Vichy and cooperates with the Nazis. French overseas colonies split between allegiance to the legal government of Vichy and declaration for the Free French Resistance, led (from London) by General Charles de Gaulle (1890–1970).

1944 D-Day, June 6: The Allies land on the beaches of Normandy and successfully invade France. Additional Allied forces land in Provence. Paris is liberated in August 1944, and France declares full allegiance to the Allies.

1944–46 A provisional government takes power under General de Gaulle; American aid assists French recovery.

The Fourth Republic

1946 France adopts a new constitution; French women gain the right to vote.

1946–54 In the Indochinese War, France is unable to regain control of its colonies in Southeast Asia. The 1954 Geneva Agreement establishes two governments in Vietnam: one in the north, under the Communist leader Ho Chi Minh, and one in the south, under the emperor Bao Dai. U.S. involvement eventually leads to French withdrawal.

1954–62 The Algerian Revolution achieves Algeria's independence from France. Other French African colonies gain independence.

1957 The Treaty of Rome establishes the European Economic Community (now known as the European Union—EU) with France as one of its members.

The Fifth Republic

1958–68 De Gaulle is the first president under a new constitution; he resigns in 1968 after widespread disturbances begun by student riots in Paris.

1976 The first supersonic transatlantic passenger service begins with the Anglo-French Concorde.

1981 François Mitterrand (1916–1996) is elected the first Socialist president of France since World War II.

1988 Mitterrand is elected for a second term.

1990 TGV (*Trains à Grande Vitesse*) train clocks a world record—515 kph (322 mph)—on a practice run. Channel Tunnel linkup between France and England begun.

1995 Jacques Chirac, mayor of Paris, is elected president.

1996 Mitterrand dies.

1997 President Chirac calls early elections, a Socialist coalition wins a majority, and Lionel Jospin is appointed prime minister.

1998 France hosts (and wins) the World Cup soccer tournament, with matches in Marseille and other parts of the country.

POSTCARDS FROM SUMMER

Portraits

Market Morning

For me, moments that make up the texture of daily life define the character of Provence as much as the history or the landscape. And if I had to choose a single example of what I missed most while living in America, it would be a country market; nothing out of the ordinary, just the usual collection of stalls that are set up each week in every town from Apt to Vaison-la-Romaine.

They have an instant visual charm, these markets, with their bursts of vividly colored flowers and vegetables and their handwritten signs, the stalls shaded by ancient plane trees or tucked up against even older stone walls. They might have been artistically arranged for a postcard photographer, or for the high season, to be dismantled and forgotten at the end of summer. But you will find them in January as in August, because their bread and butter come from local inhabitants. The tourist is a dollop of jam. Welcome, but not essential.

Stall-holders and customers know each other, and so shopping tends to be slow and social. Old Jean-Claude's brand new smile is much admired while he selects some cheese, and there is some debate as to the precisely appropriate texture, given his recently fitted dentures. A Brie would be too sticky. A Mimolette, too hard. Perhaps some Beaufort would be best, until the new teeth have had a chance to settle in. Madame Dalmasso is plunged into a state of profound suspicion by the tomatoes. It is too early in the year for these to be local tomatoes. Where have they come from? Why hasn't their place of birth been written on the sign? After some investigation—a squeeze, a sniff, the lips pursed—she decides to throw caution to the wind and try half a kilo. A bearded man wanders back to his stall, a glass of rosé in one hand and an infant's feeding bottle in the other. The bottle is for a baby *sanglier* that he has adopted, a tiny wild boar, its black snout twitching at the scent of milk. The flower lady gives my wife her change, then ducks under her stall to reappear with two freshly laid eggs which she gift wraps in a twist of newspaper. On the other side of the square, the tables outside the café are filling up. Above the hiss and clatter of the espresso machine, a voice from Radio Monte Carlo, in raptures of enthusiasm, describes this week's competition. Where do they find these people who never have to stop for breath? Four old men sit in a row on a low stone wall, waiting for the market to end and the square to be cleared so that they can play *boules*. A dog sits up on the wall next to them. All he needs is a flat cap and he'd look just like the men, patient and wrinkled.

As the stall-holders begin to pack up, there is an almost tangible feeling of anticipation. Lunch is in the air, and today it is warm enough to eat outside.

Connoisseurs At Every Turn

One Sunday last summer, my wife came back from Coustellet market still shaking her head. She had been drawn to one of the stalls by a tray of *courgette* (squash) flowers, which are delicious either stuffed or deep-fried in light batter, a favorite late-summer recipe. I'd like half a kilo of those, she said.

But nothing is that simple. The stall-holder snapped off a plastic bag from a roll behind the stall. "Of course, Madame," he said. "Male or female?"

More recently, one of our guests, a man prone to the extravagant gesture while talking, knocked a glass of red wine over his trousers. The next day he took them to the dry cleaners.

Madame spread the trousers on the counter, examining the stains with a professional eye and a discouraging shake of the head. It was possible, she said, that the stains could be removed, but that would depend on the wine. Was it a Châteauneuf or one of the lighter Luberon reds? Amazed that he couldn't remember, she then gave him a short lecture on the staining capabilities of various wines, according to their tannin content, and seemed ready to move on to particular vintages when the arrival of another customer distracted her.

Our friend returned to the house greatly impressed. He said he had spilled wine on his trousers all over Europe, and in several major cities in the United States. But never had the provenance of his stains been so thoroughly questioned. Next time this happened, he said, he would be sure to take the wine label and perhaps a few tasting notes in with his trousers.

Pretending to Read

If there is a single Provençal tradition that every visitor should experience at least once, it is the siesta, taken externally.

Oddly enough, we have often found it very difficult to convince our guests that this is the healthy, sane, and refreshing way to spend a hot afternoon. They have arrived in Provence with their work ethics intact and their Anglo-Saxon distrust of self-indulgence poised to resist undisciplined, slightly decadent Mediterranean habits. Fear of inactivity comes bubbling to the surface. We haven't traveled all this way, they say, to do *nothing*.

I try to point out the mental and digestive benefits of doing nothing, but my advice falls on suspicious ears. The lunatic idea of an after-lunch game of tennis, however, is welcomed. Don't ask me why. I can only assume that the physical labor and potentially fatal strains on the heart involved in running after a ball in hundred-degree weather have some kind of perverse attraction. When reasoned argument fails to persuade the players of the risks they're taking,

I'm obliged to call Monsieur Contini, our local Florence Nightingale. I ask him to come and park his ambulance next to the tennis court, and to leave the engine running. That will almost always bring the game to an end, and we are proud that we haven't lost any players yet. But there is still the problem of finding a civilized distraction for them that won't induce feelings of guilt and long faces around the dinner table.

The solution, we've discovered, is to give them a literary excuse, an opportunity to add to their knowledge and enrich their minds by reading a book.

The choice of the book is all-important. Thrillers, adventure stories, and bodice-rippers won't do; they don't have enough weight, either mentally or physically. An improving tone is what's needed here, something that you've been meaning to read—something you feel you *ought* to read—if only you could find the time. There are hundreds of suitable titles and authors, and we have a small selection of them, which is known as the Hammock Library. It includes Trollopes, Brontës, Austens, Hardys, Balzacs, Tolstoys, and Dostoevskys. But the book that has never failed— ever—in its appointed task is the three-volume boxed set of Edward Gibbon's *Decline and Fall of the Roman Empire*.

Tuck a volume under your arm and make your way through the trees to the shaded corner of the garden that overlooks the valley. Roll gently into the hammock, adjust the pillow, and let Gibbon come to rest on your stomach. Take in the sounds: The *cigales* are hard at it in the bushes, their tireless, scratchy, strangely soothing chirrup rising and falling in the warm afternoon air. Somewhere in the distance a dog barks—a half-hearted, heat-muffled bark that tails off into a falsetto yawn. Underneath the hammock, there is a hurried rustle in the dried grass as a lizard seizes a bug.

Supporting your elbows on the sides of the hammock, you lift Gibbon into the reading position. How heavy he is. Beyond the edges of the open book you see your toes, the rigging of the hammock, the motionless leaves of the scrub oak, and the long, blue panorama of the Luberon. A buzzard quarters the sky in lazy, graceful curves, its wings barely moving. Gibbon feels as though he's gained weight. He declines and falls back to his resting place on your stomach and, as many have done before you in similar circumstances, you decide to allow yourself a brief doze, no longer than five minutes, before getting to grips with the Roman Empire.

Two hours later you wake up. The light on the mountain is beginning to change, a rim of sky above the crest turning from blue to violet. Gibbon is sprawled, pages akimbo, beneath the hammock where he fell. You dust him off, placing a bookmark at page 135 for the sake of appearances, before taking him back through the trees to the pool. A quick plunge is followed by the most wonderful sense of well-being, and you realize that a siesta isn't such a bad idea after all.

By Peter Mayle

In Encore Provence, *Peter Mayle's third collection of stories about his life in Provence, the writer evokes the local characters, explorations, and, of course, cuisine.*

STONE, SUN, AND SEA: PROVENCE PRIMORDIAL

THE ROASTED RED ROOFS skew downhill at Cubist angles, sunbleached and mottled with age. Stone and stucco walls emerge from the bedrock all of a hue—amber, saffron, honey. The sky is a prism, scoured to clarity by the juggernaut winds of the mistral; it radiates an azure of palpable intensity and bottomless depth. A rhythm of Romanesque tiles overlaps in sensual snaking rows; they were, after all, mixed from the wet clay and molded over the thighs of women, and like their models are as alike and as varied as the reeds in a Pan pipe. Their broad horizontal flow forms a foil for the dark, thrusting verticals of the funeral cypress and the ephemeral, feminine puff of the silvery olive. In the fields behind, white-hot at midday, chill and spare at night, you crunch through an abundance of wild thyme, rosemary, and lavender dried in the arid breeze, their acrid-sweet scent cutting through the crystal air like smelling salts. Sheep bells tinkle behind dry rock walls and churchbells sound across valleys as easily as over the village wall; in the distance is the pulsing roar of the sea. Nowhere in France, and rarely in the Western world, can you touch antiquity with this intimacy—its exoticism, its purity, eternal and alive. Provence and the Côte d'Azur: together they are, as the French say, primordial.

Basking luxuriously along the sunny southern flank of France, bordered to the east by Italy, sheltered to the northeast by the Alps, and leaning west and southwest toward its Spanish-influenced neighbors in Languedoc and the Basque country, Provence and its famous coast are to the Mediterranean as Eve was to Adam's rib, begotten, as it were, by the Fertile Crescent. The Greeks and Phocaeans first brought classical culture to the Celt-like Ligurian natives of the coast in 600 BC when they founded Massilia (Marseille), which thrived as a cosmopolitan colony—the Athens of a nascent Europe—until their alliance with the upstart Romans in Aix turned sour.

Julius Caesar himself claimed Marseille in 49 BC, and thus it came to be Provincia Romana, the first Roman stronghold in Gaul. The best of Latin culture flourished here until the fall of the Empire, some of it outliving Rome. Under Roman rule, the *indigenes* (natives) were transformed (as one period writer had it) from "mustachioed, abundantly hairy, exuburant, audacious, thoughtless, boastful, passionate warriors" into disciplined hard workers—at least temporarily. In its wake, Rome left its physical mark as well: the theater and triumphal arch in Orange; the amphitheaters in Nîmes and Arles; the magnificent aqueduct bridge called the Pont du Gard; the mausoleum, arch, and village ruins in St-Rémy; the villas and baths in Vaison-le-Romaine—these monuments, still standing today, are considered among the best of their kind in existence, easily rivaling the Colosseum in Rome. The Maison Carrée in Nîmes, built by Agrippa in 16 BC, remains as pure an homage to their Greek forebears as the Romans ever produced. Vivid details in Roman artifacts bring the stories to life: the creamy marble bust of Octavian found in Arles shows a peach-fuzz beard on his all-too-young face—a Roman sign of mourning for the assassination of Julius Caesar.

Yet the noble remains of Rome have taken on a patina and given way to the more modest culture of modern Provence, where the village shops shutter down for the *sieste,* matrons pinch melons with the concentration of wine tasters in Bordeaux, and the menfolk hunch earnestly over a milky glass of pastis and size up the angle of a rolling *pétanque* ball with the skepticism and discretion of a federal judge. In this modern province, Provence, the olives blacken at their own pace to onyx, then ebony, and the melons plump with juice drawn deep under the rocky Alpilles; the world moves slowly in the heat.

Until the cell phone rings. Then the "New South" shows its well-tanned profile as one of the most coveted regions for tourism in France—even, no, especially, by the French. Today Provence and its Côte d'Azur implies a lazy, laissez-faire lifestyle, a barefoot idyll, three-hour lunches, sultry terrace nights, and a splash in the Mediterranean . . . but *branché,* plugged in, connected by phones and freeways and airports and the TGV to Paris and the world. Many a pale, embittered northerner has found new

lust for life in its chic contemporary pulse, converting old *mas* (farmhouses) into summer homes, and opening restaurants and hotels that out-Provence Provence.

These vacation retreats brim over with Provençal architecture (roughly construed in shades of ochre and pink), Provençal decor (sophisticated country prints, cheery-colored pottery, and curves of bronzed iron), and Provençal cuisine (olive oil, garlic, grilled vegetables, and fish). And it doesn't just stop at the borders: the Provence formula is a world-wide fashion now, a panacea of sunshine that brightens the darkest streets of both hemispheres. If the '80s were about Italy, from the dawning of fettuccine Alfredo to Memphis high-tech design to the wholesale invasion of Tuscan villas, the '90s were the Provençal Renaissance—and the fashion shows no sign of abating.

It's a post-industrial phenomenon, this worship of the southern *soleil,* launched by northern aristocrats fleeing the fog and coal smog on which they blamed their pallor, their lassitude, and their very real tuberculosis. The light was a blessing, the Mediterranean breezes a relief, and railroads and steamers cut swaths to the coast, first carrying the sickly, then the privileged and adventurous, then the creative, and ultimately the glamorous to its primal combination of light, rock, and sea.

Everyone from Russian princes to American robber barons to writers and thinkers flocked to the southern coast, constructing a fantasy world of gleaming-white villas, of turquoise swimming pools, and balustrades framing Technicolor sunsets. The Lost Generation found a new home here under the palms—Hemingway, Zelda and Scott Fitzgerald, nurturing a brood of bitter wits like Dorothy Parker, John Dos Passos, and Gertrude Stein and Alice B. Toklas.

And the whole of 20th-century art seemed to bloom under its sun—Picasso, Matisse, Cézanne, van Gogh, Chagall, Monet, Léger, and Miró. The crystalline light and elemental forms inspired them, and the *volupté* of the Mediterranean saturates their work—sensual fruit, lush flowers, fundamental forms, light and color analyzed, interpreted, transformed, revealed. They, like the literati before them, found in this primeval setting the peace and stimulation to create.

Then came the movie stars, trading the palm trees of Hollywood for the palm trees of the Riviera. Grace Kelly married a prince and led her own tiny principality on a cliff over the sparkling blue waters of Monaco; a tousled and tanned Robert Mitchum was arrested for smoking marijuana and swimming with a topless starlet in Cannes. A teenage Brigitte Bardot moved heaven and earth when she swayed, flat-footed and full-lipped, through *And God Created Woman* in St-Tropez.

And the world followed, blessed with long vacations, easy air travel, and post-war prosperity. On the slim, rocky beaches of the coast were nurtured the first Perfect Tans, cultivated with tantalizing exhibitionism on every flauntable inch of skin. And still today, oblivious to the ozone hole, rank on rank of nearly bare bodies press flank to flank on the Mediterranean shore.

Yet caveat emptor—the glamour of the Côte d'Azur has, for the most part, been crowded down to the shoreline and swept out to sea: honky-tonk tourist traps, candy-pink duplexes, and projectlike highrises dominate much of the region, while the wealthy hoard their seaside serenity in private, isolated villas. At greasy brasseries along the waterfront, sun-burned visitors and leathery locals fight for the waiter's attention just to gulp down a " 'ot dog" and a luke-warm Coke, or to strain through the canned crab in a mass-produced bour-ride. Only off-season—early spring, late fall, even fine mid-winter days—can you experience the healing balm of the gentle sun, the mesmerizing rhythm of the waves, the squeaky-clean breeze that flows steady and sure from the infinite blue horizon.

To find the grace and antiquity of the region, and the sun if not the seaside, you'll want to retreat to the noble city old-towns—Nice, Marseille, Aix, and Avignon—and the slow-paced villages, both nestled along the waterfront and rising like ziggurats on stony hilltops behind the coast. Here you'll discover the palpable light, the honeyed hues, the rough-hewn geometry that inspired van Gogh and Cézanne, Picasso and Matisse.

Anywhere in this ancient region you may share their epiphany, whether standing humbled inside the 5th-century baptistery in St-Saveur in Aix; breakfasting on a wrought-iron balcony overlooking turquoise Mediterranean tides; contemplating the orbs and linear perspective of a melon field outside Cavaillon; or sipping the sea-perfumed elixir of a great bouillabaisse (surely the Phocaeans sipped something similar 2,600 years ago) along the docks of Marseille. Evocative, earthy, eternal, primordial—like a woven rope of garlic, Provence and its coast are the essence of Latin France.

By Nancy Coons

BOOKS AND VIDEOS

To set the tone for your *séjour* (stay) in the south of France, take time to look into literature and films set in the region. A few choice reads by Lost Generation expatriates include: F. Scott Fitzgerald's *Tender Is the Night,* in which Dick and Nicole Diver wallow in jaded decadence in Juan-les-Pins, and John Dos Passos' *The Best Times,* written in and about Antibes. For some background on the heady 1920s, try Amanda Vaill's *Everybody Was So Young: Gerald and Sara Murphy, a Lost Generation Love Story.* The Murphys were a wealthy American couple who became legendary Riviera hosts to the era's artists and writers. Mary Blume's *Côte d'Azur: Inventing the French Riviera,* is a wry, dry history of the region's rebirth as a glamour mecca in the 20th-century. Henry Miller wrote to Anaïs Nin in *Letters to Anaïs Nin* of his sojourns on the Riviera.

Peter Mayle put the Luberon on the map with his essays on southern bliss and culture shock in *A Year in Provence, Toujours Provence,* and *Encore Provence. A Dog's Life* tells more Provençal stories from the point of view of his dog. His novels *Chasing Cézanne, Hotel Pastis,* and *Anything Considered* also evoke the region.

Prodigious writer M.F.K. Fisher wonderfully describes her experiences in the south of France; food plays a large role in her evocative work. *Two Towns in Provence* pairs essays on Aix-en-Provence and Marseilles. Many of her autobiographical stories also include observations or anecdotes on Provence. In A.S. Byatt's short story collection *Elementals: Stories of Fire and Ice,* several tales take place in Provence. W.S. Merwin's *The Lost Upland* describes the author's life in rural southwestern

France; it's out of print, but well worth looking up in a library.

Provence produced several literary stars, from the epic poetry of Frédéric Mistral *(Miranda),* father of the revival of the Provençal language, to the austere novels of Jean Giono—*Regain* and *Jean Le Bleu*—dark with the chill of Haute Provence. Alphonse Daudet wrote folklore and tall tales from his beloved mill in Fontvieille in *Lettres de Mon Moulin.*

Changing hats from playwright to screenwriter to director to novelist to memoirist, Marcel Pagnol was the quintessential raconteur, a great storyteller with a gift for evoking the sensations and smells of Provence as well as the lilting language. The original plays of his Marseille trilogy—*Marius, Fanny,* and *César*—were later developed into films thick with the tried-and-true Midi accent of the Provençal actor Raimu. And there are a dozen other films of equal charm, including his own version of *Manon des Sources (Manon of the Springs),* with his wife Jacqueline cast as the young goat girl. He wrote four volumes of memoirs, the *Souvenirs d'un Enfance.* Other directors' efforts to evoke his atmospheric stories include Claude Berri's *Jean de Florette* and *Manon des Sources* (1986), filmed in the Luberon, as well as Yves Robert's version of *La Gloire de Mon Père (My Father's Glory,* 1990) and *Le Château de Ma Mère (My Mother's Château,* 1990).

To recapture the '60s glamour of the Riviera, rent a video of Hitchcock's suspense classic *To Catch a Thief* (1955), with Cary Grant and Grace Kelly; Roger Vadim's *And God Created Woman* (1957), which in turn created Brigitte Bardot and St-Tropez; *La Cage aux Folles* (1978), with scenes in the market, port, and old

Books and Videos

town of St-Tropez; and *Two for the Road* (1967), with Albert Finney and Audrey Hepburn, whose yearly vacation in France—for better, for worse—passes by the south. In *The Horseman on the Roof* (1995), Juliette Binoche and Olivier Martinez star as 19th-century travelers trying to cross Provence during a cholera epidemic. *Marius et Jeannette* (1998), directed by Robert Guedidguan, is set in working-class L'Estaque, outside Marseille.

WORDS AND PHRASES

One of the trickiest French sounds to pronounce is the nasal final *n* sound (whether or not the *n* is actually the last letter of the word). You should try to pronounce it as a sort of nasal grunt—as in "huh." The vowel that precedes the *n* will govern the vowel sound of the word, and in this list we precede the final *n* with an *h* to remind you to be nasal.

Another problem sound is the ubiquitous but untransliterable *eu,* as in *bleu* (blue) or *deux* (two), and the very similar sound in *je* (I), *ce* (this), and *de* (of). The closest equivalent might be the vowel sound in "put," but rounded.

English	French	Pronunciation
Basics		
Yes/no	Oui/non	wee/nohn
Please	S'il vous plaît	seel voo **play**
Thank you	Merci	mair-**see**
You're welcome	De rien	deh ree-**ehn**
That's all right	Il n'y a pas de quoi	eel nee ah pah de **kwah**
Excuse me, sorry	Pardon	pahr-**dohn**
Sorry!	Désolé(e)	day-zoh-**lay**
Good morning/ afternoon	Bonjour	bohn-**zhoor**
Good evening	Bonsoir	bohn-**swahr**
Goodbye	Au revoir	o ruh-**vwahr**
Mr. (Sir)	Monsieur	muh-**syuh**
Mrs. (Ma'am)	Madame	ma-**dam**
Miss	Mademoiselle	mad-mwa-**zel**
Pleased to meet you	Enchanté(e)	ohn-shahn-**tay**
How are you?	Comment ça va?	kuh-mahn-sa-**va**
Very well, thanks	Très bien, merci	tray bee-ehn, mair-**see**
And you?	Et vous?	ay **voo**?
Numbers		
one	un	uhn
two	deux	deuh
three	trois	twah
four	quatre	**kaht**-ruh
five	cinq	sank
six	six	seess
seven	sept	set
eight	huit	wheat
nine	neuf	nuff
ten	dix	deess
eleven	onze	ohnz

Vocabulary

twelve	douze	dooz
thirteen	treize	trehz
fourteen	quatorze	kah-**torz**
fifteen	quinze	kanz
sixteen	seize	sez
seventeen	dix-sept	deez-**set**
eighteen	dix-huit	deez-**wheat**
nineteen	dix-neuf	deez-**nuff**
twenty	vingt	vehn
twenty-one	vingt-et-un	vehnt-ay-**uhn**
thirty	trente	trahnt
forty	quarante	ka-**rahnt**
fifty	cinquante	sang-**kahnt**
sixty	soixante	swa-**sahnt**
seventy	soixante-dix	swa-sahnt-**deess**
eighty	quatre-vingts	kaht-ruh-**vehn**
ninety	quatre-vingt-dix	kaht-ruh-vehn-**deess**
one-hundred	cent	sahn
one-thousand	mille	meel

Colors

black	noir	nwahr
blue	bleu	bleuh
brown	brun/marron	bruhn/mar-**rohn**
green	vert	vair
orange	orange	o-**rahnj**
pink	rose	rose
red	rouge	rooje
violet	violette	vee-o-**let**
white	blanc	blahnk
yellow	jaune	zhone

Days of the Week

Sunday	dimanche	**dee**-mahnsh
Monday	lundi	**luhn**-dee
Tuesday	mardi	**mahr**-dee
Wednesday	mercredi	**mair**-kruh-dee
Thursday	jeudi	**zhuh**-dee
Friday	vendredi	**vawn**-druh-dee
Saturday	samedi	**sahm**-dee

Months

January	janvier	**zhahn**-vee-ay
February	février	**feh**-vree-ay
March	mars	marce
April	avril	a-**vreel**

May	mai	meh
June	juin	zhwehn
July	juillet	**zhwee**-ay
August	août	oot
September	septembre	sep-**tahm**-bruh
October	octobre	awk-**to**-bruh
November	novembre	no-**vahm**-bruh
December	décembre	day-**sahm**-bruh

Useful Phrases

Do you speak . . . English?	Parlez-vous . . . anglais?	par-lay **voo** **ahn**-glay
I don't speak . . . French	Je ne parle pas . . . français	zhuh nuh parl **pah** frahn-**say**
I don't understand	Je ne comprends pas	zhuh nuh kohm-prahn **pah**
I understand	Je comprends	zhuh kohm-**prahn**
I don't know	Je ne sais pas	zhuh nuh say **pah**
I'm American/ British	Je suis américain/ anglais	zhuh sweez a-may-ree-**kehn**/ahn-**glay**
What's your name?	Comment vous appelez-vous?	ko-mahn voo za-pell-ay-**voo**
My name is . . .	Je m'appelle . . .	zhuh ma-**pell** . . .
What time is it?	Quelle heure est-il?	kel air eh-**teel**
How?	Comment?	ko-**mahn**
When?	Quand?	kahn
Yesterday	Hier	yair
Today	Aujourd'hui	o-zhoor-**dwee**
Tomorrow	Demain	duh-**mehn**
This morning/ afternoon	Ce matin/cet après-midi	suh ma-**tehn**/set ah-pray-mee-**dee**
Tonight	Ce soir	suh **swahr**
What?	Quoi?	kwah
What is it?	Qu'est-ce que c'est?	kess-kuh-**say**
Why?	Pourquoi?	**poor**-kwa
Who?	Qui?	kee
Where is . . .	Où se trouve . . .	oo suh **troov**
the train station?	la gare?	la gar
the subway?	la station de?	la sta-**syon** duh
station?	métro?	may-**tro**
the bus stop?	l'arrêt de bus?	la-**ray** duh **booss**
the airport?	l'aérogare?	lay-ro-**gar**
the post office?	la poste?	la post
the bank?	la banque?	la bahnk
the hotel?	l'hôtel?	lo-**tel**
the store?	le magasin?	luh ma-ga-**zehn**

the cashier?	la caisse?	la **kess**
the museum?	le musée?	luh mew-**zay**
the hospital?	l'hôpital?	lo-pee-**tahl**
the elevator?	l'ascenseur?	la-sahn-**seuhr**
the telephone?	le téléphone?	luh tay-lay-**phone**
Where are the rest rooms?	Où sont les toilettes?	oo sohn lay twah-**let**
Here/there	Ici/là	ee-**see**/la
Left/right	A gauche/à droite	a goash/a drwaht
Straight ahead	Tout droit	too drwah
Is it near/far?	C'est près/loin?	say pray/lwehn
I'd like . . .	Je voudrais . . .	zhuh voo-**dray**
a room	une chambre	ewn **shahm**-bruh
the key	la clé	la clay
a newspaper	un journal	uhn zhoor-**nahl**
a stamp	un timbre	uhn **tam**-bruh
I'd like to buy . . .	Je voudrais acheter . . .	zhuh voo-**dray ahsh**-tay
a cigar	un cigare	uhn see-**gar**
cigarettes	des cigarettes	day see-ga-**ret**
matches	des allumettes	days a-loo-**met**
dictionary	un dictionnaire	uhn deek-see-oh-**nare**
soap	du savon	dew sah-**vohn**
city map	un plan de ville	uhn plahn de **veel**
road map	une carte routière	ewn cart roo-tee-**air**
magazine	une revue	ewn reh-**vu**
envelopes	des enveloppes	dayz ahn-veh-**lope**
writing paper	du papier à lettres	dew pa-pee-**ay** a **let**-ruh
airmail writing paper	du papier avion	dew pa-pee-**ay** a-vee-**ohn**
postcard	une carte postale	ewn cart pos-**tal**
How much is it?	C'est combien?	say comb-bee-**ehn**
It's expensive/cheap	C'est cher/pas cher	say share/pa share
A little/a lot	Un peu/beaucoup	uhn peuh/bo-**koo**
More/less	Plus/moins	plu/mwehn
Enough/too (much)	Assez/trop	a-say/tro
I am ill/sick	Je suis malade	zhuh swee ma-**lahd**
Call a doctor	Appelez un médecin	a-play uhn mayd-**sehn**
Help!	Au secours!	o suh-**koor**
Stop!	Arrêtez!	a-reh-**tay**
Fire!	Au feu!	o fuh
Caution!/Look out!	Attention!	a-tahn-see-**ohn**

Dining Out

A bottle of . . .	une bouteille de . . .	ewn boo-**tay** duh
A cup of . . .	une tasse de . . .	ewn **tass** duh
A glass of . . .	un verre de . . .	uhn **vair** duh
Ashtray	un cendrier	uhn sahn-dree-**ay**
Bill/check	l'addition	la-dee-see-**ohn**
Bread	du pain	dew pan
Breakfast	le petit-déjeuner	luh puh-**tee** day-zhuh-**nay**
Butter	du beurre	dew burr
Cheers!	A votre santé!	ah vo-truh sahn-**tay**
Cocktail/aperitif	un apéritif	uhn ah-pay-ree-**teef**
Dinner	le dîner	luh dee-**nay**
Special of the day	le plat du jour	luh plah dew **zhoor**
Enjoy!	Bon appétit!	bohn a-pay-**tee**
Fixed-price menu	le menu	luh may-**new**
Fork	une fourchette	ewn four-**shet**
I am diabetic	Je suis diabétique	zhuh swee dee-ah-bay-**teek**
I am on a diet	Je suis au régime	zhuh sweez oray-**jeem**
I am vegetarian	Je suis végétarien(ne)	zhuh swee vay-zhay-ta-ree-**en**
I cannot eat . . .	Je ne peux pas manger de . . .	zhuh nuh **puh** pah mahn-**jay** deh
I'd like to order	Je voudrais commander	zhuh voo-**dray** ko-mahn-**day**
I'm hungry/thirsty	J'ai faim/soif	zhay fahm/swahf
Is service/the tip included?	Le service est-il compris?	luh sair-**veess** ay-teel com-**pree**
It's good/bad	C'est bon/mauvais	say bohn/mo-**vay**
It's hot/cold	C'est chaud/froid	say sho/frwah
Knife	un couteau	uhn koo-**toe**
Lunch	le déjeuner	luh day-zhuh-**nay**
Menu	la carte	la cart
Napkin	une serviette	ewn sair-vee-**et**
Pepper	du poivre	dew **pwah**-vruh
Plate	une assiette	ewn a-see-**et**
Please give me . . .	Merci de me donner . . .	Mair-**see** deh meh doe-**nay**
Salt	du sel	dew sell
Spoon	une cuillère	ewn kwee-**air**
Sugar	du sucre	dew **sook**-ruh
Waiter!/Waitress!	Monsieur!/Mademoiselle!	muh-**syuh**/mad-mwa-**zel**
Wine list	la carte des vins	la **cart** day van

ESSENTIAL INFORMATION

AIR TRAVEL

Most airlines fly to Paris and have connecting flights to the south of France on domestic airlines. The one exception is Delta, which has frequent nonstop flights to Nice from New York.

BOOKING

When you book **look for nonstop flights** and **remember that "direct" flights stop at least once.** Try to avoid connecting flights, which require a change of plane.

CARRIERS

Delta Airlines has daily direct flights from New York to Nice. Air France serves Nice and Marseille airports with daily flights from Paris and London.

➤ DOMESTIC AIRLINES: **Air France** (☎ 800/237–2747 in the U.S.; 08–02–80–28–02 in France) flies from Paris to Avignon, Marseille, Nice, Toulon, and other cities in the south of France. **Air Liberté** (☎ 01–42–86–06–49 or 08–03–80–58–05) flies from Paris to Nice and Toulon. **AOM** (☎ 01–49–79–12–34 or 08–03–00–12–34) flies from Paris to Nice, Marseille, and Toulon.

➤ MAJOR AIRLINES: **Air France** (☎ 800/237–2747 in the U.S.; 08–02–80–28–02 in France) flies to Paris Charles de Gaulle and has connecting flights on its domestic airline to Avignon, Marseille, Nice, and Toulon. **American Airlines** (☎ 800/433–7300 in the U.S.; 01–42–99–99–01 or 08–01–87–28–72 in France) flies to Paris Charles de Gaulle and Orly and connects with domestic airline flights to Marseille and Nice. **Continental** (☎ 800/231–0856 in the U.S.; 01–42–99–09–09 in France) flies to Paris Charles de Gaulle and connects with domestic airline flights to the south. **Delta** (☎ 800/241–4141 in the U.S.; 01–47–68–92–92 in France) flies to

Paris Charles de Gaulle and is the only airline with nonstop flights from the U.S. to Nice (availability varies according to time of year). **Northwest** (☎ 800/225–2525 in the U.S.; 01–42–66–90–00 in France) flies to Paris Charles de Gaulle and connects with domestic airline flights to the south. **TWA** (☎ 800/892–4141 in the U.S.; 01–49–19–20–00 in France) flies to Paris Charles de Gaulle and connects with domestic airline flights to the south. **United** (☎ 800/538–2929 in the U.S.; 08–01–72–72–72 in France) flies to Paris Charles de Gaulle and connects with domestic airline flights to the south. **US Airways** (☎ 800/428–4322 in the U.S.; 01–49–10–29–00 in France) flies to Paris Charles de Gaulle and connects with domestic airline flights to the south.

➤ FROM THE U.K.: **Air France** (☎ 0181/742–6600 in the U.K.; 08–02–80–28–02 in France). **British Airways** (☎ 0990/074–074 in the U.K.; 08–02–80–29–02 in France). **British Midland** (☎ 0345/554–554 in the U.K.; 01–48–62–55–65 in France). **Easyjet** (☎ 0990/292–929 in the U.K.; 04–93–21–48–33 in France) runs scheduled services to Nice from Luton and Liverpool.

CHECK-IN & BOARDING

To enter France, you need to **carry your passport.** You will be asked to show it when you check in. For more information, *see* Passports & Visas, *below.*

Assuming that not everyone with a ticket will show up, airlines routinely overbook planes. When everyone does, airlines ask for volunteers to give up their seats. In return, these volunteers usually get a certificate for a free flight and are rebooked on the next flight out. If there are not enough volunteers, the airline must choose who will be denied boarding. The first to get bumped are passengers who checked in late and those flying on discounted tickets, so **get to the gate and check in as early as possible,** especially during peak periods.

Always **bring a government-issued photo I.D. to the airport.** You may be asked to show it before you are allowed to check in.

CUTTING COSTS

The least expensive airfares to France must usually be purchased in advance and are nonrefundable. It's smart to **call a number of airlines, and when you are quoted a good price, book it on the spot**—the same fare may not be available the next day. Always **check different routings** and look into using different airports. Travel agents, especially low-fare specialists (☞ Discounts & Deals, *below*), are helpful.

Consolidators are another good source. They buy tickets for scheduled international flights at reduced rates from the airlines, then sell them at prices that beat the best fare available directly from the airlines, usually without restrictions. Sometimes you can even get your money back if you need to return the ticket. Carefully read the fine print detailing penalties for changes and cancellations, and **confirm your consolidator reservation with the airline.**

➤ CONSOLIDATORS: **Cheap Tickets** (☎ 800/377–1000). **Discount Airline Ticket Service** (☎ 800/576–1600). **Unitravel** (☎ 800/325–2222). **Up & Away Travel** (☎ 212/889–2345). **World Travel Network** (☎ 800/409–6753).

DISCOUNT PASSES

You can save on air travel within Europe if you plan on traveling to and from Paris aboard Air France. As part of their Euro Flyer program, you then can buy between three and nine flight coupons, valid on flights to more than 100 European cities including many French cities. At $120 each (April–September) and $99 each (October–April 1), these coupons are a good deal, and the fine print still allows you plenty of freedom.

ENJOYING THE FLIGHT

For more legroom, **request an emergency-aisle seat.** Don't sit in the row in front of the emergency aisle or in front of a bulkhead, where seats may not recline. If you have dietary concerns, **ask for special meals when booking.** These can be vegetarian, low-cholesterol, or kosher, for example. On long flights, try to maintain a normal routine, to help fight jet lag. At night, **get some sleep.** By day, **eat light meals, drink water** (not alcohol), and **move around the cabin** to stretch your legs.

FLYING TIMES

Flying time to Paris is 7½ hours from New York, 9 hours from Chicago, and 11 hours from Los Angeles. Flying time between Paris and Nice is approximately 1 hour.

HOW TO COMPLAIN

If your baggage goes astray or your flight goes awry, complain right away. Most carriers require that you **file a claim immediately.**

➤ AIRLINE COMPLAINTS: U.S. Department of Transportation **Aviation Consumer Protection Division** (✉ C-75, Room 4107, Washington, DC 20590, ☎ 202/366–2220, airconsumer@ost.dot.gov, www.dot.gov/airconsumer). **Federal Aviation Administration Consumer Hotline** (☎ 800/322–7873).

RECONFIRMING

It is wise, given the number of strikes in France, to call the day before your flight to reconfirm.

AIRPORTS

The major gateways to France are Paris's Orly and Charles de Gaulle airports. Nice, Marseille, and Montpellier airports are also served by frequent flights from Paris and London, and daily connections from Paris arrive at the smaller airports in Avignon and Nîmes.

➤ AIRPORT INFORMATION: **Avignon** (☎ 04–90–81–51–51). **Charles de Gaulle** (☎ 01–48–62–12–12). **Marseille** (☎ 04–42–14–14–14). **Montpellier** (☎ 04–67–20–85–00). **Nice** (☎ 04–93–21–30–30). **Nîmes** (☎ 04–66–70–06–88). **Orly** (☎ 01–49–75–15–15).

DUTY-FREE SHOPPING

Paris airports offer a wide selection of shops, ranging from gourmet food and wine stores to the Sonia Rykiel boutique and a Virgin Megastore.

BEACHES

The beaches in Provence can vary from fine sand to small pebble to rocky, the latter being the least crowded but requiring mattresses for comfortable sun bathing.

If you're planning to devote a lot of time to beaches and haven't tackled the French coast before, get to **know the distinction between private and public.** All along the coast, the waterfront is carved up into private frontage, roped off and advertised by coordinated color awnings, parasols, and mattresses. These private beaches usually offer full restaurant and bar service, and rent mattresses, umbrellas, and lounge chairs by the day and half-day. Dressing rooms and showers are included; some even rent private cabanas. Prices can run from 60 francs to 120 francs/€9.15 to €18.30 or more a day. Private beaches compete with each other not only via fashionable cuisine and flashy colors, but by offering entertainment—children's wading pools, waterskiing, or parasailing.

But interspliced between these commercial beaches is plenty of public space, with open access and (usually) the necessary comforts of toilets and cold rinse "showers" for washing off the salt. At these you must provide your own mattress or mat (indispensable on the rocks) and you can profit from the democratic bar service provided by enterprising vendors who cruise the waterfront with drinks and snacks. Or better yet, have lunch at one of the many shaded snack bars that line the beach, serving fresh salads and sandwiches.

BIKE TRAVEL

The French are great bicycling enthusiasts—witness the Tour de France—and there are tremendous opportunities to practice this Gallic sport in the south. From the Vaucluse, where cyclists pedal through the Luberon, to the Côte d'Azur, where they crisscross the Esterel over the sea,

Provence and the coast provide good biking conditions and multiple options for rental and transport. For 44 francs/€6.70 a day (55 francs/€8.40 for a 10-speed touring bike) you can rent bikes from many train stations; you need to show your passport and leave a deposit of 1,000 francs/€152 or a Visa or MasterCard. Mountain bikes (known as VTT or *vélo touts terrains*) can be rented from many shops, as well as from some train stations. Bikes may be taken as accompanied luggage from any station in France; some trains in rural areas don't even charge for this. Tourist offices supply details on the more than 200 local shops that rent bikes, or you can get the SNCF brochure "Guide du Train et du Vélo" from any station. Contact the Fédération Française de Cyclotourisme for information on bicycling routes in Provence and the Côte d'Azur. For more bicycling trips, *see* Theme Trips *in* Tour Operators, *below.*

➤ BICYCLING INFORMATION: **Fédération Française de Cyclotourisme** (✉ 8 rue Jean-Marie-Jégo, 75013 Paris, ☎ 01–44–16–88–88). **Institut Géographique National** (✉ IGN, 107 rue La Boétie, 75008 Paris, ☎ 01–43–98–80–00).

Comité Départemental de Cyclisme des Bouches du Rhône (✉ 184 av. Poilus, 13013 Marseille, ☎ 04–91–06–63–99).

BIKE MAPS

The yellow Michelin maps (1:200,000 scale) are fine for roads, but for off-road bicycling you may want to get one of the Institut Géographique National's detailed, large-scale maps. Try their blue series (1:25,000) or orange series (1:50,000).

BIKES IN FLIGHT

Most airlines accommodate bikes as luggage, provided they are dismantled and boxed. For bike boxes, often free at bike shops, you'll pay about $5 (at least $100 for bike bags) from airlines. International travelers can sometimes substitute a bike for a piece of checked luggage at no charge; otherwise, the cost is about $100. Domestic and Canadian airlines charge $25–$50.

BOAT & FERRY TRAVEL

Ferries leave various Provence ports for the island of Corsica daily. From Marseille you can take a night ferry, with berth, that arrives in Ajaccio in the morning. The crossing is faster from Nice, approximately 4 ½ hours. Ferries to the island of Porquerolles leave the port of Hyères and take one hour.

FARES & SCHEDULES

Departure times and fares vary daily for Corsica. **It is important to book ahead,** which can now be done via the Internet or through a travel agent. During the summer there can be up to five departures daily (on weekends) from Nice starting at 7:30 AM. There are up to three departures from Marseille, all in the evening. Fares vary depending on the day of travel and the length of your vehicle. Travel at nonpeak times can save up to 50% if you can decipher the schedule and tariff booklet. Ferries servicing the Île de Porquerolles leave from Hyères and Toulon daily, depending on the season. Some ferries make the crossing only in the summer, so be sure to check the latest schedule—or consult a travel agent.

➤ BOAT & FERRY INFORMATION: For Corsica, contact **SNCM Ferryterranee** (☎ 08–36–67–95–00 www.sncm.fr/). For Porquerolles, contact **TLV** (☎ 04–94–57–44–07, www.tlv-tvm.com).

BUS TRAVEL

France's excellent train service means that long-distance buses are rare; regional buses are found mainly where train service is spotty. The weakest rail links in the south lie in the Luberon region of the Vaucluse, in the Alpilles, and in the backcountry of the Haut Var, Haute Provence, and the pre-Alpes behind Nice. To explore these lovely regions, you must **work closely with a bus schedule** (available at most train stations) and plan connections carefully. Don't plan on too much multistop sightseeing if you're limited to bus connections, as they rarely dovetail with your plans. To visit the popular hill towns just behind the Côte d'Azur—Grasse, St-Paul, Vence, and Biot—you can catch a regional bus or watch for commer-

cial bus excursions advertised in the bigger coastal resorts. Tourist offices provide information on accompanied excursions. Excursions and bus holidays are organized by the SNCF and a plethora of private tour companies. Ask for a brochure at any major travel agent or contact France-Tourisme.

Bus tours from the U.K. generally depart from London, traveling via Hovercraft or ferry from London to Paris.

➤ TO THE U.K. AND OTHER EUROPEAN COUNTRIES: **Eurolines** (✉ 28 av. Général-de-Gaulle, Bagnolet, ☎ 01–43–54–11–99 or 08–36–69–52–52 in France; 0171/730–3499 in the U.K.).

➤ WITHIN FRANCE: **SNCF** (✉ 88 rue St-Lazare, 75009 Paris, ☎ 08–36–35–35–35 in English).

BUSINESS HOURS

BANKS & OFFICES

Bank hours vary from branch to branch, but are usually open weekdays, generally from 8:30 to 5. Most take a one-hour, or even a 90-minute, lunch break.

GAS STATIONS

Gas stations on the autoroutes are generally open 24 hours. In towns, gas stations close at 8 PM, with the occasional station staying open until 10 PM.

MUSEUMS & SIGHTS

Museum hours are somewhat lax in the south, with seasonal variations and a tendency to change slightly and often. Usual opening times are from 9:30 or 10 to 5 or 6, but many close for lunch (noon–2). To allow for long terrace lunches and an afternoon lag in business due to beach time, the lunch hour may be even longer in summer, with some later evening hours to compensate. Most museums are closed one day a week (generally Monday or Tuesday) and on national holidays: **check museum hours before you go.**

SHOPS

Large stores in big towns are open from 9 or 9:30 until 7 or 8. Smaller shops often open earlier (8 AM) and close later (8 PM) but take a lengthy lunch break (1 to 4 or 4:30) in the south of France. Corner groceries frequently stay open until around 10 PM.

CAMERAS & PHOTOGRAPHY

As you come upon view after gorgeous view in these regions, reaching for your camera may become a knee-jerk reaction. A few general ideas can help you capture some stunning shots. **Consider the light**—that famous Provençal light which mesmerized so many artists. Pay attention to the light's direction and quality, and try to match your subject with it. Strong sunlight makes for sharp contrast while sidelight accentuates surface textures. So, for instance, a photo of a Roman ruin at bright noon could emphasize its graphic shape while softer, late-afternoon light could pick up the texture of the stone. **Look for detail,** whether you're taking a close-up or trying to find an interesting way to snap a monument. Markets are a terrific place to get an evocative picture; look for bright colors and special wares, like unusual produce or local crafts.

➤ PHOTO HELP: **Kodak Information Center** (☎ 800/242–2424). *Kodak Guide to Shooting Great Travel Pictures,* available in bookstores or from Fodor's Travel Publications (☎ 800/533–6478; $18 plus $5.50 shipping).

EQUIPMENT PRECAUTIONS

Always **keep your film and tape out of the sun.** Carry an extra supply of batteries, and **be prepared to turn on your camera or camcorder** to prove to security personnel that the device is real. Always **ask for hand inspection of film,** which becomes clouded after repeated exposure to airport X-ray machines, and **keep videotapes away from metal detectors.**

FILM & DEVELOPING

For fast, professional film developing and service, use the FNAC stores, which can be found in any large Provençal town.

CAR RENTAL

Though renting a car in France is expensive—up to twice as much as in the United States—as is gas (about 8 francs/€1.22 per liter at press time), it may pay off if you are traveling with two or more people. In addition, renting a car gives you the freedom to move around at your own pace that the train does not. Rates begin at about $50 a day and $265 per week for an economy car with a manual transmission. Mileage is extra, but there are often multiday packages or weekly rates including some number of kilometers. Be careful to check whether the price includes the 20.6% VAT tax or, if you pick it up from the airport, the airport tax.

If you're flying into Paris, it may be more economical to connect via a smaller airline directly to Nice or Marseille, then rent your car in the south. Or consider a rail-drive pass with one of the larger car-rental companies, which allow a few days' rail travel—say, from Paris to Nice—and a block of car-rental time. By using the train to cover the long distances, then exploring the region in depth by car, you can make the most of both styles of transit.

➤ MAJOR AGENCIES: **Alamo** (☎ 800/522–9696; 020/8759–6200 in the U.K.). **Avis** (☎ 800/331–1212; 800/879–2847 in Canada; 02/9353–9000 in Australia; 09/525–1982 in New Zealand; 0870/606–0100 in the U.K.). **Budget** (☎ 800/527–0700; 0870/607–5000 in the U.K., through affiliate Europcar). **Dollar** (☎ 800/800–6000; 0124/622–0111 in the U.K., through affiliate Sixt Kenning; 02/9223–1444 in Australia). **Hertz** (☎ 800/654–3001; 800/263–0600 in Canada; 020/8897–2072 in the U.K.; 02/9669–2444 in Australia; 09/256–8690 in New Zealand) **National Car Rental** (☎ 800/227–7368; 020/8680–4800 in the U.K., where it is known as National Europe).

CUTTING COSTS

To get the best deal, **book through a travel agent who will shop around.** Also **price local car-rental companies,** although the service and maintenance may not be as good as those of a major player. Remember to ask about required deposits, cancellation penalties, and drop-off charges if you're planning to pick up the car in one city and leave it in another. If you're traveling during a holiday period, also make sure that a confirmed reservation guarantees you a car.

Do **look into wholesalers,** companies that do not own fleets but rent in bulk from those that do and often offer better rates than traditional car-rental operations. Payment must be made before you leave home.

➤ LONG-TERM LEASING: **Renault Eurodrive** (☎ 800/221–1052 east; 800/477–7716 west; 800/777–7131 FL and Puerto Rico).

➤ WHOLESALERS: **Auto Europe** (☎ 207/842–2000 or 800/223–5555, ℻ 800/235–6321, www.autoeurope. com).

INSURANCE

When driving a rented car you are generally responsible for any damage to or loss of the vehicle. Before you rent see what coverage your personal auto-insurance policy and credit cards already provide.

Before you buy collision coverage, check your existing policies—you may already be covered. However, collision policies that car-rental companies sell for European rentals usually do not include stolen-vehicle coverage.

REQUIREMENTS & RESTRICTIONS

In France your own driver's license is acceptable. You don't need an International Driver's Permit, unless you are planning on a long-term stay; you can get one from the American or Canadian automobile association, and, in the United Kingdom, from the Automobile Association or Royal Automobile Club.

SURCHARGES

Before you pick up a car in one city and leave it in another, **ask about drop-off charges or one-way service fees,** which can be substantial. Note, too, that some rental agencies charge extra if you return the car before the time specified in your contract. To avoid a hefty refueling fee, **fill the tank just before you turn in the car,** but be aware that gas stations near the rental outlet may overcharge.

CAR TRAVEL

Car travel is the best way to see Provence, especially since the famous hilltop villages see a bus only once a day. Road conditions in Provence are above average and potholes are rare, especially on highways. France's roads are classified into five types, numbered and prefixed *A, N, D, C,* or *V.* For the fastest roads between two points, **look for roads marked A for autoroutes.** A *péage* (toll) must be paid on most expressways: the rate varies but can be steep. At your first toll stop you will simply retrieve a ticket, and at the next toll you will pay. You may pay by debit card, as long as the toll is over 10 francs/ €1.50.

The *N* (Route Nationale) roads, which are sometimes divided highways, are the route of choice for heavy freight trucks, and are often lined with industry and large chain stores. More scenic, though less trafficked than the RNs are the *D* (Route Départementale) roads, often also wide and fast. Don't be daunted by smaller (*C* and *V*) roads, either; they're often the most scenic.

Though routes are numbered, the French generally guide themselves from city to city and town to town by destination name. When reading a map, keep one eye on the next big city toward your destination as well as the next small town; most snap decisions will have to be based on town names, not road numbers.

Negotiating the back roads requires a careful mix of map and sign reading, often at high speeds around suburban *giratoires* (rotaries). But by the time you head out into the hills and the tiny roads—one of the best parts of Provence and the Côte d'Azur—give yourself over to road signs and pure faith: As is the case throughout France, directions are indicated by village name only, with route numbers given as a small-print after-thought. Of course, this means you have to recognize the minor villages en route.

To leave Paris by car, figure out which of the *portes* (gates) corresponds to the direction you are going. Major highways connect to Paris at these points, and directions are indicated by major cities. For instance, heading north, look for Porte d'Orléans (direction Lyon and Bordeaux); heading south, follow Avignon, and after Avignon follow Nice and/or Marseille. It's best to **steer clear of rush hours** (7–9:30 AM and 4:30–7:30 PM), although this is only a real concern between Aix and Marseille and around Nice.

EMERGENCY SERVICES

If your car breaks down on an expressway, **go to a roadside emergency telephone (yellow boxes)** and call for assistance. If you have a breakdown anywhere else, find the nearest garage or contact the police (dial 17).

GASOLINE

Gas is expensive, especially on expressways and in rural areas. When possible, **buy gas before you get on the expressway** and keep an eye on pump prices as you go. These vary enormously; anything from 5.80 to 8 francs/88 European cents to €1.22 per liter. The cheapest gas can be found at *hypermarchés* (very large supermarkets) but expect long lineups. It is possible to go for many miles in the country without passing a gas station—**don't let your tank get too low in rural areas.** If you are worried about your budget, ask for a diesel car; diesel fuel at gas pumps can be labeled as *diesel, gasoil,* or *gazoil.* Unleaded gas will be labeled as *sans plomb* (SP95 for regular unleaded and SP98 for super unleaded). Be careful, as many gas stations still sell leaded gas, called *super.*

PARKING

Parking can be difficult in large towns; your best option (especially in a metropolis like Nice or Marseille) is to duck into the parking garage nearest the neighborhood you want to visit. Carry the ticket with you, and pay at the vending-machine-style ticket dispenser before you go back to your car. On the street, meters and ticket machines (pay and display) are common. Until January 2002, make sure you **have a supply of 1-, 2-, 5-, and 10-franc coins. Be sure to check the signs before you park, as rules

vary.** Street parking is free over the lunch hour (noon–2 PM).

Be careful when parking your car overnight, especially in town and village squares; if your car is still there in the early morning on a market day, it will be towed. In smaller towns, parking may be permitted on one side of the street only—alternating every two weeks—so pay attention to signs.

The coastal area of Provence—especially the Camargue and the Calanques—as well as overlooks along the Côte d'Azur are extremely vulnerable to car break-ins, and the parking lots are often littered with broken windshield glass. It's important that you **never leave valuables visible in the car,** and think twice about leaving them in the trunk. Any theft should be reported formally to the police.

ROAD MAPS

If you plan to drive through France, **get a yellow Michelin map** for each region you'll be visiting. The maps are available from most bookshops and news agents.

RULES OF THE ROAD

In France, **you may use your own driver's license,** but you must be able to prove you have third-party insurance. Drive on the right and **yield to drivers coming from streets to the right.** However, this rule does not necessarily apply at roundabouts, where you are obligated to yield to those already within (to your left)—but should watch out for just about everyone. You must **wear your seat belt,** and children under 10 may not travel in the front seat. Speed limits are 130 kph (80 mph) on expressways, 110 kph (70 mph) on divided highways, 90 kph (55 mph) on other roads, 50 kph (30 mph) in towns. French drivers break these limits and police dish out hefty on-the-spot fines with equal abandon.

CHILDREN IN PROVENCE AND THE CÔTE D'AZUR

If you are renting a car, don't forget to **arrange for a car seat** when you reserve.

FLYING

If your children are two or older, **ask about children's airfares.** As a general rule, infants under two not occupying a seat fly at greatly reduced fares or even for free. When booking, **confirm carry-on allowances** if you're traveling with infants. In general, for babies charged 10% of the adult fare you are allowed one carry-on bag and a collapsible stroller; if the flight is full, the stroller may have to be checked or you may be limited to less.

Experts agree that it's a good idea to use safety seats aloft for children weighing less than 40 pounds. Airlines set their own policies: U.S. carriers usually require that the child be ticketed, even if he or she is young enough to ride free, since the seats must be strapped into regular seats. Do **check your airline's policy about using safety seats during takeoff and landing.** And since safety seats are not allowed just everywhere in the plane, get your seat assignments early.

When reserving, **request children's meals or a freestanding bassinet** if you need them. But note that bulkhead seats, where you must sit to use the bassinet, may lack an overhead bin or storage space on the floor.

FOOD

The best restaurants in France do not welcome small children; except for the traditional family Sunday-noon dinner, fine dining is considered an adult pastime. Aim for more modest *auberges* (country inns), and if there's a choice **consider having your meal in the café or bar** rather than in the linen-and-goblet filled dining room. In cities, brasseries offer a casual option and the flexible meal times that children often require. Many mainstream restaurants have highchairs and serve children's portions *(menu enfant),* usually spaghetti or the ubiquitous *steak-frites,* a mountain of fries with a thin steak or fat patty of ground beef, usually extremely rare. If you're queasy about this, ask for it *bien cuit* (well done). Also popular with kids is the *croque monsieur,* a grilled ham-and-cheese sandwich.

If your children go to bed early, opt for your hot meal at noon (there are cheaper prix-fixe menus, too) and consider having a sandwich, quiche, or pizza at a café or brasserie in the early evening; full-service restaurants usually do not serve before 7 PM.

LODGING

Most hotels in Provence and the Côte d'Azur allow children under a certain age to stay in their parents' room at no extra charge, but others charge for them as extra adults; be sure to **find out the cutoff age for children's discounts.**

If you're planning to stay in hotels, be sure to book ahead. Many small hotels have only one or two rooms that sleep four (triples are much more common); if there are more of you, you'll have to book two neighboring rooms or a suite. If you want a family-size room or a pair of adjoining rooms, book ahead. Larger hotels will often provide cribs free to guests with young children, which is not usually the case at inns and smaller hotels.

Another option: **consider a gîte, a short-term apartment or house rental,** or a home exchange. *See* Lodging, *below* for information about rental and home exchange organizations.

SIGHTS & ATTRACTIONS

There are plenty of diversions for the young, and almost all museums and movie theaters offer discounted rates to children. Playgrounds can be found off many toll roads. Places that are especially appealing to children are indicated by a rubber duckie icon in the margin.

SUPPLIES & EQUIPMENT

Supermarkets carry several major brands of diapers (*couches à jeter*), universally referred to as Pampers (pawm-paires). Junior sizes are hard to come by, as the French toilet-train early. There's always plenty of baby food, and pharmacies provide the essentials.

TRANSPORTATION

The SNCF allows children under 4 to travel free (provided they don't occupy a seat) and children 4 to 11 to travel at half fare. The Carte Kiwi (285 francs/€43) allows children under 16 and as many as four accompanying adults to make four journeys at 25%–50% off.

Changing compartments for infants are available on all TGVs, although not on all local trains.

COMPUTERS ON THE ROAD

If you use a major Internet provider, getting on-line in major cities in the south of France shouldn't be difficult. Call your Internet provider to get local access numbers. Some hotels even have in-room modem lines. You may, however, need an adapter for your computer. Internet cafés are becoming a popular site in Provençal cities, but there is no easy way to find them except by word of mouth, or by popping into a computer store and asking for a web café location.

➤ ACCESS NUMBERS IN PARIS: **AOL** (☎ 01–71–70–44–44 or customer service at 01–71–71–71–71). **Compuserve** (☎ 08–03–00–60–00 or customer service at 03–21–13–49–49).

CONSUMER PROTECTION

Whenever shopping or buying travel services in Provence and the Côte d'Azur, **pay with a major credit card** so you can cancel payment or get reimbursed if there's a problem. If you're doing business with a particular company for the first time, **contact your local Better Business Bureau and the attorney general's offices** in your own state and the company's home state, as well. Have any complaints been filed? Finally, if you're buying a package or tour, always **consider travel insurance** that includes default coverage (☞ Insurance, *below*).

➤ BBBs: **Council of Better Business Bureaus** (✉ 4200 Wilson Blvd., Suite 800, Arlington, VA 22203, ☎ 703/276–0100, FAX 703/525–8277, www.bbb.org).

CUSTOMS & DUTIES

When shopping, **keep receipts** for all purchases. Upon reentering the country, **be ready to show customs officials what you've bought.** If you feel a duty is incorrect or object to the way your clearance was handled, note the inspector's badge number and ask to see a supervisor. If the problem isn't resolved, write to the appropriate authorities, beginning with the port director at your point of entry.

IN FRANCE

There are two levels of duty-free allowance for travelers entering France: one for goods obtained (tax paid) within another European Union (EU) country and the other for goods obtained anywhere outside the EU or for goods purchased in a duty-free shop within the EU.

In the first category, you may import duty-free: 300 cigarettes or 150 cigarillos or 75 cigars or 400 grams of tobacco; 5 liters of table wine and (1) 1½ liters of alcohol over 22% volume (most spirits), (2) 3 liters of alcohol under 22% by volume (fortified or sparkling wine), or (3) 3 more liters of table wine; 90 milliliters of perfume; 375 milliliters of toilet water; and other goods to the value of 2,400 francs/€366 (620 francs/€95 for those under 15).

In the second category, you may import duty-free: 200 cigarettes or 100 cigarillos or 50 cigars or 250 grams of tobacco (these allowances are doubled if you live outside Europe); 2 liters of wine and (1) 1 liter of alcohol over 22% volume (most spirits), (2) 2 liters of alcohol under 22% volume (fortified or sparkling wine), or (3) 2 more liters of table wine; 60 milliliters of perfume; 250 milliliters of toilet water; and other goods to the value of 300 francs/€46 (150 francs/€23 for those under 15).

IN AUSTRALIA

Australian residents who are 18 or older may bring home $A400 worth of souvenirs and gifts (including jewelry), 250 cigarettes or 250 grams of tobacco, and 1,125 ml of alcohol (including wine, beer, and spirits). Residents under 18 may bring back $A200 worth of goods. Prohibited items include meat products. Seeds, plants, and fruits need to be declared upon arrival.

➤ INFORMATION: **Australian Customs Service** (Regional Director, ✉ Box 8, Sydney, NSW 2001, Australia, ☎ 02/9213–2000, FAX 02/9213–4000, www.customs.gov.au).

IN CANADA

Canadian residents who have been out of Canada for at least 7 days may bring home C$500 worth of goods duty-free. If you've been away less than 7 days but more than 48 hours, the duty-free allowance drops to C$200; if your trip lasts 24–48 hours, the allowance is C$50. You may not pool allowances with family members. Goods claimed under the C$500 exemption may follow you by mail; those claimed under the lesser exemptions must accompany you. Alcohol and tobacco products may be included in the 7-day and 48-hour exemptions but not in the 24-hour exemption. If you meet the age requirements of the province or territory through which you reenter Canada, you may bring in, duty-free, 1.14 liters (40 imperial ounces) of wine or liquor *or* 24 12-ounce cans or bottles of beer or ale. If you are 16 or older you may bring in, duty-free, 200 cigarettes and 50 cigars. Check ahead of time with Revenue Canada or the Department of Agriculture for policies regarding meat products, seeds, plants, and fruits.

You may send an unlimited number of gifts worth up to C$60 each duty-free to Canada. Label the package UNSOLICITED GIFT—VALUE UNDER $60. Alcohol and tobacco are excluded.

➤ INFORMATION: **Revenue Canada** (✉ 2265 St. Laurent Blvd. S, Ottawa, Ontario K1G 4K3, Canada, ☎ 613/993–0534; 800/461–9999 in Canada, FAX 613/991–4126, www.ccra-adrc.gc.ca).

IN NEW ZEALAND

Homeward-bound residents 17 or older may bring back $700 worth of souvenirs and gifts. Your duty-free allowance also includes 4.5 liters of wine or beer; one 1,125-ml bottle of spirits; and either 200 cigarettes, 250 grams of tobacco, 50 cigars, or a combination of the three up to 250 grams. Prohibited items include meat products, seeds, plants, and fruits.

➤ INFORMATION: **New Zealand Customs** (Custom House, ✉ 50 Anzac Ave., Box 29, Auckland, New Zealand, ☎ 09/300–5399, FAX 09/359–6730, www.customs.govt.nz).

IN THE U.K.

If you are a U.K. resident and your journey was wholly within the European Union (EU), you won't have to pass through customs when you return to the United Kingdom. If you plan to bring back large quantities of alcohol or tobacco, check EU limits beforehand.

➤ INFORMATION: **HM Customs and Excise** (✉ Dorset House, Stamford St., Bromley, Kent BR1 1XX, U.K., ☎ 020/7202–4227, www.hmce.gov.uk).

IN THE U.S.

U.S. residents who have been out of the country for at least 48 hours (and who have not used the $400 allowance or any part of it in the past 30 days) may bring home $400 worth of foreign goods duty-free.

U.S. residents 21 and older may bring back 1 liter of alcohol duty-free. In addition, regardless of your age, you are allowed 200 cigarettes and 100 non-Cuban cigars. Antiques, which the U.S. Customs Service defines as objects more than 100 years old, enter duty-free, as do original works of art done entirely by hand, including paintings, drawings, and sculptures.

You may also mail or ship packages home duty-free: up to $200 worth of goods for personal use, with a limit of one parcel per addressee per day (except alcohol or tobacco products or perfume worth more than $5); label the package PERSONAL USE and attach a list of its contents and their retail value. Do not label the package UNSOLICITED GIFT or your duty-free exemption will drop to $100. Mailed items do not affect your duty-free allowance on your return.

➤ INFORMATION: **U.S. Customs Service** (✉ 1300 Pennsylvania Ave. NW, Washington, DC 20229, www.customs.gov; inquiries ☎ 202/354–1000; complaints c/o ✉ 1300 Pennsylvania Ave. NW, Room 5.4D, Washington, DC 20229; registration of equipment c/o ✉ Resource Management, ☎ 202/354–1000).

DINING

The sooner you relax and go with the French flow, the more you'll enjoy your stay. Expect to spend at least two hours for lunch in a restaurant, savoring three courses and talking over the wine; dinner lasts even longer. If you keep one eye on your watch and the other on the waiter, you'll miss the point and spoil your own fun.

If you're antsy to get to the next museum, or if you plan to spend the evening dining in grand style, consider lunching in a brasserie, where quick, one-plate lunches and full salads are available. Cafés often serve *casse croûtes* (snacks), including sandwiches, which are simply baguettes lightly filled with ham or cheese; or *croques monsieurs,* grilled ham and cheese open-face sandwiches with a minimum of grease. Bakeries and *traiteurs* (delis) often sell savory items like quiches, tiny pizzas, or pastries filled with pâté. On the Côte d'Azur, you can profit from a wealth of street food, from the chickpea-based crêpes called *socca* to *pissaladière* (onion-olive pizza) and *pan bagnat* (a tuna-and-egg-stuffed pita-style bun).

You may benefit from a few pointers on French dining etiquette. Diners in France don't negotiate their orders much, so don't expect serene smiles when you ask for sauce on the side. Order your coffee after dessert, not with it. When you're ready for the check, ask for it. No professional waiter would dare put a bill on your table while you're still enjoying the last sip of coffee. And don't ask for a doggy bag; it's just not done.

Also a word on the great mineral-water war: the French usually drink wine or mineral water—not soda or coffee—with their food. You may ask for a carafe of tap water, but not always. In general, diners order mineral water if they don't order wine. It's not that the tap water is unsafe; it's usually fine—just not as tasty as Evian or slightly fizzy Badoit.

One of the wonderful aspects of breakfast in Provence and on the Côte d'Azur is eating outdoors, whether on the restaurant terrace or on your own tiny balcony. Breakfasts are light, consisting of croissants and bread, jam and butter, and wonderful coffee.

More hotels are also serving yogurt, fruit juice, cereal, cheese, and even eggs upon request.

There is no need to wear a tie and jacket at most restaurants (unless specified), even fancy ones. For more on what to wear in the south of France, *see* Packing for Provence & the Côte d'Azur, *below.*

Restaurants along the coast are generally more expensive than those inland; basic regional fixed-price menus average about 90 francs to 125 francs/€14 to €19, though the high end of this figure represents the usual cost of seafood so often featured on restaurant menus. In high summer reserve at popular restaurants, especially if you want a coveted outdoor table.

The restaurants we list in this guide are the cream of the crop in each price category. Properties indicated by an ✕▣ are lodging establishments whose restaurant warrants a special trip.

MEALTIMES

You'll notice here more than anywhere in France that the lunch hour begins after 1; some places don't even open before that. If you don't mind being a gauche foreigner, eating at noon is one way to get into those sought-after restaurants that do open at 12. If you want to really do as the Romans do, reserve for a lunch at 1 or 1:30.

Breakfast usually is served from 8:30 to 10:30; if you want it earlier, arrange a time the night before. Dinner is usually eaten after 8.

Unless otherwise noted, the restaurants listed in this guide are open daily for lunch and dinner.

RESERVATIONS & DRESS

Reservations are always a good idea: we mention them only when they're essential or not accepted. Book as far ahead as you can, and reconfirm as soon as you arrive. We mention dress only when men are required to wear a jacket or a jacket and tie.

WINE & SPIRITS

Provence has several wine appellations (AOCs) that vary in size from the vast AOC Côtes de Provence (which covers most of eastern Provence), to the tiny AOC Palette, which has only one major estate. The hearty red and white wines of AOC Châteauneuf-du-Pape have been famous since Pope Clement V sought them out in the early 14th century. Many Provençals prefer to drink light, dry rosé wines, which they buy in five- or ten-liter jugs at the local wine cooperative. The fresh, white wines that are made in the hills surrounding the coastal resort of Cassis (not to be confused with the black currant syrup of the same name) are also very fine. Apéatif time is extremely popular, the preferred drink being *pastis* (an amber-colored liquor distilled with anise and secret herbs) or a glass of champagne (*une coupe de champagne*).

DISABILITIES & ACCESSIBILITY

Although the French government is doing much to ensure that public facilities provide for visitors with disabilities, it still has a long way to go. A number of monuments, hotels, and museums—especially those constructed within the past decade—are equipped with ramps, elevators, and special toilet facilities.

Certain larger towns publish their own city guides for handicapped persons, available at tourist offices. These guides list accessible restaurants and hotels, and some even mark the handicapped parking spaces in town. Beware, however, that drivers in Provence have little respect for handicapped-designated parking spots, especially those in the center of town, so you may find them taken. Bring your own handicapped sticker with you from home since there is a fair amount of red tape to obtain one in France.

If you have a hearing aid, bring batteries with you, as battery types are not coded in the same way. When buying replacements, carry the dead battery with you for a perfect match.

➤ LOCAL RESOURCES: **Association des Paralysés de France** (✉ 9 bd. Auguste-Blanqui, 75013 Paris, ☎ 01–53–62–84–00) for a list of Paris hotels. **Comité Nationale Français de Liaison pour la Réadaptation des Handicapés** (✉ 236-B rue de Tolbiac, 75013 Paris, ☎ 01–53–80–66–66).

LODGING

Tourist offices will have listings of hotels that cater to handicapped persons. Lists of regional hotels include a symbol to indicate which hotels have rooms that are accessible to people using wheelchairs. However quaint, auberges in historic buildings will probably not have handicapped facilities, and often the bathrooms are about the size of a postage stamp, difficult for those with mobility problems to negotiate.

RESERVATIONS

When discussing accessibility with an operator or reservations agent, **ask hard questions.** Are there any stairs, inside *or* out? Are there grab bars next to the toilet *and* in the shower/tub? How wide is the doorway to the room? To the bathroom? For the most extensive facilities meeting the latest legal specifications, **opt for newer accommodations.**

TRANSPORTATION

The SNCF has special cars on some trains that have been reserved exclusively for people using wheelchairs and can arrange for those passengers to be escorted on and off trains and assisted in making connections (the latter service must, however, be requested in advance).

➤ COMPLAINTS: **Disability Rights Section** (✉ U.S. Department of Justice, Civil Rights Division, Box 66738, Washington, DC 20035-6738, ☎ 202/514–0301 or 800/514–0301; 202/514–0383 TTY; 800/514–0383 TTY, ℻ 202/307–1198, www.usdoj.gov/crt/ada/adahom1.htm) for general complaints. **Aviation Consumer Protection Division** (☞ Air Travel, *above*) for airline-related problems. **Civil Rights Office** (✉ U.S. Department of Transportation, Departmental Office of Civil Rights, S-30, 400 7th St. SW, Room 10215, Washington, DC 20590, ☎ 202/366–4648, ℻ 202/366–9371) for problems with surface transportation.

TRAVEL AGENCIES

In the United States, the Americans with Disabilities Act requires that travel firms serve the needs of all travelers. Some agencies specialize in working with people with disabilities.

➤ TRAVELERS WITH MOBILITY PROBLEMS: **Access Adventures** (✉ 206 Chestnut Ridge Rd., Scottsville, NY 14624, ☎ 716/889–9096, dltravel@ prodigy.net), run by a former physical-rehabilitation counselor. **Flying Wheels Travel** (✉ 143 W. Bridge St., Box 382, Owatonna, MN 55060, ☎ 507/451–5005 or 800/535–6790, FAX 507/451–1685, thq@ll.net, www. flyingwheels.com).

DISCOUNTS & DEALS

Be a smart shopper and **compare all your options** before making decisions. A plane ticket bought with a promotional coupon from travel clubs, coupon books, and direct-mail offers may not be cheaper than the least expensive fare from a discount ticket agency. And always keep in mind that what you get is just as important as what you save.

DISCOUNT RESERVATIONS

To save money, **look into discount reservations services** with toll-free numbers, which use their buying power to get a better price on hotels, airline tickets, even car rentals. When booking a room, always **call the hotel's local toll-free number** (if one is available) rather than the central reservations number—you'll often get a better price. Always ask about special packages or corporate rates.

When shopping for the best deal on hotels and car rentals, **look for guaranteed exchange rates,** which protect you against a falling dollar. With your rate locked in, you won't pay more, even if the price goes up in the local currency.

➤ AIRLINE TICKETS: ☎ **800/FLY–ASAP.**

➤ HOTEL ROOMS: **Steigenberger Reservation Service** (☎ 800/223–5652, www.srs-worldhotels.com). **Travel Interlink** (☎ 800/888–5898, www.travelinterlink.com).

PACKAGE DEALS

Don't confuse packages and guided tours. When you buy a package, you travel on your own, just as though you had planned the trip yourself. Fly/drive packages, which combine airfare and car rental, are often a good deal. If you **buy a rail/drive pass,** you may save on train tickets and car rentals. All Eurail- and Europass holders get a discount on Eurostar fares through the Channel Tunnel.

ELECTRICITY

To use your U.S.-purchased electric-powered equipment, **bring a converter and adapter.** The electrical current in France is 220 volts, 50 cycles alternating current (AC). French electrical outlets have two round holes ("female") and a "male" ground; your appliances must either have a slender, two-prong plug that bypasses that ground, or a plug with two round prongs and a hole.

If your appliances are dual-voltage, you'll need only an adapter. Don't use 110-volt outlets marked FOR SHAVERS ONLY for high-wattage appliances such as blow-dryers. Most laptops operate equally well on 110 and 220 volts and so require only an adapter.

EMBASSIES

If you need assistance in an emergency you can go to your country's embassy or consulate. Proof of identity and citizenship are generally required to enter. If your passport has been stolen, get a police report then contact your embassy for assistance.

➤ AUSTRALIA: **Australian Embassy** (✉ 4 rue Jean-Rey, Paris, 15ᵉ, ☎ 01–40–59–33–00, métro Bir Hakeim, ☉ weekdays 9:15–12:15).

➤ CANADA: **Canadian Embassy** (✉ 35 av. Montaigne, Paris, 8ᵉ, ☎ 01–44–43–29–00, métro Franklin-D.-Roosevelt, ☉ weekdays 8:30–11).

➤ NEW ZEALAND: **New Zealand Embassy** (✉ 7 ter rue Léonardo da Vinci, Paris, 16ᵉ, métro Victor Hugo ☎ 01–45–00–24–11, ☉ weekdays 9–1).

➤ UNITED KINGDOM: **U.K. Embassy** (✉ 35 rue du Faubourg-St-Honoré, Paris, 8ᵉ, ☎ 01–44–51–31–00, métro Madeleine, ☉ weekdays 9:30–12:30 and 2:30–5; ✉ 24 av. du Prado, Marseille, ☎ 04–91–15–72–10 for

24-hour emergency help; ⊙ weekdays 9–noon and 2–5).

➤ UNITED STATES: **U.S. Embassy** (✉ 2 rue St-Florentin, Paris, 1ᵉʳ, ☎ 01–43–12–22–22 in English; 01–43–12–23–47 in emergencies, métro Concorde, ⊙ weekdays 9–3; ✉ 12 bd. Paul Peytral, Marseille, ☎ 04–91–54–92–00, ⊙ weekdays 8:30–12:30 and 1:30–5:30 and until 4:30 on Friday).

EMERGENCIES

France's emergency services are conveniently streamlined and universal, so no matter where you are in the country, you can dial the same phone numbers, listed below. Every town and village has a *médecin de garde* (on-duty doctor) for flus, sprains, tetanus shots, etc. To find out who's on any given evening, call any *généraliste* (general practitioner) and a recording will refer you. If you need an x-ray or emergency treatment, call the ambulance number (☎ 15) and you'll be whisked to the hospital of your choice—or the nearest one. Note that outside of Paris it may be difficult to find English-speaking doctors.

In case of fire, hotels are required to post emergency exit maps inside every room door and multilingual instructions.

➤ CONTACTS: **Ambulance** (☎ 15). **Fire Department** (☎ 18). **Police** (☎ 17).

ENGLISH-LANGUAGE MEDIA

BOOKS

Books in English—usually best-sellers and classics—can be found in the larger bookstores in French cities.

NEWSPAPERS & MAGAZINES

The *International Herald Tribune* can be found at most newsstands, even in small villages. Train stations and airports are the best bets for finding foreign-language magazines and newspapers.

RADIO & TELEVISION

The Côte d'Azur area has a few radio stations that broadcast the BBC and other English-language programs. Tune into **Radio International Côte d'Azur** at 100.5, 100.7, or 100.9 FM, depending where along the Mediterranean coast you are. **The Breeze** also broadcasts the BBC at certain hours at 88.4 FM.

ETIQUETTE & BEHAVIOR

It is considered impolite not to smile and say hello when entering a store in Provence. You must also say goodbye and thank you, even if you have not made a purchase. In restaurants it is quite normal to nod and smile at the people next to you and wish them "bon appétit."

GAY & LESBIAN TRAVEL

In Provence and the Côte d'Azur, the gay and lesbian communities are low-key and reserved in public, although active and easily accessible to visitors. Discos and nightclubs are numerous and popular. To find out where they are, look for the *Guide Gay Grand Sud* for men and the *Guide Lesbien,* available in most gay and lesbian bars and clubs.

➤ GAY- AND LESBIAN-FRIENDLY TRAVEL AGENCY IN FRANCE: **Mistral Tours** (✉ 4 rue Pissantour, 13150 Boulbon, ☎ FAX 04–90–43–86–90) has preplanned packages with specific cultural themes—van Gogh in Provence, say, or Roman Provence—and can include hikes and bike tours.

➤ GAY- & LESBIAN-FRIENDLY TRAVEL AGENCIES: **Different Roads Travel** (✉ 8383 Wilshire Blvd., Suite 902, Beverly Hills, CA 90211, ☎ 323/651–5557 or 800/429–8747, FAX 323/651–3678, leigh@west.tzell.com). **Kennedy Travel** (✉ 314 Jericho Turnpike, Floral Park, NY 11001, ☎ 516/352–4888 or 800/237–7433, FAX 516/354–8849, kennedytravel1@yahoo.com, www.kennedytravel.com). **Now Voyager** (✉ 4406 18th St., San Francisco, CA 94114, ☎ 415/626–1169 or 800/255–6951, FAX 415/626–8626, www.nowvoyager.com). **Skylink Travel and Tour** (✉ 1006 Mendocino Ave., Santa Rosa, CA 95401, ☎ 707/546–9888 or 800/225–5759, FAX 707/546–9891, skylinktvl@aol.com, www.skylinktravel.com), serving lesbian travelers.

HEALTH

See Emergencies, *above.*

DOCTORS & HOSPITALS

For information on doctors and hospitals throughout Provence and the Côte d'Azur, *see* A to Z sections *in* individual chapters.

OVER-THE-COUNTER REMEDIES

For a headache *(mal à la tête)* ask the pharmacist for *aspirine* (aspirin) or *doliprane* (Tylenol). For gas pains, ask for *smecta*, and for menstrual cramps you will be given *spasfon*. For car and boat sickness, *primperan*. For cuts, scrapes, and other minor "ouchies," which the French call "bobos," you will be given a disinfectant spray called *Bétadine*. *Gel d'Apis* treats mosquito bites (you may need this if you are traveling in the Carmargue). Sore throats are treated with lozenges called *pastilles* and cough syrup is *sirop*. Diarrhea *(diarrhée)* is treated with *Immodium*.

HIKING

There are many good places to hike in Provence and the Côte d'Azur, especially along the extensive network of mapped-out *Grands Randonnées* (GRs or Big Trails) that range from easy to challenging. For details on hiking in France and guides to GRs in specific areas, contact the Club Alpin Français or the Fédération Française de la Randonnée Pédestre, which also publishes good topographical maps. The IGN maps sold in many bookshops are also invaluable (☞ Bicycling, *above*).

Note that some of the best hiking wilderness along the coast—especially around the Calanques between Marseille and Cassis, and the Esterel between Fréjus and Cannes—are closed in July and August because of wildfire danger. Before you plan a summer of seaside hikes, **check with local tourist offices to confirm that trails are open.**

➤ HIKING ORGANIZATIONS: **Club Alpin Français** (✉ 24 av. Laumière, 13150 Paris, ☎ 01–53–72–88–00). **Comité Départemental de Randonée Pedestre Bouches-du-Rhône** (✉ 24 av. Prado, 13006 Marseille, ☎ 04–91–81–12–08). **Comité Départemental de Randonée Pedestre Alpes-Maritime** (✉ 83 av. Joseph-Raybaud, 06300 Nice, ☎ 04–93–13–07–60).

Comité Départemental de Randonée Pedestre Var (✉ L'Helianthe, 142 rue Emile Olivier La Rode, 83000 Toulon, ☎ 04–94–42–15–01). **Comité Départemental de Randonée Pedestre Vaucluse** (Daniel Locci, Les Fontaines du Levant, ✉ 63 av. César-Franck, 84000 Avignon, ☎ 04–90–85–65–04; written requests only). **Fédération Française de la Randonnée Pédestre** (✉ 14 rue Riquet, 75019 Paris, ☎ 01–44–89–93–90, ℻ 01–40–35–85–48, ffrp. paris@wannado.fr).

HOLIDAYS

With 11 national *jours feriés* (holidays) and 5 weeks of paid vacation, the French have their share of repose. In May, there is a holiday nearly every week, so be prepared for stores, banks, and museums to shut their doors for days at a time. Be sure to **call museums, restaurants, and hotels in advance to make sure they will be open.**

Dates in 2001 and 2002: January 1 (New Year's Day); April 15, March 31 (Easter Monday); May 1 (Labor Day); May 8 (VE Day); May 24, May 9 (Ascension); June 3, May 19 (Pentecost Monday); July 14 (Bastille Day); August 15 (Assumption); November 1 (All Saints); November 11 (Armistice); December 25 (Christmas).

It's also useful to bear in mind France's school vacations, which tend to unleash hordes of families and *classes de mer* (school trips to the coast) on museums, castles, and family hotels. School vacations are divided by region and are spread out over about three weeks in late October–November, Christmas–New Year's, again in February, and finally in April.

INSURANCE

The most useful travel-insurance plan is a comprehensive policy that includes coverage for trip cancellation and interruption, default, trip delay, and medical expenses (with a waiver for preexisting conditions).

Without insurance you will lose all or most of your money if you cancel your trip, regardless of the reason. Default insurance covers you if your tour operator, airline, or cruise line goes out of business. Trip-delay covers expenses that arise because of bad weather or mechanical delays. Study the fine print when comparing policies.

If you're traveling internationally, a key component of travel insurance is coverage for medical bills incurred if you get sick on the road. Such expenses are not generally covered by Medicare or private policies. U.K. residents can buy a travel-insurance policy valid for most vacations taken during the year in which it's purchased (but check preexisting-condition coverage). British and Australian citizens need extra medical coverage when traveling overseas.

Always **buy travel policies directly from the insurance company**; if you buy them from a cruise line, airline, or tour operator that goes out of business you probably will not be covered for the agency or operator's default, a major risk. Before making any purchase, **review your existing health and home-owner's policies** to find what they cover away from home.

➤ TRAVEL INSURERS: In the U.S.: **Access America** (⊠ 6600 W. Broad St., Richmond, VA 23230, ☎ 804/285–3300 or 800/284–8300, FAX 804/673–1586, www.previewtravel.com), **Travel Guard International** (⊠ 1145 Clark St., Stevens Point, WI 54481, ☎ 715/345–0505 or 800/826–1300, FAX 800/955–8785, www.noelgroup.com).

➤ INSURANCE INFORMATION: In the U.K.: **Association of British Insurers** (⊠ 51–55 Gresham St., London EC2V 7HQ, U.K., ☎ 020/7600–3333, FAX 020/7696–8999, info@abi.org.uk, www.abi.org.uk). In Canada: **Voyager Insurance** (⊠ 44 Peel Center Dr., Brampton, Ontario L6T 4M8, Canada, ☎ 905/791–8700, 800/668–4342 in Canada). In Australia: **Insurance Council of Australia** (☎ 03/9614–1077, FAX 03/9614–7924). In New Zealand: **Insurance Council of New Zealand** (⊠ Box 474, Wellington, New Zealand, ☎ 04/472–5230, FAX 04/473–3011, www.icnz.org.nz).

LANGUAGE

Although many French people, especially in major tourist areas, speak some English, it's important to remember that you are going to France and that people speak French. However, generally at least one person in most hotels can explain things to you in English (unless you are in a very rural area). Be patient, and speak English slowly.

The French may appear prickly at first to English-speaking visitors. But it usually helps if you **make an effort to speak a little French.** So even if your own French is terrible, try to master a few words. A simple, friendly "bonjour" (hello) will do, as will asking if the person you are greeting speaks English ("Parlez-vous anglais?").

LANGUAGES FOR TRAVELERS

A phrase book and language-tape set can help get you started.

➤ PHRASE BOOKS & LANGUAGE-TAPE SETS: *Fodor's French for Travelers* (☎ 800/733–3000 in the U.S.; 800/668–4247 in Canada; $7 for phrasebook, $16.95 for audio set).

LODGING

Provence and the Côte d'Azur may be the most accommodating region in France, with every kind of hotel, country inn, converted *mas* (Provençal farmhouse), luxury palace, bed-and-breakfast, and vacation rental imaginable. Consider the kind of vacation you want to spend—going native in a country *gîte* (rental house), being pampered in a luxury penthouse over the Mediterranean in Cannes, or getting to know the locals in a cozy B&B. Then check the Fodor's recommendations in each chapter, or contact the local tourist offices for more specific information.

The lodgings we list are the cream of the crop in each price category. We always list the facilities that are available—but we don't specify whether they cost extra: when pricing accommodations, always ask what's included and what costs extra. Properties marked ✕⊡ are lodging establishments whose restaurants warrant a special trip.

APARTMENT & VILLA RENTALS

If you want a home base that's roomy enough for a family or group and comes with cooking facilities, **con-**

sider a furnished rental. Renting an apartment or a *gîte rural*—a furnished house in the country—for a week or month can save you money if you're traveling with family or with a group. It's possible to even rent quite luxurious properties.

The national rental network, the Fédération Nationale des Gîtes de France, rents rural homes with regional flavor, often restored farmhouses or village row houses in pretty country settings (☞ Close-Up: "The Gîte Way," *in* Chapter 2) . In fact, the system grew out of a subsidized movement to salvage wonderful old houses falling to ruin. Gîtes-de-France are nearly always maintained by on-site owners, who greet you on your arrival and provide information on groceries, doctors, and nearby attractions.

A nationwide catalogue (105 francs/€16) is available from the Fédération Nationale des Gîtes de France listing gîtes ruraux for rent. Called "Nouveaux Gîtes Ruraux," the catalogue only lists the newest additions to the network because a comprehensive nationwide listing of all gîtes wouldn't fit between two covers. If you know what region you want to stay in, contact the departmental branch directly and order a photo catalogue that lists every property. If you specify which dates you plan to visit, the office will narrow down the choice to rentals available for those days. ☞ Vacation Rentals *in* A to Z sections of each chapter for how to contact regional offices.

Individual tourist offices often publish lists of *locations meublés* (furnished rentals); these are often inspected by the tourist office and rated by comfort standards. Usually they are booked directly through the individual owner, which generally requires some knowledge of French. Rentals that are not classified or rated by the tourist office should be undertaken with trepidation, and can fall well below your minimum standard of comfort.

Vacation rentals in France always book from Saturday to Saturday (with some offering weekend rates off-season). Most do not include bed linens and towels, but make them available for an additional fee. Always check on policies on pets and children, and specify if you need an enclosed garden for toddlers, a washing machine, a fireplace, etc. If you plan to have overnight guests during your stay, let the owner know; there may be additional charges. Insurance restrictions prohibit loading in guests beyond the specified capacity.

➤ INTERNATIONAL AGENTS: **At Home Abroad** (✉ 405 E. 56th St., Suite 6H, New York, NY 10022, ☎ 212/421–9165, FAX 212/752–1591, athomabrod@aol.com, http://member. aol.com/athomabrod/index.html). **Drawbridge to Europe** (✉ 102 Granite St., Ashland, OR 97520, ☎ 541/482–7778 or 888/268–1148, FAX 541/482–7779, requests@ drawbridgetoeurope.com, www.drawbridgetoeurope.com). **Hideaways International** (✉ 767 Islington St., Portsmouth, NH 03801, ☎ 603/430–4433 or 800/843–4433, FAX 603/430–4444, www.hideaways. com; membership $99).

Hometours International (✉ Box 11503, Knoxville, TN 37939, ☎ 865/690–8484 or 800/367–4668, hometours@aol.com, http://thor.he.net/ áhometour/). **Interhome** (✉ 1990 N.E. 163rd St., Suite 110, N. Miami Beach, FL 33162, ☎ 305/940–2299 or 800/882–6864, FAX 305/940–2911, interhomeu@aol.com, www. interhome.com). **Vacation Home Rentals Worldwide** (✉ 235 Kensington Ave., Norwood, NJ 07648, ☎ 201/767–9393 or 800/633–3284, FAX 201/767–5510, vhrww@juno.com, www.vhrww.com). **Villanet** (✉ 7939 LakeView La., Mercer Island, WA 98040, ☎ 206/236–1740 or 800/964–1891, FAX 206/236–1741, info@rentavilla.com, www. rentavilla.com). **Villas and Apartments Abroad** (✉ 1270 Avenue of the Americas, 15th floor, New York, NY 10020, ☎ 212/897–5045 or 800/433–3020, FAX 212/897–5039, vaa@ altour.com, www.vaanyc.com).

➤ LOCAL AGENTS: **Gîtes de France** (✉ 59 rue St-Lazare, 75009 Paris Cedex 09, ☎ 01–49–70–75–75, FAX 01–42–81–28–53, www.gites–de–france.fr). **French Government Tourist Office** (☞ Visitor Information, *below*) is another source for information about vacation rentals.

B&BS

Bed-and-breakfasts, known in France as *chambres d'hôte,* are common in rural Provence, and less so along the Côte d'Azur. Check local tourist offices for details or contact Gîtes de France, the national vacation-lodging organization that lists B&Bs all over the country, from rustic to more luxurious. Often *table d'hôte* dinners (meals cooked by and eaten with the owners) can be arranged for an extra, fairly nominal fee. Note that in B&Bs, unlike hotels, it is more likely that the owners will only speak French. Staying in one may, however, give you more of an opportunity to meet French people.

➤ B&B GUIDES: **Karen Brown's France: Charming Bed & Breakfasts** and **Rivages Bed & Breakfasts of Character and Charm in France** available in bookstores or from Fodor's Travel Publications (☎ 800/ 533–6478).

➤ RESERVATION SERVICES: **Gîtes de France** (✉ 59 rue St-Lazare, 75009 Paris Cedex 09, ☎ 01–49–70–75–75, FAX 01–42–81–28–53); request the brochure, "Chambres d'Hôtes: Campagne, Mer et Montagne," which covers Provence, the Alps, and the Côte d'Azur.

CAMPING

French campsites have a good reputation for organization and amenities but are crowded in July and August. Many campsites welcome reservations, and in summer, it makes sense to book in advance. Most parks are closed from November 1st until April 1st, but it depends on the park, so make enquiries before setting out. The Fédération Française de Camping et de Caravaning publishes a guide to France's campsites (in French only); they'll send it to you for 102 francs/€16.

➤ CAMPING INFORMATION: **Fédération Française de Camping et de Caravaning** (✉ 78 rue de Rivoli, 75004 Paris, ☎ 01–42–72–84–08, www. camping-fr.com).

HOME EXCHANGES

If you would like to exchange your home for someone else's **join a home-exchange organization,** which will send you its updated listings of available exchanges for a year and will include your own listing in at least one of them. It's up to you to make specific arrangements.

➤ EXCHANGE CLUBS: **HomeLink International** (✉ Box 650, Key West, FL 33041, ☎ 305/294–7766 or 800/ 638–3841, FAX 305/294–1448; $88 per year). **Intervac U.S.** (✉ Box 590504, San Francisco, CA 94159, ☎ 800/756–4663, FAX 415/435–7440; $83 per year).

➤ EXCHANGE LISTINGS: **FUSAC** (✉ 26 rue Bénard, 75014 Paris, ☎ 01–56– 53–54–54; ✉ Box 115, Cooper Station, New York, NY, 10276, ☎ 212/929–2929).

HOSTELS

No matter what your age, you can **save on lodging costs by staying at hostels.** In some 5,000 locations in more than 70 countries around the world, Hostelling International (HI), the umbrella group for a number of national youth-hostel associations, offers single-sex, dorm-style beds and, at many hostels, rooms for couples and family accommodations. Membership in any HI national hostel association, open to travelers of all ages, allows you to stay in HI-affiliated hostels at member rates; one-year membership is about $25 for adults (C$26.75 in Canada, £9.30 in the U.K., $30 in Australia, and $30 in New Zealand); hostels run about $10–$25 per night. Members have priority if the hostel is full; they're also eligible for discounts around the world, even on rail and bus travel in some countries.

➤ BEST OPTIONS: **Relais International de la Jeunesse** (✉ bd. de la Garoupe, 06600 Cap d'Antibes, ☎ 04–93–61– 34–40, FAX 04–93–34–89–88). **HI Youth Hostel** (✉ 3 av. Marcel-Pagnol, 13100 Aix-en-Provence, ☎ 04– 42–20–15–99). **HI Youth Hostel** (✉ La Fontasse, 13260 Cassis, ☎ 04– 42–01–02–72). **Hameau Champfleury** (✉ 33 av. Eisenhower, Avignon, ☎ 04–90–85–35–02).**Clairvallon Relais International de la Jeunesse** (✉ 26 av. Scudéri, 06000 Nice, ☎ 04–93–81– 27–63, FAX 04–93–53–35–88).

➤ ORGANIZATIONS: **Hostelling International—American Youth Hostels**

(✉ 733 15th St. NW, Suite 840, Washington, DC 20005, ☎ 202/783–6161, FAX 202/783–6171, hiayhserv@hiayh.org, www.hiayh. org). **Hostelling International— Canada** (✉ 400–205 Catherine St., Ottawa, Ontario K2P 1C3, Canada, ☎ 613/237–7884, FAX 613/237–7868, info@hostellingintl.ca, www. hostellingintl.ca). **Youth Hostel Association of England and Wales** (✉ Trevelyan House, 8 St. Stephen's Hill, St. Albans, Hertfordshire AL1 2DY, U.K., ☎ 0870/8708808, FAX 01727/844126, customerservices@yha. org.uk, www.yha.org.uk). **Australian Youth Hostel Association** (✉ 10 Mallett St., Camperdown, NSW 2050, Australia, ☎ 02/9565–1699, FAX 02/9565–1325, www.yha.com.au). **Youth Hostels Association of New Zealand** (✉ Box 436, Christchurch, New Zealand, ☎ 03/379–9970, FAX 03/365–4476, info@yha.org.nz, www.yha.org.nz).

HOTELS

Hotels are officially classified from one-star to four-star-deluxe. Prices must, by law, be posted at the hotel entrance and should include taxes and service. Rates are always by room, not per person. Remember that in France the first floor is one floor up (our second floor), and the higher up you go the quieter the street noise will be.

You should always **check what bathroom facilities the price includes,** if any. Because replumbing drains is often prohibitive, if not impossible, old hotels may have added bathrooms—often with *douches* (showers), not *baignoires* (tubs)—to the guest rooms, but not toilets. If you want a private bathroom, state your preference for shower or tub—the latter always costs more. Unless otherwise noted, lodging listings in this book include a private bathroom with a shower *or* tub.

When making your reservation, **ask for a *grand lit* if you want a double bed.** The quality of accommodations, particularly in older properties and even in luxury hotels, can vary greatly from room to room, as hotels are often renovated floor by floor; **if you don't like the room you're given, ask to see another.**

If you're counting on air-conditioning you should **make sure, in advance, that your hotel room is *climatisé*** (air-conditioned). As the French generally haven't fallen in step with American tastes for cold air in a heat wave, air-conditioning is not a given, even at hotels in inland Provence far from sea breezes. If air-conditioning is not noted in a hotel review, don't assume there will be air-conditioning. And when you throw open the windows, **don't expect screens** (*moustiquaires*). Nowhere in Europe are they standard equipment, and the only exceptions are found occasionally in the Camargue marshlands, where mosquitoes are actually a problem.

Breakfast is not always included in the price, but you are sometimes expected to have it and are occasionally charged for it regardless. Make sure to inform the hotel if you are not going to be breakfasting there. In smaller rural hotels you may be expected to have your evening meal at the hotel, too.

Logis de France hotels are small and inexpensive and can be relied on for comfort, character, and regional cuisine. Look for its distinctive yellow and green sign. The Logis de France paperback guide is widely available in bookshops (100 francs/€15) or from Logis de France.

Relais & Châteaux, Small Luxury Hotels of the World, and Leading Hotels of the World are three prestigious international groups with numerous converted châteaux and manor houses among their members. Not as luxurious, but strong on charm, is the Châteaux et Hôtels Independents group, which, despite the name, has banded together and published its own catalog.

It's always a good idea to **make hotel reservations as far in advance as possible,** especially in late spring, summer, or fall. If you arrive without a reservation, however, the tourist office may be able to help.

➤ HOTEL DIRECTORIES: **Châteaux et Hôtels Independents** (✉ 12 rue Auber 75009 Paris, ☎ 01–40–07–00–20, FAX 01–40–07–00–30). **Leading Hotels of the World** (✉ 99 Park Ave., New York, NY 10016, ☎ 212/838–7874,

FAX 212/758–7367). **Logis de France** (✉ 83 av. d'Italie, 75013 Paris, ☎ 01–45–84–70–00, FAX 01–45–83–59–66). **Relais & Châteaux** (✉ 15 rue Galvani, 75017 Paris, ☎ 01–45–72–96–50 or 08–25–32–32–32, FAX 01–45–72–96–69; ✉ 11 E. 44th St., Suite 707, New York, NY 10017, ☎ 212/856–0115 or 800–735–2478, FAX 212/856–0193, www.relaischateaux.fr). **Small Luxury Hotels of the World** (✉ 1716 Banks St., Houston, TX 77098, ☎ 713/522–9512; 800/525–4800 in the U.S., FAX 713/524–7412; ✉ James House, Bridge St., Leatherhead, Surrey, KT22 7EP, England, ☎ 44/01372–361873, FAX 44/01372–361874).

MAIL & SHIPPING

In this book, the postal code precedes the city or town in French mailing addresses, in keeping with the way envelopes are addressed in France.

POSTAL RATES

Letters and postcards to the United States and Canada cost 4.40 francs/67 European cents (about 75¢) for 20 grams. Letters and postcards to the United Kingdom cost 3 francs/50 European cents (about 33p) for up to 20 grams. Letters and postcards within France and the rest of Europe cost 3 francs/50 European cents. Stamps can be bought in post offices (La Poste) and cafés sporting a red TABAC sign outside.

RECEIVING MAIL

If you're uncertain where you'll be staying, **have mail sent to the local post office,** addressed as "poste restante," or to American Express, but remember that during peak seasons, American Express may refuse to accept mail. Bring your passport along to collect your mail.

MONEY MATTERS

The following prices are to give you an idea of costs. Note that it is less expensive to eat or drink standing at a café or bar counter than it is to sit at a table. Two prices are listed, *au comptoir* (at the counter) and *à salle* (at a table). Coffee in a bar: 6 francs to 7 francs/91 European cents to €1.07 (standing), 10 francs to 30 francs/ €1.52 to €4.57 (seated); beer in a bar: 10 francs/€1.52 (standing), 15 francs to 40 francs/€2.29 to €6.10

(seated); Coca-Cola: 6 francs to 10 francs/91 European cents to €1.52 a can; ham sandwich: 15 francs to 25 francs/€2.29 to €3.81; one-mile taxi ride: 35 francs/€5.34; movie: 50 francs/€7.60 (sometimes 15%–35% less expensive on Monday and Wednesday); foreign newspaper: 10 francs to 15 francs/€1.52 to €2.29.

Prices throughout this guide are given for adults in francs and in euros; the euro prices have been estimated. Substantially reduced fees are almost always available for children, students, and senior citizens. For information on taxes, *see* Taxes, *below.*

ATMS

ATMs are fairly common in major cities and larger towns and are one of the easiest ways to get cash; don't, however, count on finding ATMs in smaller towns and very rural areas. Banks usually offer excellent, wholesale exchange rates through ATMs.

To get cash at ATMs in France, **your PIN must be four digits long.** You may have more luck with ATMs if you are using a credit card or a debit card that is also a Visa or MasterCard, rather than just your bank card. Note, too, that you may be charged by your bank for using ATMs overseas; inquire at your bank about charges.

Using a debit card (with a Visa or MasterCard symbol on it) makes it easier to find ATMs that you can use.

Before you go, it's a good idea to **get a list of ATM locations that you can use** in France from your bank.

CREDIT CARDS

Many restaurants and stores take both credit and debit cards, though there is often a 100-franc minimum.

Throughout this guide, the following abbreviations are used: AE, American Express; DC, Diner's Club; MC, MasterCard; and V, Visa.

➤ REPORTING LOST CARDS: **American Express,** ☎ 01–47–77–72–00. **Diner's Club,** ☎ 01–49–06–17–50. **MasterCard,** ☎ 0800/90–1387. **Visa,** ☎ 0800/90–1179.

CURRENCY

The main units of currency in France have been the franc (fr) and the centime, with bills in denominations of 20, 50, 100, 200, and 500 francs; coins of 1, 2, 5, 10, and 20 francs, and 5, 10, 20, and 50 centimes. From January 1, 2002, the single European Union (EU) currency, the euro, takes over. Under the euro system, there are eight coins: 2 and 1 euros, plus 1, 2, 5, 10, 20, and 50 cents. On all coins, one side has the value of the euro on it and the other side has the national symbol of one of the countries participating in monetary union. There are seven notes: 5, 10, 20, 50, 100, 200, and 500 euros. Notes are the same for all countries.

Transactions not involving cash already are being executed in euros. Remaining francs will stay in circulation up to July 1, 2002, but from January 1, 2002, participating European national currencies will no longer be listed on foreign-exchange markets. The rates of conversion between the euro and local currencies have already been fixed (6.55957 francs to 1 euro), eliminating commission charges in currency exchange.

At press time (autumn of 2000), the exchange rate was about 7.60 francs to US$1, 5.20 to C$1, 10.90 to the pound sterling, 4.20 to A$1, 3.20 to NZ$1, and 8.30 to the Irish punt. For the euro, the exchange rate was about €1.15 to US$1, 77 European cents to C$1, 62 European cents to A$1, 51 European cents to NZ$1, €1.66 to the pound sterling, and €1.27 to the Irish punt.

Slowly but surely, the euro has been becoming a part of daily European life; for every item purchased—be it a piece of gum or a car—the price, by law, must be listed in both francs and euros.

CURRENCY EXCHANGE

There is a variety of ways to exchange money, though you have greater options in major cities than in rural areas. In general, **go to the Banque de France for the best rates** of all the banks. However, banks don't always offer great exchange rates. There is a fee for exchanging currency, which will vary from bank to bank, but it is usually close to a 35-franc/€5.35 flat fee, plus 4%.

Another option is to compare rates between booths and banks and **look for exchange booths that clearly state "no commission."** If you are exchanging a large amount of money, you may be able to get a better deal; it's worth asking. Exchange booths in airports, train stations, hotels, and stores generally offer the worst rates, though you may find their hours more convenient.

Although fees charged for ATM transactions may be higher abroad than at home (you may want to check on this before leaving), ATM exchange rates are often excellent, because they are based on wholesale rates offered only by major banks. ATMs are also convenient and are found in large cities and towns, and in major airports and train stations (☞ ATMs, *above* for more information).

If you are concerned that you may not be able to use your bank or debit card at the airport or train station when you first arrive, or you want to avoid lines at airport or train station exchange booths, **get a bit of local currency before you leave home.**

➤ EXCHANGE SERVICES: **International Currency Express** (☎ 888/278–6628 for orders, www.foreignmoney.com). **Thomas Cook Currency Services** (☎ 800/287–7362 for telephone orders and retail locations, www.us.thomascook.com).

TRAVELER'S CHECKS

Do you need traveler's checks? It depends on where you're headed. If you're going to rural areas and small towns, go with cash; traveler's checks are best used in cities. Lost or stolen checks can usually be replaced within 24 hours. To ensure a speedy refund, buy your own traveler's checks—don't let someone else pay for them: irregularities like this can cause delays. The person who bought the checks should make the call to request a refund.

With the presence of banking machines in even the smallest Provençal towns, traveler's checks are fast becoming obsolete. Store clerks are often unwilling to deal with them, and even some banks now refuse to cash them. Add to this that you will be given a better exchange rate at an ATM, and you might want to consider other options.

OUTDOORS & SPORTS

Provence and the Côte d'Azur have no shortage of sports facilities. Seaside resorts are well equipped for water sports, such as windsurfing, waterskiing, diving, and jetskiing, and private and public beaches compete to please the crowds. In inland Provence, there are public swimming pools in almost every town.

Bicycling (☞ Bicycling, *above*) and hiking (☞ Hiking, *above*) are popular, especially in the Vaucluse and the hills behind the Côte d'Azur.

Équitation (horseback riding) is possible in many rural areas; a horseback tour of the Camargue is de rigeur. The rivers draining off the Alps offer excellent fishing (check locally for authorization rights), canoeing, and kayaking.

Tennis is phenomenally popular, and courts are everywhere. Try to find a typical *terre battue* (clay court) if you can.

The French are not so keen on jogging, but you'll have no difficulty locating a suitable local park or avenue.

Golf is probably the most popular sport along the coast, with dozens of slickly maintained, beautifully landscaped courses stretching from St-Tropez to Menton. *See* individual chapters for specific outdoor activities and sports listings.

PACKING

Although you'll usually have no trouble finding a baggage cart at the airport, luggage restrictions on international flights are tight and baggage carts at railroad stations are not always available, so **pack light.** Even hotel staffs are becoming less and less tolerant of heavy suitcases and heaps of luggage worthy of a *Queen Mary* crossing.

Over the years, casual dress has become more acceptable, although the resorts along the Côte d'Azur and in the Luberon and Aix-en-Provence are still synonymous with smart dressers and fashion-plates.

Jeans are very common, though they, too, are worn stylishly, with a nice button-down shirt, polo, or T-shirt without writing. Shorts, though longish per current trends, are now a popular item for the younger crowd in most cities. More and more people are wearing sneakers, although you may still stand out as a tourist with them on, especially if you wear them when you go out at night.

There is no need to wear a tie and jacket at most restaurants (unless specified), even fancy ones, though you should still try to look nice. Most casinos and upscale nightclubs along the Côte d'Azur, however, require jackets and ties.

For beach resorts, take a decent cover-up; wearing your bathing suit on the street is frowned upon.

Most of France is hot in the summer, cool in the winter. Since it rains all year round, **bring a raincoat and umbrella.** You'll need a sweater or warm jacket for the Mediterranean in winter, and you should also bring hats, scarves, and gloves.

If you are staying in budget hotels, **take along soap; many hotels either do not provide it or give you a very limited amount.** You might also want to bring a washcloth.

In your carry-on luggage, **pack an extra pair of eyeglasses or contact lenses** and **enough of any medication you take** to last the entire trip. You may also ask your doctor to write a spare prescription using the drug's generic name, since brand names may vary from country to country. In luggage to be checked, **never pack prescription drugs or valuables.** To avoid customs delays, carry medications in their original packaging. And don't forget to carry with you the addresses of offices that handle refunds of lost traveler's checks.

CHECKING LUGGAGE

How many carry-on bags you can bring with you is up to the airline. Most allow two, but not always, so make sure that everything you carry aboard will fit under your seat or in the overhead bin, and get to the gate early. Note that if you have a seat at the back of the plane, you'll probably board first, while the overhead bins are still empty.

If you are flying internationally, note that baggage allowances may be determined not by piece but by weight—generally 88 pounds (40 kilograms) in first class, 66 pounds (30 kilograms) in business class, and 44 pounds (20 kilograms) in economy.

Airline liability for baggage is limited to $1,250 per person on flights within the United States. On international flights it amounts to $9.07 per pound or $20 per kilogram for checked baggage (roughly $640 per 70-pound bag) and $400 per passenger for unchecked baggage. You can buy additional coverage at check-in for about $10 per $1,000 of coverage, but it excludes a rather extensive list of items, shown on your airline ticket.

Before departure, **itemize your bags' contents** and their worth, and label the bags with your name, address, and phone number. (If you use your home address, cover it so potential thieves can't see it readily.) Inside each bag, **pack a copy of your itinerary.** At check-in, **make sure that each bag is correctly tagged** with the destination airport's three-letter code. If your bags arrive damaged or fail to arrive at all, file a written report with the airline before leaving the airport.

PASSPORTS & VISAS

When traveling internationally, **carry your passport** even if you don't need one (it's always the best form of I.D.) and **make two photocopies of the data page** (one for someone at home and another for you, carried separately from your passport). If you lose your passport, promptly call the nearest embassy or consulate and the local police.

ENTERING FRANCE

All Australian, Canadian, New Zealand, U.K, and U.S. citizens, even infants, need only a valid passport to enter France for stays of up to 90 days.

PASSPORT OFFICES

The best time to apply for a passport or to renew is during the fall and winter. Before any trip, check your passport's expiration date, and, if necessary, renew it as soon as possible.

➤ AUSTRALIAN CITIZENS: **Australian Passport Office** (☏ 131–232, www.dfat.gov.au/passports).

➤ CANADIAN CITIZENS: **Passport Office** (☏ 819/994–3500; 800/567–6868 in Canada, www.dfait-maeci.gc.ca/passport).

➤ NEW ZEALAND CITIZENS: **New Zealand Passport Office** (☏ 04/494–0700, www.passports.govt.nz).

➤ U.K. CITIZENS: **London Passport Office** (☏ 0870/521–0410, www.ukpa.gov.uk) for fees and documentation requirements and to request an emergency passport.

➤ U.S. CITIZENS: **National Passport Information Center** (☏ 900/225–5674; calls are 35¢ per minute for automated service, $1.05 per minute for operator service; www.travel.state.gov/npicinfo.html).

REST ROOMS

Finding a *toilette* in Provence is not difficult—even the smallest bar will have a tiny, and usually clean, toilet. But you must be a paying customer to use the facilities. In larger towns and cities there are often public toilets with an attendant busily cleaning the rest room. The charge is between 1 and 2 francs/15 European cents to 30 cents, and is well worth it. Small villages have public toilets, usually next to the boules court, but one must be very brave to enter.

SAFETY

Car break-ins have become part of daily life in the south, especially in the isolated parking lots where hikers set off to explore for the day. Be especially careful around the marshes of the Camargue, the departure point for the Iles d'Hyères ferries, the rocky Esterel between Fréjus and Cannes, and the coastal path around St-Tropez: **take valuables with you and, if possible, leave your luggage at your hotel.**

Also beware of petty theft—purse snatching and pickpocketing. Use common sense: avoid pulling out a lot of money in public, and wear a handbag with long straps that you can sling across your body, bandolier-style, with a zippered compartment for your money and passport. It's also a good idea to wear a money belt. Men should keep their wallets up front, as safely tucked away as possible.

Although cities in Provence are safe during the day, one should take caution at night, especially in port towns such as Marseilles, Nice, and Toulon. Avignon also has a high crime rate, and tourists should be alert and walk purposefully through town at night.

Women traveling alone may find themselves subjected to a bit of cat-calling or whistling from time to time. The best reaction is no reaction.

SENIOR-CITIZEN TRAVEL

Older travelers to France can take advantage of many discounts, such as reduced admissions of 20%–50% to museums and movie theaters. Seniors 60 and older should **buy a Carte Vermeil,** which entitles the bearer to discounts on rail travel outside Paris (☞ Train Travel, *below*).

➤ EDUCATIONAL PROGRAMS: **Elderhostel** (✉ 75 Federal St., 3rd floor, Boston, MA 02110, ☎ 877/426–8056, ℻ 877/426–2166, www.elderhostel.org). **Interhostel** (✉ University of New Hampshire, 6 Garrison Ave., Durham, NH 03824, ☎ 603/862–1147 or 800/733–9753, ℻ 603/862–1113, learn.dce@unh.edu, www.learn.unh.edu).

SHOPPING

People don't usually bargain in shops where prices are clearly marked. But at outdoor and flea markets and in antiques stores, bargaining is a way of life. If you're thinking of buying several items, you've nothing to lose by cheerfully suggesting to the proprietor, *"Vous me faites un prix?"* ("How about a discount?").

A number of shops offer VAT taxes to foreign shoppers (☞ Taxes, *below*).

CLOTHING SIZES

To figure out the French equivalent of U.S. clothing and shoe sizes, do the following, simple calculations.

To change U.S. men's suit sizes to French suit sizes, add 10 to the U.S. suit size. For example, a U.S. size 42 is a French size 52.

French men's collar sizes vary in their relation to U.S. collar sizes. But you can get the approximate size by multiplying the U.S. collar size by 2 and adding 8. For example, a U.S. size 15 is a French size 38. A U.S. size 15½ is a French size 39 or 40.

French men's shoe sizes vary in their relation to U.S. shoe sizes. A U.S. men's size 7½ is a French size 40; an 8½ is a 41; a 9½ is a 42.

To change U.S. dress/coat/blouse sizes to French sizes, add 30 to the U.S. size. For example, a U.S. women's size 8 is a French size 38 and a U.S. size 10 is a French size 40.

To change U.S. women's shoe sizes to French shoe sizes, add approximately 31 to the U.S. shoe size. For example, a U.S. size 7 is a French size 38.

KEY DESTINATIONS

Markets in Provence are fabulous, the best markets days being Wednesday in St-Rémy; Tuesday, Thursday, and Saturday in Aix-en-Provence; and the antiques market on Sundays in L'Isle-sur-la-Sorgue. Many *artisanal* items can be found in the markets, such as olive oil soaps and soaps of varying fragrances, as well as mass-produced items such as fabrics which come in a multitude of colors and patterns inspired by the light and color of Provence. Upscale shopping is concentrated in the towns along the Côte d'Azur. Cannes' main street, La Croisette, is full of designer boutiques, as are smaller towns such as St. Tropez and Aix-en-Provence.

SMOKING

No-smoking signs and designated areas are slowly coming to Provence. Some upscale restaurants and brasseries now have no-smoking rooms, but often these postings are ignored by your fellow Provençal diners. Cafés are, and probably always will be, havens for smokers. Cigarettes are expensive in France, from 20 francs/€3.05 a pack, so smoking travelers may want to stock up at the duty-free before departure.

STUDENTS IN PROVENCE
AND THE CÔTE D'AZUR

There are a number of universities in Provence, but the two cities where the college-age population really stands out are Aix-en-Provence and Montpellier.

There are bargains for students holding a valid college or international student I.D. almost everywhere in the south of France, on train and plane fares, and for movie and museum tickets. So, **carry your valid university or international I.D. card with you at all times so you can get discounts.**

➤ I.D.s & SERVICES: **Council Travel** (CIEE; ✉ 205 E. 42nd St., 14th floor, New York, NY 10017, ☎ 212/822–2700 or 888/268–6245, FAX 212/822–2699, info@councilexchanges.org, www.councilexchanges.org) for mail orders only, in the U.S. **Travel Cuts** (✉ 187 College St., Toronto, Ontario M5T 1P7, Canada, ☎ 416/979–2406 or 800/667–2887 in Canada, www.travelcuts.com).

TAXES

All taxes must be included in posted prices in France. The initials TTC (*toutes taxes comprises*—taxes included) sometimes appear on price lists but, strictly speaking, are superfluous. By law, **restaurant and hotel prices must include 20.6% taxes and a service charge.** If they show up as extra charges on your bill, complain.

VALUE-ADDED TAX

A number of shops offer VAT refunds to foreign shoppers. You are entitled to an Export Discount of 20.6%, depending on the item purchased, but it is often applicable only if your purchases in the same store reach a minimum of 2,800 francs/€427 (for U.K. and EU residents) or 1,200 francs/€183 (other residents, including U.S. and Canadian residents). Remember to **ask for the refund,** as some stores—especially larger ones—offer the service only upon request.

Global Refund is a V.A.T. refund service that makes getting your money back hassle-free. The service is available Europe-wide at 130,000 affiliated stores. In participating stores, **ask for the Global Refund refund form** (called a Shopping Cheque). Have it stamped like any customs form by customs officials when you leave the European Union (be ready to show customs officials what you've bought). Then take the form to one of the more than 700 Global Refund counters—conveniently located at every major airport and border crossing—and your money will be refunded on the spot in the form of cash, check, or a refund to your credit-card account (minus a small percentage for processing).

➤ V.A.T. REFUNDS: **Global Refund** (✉ 707 Summer St., Stamford, CT 06901, ☎ 800/566–9828, FAX 203/674–8709, taxfree@us.globalrefund.com, www.globalrefund.com).

TELEPHONES

AREA & COUNTRY CODES

The country code for France is 33. All phone numbers in France have a two-digit prefix determined by zone: Paris and the Ile de France, 01; the northwest, 02; the northeast, 03; the southeast, 04; and the southwest, 05. Numbers beginning with 08 are either toll-free or toll calls (with an additional charge on top of making the call).

DIRECTORY & OPERATOR ASSISTANCE

To find a number in France, **dial 12 for information.** For international inquiries, dial 00–33–12 plus 11 for the U.S., 44 for the U.K.

Another source of information is the Minitel, an on-line network similar to the Internet. You can find one—they look like a small computer terminal—in most post offices. Available (free for the first three minutes) is an on-line phone book covering the entire country. To find simple telephone information in France, hit the *appel* (call) key, then the number 3611. When prompted, type the name you are looking for and hit *envoi* (return). This information number is also useful for tracking down services: choose *activité* (activity), tap in *piscine* (swimming pool), then Chartres, for example, and it will give you a list of all the pools in Chartres. Go to other lines or pages by hitting the *suite* (next) key. Newer models will connect automatically when you hit the book-icon key. To disconnect, hit *fin* (end).

INTERNATIONAL CALLS FROM FRANCE

To call out of France, dial 00 and wait for the tone, then dial the country code (1 for the United States and Canada, 44 for the United Kingdom, 61 for Australia, 64 for New Zealand) and the area code (minus any initial 0) and number. Expect to be overcharged if you call from your hotel.

LOCAL CALLS

To make calls in the same city or town, or in the same region, dial the full 10-digit number.

LONG-DISTANCE CALLS

To call any region in France from another region, dial the full 10-digit number (including the two-digit prefix).

LONG-DISTANCE SERVICES

AT&T, MCI, and Sprint access codes make calling long distance relatively convenient, but you may find the local access number blocked in many hotel rooms. First ask the hotel operator to connect you. If the hotel operator balks, ask for an international operator, or dial the international operator yourself. One way to improve your odds of getting connected to your long-distance carrier is to travel with more than one company's calling card (a hotel may block Sprint, for example, but not MCI). If all else fails, call from a pay phone.

➤ ACCESS CODES: **AT&T Direct** (☏ 08–00–99–00–11; 800/874–4000 for information). **MCI Call USA** (☏ 08–00–99–00–19; 800/444–4444 for information). **Sprint Express** (☏ 08–00–99–00–87; 800/793–1153 for information).

PHONE CARDS

Most French pay phones are operated by *télécartes* (phone cards), which you can buy from post offices, métro stations, and some tabacs (tobacco shops) for a cost of 40.60 francs/€6.19 for 50 units and 97.50 francs/€14.86 for 120. Coin-operated pay phones are scarce, existing only in cafés (who can set their own rates) and post offices. Phone cards are accepted everywhere else. The easiest but most expensive way to phone is to use your own Visa card, which is accepted in all phone booths and works like a télécarte.

PUBLIC PHONES

Telephone booths can almost always be found at post offices, and often in

cafés. A local call costs 74 centimes/11 European cents for every three minutes; half-price rates apply weekdays between 9:30 PM and 8 AM, from 1:30 PM Saturday, and all day Sunday.

TIME

The time difference between New York and France is 6 hours; when it's 1 PM in New York, it's 7 PM in France. France is 1 hour ahead of London. The time difference between France and Sydney is 8 to 9 hours, depending on when daylight savings time is or is not in effect.

TIPPING

The French have a clear idea of when they should be tipped. Bills in bars and restaurants include service, but it is customary to **round out your bill with some small change** unless you're dissatisfied. The amount of this varies: anywhere from 50 centimes/8 European cents if you've merely bought a beer, to 10 francs/€1.50 after a meal. Tip taxi drivers and hairdressers about 10%. In some theaters and hotels, coat check attendants may expect nothing (if there is a sign saying POURBOIRE INTERDIT—tips forbidden); otherwise give them 2 francs to 5 francs/30 European cents to 76 cents. Washroom attendants usually get 2 francs, though the sum is often posted.

If you stay in a hotel for more than two or three days, it is customary to leave something for the chambermaid—about 10 francs/€1.50 per day. In expensive hotels you may well call on the services of a baggage porter (bell boy) and hotel porter and possibly the telephone receptionist. All expect a tip: Plan on about 10 francs per item for the baggage boy, but the other tips will depend on how much you've used their services—common sense must guide you here. In hotels that provide room service, give 5 francs/76 European cents to the waiter (this does not apply to breakfast served in your room). If the chambermaid does some pressing or laundering for you, give her 5 francs on top of the charge made.

Gas-station attendants get nothing for gas or oil, and 5 or 10 francs/76 cents or €1.50 for checking tires. Train and airport porters get a fixed 6 to 10 francs/91 cents to €1.50 per bag, but you're better off getting your own baggage cart if you can (a 10-franc coin—refundable—has been necessary in train stations only). Museum guides should get 5 to 10 francs/76 cents to €1.50 after a guided tour, and it is standard practice to tip tour guides (and bus drivers) 10 francs or more after an excursion, depending on its length.

TOURS & PACKAGES

Because everything is prearranged on a prepackaged tour or independent vacation, you'll spend less time planning—and often get it all at a good price.

BOOKING WITH AN AGENT

Travel agents are excellent resources. But it's a good idea to collect brochures from several agencies as some agents' suggestions may be influenced by relationships with tour and package firms that reward them for volume sales. If you have a special interest, **find an agent with expertise in that area**; ASTA (☞ Travel Agencies, *below*) has a database of specialists worldwide.

Make sure your travel agent knows the accommodations and other services of the place they're recommending. Ask about the hotel's location, room size, beds, and whether it has a pool, room service, or programs for children, if you care about these. Has your agent been there in person or sent others whom you can contact?

Do some homework on your own, too: local tourism boards can provide information about lesser-known and small-niche operators, some of which may sell only direct.

BUYER BEWARE

Each year consumers are stranded or lose their money when tour operators—even large ones with excellent reputations—go out of business. So **check out the operator.** Ask several travel agents about its reputation, and try to **book with a company that has a consumer-protection program.** (Look for information in the company's brochure.) In the United States, members of the National Tour Association and the United States Tour Operators Association are required to set aside

funds to cover your payments and travel arrangements in the event that the company defaults. It's also a good idea to choose a company that participates in the American Society of Travel Agents' Tour Operator Program (TOP); ASTA will act as mediator in any disputes between you and your tour operator.

Remember that the more your package or tour includes the better you can predict the ultimate cost of your vacation. Make sure you know exactly what is covered, and **beware of hidden costs.** Are taxes, tips, and transfers included? Entertainment and excursions? These can add up.

➤ TOUR-OPERATOR RECOMMENDATIONS: **American Society of Travel Agents** (☞ Travel Agencies, *below*). **National Tour Association** (NTA; ⊠ 546 E. Main St., Lexington, KY 40508, ☎ 859/226–4444 or 800/682–8886, www.ntaonline.com). **United States Tour Operators Association** (USTOA; ⊠ 342 Madison Ave., Suite 1522, New York, NY 10173, ☎ 212/599–6599 or 800/468–7862, ℻ 212/599–6744, ustoa@aol.com, www.ustoa.com).

GROUP TOURS

Among companies that sell tours to Provence and the Riviera, the following are nationally known, have a proven reputation, and offer plenty of options. The classifications used below represent different price categories, and you'll probably encounter these terms when talking to a travel agent or tour operator. The key difference is usually in accommodations, which run from budget to better, and better-yet to best.

➤ SUPER-DELUXE: **Abercrombie & Kent** (⊠ 1520 Kensington Rd., Oak Brook, IL 60521-2141, ☎ 630/954–2944 or 800/323–7308, ℻ 630/954–3324, www.abercrombiekent.com). **Travcoa** (⊠ Box 2630, 2350 S.E. Bristol St., Newport Beach, CA 92660, ☎ 949/476–2800 or 800/992–2003, ℻ 949/476–2538, www.travcoa.com).

➤ DELUXE: **Maupintour** (⊠ 1515 St. Andrews Dr., Lawrence, KS 66047, ☎ 785/843–1211 or 800/255–4266, ℻ 785/843–8351, www.maupintour.com). **Tauck Tours** (⊠

Box 5027, 276 Post Rd. W, Westport, CT 06881-5027, ☎ 203/226–6911 or 800/468–2825, FAX 203/221–6866).

➤ FIRST-CLASS: **Caravan Tours** (✉ 401 N. Michigan Ave., Chicago, IL 60611, ☎ 312/321–9800 or 800/227–2826, FAX 312/321–9845). **Collette Tours** (✉ 162 Middle St., Pawtucket, RI 02860, ☎ 401/728–3805 or 800/340–5158, FAX 401/728–4745, www.collettetours.com). **Insight International Tours** (✉ 745 Atlantic Ave., #720, Boston, MA 02111, ☎ 617/482–2000 or 800/582–8380, FAX 617/482–2884 or 800/622–5015, www.insighttours.com). **Trafalgar Tours** (✉ 11 E. 26th St., New York, NY 10010, ☎ 212/689–8977 or 800/854–0103, FAX 800/457–6644, www. trafalgartours.com).

➤ BUDGET: **Tours of Provence** (1700 Glen Bar Sq., Denver, CO 80215, ☎ 303/275–9899, ww.toursofprovence. com). **Trafalgar** (☞ *above*).

PACKAGES

Like group tours, independent vacation packages are available from major tour operators and airlines. The companies listed below offer vacation packages in a broad price range.

➤ AIR/HOTEL: **American Airlines Vacations** (☎ 800/321–2121 or 800/427–3311, www.aavacations.com). **DER Travel Services** (✉ 9501 W. Devon Ave., Rosemont, IL 60018, ☎ 800/937–1235, FAX 847/692–4141; 800/282–7474; 800/860–9944 for brochures, www.dertravel.com). **4th Dimension Tours** (✉ 1150 NW 72nd Ave., #250, Miami, FL 33126, ☎ 305/279–0014 or 800/644–0438, FAX 305/273–9777). **Untours** (✉ Box 405, Media, PA 19063, ☎ 888/868–6871, FAX 610/565–5142, www.untours.com).

➤ FROM THE U.K.: **Cresta Holidays** (✉ Tabley Ct., Victoria St., Altrincham, Cheshire WA14 1EZ, ☎ 0870/161–0910 or 0870/161–0909, www.crestaholidays.co.uk) for hotel and apartment holidays. **Invitation to France** (✉ 161 Fulham Rd., London SW3 6SN, ☎ 020/7581–8946, FAX 020/7225–2491) for châteaux and country-house hotels.

THEME TRIPS

➤ ART AND ARCHITECTURE: **Architectour** (601 California St., 16th Fl., San Francisco, CA 94108, ☎ 415/788–0544 or 800/272–8808, FAX 415/788–0554, www.arctour.com). **Endless Beginnings Tours** (✉ 12650 Sabre Springs Pkwy., Ste. 207-105, San Diego, CA 92128, ☎ 858/566–4166 or 800/822–7855, FAX 858/679–5376).

➤ BICYCLING: **Backroads** (✉ 801 Cedar St., Berkeley, CA 94710-1800, ☎ 510/527–1555 or 800/462–2848, FAX 510/527–1444, www.backroads. com). **Bike Riders Tours** (✉ Box 130254, Boston, MA 02113, ☎ 800/245–2229 or 800/473–7040, www.bikeriderstours.com). **Butterfield & Robinson** (✉ 70 Bond St., Toronto, Ontario, Canada M5B 1X3, ☎ 416/864–1354 or 800/678–1147, FAX 416/864–0541, www. butterfieldandrobinson.com). **Chateaux Bike Tours** (✉ Box 5706, Denver, CO 80217, ☎ 303/393–6910 or 800/678–2453, FAX 303/393–6801, www.chateauxbiketours.com). **Euro-Bike Tours** (✉ Box 990, De Kalb, IL 60115, ☎ 815/758–8851 or 800/321–6060, www.eurobike.com). **Europeds** (✉ 761 Lighthouse Ave., Monterey, CA 93940, ☎ 800/321–9552, FAX 408/655–4501, www. europeds.com). **Himalayan Travel** (✉ 110 Prospect St., Stamford, CT 06901, ☎ 203/359–3711 or 800/225–2380, FAX 203/359–3669). **Mountain Travel-Sobek** (✉ 6420 Fairmount Ave., El Cerrito, CA 94530, ☎ 510/527–8100 or 888/687–6235; 44/1494/44–8901 in the U.K.; FAX 510/525–7710; 44/1494/46–5526 in the U.K., www.mtsobek. com). **Naturequest** (✉ 30872 S. Coast Hwy., PMB 185, Laguna Beach, CA 92651, ☎ 949/499–9561 or 800/369–3033, FAX 949/499–0812, www.naturequesttours.com). **Rocky Mountain Cycle Tours** (✉ 333 Baker St., Nelson, BC, Canada V1L 4H6, ☎ 604/354–1241 or 800/661–2453, FAX 604/898–8489). **Tours of Provence** (☞ Group Tours, *above*). **Vermont Bicycle Touring** (✉ Box 711, Bristol, VT, 05443-0711, ☎ 802/453–4811 or 800/245–3868, FAX 802/453–4806).

➤ CUSTOMIZED PACKAGES: **Abercrombie & Kent** (☞ Group Tours, *above*). **Five Star Touring** (✉ 60 E. 42nd St.,

#612, New York, NY 10165, ☎ 212/818–9140 or 800/792–7827, FAX 212/818–9142). **French Experience** (✉ 370 Lexington Ave., Suite 812, New York, NY 10017, ☎ 212/986–1115, FAX 212/986–3808, www.frenchexperience.com).

➤ FOOD AND WINE: **Cuisine International** (✉ Box 25228, Dallas, TX 75225, ☎ 214/373–1161, FAX 214/373–1162, www.cuisineinternational.com). **European Culinary Adventures** (✉ 5 Ledgewood Way, Suite 6, Peabody, MA 01960, ☎ 978/535–5738 or 800/852–2625, FAX 978/535–5738). **France In Your Glass** (✉ 814 35th Ave., Seattle, WA 98122, ☎ 206/325–4324 or 800/578–0903, FAX 800/842–4618, www.inyourglass.com). **The International Kitchen** (✉ 55 E. Monroe, Suite 2840, Chicago, IL 60603, ☎ 312/726–4525 or 800/945–8606, FAX 312/803–1593, www.theinternationalkitchen.com). **Tours of Provence** (☞ Group Tours, *above*).

➤ GOLF: **Cresta Holidays** (☞ Packages, *above*). **Golf International** (✉ 14 E. 38th St., New York, NY 10016, ☎ 212/986–9176 or 800/833–1389, FAX 212/986–3720). **ITC and Golf Tours** (✉ 4134 Atlantic Ave., #205, Long Beach, CA 90807, ☎ 310/595–6905 or 800/257–4981).

➤ HOMES AND GARDENS: **Expo Garden Tours** (✉ 33 Fox Crossing, Litchfield, CT 06759, ☎ 203/938–0410 or 800/448–2685, FAX 860/567–0381, www.bostongardens.com/expogardentours).

➤ HORSEBACK RIDING: **Cross Country International Equestrian Vacations** (✉ Box 1170, Millbrook, NY 12545, ☎ 800/828–8768, FAX 914/677–6077, www.equestrianvacations.com). **Equitour FITS Equestrian** (✉ Box 807, Dubois, WY 82513, ☎ 307/455–3363 or 800/545–0019, FAX 307/455–2354, www.ridingtours.com).

➤ LEARNING: **IST Cultural Tours** (✉ 225 W. 34th St., New York, NY 10122, ☎ 212/563–1202 or 800/833–2111, FAX 212/594–6953, www.istculturaltours.com). **Smithsonian Study Tours and Seminars** (✉ 1100 Jefferson Dr. SW, Room 3045, MRC 702, Washington, DC 20560, ☎ 202/357–4700 or 877/338–8687, FAX 202/633–9250, www.smithsonianstudytours.si.edu).

➤ SPAS: **Great Spas of the World** (✉ 55 John St., New York, NY 10038, ☎ 212/267–5500 or 800/772–8463, FAX 212/889–8167, www.spatime.com). **Spa-Finders** (✉ 91 5th Ave., #301, New York, NY 10003-3039, ☎ 212/924–6800 or 800/255–7727, www.spafinders.com). **Spa Trek Travel** (✉ 475 Park Ave. S, 34th fl., New York, NY 10016, ☎ 212/779–3480 or 800/272–3480, FAX 212/779–3471).

➤ TOUR RESOURCES: **Maison de la France** (☞ Visitor Information, *below*) publishes many brochures on theme trips in France including "In the Footsteps of the Painters of Light in Provence" and "France for the Jewish Traveler." **Travel Contacts** (✉ Box 173, Camberley, GU15 1YE, England, ☎ (44)1252/68–1093, FAX (44)1252/68–1095) represents over 120 tour operators in Europe.

➤ WALKING: **Abercrombie & Kent** (☞ Group Tours, *above*). **Backroads** (☞ Bicycling, *above*). **Butterfield & Robinson** (☞ Bicycling, *above*). **Country Walkers** (✉ Box 180, Waterbury, VT 05676, ☎ 802/244–1387 or 800/464–9255, FAX 802/244–5661 www.gorp.com/countrywalkers). **Euro-Bike Tours** (☞ Bicycling, *above*). **Europeds** (☞ Bicycling, *above*). **Himalayan Travel** (☞ Bicycling, *above*). **Maupintour** (Group Tours, *above*). **Mountain Travel-Sobek** (☞ Bicycling,, *above*). **Naturequest** (☞ Bicycling, *above*). **Overseas Adventure Travel** (✉ 625 Mt. Auburn St., Cambridge, MA 02138, ☎ 800/493–6824, FAX 617/876–0455, www.oattravel.com). **Wilderness Travel** (✉ 1102 Ninth St., Berkeley, CA 94710, ☎ 510/558–2488 or 800/368–2794, FAX 510/558–2489 www.wildernesstravel.com).

➤ YACHT CHARTERS: **Lynn Jachney Charters** (✉ Box 302, Marblehead, MA 01945, ☎ 617/639–0787 or 800/223–2050, FAX 617/639–0216, www.lynnjachneycharters.com). **The Moorings** (✉ 19345 U.S. Hwy. 19 N, 4th fl., Clearwater, FL 34624, ☎ 888/952–8420 or 800/535–7289, www.moorings.com. **Ocean Voyages** (✉ 1709 Bridgeway, Sausalito, CA 94965, ☎ 415/332–4681 or 800/

299–4444, FAX 415/332–7460, www. oceanvoyages.com).

TRAIN TRAVEL

The SNCF is recognized as Europe's best national rail service: it's fast, punctual, comfortable, and comprehensive. You can get to Provence and the coast from all points west, north, and east, though lines out of Paris are by far the most direct. There are various options: local trains, overnight trains with sleeping accommodations, and the high-speed TGV, the *Trains à Grande Vitesse* (High-Speed Trains).

For overnight accommodations, you have the choice between high-priced *wagons-lits* (sleeping cars) and affordable *couchettes* (bunks, six to a compartment in second class, four to a compartment in first, with sheets and pillow provided, priced at around 90 francs/€14).

The TGVs average 255 kph/160 mph on the Lyon/southeast line, but after Valence, they slow to local-train speeds. It's still the fastest way south—you can get from Paris to Avignon in 3½ hours, and from Paris to Nice in 6½ hours. As with other main-line trains, a small supplement may be assessed during peak hours. The laying of high-speed rails from Valence to Avignon and on to Nice will cut travel time considerably; the project is supposed to be completed by June of 2001. All trains into Provence from Paris leave from the Gare du Lyon station.

Certain models of the TGV, called a "train duplex," offer luxurious, state-of-the-art comfort, with double-decker seating and panoramic views. When one of these passes along the coast—especially from Nice to Menton—it makes for a dramatic sightseeing excursion, though it pokes along at a local-train snail's pace. Ask about duplex trains when you're connecting from one coastal city to another (Marseille–Toulon–Fréjus–Cannes–Nice–Menton).

Once you're in the south, though, choose your home base carefully. Places in hill country and the mountains—the Luberon, the Alpilles, and the backcountry hills behind Nice—are not accessible by train, and you'll have to get around by bus or rental car.

If you are traveling from Paris or any other terminus, **get to the station half an hour before departure** to ensure that you'll have a good seat.

Before boarding, you must **punch your ticket (but not EurailPass) in one of the orange machines** at the entrance to the platforms, or else the ticket collector will fine you 100 francs/€15 on the spot.

CLASSES

Traveling first class can cost about 50 percent more than second class, but, with the exception of wider seats, you won't get many more amenities. You'll still need to purchase food, although in first class you can order a hot meal, served on china, if you're willing to pay quite a high price for it.

CUTTING COSTS

If you plan to travel outside of Paris by train, **consider purchasing a France Rail Pass,** which allows three days of unlimited train travel in a one-month period. Prices begin at $130 for two adults traveling together in second class and $165 second class for a solo traveler. First-class rates are $156 for two adults and $195 for a solo traveler. Additional days may be added for $30 a day in either class. Other options include the France Rail 'n Drive Pass (combining rail and rental car), France Rail 'n Fly Pass (rail travel and one air travel journey within France), and the France Fly Rail 'n Drive Pass (a rail, air, and rental car program all in one).

France is one of 17 countries in which you can **use EurailPasses,** which provide unlimited first-class rail travel, in all of the participating countries, for the duration of the pass. If you plan to rack up the miles, get a standard pass. These are available for 15 days ($522), 21 days ($678), one month ($838), two months ($1,148), and three months ($1,468). If your plans call for only limited train travel, **look into a Europass,** which costs less money than a EurailPass. Unlike EurailPasses, however, you get a limited number of travel days, in a limited number of countries, during a specified time period. For example, a two-month Europass ($316) allows between 5 and 15 days of rail travel, but costs $200 less than the least expensive EurailPass. Keep in mind, however, that the Europass is good only in France, Germany, Italy, Spain, and Switzerland, and the number of countries you can visit is further limited by the type of pass you buy.

In addition to standard EurailPasses, **ask about special rail-pass plans.** Among these are the Eurail Youthpass (for those under age 26), the Eurail Saverpass (which gives a discount for two or more people traveling together), a Eurail Flexipass (which allows a certain number of travel days within a set period), the Euraildrive Pass and the Europass Drive (train and rental car).

Whichever of the above you choose, remember that you must **purchase your pass at home before leaving for Europe.**

Don't assume that your rail pass guarantee you a seat on the train you wish to ride. You need to **book seats ahead even if you are using a rail pass;** seat reservations are required on high-speed trains, and are a good idea on trains that may be crowded—particularly in summer on popular routes. You will also need a reservation for sleeping accommodations.

➤ TICKET AGENTS: Eurail- and Europasses are available through travel agents and a few authorized organizations. **CIT Tours Corp.** (⊠ 15 West 44th St., 10th floor, New York, NY 10036, ☎ 800/248–7245 for rail; 800/248–8687 for tours and hotels). **DER Travel Services** (⊠ 9501 W. Devon Ave., Rosemont, IL 60018, ☎ 800/782–2424). **Rail Europe** (⊠ 226–230 Westchester Ave., White Plains, NY 10604, ☎ 800/438–7245, ℻ 800/432–1329; ⊠ 2087 Dundas E., Suite 105, Mississauga, Ontario L4X 1M2, ☎ 905/602–4195).

FARES & SCHEDULES

If you know what station you'll depart from, you can get a free train schedule there (while supplies last), or you can access the new multilingual computerized schedule information network at any Paris station and at larger stations (Marseille and Nice). You can also make reservations and buy your ticket while at the computer.

➤ TRAIN INFORMATION: SNCF (☎ 08–36–35–35–35); note that a per minute charge is assessed.

➤ WEB SITES: **Eurail/Eurostar** (www. eurail.com/). SNCF (www.sncf.fr/ indexe.htm).

FRENCH RAIL PASSES

SNCF offers a number of discount rail passes available only for purchase in France. When traveling together, **two people (who don't have to be a couple) can save money with the Prix Découverte à Deux.** You'll get a 25% discount during "périodes bleus" (blue periods; weekdays and not on or near any holidays). Note that you have to be with the person you said you would be traveling with.

You can **get a reduced fare if you are a senior citizen (over 60)** with the Carte Vermeil. There are two options: The first, the Carte Vermeil Quatre Temps, costs 143 francs/€21.80 and gives you a reduction on four trips of 50% off in the blue periods and 20% off during the more crowded "périodes blanches" (white periods; weekends or on or around holidays). The second, the Carte Vermeil Plein Temps, is 279 francs/€42.50 and allows you, for one year, an unlimited number of 30% reductions on trips within France and a 30% discount on trips outside of France.

With the Carte Kiwi, **children under 16 can get 25–50% off** four trips for 285 francs/€43, or for a full year of travel for 444 francs/€68. There's a wonderful bonus, too: up to four accompanying passengers, whether blood relatives or not, get the discount, too.

If you purchase an individual ticket from SNCF in France and you're under 26, you will automatically get a 25% reduction (a valid ID, such as an ISIC card or your passport, is necessary). If you're going to be using the train quite a bit during your stay in France and **if you're under 26, consider buying the Carte 12–25** (270 francs/€41), which offers unlimited 50% reductions for one year (provided that there's space available at that price, otherwise you'll just get the standard 25% discount).

If you don't benefit from any of these reductions and **if you plan on traveling at least 1,000 km (620 mi) round-trip (including several stops), look into purchasing a Billet Séjour.** This ticket gives you a 25% reduction if you stay over a Sunday and if you travel only during blue periods. It may be a major organizational feat, but you can save a lot of cash this way.

RESERVATIONS

You must **always make a seat reservation for the TGV**—easily obtained at the ticket window or from an automatic machine. Seat reservations are reassuring but seldom necessary on other main-line French trains, except at certain busy holiday times.

TRANSPORTATION AROUND PROVENCE AND THE CÔTE D'AZUR

It's possible to have a satisfying initiation to this broad region by train alone. There are sweeping, comprehensive connections all the way from Montpellier to Avignon to Marseille and on to the full length of the Italian coast. There are good regional bus networks, too, that connect out of train stations, but they're not very efficient for village-hopping and multistop sightseeing, as their schedules rarely intersect with yours. And sooner or later you may feel restless and want to burrow inland a bit, and here the trains are much more limited. A rental car is an obvious solution, but if you've flown into Paris, it's a long drive south (7 hours). For an extended vacation in the region, a rail-drive pass allows you to cover a few direct rail trajectories between bases, then take a rental car onto the back roads and byways. Or you could fly to the south of France and rent a car from the airport. If you really want to sit back and let someone else do the work, consider a holiday bus excursion, where the tour company books all lodging and meals and guides you from sight to sight.

TRAVEL AGENCIES

A good travel agent puts your needs first. Look for an agency that has been in business at least five years, emphasizes customer service, and has someone on staff who specializes in your destination. In addition, **make sure the agency belongs to a professional trade organization.** The American Society of Travel Agents (ASTA), with 27,000 agents in some 170 countries, is the largest and most influential in the field. Operating under the motto "Integrity in Travel," it maintains and enforces a strict code of ethics and will step in to help mediate any agent-client disputes if necessary. ASTA also maintains a Web site that includes a directory of agents. (If a travel agency is also acting as your tour operator, *see* Buyer Beware *in* Tours & Packages, *above*.)

➤ LOCAL AGENT REFERRALS: **American Society of Travel Agents** (ASTA; ☎ 800/965–2782 24-hr hot line, FAX 703/684–8319, www.astanet. com). **Association of British Travel Agents** (⊠ 68–71 Newman St., London W1P 4AH, U.K., ☎ 020/7637–2444, FAX 020/7637–0713, information£abta.co.uk, www. abtanet.com). **Association of Canadian Travel Agents** (⊠ 1729 Bank St., Suite 201, Ottawa, Ontario K1V 7Z5, Canada, ☎ 613/237–3657, FAX 613/521–0805, acta.ntl@sympatico.ca). **Australian Federation of Travel Agents** (⊠ Level 3, 309 Pitt St., Sydney 2000, Australia, ☎ 02/9264–3299, FAX 02/9264–1085, www.afta.com.au). **Travel Agents' Association of New Zealand** (⊠ Box 1888, Wellington 10033, New Zealand, ☎ 04/499–0104, FAX 04/499–0827, taanz@tiasnet.co.nz).

➤ FRANCE-FOCUSED AGENCY: **New Frontiers** (⊠ 12 E. 33 St., 11th floor, New York, NY 10016, ☎ 800/366–6387 or 212/779-0600, FAX 212/779–1007) books domestic air flights, trains, car rentals, and hotels in France.

VISITOR INFORMATION

See the A to Z sections *in* individual chapters for local tourist office telephone numbers and addresses.

➤ TOURIST INFORMATION: **France On-Call** (☎ 202/659–7779; ⊙ Mon.–Fri. 9–9). **Chicago** (⊠ 676 N. Michigan Ave., Chicago, IL 60611, ☎ 312/751–7800). **Los Angeles** (⊠ 9454 Wilshire Blvd., Suite 715, Beverly Hills, CA 90212, ☎ 310/271–6665, FAX 310/276–2835). **New York City** (⊠ 444 Madison Ave., 16th floor, New York, NY 10022, ☎ 212/838–7800). **Canada** (⊠ 1981 Ave. McGill College, Suite 490, Montréal, Québec H3A 2W9, ☎ 514/288–4264, FAX 514/845–4868. **U.K.** (⊠ 178 Piccadilly, London W1V OAL, ☎ 171/629–2869, FAX 0171/493–6594).

➤ REGIONAL TOURIST OFFICE: The mother lode of general information on the region covered in this book is the **Comité Régional du Tourisme de Provence-Alpes-Côtes d'Azur** (PACA, Regional Committee on Tourism in Provence, the Alps, and the Côte d'Azur, ✉ 12 pl. Joliette, 13002 Marseille, ☎ 04–91–56–47–00, FAX 04–91–56–66–61).

➤ U.S. GOVERNMENT ADVISORIES: **U.S. Department of State** (✉ Overseas Citizens Services Office, Room 4811 N.S., 2201 C St. NW, Washington, DC 20520, ☎ 202/647–5225 for interactive hot line, 301/946–4400 for computer bulletin board, FAX 202/647–3000 for interactive hot line); enclose a self-addressed, stamped, business-size envelope.

WEB SITES

Do check out the World Wide Web when you're planning. You'll find everything from current weather forecasts to virtual tours of famous cities. Fodor's Web site, www.fodors.com, is a great place to start your on-line travels. When you see a 🐝 in this book, go to www.fodors.com/urls for an up-to-date link to that destination's site. For more information specifically on Provence and the Côte d'Azur, visit: **Eurail/Eurostar** (www.eurail.com/); **French Youth Hostel Federation** (ww.fuaj.org); **Maison de la France/French Government Tourist Office** (www.francetourism.com and www.maison-de-la-france.com: 8000/); **Monaco Tourist Office** (www.monaco.mc/usa/); **Provence Tourist Office** (www.visitprovence.com); **Riviera Tourist Office** (www.crt-riviera.fr/); and **SNCF** (www.sncf.fr/indexe.htm).

WHEN TO GO

July and August in Provence and the Côte d'Azur can be stifling, not only because of the intense heat but the crowds of tourists and vacationers. June and September are the best months to be in the region, as both are free of the midsummer crowds and the weather is summer-balmy. June offers the advantage of long daylight hours, while cheaper prices and many warm days, often lasting well into October, make September attractive. Try to avoid the second half of July and all of August, when almost all of France goes on vacation. Huge crowds jam the roads and beaches, and prices are jacked up in resorts. Don't travel on or around July 14 and August 1, 15, and 31, when every French family is either going on vacation or driving home. Watch out for May, riddled with church holidays—one a week—and the museum closings they entail. Anytime between March and November will offer you a good chance to soak up the sun on the Côte d'Azur. After All Saints (November 1) the whole region begins to shutter down for winter, and won't open its main resort hotels until Easter. Still, off-season has its charms—the pétanque games are truly just the town folks' game, the most touristy hill towns are virtually abandoned, and when it's nice out—more often than not—you can bask in direct sun in the cafés.

CLIMATE

➤ FORECASTS: **Weather Channel Connection** (☎ 900/932–8437), 95¢ per minute from a Touch-Tone phone. Weather conditions in France can be checked on the Web, at www.meteo.fr

What follows are average daily temperatures for Provence and the Côte d'Azur

NICE

Jan.	55F	13C	May	68F	20C	Sept.	77F	25C
	39	4		55	13		61	16
Feb.	55F	13C	June	75F	24C	Oct.	70F	21C
	41	5		61	16		54	12
Mar.	59F	15C	July	81F	27C	Nov.	63F	17C
	45	7		64	18		46	8
Apr.	64F	18C	Aug.	81F	27C	Dec.	55F	13C
	46	8		64	18		41	5

Provence and the Côte d'Azur

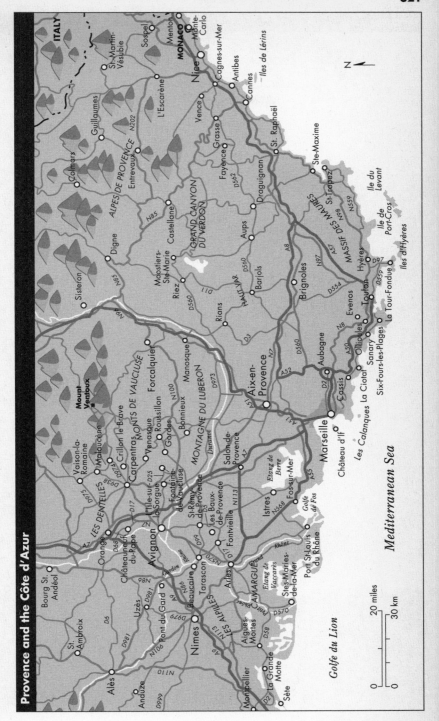

France

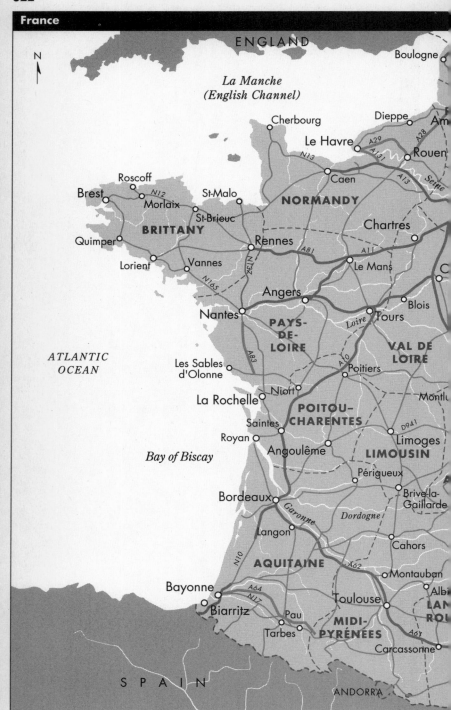

N

ENGLAND

*La Manche
(English Channel)*

Boulogne

Cherbourg

Dieppe

Am

Le Havre

N13

A29

A131

A28

Rouen

Seine

A13

Caen

Roscoff

N12

St-Malo

NORMANDY

Chartres

Brest

Morlaix

St-Brieuc

Quimper

BRITTANY

Rennes

A81

A11

Le Mans

C

Lorient

Vannes

N165

N137

Angers

Blois

Nantes

Tours

VAL DE
LOIRE

*ATLANTIC
OCEAN*

PAYS-
DE-
LOIRE

Loire

A83

A10

Poitiers

Montl

Les Sables
d'Olonne

Niort

La Rochelle

POITOU-
CHARENTES

D941

Saintes

Limoges

Royan

Angoulême

LIMOUSIN

Bay of Biscay

Périgueux

Brive-la-
Gaillarde

Bordeaux

Garonne

Dordogne

Langon

Cahors

N10

AQUITAINE

A62

Montauban

Bayonne

A64

Toulouse

Albi

Biarritz

N17

Pau

MIDI-
PYRÉNÉES

LAN
ROU

Tarbes

A61

Carcassonne

SPAIN

ANDORRA

INDEX

Icons and Symbols

★   Our special recommendations

✕   Restaurant

🏠   Lodging establishment

✕🏠   Lodging establishment whose restaurant warrants a special trip

🦆   Good for kids (rubber duck)

☞   Sends you to another section of the guide for more information

✉   Address

☎   Telephone number

🕐   Opening and closing times

💷   Admission prices

🖃   Sends you to www.fodors.com/urls for up-to-date links to the property's Web site

Numbers in white and black circles ③ ❸ that appear on the maps, in the margins, and within the tours correspond to one another.

A

Abbaye de Montmajour, *43*
Abbaye de Sénanque, *90–91*
Abbaye du Thoronet, *182–183*
Abbaye St-Victor, *126*
Agay, *168–169*
Aiglon ✕🏠, *259–260*
Aïgo Boulido ✕, *76*
Aigues-Mortes, *28–29*
Air travel. ☞ Plane travel
Airports, *289–290*
Aix, Marseille, and the Central Coast, *102–151*
beaches, 102
bed-and-breakfasts, 149
car rentals, 149
children, attractions for, 124–125
dining and lodging, 102–103, 110, 113–117, 130–136, 141, 142–143, 145, 147, 149, 150
festivals, 117, 136
guided tours, 149–150
itineraries, 104, 106
nightlife and the arts, 117, 136–137
outdoor activities and sports, 102, 103, 117–118, 137, 143, 147
price categories, 103
shopping, 118–119, 137–138

transportation, 148–149
vacation rentals, 150
visitor information, 150–151
web sites, 104
when to go, 106
wine, 104
Aix-en-Provence, *106–119, 149, 150–151.* ☞ *Also* Aix, Marseilles, and the Central Coast
Cours Mirabeau, 110–111
Place d'Albertas, 113
Albert Ier 🏠, *200*
Alexandra 🏠, *255*
Alizé 🏠, *135–136*
Alpilles, Arles, and the Camargue, *18–56*
Alpilles, 44–53
architecture and antiquities, 18
Arles, 32–41
bed-and-breakfasts, 56
the Camargue area, 27–32
car rentals, 54
children, attractions for, 27, 30, 46
dining and lodging, 19, 25–27, 29, 30, 32, 37, 39–41, 44, 45, 46–48, 50–52, 55–56
festivals, 27, 29, 41, 52–53
guided tours, 55
itineraries, 20–21
Languedoc Frontier, 21–27
nightlife and the arts, 41, 53
outdoor activities and sports, 18, 19, 27, 30, 48
price categories, 19
shopping, 27, 41, 44, 48, 53
transportation, 54
travel agencies, 55
vacation rentals, 55–56
visitor information, 56
web sites, 20
when to tour, 21
Amphithéâtre 🏠, *37*
Amusement parks, *215*
Ancienne Halle aux Grains, *109*
Antibes, *207–212, 262, 263*
Antiquities
Aix-en-Provence, 113
Alpilles, Arles, and the Camargue, 18
Antibes, 209
Arles, 34–35, 36, 37
Buoux, 96
Fréjus, 165
La Turbie, 249
Marseille, 123, 124
Nîmes, 23, 24–25
Orange, 74–76
Pont du Gard, 22
Riez, 180
St-Rémy-de-Provence, 49, 50
Vaison-la-Romaine, 80, 81

Apartment and villa rentals, *303–304*
Apt, *97*
Aquarium, *253*
Aquatropic (swimming pool), *27*
Arc de Triomphe (Orange), *75–76*
Arc Triomphal (St-Rémy-de-Provence), *49*
Arène 🏠, *76*
Arènes (Arles), *34–35*
Arènes (Fréjus), *165*
Arènes (Nîmes), *23*
Arlatan 🏠, *40*
Arles, *32–41, 55, 56.* ☞ *Also* Alpilles, Arles, and the Camargue
Arnaud ✕, *205*
Arrière-pays Niçoise, *239–244*
Art and architecture tours, *315*
Art galleries and museums
Aix-en-Provence, 109–110, 112
Antibes, 208–209
Arles, 36
Aubagne, 139
Avignon, 65, 66
Biot, 215
Cagnes-sur-Mer, 216, 217
Cannes, 195
Grasse, 204, 205
Les Baux-de-Provence, 46
Marseille, 123, 129
Menton, 259
Nice, 227, 229, 231
Nîmes, 23, 24, 25
St-Paul, 218
St-Tropez, 159
Vallauris, 207
Villeneuve-lès-Avignon, 73
Art in non-museum settings
Aix-en-Provence, 109, 110, 111
Avignon, 66–67
Notre-Dame-des-Fontaines, 241
Atelier Cézanne, *109–110*
Ateliers Thérèse Neveu, *139*
ATMs, *307*
Aubagne, *138–139, 141, 147, 151*
Au Bec Fin ✕, *198*
Auberge de la Fontaine ✕🏠, *78*
Auberge de la Madone ✕🏠, *249*
Auberge de la Reine Jeanne ✕🏠, *51–52*
Auberge des Seguins ✕🏠, *96*
Auberge des Seigneurs 🏠, *221*

NOTES

NOTES

FODOR'S PROVENCE AND THE CÔTE D'AZUR

EDITORS: Julie Mazur, Jennifer J. Paull, Christine M. Swiac

Editorial Contributors: Nancy Coons, Melisse Gelula, Mary Lou Longworth, Helayne Schiff, Alice Thompson

Editorial Production: Ira-Neil Dittersdorf

Maps: David Lindroth, *cartographer*; Robert Blake and Rebecca Baer, *map editors*

Design: Fabrizio La Rocca, *creative director*; Guido Caroti, *art director*; Jolie Novak, *senior picture editor*; Melanie Marin, *photo editor*

Cover Design: Pentagram

Production/Manufacturing: Angela L. McLean

COPYRIGHT

ISBN 0–679–00677–X

ISSN 1532–6829

SPECIAL SALES

IMPORTANT TIP

Although all prices, opening times, and other details in this book are based on information supplied to us at press time, changes occur all the time in the travel world, and Fodor's cannot accept responsibility for facts that become outdated or for inadvertent errors or omissions. So always confirm information when it matters, especially if you're making a detour to visit a specific place.

PHOTOGRAPHY

Sonja Bullaty, cover. *(Sunflower and lavender field, Mt. Ventoux region)*

Carlton InterContinental Cannes, *2 top left, 2 bottom left, 3 top right.*

Corbis, *2 top right, 3 bottom right, 6A, 14A.*

DIAF: *J.C. Gerard, 10C. Rosine Mazin, 10A. Camille Moirenc, 4–5, 8A, 8C, 9D, 12A, 13E, 15B. Eric Planchard, 9E. Giovanni Simeone, 13D. Daniel Thierry, 15C.*

Owen Franken, *1, 6B, 6C, 7A, 7 center, 7B, 8B, 9F, 10B, 12B, 16.*

Liaison Agency: *Benainous-Duclos, 3 top left.*

PhotoDisc, *2 bottom right, 3 bottom left.*

Tourisme de la Provence d'Azur, *2 bottom center.*

Nik Wheeler, *11D, 12C, 13F.*

ABOUT OUR WRITERS

Every vacation is important. So here at Fodor's we've pulled out all stops in preparing *Fodor's Provence and the Côte d'Azur*. To help you zero in on what to see in Provence and the Côte d'Azur, we've gathered some wonderful color photos of the key sights in this region. To show you how to put it all together, we've created great itineraries and neighborhood walks. And to direct you to the places that are truly worth your time and money, we've rallied the the team of endearingly picky know-it-alls we're pleased to call our writers. Having seen all corners of the regions they cover for us, they're real experts. If you knew them, you'd poll them for tips yourself.

Nancy Coons has adopted Provence and its coast as a kind of home-away-from-home, commuting on a regular basis from her farmhouse in Lorraine. In addition to working on this book, she collaborated with photographer Owen Franken to create two travel dreambooks—*Escape to Provence* and the forthcoming *Escape to the Riviera*—for Fodor's, trekking behind migrating sheep, harvesting grapes, whale-watching with the Monaco oceanography team, and testing the waters off Porquerolles as part of her research. She has worked on many other Fodor's projects, covering Switzerland, Luxembourg, Belgium, Alsace, and her own Lorraine, and her writing on European culture and food has appeared in *The Wall Street Journal, Opera News,* and *National Geographic Traveler.* When she isn't com-

muting south, she sings as part of an a cappella ensemble, performing in embassies, châteaux, and—in full costume—her village's medieval fair. Her husband, Mark Olson, and their daughters, Elodie and Alice, accompany her on her travels when French school holidays permit, which is often.

Since moving to France in 1997, **Mary Lou Longworth,** who previously was a graduate student of art history in California, has written for *The Washington Post, Wine Spectator, Bon Appetit,* Canada's *The Globe and Mail,* the *London Times,* and the *Independent* of London. In addition, she has embarked on a career in art photography, and her work has been shown in Aix and Arles. She updated the Smart Travel Tips section of this book.

Don't Forget to Write

Keeping a travel guide fresh and up-to-date is a big job. So we love your feedback—positive and negative—and follow up on all suggestions. Contact the Provence and the Côte d'Azur editor at editors@fodors.com or c/o Fodor's, 280 Park Avenue, New York, NY 10017. And have a wonderful trip!

Karen Cure

Karen Cure
Editorial Director